Whitman's Code:
A New Bible

Volume I:
Song of Myself
&
24 Canticles

M.C. Gardner

©2015 by M.C. Gardner. All rights reserved.
All reproduction or transmission
is prohibited without the consent of the author.
Printed in the United States of America.
Reg. WGA 2013
ISBN 978-0-9745042-3-0
For more information please email
anotheramericaliterary@anotheramerica.org.

Second edition, updated.
Published by Patcheny Press
in collaboration with anotheramerica.org.

www.patcheny.com

Cover:
Engraving of Walt Whitman, frontispiece to Leaves of Grass 1855.
Cover & Endpaper:
Walt Whitman, Engraving on Paper, Gustave Kruell, no date.

Whitman's Code:
A New Bible

Volume I:
Song of Myself
&
24 Canticles

M.C. Gardner

Acknowledgments

I have availed myself of dozens of predecessors in accumulating a 19th-century biography so vibrantly alive that death was the merest impediment.

I wish to particularly acknowledge The Walt Whitman Archive; The Norton Critical Edition of *Leaves of Grass and Other Writings;* NYU's *Leaves of Grass: A Textual Variorum of the Printed Poems;* and finally the support of my beloved and better by much more than half, Barbara.

— *M.C. Gardner*

Pro and Contra

Whitman enters on the last phase of spiritual triumph. He really arrives at that stage of infinity which the seers sought. By subjecting the deepest centres of the lower self, he attains the maximum consciousness in the higher self: a degree of extensive consciousness greater, perhaps, than any man in the modern world.

— *D. H. Lawrence*

It is no discredit to Walt Whitman that he wrote *Leaves of Grass,* only that he did not burn it afterwards.

— *Colonel T. W. Higginson*

Contents

Foreword		13
Prologue: Song of Myself		21
1.	I Celebrate Myself	23
2.	Houses and Rooms	30
3.	I Have Heard	39
4.	Trippers and Askers	41
5.	I Believe in You My Soul	45
6.	A Child Said ...	49
7.	Has Anyone Supposed?	56
8.	The Little One Sleeps	60
9.	The Big Doors	62
10.	Alone Far in the Wilds	63
11.	Twenty-Eight Young Men	72
12.	The Butcher Boy	82
13.	The Negro Holds Firmly	83
14.	The Wild Gander	85
15.	The Pure Contralto	87
16.	I Am of the Old and Young	98
17.	These Are Really	102
18.	With Music Strong	108
19.	This Is the Meal	115
20.	Who Goes There?	141
21.	I Am the Poet	144
22.	You Sea!	145
23.	Endless Unfolding	147
24.	Walt Whitman, a Kosmos	149
25.	Dazzling and Tremendous	153
26.	Now I Will Do Nothing	157
27.	To Be	163
28.	Is This Then a Touch?	163
29.	Blind Loving	165
30.	All Truths	165
31.	I Believe	173

32.	I Think	176
33.	Space and Time	183
34.	Now I Tell What I Knew	200
35.	Would You Hear	203
36.	Stretch'd and Still	205
37.	You Laggards	208
38.	Enough!	209
39.	The Friendly and Flowing	211
40.	Flaunt of the Sunshine	213
41.	I Am He Bringing Help	217
42.	A Call	220
43.	I Do Not Despise	225
44.	It Is Time	229
45.	O Span of Youth	233
46.	I Know	237
47.	I Am the Teacher	240
48.	I Have Said	244
49.	And As to You Death	247
50.	There Is That in Me	249
51.	The Past and Present	251
52.	The Spotted Hawk	252
Emerson		254
24 Canticles of Day & Night		318
Ante Meridiem		324
1.	Starting From Paumanok	325
2.	A Broadway Pageant (1860)	357
3.	By Blue Ontario's Shore	365
4.	Reversals	403
5.	Proud Music of the Storm	412
6.	Passage to India	429
7.	Prayer of Columbus	453
8.	The Sleepers	462
9.	Transpositions	490
10.	To Think of Time	491
11.	Thou Mother ...	510
12.	A Paumanok Picture	524

Post Meridiem		525
13.	Salut Au Monde!	526
14.	Song of the Open Road	548
15.	Crossing Brooklyn Ferry	578
16.	Song of the Answerer	604
17.	Our Old Feuillage	616
18.	A Song of Joys	627
19.	Song of the Broad-Axe	642
20.	Song of the Exposition	668
21.	Song of the Redwood-Tree	691
22.	A Song of Occupations	704
23.	A Song of the Rolling Earth	722
24.	Youth, Day, Old Age…	741

Each Hour	742
Passage to India Redux	757
Anatomy of a Code	771
Appendix	790
1. Birthplace	790
2. Parents	791
3. 328 Mickle Street	792
4. Circle	793
5. Anne Gilchrist	794
6. Whitman's Letter to Anne Gilchrist	795
7. Preface to Preface	796
8. Preface to 1855's *Leaves of Grass*, Table of Contents	847
9. Emerson's Inaugural Letter	828
10. Preface, 1856 Edition	831
11. 1856 Cover Art & Spine	846
12. 1856 Edition of *Leaves of Grass*, Table of Contents	847
13. "The Swimmers"	849
14. Deathbed Edition, Table of Contents	850
15. A Backward Glance	867
Dusk	899
Bibliography	900
Index	908
Notes	931

> Horace, I made the puzzle:
> it's not my business to solve...
>
> — *Walt Whitman*

FOREWORD

Leaves of Grass is a sprawling masterpiece and an exquisite puzzle. Walt Whitman published the first edition of its wonderful sprawl in 1855 — the puzzle, however, absorbed him for the remainder of his life. His *Deathbed* edition provided one solution. *Whitman's Code: A New Bible* considers another and, as noted in the *Forward* to volume II, this study will also proffer an additional and parallel vantage that was espied as the present exegis neared its completion. It is something of a marvel that it and the principal argument of this book have both been overlooked for more than a century. The first entails the displacement of a number of his poems, but the second is subversive enough to leave Whitman's masterpiece precisely as he bequeathed it in the early evening of Saturday, March 26, 1892 — the day he died.[1]

For purposes of this introduction and the initial insight upon which it is predicated, let it suffice to say that anyone regarding the poet's *solution* will discover that by the third edition of *Leaves of Grass* (1860) it contained two different categories of poems — the *solo canticles*[2] and the poems collected in *thematic clusters*. Whitman shuffled these disparate elements throughout the multiple editions of his *Leaves*. The appendices of Volumes I and II illustrate numerous examples of their variegated order. My solution is not the poet's — but it is simpler. I've separated the two categories into separate books. Two pieces to the code (Volume I: Prologue & 24 Solo Canticles and Volume II: 365 Poems of the Collected Clusters).

Two volumes in a twenty-first century compendium of a nineteenth-century masterpiece—each book based on deciphering a cryptic note recorded by Whitman in 1857. The puzzle is first reported in R.M. Bucke's *Notes and Fragments*.[3] Richard Maurice Bucke was a friend, an MD and one of the three executors to Whitman's estate.[4] The fragments are notebooks left by the poet and subsequently published by the doctor. Therein you will find Whitman's ambitious plan to write a *New Bible—a* volume of poetry suggesting the 365 days of the year:

> The Great Construction of the New Bible. Not to be diverted from the principal object—the main life work—the three hundred and sixty-five—it ought to be ready in 1859...[5]

These 365 poems[6] I discovered to be hiding in plain sight in the collected clusters and annexes of his *poem*.[7] The remainder of the canonical work[8] is in the 25 major poems strewn *between* the thematic collections. I've assembled these major poems in a Prologue, suggestive of Whitman's year—the 52 Cantos of *Song of Myself,* and the remaining 24 into a group suggestive of the hours of his day. The 25 canticles are the basis for Volume I, and the 365 poems—the basis for Volume II— two *Testaments*[9] aligning Whitman and his poetry with the infinite and eternal by which God takes our terrestrial measure.[10]

Leaves of Grass is one of the essential documents of nineteenth century American letters. In its subsequent European translations it became, as well, one of the preeminent pieces of world literature. Whitman (like the Buddha before him) addresses two distinct ways of viewing the world.

One is a deeply personal reflection on his own desires and limitations. The other is his identification with an Absolute sensibility extending through the whole of time and space. This second is thought, by some critics, to be a poetic convention or metaphysical retrenchment of Ralph Waldo Emerson's *Oversoul*. Indeed, the poet himself would often doubt his worthiness of the proffered vision. Those doubts are among the most moving elements of a biography that continues assemblage into its second century. Hereafter are also the reports of his contemporaries, pro and contra. Only hinted at are the testimonies of the tens of thousands who were succored by the poet during the cataclysm of the American Civil War. In "The Sleepers", in the decade before the war, he imagines himself ministering to the broken and wounded of the world:

> I stand in the dark with drooping eyes
> > by the worst suffering and the most restless,
>
> I pass my hands soothingly to and fro a
> > few inches from them,
> > The restless sink in their beds, they fitfully sleep…[11]

Within five years he becomes that ministering angel. In the first edition of *Leaves* he also imagines amputated limbs dropping *horribly in a pail* [12] and then he becomes, as well, witness to countless amputations. In "The Wound Dresser" he remembers such a soldier:

> One turns to me his appealing eyes —
> > poor boy! I never knew you,
>
> Yet, I think I could not refuse this
> > moment to die for you if that would save you.[13]

His readers are invited to share his mystic vision:

> I celebrate and sing myself,
> What I shall assume you shall assume,
> For every atom belonging to me as well
>   belongs to you.[14]

The poet is making an extraordinary assertion.[15] To wit: his readers and the poet are the same entity. Whitman will exclaim the universe (as befitting its name) to be a singular manifest—each of us its expression. On Sinai, before a bush that burned, Moses heard it exclaim *I AM*.[16] In the East it is intoned in sonorous morning prayers as *AUM*.

How are we to configure the obvious plurality of the world with this tautological assertion? Whitman's mentor, Emerson suggests an exceptional metaphor. He likens variegated humanity to the figures in a tapestry. Here frolic courtiers on the Isle of Cythera; there a shepherd tends his grazing sheep; in one corner a minstrel strums a lute; in another, a child's kite skirts the heavens; still further on, the frozen cloth reveals two lovers enraptured in an endless kiss. The tapestry could be extended to envelop every creature and entity in the world. Emerson's point of vision was, however, on the reverse side of the fabric. There a diversity of individuals dissolved in a kaleidoscope of twisting and interweaving yarns. Think of these innumerable threads as the essential energy humming throughout the fabric of space-time. Think of your life as composed of the same. Whitman believes that each life was not only *itself* but every other life, as well—*the universe sitting in smiling repose*.[17]

These myriad eyes are no less than Deity assessing Creation. In the thirteenth century, Meister Eckhart had claimed:
> The eye with which God sees me is the same eye with which I see him, my eye and his eye are one.

In Emerson's *Divinity School Address* he wondered:

> In how many churches was man made sensible that the earth and heavens are passing into his mind?

Echoing Eckhart he suggests:

> I become a transparent eyeball; I am nothing; I see all; the currents of the Universal Being circulate through me; I am part and parcel of God.[18]

Nietzsche asserts that all the lives of history are he. Schopenhauer believes that each assertion of an *I* (throughout time) is his own proclamation of identity. Bergson relates epiphanies wherein the whole of his life was presented in complete and singular plenitude. Proust's *À la recherche du temps perdu* asserts that same vision. Joyce collapses the nearly 800 pages of *Ulysses* into a single Dublin day. [19] The Irishman hears: "…the ruin of all space, shattered glass and toppling masonry and time, one final flame."[20] He further avers: "Any object, intensely regarded, may be a gate of access to the incorruptible eon of the gods."[21] Our own sage of Concord asserts that "We see God face to face every hour[22]…all the laws of nature may be read in the smallest fact."[23]

His friend Carlyle had earlier written: "... all objects are as windows, through which the philosophic eye looks into Infinitude itself."[24] Whitman concurs with them all. At the moment of his supreme enlightenment he sees Deity in the limitless "...leaves stiff or dropping in the fields, and brown ants in the little wells beneath them and mossy scabs of the worm fence, heap'd stones, elder, mullein and poke weed."[25]

Each of these men asserts the minutiae of a moment are equal to the largess of the infinite. We can little escape the movement of time — what Plato calls *the moving image of Eternity* — the flux that attends all things. However, this seeming chaos is predicated on a permanence that is, on rare occasions, glimpsed — Eliot's *still point of the turning world.*[26] Removing the strictures of time and space from the quotidian — from any person or thing — reveals the features of a totality that is the face of the Divine — the whole of the earth and heaven passing through our minds. Emerson *lifted the curtain on the common and saw that the gods were sitting disguised in every company.*[27]

He reported that such was the case when he read a small volume of verse that had come his way shortly after its 1855 publication. *Leaves of Grass* is one of the great intellectual and sensuous experiences of a lifetime. It is presented in its entirety in Volumes I & II of this compendium. Ninety-three percent of Whitman's poems[28] are confined by *cluster*.[29] The order of the clusters and the order of the poems within the clusters remain exactly as the poet decreed — I've simply collected the seven percent remainder (the solo canticles) into a *cluster* of their own.[30]

I have, as well, attempted to restrict my commentary in each volume to before or after the individual poems or cantos within the poems.[31] Aside from canticle and song, these pages also collect the elements of a lifetime recorded in word, deed, and photograph. In 1855 Whitman publishes 12 untitled[32] poems—a collection without a specifically named author.[33] Five hundred lines into the book he introduces its main character: *Walt Whitman,* [34] *an American, one of the roughs, a kosmos* — a character that he conflates with the totality of space: *Space! My Soul!* [35] and the ubiquity of time: *I am the clock myself.* [36]

In the second edition of 1856 he gives up the conceit of a single untitled poem, adds an additional 20 pieces and identifies the offerings by placing the word "Poem" in each respective title. With such concoctions as "Liberty Poem for Asia, Africa, Europe, America, Australia, Cuba, and the Archipelagoes of the Sea", this proves to be an unwieldy solution to the ramble of his verse. In "Anatomy of a Code" I argue that an 1857 notebook entry concerning time ("I accept time absolutely") inaugurates, in the least, an unconscious scheme that concludes only with the final poems added to his *Leaves* at his lifetime's end. The first poem of the initial unnamed 12 he entitles *Song of Myself.* [37] He divides this seminal work into 52 sections.[38] 1860's "Calamus" section is based on a 12-part precursor called *Live Oak with Moss*. In the cluster-setting 1881 edition he devises and names 12 clusters to thematically contain his poems. In the first cluster of those 12 he assembles 24 short *Inscriptions* to announce his poetic agenda. We find also that, besides the solo *Song of Myself,* the poet leaves an additional 24 poems uncollected by thematic cluster (although twelve of these were collected in an untitled group).

We begin to suspect that the numbers 12, 24, and 52 are of some importance to the poet.[39] Then we discover that in his *Deathbed* edition of 1891/92 the total number of poems (all unnumbered by the poet) which he compiled by cluster and annex is 365. [40]

If it is merely a coincidence that in 1857 he proposed to write a body of 365 poems and that in his final edition he had done so, it is a remarkable coincidence, indeed.[41] *Whitman's Code: A New Bible* details a discovery that his *Deathbed* edition had heretofore disguised.[42] It is a configuration he prophetically envisioned and now it is bequeathed in the two volumes presented. [43]

Whitman imagines a reader a century hence: "I that was once visible am become invisible. Now it is you, compact, visible realizing my poems, seeking me. Fancying how happy you were if I could be with you and become your comrade. Be not too certain but I am now with you." [44]

I wouldn't put it past him.

M.C. GARDNER

PROLOGUE: SONG OF MYSELF

*"It was and is one of Whitman's masterpieces,
if not the chief one it had the right position
for the book..."*

Mark Van Doren

1. I Celebrate Myself
2. Houses and Room
3. I Have Heard
4. Trippers and Askers
5. I Believe in You My Soul
6. A Child Said *What Is the Grass*?
7. Has Anyone Supposed?
8. The Little One Sleeps in the Cradle
9. The Big Doors of the Country Barn
10. Alone Far in the Wilds
11. Twenty-eight Young Men
12. The Butcher Boy
13. The Negro
14. The Wild Gander
15. The Pure Contralto
16. I Am of Old and Young
17. These Are Really the Thoughts
18. With Music Strong I Come
19. This is the Meal
20. Who Goes There?
21. I Am the Poet
22. You Sea!
23. Endless Unfold of Words

24. Walt Whitman, a Kosmos
25. Dazzling and Tremendous
26. Now I Will Do Nothing But Listen
27. To Be In Any Form
28. Is This Then a Touch?
29. Blind Loving Wrestling Touch
30. All Truths
31. I Believe
32. I Think
33. Space and Time
34. Now I Tell
35. Would You Hear
36. Stretched and Still
37. You Laggards
38. Enough
39. The Friendly Flowering Savage
40. Flaunt of Sunshine
41. I Am He
42. A Call
43. I Do Not Despise
44. It is Time
45. O Span of Youth
46. I Know
47. I Am the Teacher
48. I Have Said
49. And As to You Death
50. There Is That Part of Me
51. The Past and the Present
52. The Spotted Hawk

I Celebrate Myself

(1855)

I celebrate myself, and sing myself,	
And what I assume you shall assume,	1
For every atom belonging to me as good belongs to you.	
I loafe and invite my soul,	
I lean and loafe at my ease observing a spear of summer grass.	5
My tongue, every atom of my blood, formed from this soil, this air,	6
Born here of parents born here from parents the same, and their parents the same,	
I, now thirty-seven years old in perfect health begin,	
Hoping to cease not till death.	
Creeds and schools in abeyance,	10
Retiring back awhile sufficed at what they are, but never forgotten,	
I harbor for good or bad, I permit to speak at every hazard,	
Nature without check with original energy.	13

Perhaps only "Call me Ishmael" bespeaks as grand a commencement. In the opening three words of their respective masterpieces, both Melville and Whitman announce two of the three greatest adventures in American letters.

The opening of the third, *Huckleberry Finn*, resonates with the same question of identity: "YOU don't know about me..." Each author will assert his central character to be emblematic of mankind.[45] Whitman's poem, as here recorded, reflects the ultimate version to which the poet laid his hand. It was divided into 52 sections in 1867. I have attempted (for the most part) to restrict my commentary between cantos. The reader will do well to note that in such an instance a line number will immediately precede the interjection and a succeeding numeration will immediately follow at the resumption of the poetic text. This practice should allow the navigation of individual poems with minimal invasion to their flow and coherence.[46]

The first line of the inaugural *Leaves of Grass* was a celebration of himself: "I celebrate myself;" later the poet would see this poem as the proclamation of a national epic and would add: "and sing myself;" as earlier poets would evoke a muse from Homer's: "Sing, O goddess, the anger of Achilles son of Peleus, that brought countless ills upon the Achaeans," to Milton's "Sing, Heavenly Muse, that on the secret top / Of Oreb or of Sinai, didst inspire / That shepherd, who first taught the chosen seed, / In the beginning how the Heavens and Earth / Rose out of Chaos." Lines 6 through 13 were also subsequently added to the original poem.

As in Milton, Whitman's seminal line also evokes Genesis. The first six syllables: "I celebrate myself," are for the poet little different than the first six of the King James translation: "In the beginning God..." Whitman knew his project was large and its hugeness brought harsh words from critics who felt him presumptuous or else felt themselves diminished by his imposing facade.

He announced his desire for size in the preface of the first edition:

> The largeness of nature or the nation were monstrous without a corresponding largeness and generosity of the spirit of the citizen...The American poets are to enclose old and new for America is the race of races. Of them a bard is to be commensurate with a people...His spirit responds to his country's spirit...he incarnates its geography and natural life and rivers and lakes...Here at last is something in the doings of man that corresponds with the broadcast doings of day and night...The greatest poet hardly knows pettiness or triviality. If he breathes into anything that was before thought small it dilates with the grandeur and life of the universe.

Note that the poet again alludes to his *Genesis Project* in "something in the doings of man that corresponds with the broadcast doings of day and night...it dilates with the grandeur and life of the universe." He will more than once in his musings imagine that he was at the beginning of all things—"Afar down I see the huge first Nothing, I know I was even there..." What will come to be considered the second Canto begins with the line: "Houses and rooms are full of perfumes....the shelves are crowded with perfumes," and concludes with "You shall listen to all sides and filter them from yourself." The only difference between the inclusive lines of the second Canto and the '55 edition are in punctuation.

Song of Myself represented more than half of the 1855 edition's 2315 lines.[47] It is as complex and garrulous as the poet himself. Critics have resorted to a variety of schemes to reign in the poem's magnificent ramblings.[48] Each of these explications has much to recommend it no matter how forbidding each initially appears. For the abstrusely challenged my delineation will appear comfortably familiar. Each Canto of the poem is treated as a separate week of the 52 in a year.[49]

The poet loafs and invites his *soul* as he observes a spear of summer grass. One can imagine the poet observing the grass both as the naturalist Aristotle and, as well, as the idealist Plato (his soul) considering its archetype in eternity. The poet returns to time as he contemplates his own mortality: "I, now thirty-seven years old in perfect health begin, / Hoping to cease not till death."

Given the seminal importance the 52 sections of *Song of Myself* I have taken it upon myself to give each Canto a title. This was, more often than not, Whitman's practice for the majority of his poems--the titles mirror the first line. Here, in the first three lines of *Song of Myself* the poet exudes a vitality and assurance that could retire legions of psychiatrists. If you celebrate yourself you are, ipso facto, worthy of celebration. If you assure your fellow citizens that such is true of them, as well—there is nothing about you to which they could feel inferior and nothing of which you would suppose they were. For Victorian and Puritanical sensibilities, Whitman was initially regarded (when regarded at all) simply as a lewd vulgarian. He was thought as destructive to the morality of the period as the proverbial bovine in a China shop.

Sex was a participant sport engaged only under the cover of darkness—in the boudoir or the brothel, but certainly not in the open air's cleansing sunlight. To display nature *in Nature* was viewed as unnatural, aberrant, and likely, criminal.

Numerous critics suggested the poet should be hog-tied, whipped, shot, hanged and/or all of the above. The rawness of the nerve he touched was in direct proportion to the anger and derision that was heaped upon him. Whitman would never have much money. He knew that *pocketless* of a dime he could purchase the pick of the earth. Along with Elias Hicks and Meister Eckhart he believed that the world was an overflow of God's goodness and that those who partake of that goodness each come home richer than when they set out:

> And everything which such persons leave in multiplicity will always be returned to them in simplicity, for they find both themselves and everything else in the now of unity. And those who go out in this way come home much nobler than when they went out. Such persons live now in bare freedom and complete emptiness, having no need to possess or acquire anything, whether little or much. For everything belonging to God belongs to them.[50]

Whitman's father died on July 11, 1855—a few days after the inaugural publication of his *Leaves*. The poet remained the primary support for his mother and invalid brother throughout their respective lifetimes.

He hoped his poetry would produce sufficient income to provide for them each—realistically he knew he would have to supplement his literary activities with other ventures. He also believed his most valuable commodity was himself. It was out of his personality that he created *Walt Whitman*, a Bunyan-like colossus that could cross a county in a stride or two. Near the end of his life he looked back on the efforts that had consumed it:

> This was a feeling or ambition to articulate and faithfully express in literary or poetic form, and uncompromisingly, my own physical, emotional, moral intellectual and aesthetic Personality, in the midst of tallying, the momentous spirit and facts of its immediate days, and of current America—and to exploit that Personality, identified with place and date, in a far more candid and comprehensive sense than any hitherto poem or book.[51]

Epictetus knew that ownership of anything, other than oneself, was an illusion: "Never say you lost something, rather say you borrowed it for a time and then returned it,"—this from a Greek slave (much beloved by Whitman) whose era shortly preceded that of the Stoic Roman Emperor Marcus Aurelius.

Horace Traubel records the poet's account of the same precept:

> The ignorant man is demented with the madness of owning things—of having by warranty deeds and court clerk's records, the right to mortgage, sell, give away or raise money on certain possessions—but the wisest soul knows that no object can really be owned by one man or woman any more than another.[52]

Whitman knew that each atom of the earth "belonging to me as well belongs to you." He was not seized by the "mania of owning things." He could take the time to "lean and loafe" at his ease to observe a spear of summer grass. He knew that he was formed by the same globe that produces the grass. He knew that the air he breathed was breathed by his parents before him and their parents before them. From this humble genealogy, at age thirty seven, he will trace his lineage to the stars and to the origins of the universe itself. In order to empirically observe, without prejudice, he will hold "all schools and creeds in abeyance." He will harbor for good or bad, and hazard any voice to be heard—for the "world is nature without check, with original energy." Emerson's council in *Nature,* was for "every a man in proportion to his energy to take the world into himself." Even as Whitman "retires back a little", he knows that his mentor's words "sufficed for themselves", as did the words of the *Bhagavad Gita* and the Bible did in their time—"each will never be forgotten." For Whitman, the world is the outward manifestation of an inner desire. This interior intention he calls the "Me myself," It makes its first appearance in line 65 of the '55 edition and in line 74 of **Song of Myself** as adjusted in the final disposition of the *Deathbed* edition's 4th Canto.

The *Me myself* is derivative of the Hindu *Atman* and also of Kant's *thing in itself,* which for Schopenhauer was *the will,* for Nietzsche *the will to power* and for Whitman's mentor the ultimate fact: *the resolution of all into the everblessed one.*[53] In the Upanishads the *everblessed one* is identified as the god[54] and foundational principal, Brahman, *one without second.*

Here, at the inception of a spiritual odyssey no less wondrous than that of which another poet sang twenty-seven hundred years before, Whitman invites his audience to lean and loaf and contemplate the shared and sheer miracle of *being and becoming, time and eternity, Atman and Brahman* — in a single spear of summer grass.

2. Houses and Rooms

> Houses and rooms are full of perfumes, the shelves are crowded with perfumes, 14
> I breathe the fragrance myself and know it and like it,
> The distillation would intoxicate me also, but I shall not let it.
>
> The atmosphere is not a perfume, it has no taste of the distillation, it is odorless,
> It is for my mouth forever, I am in love with it,
> I will go to the bank by the wood and become undisguised and naked,
> I am mad for it to be in contact with me.

The smoke of my own breath
Echoes, ripples, buzz'd whispers, love root, silk thread, crotch and vine, 22
My respiration and inspiration, the beating of my heart, the passing of blood and air through my lungs, 23
The sniff of green leaves and dry leaves, and of the shore and the dark-color'd sea-rocks, and of hay in the barn,
The sound of the blech'd words of my voice loos'd to the eddies of the wind,
A few light kisses, a few embraces, a reaching round of arms,
The play of shine and shade on the trees as the supple boughs wag,
The delight alone or in the rush of the streets, or along the field and hillsides,
The feeling of health, the full-noon trill, the song of me rising from bed and meeting the sun.

Have reckon'd a thousand acres much? Have you reckon'd the earth much?
Have you practis'd so long to learn to read?
Have you felt so proud to get at the meaning of poems?

Stop this day and night with me and you shall possess the origin of all poems, 33

> You shall posses the good of the earth
>   and sun (there are millions of suns
>   left,) 34
> You shall no longer take things at
>   second or third hand, nor look
>   through the eyes of the dead, nor
>   feed on the specters in books,
> You shall not look through my eyes
>   either, not take things from me,
> You shall listen to all sides and filter
>   through them from yourself. 37

In *Houses and Rooms* (immediately above), the second Canto of his *Song*, Whitman begins the first of his radical, sensuous tallies — the eternal record of time's moving image. From the artificial fragrance on a shelf he moves to the odorless fragrance of the air: "I am in love with it." After shedding his clothes by the river bank he takes a visual tally of the smoke of his breath and then an aural tally of echoes and whispers. Then, somewhat shocking to Victorian sensibilities (even to this day), he masturbates. He acknowledges his *love root; silk-thread* (ejaculate); *crotch and vine* (Line 22 above) — further noting: "my respiration, and inspiration, the beating of my heart, the passing of blood and air through my lungs."(Line 23 above)

From the sensuality of the first two stanzas he moves to the intellectual in stanzas three and four. He challenges the idea of extension — *do you reckon a thousand acres much? Have you reckon'd the earth much?* (Line 30 above) Do you read? Can you read and comprehend a poem? Then he prophetically challenges his readers to stop with him — and promises that they shall *possess the origin of all poems.* (Line 33 above)

Most poets aver that once a poem takes flight its meaning is commingled with the life of its reader. Whitman offers the good of the earth and sun: "there are millions of suns left." (Line 34 above) Those millions are living poems — not dead leavings in old tomes — they are even more alive than the poems in the poet's tome itself:

> You shall not look through my eyes either, not take things from me,
> You shall listen to all sides and filter them from yourself.

One might hear a note or two from Emerson's *Self-Reliance*:

> Society everywhere is in conspiracy against the manhood of every one of its members...Whoso would be a man, must be a non-conformist. He who would gather immortal palms must not be hindered by the name of goodness. Nothing is at last sacred but the integrity of your own mind.

Whitman would add to Emerson's last line: "...and the integrity of your own body" — by which the poet, not hindered by Victorian standards of morality, would also forcibly assert — sex. Sex and death are among the few subjects little addressed in what would otherwise be the all encompassing sagas of the *Emerson Essay*. Emerson was too profoundly a New Englander to believe procreation a proper topic of poetic fancy. One of Emerson's chroniclers suggested to one of Whitman's[55]: "...he disliked Whitman's too frequent mention of the organ of generation."

In a famous walk with Whitman around the Boston Commons he was unable to dissuade the younger poet of just that view—Whitman refused to bowdlerize his book. Some years after Emerson's death Whitman would reflect:

> They never realized how pervasive and vital to the life-blood of the book was the procreational element...*Leaves of Grass* is avowedly the song of Sex...the espousing principle of those lines so gives breath of life (generation, time, and becoming)[56] to my whole scheme that the bulk of the pieces might as well have been left unwritten were those lines omitted...the lines I allude to, and the spirit in which they are spoken, permeate all *Leaves of Grass* and the work must stand or fall with them.[57]

As will be noted further along, he would allow and then subsequently regret the liberties that William Michael Rossetti would take by deleting some of his greatest poems from the first presentation of his *Leaves* in England. Most of the deletions were of the "procreational element." As to death, readers of Emerson's Journal of March 29, 1831 will never forget the inconsolable cleric's visit to Ellen's mausoleum and the Poe-like gesture of flinging open her coffin—whether a morbid fantasy or a nightmarish memory has never been determined. His marriage to Lydia Jackson produced four children. His first born, Waldo, contracted and died of scarlet fever in 1842: "And he, the wondrous child,/Whose silver warble wild/Outvalued every pulsing sound/Within the air's cerulean round..."

[58] Excepting the heart-rending lyrics of *Threnody*, no one would argue either sex or death Emersonian mainstays. In the third Canto ("I Have Heard"), Whitman celebrates the "Urge and urge and urge, / Always the procreant urge of the world...always sex."(Line 44 below) As he discovered of masturbation in his *Paumanok* youth and in the "Calamus" intimacies of his young manhood — the urge was not always procreant — but nonetheless, it was not be denied, whatever its guise or manifest.

The third week (Canto 3) of his *Song* embraces the *amative* commingling of man and woman, the *adhesive*[59] connection between loving men and the Taoist and Tantric commingling of nature. Whitman's reading of Hegel's dialectic elicits:

> Clear and sweet is my soul and clear and sweet is all that is not my soul.
>
> Lack one lacks both and the unseen is proved by the seen,
> Till that becomes unseen and receives proof in its turn.

Emerson, of course, is never far afield:

> An inevitable dualism bisects nature so that each thing is a half and suggests another to make it whole...There is a crack in everything[60] God hath made...We can no more have things and get the sensual good by itself , than we can get an inside without an outside or a light without a shadow... All things are double... curses always recoil on him

> who imprecates them—if you put a chain around the neck of a slave the other end fastens around your own... the exclusionist in religion does not see that he shuts the door of heaven on himself.[61]

Whitman also proclaims his attraction to other men: "any man hearty and clean." There is some question about his bedfellow who "sleeps by his side through the night and who withdraws at the peep of day with stealthy tread." Does he depart in stealth to not awaken the poet or not to be discovered departing?

Whitman is almost violent in protest (Line 62 when the poem resumes):

> Shall I postpone my acceptance and realization and scream at my eyes,
> That they turn from gazing down the road,
> And forthwith cipher and show me to a cent,
> Exactly the value of one and exactly the value of two, and which is ahead?

As we will see below, the 1855 edition of his poetry reports the bedfellow to be God:

> As God[62] comes a loving bedfellow and sleeps at my side all night and close on the peep of the day.

It's a fair bet you won't find *that* in Emerson. Ralph Waldo, in fact, showed more concern about Whitman's poetic relations with women than his dalliances with men, be they God or longshoremen. Emerson urged the suppression of the "Children of Adam" cluster—not the male camaraderie of "Calamus". Same-sex closeness was not considered an aberration in fifth century Greece BCE nor in nineteenth-century America. Ishmael was not concerned with sharing a bed at the Spouter-Inn with Queequeg—except for possible cannibalism on the harpooner's part. Biographers of Whitman either apologize for or salute his relationships with Fred Vaughan, Peter Doyle, Harry Stafford and perhaps, Warren Fritzinger.

There are no Mathew Brady daguerreotypes documenting *inflagranti delicto*—but it is clear that these relationships were more emotionally devastating than any the poet ever had with a woman. For Whitman is "forthwith a cipher" and believes that relations between men and men are as natural as those between women and men:

> Exactly the value of one and exactly
> value of two, and which is ahead?

Given the poet's stature it is not surprising that many have had a vested interest in sorting out the poet's sexual proclivities. Oscar Wilde seemed satisfied to this end and reported having kissed Whitman on the lips.[63] At the end of his long life, the poet and gay activist Edward Carpenter recounted an erotic encounter with Whitman when Carpenter had visited the poet as a young man. This was a confession reported through the offices of another, so it is tantalizing hearsay.

A more scandalous claim was published in *Walt Whitman at Southold* in 1939. Southold is a fishing town in Northeastern Long Island. The book was authored by the town historian, Wayland Jefferson. It recounts a lurid oral testimony from ancient mariners whose ancestors were students of Whitman's in 1840. As the tale is told, Whitman was declared a sodomite from the pulpit of the First Presbyterian Church by the Reverend Ralph Smith. With torches in hand, the townspeople hunted down the poet as if he were Frankenstein's monster incarnate. He was beaten, tarred and feathered, and run out of town. If the story is short on truth it might go some way to suggest why Whitman did not long continue his career as a teacher.

Shortly before his death the poet proclaimed that any homosexual (morbid) inferences to the "Calamus" cluster were mistaken, and "disavowed by me and even damnable."

> I am fain to hope the pages themselves are not to be even mention'd for such gratuitous and quite at the time entirely undreamed and unreck'd possibility of morbid inferences—wh'are disavowed by me and even damnable.[64]

Earlier in the twentieth century (1905), British author Henry Bryan Binns alleged that an affair with a New Orleans woman was the inspiration for Whitman's poetry. Whitman claimed to have fathered numerous children but that claim was probably truer of his literary persona than of Walter Whitman Jr. the author of *Leaves of Grass*. David S. Reynolds notes in *Walt Whitman's America*:

His sister Mary had five children: although next to nothing is known about her, we know for certain five more things about her sex life than about Walt's.[65]

The third and fourth Cantos now proceed. The excluded line from the 1855 edition : "As God[66] comes a loving bedfellow and sleeps at my side all night and close on the peep of the day…" appears in italics between lines 59 and 60.

3. I Have Heard

> I have heard what the talkers were talking, the talk of the beginning and the end,   38
> But I do not talk of the beginning or the end.
>
> There was never any more inception than there is now,
> Nor any more youth or age than there is now,
> And will never be any more perfection than there is now,
> Nor any more heaven or hell than there is now.
>
> Urge and urge and urge,   44
> Always the procreant urge of the world.

Out of the dimness opposite equals advance, always substance and increase, always sex, 46
Always a knit of identity, always distinction, always a breed of life.

To elaborate is no avail, learn'd and unlearn'd feel that it is so.

Sure as the most certain sure, plumb in the uprights, well entretied, braced in the beams,
Stout as a horse, affectionate, haughty, electrical,
I and this mystery here we stand.

Clear and sweet is my soul and clear and sweet is all that is not my soul.
Lack one lacks both and the unseen is proved by the seen, 53
Till that becomes unseen and receives proof in its turn.

Showing the best and dividing it from the worst age vexes age,
Knowing the perfect fitness and equanimity of things, while they discuss I am silent, and go and bathe and admire myself.

Welcome is every organ and attribute of me, and of any man hearty and clean,

Not an inch nor a particle of an inch is
    vile, and none shall be less familiar
    than the rest.

I am satisfied — I see, dance, laugh, sing;   59
As God comes a loving bedfellow and sleeps
    at my side all night and close on the
    peep of the day.
As the hugging and loving bed-fellow
    sleeps at my side through the night
    and withdraws at the peep of the
    day with stealthy tread,   60
Leaving me baskets cover'd with white
    towels swelling the house with
    plenty,
Shall I postpone my acceptance and
    realization and scream at my eyes,   62
That they turn from gazing after and
    down the road,
And forthwith cipher and show me to a
    cent,
Exactly the value of one and exactly the
    value of two, and which is ahead.   65

4. Trippers and Askers

Trippers and askers surround me,   66
People I meet, the effect upon me of my
    early life or the ward and city I live
    in, or the nation,
The latest dates, discoveries, inventions,
    societies, authors old and new,
My dinner, dress, associates, looks,
    compliments, dues,

> The real or fancied indifference of some man or woman I love,
> The sickness of one of my folks or of myself, or ill-doing or loss or lack of money, or depressions or exaltations,
> Battles, the horrors of fratricidal war, the fever of doubtful news, the fitful events;
> These come to me day and nights and go from me again,
> But they are not the Me myself. 74
>
> Apart from the pulling and hauling stand what I am,
> Stands amused, complacent, compassionating, idle, unitary,
> Look s down, is erect, or bends an arm on an impalpable certain rest,
> Looking with side-curved head curious what will come next,
> Both in and out of the game and watching and wondering at it. 79
>
> Backward I see in my own days where I sweated through fog, with linguists and contenders,
> I have no mocking or arguments, I witness and wait. 81

If one hadn't suspected genius in the first three *weeks* (Cantos) of his poem, here, as the month concludes, in *Trippers and Askers*, we find ourselves with the obvious presentation of it — we have begun to realize that many of the 52 Cantos are masterpieces in themselves.

Aside from an epic, we mostly encounter poems as brevities. We hurry through Whitman's extended verse at our own peril. Each line is pregnant with outlandish subtleties—if we seek to speed through them they will be compromised. It is not overly extravagant to read a Canto a week during the fifty-two weeks that the poems together mirror. Here, in the sixteen lines of "Trippers and Askers", is a developmental biography of the poet's consciousness. He is pummeled no less by the winds of fortune than those that assail us all: The people he meets; the city and ward wherein he lives; the discoveries; inventions; authors (old and new); his infatuations; the health of his parents; the loss or lack of money; war; doubtful news and fitful events—a universal summary with which all can relate—each comes to him and departs—none are the "Me myself." (Line 74 above) Behind the events of his biography is the *being* that scans the events. For most of us the events are preeminent and prevail—for the select among us, the *being* behind the objects surveyed is also identity.

It is among the major epiphanies that Whitman and Emerson shared. This is Emerson from two different Essays directed to the same end:

> I conceive a man as always spoken to from behind, and unable to turn his head and see the speaker. In all the millions who have heard the voice, none ever saw the face...the well known voice speaks in all languages, governs all men, and none ever got a glimpse of its form. If a man will exactly obey it, it will adopt him, so that he shall not any longer separate it from himself.[67]

> The consciousness of each man is a sliding scale, which identifies him now (with) the First Cause, and now with the flesh of his body...the baffled intellect must still kneel before this cause, which refuses to be named...In our more correct writing we to give to this the name of Being, that we thereby confess that we have arrived as far as we can go. Suffice it for the joy of the universe that we have not arrived at a wall, but at interminable oceans.[68]

In the *Advaita Vedanta* of Shankara, the dualism of Brahman (all encompassing being) and Atman (the self) is an illusion. The path of consciousness is first to recognize the duality and then to dissolve it. Whitman sees that the attributes of his life are not the totality of his experience: "Apart from the pulling and hauling stands what I am." *That* "I am" is the face on Sinai which Moses was forbidden to see. In Whitman it becomes the *witness*—he, who with bent arm or side curved-head, stands amused, idle unitary—curious of what will come next—both in and out of the game, watching and wondering. The "trippers and askers" of the first line are recapitulated as "linguists and contenders" in the next to last. But the poet is unassailable and now beyond the fray:

> I have no mocking or agreement, I witness and wait.

In one of Whitman's most magnificent conceits he remembers the occasion of his *illumination*. The 5th Canto, *I Believe in You My Soul* is one of the wonders of World Literature.

Read lines 82-99 slowly and savor—I will then return to my commentary and suggest you read it again.

5. I Believe In You My Soul

> I believe in you my soul, the other I am must not abase itself to you,
> And you must not be abased to the other.   82
>
> Loafe with me on the grass, loose the stop from your throat,
> Not words, not music, or rhyme I want, not custom or lecture, not even the best,
> Only the lull I like, the hum of your valued voice.
>
> I mind how once we lay such a transparent summer morning,   87
> How you settled your head athwart my hips and gently turned over upon me,   88
> And parted the shirt from my bosom-bone and plunged your tongue to my bare-stript heart,   89
> And reach'd till you felt my beard, and reached till you held my feet.   90
> Swiftly arose and spread around me the peace and knowledge that pass all the argument of the earth,   91
> And I know that the hand of God is the promise of my own,   92

> And that all the men ever born are also my brothers, and the women, my sisters and lovers, 93
> And that the kelson of the creation is love,
> And limitless are leaves stiff or dropping in the fields
> And brown ants in the little wells beneath them,
> And mossy scabs of the worm fence, heap'd stones, elder, mullein and poke-weed. 98

As the poet would have it, he discovered his *soul* when *it* parted his shirt and plunged its tongue to his bare-stript heart (Line 89 above). His friend Richard Maurice Bucke relates that the date of this experience was either June of '53 or '54: "I mind how once we lay such a transparent summer morning." In the original '55 version of the line the poet had written: "I mind how we lay in June, such a transparent summer morning." This gives credence to Bucke's dating—but the key word is *transparent,* which is preserved in both versions. The dissolution of boundaries is one of the central insights reported in mystical vision: "If the reason be stimulated to more earnest vision, outlines and surfaces become transparent and are no longer seen."[69] It is also a major tenet in twentieth century physics where it is noted that a major characteristic of matter is the space between the molecules and the atoms themselves. Matter is as much a whirling dervish as any enraptured Sufi. The correspondence between Whitman's experience and the mystical report of the 16th Century's St. Teresa of Avila is one of the most striking of the mystic record:

> I saw in his hand a long spear of gold, and at the iron's point there seemed to be a little fire. He appeared to me to be thrusting it at times into my heart, and to pierce my very entrails; when he drew it out, he seemed to draw them out also, and to leave me all on fire with a great love of God. The pain was so great, that it made me moan; and yet so surpassing was the sweetness of this excessive pain, that I could not wish to be rid of it. The soul is satisfied now with nothing less than God. The pain is not bodily, but spiritual; though the body has its share in it. It is a caressing of love so sweet which now takes place between the soul and God...

In the earlier ecstasy, the saint is companioned by an angel that repeatedly plunges a long spear of gold into her heart. Even without the detail of the *fire at its tip* and her sensous *moan*, the erotic component is unmistakable. In Bernini's magnificent sculpture, Teresa swoons in ecstasy as she is showered by the golden rays of God's love. Not content to only elucidate the players in the drama, Whitman imagines an erotic encounter between them, as well. In line 52 of the '55 edition, God had slipped stealthily from his bed. Here, in the fifth Canto, his Soul outrageously plunges its tongue into the poet's bare-stript heart and reaches to feel him from beard to foot. Whitman's *soul* is a passionate contortionist—but the point of each episode is that their respective spiritual/erotic encounters has given them both a knowledge of the glory and love of God—which for Whitman is the "kelson of creation," and for the Zen master, Hakuin—"the lotus land of purity / and the body of the Buddha."

The ecstasy between material and spiritual is presented, here, at its apex — the poet knows that the hand of God is the promise of his own and that the spirit of God is the brother of his own. He sees that *limitless are the leaves stiff or dropping in the fields* [70] and as Emerson suggested:

> The true doctrine of omnipresence is that God reappears with all his parts in every moss and cobweb...[71]

From Meister Eckhart we have:

> Any flea, as it is in God, is nobler than the highest angels in the heavens...[72]

The younger poet agrees with both and concludes:

> And mossy scabs of the worm fence, heaped stones, elder, mullein and poke weed.

And then, in a beautifully designed or happy accident of poetry the concluding image of one masterful canto matches the opening image of another — as we close with poke weed in Canto 5 so we open with the grass in Canto 6. "A child said *What is the grass?*" is the premier signature line in all of Whitman and, perhaps, in American Literature. The path to wisdom is only approached on the occasion of doubt. In this seminal line, the poet calls into question the fundamentals of epistemology and ontology: What do we know and of what is it comprised? The supreme genius of the question is in conflating the child's query with the poet's doubt: "How could I answer the child?" You will search rigorously through the world's wisdom literature to find as succinct a posture:

> "Then I beheld all the work of God, that man cannot find out the work that is done under the sun: because however much a man labor to seek it out, yet he shall not find it..."[73]

The same could be said of the 6th Canto. You can behold the work on the printed page but to understand how it came to be there, how he came to put there, *however much a man labor to seek it out, yet he shall not find it.*

I invite you to ponder the wonder, power and expressive beauty of the printed word. Had the poet left us with nothing other than these 32 lines he would still remain revered in our collective memory.

6. A Child Said ...

A child said *What is the grass?* fetching it to me with full hands;	99
How could I answer the child? I do not know any more than he.	100
I guess it must be the flag of my disposition out of hopeful green stuff woven.	101
Or I guess it is the handkerchief of the Lord,	
A scented gift and remembrance designedly dropt,	
Bearing the owner's name someway in the corners, that we may see and remark, and say whose?	104

Or I guess the grass is itself a child, the
 produced babe of the vegetation.

Or I guess it is a uniform hieroglyphic,
And it means, Sprouting alike in broad
 zones and narrow zones,
Growing among black folks as among
 white,
Kanuck, Tuckahoe, Congressman, Cuff,
 I give them the same, I receive them
 the same.

And now it seems to me the beautiful
 uncut hair of graves.   110

Tenderly will I use you curling grass,
It may be that you transpire from the
 breasts of young men,
It may be if I had known them I would
 have love them,
It may be that you are from old people,
 or from offspring taken soon out of
 their mother's laps,
And here you are there mother's laps.

This grass is very dark to be from the
 white heads of old mothers,
Darker than the colorless beards of old
 men,
Dark to come from under the faint red
 roofs of mouths.

O I perceive after all so many uttering
 tongues,

And I perceive they do not come from
   the roofs of mouths for nothing.

I wish I could translate the hints about
   the dead young men and women,
And the hints about old men and
   mothers, and the offspring taken
   soon out of their laps.

What do you think has become of the
   young and old men?
And what do you think has become of
   the women and children?

They are alive and well somewhere,
The smallest sprout shows there is really
   no death, 126
And if ever there was it led forward life,
   and does not wait at the end to
   arrest it,
And ceas'd the moment life appear'd.

All goes onward and outward, nothing
   collapses,
And to die is different from what any
   one supposed, and luckier. 130

The first metaphor, *the flag of my disposition*, links the grass to the poet, himself. The more he searches his soul, behind the elusive "Me-myself", the more he comes to discover it in the world about himself — the interior *Being* mirrored in the totality of its outward reflection.

He is not alone in his conjecture: *Then shall also the Son be subjected to Him who put all things under him that God may be all in all* and *All things are united with one another, all in all* [74] and *As I am. All or not at all.* [75] And so we move from Saint Paul to Meister Eckhart to James Joyce, above--to Waldo Emerson, below, to conclude our *omnific* catechism:

> That only which we have within, can we see without. If we meet no gods, it is because we harbor none. If there is grandeur in you, you will find grandeur in porters and sweeps. He is only rightly immortal to whom all things are immortal.[76]

In the Chandogya Upanishad a famous dialogue is presented between Shvetaketu and his father, Uddalaka:

> Uddalaka
> But did you ask your teacher for the spiritual wisdom which enables you to hear the unheard, think the unthought, and know the unknown?
>
> Shvetaketu
> What is that wisdom, father?
>
> Uddalaka
> ...In the beginning was only being, one without second. Out of himself he brought forth the Cosmos and entered into everything in it. There is nothing that does not come from him. Of everything he is the inmost Self. He is the truth, he is the Self supreme:

Tat tvam asi.
You are that,

Shvetaketu, You are that.

Tat Tvam Asi is a mahatakyu or great saying from Hindu scriptures. Whitman would have had difficulty missing it during his earlier study of the Vedas—even the poet would rarely be as succinct. It should be noted that Whitman's question concerning the grass was asked by a child. It would not have been out of place in this ancient dialogue. Grass is emblematic of time and mortality. It is among the poet's best known metaphors. It is by contemplation of its ubiquitous, humble and fleeting nature that he is ferried into the eternal. Eckhart had grasped the same truth half a millennium earlier:

> Our life may be very small but if we grasp it to the extent that it is *being* then it is more noble than anything that has attained life. I am certain that if a soul only knew the smallest object that has being, that soul would never turn away from it, not even for a moment. If we were to know the smallest object as it is in God—say, if we were to know only a flower that has being in God—this object would be more noble than the whole world. To know the smallest object in God—to the extent that it is in *being*—is better than it would be for someone to know an angel.[77]

Shortly before the American Revolution Goethe published *The Sorrows of Young Werther*.

The young Goethe was greatly moved and influenced by the pantheism of Spinoza. Whitman's conception is closer to *panentheism*. For the Dutchman, there was only one substance and the seeming entities within that substance are attributes of it. In panentheism any entity embodies the whole and is not merely an adjunct to it. Goethe's hero is a romantic who will set off a wave of suicides by taking his own life for the unrequited love of a young lady he meets in the village of Wahlheim. Before taking that final *final* step Werther becomes contemplative of the whole world he finds within the blades of grass:

> I lie in the high grass near the tumbling brook and the earth near me is covered with a thousand small grass blades; completely absorbing and engrossing, I feel the myriads of a whole little world among the blades...then I pine and think: Oh, if thou couldst express that, couldst breathe out on paper what lives so warmly in thee!

The next stanza in Whitman's poem is a statement, *Or I guess it is the handkerchief of the Lord* which the poet adroitly turns into the question of "Whose?" (Line 104 above). The poet alternates single line stanzas with multiple line stanzas in the first of half of the sixth Canto. Notice that the single lines go from Whitman's disposition of *the produced babe of vegetation* to *the beautiful uncut hair of graves* — from cradle to corpse. Of all the great opposites that Whitman considers none is dearer to him than the opposition of life and death. It will be the basis of some of his most celebrated images and few more than here:

> Tenderly will I use you curling grass.
> It may be that you transpire from the breast of young men,
> It may be I had known them I would have loved them
> It may be you are from old people, or from offspring taken soon out of their mother's laps
> And here you are the mother's laps.

The juxtapositions he achieves in his contemplation of the grass are astonishing! From babe to old age—from grave to mother's laps—and then, from the red roofs of mouths: "And I perceive that they do not come from the roofs of mouths for nothing."

The grass grows from dead mouths so that those mouths can give witness or "hints about the dead young men and women, / And hints about old men and mothers, and offspring taken soon out of their laps." The equation of mortality with grass is, once again, a timeless metaphor: "...all flesh is grass...surely the people is grass. The grass withereth and the flower fadeth, but the word of God shall stand forever." [78] Whitman was to take no little inspiration from the dance and cadence of the King James, in general and Isaiah, in particular. Here in the sixth Canto of his celebrated *Song*, the poet peers into the abyss of man's greatest doubt and offers the balm of simple wisdom:

> The smallest sprout shows there is really no death. / And if ever there was it led forward life, and does not wait at the end to arrest it, / And ceased the moment life appear'd.

We hear here also the echo of Eckhart:

> We esteem dying in God so that he may remove us to a being better than life — a form of being in which our life goes on living to the extent that our life becomes being. People should go willingly toward death so that a better form of being will be theirs. To God nothing dies, for all things live in him.[79]

The seventh Canto continues the meditation on death. His readers are assured of the immortality of which he speaks: *They do not know how immortal, but I know.* (Line 138 below). Even at this early juncture, we suspect he very well might. It is a cherished theme that the poet will return to time and again. None of the world's great poets has staked out the poetry of death to so render its cadence into hope and affirmation.

7. Has Anyone Supposed?

> Has anyone supposed it lucky to be born? 131
> I hasten to inform him or her it is just as lucky to die, and I know it.
>
> I pass death with the dying and birth with the new washed babe, and am not contained between my hat and my boots, 133
> And pursue manifold objects, no two alike, and everyone good,

The earth good and the stars good, and
their adjuncts all good.

I am not an earth nor an adjunct of the
earth,
I am the mate and companion of people,
all just as immortal as and
fathomless as myself,
(They do not know how immortal, but I
know.) 138

Every kind for itself and its own, for me
mine male and female,
For me those that have been boys and
that love women,
For me the man that is proud and feels
how it stings to be slighted.

For me the sweet-heart and the old
maid, for me mothers and the
mothers of mothers,
For me lips that have smiled, eyes that
have shed tears,
For me children and the begetters of
children.

Undrape! you are not guilty to me, nor
stale nor discarded, 145
I see through the broadcloth and
gingham whether or no,
And am around, tenacious, acquisitive,
tireless, and cannot be shaken away. 147

Whitman knows that the surface of his skin is not a dividing line but rather a porous filter through which flows the world—a flow from which he is not distinct: "I am not contained between my hat and my boots." (Line 133 above).

This last is certainly among the more amusing *mahatakyus* of the work we are considering—and yet, this folksy aphorism takes us distantly beyond the empiricism that defines our world. Here the poet suggests there is more to your *being* than flesh adhering to bone— you are, so he asserts, wired into the entirety of the cosmos. This is also the contention of Meister Eckhart:

> The more God is in all things, the more He is outside them. The more He is within, the more without.[80]

And also that of the English mystic, William Law:

> But there is a root of depth of thee from whence all these faculties come forth, as lines from a centre or as branches from the body of a tree. This depth is called the centre, the fund or the bottom of the soul. This depth is unity, the eternity of thy soul.[81]

As such, he is becoming increasingly all-embracing: "You are not guilty to me, nor stale, nor discarded." This is a theme to which he will return and expand. He combines a fascinating blend of the spiritual and sexual. Meister Eckhart would often use the metaphor of God as a bride or mother:

> God from all eternity has given birth to his only begotten Son and continues to give birth now and into all future eternities—so teaches a master—and so God lies in the maternity bed like a woman who has given birth.[82]

"Undrape" (145 above) is a command of truth—but also a sensual declaration. He can see through the broadcloth and gingham to the naked truth and to the truth of naked flesh. In both instances he remains tenacious and cannot be shaken away. The eighth Canto begins a series of *Witness* scenes that concludes at the end of the fifteenth. In the first of three stanzas the poet begins with an infant: *The little one sleeps in its cradle* (line 148 below)—moves on to the second and adolescence: *The youngster and the red-faced girl* (line 150 below)—and then concludes in the 3rd with death: *The suicide sprawls on the bloody floor of the bedroom* (Line 152 below).

To the *witness* all events are equal in nature. As Emerson reminds us:

> Those roses under my window make no reference to former roses or better ones; they are for what they are; they exist with God today. There is no time in them. There is simply the rose; it is perfect in every moment of its existence.[83]

One might as well imagine a mountain "bad" for not being high enough. Whitman simply notes where the suicide sprawls—and then moves on. *The Theologia Germanica* notes:

> Goodness needeth not enter into the soul, for it is there already, only it is unperceived.

And, as well, Sen T'sen: "When the Ten Thousand things are viewed in their oneness, we return to the Origin and remain where we have always been.[84]" "The blab of the pave" begins a litany of existential experience that could be found in any village, town or city of his day. Each of them, from the *sluff* of "boot soles" to "the arrest of criminals" and "adulterous offers made," simply and exquisitely is recorded by the *witness*. My favorite is the recognition of the "buried speech that is always vibrating here, what howls restrain'd by decorum" — Pinter's silence meets Ginsberg's *Howl*. The poet minds them "or the show or resonance of them — I come and I depart."

8. The Little One Sleeps

> The little one sleeps in the cradle, 148
> I lift the gauze and look a long time, and silently brush away flies with my hand.

> The youngster and the red-faced girl turn aside up the bushy hill, 150
> I peeringly view them from the top.

> The suicide sprawls on the bloody floor of the bedroom, 152
> I witness the corpse with its dappled hair, I note where the pistol has fallen.

The blab of the pave, tires of the carts, sluff of boot-soles, talk of the promenaders,
The heavy omnibus, the driver with his interrogating thumb, the clank of the shod horses on the granite floor.
The snow-sleighs, clinking, shouted jokes, pelts of snow balls,
The hurrahs for popular favorites, the furry of the rous'd mobs,
The flap of the curtain'd litter, a sick man inside borne to the hospital,
The meeting of enemies, the sudden oath, the blows, the fall,
The excited crowd, the policeman with his star quickly working his passage to the center of the crowd,
The impassive stones that receive and return so many echoes,
What groans of over-fed or half starv'd who fall sun struck or in fits,
What exclamations of women taken suddenly who hurry home and give birth to babes,
What living and buried speech is always vibrating here, what howls restrain'd by decorum,
Arrests of criminals, slights, adulterous offers made, acceptances, rejections with convex lips,
I mind them or the show or resonance of them—I come and depart. 166

The 9th Canto is an example of a verse painting. Whitman enjoyed visiting galleries.

We will find examples of an exquisite painterly eye through out his *Leaves*. Canto 9 is a propitious beginning:

9. The Big Doors

> The big doors of the country barn stand open and ready, 167
> The dried grass of the harvest-time loads the slow-drawn wagon,
> The clear light plays on the brown gray and green intertinged,
> The armfuls are pack'd to the sagging mow.
>
> I am there, I help, I came stretch'd atop of the load,
> I felt its soft jolts, one leg reclined on the other,
> I jump from the cross-beams and seize the clover and timothy,
> And roll head over heals and tangle my hair full of wisps. 174

Constable's *The Hay Wain* is a possible progenitor of the poet's idyll. Whitman will employ actual paintings in his word pictures. In this instance the painting in question is more likely William Sidney Mount's *Farmer's Nooning*. Constable's painting is among the most famous of English landscapes and was produced in 1821. Certainly we have the dried grass of harvest time and a slow-drawn wagon and clearly the brown gray and the green of the stream are "intertinged."

In *Mount's* 1836 depiction a group of five young men enjoy the shade of a lone birch while a black farmhand lounges upon the premier seating of the hay wagon. It is left to the reader to imagine the poet rolling head over heels with a tangle of wisps in his hair. Whitman's experience was composed of anything that came within his ken—the books he read, the operas he heard and the museums he visited. One can imagine him standing next to sketch artists copying masterworks while making his own *word sketches* of the same paintings. After one of his last visits with Emerson he viewed a Millet collection in Boston. Millet's paintings of peasants, farmers and people from the countryside of France were sure to please the poet of the common man:

> Never before have I been so penetrated by this kind of expression. Will America ever have such an artist out of her own gestation, body, soul?[85]

10. Alone Far in the Wilds

> Alone far in the wilds and mountains I hunt. 175
> Wandering amazed at my own lightness and glee,
> In the late afternoon choosing a safe spot to pass the night,
> Kindling a fire a broiling the fresh-kill'd game,
> Falling asleep on the gather'd leaves with my dog and gun by my side.

The Yankee clipper is under her sky-
 sails, she cuts the sparkle and the
 scud,
My eyes settle the land, I bend at her
 prow or shout joyously from the
 deck.
The boatmen and the clam-diggers arose
 early and stopt for me,
I tuck'd my trowser-ends in my boots
 and went and had a good time;
You should have been with us that day
 round the chowder-kettle.

I saw a marriage of the trapper in the
 open air in the far west, the bride
 was a red girl,
Her father and his friends sat near cross-
 legged and dumbly smoking, they
 had moccasins to their feet and
 large thick blanket hanging from
 their shoulders,
On a bank lounged the trapper, he was
 drest mostly in skins, his luxuriant
 beard and curls protected his neck,
 he held his bride by the hand,
She had long eyelashes, her head was
 bare, her coarse straight locks
 descended upon her voluptuous
 limbs and reach'd to her feet.

The runaway slave came to my house
 and stopt outside,
I heard his motions crackling the twigs
 of the woodpile,

> Through the swung half-door of the
>   kitchen I saw him limpsy and week,
> And went where he sat on a log and led
>   him in and assured him,   193
> And brought water and fill'd a tub for
>   his seated body and bruis'd feet,
> And gave him a room that entered from
>   my own, and gave him some coarse
>   clean clothes,
> And remember putting plasters on the
>   galls of his neck and ankles,   196
> He staid with me a week before he was
>   recuperated and pass'd north,
> I had him sit next me at table, my fire-
>   locked lean'd in the corner.   198

The marriage of the trapper and the squaw cited above has been identified as *The Trapper's Bride* by Alfred Jacob Miller. In 1889 *Harper's* paid Whitman twenty-five dollars to write a companion poem to George Inness' *The Valley of the Shadow of Death*. The poem, which he called *Death's Valley*, and the painting were printed in the magazine the month following the poet's death in March of '92. It, along with a companion poem entitled *On the Same Picture*, was one of the three last poems collected in "Old Age Echoes". Less a verse painting than a verse drama is Whitman's report (imaginary or otherwise) of the visit of a runaway slave. His nursing of the slave's wounds: "putting plasters on the galls of his neck and ankles" (line 196 above) foreshadows his years as a wound dresser in the civil war. The drama itself was taken from a notebook entry (immediately below) from which he developed the idea. Note that the poet's empathy extends beyond the slave—to a rebel at the scaffold and Lucifer tumbling from the empyrean:

> The hunted slave who flags in the race
> at last, and leans up by the fence,
> blowing and covered with sweat,
> And the twinges that sting like needles
> his breast and neck
> The murderous buck-shot and the
> bullets.
> All this I not only feel and see but am.
> I am the hunted slave . . .
> What the rebel felt gaily adjusting his
> neck to the rope noose,
> What Lucifer cursed when tumbling
> from Heaven . . . .

If there is any question as for *whom* the fire-locked leans in the corner (line 198 above), one needs only reflect on the fragment: "Now Lucifer Was Not Dead". It originally appeared as a stanza in the '55 edition of the poem that would later become the solo canticle initially entitled "Night Poem" and ultimately, "The Sleepers".

> Now Lucifer was not dead . . . . or if he
> was I am his sorrowful terrible heir;
> I have been wronged . . . . I am
> oppressed . . . I hate him that
> oppresses me,
> I will either destroy him, or he shall
> release me.
>
> Damn him! How he does defile me,
> How he informs against my brother and
> sister and takes pay for their blood,
> How he laughs when I look down the
> bend after the steamboat that carries
> away my woman.

> Now the vast bulk that is the whale's
>   bulk.... it seems mine,
> Warily, sportsman! Though I lie so
>   sleepy and sluggish, my tap is
>   death. [86]

The passage is one the most powerful stanzas later excluded from the *Leaves*. In it the poet takes up the voice of a slave and seems to anticipate both Nat Turner and John Brown's raid on Harper's Ferry: "... my tap is death." In an uncollected poem called *Pictures* the poet describes a series of portraits. Among the most telling is a black portrait: "...this head, huge, frowning, sorrowful—is Lucifer's portrait. "(But I do not deny him—though cast out and rebellious, he is my God as much as any.)"[87] Whitman had read Milton. He would know the strength of Milton's portrayal of Lucifer, as Melville had in the convergence of Milton and Shakespeare in the creation of Ahab. Whitman's sympathy to abolition is tempered, as was Lincoln's, by the desire to preserve the Union but here its depth is unmistakable: "I am oppressed... I hate him... Damn him!... takes pay for their blood... the steamboat carries away my woman."

Whitman became more conservative with advancing age. During the Reconstruction period he worked in the Attorney General's office as a clerk for a livable stipend of $1,600.00 a year. The Whitman who was to write the elegy for America's greatest President was then working for one of its worst. Andrew Johnson was the poorest and least educated of American Presidents. He was a Southerner who hated both the rich plantation owners and the slaves who were instrumental to their wealth and power:

> Blacks have less capacity for government than other races of people (they have) a constant tendency to relapse into barbarism.

Johnson later compared himself to Jesus Christ and declared that Lincoln's assassination had been ordained from on high to make him President. That alone should have set the poet off his morning cup of tea. Whitman admired Johnson's rise from poverty to power. The poet's all-embracing attitude was mostly evident in the rapture of the antebellum editions of his *Leaves*. Whitman, the grand egalitarian, became a reactionary, who in a less impassioned moment might have thought better than leaving this less than egalitarian reflection to posterity:

> As if we had not strained the voting and digestive caliber of American democracy to the utmost for the last fifty years with millions of ignorant foreigners, we have now infused a powerful percentage of blacks, with about as much intellect and caliber (in the mass) as so many baboons.[88]

Whitman would later regret the egregiousness of that proclamation. It was the cause of a serious breach between himself and his most fervent champion, William O' Connor. O'Connor had been a passionate abolitionist and continued to monitor the Negro's promise and progress into the reconstruction era. The rift lasted ten years. This is Burroughs' recollection of it:

> O'Connor became enraged at what Walt said about the unfitness of the Negroes for voting. They were in the habit of goring each other in argument like two bulls, and that time Walt was, I guess, rather brutal and insulting. It was in O'Connor's home. O'Connor fired up and turned on him. Walt took his hat and went home in a pet. Then when they met on the street the next day, Walt put out his hand; but William shied around and went on past. The iron had entered his soul. But when Walt was in trouble—over the Osgood affair—William rushed to the rescue. He opened the correspondence, and right away they got back to the old footing. He came to see Walt in '88, I think, and staid a week or more.[89]

That visit in '88 occasioned a softening of Whitman's views—near the end of his life. Traubel recorded a conversation with Whitman concerning the friendship in November of 1888:

> O'Connor was warm, earnest, eager, passionate, warrior-like for the anti-slavery idea...This in some ways served to keep us apart—though not really apart—(superficially apart). I can easily see now that I was a good deal more repelled by that devotion in William—(for with him it was the profoundest moral devotion)—than was justified. With these latter-day confirmations of

> William's balance...the latter succession of events—there has come some self-regret—some suspicion that I was extreme, at least too lethargic, in my withdrawals from William's magnificent enthusiasm... some things I did not see then I see now. After all I may have been tainted a bit, just a little with the New York feeling with regard to anti-slavery; yet I have been anti-slavery always—was then, and am now; and to all other slaveries, too, black or white, mental or physical.[90]

O'Connor would be dead within six months. We can be grateful that his "magnificent enthusiasm" resulted in the self-reflection that Traubel reported. And even with his New York "taint," Whitman's claim of being "anti-slavery always—was then, and am now," is also part of his Quaker heritage:

> The first collective protest against the slave system introduced by the English and the Spaniards into the New World, was made in 1688 by the Quaker Meeting of Germantown...They believed that the inner light was in all human beings and salvation came to those who lived in conformity with that light and was not dependent on the profession of belief in historical or pseudo-historical events, nor on the performance of certain rites, nor on the support of a particular ecclesiastical organization...

> Because Quaker theology was a form of eternity philosophy, Quaker political theory rejected war and persecution as a means to ideal ends, denounced slavery and proclaimed racial equality.[91]

Emerson's own intensity (a belated support of abolition and aversion to the South), figured in the reported dementia that afflicted him in his closing years. Whitman's attention to tens of thousands of wounded soldiers led to his early physical deterioration and the stroke of his middle age. His autopsy reported the cause of death as: "...pleurisy of the left side, consumption of the right lung, general military tuberculosis and parenchymatous nephritis." Lincoln, Emerson and Whitman were a trinity of victims, the most illustrious of the American Civil War. In light of this, it should be noted that the poet's harboring of the runaway slave immediately precedes one of his most personal and evocative cantos. The *Twenty-Eight Young Men* is Whitman's first major attempt at a parable. *Major* may seem too strong a word for story expressed in 18 lines. The tale is at once supremely sympathetic to the lonesome woman and erotically charged. At 28 years old, her age repeats the number of the young men frolicking in the pond. In the mid nineteenth century a twenty-eight year old woman would, as well, have been considered a spinster. We sense her desire and longing as she watches the twenty-eight young men bathe. Bathing can be loosely be used for swimming — but in the context and contrast of her attire's description: "richly drest aft the blinds of the windows" — they are clearly, naked. (See Appendix, Eakins' *The Swimmers*) The poet says he sees her splashing in the water though she stays secluded in her room. What happens next I will leave to the reader to discover.

Suffice it to say, in the succeeding century perhaps only Kafka and Borges could create a parable of such depth, as succinctly.

11. Twenty-Eight Young Men

> Twenty-eight young men bathe by the shore,
> Twenty-eight young men and all so friendly;
> Twenty-eight years of womanly life and all so lonesome.
>
> She owns the fine house by the rise of the bank,
> She hides handsome and richly drest aft the blinds of the windows.
>
> Which of the young men does she like the best?
> Ah, the homeliest of them is beautiful to her.
>
> Where are you off to, lady? For I see you,
> You splash in the water there yet stay stock still in your room.
>
> Dancing and laughing along the beach came the twenty-ninth bather,
> The rest did not see her, but she saw them and loved them,
> The beards of the young men glisten'd with wet, it ran from their long hair,

199

Little streams passed all over their bodies.

An unseen hand passed over their bodies,
It descended tremblingly from their temples and ribs.

The young men float on their backs, their white bellies bulge to the sun, they do not ask who seizes fast to them,
They do not know who puffs and declines with pendant and bending arch, 215
They do not think who they souse with spray. 216

Tennessee Williams:

1911-1983

It would take the passage of a hundred years for Whitman to find the audience that he sought. Tennessee Williams' Hannah Jelkes, from *Night of the Iguana,* will take up several of the themes that Whitman illustrates here in the 11th Canto of his Song. Hannah Jelkes is no less the playwright's voice than is the 29th bather of the poet's reverie.

In Williams' play the suicidal Reverend T. Shannon had been bound and secured in a hammock to keep him from taking *the long swim to China* — which from Mexico is no easy backstroke. Shannon succeeds in loosening the ties and exiting the hammock. As he moves about the verandah, Hannah attempts to distract him from near madness. They strike a bargain. He will resume his place in the hammock (without the ties) if he can ask her a question that has been on his mind. She replies: "Ask it, there's no set limit on questions here tonight." He counters with: "And no set limit on answers?" He asks her about her *love life*:

> HANNAH
> Would you mind repeating the question?
>
> SHANNON
> Have you never had in all of your life and travels any experience, any encounter, with what Larry-the-Crackpot Shannon thinks of as a love life?
> HANNAH
> There are ... worse things than chastity, Mr. Shannon.

SHANNON
Yeah, lunacy and death are both a little worse, maybe! But chastity isn't something that a beautiful woman or an attractive man fall into like a booby trap or an overgrown gopher-hole is it? I still think you are welching on the bargain and I...

HANNAH
Mr. Shannon, this night is just as difficult for me to get through as it is for you. But its you that are welching on the bargain, you're not staying in the hammock. Lie back down in the hammock. Now. Yes. Yes, I've had two experiences, well encounters, with...

SHANNON
Two did you say?

HANNAH
Yes, I said two. And I wasn't exaggerating and don't say "fantastic" before I've told you both stories. When I was sixteen, your favorite age, Mr. Shannon, my grandfather, Nonno, gave me thirty cents, my pay for my secretarial and housekeeping duties. Twenty-five cents for admission to the Nantucket Movie Theater and five cents extra for a bag of popcorn, Mr. Shannon. I'd sit at the back of the almost empty movie theater so that my munching of the popcorn would not disturb the other

patrons. Well one afternoon a young man sat down beside me…and pushed his knee against mine…and I moved over two seats but he moved over beside me and continued his…pressure! I jumped up and screamed, Mr. Shannon. He was arrested for molesting a minor.

SHANNON
Is he still in the Nantucket jail?

HANNAH
No. I got him out. I told the police it was a Clara Bow picture — it was a Clara Bow picture — and I was just overexcited.

SHANNON
Fantastic.

HANNAH
Yes, very! The second experience is much more recent, only two years ago when Nonno and I were operating out of the Raffles Hotel in Singapore, and doing very well there making expenses and more. One evening in the Palm Court of the Raffles we met this middle-aged sort of nondescript Australian salesman. You know — plump and bald-spotted, with a bad attempt at speaking with an upper class accent and terribly overfriendly. He was alone and looked

lonely. Grandfather said him a poem and I did a quick character sketch that was shamelessly flattering of him. He paid me more than my usual asking price and gave my grandfather five Malayan dollars, yes and he even purchased one of my watercolors. Then it was grandfather's bedtime. The Aussie salesman asked me out on a sampan with him. Well, he'd been so generous...I accepted. I did, I accepted. Grandfather went up to bed and I went out in the sampan with this ladies' underwear salesman. I noticed that he became more and more...

SHANNON

What?

HANNAH

Well...agitated...as the afterglow of the sunset faded out on the water. Well, finally, eventually, he leaned toward me...we were vis-à-vis in the sampan...and he looked intensely, passionately in my eyes and he said: "Miss Jelkes? Will you do me a favor. Will you do something for me?" "What," said I. "Well," said he, "If I turn my back, if I look the other way, will you take off some piece of your clothing and let me hold it, just hold it?

SHANNON

Fantastic!

HANNAH

Then he said, "I will just take a few seconds." "Just a few seconds for what," I asked him. He didn't say for what, but...

SHANNON

His satisfaction?

HANNAH

Yes.

SHANNON

What did he do with it?

HANNAH

He didn't move, except to seize the article he'd requested. I looked the other way when his satisfaction took place.

SHANNON

Watch out for commercial travelers in the Far East. Is that the moral, Miss Jelkes, honey?

HANNAH

Oh, no, the moral is oriental. Accept whatever situation you cannot improve.

SHANNON

"When it's inevitable, lean back and enjoy it" — is that it?

HANNAH
He'd bought a watercolor. The incident was embarrassing, not violent. I left and returned unmolested. Oh, and the funniest part of all is when we got back to the Raffles Hotel, he took the piece of apparel out of his pocket like a bashful boy producing an apple for his schoolteacher and tried to slip it into my hand in the elevator. I wouldn't accept it. I whispered: "Oh please keep it, Mr. Willoughby." He'd paid the asking price for my watercolor and somehow the little experience had been rather touching, I mean it was so lonely out there in the sampan with the violet streaks in the sky and this little middle-aged Australian making sounds like he was dying of asthma! And the planet Venus coming serenely out of a fair-weather cloud, over the Straits of Malacca…

SHANNON
And that experience…you call that a…

HANNAH
A love experience. Yes, I call it one.

SHANNON
That, that…sad, dirty little episode, you call it a…?

> **HANNAH**
> Sad it was—for the odd little man—but why do you call it "dirty"?
>
> **SHANNON**
> How did you feel when you went into your bedroom?
>
> **HANNAH**
> Confused, I... a little confused, I suppose...I'd known about loneliness—but not that degree or... depth of it.
>
> **SHANNON**
> You mean it didn't *disgust* you?
>
> **HANNAH**
> Nothing Human disgusts me unless it is unkind, violent. And I told you how gentle he was—apologetic, shy and really very *delicate* about it. However, I do grant you it was rather on the fantastic level.

It is clear that Hannah is a spokesperson for the playwright as was the more celebrated Blanche DuBois before her. It does Williams no disservice to suggest that the emotions of either spinster were his own. Both Whitman and Williams can easily envision the feelings of women because of the deep inversion that stimulates their empathy. The fact that Whitman could project his fantasy on the woman at the window makes the drama no less true to the character of his creation. And, as it is true that Whitman is the supreme poet of the autoerotic, so also Williams identified with the masturbating "middle-aged, sort of nondescript Australian salesman."

The emotional torments that both poet and playwright experienced were human torments—they are separated by a century but the years have done little to diminish the distance between them. Whitman is the 29th bather as surely as Williams is Hannah Jelkes. Whitman's "unseen hand" composes an erotic image descending from temple to ribs—he "puffs and declines with pendant and bending arch" and "the young men do not see who they souse and spray." Whitman's interest in working class males continues with the butcher boy and the blacksmith. He notes the grimed and hairy chests and *the lithe sheer of waists and massive arms*:

12. The Butcher Boy

> The butcher-boy puts off his killing-clothes, or sharpens his knife at the stall in the market. 217
> I loiter enjoying his repartee and shuffle and break-down.
>
> Blacksmiths with grimed and hairy chests environ the anvil,
> Each has his main-sledge, they are all out, there is great heat in the fire.
>
> From the cinder-strew'd threshold I follow their movements,
> The lithe sheer of their waists plays even with massive arms,
> Overhand the hammers swing, overhand so slow, overhand so sure,
> They do not hasten, each man hits in his place. 224

Whitman will as heroically champion the female as the male. His success with the former is witnessed by the numbers of women who were seduced by the poetry yet were spurned by the man. His previous observation of the butcher boy: *There is great heat in the fire,* suggests the direction of the poet's own predilections. It is a *heat* that continues below as he notes the negro's ample neck, breast and perfect limbs. "I behold the picturesque giant and love him." The thirteenth Canto also begins the poet's empathetic connection with creatures other than man. He absorbs oxen and oceans as he continues the lyrics of his *song*. The look of oxen seems more than all the print he has ever read — and this from a print-setter! The look of the bay mare, as well, shames all silliness out of him. He believes in the winged purposes of the wood drake and the duck. This pair will return as the doomed feathered lovers from Alabama in *Out of the Cradle Endlessly Rocking*. Whitman's sexual sublimation manifests itself in the deep spiritual regard he has for all of God's creatures and the creation in which they participate.

13. The Negro Holds Firmly

> The Negro holds firmly the reins of his four horses, the block swags underneath on its tied-over chain,   225
> The Negro that drives the long dray of the stone-yard, steady and tall he stands pois'd on one leg on the string-piece,
> His blue shirt exposes his ample neck and breast and loosens over his hip-band,

His glance is clam and commanding, he tosses the slouch of his hat away from his forehead,
The sun falls on his crispy hair and mustache, falls on the black of his polished and perfect limbs.

I behold the picturesque giant and love him, and I do not stop there,
I go with the team also.

In me the caresser of life wherever moving, backward as well as forward sluing,
To niches aside and junior bending, not a person or object missing,
Absorbing all to myself and for this song.

Oxen that rattle the yoke and chain or halt in the leafy shade, what is that you express in your eyes?
It seems to me more than all the print I have read in my life.

236

My tread scares the wood-drake and wood-duck on my distant and day-long ramble,
They rise together, they slowly circle around.

I believe in those winged purposes,
And acknowledge red, yellow and white playing within me,

And consider green and violet and the
    tuft crown intentional,
And do not call the tortoise worthy
    because she is not something else,
And the jay in the woods never studied
    the gamut, yet trills pretty well to
    me,
And the look of the bay mare shames
    silliness out of me.   244

Whitman's affection for nature continues in the 14th week of his song. From moose to prairie dog—to the litters and chicks of sows and turkey hens he further enlarges his reflected menagerie. He hears the *Ya-honk* of the gander and believes he finds its purpose directed toward the wintry sky. He is enamour'd of growing out of doors. He can eat and sleep with the wielders of axes and mauls and the drivers of horses. Carlyle's "It availeth a man little to rail against the sun for refusing to light his cigars," is echoed in the poet's refusal to ask the sky to come down to do his *good will* (Line 262 below).

14. The Wild Gander

The wild gander leads his flock through
    the cool night,   245
Ya-honk he says, and sounds it down to
    me like an invitation,
The pert may suppose it meaningless,
    but I listening close,
Find its purpose and place it up there
    toward the wintry sky.

The sharp-hoof'd moose of the north, the cat on the house-sill, the chickadee, the prairie-dog,
The litter of the grunting sow as they tug at her teats,
The brood of the turkey-hen and she with her half-spread wings,
I see in them and myself the same old law.

The press of my foot to the earth springs a hundred affections,
They scorn the best I can do to relate them.

I am enamour'd of growing out-doors,
Of men that live among cattle or taste of the ocean or woods,
Of the builders and steerers of ships and the wielders of axes and mauls, and the drivers of horses,
I can eat and sleep with them week in and week out.

What is commonest, cheapest, nearest, easiest, is Me,
Me going in for my chances, spending for vast returns,
Adorning myself to bestow myself on the first that will take me,
Not asking the sky to come down to my good will,
Scattering it freely forever.

At sixty-six lines the 15th Canto is the second longest section in the poem and longest up until this point. The list will seem pedestrian at times and then the poet will move us with the anticipated committal of his retarded brother Edward: *The lunatic is carried at last to the asylum...He will never sleep any more as he did in the cot of his mother' room* (Lines 273-274 below) – and then he will startle us with: *The malform'd limbs are tied to the surgeon's table, What is removed drops horribly in a pail* (Line 277 below). One is taken aback by the abruptness and the realism of the image.

When we realize that Eddie is less than three decades from committal and that Whitman is less than a decade away from his hospital service—comforting hundreds after amputations, we are moved by the vividness of a tragic prescience of both images.

The poet's eye is a wonder. The reader is challenged to savor the dozens of incisive, telling, sad, humorous, and all too human observations of which the 15th Canto is comprised. Also note that with the exception of three exclamation points the entire effort is a single sentence. *The Pure Contralto*, from whom we derive the canto's name, is only the first of a huge supporting cast:

15. The Pure Contralto

> The pure contralto sings in the organ loft, 264
> The carpenter dresses his plank, the tongue of his fore plane whistles its wild ascending lisp,

The married and unmarried children ride home to their Thanksgiving dinner,
The pilot seizes the king-pin, he heaves down with a strong arm,
The mate stands braced in the whale-boat, lance and harpoon are ready,
The duck-shooter walks by silent and cautious stretches,
The deacons are ordain'd with cross'd hands at the altar,
The spinning-girl retreats and advances to the hum of the big wheel,
The farmer stops by the bars as he walks on a First-day loafe and looks at the oats and rye,
The lunatic is carried at last to the asylum a confirm'd case,
(He will never sleep any more as he did in the cot in his mother's bed-room;)
The jour printer with gray head and gaunt jaws works at his case,
He turns his quid of tobacco while his eyes blur with the manuscript;
The malform'd limbs are tied to the surgeon's table,
What is removed drops horribly in a pail;
The quadroon girl is sold at the auction-stand, the drunkard nods by the bar-room stove,
The machinist rolls up his sleeves, the policeman travels his beat, the gate-keeper marks who pass,

The young fellow drives the express-wagon, (I love him, though I do not know him;)
The half-breed straps on his light boots to compete in the race,
The western turkey-shooting draws old and young, some lean on their rifles, some sit on logs,
Out from the crowd steps the marksman, takes his position, levels his piece;
The groups of newly-come immigrants cover the wharf or levee,
As the woolly-pates hoe in the sugar-field, the overseer views them from his saddle,
The bugle calls in the ball-room, the gentlemen run for their partners, the dancers bow to each other,
The youth lies awake in the cedar-roof'd garret and harks to the musical rain,
The Wolverine sets traps on the creek that helps fill the Huron,
The squaw wrapt in her yellow-hemm'd cloth is offering moccasins and bead-bags for sale,
The connoisseur peers along the exhibition-gallery with half-shut eyes bent sideways,
As the deck-hands make fast the steamboat the plank is thrown for the shore-going passengers,
The young sister holds out the skein while the elder sister winds it off in

a ball, and stops now and then for the knots,
The one-year wife is recovering and happy having a week ago borne her first child,
The clean-hair'd Yankee girl works with her sewing-machine or in the factory or mill,
The paving-man leans on his two-handed rammer, the reporter's lead flies swiftly over the note-book, the sign-painter is lettering with blue and gold,
The canal boy trots on the tow-path, the book-keeper counts at his desk, the shoemaker waxes his thread,
The conductor beats time for the band and all the performers follow him,
The child is baptized, the convert is making his first professions,
The regatta is spread on the bay, the race is begun, (how the white sails sparkle!)
The drover watching his drove sings out to them that would stray,
The peddler sweats with his pack on his back, (the purchaser higgling about the odd cent;)
The bride unrumples her white dress, the minute-hand of the clock moves slowly,
The opium-eater reclines with rigid head and just-open'd lips,

The prostitute draggles her shawl, her bonnet bobs on her tipsy and pimpled neck, 305
The crowd laugh at her blackguard oaths, the men jeer and wink to each other, 306
(Miserable! I do not laugh at your oaths nor jeer you;) 307
The President holding a cabinet council is surrounded by the great Secretaries,
On the piazza walk three matrons stately and friendly with twined arms,
The crew of the fish-smack pack repeated layers of halibut in the hold,
The Missourian crosses the plains toting his wares and his cattle,
As the fare-collector goes through the train he gives notice by the jingling of loose change,
The floor-men are laying the floor, the tinners are tinning the roof, the masons are calling for mortar,
In single file each shouldering his hod pass onward the laborers;
Seasons pursuing each other the indescribable crowd is gather'd, it is the fourth of Seventh-month, (what salutes of cannon and small arms!)
Seasons pursuing each other the plougher ploughs, the mower mows, and the winter-grain falls in the ground;

Off on the lakes the pike-fisher watches and waits by the hole in the frozen surface,
The stumps stand thick round the clearing, the squatter strikes deep with his axe,
Flatboatmen make fast towards dusk near the cotton-wood or pecan-trees,
Coon-seekers go through the regions of the Red river or through those drain'd by the Tennessee, or through those of the Arkansas,
Torches shine in the dark that hangs on the Chattahooche or Altamahaw,
Patriarchs sit at supper with sons and grandsons and great-grandsons around them,
In walls of adobie, in canvas tents, rest hunters and trappers after their day's sport,
The city sleeps and the country sleeps,
The living sleep for their time, the dead sleep for their time, 325
The old husband sleeps by his wife and the young husband sleeps by his wife; 326
And these tend inward to me, and I tend outward to them,
And such as it is to be of these more or less I am,
And of these one and all I weave the song of myself. 329

Is there anything more evocative than: "The living sleep for their time, the dead sleep for their time," (Line 325 above). Whitman's *Witness* is also Joyce's *Old Hill*:

> The year returns. History repeats itself.
> Ye crags and peaks I'm with you once
> again. Life, love, voyage round our own
> little world... All that old hill has seen.
> Names change: that's all.[92]

The poet's defense of a prostitute (Lines 305-307 above) is pure Whitman: *The crowd laughs at her blackguard oaths, the men jeer and wink to each other, (Miserable! I do not laugh at your oaths nor jeer you ;).* Those sentiments will emerge, again, in *To a Common Prostitute,* later in his *Leaves.* Some of the observations are quotidian, as is most of what constitutes our days. As noted, Edward was mentally and physically handicapped. His oldest brother Jesse would later be committed to an asylum. His sister Hanna's husband was violently abusive. His brother Andrew, named for the seventh president, became an alcoholic and married a prostitute. Andrew died in 1863. His widow would beg in the streets with her children and ply her *wares* in fifty-cent New York hotels and hovels.

The litany continues suggesting an inventory of which Emerson was critical. Yet the poem progresses as a day matures across the land. And here, again, we sense the ticking of Whitman's clock:

> ... and flatboatmen make fast for the
> dusk...the torches shine in the dark that
> hangs on Chattahooche...Patriarchs sit
> at supper with sons and grandsons and

> great grandsons around them...in canvas tents rest hunters and trappers...the city sleeps, the country sleeps...the living sleep for their time, the dead sleep for their time...the old husband sleeps with his wife and the young husband sleeps with his wife.

And, in the end, we realize that his witness has traversed over 180 lines from the 8th Canto's, *The little one sleeps in the cradle*, (Line 147 above), through the 15th's, *the young husband sleeps with his wife* (Line 326 above) — an astonishing performance that only becomes apparent after multiple readings of the cantos in question.Whitman reviewed six of Thomas Carlyle's books for the *Eagle*. Carlyle was profoundly pessimistic. He was darkly critical of democracy and believed there were not enough good people among the rabble from whom to select a leader. The democratic Whitman embraced all of mankind — for the Scotchman, only a select few were worthy of his adulation. He begins his book, *On Heroes, Hero-worship and the Heroic in History* with: "Universal History, the history of what man has accomplished in this world, is at bottom the History of Great Men who have worked here. They were the leaders of men, these great ones; the modelers, patterns, and in a wide sense creators, of whatsoever the general mass of man contrived to do or attain." For Carlyle, only the Hero was worthy of interest and ultimately, salvation — for the rest of mankind, damnation was favor too grand and good for them. He shared Gibbons' and Nietzsche's aversion to Christianity. He suggested it had degenerated into a vile, cloying religion of cowards. Whitman rejected Carlyle for his "cussedness and everlurking pessimism."

But Carlyle would also muse that history was an impossible discipline because there wasn't any past event that is not the off-spring of all prior events and also the cause of all future ones. That puts Whitman of "Kosmos," solidly in one aspect of the Scotchman's debt: "Sartor Resartus has all of Mr. Carlyle's strange wild ways; and all his fiery breadth and profundity of meaning." We recall Carlyle's Herr Teufelsdrockh, Professor of Things in General, from Book 1 of *Sartor Resartus*:

> Detached, separated! I say there is no such separation: nothing to be ever stranded, cast aside; but all, were it only a withered leaf, works together with all; is borne forward on the bottomless, shoeless flood of Action and lives through perpetual metamorphoses. The withered leaf is not dead and lost, there are Forces in it and around it, though working in inverse order; else how could a leaf *rot*? Despise not the rag from which makes Paper, or the litter from which the Earth makes Corn. Rightly viewed no meanest object is insignificant; all objects are as windows, through which the philosophic eye looks into Infinitude itself.[93]

And then, alone with Carlyle and the starry heavens, the vast, void night, noting the newborn and the soon to die—the reader will find, there as here, that we have come full circle from sleep to sleep—and that we might forgive an excess of inventory for the subtle beauty reiterating the poem's central thesis in the Canto's concluding lines:

> And these tend inward to me, and I tend
> outward to them,
> And such as it is to be of these more or
> less I am,
> And of these one and all I weave the
> song of myself.

The 16th Canto begins with a tabulation of opposites. He finds these within himself as he gazes outward to humanity. He is old and young; foolish and wise; maternal and paternal; child and man; coarse and fine; a Southerner soon as a Northerner. As one might imagine, we find these oppositions also in Emerson:

> Polarity, or action and reaction, we meet in every part of nature; in darkness and light; in heat and cold; in the ebb and flow of waters; in male and female...in the systole and the diastole of the heart... Super induce magnetism at one end of a needle, the opposite magnetism takes place at the other end. If the South attracts the North repels. To empty here, you must condense there. An inevitable dualism bisects nature, so that each thing is a half, and suggests another thing to make it whole; as spirit, matter; odd, even; subjective, objective; in, out; upper, under; motion rest; yea, nay.

THOMAS CARLYLE

1795-1881

16. I Am of the Old and Young

I am of old and young, of the foolish as much as the wise, 330
Regardless of others, ever regardful of others,
Maternal as well as paternal, a child as well as a man,
Stuff'd with the stuff that is coarse and stuff'd with the stuff that is fine,
One of the Nation of many nations, the smallest the same and the largest the same,
A Southerner soon as a Northerner, a planter nonchalant and hospitable down by the Oconee I live,
A Yankee bound my own way ready for trade, my joints the limberest joints on earth and the sternest joints on earth,
A Kentuckian walking the vale of the Elkhorn in my deer-skin leggings, a Louisianan or Georgian,
A boatman over lakes or bays or along coasts, a Hoosier, Badger, Buckeye,
At home on Kanadian snow-shoes or up in the bush, or with fishermen off Newfoundland,
At home in the fleet of ice-boats, sailing with the rest and tacking,
At home on the hills of Vermont or in the woods of Maine, or the Texan ranch,

Comrade of Californians, comrade of
free North-Westerners, (loving their
big proportions,)
Comrade of raftsmen and coalmen,
comrade of all who shake hands
and welcome to drink and meat,
A learner with the simplest, a teacher of
the thoughtfullest,
A novice beginning yet experient of
myriads of seasons,
Of every hue and caste am I, of every
rank and religion,
A farmer, mechanic, artist, gentleman,
sailor, Quaker,
Prisoner, fancy-man, rowdy, lawyer,
physician, priest.

I resist any thing better than my own
diversity,
Breathe the air but leave plenty after me,
And am not stuck up, and am in my
place.

(The moth and the fish-eggs are in their
place,
The bright suns I see and the dark suns I
cannot see are in their place,
The palpable is in its place and the
impalpable is in its place.) 354

The semanticists of the twentieth century have pointed out the necessity of opposites in the formulation of language. The world is divided primarily by a logic that Aristotle employed in the 4th century before the current era. $A = A$, $A \neq B$.

Those two statements are straightforward enough as long as one accepts the parameters of the A and B in question. Aristotle's distinction is used *spatially*, up and down; *socially*, success and failure; *esthetically*, the ugly and the beautiful; *morally*, good and evil; *logically*, true and false; *psychologically*, self and other; *epistemologically*, appearance and reality; and *ontologically*, being and nonbeing. Alfred Korzybski famously noted that a map is not the territory it seeks to describe. We cognitively separate a leaf from a twig and the twig from the branch and the branch from the tree in our imagination. Each of these entities could be divided inwardly into smaller composites or outwardly to the universe itself — any segment of thought is comprised of the segment and everything else — the two together are a reality of one — and such is so of any single item we so isolate.

This is Chuang Tzu of the same century as Aristotle:

> How can Tao be so obscured that there should be a distinction of true and false? How can speech be so obscured that there should be distinction between right and wrong?... But to show that what each regards as right is wrong or to show that what each regards as wrong is right, there is no better way than to use the light of nature. There is nothing that is not the "that" and nothing that is not the "this." Things do not know that they are the "that" of other things; they only know what they themselves know. Therefore I say the "that" is produced by the "this" and the "this" is produced by "that."

> This is the theory of mutual production. Nevertheless, when there is life there is death, and when there is death there is life. Where there is possibility there is impossibility... Because of the right, there is wrong, and because of the wrong there is right. Therefore the sage doesn't proceed along these lines...

Whitman's program is not only a celebration of time and eternity but also a relentless program to dissolve the opposition of self and other. For as he concludes his "witness" cantos with: "And such as it is to be of these more or less I am, / And of these one and all I weave the song of myself," so also here. He begins with the statement of opposites and then he moves to oppositions that geographically divide one American from another.

Here, Democracy meets Ontology. The poet opposes one state with another before concluding that he is "Of every hue and cast...Of every rank and religion" and even anticipates the astrophysicist's discussion of *dark matter*: "The bright suns I see and the dark suns that I cannot see are in their place, / The palpable is in its place and the impalpable is in its place."

Emerson is, again, instructive:

> Cause and effect, means and end, seed and fruit cannot be severed: for the effect already blooms in the cause, the end preexists in the means, the fruit in the seed...people suffer all their life long under the foolish superstition that they can be cheated.

> But it is impossible for a man to be cheated by anyone but himself, as it is for a thing to be and not be at the same time. There is a third silent party to all our bargains. The nature and soul of things takes on itself the guaranty of the fulfillment of every contract so that honest service cannot come to loss. If you serve an ungrateful master, serve him the more. Put God in your debt. Every stroke shall be repaid…There is a deeper fact in the soul than compensation, to wit, its own nature. The soul *is*. Under all this running sea of circumstance, whose waters ebb and flow with perfect balance lies the original abyss of real Being. Essence or God is not a relation or part, but the whole…the heart and soul of all men being one, this bitterness of His and Mine ceases. His is mine. I am my brother and my brother is me…It is the nature of the soul to appropriate all things…[94]

If you believe this thought not original with the two poets, our poet would agree:

17. These Are Really

> These are really the thoughts of all men in all ages and lands, they are not original with me,   355

> If they are not yours as much as mine
> they are nothing, or next to nothing
> If they are not the riddle and the untying of the riddle they are nothing,
> If they are not just as close as they are distant they are nothing.
>
> This is the grass that grows wherever the land is and the water is,
> This the common air that bathes the globe. 360

The 1855 edition of this part of the poem concluded with the six lines listed immediately below:

> This is the breath for America, because it is my breath,
> This is for the laws, songs, behavior,
> This is the tasteless water of Souls—this is the true sustenance.
> This is for the illiterate, and for the judges of the Supreme Court, and for the Federal capitol and the state capitols,
> And or the admirable communes of literats, composers, singers, lecturers, engineers, and savans,
> And for the endless races of work-people, farmers and seamen.

Whitman believed, to his great disappointment, that his poetry was the verse of the common man. He is correct in presuming that his thoughts are not original—few thoughts are—but the presentation of his thoughts is highly original.

It should be asserted that rather than for the common man his verse is for the *uncommon* man. It is not inconsequential that Emerson was his first champion — clearly, that itinerant sage was one of the most uncommon minds to have yet graced humanity. But there is something naively touching in the younger man's desire to voice the concerns of the rough and tumble semi-literate of his day. The kinship he felt was undeniable. The correspondence between Peter Doyle and the poet as well as those between the poet and his own family show none of the lofty tropes of his *Leaves*. Rather, they each seem as humble and humdrum as anything in nineteenth century letters. Whitman was obviously of two, if not, multiple minds. He shared a profound intimacy with the likes of Doyle and a farm boy named Harry Stafford after the war. He would often assume a fatherly or avuncular stance and address his "darlings" as sons or dear friends. His inner circle of Bucke, O'Connor, Burroughs and Traubel and his association with Emerson, Thoreau, Carpenter and Wilde bespoke something more of the minds that he had engaged with his poetry. His own family could make little of his writings. And Whitman was as likely as not to share Shakespeare's iambic with Doyle than his own Niagara of free verse.

Emerson was an American aristocrat as was his friend, Henry James Sr. His sons, William and Henry Jr., were reluctant heirs to Emerson's intellectual legacy. Whitman was a carpenter's son who will strive to emulate the measure of another carpenter's son of an earlier era. Henry James Jr., although initially critical of Whitman, came to emulate the wound dresser in his visits to soldiers' hospitals during WWI.

As often as Whitman will follow Waldo's lead, we can not quite imagine Whitman musing:

> Do not tell me, as a good man did to me today, of my obligation to put all poor men in good situations. Are they my poor? I tell thee, thou foolish philanthropist, that I grudge the dollar, the dime, the cent I give to such men as do not belong to me and to whom I do not belong. There is a class of persons that by all spiritual affinity I am bought and sold; for them I will go to prison if need be; but your miscellaneous popular charities; the education at college of fools, the building of meeting houses to the vain end to which many now stand; alms to sots, and the thousand-fold Relief Societies: — though I sometimes succumb a give the dollar, it is a wicked dollar, which by and by I shall have the manhood to withhold.[95]

And again:

> Mankind divides itself into two classes — benefactors and malefactors. The second class is vast, the first a handful. A person seldom falls sick but the bystanders are animated with the faint hope he will die…Masses are rude, lame, unmade, pernicious in their demands and influence, and need not to be flattered but schooled.

> I wish not to concede anything to them, but to tame, drill, divide and break them up...the worst of charity is that lives you are asked to preserve are not worth preserving.[96]
>
> The visions of good men are good; it is the undisciplined will that is whipped with bad thoughts and bad fortunes. When we break the laws we lose our hold on the central reality. Like sick men in hospitals, we change only from bed to bed, from one folly to another; and it cannot signify much what becomes of such castaways, wailing, stupid, comatose creatures, lifted from bed to bed, from the nothing of life to the nothing of death.

Whitman's youngest sibling, his brother Edward, was born in 1836. *Eddy*, the last of the Whitman children, was retarded and an invalid who suffered seizures (probably epileptic) throughout his life. Whitman shared a bed with him through the late 1850s. He felt personally responsible for the boy after his father's death. He paid for Edward's upkeep in a variety of homes and would also make provision for the boy in each of the wills he would later draw. In his poem *Faces* he writes in horrific irony of the face of an advertising man falling in an epileptic fit:

> ... its wordless tongue gives out the unearthly cry, Its veins down the neck distend... its eyes roll till they show nothing but their whites, Its teeth grit ...

the palms of the hands are cut by the
turned in nails, the man falls struggling
and foaming to the ground while he
speculates well.[97]

Later in the poem he speaks specifically of his brothers' ailments: "I knew of the agents that emptied and broke my brother."[98] On August 1, 1888 Edward's seizures worsened and he was placed in the Blackwoodtown Insane Asylum in New Jersey. Whitman, also gravely ill, continued his payments of support. In another strange prescience from the '55 edition he writes:

> I saw the face of the most smeared and
> slobbering idiot they had at the
> asylum.[99]

In the year before his death, belying the chill of Emerson's "… it can not matter much," he visited the youngest of his siblings only to discover that the boy's hair had turned as white as his own and the stone visage of the retarded invalid stared in icy silence back at the solicitude of his broken older brother. For Whitman each man is the riddle and the untying of the riddle, each is the grass that grows wherever the land is and the water is — the common man is the common air that bathes the globe.

Before we leave the wintery judgments of his mentor we would do well to remember that Emerson was no stranger to tragedy. His first bride of three years, Ellen, died of tuberculosis in 1832 at the age of nineteen. As earlier noted, his son Waldo died of scarlet fever a decade later. Each death left his fabled serenity in tatters — he was inconsolable for months after each loss.

And like Whitman, Emerson cared for a retarded brother, Robert Bulkily Emerson, until his death in 1859. In "Spiritual Laws" he quotes an old adage that shows he was abundantly clear of his own short-comings:

> My children, you will never see anything worse than yourselves...as in dreams, so in the scarcely less fluid events of the world every man sees himself as a colossal, without knowing it is himself. The good compared to the evil which he sees is his own good to his own evil.

Whitman's "With Music Strong" again invokes the spirit of the *Bhagavad Gita*. He understands that you don't have victors without the fallen and defeated: "battles are lost in the same spirit they are won."

18. With Music Strong

> With music strong I come, with my cornets and my drums, 361
> I play not marches for accepted victors only, I play marches for conquer'd and slain persons. 362
>
> Have you heard that it was good to gain the day?
> I also say it is good to fall, battles are lost in the same spirit in which they are won. 364
>
> I beat and pound for the dead,

> I blow through my embouchures my loudest and gayest for them.
>
> Vivas to those who have fail'd!
> And to those whose war-vessels sank in the sea!
> And to those themselves who sank in the sea!
> And to all generals that lost engagements, and all overcome heroes!
> And the numberless unknown heroes equal to the greatest heroes known! 371

That he sides with the defeated puts him at odds with the capitalist spirit that celebrates only the winners on Wall Street. This from a "Thought" in *Autumn Rivulets*:

> To me all that those persons have arrived at sinks away from them, except as it results to their bodies and souls...
> And often to me they are alive after what custom has served them and nothing more...
> And often to me they are sad, hasty, unwaked sonnambules walking the dusk. 100

Whitman will never invest in the market nor be paid very much for his poetry; perhaps as a rich man he would have had to face the dilemma of *camels, eyes* and *needles*:

> Hast never come to thee an hour, / A sudden gleam divine precipitating, bursting all these bubbles, fashions, wealth? / These eager business aims — books, politics, art, amours, / To utter nothingness? [101]

As the second oldest and most competent of his siblings, he took up the mantle of provider. He will die a poor man but will borrow enough money to secure a large enough mausoleum to house those of his family that preceded him and those that will follow. The tomb episode doggedly hounded the poet's reputation. Whitman, at the time, was a near invalid and living off meager royalties and occasional small gifts from his friends. In a letter to R.M. Bucke in August of 1890 he alludes to the design of the tomb being based on a drawing by William Blake. The critic Higginson made much hoo-ha about monies still owed the stone masons at the time of Whitman's death and other debts that had gone unpaid by the poet. His friend Burroughs indicated that although he did, on occasion, receive gifts from admirers, they were never enough to end his financial woes:

> When Fields gave me this one hundred dollars to send him it struck him at just the right time. Fields gave Aldrich $10,000, and other authors, $10,000. But everyone enlarges on the help given Walt. They gave Aldrich and Howells and Sarah Orne Jewett purses of $5,000, and more, and *they* didn't need it. Mark Twain was helped tremendously by his wealthy friends.

> Walt had Eddie, his imbecile brother, to provide for, and was always fearing Eddie would be neglected after his death...It is ridiculous—the hullabaloo they make about the money given Walt.[102]

It is instructive to hear from Burroughs, a reminiscence going the other way: "Walt is very often lacking in the merest rudiments of common courtesy." He reports that the poet once pocketed two dollars from an Iowa man who requested an autograph, but Whitman never sent the autograph! [103]

By way of retort, Traubel reports this from the poet:

> You don't know, Horace, he said, what a good investment that stove has been: I take a few of the autograph fellows, put a match on top of them, apply a match: then the fire is here. It is a great resource in time of trouble.[104]

During the filming of *North by Northwest* Eva Marie Saint reported that co-star Cary Grant (perhaps remembering his childhood poverty as *Archie Leach*) would charge a quarter to any fan who had the temerity to approach him for an autograph.

As to the more serious allegations regarding the tomb, Whitman chose Camden's Harleigh Cemetery, or it might be more accurate to say the cemetery chose the poet:

Harleigh was among the first landscaped parks of its kind and the owners of the cemetery offered Camden's most illustrious poet a plot for the payment of a poem. If Whitman ever managed the desired poem it never made its way into *Leaves of Grass* — perhaps Whitman's remains were poem enough. The natural ambience of Harleigh appealed to Whitman. He selected a lot that was 20 feet by 30 feet — much larger than Shakespeare's "two paces of the vilest earth."

Whitman had something a little grander in mind. As noted it was inspired by a drawing by William Blake. However much he denied Blake's influence in his poems here it was acknowledged and certain. The tomb measured 15 feet high by 15 feet wide by 20 feet deep. In would consume 72 tons of Massachusetts granite and 15,000 bricks.

Although its amenities were few, it would eventually house, along with the poet, his father and mother, his sister, Hannah, his brother, George and wife, and finally return the closeted little Edward to his family's eternal circle and care. Whitman paid a total of $1,500 in payments over the first year. Less than a year and a half before his death, he was shocked to receive a closing bill for $2,500.00 and balked at the inflated balance. It was here that the rumors started stirring.

His friend, the lawyer Thomas Harned (who, along with Burroughs and Bucke, was an executor of the estate) sought to quell the old stories — two and a half decades after Whitman's interment in his granite accommodation.

The statement that W.W's friends raised a fund of $5,000.00 to go to the purchase of a home that Walt diverted it to the building of a tomb is out of whole cloth. Whitman already had a home clear, and he paid $1,700.00 for it out of his royalties. At a later period some New England friends sent him $700.00 to buy a seashore bungalow, but he preferred to stay in Camden... Walt never thought of a tomb until ten years after his mother's death. Through me the Harleigh Cemetery Company gave him a lot. I hold the deed in my hand, dated April 15, 1890 less than two years before his death. I went with him when he selected the lot. It was on a slight rising ground and he said to me, 'I think I will go into the woods.' Some stone masons got him to order the tomb which he thought would cost a few hundred dollars. They had $1,500.00 out of him. About a year before he died I found him greatly worried. An enormous bill was presented to him. He had hived some money from various sources, and was keeping it to make sure that his invalid brother, Eddie, should be properly cared for. I took the bill, and told the stone masons they could take their damned old tomb—that they had no right to impose on a man who had no idea of values. A few days after, I told Walt not to bother his head about the matter...suffice it to say that the bill was greatly reduced and settled. About this time he conceived the idea to have immediate relatives buried in the tomb, and now all eight spaces are filled. You know how attached he was to his family. I laughed at the idea of the tomb at the time, but Walt had the right vision...[105]

Despite the fuss over the mausoleum, Walt's sentiments were more akin to the beatitudes of Eckhart:

> Empty yourself of all that is yours and give yourself over to God. Make God to be your own as he is for himself his own, and he will be God for you as he is for himself, and nothing less. What is truly mine I have received from no one. If I have it from someone else it is not mine, it is hers or his from whom I have it...all goodness flows out from the overflow of the goodness of God. "Such a person comes home richer" than when he went out. Those who go out from themselves in this way will be given themselves more fully. And everything which such persons leave in multiplicity will always be returned to them in simplicity, for they find both themselves and everything else in the present now of unity. And those who go out in this way come home much nobler than they went out.

> Such persons live now in bare freedom and complete emptiness, having no need to possess or acquire anything, whether little or much. For everything belonging to God belongs to them.[106]

Whitman's identification with the defeated continues in the 19th Canto—"This Is the Meal". The meal is eaten at a table that he sets for all—yet he names (almost exclusively) the dispossessed: the kept-woman, sponger, thief, the slave, the venerealee—there shall no difference between them and the rest. He sees within the eyes of the lonely and lost a shared consciousness: "This is the far-off depth and height reflecting my own face, / This is the thoughtful merge of myself and outlet again." His great theme of the miraculous in the commonplace is taken up again with: "Do you take it I would astonish? Does the daylight astonish?" He concludes with his enchanting theme of intimacy: "This hour I will tell you things in confidence, I might not tell everyone, but I will tell you." (Line 388 below)

19. This Is the Meal

> This is the meal equally set, this the meat for natural hunger,   372
> It is for the wicked just same as the righteous, I make appointments with all,   373
> I will not have a single person slighted or left away,
> The kept-woman, sponger, thief, are hereby invited,

The heavy-lipp'd slave is invited, the
   venerealee is invited;
There shall be no difference between
   them and the rest.

This is the press of a bashful hand, this
   the float and odor of hair,
This the touch of my lips to yours, this
   the murmur of yearning,
This the far-off depth and height
   reflecting my own face,
This the thoughtful merge of myself,
   and the outlet again.

Do you guess I have some intricate
   purpose? 382
Well I have, for the Fourth-month
   showers have, and the mica on the
   side of a rock has.

Do you take it I would astonish? 384
Does the daylight astonish? does the
   early redstart twittering through the
   woods? 385
Do I astonish more than they?

This hour I tell things in confidence,
I might not tell everybody, but I will tell
   you. 388

The next twelve Cantos of the poem are comprised of 320 lines—approaching a near fourth of the poem's 1,345. They are of a piece and will be treated in a freer format than those discussed previously.

These lines are a precursor to the messianic 33rd Canto which will follow thereafter. They compete quite nicely with the skeptical aphorisms of Solomon that we know as *Ecclesiastes* — except the exquisite pessimism of the *Preacher* is darker than all but a handful of Whitman's observations. In the 12th Canto of *Starting From Paumanok* the poet takes aim at the Preacher's contention that everything is meaningless and chasing after wind:

> And I will show that there is no imperfection in the present, and can be none in the future,
> And I will show that whatever happens to anyone it may be turn'd to beautiful results…[107]

Whitman had earlier stipulated that to die was different than what any had supposed and luckier. *Ecclesiastes* is at once similar but remains a universe apart:

> "I praised the dead which are already dead more than the living which are yet alive…yea better than both did I esteem him which hath not yet been, who hath not seen the evil work that is done under the sun."

The first Canto of the next twelve begins with a series of questions: "Who goes there? How is it I extract strength from the beef I eat? What is man? What am I? What are you? Why should I pray? (Line 398 below) Why should I venerate and be ceremonious?" These are followed by a series of affirmations:

"I know I am solid and sound. I know I am deathless. (Line 406 below) I know the amplitude of time." Intermixed with these are some of his most notable aphorisms: "I wear my hat as I please indoors or out... I find no sweeter fat than sticks to my own bones... To me the converging objects of the universe perpetually flow... All are written to me and I must get at what the writing means. I reckon I am no prouder than the level I plant my house by... I exist. I am, that is enough..." In the 21st Canto the affirmations continue: "I am the poet of the body and I am the poet of the Soul... I am the poet of the woman the same as the man. I chant the chant of dilation or pride... We have been ducking and deprecating enough, I show that size is only development." (Line 430 below). He then suggests that to be the President is a trifle and that each will arrive there the same and pass on. He then imagines in his dilation and pride that he becomes a lover of the night: "Press close bare-bosom'd night.../ Night of the south winds.../ mad naked summer night." His apotheosis continues as lover of the earth with the ineffable: "O voluptuous cool-breathed earth. Earth of the slumbering liquid trees... rich apple-blossomed earth..." (Lines 435-445 below). In the 22nd Canto his lover becomes the sea: "I resign myself to you also — I guess what you mean...I believe you refuse to go back without feeling of me...dash me with amorous wet... Sea breathing broad and convulsive breaths..." The opposites are, once again, engaged: "I too am of one phase and all phases... Partaker of influx and efflux...extoller of armies and those that sleep in each other's arms...I am not the poet of goodness only, I do not decline to be the poet of wickedness also..." and then he reconciles the differences: "I find one side a balance and the antipodal side a balance...The wonder is always how there can be a mean man or an infidel."

The influence of Hegel is often cited in connection to the oppositions: *...one side a balance and the antipodal side a balance*. The dialectic of *thesis, antithesis and synthesis* is at work in the poet's thought. Reference is made to the German philosopher in several poems of late composition and his influence appears early in Whitman's *Democratic Vistas* in one of the greatest challenges ever presented to the American Republic:

> But precluding no longer, let me strike the key-note of the following strain. First premising that, though the passages of it have been written at widely different times, (it is, in fact, a collection of memoranda, perhaps for future designers, comprehenders) and though it may be open to the charge of one part contradicting another—for there are opposite sides to the great question of democracy, as to every great question—I feel the parts harmoniously blended in my own realization and convictions, and present them to be read only in such oneness, each page and each claim and assertion modified and temper'd by the others...I will not gloss over the appalling dangers of universal suffrage in the United States. In fact, it is to admit and face these dangers I am writing.

Whitman was to anticipate and decry the materialism of the coming *Gilded Age*. One of the great dangers of capitalism is the desire of wealth and the lopsided nature of its distribution.

The poet was an enthusiast of *spiritual gold*. This he accumulated on his long walks on the seashore or during his daydreams under any tree throughout Long Island that afforded him its welcome shade:

> Mrs. Brenton always emphasized, when speaking of Walt Whitman that he was inordinately indolent and lazy and had a very profound disinclination to work...When Whitman would come from the printing office and finish the mid-day dinner he would go out into the garden, lie on his back under the apple tree, and forget everything about going back to work...as he gazed up at the blossoms and the sky...
>
> Mr. Brenton would wait for him at the office for an hour or two and then send the "printer's devil" up to see what had become of him. He would invariably be found still lying on his back on the grass looking into the tree entirely oblivious of the fact that he was expected to be at work.[108]

Whitman was not preternaturally disposed to work. He arrived in New York during a great expansion in the Newspaper business. He was thought well enough to become editor at Brooklyn's *Daily Eagle* in 1846. His journalism career spanned the fifteen years prior to the appearance of *Leaves of Grass*. He worked for *The Long Islander*, Brooklyn's *Evening Star*, The Brooklyn *Freeman*, The *New York Sunday Dispatch* and New York's *Aurora*.

He was sometimes fired for being at odds with the owners of the papers and sometimes dismissed for enjoying a work ethic that would find him, as above, under an apple tree or strolling nattily down the bustling avenues of Manhattan: Few of such oscitant inclinations have left us so much:

> (He) usually wore a frock coat and high hat, carried a small cane, and the lapel of his coat was almost invariably ornamented with a boutonniere...it was Mr. Whitman's habit to stroll down Broadway to the Battery, spending an hour or two amid the trees and enjoying the water view, returning to the office location about 2 or 3 o'clock in the afternoon.[109]

Herrick, of the *Aurora*, said of his fledgling editor: "There is a man about our office so lazy that it takes two men to open his jaws when he speaks...what can be done with him?"[110] Earlier the *Eagle's* editors couldn't resist commenting on a story suggesting that Whitman had been fired for kicking a conservative opponent down a flight of stairs: (Whitman is) "slow, indolent, heavy, discourteous and without steady principles...whoever knows him will laugh at the idea of his kicking anybody, much less a prominent politician. He is too indolent to kick a musketo (sic)".[111] Whitman's *American Dream* would not be shared by most Americans — just as Christ's admonitions against material wealth remain only a lofty ideal for most Christians. As he imagines that *Leaves of Grass* will become the New Bible he announces his own "New Testament" in the preface of the inaugural edition:

> This is what you shall do: Love the earth and sun and animals, despise riches, give alms to everyone that asks, stand up for the stupid and crazy, devote your income and labor to others, hate tyrants, argue not concerning God. Have patience and indulgence toward people, take off your hat to nothing known or unknown or to any man or number of men, go freely with powerful uneducated persons and with the young and with the mothers of families, read these leaves in the open air every season of every year of your life, re-examine all you have been told at school or church or in any book, dismiss whatever insults your own soul, and your very flesh shall be a great poem and have the richest fluency not only in words but in the silent lines of its lips and face and between the lashes of your eyes and in every motion and joint of your body.

Then, as if taking up the mantle of an Old Testament prophet, he counsels against the unflagging materialism he sees rampant in his democratic masses:

> Our country seems to be threatened with a sort of ossification of the spirit. Amid all the advanced grandeur of these times beyond any other which we know—amid the never enough praised spread of common education and common newspapers and books—amid

> the universal accessibility of riches and personal comforts—the wonderful inventions—the cheap swift travel bringing far nations together—that current that bears us is one broadly and deeply materialistic and infidel. It is the very worst of infidelity because it suspects not itself but proceeds to not believe the people of these days are happy. The public countenance lacks its bloom of love and its freshness of faith—for want of these it is as cadaverous as a corpse.

His early reading of Count Volney's *Ruins: or Meditation on the Revolutions of Empires,* along with his father's copy of Paine's *The Age of Reason* would develop his early distaste for the formality of organized religion. His parents' enthusiasm for Elias Hicks' radical Quakerism would further distance him from any institutional claim to preeminence or superiority. Hicks' declaration that the primary end of man is to enjoy the gift of life to the fullest would, as well, become a great theme shared by the poet. Earlier the Quaker founder George Fox had declared that:

> Everyman was enlightened by the Divine Light of Christ and saw it shine through all; and believed it came out of Condemnation and came to the Light of Life, and became the Children of it; and they that hated it and did not believe in it, were condemned by it, though they made a profession of Christ.

> This I saw in the pure Opening of Light,
> without the help of any man.

American Quaker William Penn declared: "There is something nearer to us than the Scriptures, to wit, the Word in the heart from which all scriptures come." Whitman's reference to *not removing his hat to anyone known or unknown* is a Quaker sensibility. Fanny Wright's *A Few Days in Athens* was also a prominent volume in his father's library. Walt Senior's sternness moved his young son to become more emotionally entwined with his mother. He would little acknowledge his father in his later writings as he was also prone to forget a good deal of his debt to Emerson—but both had an abiding influence on the development of his intellect. Wright's book centers on a debate between the Stoic and the Epicurean School of Athens. It would be the basis of his later interest in the Lucretian Roman School of Epicurean thought.

Both Epicurus and Lucretius believed that religion was among the chief impediments to man's happiness. They were both advocates of pleasure: *an avoidance of pain in the pursuit of a rightful happiness*. This limited definition of pleasure was ignored by their critics. Epicureans, like Whitman and Henry Miller thereafter would be charged with absolute depravity. Miller and Whitman shared the world's stage for exactly three months. Miller came into the world on the 26th of December, 1891 and the poet departed on March 26, 1892.

HENRY MILLER

1891-1980

This is Miller's indictment of Western Civilization in the decade after WWI:

There is something more involved—not just manhood perhaps but will. It's like a man in the trenches again: he doesn't know any more why he should go on living, because if he escapes now he'll only be caught later, but he goes on just the same, and even though he has the soul of a cockroach and has admitted as much to himself, give him a gun or a knife or even just his bare nails and he'll go on slaughtering, he'd slaughter a million men rather than ask himself why...He's like a machine throwing out newspapers, millions and billions of them every day, and the front page is loaded with catastrophes, with riots, murders, explosions, collisions, but he doesn't feel anything...if somebody doesn't turn the switch off; he'll never know what it means to die; you can't die if your own proper body has been stolen...you can go to the trenches and be blown to bits; nothing will create that spark of passion if there isn't the intervention of a human hand. Somebody has to put his hand into the machine and let it be wrenched off...somebody has to do this without hope of reward...somebody whose chest is so thin that a medal would make him a hunchback...Otherwise this show'll go on forever. There is no way out of this mess.[112]

And this is Walt Whitman's indictment of the United States in the decade after the Civil War:

> To him or her within whose thought rages the battle, advancing, retreating, between democracy's convictions, aspirations and the people's crudeness, vice, caprices, I mainly write this essay. I shall use the words America and democracy as convertible terms. Not an ordinary one is the issue. The United States are destined either to surmount the gorgeous history of feudalism, or else prove the most tremendous failure of all time.[113]

IMMANUEL KANT:

1724 – 1804

Immanuel Kant was to play a great role in the American Transcendentalism of George Ripley. Emerson's *Nature* essay of 1836 was a foundational document. Transcendentalism was a philosophic adjunct of Unitarianism. Unitarianism arose at the end of the eighteenth century as a protest movement to the intolerance of Puritanism and American Calvinism. Both Ripley and Emerson were originally Unitarian ministers.

Emerson resigned over disagreements about the nature of Jesus and the claims attendant to the sacraments. Ripley remained a minister until his resignation in 1840 and the beginning of the socialist experiment of Brook Farm. In the 1830s many of the Unitarians had adopted elements of the philosophic idealism inherent in the teachings of Immanuel Kant.

In his essay on Plato, Emerson asserts:

> The knowledge that this spirit, which is essentially one, is in one's own and in all other bodies, is the wisdom of one who knows the unity of things...the nature of the Great Spirit is single, though its forms be manifold, arising from the consequences of acts. If speculation tends thus to a terrific unity, in which all things are absorbed, action tends directly backwards to diversity. The first is the course or gravitation of mind; the second is the power of nature. Nature is manifold. The unity absorbs, and melts and reduces. Nature opens and creates.

> These two principles reappear and interpenetrate all things… 1. Unity, or Identity; and, 2. Variety; We unite all things by perceiving the law which pervades them; by perceiving the superficial differences and the profound resemblances. But every mental act — this very perception of identity or oneness, recognizes the difference of things. Oneness and otherness. It is impossible to speak or to think without embracing both.

The Prussian thinker had earlier declared: "all knowledge is transcendental which is concerned not with objects but with our mode of knowing objects." When the physicality of objects is thrown into doubt there remains only the mind that configures what it comes to know: "The human mind can claim no direct mirror like knowledge of the objective world, for the object it experiences has already been structured by the subject's own internal organization."[114] Whitman was to see these two poles of transcendental thought under the manifest of a single mind — what Emerson called the *Oversoul* and Whitman, simply *the soul*. Each of these poets was influenced by the Hindu scriptures with which they were familiar. Eastern consciousness more comfortable and cognitive of the *one* — as opposed to the Western conscious connection to the *many*. Emerson suggests: *Oneness and otherness… It is impossible to speak or to think without embracing both.* And Whitman concurs: *I find one side a balance and the antipodal a side a balance.* (Line 470 below)

WHITMAN'S CODE: A NEW BIBLE, VOLUME I
M.C. GARDNER

Whitman will claim to contain multitudes—but he primarily sees himself as a trinity: Walt Whitman, Me myself, and the Soul—as in the more celebrated Catholic Trinity, these three are one. Such distinctions as not set or completely certain—sometimes they spill over into each other. Earlier in the century the composer Robert Schumann divided himself into a trinity comprised of a passionate Beethovenian (Florestan); a dreamy poetic introvert (Eusebius); and mixture of the masculine and feminine of he and his wife Clara. He called this personality *Master RARO* (claRA and RObert combined). Schumann was later afflicted by hearing a single note of music and angelic visions. When these turned demonic he attempted suicide by leaping into the Rhine. At his own request he was committed to a hospital for the insane and died two years later in July of 1856—one year after Whitman formulated his own trinity in the publication *Leaves of Grass*.

Walt Whitman (the "rough" of his poems) is a public persona and a poetic creation. That literary character is a god-like being that looks down the corridors of time and who is *not contained between his hat and his boots* or by any spatial restrictions—"my elbows rest in sea-gaps I skirt sierra, my palms cover continents.". He is also the generous lover who is happy to share his seed with the countless lucky women within whom he would willingly bestow it. The second being in his cartography is the "Me Myself." This is the interior man—a man who very possibly shared his seed with no one—at least no one that could bear him the athletic sons and daughters of his beloved states. He appears in the poems when he is most heart-breakingly human.

The wounded lover of the Calamus cluster—"For the one I love most lay sleeping by me under the same cover in the cool night," —the diffident poet adrift in Sea-Drift:

"I have not once had the least idea who or what I am...I perceive I have not really understood anything..." This is the Whitman that is "both in and out of the game" as he hustles his poems to print or stares in silent wonder at all he surveys:

> The suicide sprawls on the bloody floor of the bedroom,
> I witness the corpse with its dabbled hair, I note where the pistol has fallen.

The third being of his quintessential triad is the *Soul*. This is the deepest of the three and is shared by any and all who participate in *being*—inanimate rocks, the teeming millions of the globe or the spinning billions of the galaxies. It is by virtue of the *Soul* that his trinity can overlap.

The public persona is a fiction but by his understanding of the soul he can also believe the "Me Myself" to be the being of his own creation. In fact, that is one of his primary themes—that each of us is *that* Being, besides being the face we show the world or the one we share only with ourselves. Whitman is the *one*—his beloved democracy is the *many* of whom he is also all others—"I am the man, I suffered, I was there...all of these I feel or am."

Plato said that time is the moving image of eternity. Kant had stipulated that time and extension (space) were structures of the mind. In the 23rd Canto, Whitman declares: "I accept time absolutely. It alone is without flaw, it alone rounds and completes all." He then salutes science: "Hurrah for positive science! Long live exact demonstration! Gentleman, to you the first honors always!"

The impact of those exclamations is as close as the poet comes to sarcasm: "Your facts are useful, and yet they are not my dwelling...and more the reminders they of life untold." Blake is less than two decades in his grave and yet he seems to stir here, upon the page. The Englishman's war with Sir Isaac Newton is renewed in Whitman's "And beat the gong of revolt, and stop with fugitives and them that plot and conspire." In Blake, the revolution pitted the Imagination against Urizen (your reason). In Emerson, the agons are knowledge against piety:

> ...cleave to God against the name of God. When he has once known the oracle he will need no priest...I think that philosophy is still rude and elementary. It will one day be taught by poets.[115]

And so also we hear Wallace Stevens strumming his *Blue Guitar:*

> Throw away the light, the definitions,
> and say what you see in the dark.

> That it is this or that it is that,
> But do not use the rotted names
>
> How should you walk in that space and
>   know
> Nothing of the madness of space,
>
> Nothing of its jocular procreations?
> Throw the lights away.
>
> Between you and the shapes you take
> When the crust of shape has been
>   destroyed.
>
> You as you are? You are yourself
> The blue guitar surprises you.[116]

In Canto 24 Whitman advises his readers to unscrew the locks from the doors and the doors from the jambs. He has arrived and the poet is nothing less than the Kosmos. Kosmos was the name of Alexander von Humboldt's classic integration of all the sciences. It's volumes were translated and published in America as: *Cosmos: A sketch of a Physical Description of the Universe*, over a twenty year period starting in 1845. It was one of the publishing events of its era and had sold over eighty-thousand copies by 1851.

It should be remembered that Josiah Holbrook's 1826 experiment of a lecture circuit, the *American Lyceum* in Connecticut, had become a national institution by the late 1840s. Whitman had made plans to join the circuit before attempting to become our national poet-prophet.

People were hungry for knowledge in a way that is difficult for our entertainment oriented culture to presently comprehend. Whitman reviewed a new edition of William Paley's 1802 *Natural Theology* in 1847:

> If the undevout astronomer is mad, the undevout physiologist is equally so. For all the great harmony of purpose evinced in the structure and movement of the worlds, is evinced—to our mind quite as wonderfully—in the structure and frame of animals and other growing life. Dr. Paley's *Natural Theology* but systematizes this great point.[117]

The great harmony of purpose is also the argument for *Creationism, the Argument from Design*. This was a period when the believing public and the preaching pulpit were disturbed over the discovery of fossils millions of years of age, evidently in conflict with *Genesis*. The British zoologist, Phillip Henry Grosse wrote *Omphalos, An Attempt to Untie the Geological Knot* two years after the publication of *Leaves of Grass*. Grosse is remembered for numerous books on marine biology and as the creator of the aquarium. He published his book *The Aquarium* in 1854. The Omphalos Argument was resurrected the twentieth century when Darrow and Bryan took teleological aim at each other in the 1925 Scopes trial in Clark County, Tennessee. Omphalos is Greek for navel. It has been suggested, down the centuries, that Adam had no navel, being created by God and not by the exigencies of flesh. Grosse argued that Adam did, in fact, have a navel but it was devised to make it look as if Adam had been "naturally" conceived.

Extrapolating from this premise he suggested that God also created fully grown trees that would show evidence of growing (rings) even though such growth had never occurred. It was but a small step to show that animals predating *Genesis* need not have existed at all but merely appeared to exist before Creation. Had Grosse known of DNA he could have as effectively argued that Joseph's half of the DNA in Jesus was not evidence of paternity — God had just arranged that it appear so.

Bertrand Russell lent the theory a certain mock respect when he suggested: "'there is no logical impossibility in the hypothesis that the world sprang into being five minutes ago, exactly as it then was, with a population that "remembered" a wholly unreal past. [118] Chateaubriand's post-revolution apologia to Christianity anticipated Grosse's conception by a half century: "God might have created, and doubtless did create, the world with all the marks of antiquity and completeness which it now exhibits."[119] Catholic monks of the medieval period believed the omphalos was God's mark of our humanity. Joyce imagined placing a phone call to Eden to so confirm it.

> The cords all link back, strand entwining cable of all flesh. That is why the mystic monks. Will you be as gods? Gaze in your omphalos. Hello, Kinch here. Put me on to Edenville. Aleph, alpha: nought, nought one. [120]

Two Rabbis of our own day continue the contention. This is Rabbi David Gottlieb:

> The bones, artifacts, partially decayed radium, potassium-argon, uranium, the red-shifted light from space, etc. — all of it points to a greater age which nevertheless is not true.[121]

Rabbi Nathan Slifkin begs to differ:

> God essentially created two conflicting accounts of Creation: one in nature, and one in the Torah. How can it be determined which is the real story, and which is the fake designed to mislead us? One could equally propose that it is nature which presents the real story, and that the Torah was devised by God to test us with a fake history! One has to be able to rely on God's truthfulness if religion is to function. Or, to put it another way — if God went to enormous lengths to convince us that the world is billions of years old, who are we to disagree?[122]

Who indeed? *Natural Theology* was soon to be supplanted by *Natural Selection*. Darwin's *On the Origin of Species by Means of Natural Selection, or The Preservation of Favored Races in the Struggle for Life* kept the *Natural* but did away with the *Theology*. Whitman saw, as did Spinoza two centuries before him, the divinity in all things. Both were *God-intoxicated*. Pantheism is, however, ill regarded by Theists. If one believes the Divine is evinced on the good green earth, one is not as likely to believe *It* ensconced in the gold of the starry Heavens.

In "Whoever degrades another, degrades me," we hear the echo of that other carpenter's son: "In so much you do it to the least of these you do also unto me." The poet then becomes even more emphatic as he announces his own Divinity:

> By God I will accept nothing which all cannot have their counterpart on the same terms...Divine I am on the inside and out and I make holy whatever I touch or am touch'd from, the scent of these armpits aroma finer than prayer, this head more than churches, bibles, and all creeds.

Canto 24 is one of the great celebratory songs of the *self* in *Song of Myself*. Each of its 61 lines is worthy of thought—though in 1855 each was thought more worthy of flame. The first two words are the poet's name which he declares a Kosmos. The second line delineates: "Turbulent, fleshy, sensual, eating, drinking and breeding." His command to "Unscrew the locks from the door!" must have struck many a reader with horror—for, aside from his own turbulent flesh, he represents the pariahs of mankind: "Through me many long dumb voices...prisoners and slaves...the diseased and despairing...thieves and dwarfs...the deform'd, trivial, flat, foolish, despised...Fog in the air, beetles rolling balls of dung." He then brings things down to a more personal level—he will not be silent or circumscribed by society's mores: "I do not press my fingers across my mouth...Through me forbidden voices, Voices of sexes, lusts, voices veiled and I remove the veil, / Voices indecent by me clarified and transfigur'd."

He moves from the beetle's dung to his own: "I keep as delicate around the bowels as around the head and heart." And then in the nineteenth century equivalent to dropping an "f-bomb," he asserts: "Copulation is no more rank than death is." And, as if one need further convincing, he suggests that: "I believe in the flesh and the appetites."

The remainder of Canto 24 is a glorious rant and spit in the eye of worship believed only legitimately found in a church pew. Even at this juncture we should remember that the poet closed the previous canto with: "The wonder is always and always how there can be a mean man or an infidel…" (Line 476 below), even as he shortly declares that he is "Divine am I inside and out, and I make holy whatever I touch or am touch'd from…" (Line 524 below).

Who but Whitman would imagine his penis as a *timorous pond-snipe*? Who but Whitman would give us a *Nest of guarded duplicate eggs*, for a pair of testicles? Who but Whitman would imagine the wind as genitals rubbing against him? Who but Whitman would see his *upward libidinous prongs suffusing the heavens with seas of bright juice*? This Canto is a miracle of his delight in miracles. Between lines 528 and 543 he ticks off a heady catalogue of seventeen of them concluding each line with the musical refrain of "it shall be you!"

These and others are such subversive and wild lyrics that I've grouped a selection of them below. They will appear again in their proper place and stanzas hereafter.

> Divine am I inside and out, and I make holy whatever I touch or am touch'd from, The scent of these arm-pits aroma finer than prayer, The head more than churches, bibles, and all the creeds. If I worship one thing more than another it shall be the spread of my own body, or any part of it...Firm masculine colter it shall be you...You my rich blood! You milky stream pale strippings of my life! Breast that presses against other breast...Root of wash'd sweet flag! Timorous pond-snipe! Nest of guarded duplicate eggs! It shall be you!...Mix'd tusseled hay of head, beard, brawn, it shall be you! You sweaty brooks and dews it shall be you! Winds whose soft tickling genitals rub against me it shall be you!... Something I cannot see puts upward libidinous prongs. Seas of bright juice suffuse heaven.

The poet then dotes on himself: "...there is a lot me and all so luscious, each moment and whatever happens fills me with joys... a morning glory at my window satisfies me more than all the metaphysics of books." He concludes the 25th Canto with "Writing and talk do not prove me. I carry the plenum of proof and everything else in my face. With the hush of my lips I wholly confound the skeptic." In the 26th Canto he advocates for hearing. The mystic, in an effort to seek his most interior state, allows all outward sounds to flood his consciousness without encumbrance.

I hear bravuras of birds, bustles of growing wheat, gossip of flames, clack of sticks cooking my meals, I hear the sound I love, the human voice. I hear all sounds running together combined, fused or following, Sounds of the city and sounds out of the city, sounds of the day and night... I hear the violin cello, the keyed cornet... I hear the chorus, it is grand opera, a tenor large, the train'd soprano, the orchestra—it sails me I dab with bare feet, I am cut by indolent hale, I lose my breathe, my windpipe throttled in fakes of death, At length let up again to feel the puzzle of puzzles and that we call Being.

The reader is now encouraged to linger and loaf through Cantos 20-25 of which we have only hinted—to further engage *the puzzle of puzzles and that we call Being* in the succeeding twenty-sixth.

20. Who Goes There?

Who goes there? hankering, gross, mystical, nude; 389
How is it I extract strength from the beef I eat?

What is a man anyhow? what am I? what are you?

All I mark as my own you shall offset it with your own,

Else it were time lost listening to me.

I do not snivel that snivel the world over,
That months are vacuums and the ground but wallow and filth.

Whimpering and truckling fold with powders for invalids, conformity goes to the fourth-remov'd,
I wear my hat as I please indoors or out.

Why should I pray? why should I venerate and be ceremonious? 398

Having pried through the strata, analyzed to a hair, counsel'd with doctors and calculated close,
I find no sweeter fat than sticks to my own bones. 400

In all people I see myself, none more and not one a barley-corn less,
And the good or bad I say of myself I say of them.

I know I am solid and sound,
To me the converging objects of the universe perpetually flow, 404
All are written to me, and I must get what the writing means.

I know I am deathless, 406
I know this orbit of mine cannot be swept by a carpenter's compass,

I know I shall not pass like a child's carlacue cut with a burnt stick at night.

I know I am august,
I do not trouble my spirit to vindicate itself or be understood,
I see that the elementary laws never apologize,
(I reckon I behave no prouder than the level I plant my house by, after all.) 412

I exist as I am, that is enough,
If no other in the world be aware I sit content,
And if each and all be aware I sit content.

One world is aware and by far the largest to me, and that is myself,
And whether I come to my own to-day or in ten thousand or ten million years,
I can cheerfully take it now, or with equal cheerfulness I can wait.

My foothold is tenon'd and mortis'd in granite,
I laugh at what you call dissolution,
And I know the amplitude of time. 421

21. I Am the Poet

> I am the poet of the Body and I am the poet of the Soul,   422
> The pleasures of heaven are with me and the pains of hell are with me,
> The first I graft and increase upon myself, the latter I translate into a new tongue.
>
> I am the poet of the woman the same as the man,   425
> And I say it is as great to be a woman as to be a man,
> And I say there is nothing greater than the mother of men.
>
> I chant the chant of dilation or pride,
> We have had ducking and deprecating about enough,
> I show that size is only development.   430
>
> Have you outstript the rest? are you the President?
> It is a trifle, they will more than arrive there every one, and still pass on.   432
>
> I am he that walks with the tender and growing night,   433
> I call to the earth and sea half-held by the night.
>
> Press close bare-bosom'd night—press close magnetic nourishing night!   435

Night of south winds—night of the large few stars!
Still nodding night—mad naked summer night. 436

Smile O voluptuous cool-breath'd earth!
Earth of the slumbering and liquid trees!
 439

Earth of departed sunset—earth of the mountains misty-topt!
Earth of the vitreous pour of the full moon just tinged with blue!
Earth of shine and dark mottling the tide of the river!
Earth of the limpid gray of clouds brighter and clearer for my sake!
Far-swooping elbow'd earth—rich apple-blossom'd earth! 444
Smile, for your lover comes. 445

Prodigal, you have given me love— therefore I to you give love!
O unspeakable passionate love. 446

22. You Sea!

You sea! I resign myself to you also—I guess what you mean, 447
I behold from the beach your crooked fingers,
I believe you refuse to go back without feeling of me,

We must have a turn together, I undress, hurry me out of sight of the land,
Cushion me soft, rock me in billowy drowse,
Dash me with amorous wet, I can repay you. 453

Sea of stretch'd ground-swells,
Sea breathing broad and convulsive breaths,
Sea of the brine of life and of unshovell'd yet always-ready graves,
Howler and scooper of storms, capricious and dainty sea,
I am integral with you, I too am of one phase and of all phases. 457

Partaker of influx and efflux I, extoller of hate and conciliation,
Extoller of armies and those that sleep in each others' arms.

I am he attesting sympathy,
(Shall I make my list of things in the house and skip the house that supports them?)
I am not the poet of goodness only, I do not decline to be the poet of wickedness also. 462

What blurt is this about virtue and about vice?

Evil propels me and reform of evil
  propels me, I stand indifferent,
My gait is no fault-finder's or rejecter's
  gait,
I moisten the roots of all that has grown.

Did you fear some scrofula out of the
  unflagging pregnancy?
Did you guess the celestial laws are yet
  to be work'd over and rectified?

I find one side a balance and the
  antipodal side a balance, 470
Soft doctrine as steady help as stable
  doctrine, 471
Thoughts and deeds of the present our
  rouse and early start.

This minute that comes to me over the
  past decillions,
There is no better than it and now. 474

What behaved well in the past or
  behaves well to-day is not such a
  wonder,
The wonder is always and always how
  there can be a mean man or an
  infidel. 476

23. Endless Unfolding

Endless unfolding of words of ages! 477
And mine a word of the modern, the
  word En-Masse.

A word of the faith that never balks,
Here or henceforward it is all the same to me, I accept Time absolutely. 480

It alone is without flaw, it alone rounds and completes all, 481
That mystic baffling wonder alone completes all. 482

I accept Reality and dare not question it,
Materialism first and last imbuing.

Hurrah for positive science! long live exact demonstration! 485
Fetch stonecrop mixt with cedar and branches of lilac,
This is the lexicographer, this the chemist, this made a grammar of the old cartouches,
These mariners put the ship through dangerous unknown seas.
This is the geologist, this works with the scalper, and this is a mathematician.

Gentlemen, to you the first honors always! 490
Your facts are useful, and yet they are not my dwelling,
I but enter by them to an area of my dwelling.
Less the reminders of properties told my words,
And more the reminders they of life untold, and of freedom and extrication,

And make short account of neuters and geldings, and favor men and women fully equipt,
And beat the gong of revolt, and stop with fugitives and them that plot and conspire. 492

24. Walt Whitman, a Kosmos

Walt Whitman, a kosmos, of Manhattan the son, [123] 493
Turbulent, fleshy, sensual, eating, drinking and breeding,
No sentimentalist, no stander above men and women or apart from them,
No more modest than immodest.

Unscrew the locks from the doors! 497
Unscrew the doors themselves from their jambs! 498

Whoever degrades another degrades me, 499
And whatever is done or said returns at last to me.

Through me the afflatus surging and surging, through me the current and index.
I speak the pass-word primeval, I give the sign of democracy,

By God! I will accept nothing which all
cannot have their counterpart of on
the same terms. 503

Through me many long dumb voices, 504
Voices of the interminable generations
of prisoners and slaves,
Voices of the diseas'd and despairing
and of thieves and dwarfs, 506
Voices of cycles of preparation and
accretion,
And of the threads that connect the
stars, and of wombs and of the
father-stuff, 508
And of the rights of them the others are
down upon,
Of the deform'd, trivial, flat, foolish,
despised, 510
Fog in the air, beetles rolling balls of
dung.

Through me forbidden voices, 512
Voices of sexes and lusts, voices veil'd
and I remove the veil,
Voices indecent by me clarified and
transfigur'd.

I do not press my fingers across my
mouth, 515
I keep as delicate around the bowels as
around the head and heart,
Copulation is no more rank to me than
death is. 521

I believe in the flesh and the appetites,

Seeing, hearing, feeling, are miracles, and each part and tag of me is a miracle.

Divine am I inside and out, and I make holy whatever I touch or am touch'd from, 524
The scent of these arm-pits aroma finer than prayer, 525
This head more than churches, bibles, and all the creeds. 526

If I worship one thing more than another it shall be the spread of my own body, or any part of it, 527
Translucent mould of me it shall be you!
Shaded ledges and rests it shall be you!
Firm masculine colter it shall be you!
Whatever goes to the tilth of me it shall be you!
You my rich blood! your milky stream pale strippings of my life!
Breast that presses against other breasts it shall be you!
My brain it shall be your occult convolutions!
Root of wash'd sweet-flag! timorous pond-snipe! nest of guarded duplicate eggs! it shall be you!
Mix'd tussled hay of head, beard, brawn, it shall be you!
Trickling sap of maple, fibre of manly wheat, it shall be you!
Sun so generous it shall be you!

Vapors lighting and shading my face it
  shall be you!
You sweaty brooks and dews it shall be
  you!
Winds whose soft-tickling genitals rub
  against me it shall be you! 541
Broad muscular fields, branches of live
  oak, loving lounger in my winding
  paths, it shall be you!
Hands I have taken, face I have kiss'd,
  mortal I have ever touch'd, it shall
  be you. 543

I dote on myself, there is that lot of me
  and all so luscious, 544
Each moment and whatever happens
  thrills me with joy,
I cannot tell how my ankles bend, nor
  whence the cause of my faintest
  wish,
Nor the cause of the friendship I emit,
  nor the cause of the friendship I take
  again.

That I walk up my stoop, I pause to
  consider if it really be,
A morning-glory at my window satisfies
  me more than the metaphysics of
  books. 549

To behold the day-break!
The little light fades the immense and
  diaphanous shadows,
The air tastes good to my palate.

Hefts of the moving world at innocent gambols silently rising freshly exuding,
Scooting obliquely high and low.

Something I cannot see puts upward libidinous prongs, 555
Seas of bright juice suffuse heaven. 556

The earth by the sky staid with, the daily close of their junction,
The heav'd challenge from the east that moment over my head,
The mocking taunt, See then whether you shall be master! 559

25. Dazzling and Tremendous

Dazzling and tremendous how quick the sun-rise would kill me, 560
If I could not now and always send sun-rise out of me. 561

We also ascend dazzling and tremendous as the sun,
We found our own O my soul in the calm and cool of the daybreak. 563

My voice goes after what my eyes cannot reach,
With the twirl of my tongue I encompass worlds and volumes of worlds. 565

Speech is the twin of my vision, it is
  unequal to measure itself,
It provokes me forever, it says
  sarcastically,
Walt you contain enough, why don't
  you let it out then? 568

Come now I will not be tantalized, you
  conceive too much of articulation,
Do you not know O speech how the
  buds beneath you are folded?
Waiting in gloom, protected by frost,
The dirt receding before my prophetical
  screams,
I underlying causes to balance them at
  last,
My knowledge my live parts, it keeping
  tally with the meaning of all things,
Happiness, (which whoever hears me
  let him or her set out in search of
  this day.) 575

My final merit I refuse you, I refuse
  putting from me what I really am,
Encompass worlds, but never try to
  encompass me,
I crowd your sleekest and best by
  simply looking toward you.

Writing and talk do not prove me,
I carry the plenum of proof and every
  thing else in my face,
With the hush of my lips I wholly
  confound the skeptic. 581

WHITMAN'S CODE: A NEW BIBLE, VOLUME I
M.C. GARDNER

In the years preceding the publication of the '55 edition, the poet's most enrapturing experiences occurred at the opera. There the disappointments of the day were dissolved in the arias that enveloped his imagination in the night. The power of the tenor and the purring legato of a soprano would transport him to interior expanses that he had only experienced in his youthful reveries by the sea. In early sketchbooks he dabbled with lines that would one day become *Leaves*. There we find an apostrophe to the opera, portions of which *do* end up in the inaugural poem and the canto we are now considering:

> I want the tenor, large and fresh as the creation, the orbed parting of whose mouth shall lift over my head the sluices of all delight yet discovered for our race—I want the soprano that lithely overleaps the stars, and convulses me like the love-grips of her in whose arms I lay last night—I want an infinite chorus and orchestrium, wide as the orbit of Uranus, true as the hours of the day, and filling my capacities to receive, as thoroughly as the sea fills its scooped out sands—I want the chanted hymn whose tremendous sentiment shall uncage in my breast a thousand wide-winged strengths and unknown ardors and terrible ecstasies—putting me through the flights of all passions—dilating me beyond time and air—Startling me with the overture of some unnameable horror —calmly sailing me

> all day on a bright river with lazy slapping waves—stabbing my heart with myriads of forked distractions more furious than hail or lightning—lulling me drowsily with honeyed morphine—tightening the fakes of death about my throat, awakening me again to know by that comparison, the most positive wonder in the world, and that's what we call life.

The prose in this passage is so cosmically vital that we perceive that it is on the threshold of bursting into song—the inaugural '55 edition of *Leaves of Grass*. For Whitman, opera, sexuality and spirituality are deeply entwined. Many of the preceding lines will make their way into Section 26. Among the most provocative is: "I want the soprano that lithely overleaps the stars, and convulses me like the love-grips of her in whose arms I lay last night..."

The 1853 concerts of Marietta Alboni were still fresh in his mind. Inspired by one of the great divas of the age, the poet's imagination even overleaps his sexual proclivities to land in the arms of a woman. Whitman will remove the *convulsive love-gripping* lines from subsequent editions of the poem. Here in Canto 26 it follows the replacement line 603: "I hear the train'd soprano (what work with hers is this?" It is for such deletions and replacements that Malcolm Cowley argues that the '55 edition is superior to those which succeeded it. Line 604 continues the final disposition of the *Deathbed* text.

The sexual and cosmic leaps of the prose passage anticipate Henry Miller's posturings in *Tropic of Cancer*. It is not difficult to hear a distinct echo of the earlier writer and the ticking of the *Whitman Clock* in Miller's embrace of time and eternity:

> If any man ever dared to translate all that is in his heart, to put down what is really his experience, what is truly his truth, the world would go to smash, that it would be blown to smithereens and no god, no accident, no will could ever again assemble the pieces...Today I am proud to say that I am inhuman, that I belong not to men and governments, that I have nothing to do with creeds and principles, I have nothing to do with the creaking machinery of humanity—I belong to the earth...I am inhuman! I say it with a mad hallucinated grin, and I will keep saying it though it rain crocodiles...I love everything that flows, everything that has time in it and becoming...

Note, that after Whitman's ecstatic lines he, as well, contemplates *being*: "At length let up again to feel the puzzle of puzzles, / And that we call being." (Line 610 below)

26. Now I Will Do Nothing

Now I will do nothing but listen,   582

To accrue what I hear into this song, to
let sounds contribute toward it.

I hear bravuras of birds, bustle of
growing wheat, gossip of flames,
clack of sticks cooking my meals,
I hear the sound I love, the sound of the
human voice,
I hear all sounds running together,
combined, fused or following, 586
Sounds of the city and sounds out of the
city, sounds of the day and night,
Talkative young ones to those that like
them, the loud laugh of work-
people at their meals,
The angry base of disjointed friendship,
the faint tones of the sick,
The judge with hands tight to the desk,
his pallid lips pronouncing a death-
sentence,
The heave'e'yo of stevedores unlading
ships by the wharves, the refrain of
the anchor-lifters,
The ring of alarm-bells, the cry of fire,
the whirr of swift-streaking engines
and hose-carts with premonitory
tinkles and color'd lights,
The steam-whistle, the solid roll of the
train of approaching cars,
The slow march play'd at the head of the
association marching two and two,
(They go to guard some corpse, the flag-
tops are draped with black muslin.)

I hear the violoncello, ('tis the young
    man's heart's complaint,)   594
I hear the key'd cornet, it glides quickly
    in through my ears,
It shakes mad-sweet pangs through my
    belly and breast.   596

I hear the chorus, it is a grand opera,   597
Ah this indeed is music — this suits me.   598

A tenor large and fresh as the creation
    fills me,
The orbic flex of his mouth is pouring
    and filling me full.

I hear the train'd soprano (what work
    with hers is this?)
*I hear the train'd soprano...she convulses
    me like the climax of my love grip.*
The orchestra whirls me wider than
    Uranus flies,   604
It wrenches such ardors from me I did
    not know I possess'd them,   605
It sails me, I dab with bare feet, they are
    lick'd by the indolent waves,
I am cut by bitter and angry hail, I lose
    my breath,
Steep'd amid honey'd morphine, my
    windpipe throttled in fakes of
    death,   608
At length let up again to feel the puzzle
    of puzzles,
And that we call Being.   610

Canto 26 is a warm up for the themes he will later develop in *Proud Music of the Storm*. Here, in the 26th Canto, we are introduced to the depths that music stirs within him: *I hear the violincello, 'tis the young man's heart's complaint* and the *cornet glides quickly in through my ears, It shakes mad-sweet pangs through my belly and breast.* (Lines 596-598 above) The opera: *It is a grand opera* – He hears the chorus, the tenor, the trained soprano and *the orchestra whirls me wider than Uranus flies.* (Lines 599-604 above) It wrenches ardors out of him that he didn't know he possessed. He loses his breath, it drives him to a near drug induced madness:

> Steep'd amid hony'd morphine, my windpipe throttled in fakes of death.
> (Lines 604- 608 above)

At the beginning of the 27th section the poet anticipates Nietzsche's doctrine of the *Eternal Return* and configures time's movement within eternity's rondure: *Round and round we go, all of us, and ever come back thither.* (Line 611 below) If you are having a bad day the thought of the eternal return is a dreary speculation, at best and damnation, at worst. Goethe's Faust was possessed of such restless striving that he could not imagine an instant of time to which he might say: "Linger awhile, thou art so fair." But the rapture that finds eternity in every moment welcomes rather than fears its return.

This, in fact, was Nietzsche's notion of happiness – the desire to say to every moment: Linger forever and forever return, for *thou art so fair*. Aside from its poetic (or horrific) possibility, Bertrand Russell suggests a logical one:

> The hypothesis that history is a cycle can be expressed as follows: form the group of all qualities contemporaneous with a given quality; in certain cases the whole of this group precedes itself. [124]

In Cantos 27, 28 and 29 Whitman turns from the last section's sense of hearing to the sense of touch. He has instant conductors all over his skin *that seize every object and lead it harmlessly through me...To touch my person to someone else's is about as much as I can stand...Is this then a touch?...Flames and ether making a treacherous rush for my veins.*

When he discusses the *treacherous tip of himself reaching and crowding to help them...* the Victorian sensibilities of the era found they were exploring body-scapes admissible only in smoke-choked brothels and torrid dreams. In *Calamus* he boldly celebrates same sex camaraderie. Here his touch is directed to himself and although he is his own most successful paramour, he finds the exigencies of masturbation almost as troubling: *Is this then a touch quivering me to a new identity...Flames and ether making a rush for my veins, Treacherous tip of me reaching and crowding. My flesh and blood playing out lightning to strike what is hardly different from myself...unbuttoning my clothes holding me by my bare waist...the sentries desert every part of me they have left me helpless to a red marauder, I am given up by traitors... I talk wildly I have lost my wits. I and nobody else am the greatest traitor, I went first to the headland, my own hands carried me there.* (Lines 619–639 below) The headland is both the *red marauder* of his genitalia and the furthest reach of the land into the sea.

It is the last of terra firma before the uncharted regions of the deep: *You villain touch! What are you doing? My breath is tight in its throat, unclench your floodgates, you are too much for me...* (Lines 640-641 below). D.H. Lawrence saw that Whitman attained the heights of consciousness because he had little truck with repression:

> By subjecting the *deepest centres* of the lower self, he attains the maximum consciousness in the higher self: a degree of extensive consciousness greater, perhaps, than any man in the modern world.

Canto 28 is a *masturbation sonata* written by the poet in great perturbation — it is other-worldly music reflecting a taboo that is universally experienced, and therefore an odd taboo, indeed. In Canto 29 he continues his tally of touch. There he addresses the pain of separation, either from his own auto-erotic passion or that which he shares with another: "Parting track'd by arriving, perpetual payment of perpetual loan." As to the gender of the lover, the metaphors: "Blind loving wrestling touch, sheath'd hooded sharp-tooth'd touch!, ...Rich showering rain and landscapes projected masculine, full-sized and golden...," (lines 642-647 below) leave little ambiguity. Taken together, with the *Kosmic* prelude of the 24th Canto, the introductory phrases of the 27th, the rising arpeggios of the 28th, and the climatic conclusion of the 29th -- these four movements become a startling symphony of the sensual word — excepting Wagner's *Tristan*, there few things quite like it in the spiritual ecstasies of the world.

27. To Be

To be in any form, what is that?   611
(Round and round we go, all of us, and
    ever come back thither,)   612
If nothing lay more develop'd the
    quahaug in its callous shell were
    enough.   613

Mine is no callous shell,
I have instant conductors all over me
    whether I pass or stop,   615
They seize every object and lead it
    harmlessly through me.

I merely stir, press, feel with my fingers,
    and am happy,
To touch my person to some one else's is
    about as much as I can stand.   618

28. Is This Then a Touch?

Is this then a touch? quivering me to a
    new identity,   619
Flames and ether making a rush for my
    veins,   620
Treacherous tip of me reaching and
    crowding to help them,   621
My flesh and blood playing out
    lightning to strike what is hardly
    different from myself,
On all sides prurient provokers
    stiffening my limbs,

Straining the udder of my heart for its
   withheld drip, 624
Behaving licentious toward me, taking
   no denial,
Depriving me of my best as for a
   purpose,
Unbuttoning my clothes, holding me by
   the bare waist, 627
Deluding my confusion with the calm of
   the sunlight and
   pasture-fields,
Immodestly sliding the fellow-senses
   away,
They bribed to swap off with touch and
   go and graze at the edges of me,
No consideration, no regard for my
   draining strength or my anger,
Fetching the rest of the herd around to
   enjoy them a while,
Then all uniting to stand on a headland
   and worry me. 633

The sentries desert every other part of
   me, 634
They have left me helpless to a red
   marauder, 635
They all come to the headland to
   witness and assist against me. 636

I am given up by traitors, 636
I talk wildly, I have lost my wits, I and
   nobody else am the greatest traitor,
I went myself first to the headland, my
   own hands carried me there.

> You villain touch! what are you doing?
> my breath is tight in its throat, 640
> Unclench your floodgates, you are too
> much for me. 641

29. Blind Loving

> Blind loving wrestling touch, sheath'd
> hooded sharp-tooth'd touch! 642
> Did it make you ache so, leaving me?
> Parting track'd by arriving, perpetual
> payment of perpetual loan,
> Rich showering rain, and recompense
> richer afterward.
> Sprouts take and accumulate, stand by
> the curb prolific and vital,
> Landscapes projected masculine, full-
> sized and golden. 647

The tactile is reprised in the last line of the first stanza of Section 30: "What is more or less than a touch?" Touch is traditionally a *touchstone* to truth. To get a handle on things is to get to know them up close—to get to know them *first hand*. It is also whereby we can assert personal knowledge—what we know to be the case from our grasp and embrace of the experience of which we testify. The 30th Canto is among the poet's most radical assertions on truth, belief and thought:

30. All Truths

> All truths wait in all things, 648

> They neither hasten their own delivery nor resist it,
> They do not need the obstetric forceps of the surgeon,
> The insignificant is as big to me as any, 651
> (What is less or more than a touch?) 652
>
> Logic and sermons never convince, The damp of the night drives deeper into my soul. 653
>
> (Only what proves itself to every man and woman is so,
> Only what nobody denies is so.) 655
>
> A minute and a drop of me settle my brain,
> I believe the soggy clods shall become lovers and lamps, 658
> And a compend of compends is the meat of a man or woman,
> And a summit and flower there is the feeling they have for each other, 660
> And they are to branch boundlessly out of that lesson until it becomes omnific, 661
> And until one and all shall delight us, and we them. 662

Whitman's "All truths wait in all things[125]," is neighbor to Emerson's "All the laws of nature may be read in the smallest fact." Both are preceded by two millennia of Buddhist conjecture. For the Hua Yen Buddhist, the *Gandavyhua Sutra* is the summit of Buddhism.

The *Gandavyhua* is the 39th and concluding volume of a larger collection called the *Avatamsaka Sutra*. This conclusion documents the visit of the pilgrim Sudhana to the "Tower of Maitreya". As the door opens he sees:

> ...the tower immensely vast and wide, hundreds of thousands of leagues wide, as measureless as the sky, as vast as all space adorned with countless attributes...canopies, banners, pennants, jewels, garlands of pearls and gems...showers of gold dust...arches, turrets, mirrors... images of enlightening beings...lotus ponds...arrays of all kinds of jewels... Also inside the great tower he saw hundreds of thousands of other towers similarly arrayed; he saw those towers as infinitely vast as space, evenly arrayed in all directions... Yet these towers were not mixed up with one another, being mutually distinct, while appearing reflected in each and every object of the other towers...just as a monk in the trance absorption in one of the points of totality is single-minded and undivided whether walking, standing still, sitting, or reclining, and sees and experiences the whole world through entry into the sphere of total absorption in whatever point of totality he is focused on, by the marvel of meditation, in the same way Sudhana saw all those arrays of whatever object he immersed himself in.[126]

BOROBUDUR

Photograph: by Jean-Marie Hullot

The vast temple complex of Borobudur at Magelang, on the island of Java, is an architectural statement of this same great theme. It was constructed in the 9th century CE and was a site of Buddhist pilgrimage for two centuries. It then was lost to the jungle overgrowth for eight hundred years until unearthed from superstition and legend shortly before Whitman's birth in the second decade of the nineteenth century. Under the direction of the British Governor-General Thomas Stamford Raffles, the Dutch engineer H.C. Cornelius and two hundred Javanese, the excavation commenced in 1814. It was finished twenty years later and is truly one of the great architectural restorations of the nineteenth century. The temple sits on a direct line with two other temples, Mendut and Pawon, completing the tri-body symbolism of the Mahayana Buddha.

Borobudur is a complex shrine or stupa that also doubles as the *Tower of Maitreya*—a huge architectural depiction of the body of Buddha and the body of the Universe. In Buddhism and in Whitman these are interchangeable terms of exact equivalence. The Buddhist Cosmos is depicted in the structure itself and fifteen hundred narrative bas reliefs that wind around the slowly ascending levels. The square base is considered the foot of the Buddha. Beyond the foot, the five ascending squares suggest the ascending structure of the physical body. The physical structure is succeeded by three circles representing the psychic structures of the Buddha. This culminates in the central stupa, spire and point around which the universe revolves, is reflected and contained. Aside from repeating the Triple body of the Buddha, the three levels also represent the world of sentient desire, Kamadhatu, the world of form,

Rupadhatu, and the world of the formless, Arupadhatu—anticipating Whitman's own cartography. More to the point are the "Stations of Sudhana". These mirror Sudhana's advancement toward the enlightenment he achieves in the Tower. The Stations are suggested by his pilgrimage to 52 enlightened beings in the pages of the *Gandavyhua*; in 52 galleries approaching the summit of Borobudur; and in the 52 Cantos of *Song of Myself*.

The philosopher emperor, Marcus Aurelius had a similar epiphany:

> To see the things of the present moment is to see all that is present now, all that has been since time began and all that shall be until the world's end...[127]

A thousand years later Meister Eckhart would concur:

> When is a man in mere understanding? I answer, 'When a man sees one thing separated from another.' And when is a man above mere understanding? That I can tell you: 'When a man sees all in all, then a man stands beyond mere understanding...I say that in the kingdom of heaven everything is in everything else, and everything is one, and everything is ours...this knowledge is without time and space and without here and now...

> In this life all things are one, and all things are united with one another, all in all and all in all.[128]

From the Zen perspective we have the reflection of Huang Po:

> Do not build up your views upon your senses and thoughts, but at the same time do not seek the mind away from your senses and thoughts, do not try to grasp reality by rejecting your senses and thoughts. When you are neither attached to, nor detached from them, then you enjoy your perfect unobserved freedom, then you have your seat of enlightenment.

And finally we'll let D.T. Suzuki have the final word on this point:

> When this is done, the world of the Gandavyhua ceases to be a mystery, a realm devoid of form and corporeality, for it now overlaps this earthly world; no it becomes 'That art it,' and there is a perfect fusion of the two. The Dharmadhatu is the Lokadhatu, and its inhabitants—that is all the Bodhisattvas, including the Buddhas—are ourselves, and their doings are our doings. They looked so full of mystery, they were miracles, so long as they were observed from this earthly end, where we

> imagined that there was something really at the other end; but as soon as the dividing-wall constructed by our imagination is removed, Samantabdhadra's arms raised to save sentient beings become our own, which are now engaged in passing salt to a friend at the table, and Maitreya's opening the Vairocana Tower for Sudhana is our ushering a caller into the parlor for a friendly chat.[129]

Each of these authors proclaim: "All truths wait in all things." Whitman further extrapolates: "I believe the soggy clods shall become lovers and lamps..." If all things are one thing, then it follows that *in time* everything becomes everything else: "And they are to branch boundlessly out of that lesson until it becomes omnific." We find this same assertion throughout Joyce:

> The voices blend and fuse in clouded silence: silence that is the infinite of space: and swiftly, silently the soul is wafted over regions of cycles of cycles of generations that have lived. A region where grey twilight ever descends, never falls on wide sagegreen pasturefields, shedding her dusk, scattering a perennial dew of stars.[130]

It is in this belief that the most mundane item or quotidian moment is fraught with the significance of revelation. It is only in the silence of the mind that it is experienced and explored.

The 31st Canto is a litany of the miraculous from that exploration: Grass is a journey work of the stars, an ant, a grain of sand and the egg of a wren are each perfect — and *the running blackberry would adorn the parlors of heaven*. In vain the creatures of the earth can not evade him:

> In vain the razor-bill'd auk sails far
> north to Labrador, I follow quickly, I
> ascend to the nest in the fissure in the
> cliff.

Pretend these declarations and those of the 32nd Canto's "I Think" are your own. Take these words as a personal credo and say them out loud. Be careful, wary reader — you may discover that as you believe and think, you find that you are — *tat tvam asi*...

31. I Believe

> I believe a leaf of grass is no less than
> the journey work of the stars,   663
> And the pismire is equally perfect, and a
> grain of sand, and the egg of the
> wren,
> And the tree-toad is a chef-d'oeuvre for
> the highest,
> And the running blackberry would
> adorn the parlors of heaven,
> And the narrowest hinge in my hand
> puts to scorn all machinery,
> And the cow crunching with depress'd
> head surpasses any statue,

And a mouse is miracle enough to stagger sextillions of infidels. 669

I find I incorporate gneiss, coal, long-threaded moss, fruits, grains, esculent roots,
And am stucco'd with quadrupeds and birds all over,
And have distanced what is behind me for good reasons,
But call any thing back again when I desire it.

In vain the speeding or shyness,
In vain the plutonic rocks send their old heat against my approach,
In vain the mastodon retreats beneath its own powder'd bones,
In vain objects stand leagues off and assume manifold shapes,
In vain the ocean settling in hollows and the great monsters lying low,
In vain the buzzard houses herself with the sky,
In vain the snake slides through the creepers and logs,
In vain the elk takes to the inner passes of the woods,
In vain the razor-bill'd auk sails far north to Labrador,
I follow quickly, I ascend to the nest in the fissure of the cliff. 683

Whitman found solace in the wide berth of his reading. He reviewed Justus Liebig's *Chemistry in Its Application to Physiology and Agriculture* for the Eagle: "Chemistry which involves the essences of creation, and the changes, and the growths, and the formulations and decays of so large a constituent part of the earth, and the things thereof!" Here, in science, was life-everlasting. All is a vast recycling organism. In chemical reactions forms are transmuted, move in and through the new life formed from the old.

The very leaves of the grass was the uncut hair of graves and showed their really was no death, in any final sense of the word. His reverence for animals continues in one of most popular and duly famed sections of *Song of Myself*--the 32nd Canto: "I think I could turn and live with the animals, they are so placid and self contained, I stand and look at them long and long." (Lines 684-685 below) His next assertions are a critique of nineteenth century religious practice: "They do not sweat and wine about their condition, they do not lie awake in the dark and weep for their sins, They do not make me sick discussing their duty to God... not one kneels to another, nor to his kind that lived thousands of years ago."(Lines 686-691 below) Emerson's most controversial statements were contained in his *An Address*, delivered to Divinity College in Cambridge:

> That which shows God in me fortifies me. That which shows God out of me makes me a wart... Men have come to speak of revelation as somewhat long ago given and done, as if God was dead...

> The need was never greater for new revelation than now... faith should blend with the light of the rising and setting sun, with the flying cloud, the singing bird and the breath of flowers...
>
> The assumption that the age of inspiration is past, that the Bible closed; the fear of degrading the character of Jesus by representing him as a man; indicate the falseness of our theology.

And then, almost two decades before he read Whitman's book and perhaps why he read the book with such evident joy—he anticipates the appearance of the younger poet:

> I look for the new teacher that shall follow so far those shining laws that he shall see them come full circle; shall see their rounding complete grace; shall see the world to be the mirror of the soul...[131]

32. I Think

> I think I could turn and live with
>   animals, they are so placid and self-
>   contain'd,   684
> I stand and look at them long and long.
>
> They do not sweat and whine about
>   their condition,   686

They do not lie awake in the dark and
    weep for their sins, 687
They do not make me sick discussing
    their duty to God,
Not one is dissatisfied, not one is
    demented with the mania of owning
    things, 689
Not one kneels to another, nor to his
    kind that lived thousands of years
    ago, 690
Not one is respectable or unhappy over
    the whole earth.

So they show their relations to me and I
    accept them,
They bring me tokens of myself, they
    evince them plainly in their
    possession. 693

I wonder where they get those tokens,
Did I pass that way huge times ago and
    negligently drop them?

Myself moving forward then and now
    and forever,
Gathering and showing more always
    and with velocity,
Infinite and omnigenous, and the like of
    these among them, 698
Not too exclusive toward the reachers of
    my remembrancers,
Picking out here one that I love, and
    now go with him on brotherly
    terms.

> A gigantic beauty of a stallion, fresh and
> responsive to my caresses, 701
> Head high in the forehead, wide between the ears,
> Limbs glossy and supple, tail dusting the ground,
> Eyes full of sparkling wickedness, ears finely cut, flexibly moving. 704
>
> His nostrils dilate as my heels embrace him,
> His well-built limbs tremble with pleasure as we race around and return.
> I but use you a minute, then I resign you, stallion,
> Why do I need your paces when I myself out-gallop them?
> Even as I stand or sit passing faster than you. 709

The other influence on this canto is the Book of Job's evocation of the horse. Whitman's lines are contained in the last three stanzas of the 32nd Canto. (Lines 701-709 above) Compare Whitman's: "A giant beauty of a stallion...Head high in the forehead...Limbs glossy and supple, tail dusting the ground...Eyes full of sparkling wickedness... His nostrils dilate as my heels embrace him." with Job's:

> Hast thou given the horse his might? Hast thou clothed his neck with the quivering mane? Hast thou made him to leap as a locust? The glory of his snorting is terrible.

> He paweth the valley, and rejoiceth in his strength... He mocketh at fear, and is not dismayed; Neither turneth he back from the sword... He swalloweth the ground with fierceness and rage; [132]

In the same way that Whitman's lines look backward to Job, they look forward to Doctor Dysart's "Horse Monologue" in Peter *Shaffer's Equus:*

> Afterwards, he says, they always embrace.
> The animal digs his sweaty brow
> into his cheek...
> and they stand in the dark for an hour...
> Like a necking couple.
> And of all nonsensical things,
> I keep thinking about the horse...
> not the boy, the horse,
> and what he might be trying to do.
> I keep seeing the huge head,
> kissing him with its chained mouth...
> nudging through the metal,
> some desire absolutely irrelevant...
> to filling its belly or propagating its own
> kind. What desire could this be?
> Not to stay a horse any longer?
> Not to remain reined up forever
> in those particular genetic strings?
> Is it possible, at moments we can't imagine,
> a horse can add its sufferings together...
> the non-stop jerks and jabs that are its daily
> life...and turn them... into grief?
> What use is grief to a horse?

We remember that earlier in his song the poet sang: *And the look of the bay mare shames silliness out of me.* (Line 244 Canto 13) What use is grief to a horse? Once again, Whitman's assertion that "All truths wait in all things." is a reassertion of Emerson's: "The true doctrine of omnipresence is that God re-appears with all his parts in every moss and cobweb."[133] In the same essay Emerson had earlier asserted: "These appearances indicate the fact that the universe is represented in every one of its particles. The world globes itself in a drop of dew." And still later:

> The heart in thee is the heart of all; not a valve, not a wall, not an intersection is there any where in nature, but one blood rolls uninterruptedly in an endless circulation through all men, as the water of the globe is all one sea and truly seen, its tide is one.[134] ...the consciousness in each man is a sliding scale, which identifies him with the First Cause, and now the flesh of his body; the life above life, in infinite degrees.[135]

Eckhart puts it this way:

> As long as I am this or that, or have this or that, I am not all things and have not all things. Become pure till you neither are nor have this or that; then you are omnipresent and, being neither this nor that, are all things...for God is here—in this very place—just as much incarnate in a human being long ago...

> And this is why he has become a human being: that he might give to you his only begotten son.[136]

Assaying those varying degrees the poet asserts that "logic and sermons never convince and that the damp of the night drives deeper in my soul." He believes: "...the soggy clods shall become lovers and lamps... and that the compend of compends is the meat of a man and a woman and a summit and flower there is the feeling they for each other and they are to branch boundlessly out of that lesson until it becomes omnific, and until one and all shall delight us, and we them — and so also the animals of the earth with which he could turn and live, share in this rich legacy: *Infinite and onigenuous, and the like of these among them.* (Line 698 above) This is the gospel according to Whitman. The poet had a keen ear for oratory and delighted in the skill of such preachers as the Congregational minister Henry Ward Beecher. Beecher was the pastor of Brooklyn's Plymouth Church, which was always filled to overflowing with excited parishioners: "He hit me so hard, fascinated to such a degree that I was afterwards willing to go far out of my way to hear him talk." Within a few years, however, he soured on conventional religion. In his August, 1856 prefatory-open-letter to Emerson he, perhaps, overstates his position:

> The churches are one vast lie; the people do not believe them, and they do not believe themselves; the priests are continually telling what they know well enough is not so, and keeping back what they know is so.

His stance is softened somewhat in a notebook entry that the truth of any religion is conferred in:

> ... the clear atmosphere above them — there all meet — previous distinctions are lost — Jew meets Hindu, and Persian, Greek, and Asiatic and European and American are joined — any one religion is as good as another. [137]

This is also the stance of Deism — the stance that Jefferson, Washington, Franklin and Paine took in their defense of the separation of church and state — which remains one of the hallmarks of America's freedom of religion, whatever its diversity. Deism arose during the scientific revolution of the 17th century and became more radically defined in the philosophic and political upheavals of the 18th. Deists believe in a transcendental creator who has neither contact with nor interest in human affairs. This lack of interference or interest puts to rest any report of contact *with* or direction *from* the transcendental being. Thus any particular claim to ascendency in matters of faith is considered more a report of ignorance than of revelation. There was no conflict between Deism and scientific thought — whereas such conflict was inherent between the exigencies of faith as adopted by a state — be it Catholic or Protestant.

In the 33rd Canto Whitman reports the apotheosis that Emerson foresaw: Space and Time reveal themselves to him — he is what he guess'd at when he loafed on the grass or walked alone on the beach under the paling stars of morning: His elbows rest in sea gaps, he skirts sierras, his palms cover continents.

Those familiar with Clarke and Kubrick's 2001 will smile at lines 791-796. In the line preceding his *Star Child* vision, he imagines "Walking the old hills of Judaea" with another *celestial child* "by his side." Whitman clips through space with Keir Dullea, *speeding through heaven and the stars* before another nativity of the infinite:

> Carrying the crescent child that carries
> its own full mother in its belly...

More remarkable than this prescient line is the confession concluding in line 797:

> I tread day and night by such roads.

I invite the reader to leisurely follow the poet in 160 lines of this, the longest Canto in his *Song*. I will renew the commentary at its conclusion. Half of it is dedicated to a catalogue's reverie. Rather than a long grocery list with which Emerson would later take exception, it is one of the great moments of the 19th century. The eighty lines of the third stanza (Lines 717-797) make it one of the most extraordinary in the poem. In the 22 stanzas of the 33rd Canto, the poet of the *one* becomes the *many*.

33. Space and Time

> Space and Time! now I see it is true,
>   what I guess'd at, [138] 710
> What I guess'd when I loaf'd on the grass,
> What I guess'd while I lay alone in my bed,

And again as I walk'd the beach under the paling stars of the morning.

My ties and ballasts leave me, my elbows rest in sea-gaps, 714
I skirt sierras, my palms cover continents, 715
I am afoot with my vision.

By the city's quadrangular houses—in log huts, camping with lumber-men,
Along the ruts of the turnpike, along the dry gulch and rivulet bed,
Weeding my onion-patch or hosing rows of carrots and parsnips, crossing savannas, trailing in forests,
Prospecting, gold-digging, girdling the trees of a new purchase,
Scorch'd ankle-deep by the hot sand, hauling my boat down the shallow river,
Where the panther walks to and fro on a limb overhead, where the buck turns furiously at the hunter,
Where the rattlesnake suns his flabby length on a rock, where the otter is feeding on fish,
Where the alligator in his tough pimples sleeps by the bayou,
Where the black bear is searching for roots or honey, where the beaver pats the mud with his paddle-shaped tall;

Over the growing sugar, over the yellow-flower'd cotton plant, over the rice in its low moist field,

Over the sharp-peak'd farm house, with its scallop'd scum and slender shoots from the gutters,

Over the western persimmon, over the long-leav'd corn, over the delicate blue-flower flax,

Over the white and brown buckwheat, a hummer and buzzer there with the rest,

Over the dusky green of the rye as it ripples and shades in the breeze;

Scaling mountains, pulling myself cautiously up, holding on by low scragged limbs,

Walking the path worn in the grass and beat through the leaves of the bush,

Where the quail is whistling betwixt the woods and the wheat-lot,

Where the bat flies in the Seventh-month eve, where the great goldbug drops through the dark,

Where the brook puts out of the roots of the old tree and flows to the meadow,

Where cattle stand and shake away flies with the tremulous shuddering of their hides,

Where the cheese-cloth hangs in the kitchen, where andirons straddle the hearth-slab, where cobwebs fall in festoons from the rafters;

Where trip-hammers crash, where the
press is whirling its cylinders,
Wherever the human heart beats with
terrible throes under its ribs, 739
Where the pear-shaped balloon is
floating aloft, (floating in it myself
and looking composedly down,)
Where the life-car is drawn on the slip-
noose, where the heat hatches pale-
green eggs in the dented sand,
Where the she-whale swims with her
calf and never forsakes it, 742
Where the steam-ship trails hind-ways
its long pennant of smoke,
Where the fin of the shark cuts like a
black chip out of the water, 744
Where the half-burn'd brig is riding on
unknown currents,
Where shells grow to her slimy deck,
where the dead are corrupting
below;
Where the dense-starr'd flag is borne at
the head of the regiments,
Approaching Manhattan up by the long-
stretching island,
Under Niagara, the cataract falling like a
veil over my countenance,
Upon a door-step, upon the horse-block
of hard wood outside,
Upon the race-course, or enjoying
picnics or jigs or a good game of
base-ball,
At he-festivals, with blackguard gibes,
ironical license, bull-dances,
drinking, laughter,

At the cider-mill tasting the sweets of the brown mash, sucking the juice through a straw,
At apple-peelings wanting kisses for all the red fruit I find,
At musters, beach-parties, friendly bees, huskings, house-raisings;
Where the mocking-bird sounds his delicious gurgles, cackles, screams, weeps,
Where the hay-rick stands in the barn-yard, where the dry-stalks are scatter'd, where the brood-cow waits in the hovel,
Where the bull advances to do his masculine work, where the stud to the mare, where the cock is treading the hen,
Where the heifers browse, where geese nip their food with short jerks,
Where sun-down shadows lengthen over the limitless and lonesome prairie,
Where herds of buffalo make a crawling spread of the square miles far and near,
Where the humming-bird shimmers, where the neck of the long-lived swan is curving and winding,
Where the laughing-gull scoots by the shore, where she laughs her near-human laugh,
Where bee-hives range on a gray bench in the garden half hid by the high weeds,

Where band-neck'd partridges roost in a ring on the ground with their heads out,
Where burial coaches enter the arch'd gates of a cemetery,
Where winter wolves bark amid wastes of snow and icicled trees,
Where the yellow-crown'd heron comes to the edge of the marsh at night and feeds upon small crabs,
Where the splash of swimmers and divers cools the warm noon,
Where the katy-did works her chromatic reed on the walnut-tree over the well,
Through patches of citrons and cucumbers with silver-wired leaves,
Through the salt-lick or orange glade, or under conical firs,
Through the gymnasium, through the curtain'd saloon, through the office or public hall;
Pleas'd with the native and pleas'd with the foreign, pleas'd with the new and old,
Pleas'd with the homely woman as well as the handsome,
Pleas'd with the quakeress as she puts off her bonnet and talks melodiously,
Pleas'd with the tune of the choir of the whitewash'd church,
Pleas'd with the earnest words of the sweating Methodist preacher,

impress'd seriously at the camp-meeting;
Looking in at the shop-windows of Broadway the whole forenoon, flatting the flesh of my nose on the thick plate glass,
Wandering the same afternoon with my face turn'd up to the clouds, or down a lane or along the beach,
My right and left arms round the sides of two friends, and I in the middle;
Coming home with the silent and dark-cheek'd bush-boy, (behind me he rides at the drape of the day,)
Far from the settlements studying the print of animals' feet, or the moccasin print,
By the cot in the hospital reaching lemonade to a feverish patient,
Nigh the coffin'd corpse when all is still, examining with a candle;
Voyaging to every port to dicker and adventure,
Hurrying with the modern crowd as eager and fickle as any,
Hot toward one I hate, ready in my madness to knife him,
Solitary at midnight in my back yard, my thoughts gone from me a long while,
Walking the old hills of Judaea with the beautiful gentle God by my side,   790
Speeding through space, speeding through heaven and the stars,   791

Speeding amid the seven satellites and the broad ring, and the diameter of eighty thousand miles,
Speeding with tail'd meteors, throwing fire-balls like the rest,
Carrying the crescent child that carries its own full mother in its belly, 794
Storming, enjoying, planning, loving, cautioning,
Backing and filling, appearing and disappearing,
I tread day and night such roads. 797

I visit the orchards of spheres and look at the product,
And look at quintillions ripen'd and look at quintillions green.

I fly those flights of a fluid and swallowing soul,
My course runs below the soundings of plummets.

I help myself to material and immaterial,
No guard can shut me off, no law prevent me.

I anchor my ship for a little while only,
My messengers continually cruise away or bring their returns to me.

I go hunting polar furs and the seal, leaping chasms with a pike-pointed

staff, clinging to topples of brittle
and blue.

I ascend to the foretruck,
I take my place late at night in the crow's-nest,
We sail the arctic sea, it is plenty light enough, 809
Through the clear atmosphere I stretch around on the wonderful beauty,
The enormous masses of ice pass me and I pass them, the scenery is plain in all directions, 811
The white-topt mountains show in the distance, I fling out my fancies toward them,
We are approaching some great battle-field in which we are soon to be engaged,
We pass the colossal outposts of the encampment, we pass with still feet and caution,
Or we are entering by the suburbs some vast and ruin'd city, 815
The blocks and fallen architecture more than all the living cities of the globe.
816

I am a free companion, I bivouac by invading watchfires,
I turn the bridgroom out of bed and stay with the bride myself, 818
I tighten her all night to my thighs and lips.

My voice is the wife's voice, the screech
   by the rail of the stairs, 820
They fetch my man's body up dripping
   and drown'd.

I understand the large hearts of heroes,
The courage of present times and all
   times,
How the skipper saw the crowded and
   rudderless wreck of the steamship,
   and Death chasing it up and down
   the storm,
How he knuckled tight and gave not
   back an inch, and was faithful of
   days and faithful of nights,
And chalk'd in large letters on a board,
   Be of good cheer, we will not desert
   you;
How he follow'd with them and tack'd
   with them three days and would not
   give it up,
How he saved the drifting company at
   last,
How the lank loose-gown'd women
   look'd when boated from the side of
   their prepared graves,
How the silent old-faced infants and the
   lifted sick, and the sharp-lipp'd
   unshaved men;
All this I swallow, it tastes good, I like it
   well, it becomes mine,
I am the man, I suffer'd, I was there. 832

The disdain and calmness of martyrs,

The mother of old, condemn'd for a
    witch, burnt with dry wood, her
    children gazing on,   834
The hounded slave that flags in the race,
    leans by the fence, blowing, cover'd
    with sweat,   835
The twinges that sting like needles his
    legs and neck, the murderous
    buckshot and the bullets,
All these I feel or am.   836

I am the hounded slave, I wince at the
    bite of the dogs,   838
Hell and despair are upon me, crack and
    again crack the marksmen,
I clutch the rails of the fence, my gore
    dribs, thinn'd with the ooze of my
    skin,
I fall on the weeds and stones,
The riders spur their unwilling horses,
    haul close,
Taunt my dizzy ears and beat me
    violently over the head with whip-
    stocks.

Agonies are one of my changes of
    garments,   844
I do not ask the wounded person how
    he feels, I myself become the
    wounded person,   845
My hurts turn livid upon me as I lean on
    a cane and observe.

I am the mash'd fireman with breast-
    bone broken,   847

Tumbling walls buried me in their debris,
Heat and smoke I inspired, I heard the yelling shouts of my comrades,
I heard the distant click of their picks and shovels,
They have clear'd the beams away, they tenderly lift me forth.

I lie in the night air in my red shirt, the pervading hush is for my sake,
Painless after all I lie exhausted but not so unhappy,
White and beautiful are the faces around me, the heads are bared of their fire-caps, 854
The kneeling crowd fades with the light of the torches.

Distant and dead resuscitate, 856
They show as the dial or move as the hands of me, I am the clock myself. 857

I am an old artillerist, I tell of my fort's bombardment,
I am there again.
Again the long roll of the drummers,
Again the attacking cannon, mortars,
Again to my listening ears the cannon responsive.

I take part, I see and hear the whole, 863
The cries, curses, roar, the plaudits for well-aim'd shots,

> The ambulanza slowly passing trailing
>   its red drip,
> Workmen searching after damages,
>   making indispensable repairs,
> The fall of grenades through the rent
>   roof, the fan-shaped explosion,
> The whizz of limbs, heads, stone, wood,
>   iron, high in the air.
>
> Again gurgles the mouth of my dying
>   general, he furiously waves with his
>   hand,
> He gasps through the clot *Mind not me –*
>   *mind – the entrenchmets*.   870

The impetuous reader will hurry through the inventory in a blur. Whitman is patient. He'll wait for a sprawl of years or decades to attempt again his seduction. For the present it will serve our purpose to revisit pieces of his vision in prose. Space and Time have been revealed to the poet.

Here the poet visits the forests of the lumbermen and prospectors. He imagines a panther overhead on a slow winding river, the angry charge of a buck, a rattlesnake on a rock, an otter on the shore, an alligator in a bayou, a beaver and a black bear. His next collections are landscapes and vistas. He takes to the air floating over the growing sugar, the rice in the low moist field, over the western persimmon, corn, flax, flower'd cotton plant, buckwheat and rye.

Each item is vividly imagined — their sheer volume is evidence of heady research and innumerable notebooks. He anchors the reveries in his own experience (imagined or otherwise): "Where the pear-shaped balloon is floating aloft, (floating in it myself and looking composedly down.)" And there aloft he sees the she-whale and the fin of its cutting a black chip out of the water. Amidst the animals and environs he spies out a farmhouse, a printer's shop and the trip hammer of the metal worker — "wherever the human heart beats with terrible throes under its ribs," and then he views a seascape with a burned-out rig riding on unknown currents, and the dead are corrupting below. Whenever we grow too complacent with the picturesque we find ourselves in a human drama: "... hot toward one I hate, ready in my madness to knife him; by the cot in the hospital reaching lemonade to a feverish patient; nigh the coffin corpse when all is still, examining with a candle."

As a counterpoint to the derision he held for those worshiping the dead of centuries ago and for the reservations noted in Emerson's *Address*, he finds himself "walking the old hills of Judea with the beautiful gentle God by my side." (Line 790 above). He then returns to his own time in the *star-child* reverie that we have already noted: Speeding amid the seven satellites and the broad ring, and the diameter of eighty-thousand miles, Speeding with tail'd meteors, throwing fireballs like the rest ... (Lines 791-797 above). He further flies "those flights of a fluid and swallowing soul. My course runs below the soundings of plummets. I help myself to material and immaterial, no guard can shut me off, no law prevent me."

He then imagines an Arctic voyage (it is plenty light enough.) "The enormous masses of ice pass me and I pass them." The voyage anticipates H.P. Lovecraft's *At the Mountains of Madness*: "We are approaching some great battle-field... we pass the colossal outposts of the encampment... we are entering by the suburbs some vast and ruin'd city, the blocks and fallen architecture more than all the living cities of the globe." (Line 816 above). And then, in the strangest of his erotic musings, he is bivouacking by invading watch-fires and then turning a bridegroom out of his bed, he ravishes his bride: "I tighten her all night to my thighs and lips."(Lines 818-819 above) And then, in the next stanza, he envisions the most startling reversal in the poem: "My voice is the wife's voice, the screech by the rail of the stairs; they fetch my man's body up dripping and drown."(Lines 820-821 above) Unless we connect the drowned man with the Arctic voyage of the previous stanzas this nightmarish episode takes place within five lines of two stanzas. The episode with the bridegroom and his wife had its origin in a tale that Whitman had heard while in the whaling village of Greenport. The story was reported in a series of travel essays that he called "Letters from a Traveling Bachelor," and to which he signed the name *Paumanok*. As Whitman reports the story some ten years earlier a hunter became lost and was invited to share the bed of a newly married couple. Turning the bridegroom from the bed and ravishing the bride is the fanciful (though odd) conceit of the poet. (Line 818 above) Whitman then describes a series of dramas almost as succinct: the skipper desperately trying to save his ship; a mother condemned as a witch (Line 834 above) burnt with dry wood, her children looking on; the hounded slave that flags in the race: "I am the hounded slave..." (Line 839 above).

> All these I feel or am... I wince at the bite of the dogs, hell and despair are upon me, crack and again crack of the marksmen, I clutch the rails of the fence, my gore dribs, thinn'd with the ooze of my skin, I fall on the stones, the riders spur their unwilling horses, haul close, Taunt my dizzy ears and beat me violently over the head with whip-stocks. Agonies are one of my garments, I do not ask the wounded person how he feels, I myself become the wounded person. I am the mash'd fireman with breast-bone broken, Tumbling walls buried me in their debris. Heat and smoke I inspired, I heard the yelling shouts of my comrades, I heard the distant click of their picks and shovels, they have cleared the beams away, they tenderly lift me forth...white and beautiful are the faces around me, the heads are bared of their fire-caps, the kneeling crowd fades with the light of the torches.

The fireman scene is clearly suggestive of a *Passion*. Coming up from the debris is the obverse of coming down from the cross—but their meaning is the same. The disciples "tenderly lift me forth." It is at this juncture that the poet imagines himself as a resurrected savior:

> Distant and dead resuscitate,

> They show as the dial or move as the
>   hands of me,
> I am the clock myself.

It is not an accident that the apotheosis takes place in the 33rd Section—the year that concludes the life of Jesus. The poet then imagines that his "Christ" continues as an old artillerist: "I am there again... In *Drum Taps'* "A Sight in Camp in the Daybreak Gray and Dim", he will view three corpses brought from the field of battle: An old man, a young man and the third: "*Christ himself, dead and divine and brother of all, and here again he lies.*" The dense complexity of these 160 lines could easily be considered a masterpiece in its own right. Whitman is reporting a cosmic illumination. That illumination leads the poet to identify with each episode and item of the meditation. It is an illumination each reader shares by vividly imagining each of the poet's lines:

> I am the man, I suffered, I was there. (832)
> All these I feel or am. (837)
> I am the hounded slave. (838)
> Agonies are one of my changes of garments. (844)
> I do not ask the wounded person how he feels, (845)
> I myself become the wounded person. (845)
> I am the mashed fireman with breast-bone broken. (847)
> Distant and dead resuscitate, they show as the hands of me, (856)
> I am the clock myself. (857)

> I take part, I see and hear the whole.
> (863)

Excepting Shakespeare, perhaps only Joyce approaches Whitman's ubiquity: "We walk through ourselves, meeting robbers, ghosts, giants, old men, young men, wives, widows, brothers-in-love. But always meeting ourselves."[139]

In the next three Cantos he tells two tales. The first is of the *murder of the four-hundred and twelve young men,* the second, an *old sea fight* — the poet tells them each better than I dare paraphrase either.

34. Now I Tell What I Knew

> Now I tell what I knew in Texas in my early youth, 871
> (I tell not the fall of Alamo,
> Not one escaped to tell the fall of Alamo,
> The hundred and fifty are dumb yet at Alamo,)
> 'Tis the tale of the murder in cold blood of four hundred and twelve young men. 875
>
> Retreating they had form'd in a hollow square with their baggage for breastworks,
> Nine hundred lives out of the surrounding enemies, nine times

their number, was the price they took in advance,
Their colonel was wounded and their ammunition gone,
They treated for an honorable capitulation, receiv'd writing and seal, gave up their arms and march'd back prisoners of war.

They were the glory of the race of rangers,
Matchless with horse, rifle, song, supper, courtship,
Large, turbulent, generous, handsome, proud, and affectionate,
Bearded, sunburnt, drest in the free costume of hunters,
Not a single one over thirty years of age.

884

The second First-day morning they were brought out in squads and massacred, it was beautiful early summer,
The work commenced about five o'clock and was over by eight.

885

None obey'd the command to kneel,
Some made a mad and helpless rush, some stood stark and straight,
A few fell at once, shot in the temple or heart, the living and dead lay together,

> The maim'd and mangled dug in the dirt, the new-comers saw them there,
> Some half-kill'd attempted to crawl away,
> These were despatch'd with bayonets or batter'd with the blunts of muskets,
> A youth not seventeen years old seiz'd his assassin till two more came to release him,
> The three were all torn and cover'd with the boy's blood.
>
> At eleven o'clock began the burning of the bodies;
> That is the tale of the murder of the four hundred and twelve young men. 896

The 34th Canto is one of the great fragments in narrative. In twenty five lines the poet dramatizes a tale that could as easily have taken twenty-five hundred. The details of betrayal, pride and murder are related unequivocally — and with complete dispassion: "Not a single over thirty years of age. They are brought out in squads and massacred. It was beautiful early summer, the work commenced at five and was over by eight..." (Lines 884-886 above). The quotidian and the tragic: "None obeyed the command to kneel, some made a mad helpless rush, some stood stark and straight, a few fell at once, shot in the temple or heart, the living and dead lay together...some half killed attempted to crawl away..." His description of one holocaust anticipates another, less than a century away. Cantos 35 and 36 relate a sea-tale as told to Whitman as a child.

He must have been very young or the great-grandfather very old for the interview to have taken place at all. The daring of the captain as his response to the request to surrender, "We have just begun our part of the fighting," sounds suspiciously like the rhetoric of John Paul Jones. "List to the yarn... as it was told to me."

We can little resist the invitation.

35. Would You Hear

Would you hear of an old-time sea-fight?	897
Would you learn who won by the light of the moon and stars?	898

List to the yarn, as my grandmother's
    father the sailor told it to me.

Our foe was no sulk in his ship I tell
    you, (said he,)
 His was the surly English pluck, and
    there is no tougher or truer, and
    never was, and never will be;
Along the lower'd eve he came horribly
    raking us.
We closed with him, the yards
    entangled, the cannon touch'd,
My captain lash'd fast with his own
hands.
We had receiv'd some eighteen pound
    shots under the water,
    On our lower-gun-deck two large

pieces had burst at the first fire,
killing all around and blowing up
overhead.

Fighting at sun-down, fighting at dark,
Ten o'clock at night, the full moon well up,
our leaks on the gain, and five feet of water
reported,
The master-at-arms loosing the prisoners
confined in the after-hold to give them a
chance for themselves.

The transit to and from the magazine is now
stopt by the sentinels,
They see so many strange faces they do not
know whom to trust.

Our frigate takes fire,
The other asks if we demand quarter?
If our colors are struck and the fighting done?
Now I laugh content, for I hear the voice of my
little captain,
We have not struck, he composedly cries, *we have
just begun our part of the fighting.*

Only three guns are in use,
One is directed by the captain himself against
the enemy's mainmast,
Two well serv'd with grape and canister silence
his musketry and clear his decks.

The tops alone second the fire of this little
battery, especially the main-top,

> They hold out bravely during the whole of the action.
>
> Not a moment's cease,
> The leaks gain fast on the pumps, the fire eats toward the powder-magazine.
>
> One of the pumps has been shot away, it is generally thought we are sinking.
>
> Serene stands the little captain,
> He is not hurried, his voice is neither high nor low,
> His eyes give more light to us than our battle-lanterns.
>
> Toward twelve there in the beams of the moon they surrender to us. 928

In the 36th Canto, the last eight lines (beginning with: *O Christ! My fit is mastering me!*) were original with the '55 text but were then excised in later editions. They have been restored below line 944 (The Deathbed text's final line) in italics.

36. Strectch'd and Still

> Stretch'd and still lies the midnight, 929
> Two great hulls motionless on the breast of the darkness,

Our vessel riddled and slowly sinking, preparations to pass to the one we have conquer'd,
The captain on the quarter-deck coldly giving his orders through a countenance white as a sheet,
Near by the corpse of the child that serv'd in the cabin,
The dead face of an old salt with long white hair and carefully curl'd whiskers,
The flames spite of all that can be done flickering aloft and below,
The husky voices of the two or three officers yet fit for duty,
Formless stacks of bodies and bodies by themselves, dabs of flesh upon the masts and spars, 937
Cut of cordage, dangle of rigging, slight shock of the soothe of waves,
Black and impassive guns, litter of powder-parcels, strong scent,
A few large stars overhead, silent and mournful shining,
Delicate sniffs of sea-breeze, smells of sedgy grass and fields by the shore, death-messages given in charge to survivors,
The hiss of the surgeon's knife, the gnawing teeth of his saw, 942
Wheeze, cluck, swash of falling blood, short wild scream, and long, dull, tapering groan,
These so, these irretrievable. 944

> *O Christ! My fit is mastering me!*
> *What the rebel said gaily adjusting his throat to the rope-noose,*
> *What the savage at the stump, his eye-sockets empty, his mouth spiriting whoops and defiance,*
> *What stills the traveler come to the vault at Mount Vernon,*
> *What sobers the Brooklyn boy as he looks down the shores of Wallabout and remembers the prison ships,*
> *What burnt the gums of the red-coat at Saratoga when he surrendered his brigades*
> *These become mine and me everyone — and they are but little,*
> *I become as much more as I like.*

Our knowledge of the coming plague of war and death and the poet's participation in Washington's tented hospitals makes: "The hiss of the surgeon's knife, the gnawing teeth of his saw, wheeze, cluck, swash of falling blood, short wild scream, and long, dull tapering groan" again sadly prescient. The deleted images look back to earlier wars as the preceding lines anticipate impending conflicts. The "O Christ!" would have offended some of his readers. And "My fit is mastering me," is likely more related to the Sufism of Jalal ad-Din Rumi than to the epilepsy of his brother, Edward. Line 945 of Canto 37 is the Deathbed Text's inaugural verse. "I become any presence or truth of humanity here," which precedes it, was from the 1855 edition. It was later excised but is restored below in italics.

Note that the idea of possession ("I am possessed!") eliminated from the previous canto is retained below in the Deathbed disposition. (End of line 946 below)

37. You Laggards

> *I become any presence or truth of humanity here,*
> You laggards there on guard! look to your arms! 945
> In at the conquer'd doors they crowd! I am possess'd! 946
> Embody all presences outlaw'd or suffering,
> See myself in prison shaped like another man,
> And feel the dull unintermitted pain. 949
>
> For me the keepers of convicts shoulder their carbines and keep watch,
> It is I let out in the morning and barr'd at night.
>
> Not a mutineer walks handcuff'd to jail but I am handcuff'd to him and walk by his side, 952
> (I am less the jolly one there, and more the silent one with sweat on my twitching lips.)
>
> Not a youngster is taken for larceny but I go up too, and am tried and sentenced. 954

> Not a cholera patient lies at the last gasp
>   but I also lie at the last gasp,
> My face is ash-color'd, my sinews gnarl,
>   away from me people retreat.
>
> Askers embody themselves in me and I
>   am embodied in them,
> I project my hat, sit shame-faced, and
>   beg.   958

In the forgoing canto the poet again imagines the plight of the lost and defeated: *If a mutineer walks handcuffed to jail... I am handcuff'd to him and walk by his side.* Whitman dies along with the dying and pleads plaintively with the destitute: *I project my hat, sit shame-faced, and beg.* In Section 38's *Enough!* he continues the litany and once again imagines himself as the Christ: "That I could forget the mockers and insults!... That I could look with a separate look at my own crucifixion and bloody crowning."

And then, in a stunning splintering he imagines that he is also the rising dead of the resurrection: "Corpses rise, gashes heal, fastenings roll from me... I troop forth replenish'd with supreme power, one of an average unending procession, Inland and sea-coast we go, and pass all boundary lines, Our swift ordinances on their way over the whole earth."

38. Enough!

> Enough! enough! enough!   959

Somehow I have been stunn'd. Stand back!
Give me a little time beyond my cuff'd head, slumbers, dreams, gaping,
I discover myself on the verge of a usual mistake.

That I could forget the mockers and insults!
That I could forget the trickling tears and the blows of the bludgeons and hammers! 964
That I could look with a separate look on my own crucifixion and bloody crowning. 965

I remember now,
I resume the overstaid fraction,
The grave of rock multiplies what has been confided to it, or to any graves,
Corpses rise, gashes heal, fastenings roll from me. 969

I troop forth replenish'd with supreme power, one of an average unending procession, 970
Inland and sea-coast we go, and pass all boundary lines,
Our swift ordinances on their way over the whole earth,
The blossoms we wear in our hats the growth of thousands of years.

Eleves, I salute you! come forward!

Continue your annotations, continue
    your questionings. 975

In Section 39 the poet wears his Rousseau on his shirt sleeves: "The friendly savage, who is he?" (Line 976 below). It is easy to see Whitman's affinity with the nobility of the *noble savage*: "Is he waiting for civilization, or past it and mastering it?" (Line 977 below)

"Wherever he goes men and women accept and desire him...behavior lawless as snow-flakes." And if we have the least doubt that the subject is the poet himself (or a subject with whom he closely identifies), we have the line: ...*words as simple as grass*... (Line 983 below).

39. The Friendly and Flowing

> The friendly and flowing savage, who is
>   he? 976
> Is he waiting for civilization, or past it
>   and mastering it?
> Is he some Southwesterner rais'd out-
>   doors? is he Kanadian?
> Is he from the Mississippi country?
>   Iowa, Oregon, California?
> The mountains? prairie-life, bush-life?
>   or sailor from the sea?
>
> Wherever he goes men and women
>   accept and desire him,
> They desire he should like them, touch
>   them, speak to them, stay with
>   them.

> Behavior lawless as snow-flakes, words simple as grass, uncomb'd head, laughter, and naivete, 983
> Slow-stepping feet, common features, common modes and emanations,
> They descend in new forms from the tips of his fingers,
> They are waited with the odor of his body or breath, they fly out of the glance of his eyes. 986

Flaunt of Sunshine is one of the grandest moments in the poet's *Song*. Whitman's agon is the Sun as he hallows his own nature: "You light surfaces only, I force surfaces and depths also." Like Emerson he does not give charity — when he gives he gives himself — he will not be denied and he will blow grit within you — he has stores of plenty and to spare — anything he has he bestows. When he proclaims that: "This day I am jetting the stuff of far more arrogant republics, there were some in the republic that thought him arrogant. His "desire" for women fit for conception on which to start bigger nimbler babes will cause him no end of trouble when a number of *fit* women take him up on the proposition. But this is a mischief caused by the desire to propagate nothing more than his own mythos. In a ghost-written letter which he composed with William O'Connor to publicize an English edition of his poems he was to write:

> All really refined persons, and the women more than the men, take to Walt Whitman. The most delicate and even

conventional lady only needs to know him to love him.

If ever the poet will claim *poetic license*, he will claim it here. O'Connor, as well, must have had second thoughts; his wife, Nelly fell in love with the poet.

The great declamation in the Canto is his messianic command to one dying: ...*thither I speed and twist the lock of the door* (Line 1008 below) and then: *By God, you shall not go down!* (Line 1013 below)

40. Flaunt of the Sunshine

> Flaunt of the sunshine I need not your
>   bask—lie over! 987
> You light surfaces only, I force surfaces
>   and depths also.
>
> Earth! you seem to look for something at
>   my hands,
> Say, old top-knot, what do you want?
>
> Man or woman, I might tell how I like
>   you, but cannot,
> And might tell what it is in me and what
>   it is in you, but cannot,
> And might tell that pining I have, that
>   pulse of my nights and days.
>
> Behold, I do not give lectures or a little
>   charity,
> When I give I give myself.

You there, impotent, loose in the knees,
Open your scarf'd chops till I blow grit within you,
Spread your palms and lift the flaps of your pockets,
I am not to be denied, I compel, I have stores plenty and to spare,
And any thing I have I bestow. 1000

I do not ask who you are, that is not important to me,
You can do nothing and be nothing but what I will infold you.

To cotton-field drudge or cleaner of privies I lean,
On his right cheek I put the family kiss,
And in my soul I swear I never will deny him.

On women fit for conception I start bigger and nimbler babes.
(This day I am jetting the stuff of far more arrogant republics.)

To any one dying, thither I speed and twist the knob of the door. 1008
Turn the bed-clothes toward the foot of the bed,
Let the physician and the priest go home.

I seize the descending man and raise him with resistless will,
O despairer, here is my neck,

> By God, you shall not go down! hang
> your whole weight upon me. 1013
>
> I dilate you with tremendous breath, I
> buoy you up,
> Every room of the house do I fill with an
> arm'd force,
> Lovers of me, bafflers of graves.
>
> Sleep—I and they keep guard all night
> Not doubt, not decease shall dare to
> lay finger upon you,
> I have embraced you, and henceforth
> possess you to myself,
> And when you rise in the morning you
> will find what I tell you is so. 1020

The 1800s was a time of great spiritual revival. Joseph Smith *spoke with God* under the noon day sun in a New York meadow. Like the Mormon prophet, Whitman believes he will one day be a god—one of the *Supremes*. Also in upstate New York Margaret and Katherine Fox heard ghostly knockings in their home near Rochester. In the 1850s they toured and gave public demonstrations of their prowess as spiritual adepts—soon they became celebrities. Flying lamps and tables then became the order of the day. Whitman was also familiar with the Poughkeepsie seer, Andrew Jackson Davis. Davis was an avid trance enthusiast and claimed the ability to time travel: "The clairvoyant sometimes sees places not as they appear now, but as they existed many years ago…the angels unroll before the spiritual sight…a grand panorama of past scenes and events."

Davis gave hundreds of trance performances in the late 1840s. Whether Whitman had a mystic experience or only the pretence of one will long be debated between his critics and followers. If only a performance, it was a damn fine one. It is often said that we become what we pretend — and there is evidence to suggest a remarkable spiritual presence that attended few others of whom we have record. Given his faith in that presence, he becomes a healer:

> Let the physician and the priest go home... I have embraced you, and henceforth possess you to myself, And when you rise in the morning you will find what I tell you is so.

In Canto 41's *I Am He Bringing Help* the poet's belief in his own powers has him "Taking myself the exact dimension of Jehovah, Kronos, Zeus... and Hercules." Western believers don't like their Jehovah (Line 1028 below) put on the same ontological stage as the pagan Kronos and Zeus. Bertrand Russell suggests why this is so:

> I do not pretend to be able to prove that there is no God. I equally cannot prove that Satan is a fiction. The Christian God may exist; so may the Gods of Olympus, or of ancient Egypt, or of Babylon. But no one of these hypotheses is more probable than any other; they lie outside the region of even probable knowledge, and therefore there is no reason to consider any of them.[140]

Whitman continues his litany of gods with Osiris, Isis, Allah, Odin, Brahma, Buddha and Mexitli and therefore offends just about everyone: "Admitting they were alive and did the work of their days." The carpenter framing a house impresses him more. Then he lists another half dozen to whom he applies his *rough deific sketches*. He doesn't object to special revelations but finds a curl of smoke or hair on the back of his hand just as curious as any revelation... *dung and dirt more admirable than was dreamed...* " (Line 1049 below) immediately preceding: "The supernatural of no account, myself waiting my time to become one of the Supremes." He concludes the canto by suggesting that through his "life-lumps" (his experience) he is already a creator.

41. I Am He Bringing Help

> I am he bringing help for the sick as
> they pant on their backs, 1021
> And for strong upright men I bring yet
> more needed help.
>
> I heard what was said of the universe,
> Heard it and heard it of several
> thousand years;
> It is middling well as far as it goes — but
> is that all?
>
> Magnifying and applying come I,
> Outbidding at the start the old cautious
> hucksters,
> Taking myself the exact dimensions of
> Jehovah, 1028

Lithographing Kronos, Zeus his son, and Hercules his grandson,
Buying drafts of Osiris, Isis, Belus, Brahma, Buddha, 1030
In my portfolio placing Manito loose, Allah on a leaf, the crucifix engraved,
With Odin and the hideous-faced Mexitli and every idol and image,
Taking them all for what they are worth and not a cent more, 1033
Admitting they were alive and did the work of their days,
(They bore mites as for unfledg'd birds who have now to rise and fly and sing for themselves,) 1035
Accepting the rough deific sketches to fill out better in myself, bestowing them freely on each man and woman I see,
Discovering as much or more in a framer framing a house, 1037
Putting higher claims for him there with his roll'd-up sleeves driving the mallet and chisel,
Not objecting to special revelations, considering a curl of smoke or a hair on the back of my hand just as curious as any revelation, 1039
Lads ahold of fire-engines and hook-and-ladder ropes no less to me than the gods of the antique wars,
Minding their voices peal through the crash of destruction,

Their brawny limbs passing safe over charr'd laths, their white foreheads whole and unhurt out of the flames;
By the mechanic's wife with her babe at her nipple interceding for every person born,
Three scythes at harvest whizzing in a row from three lusty angels with shirts bagg'd out at their waists,
The snag-tooth'd hostler with red hair redeeming sins past and to come,
Selling all he possesses, traveling on foot to fee lawyers for his brother and sit by him while he is tried for forgery;
What was strewn in the amplest strewing the square rod about me, and not filling the square rod then,
The bull and the bug never worshipp'd half enough, 1048
Dung and dirt more admirable than was dream'd,
The supernatural of no account, myself waiting my time to be one of the supremes, 1050
The day getting ready for me when I shall do as much good as the best, and be as prodigious;
By my life-lumps! becoming already a creator, 1052
Putting myself here and now to the ambush'd womb of the shadows. 1053

Joseph Smith's tenet: "that as man is God once was and as God is man may become," is herein embraced: "...becoming already a creator..." Once again he finds music to be creation's most perfect manifestation. In the 42nd Canto he proclaims to have "pass'd his prelude on the reeds within."

But the music is rather *A Call* from within for his love of those he embraces without. Aside from his refreshingly real and wicked neighbors are those whose thrum and climax he feels: "Music rolls, but not from the organ, Folks are all around me, but they are no household of mine... Ever myself and my neighbors, refreshing wicked, real... (Line 1065 below) I feel the thrum of your climax and close. (Line 1059 below) Ever love, ever the sobbing liquid of life..."(Line 1068 below). "I know perfectly well my own egotism, Know my omnivorous lines and must not write any less..." (Line 1084 below).

42. A Call

> A call in the midst of the crowd,   1054
> My own voice, orotund sweeping and final.
>
> Come my children,
> Come my boys and girls, my women, household and intimates,
> Now the performer launches his nerve, he has pass'd his prelude on the reeds within.

Easily written loose-finger'd chords—I
feel the thrum of your climax and
close.   1059

My head slues round on my neck,
Music rolls, but not from the organ,
Folks are around me, but they are no
household of mine.

Ever the hard unsunk ground,
Ever the eaters and drinkers, ever the
upward and downward sun, ever
the air and the ceaseless tides,
Ever myself and my neighbors,
refreshing, wicked, real,   1065
Ever the old inexplicable query, ever
that thorn'd thumb, that breath of
itches and thirsts,
Ever the vexer's hoot! hoot! till we find
where the sly one hides and bring
him forth,
Ever love, ever the sobbing liquid of life,

1066

Ever the bandage under the chin, ever
the trestles of death.

Here and there with dimes on the eyes
walking,
To feed the greed of the belly the brains
liberally spooning,
Tickets buying, taking, selling, but in to
the feast never once going,
Many sweating, ploughing, thrashing,
and then the chaff for payment
receiving,

A few idly owning, and they the wheat
    continually claiming.
This is the city and I am one of the
    citizens,
Whatever interests the rest interests me,
    politics, wars, markets, newspapers,
    schools,
The mayor and councils, banks, tariffs,
    steamships, factories, stocks, stores,
    real estate and personal estate.

The little plentiful manikins skipping
    around in collars and tail'd coats,
I am aware who they are, (they are
    positively not worms or fleas,)
I acknowledge the duplicates of myself,
    the weakest and shallowest is
    deathless with me,   1080
What I do and say the same waits for
    them,
Every thought that flounders in me the
    same flounders in them.

I know perfectly well my own egoism,   1083
Know my omnivorous lines and must
    not write any less,   1084
And would fetch you whoever you are
    flush with myself.

Not words of routine this song of mine,
But abruptly to question, to leap beyond
    yet nearer bring;
This printed and bound book—but the
    printer and the printing-office boy?

> The well-taken photographs—but your wife or friend close and solid in your arms?
> The black ship mail'd with iron, her mighty guns in her turrets—but the pluck of the captain and engineers?
> In the houses the dishes and fare and furniture—but the host and hostess, and the look out of their eyes?
> The sky up there—yet here or next door, or across the way?
> The saints and sages in history—but you yourself? 1093
> Sermons, creeds, theology—but the fathomless human brain,
> And what is reason? and what is love? and what is life? 1095

He acknowledges that all men are duplicates of himself—"the weakest and the shallowest is deathless with me." (Line 1080 above) And that his readers share his ubiquity he defiantly challenges:

> The saints and sages in history—(who)[141] but you yourself? (Line 1093 above)

Canto 42 was a litany to the gods. Canto 43 is a litany to belief and believers--and doubt and unbelievers. In the first half of the Canto he salutes oracles; the sun; he pow wows; he helps the Llama or Brahmin trim the lamps; drinks mead from a skull-cap; minds the Koran; accepts the Gospels and he that was crucified. Whitman accepts belief because it is affirmation.

He belongs (as do we all) to "the winders of the circuit of circuits." He is "one of that centripetal and centrifugal gang." He then considers the case of doubt. The great doubts that each man entertains are likened to the bloody flukes of a dying whale: "Frivolous, sullen, moping, angry, affected, dishearten'd, atheistical, I know every one of you, I know the sea of torment, doubt, despair and unbelief... Be at peace bloody flukes of doubters... Each who passes is considered, each who stops is considered, not a single one can it fail." The 2nd half of the Canto (Lines 1112-1133) is among the greatest in his song and hence among the greatest of the canon. Among the most haunting of these lines concern children who die or whose innocence is compromised to no seeming purpose or end: ...*the little child who peep'd in at the door, and drew back and was never heard again.* Existence can not fail even ...*the sacs merely floating with open mouths for food to slip in; nor anything in the earth...nor anything in the myriads of spheres, nor the myriads that inhabit them. Nor the present; nor the least wisp that is known*...The poet's affirmation is complete and an answer to the question of *Why* that accompanies the *sea of torment, doubt and despair* that has been reported from time immemorial and is reported in our daily newscasts --from Columbine High in Littleton, Colorado to Sandy Hook Elementary in Newtown, Connecticut--from the million slaughtered by the Interahamwe in Rwanda to the atrocities of the Taliban in Afghanistan. This is a hard lesson, for we hold loss very dear and are hesitant to relinquish the judgment we claim of its perpetrators. For the Peruvian-America author Carlos Castaneda, our judgements are the province of the *Tonal*. But the "winders of the circuits of the circuits" view things from a different vantage. Castaneda called this outre' vantage the *Nagual*.

Castaneda's claim to mystical experience has been questioned as much as Whitman's. Both give witness to a personal holocaust, whether real or imagined: the suicide sprawled on the bloody floor of the bedroom in Whitman; and the report of the death of Don Juan's son in an industrial accident in Mexico. In the *Tonal* you view the suicide and or the son crushed to death as judgments: The suicide was "self-murder", a damnable offence. The death of a son is too painful for Don Juan to witness in the discriminating judgment of the *Tonal*. He therefore employs another vantage to reconcile its placement in time and diffuse the impact of his monumental pain. Though the terminology of the authors differs their conclusions are the same. In Castaneda's parlance, judgment takes place in the *Tonal:* "The Tonal begins at birth and ends at death..." For Whitman and the Peruvian the vastness of the alternative vision beckons: "... the Nagual never ends. The Nagual has no limit."

We learn in the 43rd Canto that everything is sufficient unto itself. From the haunted *child who peeped in the door* to the skeptics thrashing in a sea of doubt, to the *least wisp of that is known*--each is reflective of the Universe— each is tautologically *All*. The affirmation of Whitman (and so also the Nagual) is an affirmation that can not fail and will never end.

43. I Do Not Despise

> I do not despise you priests, all time, the
>   world over,   1096
> My faith is the greatest of faiths and the
>   least of faiths,

Enclosing worship ancient and modern
and all between ancient and
modern,
Believing I shall come again upon the
earth after five thousand years,
Waiting responses from oracles,
honoring the gods, saluting the sun,
Making a fetish of the first rock or
stump, powwowing with sticks in
the circle of obis,
Helping the llama or Brahmin as he
trims the lamps of the idols,
Dancing yet through the streets in a
phallic procession, rapt and austere
in the woods a gymnosophist,
Drinking mead from the skull-cap, to
Shasta's and Vedas admirant,
minding the Koran, 1104
Walking the teokallis, spotted with gore
from the stone and knife, beating
the serpent-skin drum,
Accepting the Gospels, accepting him
that was crucified, knowing
assuredly that he is divine, 1106
To the mass kneeling or the puritan's
prayer rising, or sitting patiently in
a pew,
Ranting and frothing in my insane crisis,
or waiting dead-like till my spirit
arouses me,
Looking forth on pavement and land, or
outside of pavement and land,
Belonging to the winders of the circuit
of circuits. 1110

One of that centripetal and centrifugal
    gang I turn and talk like man
    leaving charges before a journey.

Down-hearted doubters dull and
    excluded,   1112
Frivolous, sullen, moping, angry,
    affected, dishearten'd, atheistical,
I know every one of you, I know the sea
    of torment, doubt, despair and
    unbelief.

How the flukes splash!   1115
How they contort rapid as lightning,
    with spasms and spouts of blood!   1116

Be at peace bloody flukes of doubters
    and sullen mopers,
I take my place among you as much as
    among any,
The past is the push of you, me, all,
    precisely the same,
And what is yet untried and afterward
    is for you, me, all, precisely the
    same.

I do not know what is untried and
    afterward,
But I know it will in its turn prove
    sufficient, and cannot fail.   1122

Each who passes is consider'd, each who
    stops is consider'd, not a single one
    can it fail.

> It cannot fail the young man who died and was buried, 1124
> Nor the young woman who died and was put by his side,
> Nor the little child that peep'd in at the door, and then drew back and was never seen again, 1126
> Nor the old man who has lived without purpose, and feels it with bitterness worse than gall, 1127
> Nor him in the poor house tubercled by rum and the bad disorder,
> Nor the numberless slaughter'd and wreck'd, nor the brutish koboo call'd the ordure of humanity, 1129
> Nor the sacs merely floating with open mouths for food to slip in,
> Nor any thing in the earth, or down in the oldest graves of the earth,
> Nor any thing in the myriads of spheres, nor the myriads of myriads that inhabit them, 1132
> Nor the present, nor the least wisp that is known. 1133

The 44th Canto is also among the most astonishing in *Song of Myself*. The poet avers that "It is time to explain myself—let us stand up." He knows that he can only be explained by all others (let *us* stand up) and all others by himself. He then waxes expansive on the theme of time and his all embracing sense of it. He informs us that we have exhausted trillions of winters and summers—at last, an exaggeration!

21st century science computes the age of the universe at 15-18 billion years). The poet assures us that there are trillions of years ahead, and trillions ahead of them. Perhaps he feels certain because: "Afar down I see the huge first Nothing, I know I was even there..." and since science concerns itself with time only after *the beginning*, who is to say his calculation of *time before time* is necessarily wrong? To claim that he was there with the "first nothing" is to greatly extend his *three score and ten*. We love the poet for the horizons he expands for us: "I am not contained between my hat and boots." Given that faith, he imagines participating in the whole concatenation of time: "I waited unseen and always, and slept through the lethargic mist, and took my time, and took no hurt from the fetid carbon. Long I was hugg'd close—long and long. Immense have been the preparations for me... Cycles ferried my cradle, rowing and rowing like cheerful boatmen, for room to me stars kept aside in their own rings, they sent influences to look after what was to hold me." Other births, as well, have brought us richness and variety: "I do not call one greater or smaller, that which fills its period and place is equal to any." With that assurance the reader is invited to proceed.

44. It Is Time

> It is time to explain myself—let us stand
>   up. 1134
>
> What is known I strip away,
> I launch all men and women forward
>   with me into the Unknown.

The clock indicates the moment — but what does eternity indicate?

We have thus far exhausted trillions of winters and summers,
There are trillions ahead, and trillions ahead of them.

Births have brought us richness and variety,
And other births will bring us richness and variety.

I do not call one greater and one smaller, 1141
That which fills its period and place is equal to any. 1142

Were mankind murderous or jealous upon you, my brother, my sister?
I am sorry for you, they are not murderous or jealous upon me,
All has been gentle with me, I keep no account with lamentation,
(What have I to do with lamentation?)

I am an acme of things accomplish'd, and I an encloser of things to be. 1148

My feet strike an apex of the apices of the stairs,
On every step bunches of ages, and larger bunches between the steps,
All below duly travel'd, and still I mount and mount.

Rise after rise bow the phantoms behind me,
Afar down I see the huge first Nothing, I know I was even there, 1153
I waited unseen and always, and slept through the lethargic mist,
And took my time, and took no hurt from the fetid carbon.

Long I was hugg'd close—long and long.

Immense have been the preparations for me, 1157
Faithful and friendly the arms that have help'd me.

Cycles ferried my cradle, rowing and rowing like cheerful boatmen,
For room to me stars kept aside in their own rings,
They sent influences to look after what was to hold me.

Before I was born out of my mother generations guided me, 1163
My embryo has never been torpid, nothing could overlay it.

For it the nebula cohered to an orb,
The long slow strata piled to rest it on,
Vast vegetables gave it sustenance,
Monstrous sauroids transported it in their mouths and deposited it with care.

> All forces have been steadily employ'd
>   to complete and delight me,
> Now on this spot I stand with my robust
>   soul.   1169

One of the wonders of Whitman is his intimacy with miracles. He truly believes that:

> "Immense have been the preparations for me..."

Before he was born out of his mother, generations guided him... for him the nebula cohered in an orb and the long slow strata was piled inch upon inch to make a stand for him to rest upon. He claims that the same meticulous preparation attended each of his readers. That each of them can come to that same transcendent understanding is whereby: Now on this spot *they stand* with their robust souls! The 45th Section continues his absorption in existence and time: "O span of youth...O manhood, balanced, florid and full." He imagines that all things are his lovers: "My lovers suffocate me, crowding my lips, thick in the pores of my skin...Crying by day, Ahoy, from the rocks of the river, swinging and chirping over my head, calling my name from the flower beds, vines, tangled underbrush, lighting on every moment of my life." Death is always near in any list of his celebrants: "And the dark hush promulges as much as any." (Line 1182 below) And Whitman uncannily anticipates Hubble's Mount Wilson observations from the next century: *Wider and wider they spread, expanding, always expanding, Outward and outward forever outward.* (Lines 1181-1195) The reader is invited to hear his or her own name in the silence between the lines that follow...

45. O Span of Youth

> O span of youth! ever-push'd elasticity! 1170
> O manhood, balanced, florid and full.
>
> My lovers suffocate me,
> Crowding my lips, thick in the pores of my skin,
> Jostling me through streets and public halls, coming naked to me at night,
> Crying by day, Ahoy! from the rocks of the river, swinging and chirping over my head,
> Calling my name from flower-beds, vines, tangled underbrush,
> Lighting on every moment of my life,
> Bussing my body with soft balsamic busses,
> Noiselessly passing handfuls out of their hearts and giving them to be mine. 1179
>
> Old age superbly rising! O welcome, ineffable grace of dying days! 1180
>
> Every condition promulges not only itself, it promulges what grows after and out of itself, 1181
> And the dark hush promulges as much as any.
>
> I open my scuttle at night and see the far-sprinkled systems,

And all I see multiplied as high as I can cipher edge but the rim of the farther systems.

Wider and wider they spread, expanding, always expanding,
Outward and outward and forever outward.

My sun has his sun and round him obediently wheels,
He joins with his partners a group of superior circuit,
And greater sets follow, making specks of the greatest inside them.

There is no stoppage and never can be stoppage,
If I, you, and the worlds, and all beneath or upon their surfaces, were this moment reduced back to a pallid float, it would not avail the long run,
We should surely bring up again where we now stand, 1192
And surely go as much farther, and then farther and farther.

A few quadrillions of eras, a few octillions of cubic leagues, do not hazard the span or make it impatient,
They are but parts, any thing is but a part. 1195

> See ever so far, there is limitless space outside of that,
> Count ever so much, there is limitless time around that.
>
> My rendezvous is appointed, it is certain,
> The Lord will be there and wait till I come on perfect terms,   1199
> The great Camerado, the lover true for whom I pine will be there.   1200

Comparatively few people of the mid-nineteenth century had any conception of the size of what we oxymoronically call the *known universe*. In Section 45 he becomes more expansive as he speaks of quadrillions of eras. His grasp of space is on surer ground as he speculates a diameter approaching octillions of cubic leagues. He would have had no conception of a light year's 6 trillion miles. His guess to the most distant of galaxies was surprisingly prescient. He suggested a measurement in octillions. If we translate the light years into miles it is surprisingly close to a twenty-first century estimate. How he knew is anybody's guess (as it must have also been his own).

To comprehend the scope of the *guess* we need to bring the variables in question to our familiar dimensions. Imagine the earth the size of a grain of sugar. Then the moon would be a mote of dust ¼ of an inch away. The sun would then be roughly equivalent to a ping pong ball at a distance ten feet from the grain of sugar. Pluto would be a speck of dust two blocks away. The nearest star would then be 500 miles away.

The edge of our galaxy would be 2,500,000 miles still more distant. And the furthermost galaxy (4.4 quadrillion light years or 25.6 of Whitman's octillion miles.) — one-trillion, five-hundred billion miles from the grain of sugar. Many more variables could be figured into this quaint assessment but the poet is more than happy to leave calculations to the astronomers while he goes out for a bracing walk under the stars. In Canto 46 he sees such speculation as trifling: "I know I have the best of time and space." Time and again in this study we will have the occasion to review the spiritual exercises of numerous Oriental classics. These scriptures or sutras attempt to open the eyes and minds of the adepts who study them. Primarily the effort is to catch a fleeting glimpse of the splendid paradises for which they yearn. If the student persists in his resolve he will come to discover that the paradise he seeks is where he presently finds himself to be. Whitman expresses that same thought:

> It is not far, it is within reach,
> Perhaps you have been on it since you
>   were born and did not know it.
> Perhaps it is everywhere on water and
>   on land.

Earlier we suggested that the child in "A child said *What is the grass*" might be an imagined son. Here in Canto 46 the child *is* his son. Whitman once said that he didn't begrudge a man his wife but he was envious of his children. Near the end of his life he claimed he had fathered a half dozen of them.

This was taken with some seriousness at the time. Subsequent studies of his known itineraries, however, reduced this possibility to one approaching zero. His imagined progeny are now seen as a comforting fiction of a consciousness slowly drifting to eternity. If we wonder what kind of parent the poet might have been (or would have wished to be) the stanza commencing with: *Shoulder your duds dear son* of the 46th Canto (line 1215 to its conclusion) is as close an answer as we are likely to find. The last line is one of the loveliest in all of Whitman.

46. I Know

> I know I have the best of time and space, and was never measured and never will be measured.   1201
>
> I tramp a perpetual journey, (come listen all!)
> My signs are a rain-proof coat, good shoes, and a staff cut from the woods,
> No friend of mine takes his ease in my chair,
> I have no chair, no church, no philosophy,   1205
> I lead no man to a dinner-table, library, exchange,
> But each man and each woman of you I lead upon a knoll,
> My left hand hooking you round the waist,

My right hand pointing to landscapes of
continents and the public road.
Not I, not any one else can travel that
road for you, 1210
You must travel it for yourself.

It is not far, it is within reach,
Perhaps you have been on it since you
were born and did not know,
Perhaps it is everywhere on water and
on land.

Shoulder your duds dear son, and I will
mine, and let us hasten forth, 1215
Wonderful cities and free nations we
shall fetch as we go.
If you tire, give me both burdens, and
rest the chuff of your hand on my
hip,
And in due time you shall repay the
same service to me,
For after we start we never lie by again.

This day before dawn I ascended a hill
and look'd at the crowded heaven,
And I said to my spirit When we
become the enfolders of those orbs,
and the pleasure and knowledge of
every thing in them, shall we be
fill'd and satisfied then?
And my spirit said No, we but level that
lift to pass and continue beyond.

You are also asking me questions and I
hear you,

> I answer that I cannot answer, you must
> find out for yourself.
>
> Sit a while dear son,
> Here are biscuits to eat and here is milk
> to drink, 1226
> But as soon as you sleep and renew
> yourself in sweet clothes, I kiss you
> with a good-by kiss and open the
> gate for your egress hence.
>
> Long enough have you dream'd
> contemptible dreams,
> Now I wash the gum from your eyes,
> You must habit yourself to the dazzle of
> the light and of every moment of
> your life.
>
> Long have you timidly waded holding a
> plank by the shore,
> Now I will you to be a bold swimmer,
> To jump off in the midst of the sea, rise
> again, nod to me, shout, and
> laughingly dash with your hair. 1233

Whitman's advice "to habit yourself to the dazzle of the light...." is also the astonishment of Leopold Bloom assaying the universe: "... the great bear and Hercules and the dragon and the whole jingbang lot. But by God, I was lost, so to speak, in the milky way." [142]

Whitman takes up the role of teacher, once again, in Section 47. Among his unique instructions we will find: *If you would understand me go to the heights or water-shore,*

The nearest gnat is an explanation, and a drop or motion of waves key, The maul, the oar, the hand-saw, second my words. (Lines 1252-1254 below)

47. I Am the Teacher

I am the teacher of athletes,   1234
He that by me spreads a wider breast than my own proves the width of my own,
He most honors my style who learns under it to destroy the teacher.   1236

The boy I love, the same becomes a man not through derived power, but in his own right,
Wicked rather than virtuous out of conformity or fear,   1238
Fond of his sweetheart, relishing well his steak,
Unrequited love or a slight cutting him worse than sharp steel cuts,
First-rate to ride, to fight, to hit the bull's eye, to sail a skiff, to sing a song or play on the banjo,
Preferring scars and the beard and faces pitted with small-pox over all latherers,
And those well-tann'd to those that keep out of the sun.

I teach straying from me, yet who can stray from me?

I follow you whoever you are from the
    present hour,
My words itch at your ears till you
    understand them.   1246

I do not say these things for a dollar or
    to fill up the time while
    I wait for a boat,
(It is you talking just as much as myself,
    I act as the tongue of you,   1247
Tied in your mouth, in mine it begins to
    be loosen'd.)

I swear I will never again mention love
    or death inside a house,
And I swear I will never translate
    myself at all, only to him or her who
    privately stays with me in the open
    air.

If you would understand me go to the
    heights or water-shore,   1252
The nearest gnat is an explanation, and
    a drop or motion of waves key,   1253
The maul, the oar, the hand-saw, second
    my words.

No shutter'd room or school can
    commune with me,
But roughs and little children better
    than they.

The young mechanic is closest to me, he
    knows me well,

> The woodman that takes his axe and jug
> with him shall take me with him all
> day,
> The farm-boy ploughing in the field
> feels good at the sound of my voice,
> In vessels that sail my words sail, I go
> with fishermen and seamen and
> love them.
>
> The soldier camp'd or upon the march is
> mine,
> On the night ere the pending battle
> many seek me, and I do not fail
> them,
> On that solemn night (it may be their
> last) those that know me seek me.
>
> My face rubs to the hunter's face when
> he lies down alone in his blanket,
> The driver thinking of me does not
> mind the jolt of his wagon,
> The young mother and old mother
> comprehend me,
> The girl and the wife rest the needle a
> moment and forget where they are,
> They and all would resume what I have
> told them. 1268

As he had in Canto 46, in 47 he speaks of the need to let his pupil go once the lesson has been learned: "He most honors my style who learns under it to destroy the teacher."

WHITMAN'S CODE: A NEW BIBLE, VOLUME I
M.C. GARDNER

In Zen Buddhism there is a saying: *Kill the Buddha if you meet him on the road* — this is known as *Cho-Butsu-Ossono-Dan* which roughly translates as *the play beyond the Buddha* — so also here. Whitman takes the metaphor further, for the poet is also pupil:

> I teach straying from me, yet who can stray from me?
> I follow you whoever you are from the present hour,
> My words itch at your ears till you understand them.
> (It is you talking just as much as myself,
> I act as the tongue of you,
> Tied in your mouth, in mine it begins to be loosen'd.)

He concludes the section with a litany of working people whom he loves: the mechanic, the woodsman, the farmboy ploughing, fishermen, seamen and the soldiers facing a coming battle: "On that solemn night (it may be their last) those that know me seek me." *Leaves of Grass* is the most empathetic tome in American Literature. The embrace of the poet is as large as his Kosmos and includes us all. In elevating the soul, Deity is not necessarily diminished. Yet I wonder how many Americans would take offense at the line: "And nothing, not God, is greater than one's self is..." Diminishment is more inherent in the thought of the wonderfully acerbic David Hume: "This world was only the first rude essay of some infant deity who afterward abandoned it, ashamed of his lame performance."[143] I assert that Whitman's project is precisely the opposite and more in the nature of Eckhart's proposition:

> I am as certain as I am that I am a man
> that nothing is so "near" to me as God.
> God is nearer to me than myself. [144]

Joyce smiles and concurs:

> Washed in the blood of the lamb,
> Come on you wine fizzling,
> ginsizzlingboozegulling existences!...
> Alexander J. Christ Dowie, that's
> yanked to glory most half this planet
> from Frisco Beach to Vladivostok.
> The Deity aint no nickel dime
> bumshow... he's the grandest
> thing yet and don't you forget it. [145]

Week 48 is Whitman's *God Canto* -- the reader is invited to judge for himself...

48. I Have Said

I have said that the soul is not more than the body,	1269
And I have said that the body is not more than the soul,	
And nothing, not God, is greater to one than one's self is,	1271
And whoever walks a furlong without sympathy walks to his own funeral drest in his shroud,	1272
And I or you pocketless of a dime may purchase the pick of the earth,	1273

And to glance with an eye or show a bean in its pod confounds the learning of all times,
And there is no trade or employment but the young man following it may become a hero,
And there is no object so soft but it makes a hub for the wheel'd universe,   1276
And I say to any man or woman, Let your soul stand cool and composed before a million universes.   1277

And I say to mankind, Be not curious about God,
For I who am curious about each am not curious about God,   1277
(No array of terms can say how much I am at peace about God and about death.)

I hear and behold God in every object, yet understand God not in the least,   1281
Nor do I understand who there can be more wonderful than myself.

Why should I wish to see God better than this day?
I see something of God each hour of the twenty-four, and each moment then,   1284
In the faces of men and women I see God, and in my own face in the glass,

> I find letters from God dropt in the street, and every one is sign'd by God's name,
> And I leave them where they are, for I know that wheresoe'er I go,
> Others will punctually come for ever and ever. 1288

As we count down the final measure of the Whitman *year* we find a suggestion of the hours that comprise the Whitman *day*: *I see something of God each hour of the twenty-four.* (Line 1284 above) This, after a rich plethora of *mahatakyus* that are a wonder of the poem (Lines 1269-1288 above and recapitulated below):

> And whoever walks a furlong without sympathy walks to his own funeral drest in his shroud,
> And I or you pocketless of a dime may purchase the pick of the earth,
> And to glance with an eye or show a bean in its pod confounds the learning of all times,
> And there is no trade or employment but the young man following it may become a hero…

One of my favorites has a corollary in Mahayana Buddhism in general, and Hua-Yen Buddhism, in particular. Later in this study we'll have the occasion to further dilate. Let it suffice to say that the concept of *Indra's Net* is exquisitely rendered by: *And there is no object so soft but it makes a hub for the wheel'd universe.*

The omnific ubiquity of " I hear and see God in every object," anticipates the omniscience of Joyce's *dio boia*:

> Whom the most Roman of Catholics call
> dio boia, hangman god, is doubtless all
> in all in all of us." [146]

In the 49th Canto the poet takes up a reality that most try *religiously* to avoid.

49. And As to You Death

> And as to you Death, and you bitter hug of mortality, it is idle to try to alarm me.   1289
>
> To his work without flinching the accoucheur comes,
> I see the elder-hand pressing receiving supporting,
> I recline by the sills of the exquisite flexible doors,
> And mark the outlet, and mark the relief and escape.
>
> And as to you Corpse I think you are good manure, but that does not offend me,   1294
> I smell the white roses sweet-scented and growing,
> I reach to the leafy lips, I reach to the polish'd breasts of melons.

> And as to you Life I reckon you are the
>   leavings of many deaths,
> (No doubt I have died myself ten
>   thousand times before.) 1298
>
> I hear you whispering there O stars of
>   heaven,
> O suns—O grass of graves—O
>   perpetual transfers and promotions,
> If you do not say any thing how can I
>   say any thing?
>
> Of the turbid pool that lies in the
>   autumn forest,
> Of the moon that descends the steeps of
>   the soughing twilight,
> Toss, sparkles of day and dusk—toss on
>   the black stems that decay in the
>   muck,
> Toss to the moaning gibberish of the dry
>   limbs.
> I ascend from the moon, I ascend from
>   the night,
> I perceive that the ghastly glimmer is
>   noonday sunbeams reflected,
> And debouch to the steady and central
>   from the offspring great or small. 1308

Whitman had learned from the *Gita* that the core of his being was deathless—however many times it would die. Whitman was also intrigued by Justus Liebig's *Chemistry in Its Application to Physiology and Agriculture*. He wrote a review for the *Eagle* in which praised the book for:

> "its elevating beautiful study…which involves the essence of creation and the changes, and the growths, and the formations of so large a constituent part of the earth, and the things thereof."

From this Whitman took the notion of the universe being a colossal recycling machine in which each of us is deposited and returned time and time again: "No doubt I have died ten thousand times before." When Whitman says "And as to you corpse I think you are good manure but that does not offend me." We find that we take little offense and perhaps are spared a portion of the fear that often attends the thought of our own dissolution. We suspect that we too might *debouch to the steady and central from the offspring great or small.* The adepts of Zen Buddhism will find themselves not far afield as they wander through Canto 50…

50. There Is That in Me

> There is that in me—I do not know what
>   it is—but I know it is in me.   1309
> Wrench'd and sweaty—calm and cool
>   then my body becomes,
> I sleep—I sleep long.
>
> I do not know it—it is without name—it
>   is a word unsaid,
> It is not in any dictionary, utterance,
>   symbol.
>
> Something it swings on more than the
>   earth I swing on,

> To it the creation is the friend whose embracing awakes me.
>
> Perhaps I might tell more. Outlines! I plead for my brothers and sister.
>
> Do you see O my brothers and sisters?
> It is not chaos or death—it is form, union, plan—it is eternal life—it is Happiness.   1318

There is *that* in the poet: "I do not know what it is—but I know it is in me—it is a word unsaid, it is not in any dictionary, utterance, symbol...it is happiness." The final two cantos complete the 52 weeks of the Whitman *year*. As we earlier described in the *Gandavyhua Sutra* and in the architectural splendor of Borobudur, the pilgrim Sudhana visits 52 enlightened beings in his search for illumination. The *final* enlightened being of the 52 is also the *first* that sent him on his journey—Sudhana discovers that his epic voyage of discovery has deposited him at the paradise of his own door-step. [147] Whitman began his voyage in celebration—"hoping not to cease till death."

At its conclusion he is invited to become vapor and dusk—he is invited by *Death*: "I depart as air, I shake my white locks at the runaway sun, / I effuse myself in eddies, and drift in lacy jags. / I bequeath myself to the dirt to grow from the grass I love, / If you want me again look for me under your bootsoles." Beginning in perfect health he now concludes in perfect death—yet, he waits for us up ahead at the side of a road that each of us must travel. We find along with another poet:

> What we call the beginning is often the end
> And to make an end is to make a beginning,
> The end is where we start from…
> We shall not cease from exploration
> And the end of all our exploring
> Will be to arrive where we started
> And know the place for the first time.[148]

The culminating cantos are short. Together they make an intimate masterpiece—I will leave the reader alone with poet—he will be good health to you and filter and fibre your blood—he has assured me there will be no need of further introduction.

51. The Past and Present

> The past and present wilt—I have fill'd them, emptied them.   1319
> And proceed to fill my next fold of the future.
>
> Listener up there! what have you to confide to me?
> Look in my face while I snuff the sidle of evening,
> (Talk honestly, no one else hears you, and I stay only a minute longer.)

Do I contradict myself?   1324
Very well then I contradict myself,
(I am large, I contain multitudes.)   1326

I concentrate toward them that are nigh,
I wait on the door-slab.

Who has done his day's work? who will
soonest be through with his supper?
Who wishes to walk with me?
Will you speak before I am gone? will
you prove already too late? 1330

52. The Spotted Hawk

The spotted hawk swoops by and
accuses me, he complains of my gab
and my loitering. 1331

I too am not a bit tamed, I too am
untranslatable,
I sound my barbaric yawps over the
roofs of the world.

The last scud of day holds back for me,
It flings my likeness after the rest and
true as any on the shadow'd wilds,
It coaxes me to the vapor and the dusk. 1336

I depart as air, I shake my white locks at
the runaway sun, 1337
I effuse my flesh in eddies, and drift it in
lacy jags. 1338

I bequeath myself to the dirt to grow
from the grass I love, 1339
If you want me again look for me under
your boot-soles. 1340

You will hardly know who I am or what
    I mean,

But I shall be good health to you
    nevertheless,
And filter and fibre your blood.   1343

Failing to fetch me at first keep
    encouraged,
Missing me one place search another,
I stop somewhere waiting for you.   1346

BEMERSON

&

THE IDEALIST LOCUS

Walt Whitman, although unique in presentation, is not original as to concept and content. Midway in the twentieth century Aldous Huxley collected a philosophic compendium he called *The Perennial Philosophy*. In conjunction with this essay I have revised a collection of my own perennials. It is entitled, *Buddha Boogie, The Tautological Paradigm*. The book was predicated on statements that would fall outside Aristotle's conception of logic. As earlier stated, Aristotle's division of the world was based on the distinction: A ≠ B. To say that A was equal to B was no different than saying A = A, a tautology familiar to anyone who has ever constructed an equation. In mystic traditions we find a very different logic operative. Since Nicaea the Christian world has asserted that God the Father, God the Son and God the Holy Spirit or *Ghost* constitute a Trinity: A=B=C which, theologically, is rendered simply as A. Curiously, this is also the conclusion of the simplest of the Prajnaparamita Sutras of Mahayana Buddhism—that a single letter contains all the wisdom of the world's texts. In the Far East, Taoists believe that all things are resolved in the Tao. In Buddhism we find that all things are Buddha-things and equally void or sunyata. In the Bhagavad Gita we hear Krishna report: "He who is free from delusion and knows me as the supreme Reality, knows all that can be known—this is the most sacred of all truths that I have taught you. Some see me one with themselves, or separate; some bow to the countless gods that are my million faces."

As I gathered these statements and scriptures I found myself often supplementing my text with lines from *Leaves of Grass*. There is no American poet that is as inclusive — the countless elements of the world and its inhabitants are *his* million faces.

Ralph Waldo Emerson 1804-1883

Clear and sweet is my soul, and clear
 and sweet is all that is not my soul.
Lacks one lacks both, and the unseen is
 proven by the seen,
Till that becomes unseen and receives
 proof in its turn.

All these tend inward to me and I tend
 outward to them,
And such as it is to be of these more or
 less I am,
And of these one and all I weave the
 song of myself.

Since Whitman is the primary focus of this study it would be redundant to isolate lines and poems that have already been discussed or are still to come. However, since the poet was a guest in the earlier writing I've decided to supplement his material with some tautological loci that are congruent to it. This material will be dispersed throughout the volumes as way stations between significant sections of the New Bible.

First we must get a handle on some difficult thoughts — difficult because they are rarely thought. However much we are preoccupied with the minutiae of any given hour we will find that the matter of which I speak is wholly present — and representative of time and eternity.

Of time we are well acquainted with clocks and calendars. The eternal is more metaphysically elusive. Spinoza suggests: "By eternity, I mean existence itself..." [149] For Spinoza and Whitman and for many a mystic voice that preceded them — the everyday passage of the day disguises the eternity in every moment. Time and Eternity are tautologically conjoined — differing sides of the same shiny penny.

Measurement in space runs a similar gauntlet — from the inch to the infinite. Once again, we are familiar with the first and less certain of the second. Over a millennium before Blake saw the Universe in a grain of sand, Fa Tsang saw it in a mote of dust. The equivalence of anything with the totality of everything is an ancient conundrum. Whitman was fascinated by Egyptian culture and all things Greek. His interest in the culture of the Nile was stimulated by the Egyptian Museum on upper Broadway. He became good friends with its proprietor, Dr. Henry Abbott:

...paid him many visits there, and had long talks with him, in connection with my readings of many books and reports on Egypt—its antiquities, history, and how things and the scenes really look, and what the old relics stand for, as near as we can now get.

From the Aegean centuries he had memorized much of Homer and was familiar with the major philosophers that Greece had produced. He was also aware of how deeply Emerson was indebted to the Idealism of the broad shouldered gentleman named Plato. The archetypes of Plato were eternal verities in which the philosopher could hang the shingles of Truth, Justice, Beauty and the Good.

To the seeker of Wisdom the only escape from the cynicism and relativity of the Sophists was found outside time's transient shadows in the clarity of the *Sun's* eternal illumination. Plato believed this transcendent realm to be the bedrock and very basis of thought itself. Its logical necessity is suggested by the purity of mathematics and its presumed application in the celestial perfection of planetary movement. Through the use of Socratic dialectic, falsity is exposed and the pre-natal memory (anamnesis) of the eternal archetypes is elicited.

Whitman is cognizant of the long historical argument between Plato and his most prominent student, Aristotle. The younger philosopher believes his master's archetypes to be a fiction. Truth is found not in a transcendent realm of Ideas, but in the fact of physical substance. His categories give substance, shape & form. Substance is a given fact. The study of its categories reveals its empirical structures pertinent to the human mind.

Substance is foundation—the categories reveal its derivative logical constituents. Thus, Achilles is the substance, man. His weight would suggest his mass or quantity. That Achilles was slower or faster than a horse or a turtle was a consequence of the categorical "relation" between the substances under consideration.

Aristotle believed that the categories were universal constructs applicable to substance and that they existed only in the empirical world. Plato found the physical world a completely transient phenomenon. It logically necessitated an eternal and unchanging counterpart.

Aristotle believed that the physical world was the only one in which Plato's Ideas (Aristotle's Universals) could have any empirical relevance. Imagine Plato as Pascal—Aristotle as Voltaire; or Plato as Pope Benedict for whom God is Great and Aristotle as the late Christopher Hitchens for whom he is, perhaps, less so. [150]

Raphael's celebrated *School of Athens* is a Renaissance masterpiece depicting the amalgamation of his own time with that of the 5th and early 4th century BCE of the Greeks. The 27 year old artist depicts celebrated geniuses of the earlier era in the guise of heroes from his own. Thus, Heraclitus is pictured in a brooding portrait of Michelangelo seated in the foreground; Euclid is depicted as Bramante surrounded by a group of students; and Apelles appears by the right column facing as Raphael, himself. The centerpiece of the drama, appearing beneath the then rising dome of St. Peter's, is the opposition of two distinctive world views:

Plato (Leonardo) directs his finger to the starry heavens and Aristotle (perhaps his rival, Michelangelo, again)[151] outstretches his forearm and fingers parallel to the solid earth. The dichotomy of heaven and earth, spirit and flesh, mind and matter—constitutes a dynamic debate that has continued unabated for two thousand-five hundred years of Western deliberation. Note that the vanishing point of Raphael's composition is precisely between the two iconic heads of that dilemma.

Raphael's *School of Athens*
1510-11.
Fresco Vatican, Stanza della Segnatura, Rome
mezzo-mondo.com

Plato and Aristotle
428-347 BCE & 384-322 BCE

Plotinus, even more profoundly, defines the spiritual prerogatives he finds in Plato. Neo-Platonism was an aid in promulgating Christian theology. Despite an esoteric argument in Book XXII called *Against the Platonists*, Augustine's distinction between the City of Man (Rome) and the City of God (Heaven) has a decidedly Platonic caste. *The City of God* was written as the *City of Man* was falling down around the ears of post Pax Romana.

For the Dominicans, Albert Magnus, Thomas Aquinas and the younger Meister Eckhart, of the High Middle Ages, Aristotle is known as *the Philosopher*. He is thought by the schoolmen to be a pre-Christian pagan. Each of these celebrated scholars seeks to integrate the recently translated texts of Aristotle and his Persian (Avicenna) and Arabic (Averroes) commentators with the Platonism of Saint Augustine.

Aquinas' mentor, Albert Magnus, believes that revelatory truth pertains to scripture and spirit. He also believes that the physical world is open to empirical observation. The first comes directly from God. The second comes from the artifact of God's creation—the world. Both are sources of God's truth, because both are of God. Each of the periods in which these men lived was energized by a new confidence of man's place in the world. Plato lives in the generation succeeding the Age of Pericles and the building of the Parthenon. Magnus, Aquinas and Eckhart lived in the generation after the first Cathedrals exploded the medieval sky. Pride of place suggests the foundation of those first spires were laid at the Abbey of St. Denis. It was during the building of the Abbey's Basilica that the Latin translation of Aristotle's work first becomes available. Theretofore, only a fraction of his work was known and then, only second-hand.

The building of the Cathedral at Chartres is begun three decades before the birth of Aquinas. It is consecrated 14 years before his demise at 49. The Cathedrals mark one of the high water marks of man's aesthetic sensibility. From their initiation at St. Denis they spread to Italy, Germany and England during the two centuries in which they were primarily built. Medieval Cathedrals have a decidedly Platonic caste. They direct the mind beyond the mundane to the celestial heights to which they soar. The rib, vault, pointed arch and the eco-skeletal of buttress, allows the stones to achieve an ethereal quality that floats above the awe of the celebrant. This otherworldly quality is further enhanced by glass stained to catch the gaze of passing sun and lambent moon.

The building projects of Acropolis and Cathedral speak to the confidence of their respective ages. Vast temple complexes are possible only to men whose feet are fastened firmly to terra firma. This is the legacy the genius of one culture bequeaths to another. In the 12th century Hugh of Saint-Victor proposes that secular learning is instrumental and yea—inaugural to mystic vision.

> Learn everything; later you will see that nothing is superfluous.

Hugh writes the first *Summae,* which becomes the impetus for Aquinas' formulation of man's relationship to God and creation. The *Summa Theologica* is an intellectual challenge of *cathedralesqe* dimensions. Aquinas attempts to wed the systems of Plato and Aristotle to the tenets of the Holy Roman Church.

The Word of God is not only written in the Scripture below and the Heavens above but, as well, in the earth, sea and sky. To know God is to know life. Nature is itself the proof of God and Holy Writ is found *in* Creation as surely as it is found in either Testament.

God is both Essence and Existence—man's existence is predicated on an Essence he shares with the Being who is both. Because the world is God's creation the study of it more readily prepares the mind for the contemplation of *Him* who created it. Aquinas' embrace of a pagan's system of logic does not sit well with many of his fellow clerics. They feel that too keen an interest in the physical world lessens the need and apprehension of the spiritual. Eckhart takes Aquinas' argument even further afield. He believes that God is found in the recesses of His creation—in the inward depths of man. When one finds God within there is less need to look for Him without—or within the hallowed sanctuary of Holy Church.

Both men are censored for these tendencies. Aquinas, however, is declared a Saint. Eckhart is condemned by Papal Bull posthumously, on March 27, 1329. Aquinas reports a beatific vision, shortly before his death. In that extraordinary report he proclaims his logical constructions in the vast tomes of his *Summa* are as significant as straw and of no directive consequence. We have no way of knowing what aspect of his teaching is seen as deficient—but clearly his vision consecrates earth as well as Heaven and will not go away. Eckhart asserts:

> God is nowhere as much as he is in the soul…and the soul means the world.

This dialectic between the physical and the spiritual is instrumental in Hegel's *Phenomenology of Spirit* and proves influential to Whitman. The Catholic philosopher Franz von Baader introduced Hegel to the writings of Eckhart: "I was with Hegel in Berlin. Once I read him a passage from Meister Eckhart, who was only a name to him. He was so excited by it that by the next day, he read me a whole lecture on Eckhart, which he ended with:

There, indeed, we have what we want!

Rhineland Mysticism rises with the Cathedrals. It follows in Eckhart's wake. It begins the tradition of honoring the earth and the God-within one's *own* Cathedral. This, on occasion, takes a twisted form. This is also the era of the Black Plague. The Bubonic bacillus kills one out of every three people in Europe. Flesh is sin and complicit in flesh's corruption. It only takes three bacilli to kill a mouse—the single bite of a flea disperses twenty thousand bacilli into a host body—flagellates roam the land. One of Eckhart's students, Heinrich Seuse, writes one of the most revered devotional tracts of the High Medieval period, *The Little Book of Eternal Wisdom*. Seuse loses his Eckhartian bearings in the face of the plague. After the manner of the flagellates he wears an undergarment festooned with hundreds of sharpened nails—a design rumored to be in preproduction by *Abercrombie and Fitch*. Seuse also wears gloves covered with tacks to keep him from disturbing the lice that make of his body a lovely home. He is said to have purposefully avoided a bath for twenty-five years.

Eckhart is more moderately influential in two lay organizations that take their names from the priest, Lambert le Bègue. The women are known as Beguines. No vows are required; the Beguines can return to society and marry if such proves a desire or option. The counterpart for the men is known as the *Beghards*. The Beghards are generally retiring members of local guilds who are at the tail-end of a lifetime's labor. They are bound together in the hope of contributing good works but also in communing with God outside the sanctity of Church. This earth and secular oriented spirituality results in science on the one hand and pantheism on the other — and becomes an under-current eventually leading to the 17th century's Royal Academy and George Fox's *Society of Friends*, later derisively known as Quakers. But prior to that, the synthesis that the Schoolmen began with Plato, Aristotle, and Christianity comes to a stunning culmination in the 15th and 16th centuries.

The stature of the 5th century Greeks is again the inspiration to the magnificence that ensues in the Renaissance. Pico della Mirandolla composes the *Oration on the Dignity of Man* and Ficino publishes the first complete translation of Plato to be found in the West. The second half of the Quattrocento sees the birth of Leonardo, Michelangelo, Giorgione, Durer, Botticelli, and Bramante. They and many others mark the cultural high-water mark of the Church's preeminence. The building of St. Peter's and the decoration and the expansion of the Vatican constitute the greatest artistic undertaking since the building of the Cathedrals at the height of the medieval period nearly three centuries before.

Along with the artists cited above we might also add Copernicus, Machiavelli, Cesare Borgia, Columbus, Magellan, Pizarro and Martin Luther. Although devout to varying degrees these men with the help of the new navigational tools, the printing press and the discovery of new worlds, begin to undermine the Divine scaffolding that supports the universal power of the Catholic Church. In the succeeding centuries both the British Empiricism of Bacon, Locke, Berkeley and Hume and the Rationalism of Decartes, Spinoza and Leibnitz divide different aspects of the Plato/Aristotle rift and further erode the authority of Rome. Whitman is born (1819) in post revolutionary America, at the end of the so-called *Age of Reason*. His father is a personal friend of Thomas Paine, who previously pens the revolutionary essay, *The Age of Reason*. Voltaire and the Encyclopediasts spend a good deal of the eighteenth century railing against the Church (Écrasez l'Infâme) and the Monarchy. The American and French Revolutions are political upheavals resulting from their literary attacks and the general revulsion to institutions that their respective peoples can no longer abide. The revolution in America and abroad is also preceded by a religious enthusiasm known as the *Great Awakening*. The Catholic Church is seen as secular as any nation and the Pope as powerful as any King. In Germany Martin Luther had inaugurated the Reformation. A decade later, Henry the VIII declares himself Supreme Head of the Church in England. Overthrowing the catholic rule of Catholicism by a king who will die riddled with Syphilis, precedes the regicides that will topple the uncontested privilege of European Royalty. Whitman is a product of the 2nd *Great Awakening*. Each of the "awakened" facets seeks a lay clergy that assists their congregants in achieving a personal relationship—a relationship without intercession—with their Savior and God. The American Bible Society is founded in 1816.

In their first few years they distribute over 100,000 Bibles. New translations of the Bible proceed apace. Congregants not only receive a personal Bible but one that is unique to their congregation. A supplementary Bible called the *Book of Mormon* is "translated" by Joseph Smith from golden plates reporting an ancient visit by Jesus Christ to South America.

William Miller's careful study of the Book of Daniel and other Biblical texts suggest that the 2nd coming is nigh at hand. The Millerites calculate that Christ's arrival is imminent and cancel all dentist appointments for October 24, 1844. The *Great Hope* up to and including October 24th becomes the *Great Disappointment* of the 25th. Miller felt his calculations might need tweaking but remained devoted to a *stairway to heaven* that never descended.

> I am still looking for the Dear Savior.... The time, as I have calculated it, is now filled up; and I expect every moment to see the Savior... I have now nothing to look for but this glorious hope.

The Millerites splinter into several groups — the most prominent being the 7th Day Adventists. A similar hope of Rapture is generated by the calculations of Harold Camping's Family Radio. Camping's calculations[152] suggest that May 21, 2011 is the big day. As this day comes and goes it is rescheduled for October 21st of the same year. As that 21st arrives and departs the goodly Harold Camping suffers a rapturous stroke and is persuaded to give his apocalyptic timetable a rest. Late in his life Whitman records a series of notes on his childhood memory of the Quaker preacher, Elias Hicks:

> As myself a little boy hearing so much of E. H., at that time, long ago, in Suffolk and Queens and Kings Counties—and more than once personally seeing the old man—and my dear, dear father and mother faithful listeners to him at the meetings—I remember how I dream'd to write perhaps a piece about E. H. and his look and discourses, however long afterward—for my parents' sake—and the dear Friends too! And the following is what has at last but all come out of it—the feeling and intention never forgotten yet! [153]

Whitman begins this reminiscence less than four years before his death. It is touching to find him reflecting so sweetly on his father: "—and my dear, dear father." We know of his life-long devotion to his mother but we have little evidence of a commensurate feeling for his namesake. The Hicks account is one of the prose pieces collected for *November Boughs*, among the last of Whitman's published writings. It recounts much of the triumph and tragedy of the unconventional preacher. Whitman is particularly interested in the "inner light" of the Quakers, which in turn, had been stimulated by the writings of Jacob Boehme. Early in the 1850s he discerns that there is no difference between these illuminations and his own.

> Now and then, at the many scores and hundreds—even thousands—of his discourses—as at this one—he was very mystical and radical, and had much to say of "the light within."

> Very likely this same *inner light,* (so dwelt upon by newer men, as by Fox and Barclay at the beginning, and all Friends and deep thinkers since and now,) is perhaps only another name for the religious conscience.
>
> In my opinion they have all diagnos'd, like superior doctors, the real inmost disease of our times, probably any times. Amid the huge inflammation call'd society, and that other inflammation call'd politics, what is there to-day of moral power and ethic sanity…

Whitman continues his attack on the moral turpitude of his fellow Americans:

> …it is certain that any mark'd or dominating National Morality, (if I may use the phrase) has not only not yet been develop'd, but that—at any rate when the point of view is turn'd on business, politics, competition, practical life, and in character and manners in our New World—there seems to be a hideous depletion, almost absence, of such moral nature.

His up-bringing in the radical Quakerism of Elias Hicks and his extensive reading regimen from Plato to Emerson make him particularly sensitive to the otherworldly perquisites of Idealism:

> Elias taught throughout, as George Fox began it, or rather reiterated and verified it, the Platonic doctrine that the ideals of character, of justice, of religious action, whenever the highest is at stake, are to be conform'd to no outside doctrine of creeds, Bibles, legislative enactments, conventionalities, or even decorums, but are to follow the inward Deity-planted law of the emotional soul.[154]

Yet, in his preoccupation with exigencies of the flesh and the physical world he is firmly grounded in an Aristotelian world. Even Elias Hicks draws the fire from the "friends" when he suggests:

> The blood of Christ—the blood of Christ—why, my friends, the actual blood of Christ in itself was no more effectual than the blood of bulls and goats—not a bit more—not a bit.[155]

In Whitman we find not only Hicks and Emerson, but also Plato and Aristotle meticulously blended. The verb "blended" is Whitman's own. In 1876 he pens a poem addressing this very dichotomy. The poem takes its title from the first line:

> When the full-grown poet came,
> Out spake pleased Nature (the round impassive globe, with all its shows of day and night,) saying, He is mine;

> But out spake too the Soul of man,
>   proud, jealous and unreconciled,
> Nay he is mine alone;
> Then the full-grown poet stood between
>   the two, and took each by the hand;
> And to-day and ever so stands, as
>   blender, uniter, tightly holding
>   hands,
> Which he will never release until he
>   reconciles the two,
> And wholly and joyously blends them.

A leaf of grass is both existential (Nature) and profoundly other-worldly[156] (Soul). He ponders both the glowing globe and starry heavens. He finds each equally full of wonder. The poet's work is a cogent blending of the *Ideal* world of the spirit and the *Material* world of the flesh — heaven and earth, Plato and Aristotle. This book is predicated on the poet's conscious or unconscious preoccupation with time: "I am the clock...I see something of God each hour of the twenty-four," and eternity: "To me the converging objects of the Universe perpetually flow, All are written to me and I must get at what the writing means."

Aside from the religious awakening of the first half of the nineteenth century there is also a significant intellectual and literary awakening that runs parallel to it. This is a form of Idealism called American Transcendentalism — a post-enlightenment form of Romanticism tied to the Lyceum movement advancing calls to culture and education in America. Dr. William Ellery Channing speaks to the issue of Americans creating their own literature and culture in *Remarks on American Literature*. Channing is a Unitarian Minister in Boston.

His statements on American Literature pre-date Emerson's call to arms in the *American Scholar* (1837) by a half a dozen years and his sermon on God's shared nearness in the soul and nature (*Likeness to God*, 1828) anticipates *Nature* by eight years and the *Divinity School Address* by a decade. His nephew, the poet Ellery Channing, is a friend of Thoreau's and closely aligns with the movement. Emerson becomes the head of the Transcendental cause with the anonymous publication of *Nature* in 1836, the *American Scholar* in '37 and the *Divinity School Address* in 1838. Joel Myerson's study on the movement puts the matter simply: "Perhaps the single most important question raised by the Transcendentalists is: 'How do we see the world?'"[157] Specifically, they believe in knowledge that transcends the senses. John Locke had earlier argued the senses were the only conveyors of reality. For Locke, the senses stimulate impressions that are then imprinted on the Tabula Rasa of the awaiting mind. In contrast, the Transcendentalists believe that the essential ordering of the collection takes place within the mind. Taking their lead from Kant who was awakened from his *dogmatic slumbers* by the radical skepticism of David Hume — they believe that there are "Transcendental" realms of knowledge that can only be accessed within a clear thinking, intuitive mind.

In the Orient these realms had been opened to the forest sages of the Upanishads. In the West we find them explored in the dialectical legacy of Socrates and Plato as recorded in *Dialogues* of the 2nd named. They include the categories Kant believed were the apriori structures of thought which are in turn linked to the eternal archetypes in the creative mind of God:

The soul knows no person but invites each to expand to the full measure of the universe...One mind is the only sovereign agent...the whole of history is in each man...I can find each era in my own mind...nothing is sacred but the integrity of your mind... None of us can harm the universe, there is a great soul over the will of every man...by lowly listening we shall hear the right word...our being is descending into us from where we know not hence—from some alien energy the visions come...There is no screen or ceiling between our heads and the infinite heavens. Every man's particular being is contained within the unity and hence made one with all other...a light shines through us to show that we are nothing and the light is all. When it shines through the intellect it is genius. When it shines through the will it is virtue. When it shines through the affection it is love...We are wiser than we know...the blindness of the intellect begins when it would be something of itself...There is less in the great to reflect upon then in lesser souls as the virtue of the pipe is to be smooth and hollow, so also here. No answer in words can reply to a question in being—the question and the answer are one. Do you think your porter or cook have no anecdotes for you.

> Everybody knows as much as a servant.
> Each mind is filled is filled with
> hieroglyphics to which a lamp may one
> day be held. All the laws of nature may
> be read in the smallest fact. Let us be
> silent for so are the Gods. [158]

And if, dear reader, you find this to be too rich an affair for a single paragraph you would be quite right—it was randomly culled from a dozen different essays by Emerson. His persuasive powers were even much more formidable on the lecture circuit, although he couldn't completely disguise the *better angels* of his nature. His son Edward Waldo reports a conversation with a servant girl who attends each of his lectures. She is asked if she understand the so called *Sage of Concord*:

> No a word, but I like to go and see him
> stand up there and look as if he thought
> every one was as good as he was.

The Transcendentalist Club is formed shortly after its foundational document, *Nature,* is published by Emerson in 1836. Other members include Amos Bronson Alcott, Margaret Fuller, Henry David Thoreau, George Ripley and a group of Unitarian ministers including William Henry Channing, Christopher Pearce Cranch and Convers Francis. Emerson resigns his pastorage in 1832 over a dispute concerning the Eucharist. A larger group, including Nathaniel Hawthorne, gathers for experiments in social engineering at Ripley's "Brook Farm" and Alcott's "Fruitlands." Aside from the renowned *Sage of Concord*, the most internationally celebrated of the group is Henry David Thoreau.

Henry David (initially David Henry until graduating Harvard) has the good fortune to be one of Emerson's closest friends. He lives with *Waldo* (Emerson's preferred appellation) and Lydian over a period of years in the 1840s (1841-43 and 1847-48). He desires to live as simply as his minimal needs dictate. In 1844 Emerson purchases land at Walden Pond and Thoreau is given, by his mentor, the opportunity to engage in his two-year experiment of *Walden*:

> In most books, the I, or first person, is omitted; in this it will be retained; that, in respect to egoism, is the main difference. We commonly do not remember that it is, after all, always the first person that is speaking. I should not talk so much about myself if there were any body else whom I knew as well. Unfortunately, I am confined to this theme by the narrowness of my experience...I trust that none will stretch the seams in putting on the coat, for it may do good service to him whom it fits...I have traveled a good deal in Concord; and every where, in shops, and offices, and fields, the inhabitants have appeared to me to be doing penance in a thousand remarkable ways...The twelve labors of Hercules were trifling in comparison with those which my neighbors have undertaken; for they were only twelve, and had an end...I see young men, my townsmen, whose misfortune it is to have inherited farms, houses, barns, cattle, and farming

tools; for these are more easily acquired than gotten rid of…The portionless, who struggle with no such unnecessary inherited encumbrances, find it labor enough to subdue and cultivate a few cubic feet of flesh. But men labor under a mistake. The better part of the man is soon ploughed into the soil as compost…He has no time to be any thing but a machine… I have no doubt that some of you who read this book are unable to pay for the dinner which you have already eaten, or for the coat and shoes which are wearing out or already worn out, and have come to this page to spend borrowed or stolen time, robbing your creditors of an hour… promising to pay tomorrow and dying today… making yourself sick, that you may lay up something against a sick day… but worst of all you are the slave-driver of yourself… as if you could kill time without injuring eternity... The greater part of what my neighbors call good I believe in my soul to be bad, and If I repent of any thing, it is very likely to be my good behavior. What demon possessed me that I behaved so well…

For many years I was self-appointed inspector of snow storms and rain storms, and did my duty faithfully; surveyor, if not of highways, then of forest paths and…ravines bridged and passable at all seasons, where the public heel had testified to their utility…

In short, I went on thus for a long time...till it became more and more evident that my townsmen would not after all admit me into the list of town officers, nor make my place a sinecure with a moderate allowance...The life which men praise and regard as successful is but one kind. Why should we exaggerate one kind at the expense of the others? ... It is not necessary that a man should earn his living by the sweat of his brow unless he sweats more than I do... We may not arrive at our port within a calculable period, but we would preserve the true course... I went to the woods because I wished to live deliberately, to front only the essential facts of life and see if I could not learn what it had to teach, and not, when I came to die, discover that I had not lived.

Henry David Thoreau
1817-1862

Most of these words of quite remarkable wisdom and wit are distilled from the first twelve pages of *Economy*, the opening chapter of Thoreau's *Walden*. Emerson gives his friend a lease of Walden unencumbered by whatever modest rent it might have delivered. During his two year stay Thoreau produces *A Week on the Concord and Merrimac Rivers* and *Walden: or Life in the Woods*. At the end of his first summer at Walden the author is arrested in Concord:

> I went to the village to get a shoe from the cobbler and was seized and put in jail...because I did not pay a tax to, or recognize the authority of, the state which buys and sells men, women, and children, like cattle at the door of its Senate house. I had gone down to the wood for other purposes. But, where ever a man goes, men will pursue and pay him with their dirty institutions and, if they can constrain him... It is true that I might have resisted forcibly with more or less effect, might have run "amok" against society but I preferred that society run amuck against me — it being the desperate party.

He spends a single night in jail. Lacking this modest defiance over funds he believed supportive of slavery and the Mexican War our collective memory might be bereft of Mahatma Gandhi and Martin Luther King. Certainly, considering its twenty pages, *Civil Disobedience* is among the most influential documents of the nineteenth century.

Both Gandhi and King would have made remarkable contributions to their respective worlds—but they would have been different worlds and likely very different gifts than those for which they remain supremely cherished. We can thank Emerson for Thoreau and Whitman. Not only for his support but also for a loving opposition that helped, as well, to formulate who they both became. Emerson was more intimate with Thoreau than Whitman—which was all to the good for he had a much shorter time with which to engage him. The tubercular Thoreau died in 1862 at the age of forty.

Amos Bronson Alcott is more popularly remembered as the father of Louisa May Alcott, author of *Little Women*. He is also a radical educator who decries the infliction of physical punishment on any student. He often says that if a child misbehaves it is the educator who should be reprimanded. He is a vegetarian and the founder of "Fruitlands," which, along with Brook Farm, is one of the noted communal experiments of the period. This is from one of his many contributions to Emerson's *The Dial*:

> Nature is quick with spirit. In eternal systole and diastole, the living tides course gladly along, incarnating organ and vessel in their mystic flow. Let her pulsations for a moment pause on their errands, and creation's self ebbs instantly into chaos and invisibility again. The visible world is the extremist wave of that spiritual flood, whose flux is life, whose reflux death, efflux thought, and conflux light. Organization is the confine of incarnation,—body the atomy of God.

Which is to say, that not all the transcendentalists were as pithy as Emerson and Thoreau. In Amos' favor, however, is the esteem in which his fellows held him:

> I should not forget that during my last winter at the pond, there was another welcome visitor...One of the last of the philosophers—Connecticut gave him to the world.
>
> I think he must be the man of the most faith of any alive. His words and attitude always assume a better state of things than other men are acquainted with, and he will be the last man to be disappointed as the ages revolve...
>
> With his hospitable intellect he embraces children, beggars, insane, and scholars, and entertains the thought of all, adding to it some breadth and elegance...
>
> He is perhaps the sanest man and has the fewest crochets of any I chance to know; A blue-robed man, whose fittest roof is the overarching sky which reflects his serenity,
>
> I do not see how he can ever die. Nature can not spare him.

Amos Bronson Alcott:

1799-1888

Of the numerous Transcendentalists, Margaret Fuller is thought to be the most well-read. She starts her study at age three and a few years later became the first woman admitted to the hallowed stacks of Harvard's library. She is primarily remembered for faithfully editing the group's quarterly journal, *The Dial*, and penning the well regarded, *Woman in the Nineteenth Century*. In 1850 she returns from Italy with (the order is uncertain) a new husband, a new child and a new manuscript on the creation of the Roman Republic. She loses each and her own life before reaching dockage in New York. Her ship capsizes after running aground on a sandbar—she was forty years old.

The loss recalls both that of Shelley earlier in the century and Lincoln, a little latter. When Lincoln was elected our 16th President he had an odd vision that he related to his wife. He reported seeing a ghostly visage as he peered within a mirror. The 2nd was his face also but possessed of a deathly pallor.[159] A week before the Assassination he saw the same face lying in State in his Presidential coffin. Both Shelley and Fuller had premonitions, as well, about deaths at sea. Shelley related that his *doppelganger* appeared before him and told him he was shortly to die. Margaret Fuller spoke of dark presentiments that also foretold her coming demise: "I am absurdly fearful and various omens have combined to give me a dark feeling... It seems to me that my future upon earth will soon close..." Thoreau (like Byron before him searching for Shelly's body on the beach near Viareggio) scanned the coast off Fire Island for any trace of Fuller. Of the three, only the child's body was recovered. The tragedy was made absurdly tragic as the accident occurred within 100 yards of the shore.

It was a major loss to the group and to the growing brilliance of what was to become an American Renaissance. This was Fuller's call to arms at the beginning of *Woman and the Nineteenth Century*:

> ...the time is come when Eurydice is to call for an Orpheus, rather than Orpheus for Eurydice; that the idea of Man, however imperfectly brought out, has been far more so than that of Woman; that she, the other half of the same thought, the other chamber of the heart of life, needs now take her turn in the full pulsation, and that improvement in the daughters will best aid in the reformation of the sons of this age.

In words which anticipate her own gender's *Emancipation Proclamation* she writes:

> Yet, then and only then will mankind be ripe for this, when inward and outward freedom for Woman as much as for Man shall be acknowledged as a right, not yielded as a concession. As the friend of the negro assumes that one man cannot by right hold another in bondage, so should the friend of Woman assume that Man cannot by right lay even well-meant restrictions on Woman. If the Negro be a soul, if the woman be a soul, appareled in flesh, to one Master only are they accountable. There is but one law for souls, and, if there is to be an interpreter of it, he must come not as man, or son of man, but as son of God.

The only known photograph of Margaret Fuller is the image below:

1810 – 1850
Daguerreotype

Transcendentalism declines after the death of Margaret Fuller. *Fruitlands* and *Brook Farm* recede into the historical memory. What survives as vitally in our own century is the work precipitated by the genius of Emerson and the writings of Thoreau, Hawthorne, Melville, Dickinson, James and the wild elephant in the room to whom Emerson had extended invitation—Walt Whitman.

In *The Poet*, Emerson suggests that America awaits a poet to whom all will be written, who will sing for "...the northern trade, the southern planting, the western clearing, Oregon and Texas are yet unsung. Yet America is a poem in our eyes; its ample geography dazzles the imagination, and it will not wait long for meters." In the ecstatic close of the essay he anticipates the very poet of whom we write:

> The world is full of renunciations and apprenticeships, and is thine; thou must pass for a fool and a churl for a long season. This is the screen and sheath in which Pan has protected his well-beloved flower, and thou shalt be known only to thine own, and they shall console thee with tenderest love...And this is the reward; that the ideal shall be real to thee and the impressions of the actual world shall fall like summer rain, copious, but not troublesome to thy invulnerable essence. Thou shalt have the whole land for thy park and manor, the sea for thy bath and navigation, without tax and without envy, the woods and the rivers thou shalt own, and thou shalt possess that wherein others are only tenants and boarders. Thou true land-lord! Sea-lord! Air-lord! Wherever snow falls or water flows or birds fly, wherever day and night meet in twilight, wherever the blue heaven is hung by clouds or sown with stars, wherever are forms with transparent boundaries, wherever are outlets into celestial space, wherever is danger and awe, and love—there is Beauty, plenteous as rain, shed for thee, and though shouldst walk the world over, thou shalt not be able to find a condition inopportune or ignoble.

If, perchance, one fails to grasp what Emerson foresees — a more prosaic list might prove useful — the correspondence is so subtle and remarkable that it might be overlooked.

1. Whitman apprentices as a type-setter, reporter, and editor at numerous newspapers.
2. With the appearance of *Leaves of Grass* he is called a quack, a fool, a beast, a churl, an egoist and worse.
3. Whitman is thought pagan — he is even thought of as a hairy goat, a pan.
4. Known only to his own — his inner circle is derisively called *hot little prophets* for their unfailing loyalty to their *god*.
5. The ideal will be real for the poet. We've already seen how *he* has seen Plato's *Ideas* in the realm of the mundane and blended the two.
6. Impressions of the world will fall like rain. No poet has complied more extensive lists and catalogues of those impressions.
7. The land shall be his manor. Ownership of the earth is one of his favorite themes.
8. He shall bathe in the sea. Bathing in the sea is one of the poet's favorite activities.
9. Wherever there are forms with transparent boundaries, there you shall find him. When he speaks of his mystic

experience he recalls that it happened on a *transparent* summer morning.
10. The heavens hung with clouds or sown with stars—there Beauty, plenteous as rain shall be shed for him. Some of his major themes are drawn from the sea, the sky and the stars.
11. And finally, nothing shall seem inopportune or ignoble—an outlook we find time and again in his poetry.

Emerson's list, at the conclusion of *The Poet,* is as close to a prognostication of Walt Whitman as one is ever likely to find. And whether Whitman the New Yorker can be said to keep proper truck with the New England Transcendentalists it is clear that the gauntlet that Emerson had tossed to the earth and ear would be claimed by Walter Whitman, Junior:

> Then the full-grown poet stood between the two, and took each by the hand;
> And to-day and ever so stands, as blender, uniter, tightly holding hands,
> Which he will never release until he reconciles the two,
> And wholly and joyously blends them.

We have spoken before[160] of this poem and its reference to blending the Ideal and Physical worlds. Let's let Whitman further dilate:

> Most writers have disclaimed the physical world and they have not over-estimated the other, or soul, but have under-

estimated the corporeal. How shall my eye separate the beauty of the blossoming buckwheat field from the stalks and heads of tangible matter? How shall I know what life is except as I see it in the flesh? I will not praise one with the other or any more than the other.

These two rivulets of thought were further *praised* in the supplement to the Centennial edition of *Leaves of Grass* in the poem, *Two Rivulets*:

> Two Rivulets side by side,
> Two blended, parallel, strolling tides,
> Companions, travelers, gossiping as they journey.
> For the Eternal Ocean bound,
> These ripples, passing surges, streams of Death and Life,
> Object and Subject hurring, whirling by,
> The Real and the Ideal,
> Alternate ebb and flow the Days and Nights
> Strands of a Trio twining, Present, Future, Past.)
> In You, whoe'er you are, my book perusing,
> In I myself—in all the World—these ripples flow,
> All, all, toward the mystic Ocean trending.
>
> (O yearnful waves! The kisses of your lips!

Your breast so broad, with open arms, O
firm, expanded shore!)

Here again, the full-grown poet blends the Ideal and the Material. This blending reveals that his days and nights are also the trinity of the past, present and future — these mirror the cartography of his soul — the blending of time and eternity. It is a notion that is found in the world's mystic traditions and given amble credence by those sympathetic to them in the scientific community, as well:

> Subject and object are only one. The barrier between them cannot be said to have broke down as a result of recent experiences in the physical sciences, for this barrier does not exist... Inconceivable as it seems to ordinary reason, you and all other conscious beings as such — are all in all. Hence this life of yours which you are living is not merely a piece of the entire existence, but is in a certain sense the whole." [161]

That the one mirrors the other is whereby the revelation of eternity is always attendant to any presentation of time, and the totality of space dimensionally present in the details of any locale. To view what we take to be other (other people, places or things) is to view the exterior structure of the *mind*. We each abide in an isolation encompassed by totality. Totality is *mind* entertaining the illusion of distinction. Being is never represented in anything less than its complete presentation.

To wonder why the world is anything in particular is at once to be offered the answer in the clarity of what is surveyed. Any moment of our being-in-the-world is a manifest of the world in our being. One of the traditional maxims of Quantum Physics is that anyone claiming to understand Quantum Physics does not understand Quantum Physics. The dynamics of the quantum world are described by probabilities. Given a large sampling-body the predictions are statistically very accurate.

It is when the numbers are reduced that the accuracy declines precipitously. The dwindling numbers reduce the observational field to the degree that the observer himself interferes with the observations in question. The same dwindling numbers in a *mystic report* diminishes the reality between the devoted to his devotional object—it declines to zero—there is no distance between the two because they are discovered to be the same entity. It is in this interconnection that the Buddha proclaims:

> I and all beings on earth together attain enlightenment at the same time.

Whitman then echoes:

> For every atom belonging to me as good belongs to you…

THE WHITMAN PORTRAITS

Rembrandt painted over fifty self-portraits. He was fascinated by the changes in his character as he advanced in age. He was a pitiless scientific observer chronicling the years of material success and then the slow merciless evidence of his material and physical decline. There is no more compelling and tragic collection of self portraits in the history of art.

Photography has it beginnings in the century following Rembrandt. In 1725 Johan Heinrich Schulze mixed a chemical substance containing chalk, nitric acid and silver. He noted that the substance turned dark when exposed to direct sunlight. Such were the chemical beginnings of Kodak and Polaroid—the storied precursors of pixels and Photoshop. The world's first photograph was produced by Joseph Nicephore Niepce a near century later—1826. The exposure took eight hours and a portion of it is produced below.

World's First Photograph:
Joesph Nicephore Niepce:

Nicephore Niepce partnered with Louis-Jacques-Mande Daguerre. Daguerre was an artist and showman that operated a variation on the camera obscura called the Diorama. The Diorama allowed the display of 72 X 46 foot canvases that were vividly realistic that suggested the depth of three dimensions. Although Daguerre did not invent the process he was later to popularize, he did work with chemicals that made the process more practical. Four years after Niepce's death the Frenchman discovered that by heating mercury the resulting vapors would develop the image on silver iodine. Niepce was nearly forgotten in the excitement of the Daguerreotype's continuing development.

It should be noted that Daguerre did, however, remember his financial obligations to Niepce's widow and son, Isodre, whom he partnered upon the death of the impoverished father, Nicephore Niepce. Whitman's preoccupation with time: "I am the clock," made him fascinated with photography's ability to make time stop. He could and often did analyze the emotional purport of what the camera recorded. He might comment on the theatricality of a portrait, his dullness of eye or the good spirits the lens had captured.

The cellist and antiquarian, Henry Scholey Saunders (1864-1951) collected all images of Whitman to which he could lay his hands. He and his wife were admirers of the poet and preserved their efforts in 1922's *Whitman Portraits*. In 1939 they privately printed *Whitman Photographs*. Whitman was of a divided mind concerning his self portraits. He discussed collecting them with his comrades but could just as easily be dismissive: "What the hell would a man want such a collection for anyway?" Using the Saunters' collection as a base, various library and university collections have preserved over one hundred and twenty-five photos documenting the last four decades of his life. Numerous other images from oil paintings to cigar box illustrations have also preserved his likeness. An *Old Crow* whiskey ad (featuring an illustration of a serenely fit Whitman a few months before his death) is reproduced in Volume II of *Whitman's Code*. The poet would have been amused at the fantasy. He was a paralytic incapacitated by numerous tumors and debilitating pain. Whitman had great respect for the aristocratic record of easel and oil but he was disposed to the Democratic ideal of a storefront studio and the nineteenth century equivalent of a *snapshot*.

WHITMAN'S CODE: A NEW BIBLE, VOLUME I
M.C. GARDNER

I have a personal interest in the work of Alexander Gardner. We both descend from a common ancestor in Scotland.[162] If I've given the edge in attribution to a *cousin* over his employer it is by way of leveling the playing field. Most of what we think of as the Civil War photography of Mathew Brady was photographed in the field by Alexander Gardner[163] and two dozen other photographers who were commissioned by Brady to document the war.

The title of Ed Folsom's[164] introduction to the photographs at The Walt Whitman Archive is, *This Heart's Geography Map*. It is taken from the eighth line of *Out from Behind This Mask*: "This heart's geography's Map, this limitless small continent, this soundless sea." Limitless, continent and sea are each tropes employed by the poet to describe himself.

The best of the photographs draw us inward to his depths. Something of their mystery is suggested in the enigmatic close of Borges' *A Personal Anthology*:

> Through the years, a man peoples a space with images of provinces, kingdoms, mountains, bays, ships, islands, fishes, rooms, tools, stars, horses, and people. Shortly before his death, he discovers that the patient labyrinth of lines traces the image of his own face.

The initial four portraits date from before the publication of *Leaves of Grass*. The first is from New Orleans, 1848.

Whitman traveled to the *Big Easy* for an editing job with the New Orleans Crescent. He made the journey with his brother Jeff. The weather did not agree with Jeff and Whitman's work schedule did not always correspond with the desires of his employers. They returned to N.Y. by riverboat within five months of their departure. The photo below appears overly posed—it is the property of the Walt Whitman House in Camden, New Jersey.

Earliest Whitman Photo:

Attribution Unknown
New Orleans, 1848
Walt Whitman House, Camden N.J.

The Journalist

This photo is from the late 1840s—of a somewhat foppish journalist who takes as much pride in his appearance as his pocketbook can afford. While working for the New York *Aurora* he was given a fashionable hat and cane for the doing a 'puff' piece for a store called Banta's at 130 Chatham street (since relocated). The print is from the late Gay Wilson Allen's collection.

Gabriel Harrison

The Samuel Hollyer (or John C. McRae) engraving[165] became the basis for the most famous frontispiece in the history of American letters. The original photo by his friend Gabriel Harrison would be worth a fortune should it turn up in a New York or New Jersey garage sale. Rather than place his name as poet on the title page of his Leaves he let the photo speak for his authorship.

In 1830 Emerson published "Nature," anonymously — Whitman's conceit was not without a celebrated precedent. The photo became controversial because *Leaves of Grass* initially gave his outraged critics no name to which to direct their ire and contention. The tilt of Whitman's head and his open collar sent people into a righteous frenzy. Even among the literati of his own camp there were those that found the pose entirely inappropriate. William Sloane Kennedy referred to the engraving as:

> "this repulsive, loaferish portrait, with its sensual mouth, (should) be dropped from future editions, or be accompanied by other and better ones that show the mature man, and not merely the defiant young revolter of thirty-seven, with a very large chip on his shoulder, no suspenders to his trousers, and his hat very much on one side."

One recalls that Melville's *Ishmael* took to the sea whenever the desire to knock men's hats from their heads became too much of a temptation. In this nineteenth century compulsion, the would-be whaler was apparently not alone. Whitman acceded to the criticism to the extent that he believed the original photo was overly provocative: "as if I was hurling bolts at somebody, full of mad oaths, saying defiantly, to hell with you!" Today's readers wonder what the hubbub was all about. It's a great image and indelibly limned in America's memory and imagination. This steel engraving is in the Bailey Collection, Ohio Wesleyan University.

Detail

Alexander Gardner

Earliest Extant Photograph of Alexander Gardner
Library of Congress

Family lore suggests that Alexander Gardner's great grandfather was brother to my great, great, great, grandfather. Whether all the links in a record extending over three centuries are as sound[166] as I am assured, I will leave to the genealogists among my siblings. Family lore also suggests that my *greatly* removed cousin was proficient with a camera. Here the ground could hardly be more certain. During the course of this study I discovered that *that* tradition – was a very grand understatement of a properly proud ancestry.

Alexander Gardner (b. 1821 in Paisley, Scotland) was early schooled in the art of a silversmith. Despite his Calvinist upbringing he sought to alter the fates of man's predetermined ends. In his twenties he bought, ran and edited a socialist newspaper, *The Glasgow Sentinel,* in Scotland. He joined a socialist enclave, after the fashion of Robert Owen, and purchased land in Iowa. His interest in photography was stimulated by *The Great Exhibition of '51* in Hyde Park. Among the photographers exhibiting was Mathew Brady, whose classically candid style would later influence his own.

When he came with his family to America he discovered that the members of the Iowa contingent were either dead or dying from tuberculosis. He settled his family in New York and shortly thereafter contacted Mathew Brady. Gardner was also a practiced chemist and proficient in the dark room. The collion wet plate was more manageable than the daguerreotype and Gardner was among its chief exponents. He was also an expert in the production of *Imperial Prints*—a process that competed with life sized oil portraits and demanded much higher prices than the smaller daguerreotypes.

He worked for Brady from 1856-1862. The famed employer came to rely more fully on his assistant as his own weakening eyesight necessitated increasingly thicker lenses. Gardner was given the plum assignment of running Brady's Washington D.C. studio prior to the war. Brady sent Alexander, his brother James and two dozen other photographers to document battle scenes and their grim aftermath. Alexander produced the most celebrated photographs of the war although, in the custom of the time, credit was given to the employer for the work submitted by the photographers. In 1862 Alexander set up his own studio and pursued the major battles of the Civil War on his own or with a talented group of photographers who followed his lead in departing from Brady's employ.

Abraham Lincoln and Walt Whitman were two of Alexander's most famous subjects. Each counted Gardner among their favorite photographers as Gardner counted each of them among his favorite subjects. Whitman was to say of the photographer:

> Gardner was a mighty good fellow — also mightily my friend; he was always loving; I feel near to him — always — to this day; years, deaths, severances, don't seem to make much difference when you once loved a man. Gardner was a real artist — had the feel of his work — the inner feel, if I may say it so... he was also beyond his craft — saw further than his camera — saw more; his pictures are an evidence of his endowment. [167]

In a strange alignment of number the surviving photographs of both Whitman and Lincoln number around 125. A letter of appreciation from the President and a selection of Gardner's portraits of Lincoln is produced in the *Memories of Mr. Lincoln* section of Volume II. Gardner was the only photographer allowed to document the execution of the four convicted conspirators of the Lincoln Assassination. He posed them with the pock-marked turret of a gunship as his backdrop. Each is photographed face forward and in profile. Later he worked with the Washington D.C. police in developing a "rogue's gallery" of their most notorious fugitives. For work in both areas he is credited with developing the "mug shot" familiar to anyone who has ever visited a post office.

Because of his frequent assistance to the Federal Government he was also the only photographer allowed to document the execution of Captain Henry Wirz. Wirz was a Swiss physician who was practicing medicine in Louisiana at the inception of the hostilities that would later consume him. He became commandant of Andersonville prison in January 1864. He is remembered as a nineteenth century *Dr. Mengele* who oversaw the highest death rate of prisoners of war from either side of the Mason Dixon. The trial was adjudicated by General Lew Wallace. Wallace was later the 11th Governor of the New Mexico Territory but he is better remembered as the author of the biblical pot-boiler, *Ben Hur*. Hundreds died daily at Andersonville from starvation and contagions as Wirz strode among the prisoners on horseback often accompanied by vicious dogs.

Photography by Chaplain J. J. Geer of the 148th Ohio volunteers documented the emaciated victims in much the same way the news cameras captured the living skeletons of Dachau and Buchenwald less than a century later. Wirz's defense was also echoed in Nuremburg at the close of that later war. Wirz protested that he was innocent and guilty of only following the orders of his superiors.

Gardner later published
Gardner's Photographic Sketchbook of the Civil War:

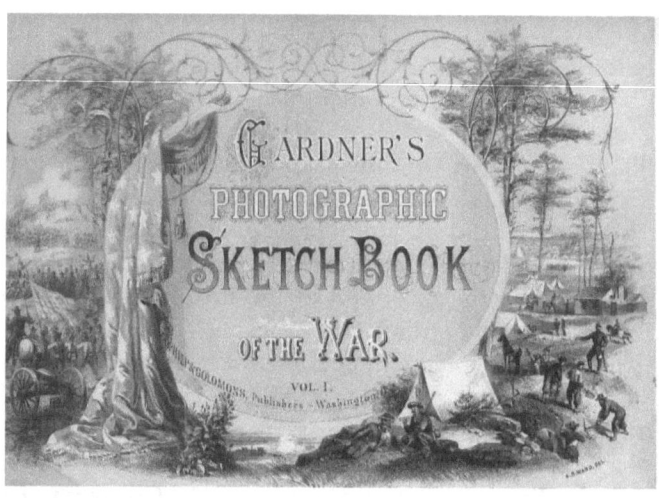

This was one of the major works of photographic art composed in the nineteenth century. It is as interesting a document for what is not shown as for what is presented. Gardner produced the positives for the 100 photographs he selected for the work's two volumes.

Over 75% of the exposures are taken and credited to other members of his photographic team, with over 40 % of that total credited to Timothy H. O'Sullivan. O'Sullivan and Gardner worked together at Gettysburg. One of the most famous exposures (credited to each at different times) was "Home of Rebel Sharpshooter." William A. Frassanito was able to establish that the body of the "Sharpshooter" was actually the body from an earlier set of exposures and had been "posed" for the celebrated shot in question.

At the height of his own photographic fame he wanted to assure credit to others which had largely been denied him while working for Mathew Brady. Brady was cited as the author for Gardner and Gibson's celebrated work documenting the grim aftermath to the battle of Antietam.

In *Gardner's Photographic Sketchbook* less than dozen photographs are of the leavings of battle. 90% of the exposures are rather of living soldiers and the environs around which so many of their comrades had fallen. Gardner produced each photograph by hand and then mounted them with an adjacent commentary on the page to their left.

By calling the book a Photographic "Sketch Book," he acknowledged that the choices he made were as an artist presenting a particular view of a remarkable era. Gardner spoke of his photographs as "leaves." Elizabeth Young concludes her essay, Verbal Battlefields (*On Alexander Gardner's Photographic Sketch Book of the Civil War*) by speaking of his negatives as Leaves of *Glass*.

After the war he was asked to document the visits of numerous Indian delegations that were lobbying Washington for their own portion of the Emancipation Proclamation. Later he was commissioned by the Kansas Pacific railroad to survey their proposed cross-country route to the Pacific. His career as a photographer lasted until the early 1870s.

The final decade of his life returned him to the altruism with which he first ventured into the New World—he devised an insurance plan that would benefit a consortium of Masons and their survivors. He died in Washington in December, 1882. Further details of the life of my illustrious cousin are produced in Volume II. A picture of the photographer, his studio and a set piece used to stage photographs follows below. The Whitman Gallery of Gardner's Whitman portraits continues, thereafter.

Alexander Gardner's Washington D.C. Studio
Witness to an Era, D. Mark Katz

Alexander Gardner's Studio & Alexander Gardner
Witness to an Era, D. Mark Katz

1860s
Alexander Gardner
Library of Congress

1862
Alexander Gardner
Feinberg Collection

Whitman enters the war in December 1862 looking for his wounded brother, George, at Fredericksburg.

1862
Alexander Gardner
Walt Whitman House Camden, N.J.

1863
Alexander Gardner
Alderman Library, University of Virginia

1863
Alexander Gardner
Alderman Library, University of Virginia

Whitman referred to this Gardner photo as the best of all. Whitman reported that it was also the artist's Thomas Eakins' favorite photograph, "always excepting his own, to be sure."

1865
Alexander Gardner
New York Public Library Collection

1865
Alexander Gardner
Alderman Library, University of Virginia

1865
Alexander Gardner
Ohio Wesleyan University, Bayley Collection

1863
Alexander Gardner
Ohio Wesleyan University, Bayley Collection

1864-1865
Alexander Gardner
"…one of my best….my mother's favorite image."
Ohio Wesleyan University, Bayley Collection

24 Canticles of Day & Night

Whitman's Code: A New Bible begins with the Volume I Prologue: The 52 Cantos of *Song of Myself* and continues with the 24 solo poems *uncollected* by cluster. Volume II is comprised of the 365 poems contained in the designated clusters and annexes of the *Deathbed* edition.

This compendium of *Leaves of Grass* is based on the poet's early ambition to construct a new Bible — *the three hundred and sixty-five*. In looking closely at the body of his poetry I discovered that with the final addition of an Epigraph the total number of poems collected in his clusters equaled 365. This left a remainder of 25 poems which were uncollected — *unclustered*, as it were. Whitman eventually entitled the inaugural poem of his first edition *Song of Myself* — and, in 1867, divided it into 52 cantos — the 52 weeks of the year — the basis for the Volume I Prologue of the Code.

This left a remainder of 24 solo poems — the 24 hours of the day — the basis for the concluding poems of Volume I: *Duly the twenty-four appear in public every day.*[168] The 24 solo poems of the Code are scattered between the *Deathbed* clusters without apparent program.[169] They are diversely placed in advancing editions of *Leaves of Grass*. Their variegated orders are listed in the Appendices of each volume and the note concluding this foreword.

I've justified my placement as best I might in the *Anatomy of a Code*. There you will find a late exhortation of the poet:

> The reader will always have his or her part to do, just as much as I have had mine. I seek less to state or display any theme or thought and more to bring you the reader into the atmosphere of the theme or thought—there to pursue your own thought.

The inaugural 1855 edition of *Leaves of Grass* contained a prose preface of 827 lines and an untitled collection of verse of 2315 lines. Of the poetry represented by those twenty-three hundred[170] over 1900 of the inaugural lines ended up *outside* the poems collected in the 1881 clusters. 5 of the 25 solo poems in his final collection were from the original untitled 12 (12 again!) of the first edition. The solo poems were of major import to the poet. Nine of the twenty-five he designates as *Songs*—a sign of affection that recalled the poet's love of opera. I call these 24 poems *Canticles* (after the Latin canticum for song)—a Biblical designation (for poetry, often long poems, excluding the Psalms) that includes them all. They contain some of Whitman's greatest poems as well as some of his most neglected.

Most of them present the difficulties attendant to length. They are inaccessible by *Tweet* and will take more than a cursory glance to fully appreciate. The most anthologized of the group is *Song of the Open Road*—easily one of the poet's signature presentations. He was also very fond of *Starting from Paumanok*. It is among his most biographical poems and he ultimately selected it to *star* as the first of his Solo selections in the 1881 order—here, it is the first poem or *hour* of the 24 comprising Whitman's *Day*.

"The Sleepers" and "To Think of Time" are among the most haunting of the 24 and each are eerily prescient of the Civil War which was to consume the nation and the poet in the succeeding decade. The greatest of the group is, arguably, 1856's "Sundown Poem" — later, "Crossing Brooklyn Ferry". It was one of Thoreau's favorites:

> That Walt Whitman, of whom I wrote you, is the most interesting fact to me at present. I have just read his second edition (which he gave me) and it has done me more good than any reading for a long time. Perhaps I remember best the *Poem of Walt Whitman* and the *Sundown Poem*. [171]

In *Song of Myself* the poet declares:

> Distant and dead resuscitate,
> They show as the dial or move as the hands of me.
> I am the clock myself.

Herein are presented the 24 Canticles of Whitman's glorious day.

Note:

At the conclusion of the 52 Cantos of *Song of Myself* (Whitman's year), a new day dawns in the a.m. (Ante Meridiem of the succeeding year) — as one day crosses into another. The first solo poem of that new day is *Starting From Paumanok*, the Indian name for his childhood home of Long Island.

It appears after the commencement of *Leaves of Grass* — the 24 Inscriptions (24 again!) — of the inaugural cluster. The succeeding 11 poems of the Ante Meridiem are: *A Broadway Pageant* which in 1881 appeared between the Birds of Passage and Sea Drift clusters.

The 3rd and 4th *hours* of Book I are *By Blue Ontario's Shore* and *Reversals* which were placed consecutively between the "Memories of President Lincoln" and the "Autumn Rivulets" group. The largest assemblage of the first 12 canticles are the six poems (5 through 10) *Proud Music of the Storm; Passage to India; Prayer of Columbus; The Sleepers; Transpositions;* and *To Think of Time*). These 6 poems were given their placement after the Autumn Rivulets cluster. The final two *hours* of the first 12 of Book I are *Thou Mother with Thy Equal Brood* and *A Paumanok Picture*. The poet had placed them after the "Whispers of Heavenly Death" cluster.

The second group of twelve *solo* poems is presented in the (Post Meridiem) — from noon to midnight of the compendium. One of the poet's later clusters is entitled *From Noon to Starry Night* — so if not exclusively Night, then from noon to starry night, as well. The poet, conveniently, grouped this second set of *solo* poems as a unit of twelve. They appear in *Leaves of Grass* after the celebrated Calamus cluster. They conclude the 2nd 12 *hours* of Book I: *Salut au Monde!; Song of the Open Road; Crossing Brooklyn Ferry; Song of the Answerer; Our Old Feuillage; A Song of Joys; Song of the Broad-Axe; Song of the Exposition; Song of the Redwood Tree; A Song of Occupations; A Song of the Rolling Earth; Youth, Old Age, and Night.*

"I see something of God each hour of the twenty-four."

Walt Whitman

24 SOLO CANTICLES
DAY & NIGHT

1. Starting From Paumanok
2. A Broadway Pageant
3. By Blue Ontario's Shore
4. Reversals
5. Proud Music of the Storm
6. Passage to India
7. Prayer of Columbus
8. The Sleepers
9. Transpositions
10. To Think of Time
11. Thou Mother with Thy Equal Brood
12. A Paumanok Picture
13. Salut Au Monde!
14. Song of the Open Road
15. Crossing Brooklyn Ferry
16. Song of the Answerer
17. Our Old Fueillage
18. A Song of Joys
19. Song of the Broad-Axe
20. Song of the Exposition
21. Song of the Redwood Tree
22. Song for Occupations
23. A Song of the Rolling Earth
24. Young, Day, Old Age and Night

Note: I am indebted to both the Variorum and the Norton Critical Edition for the origin dates of the 24. The date appears adjacent to the title of each poem if not otherwise noted.

ANTE MERIDIEM
12 SOLO CANTICLES
MIDNIGHT TO NOON

1. Starting From Paumanok
2. A Broadway Pageant
3. By Blue Ontario's Shore
4. Reversals
5. Proud Music of the Storm
6. Passage to India
7. Prayer of Columbus
8. The Sleepers
9. Transpositions
10. To Think of Time
11. Thou Mother with Thy Equal Brood
12. A Paumanok Picture

1. Starting From Paumanok

(1856)

Manuscript entries indicate that *Starting From Paumanok* was originally entitled *Premonitions*. It first appeared in 1860 under the title *Proto-Leaf*. It was christened its final title in the 1867 edition of *Leaves*. Whitman was born at West Hills, Long Island—*fish shape Paumanok*.

Other details bespeak the Whitman that the poet *created*—as Borges and other critics have established, the child of Long Island was never a miner in California (Line 5 below) nor, as in a later poem, was he witness to John Brown's execution: "I was at hand, silent I stood with teeth shut closed, I watch'd, / I stood very near you old man..."[172] This poem is one of the most autobiographical in the canon. It has long stood in the shadow of its celebrated elder brother. Nonetheless, it and *Song of Myself* are each are among the poet's greatest achievements.

Starting From Paumanok

> Starting from fish-shape Paumanok where I was born, 1
> Well-begotten, and rais'd by a perfect mother,
> After roaming many lands, lover of populous pavements,
> Dweller in Mannahatta my city, or on southern savannas,
> Or a soldier camp'd or carrying my knapsack and gun, or a miner in California, 5

> Or rude in my home in Dakota's woods, my diet meat, my drink from the spring,
> Or withdrawn to muse and meditate in some deep recess,
> Far from the clank of crowds intervals passing rapt and happy,
> Aware of the fresh free giver the flowing Missouri, aware of mighty Niagara,
> Aware of the buffalo herds grazing the plains, the hirsute and strong-breasted bull,
> Of earth, rocks, Fifth-month flowers experienced, stars, rain, snow, my amaze,
> Having studied the mocking-bird's tones and the flight of the mountain hawk,
> And heard at dawn the unrivall'd one, the hermit thrush from the swamp-cedars,
> Solitary, singing in the West, I strike up for a New World.   14

The poet declares he was a meat eater "my diet meat, my drink from the spring," then again, perhaps the carnivore is only on the printed page. Whitman was known for his frugality and simple meals would, more often than not, be his primary sustenance. In an early description he relates to drinking "strong flavored coffee and likes a supper of oysters fresh from the oyster-smack."[173]

The unrivall'd one, "the hermit thrush from the swamp cedars," will return with unrivall'd poignancy in *When Lilacs Last in the Dooryard Bloom'd*.

In the 2nd Canto the poet reports his fascination with *being*: "This then is life, here is what has come to the surface after so many throes and convulsions. How curious! How real! Underfoot the divine soil, overhead the sun. See the revolving globe." (Lines 18-21 below)

2.

    Victory, union, faith, identity, time,   15
    The indissoluble compacts, riches, mystery,
    Eternal progress, the kosmos, and the modern reports.

    This then is life,   18
    Here is what has come to the surface after so many throes and convulsions.

    How curious! how real!   20
    Underfoot the divine soil, overhead the sun.   21

    See revolving the globe,   22
    The ancestor-continents away group'd together,
    The present and future continents north and south, with the isthmus between.

    See, vast trackless spaces,

> As in a dream they change, they swiftly fill,
> Countless masses debouch upon them,
> They are now cover'd with the foremost people, arts, institutions, known.
>
> See, projected through time,
> For me an audience interminable.   30
>
> With firm and regular step they wend, they never stop,
> Successions of men, Americanos, a hundred millions,
> One generation playing its part and passing on,   33
> Another generation playing its part and passing on in its turn,
> With faces turn'd sideways or backward towards me to listen,
> With eyes retrospective towards me.   36

Projecting himself through time he anticipates that which eludes him at this early juncture in his career: "For me an audience interminable… (Line 30 above) one generation playing its part and passing on… (Line 33 above) with eyes retrospective towards me…" (Line 36 above). He continues the theme in Canto 3 "Americanos… century marches… chants of the prairies…" And then, in one of the most vivid images of his own poetry he describes it as "shooting in pulses of fire ceaseless to vivify all." (Line 44 below).

3.
> Americanos! conquerors! marches humanitarian!   37

> Foremost! century marches! Libertad! masses!
> For you a programme of chants.
> Chants of the prairies,
> Chants of the long-running Mississippi, and down to the Mexican sea,
> Chants of Ohio, Indiana, Illinois, Iowa, Wisconsin and Minnesota,
> Chants going forth from the centre from Kansas, and thence equidistant,
> Shooting in pulses of fire ceaseless to vivify all. 44

In Canto 4 he admonishes America to take his *leaves* — "for they are your own off-spring." He salutes his forerunners: "I sat studying at the feet of great masters." (Line 50 below) His *leaves* "are the children of the antique...," the new poems being the justification of the old. (Line 53 below)

4.

> Take my leaves America, take them South and take them North, 45
> Make welcome for them everywhere, for they are your own off-spring,
> Surround them East and West, for they would surround you,
> And you precedents, connect lovingly with them, for they connect lovingly with you.
>
> I conn'd old times,
> I sat studying at the feet of the great masters, 50

> Now if eligible O that the great masters
> might return and study me.
>
> In the name of these States shall I scorn
> the antique?
> Why these are the children of the
> antique to justify it. 53

Canto 5 continues his acknowledgment of debt: "I respectfully credit what you have wafted hither." It is reminiscent of Emerson's *The American Scholar*: "Our day of dependence; our long apprenticeship to the learning of other lands draws to a close." Whitman owns that such learning is "admirable." He regards "it all intently a long while, then dismissing it, I stand in my place with my own day." Early in the 1855 edition[174] he describes the rapture of enlightenment as his *soul* plunges its tongue to his bare-stript heart. At the end of this canto, his satisfier and *mistress* returns: "Yes here comes my mistress the soul." (Line 68 below)

5.

> Dead poets, philosophs, priests, 54
> Martyrs, artists, inventors, governments
> long since,
> Language-shapers on other shores,
> Nations once powerful, now reduced,
> withdrawn, or desolate,
> I dare not proceed till I respectfully
> credit what you have left wafted
> hither,
> I have perused it, own it is admirable,
> (moving awhile among it,)

> Think nothing can ever be greater,
>   nothing can ever deserve more than
>   it deserves, 60
> Regarding it all intently a long while,
>   then dismissing it,
> I stand in my place with my own day
>   here. 62
>
> Here lands female and male,
> Here the heir-ship and heiress-ship of
>   the world, here the flame of
>   materials,
> Here spirituality the translatress, the
>   openly-avow'd,
> The ever-tending, the finale of visible
>   forms,
> The satisfier, after due long-waiting
>   now advancing,
> Yes here comes my mistress the soul. 68

The soul is his nexus for combining the real with the ideal; the material with the spirit. The great divide between Plato and Aristotle is bridged by the poet: "I will make the poems of materials, for I think they are to be the most spiritual poems." (Line 71 below) The physicality of Aristotle's substance is wedded to the eternal in his teacher, Plato: "And I will make poems of my body and of mortality, for I think I shall then supply myself with the poems of immortality." The dichotomy between the ideal and the real has been at loggerheads since the two Greeks introduced it twenty-five hundred years ago. The poet will return to it throughout his poem. For the present, simply note it below — we will have occasion to treat the dualism more fully in later pages of the compendium.

The second half of the 6th Canto is a forthright exhortation of his ideal of manly love. The poet's apologists point to antebellum mores that were more accepting of male affection than our present homophobic sensibilities:

> I believe these are to found their own
>   ideal of manly love,
> I indicating it in me,
> I will therefore let flame from me the
>   burning fires that were threatening
>   to consume me,
> I will lift what has too long kept down
>   those smouldering fires,
> I will give them complete abandonment,

The poet says that he will give complete abandonment to what has been threatening to consume him. It is not known to what degree of abandonment, complete or otherwise, to which he succeeded. In pointed questions about his *actual* as opposed to poetical meanings by John Addington Symonds, he was highly elusive—even suggesting that he did not know the implications of many of his most personal poems. The Whitman who wrote these Paumanok lines was not the same Whitman who denied their intent to Symonds. The first was a revolutionary in his mid-thirties; the second, an American institution in his sixties.

6.
> The soul, 69
> Forever and forever—longer than soil is
>   brown and solid—longer than water
>   ebbs and flows.

I will make the poems of materials, for I
    think they are to be the most
    spiritual poems,   71
And I will make the poems of my body
    and of mortality,
For I think I shall then supply myself
    with the poems of my soul and of
    immortality.   73

I will make a song for these States that
    no one State may under any
    circumstances be subjected to
    another State,
And I will make a song that there shall
    be comity by day and by night
    between all the States, and between
    any two of them,
And I will make a song for the ears of
    the President, full of weapons with
    menacing points,
And behind the weapons countless
    dissatisfied faces;
And a song make I of the One form'd
    out of all,   78
The fang'd and glittering One whose
    head is over all,
Resolute warlike One including and
    over all,
(However high the head of any else that
    head is over all.)   81

I will acknowledge contemporary lands,
I will trail the whole geography of the
    globe and salute courteously every
    city large and small,

> And employments! I will put in my
>   poems that with you is heroism
>   upon land and sea,
> And I will report all heroism from an
>   American point of view. 85
>
> I will sing the song of companionship,
> I will show what alone must finally
>   compact these,
> I believe these are to found their own
>   ideal of manly love, 88
> I indicating it in me,
> I will therefore let flame from me the
>   burning fires that were threatening
>   to consume me, 89
> I will lift what has too long kept down
>   those smouldering fires,
> I will give them complete abandonment,
> I will write the evangel-poem of
>   comrades and of love, 92
> For who but I should understand love
>   with all its sorrow and joy?
> And who but I should be the poet of
>   comrades? 94

Whitman equates the material with the spiritual. The poet's handling of the theme is one of the most cogent in Western thought: *I will make the poems of materials, for I think they are to be the most spiritual poems.* (Line 71 above) From *material* he extrapolates his personal flesh and blood. This is one of his most profound themes. He will return to it throughout *Leaves of Grass*. It is the basis for the ecstatic delight of his physical being and the equation of that experience with the Divine:

> I will make the poems of my body and of mortality, For I think I shall then supply myself with the poems of my soul and of immortality. (Line 73 above)

In the East, the loftiest expressions of Mahayana Buddhism are dedicated to this same end. The Pure Land school of Buddhism is predicated on the simple utterance of *namu Amida butsu*. The pure land of its name is called Sukhavati. Sukhavati is a heavenly land that all are invited to enter.

The Pure Land worshipers believe even the single pronunciation of Amida's name will assure entrance into his paradise. Practitioners endlessly recite the mantra, *namu Amida butsu* in their daily devotionals. Amida was the god of infinite light (Amitabha) and the god of infinite time (Amitayus).

The enlightened adepts come to see with the infinite light of Amitabha that the material world of our ordinary reality *is* Suhhavati and each moment of our being, an expression of Amitayus—infinite time. Once again (with feeling):

> I will make the poems of materials, for I think they are to be the most spiritual poems,
> And I will make the poems of my body and of mortality,
> For I think I shall then supply myself with the poems of my soul and of immortality.

In Cantos 7 and 8 he tackles good, evil, and religion. He asserts that he is as much evil as good: "I commemorate that part also." In an era that speaks and believes fervently in an *axis of evil* it is helpful to be reminded that our certainties can be subject to question. Rather than undermine religion he further asserts that *no man has ever been half devout enough, or worship'd half enough.* In writing a *New Bible* we shouldn't be surprised to find him inaugurating a *New Religion*: "I descend into the arena." When the poet declares: "Each is not for its own sake," he gives a hint to his notion of good and evil. The good is predicated on our compassion for others—evil on the lack thereof. These are judgments of a given place and time. Whitman, however, takes a more expansive view. He is an advocate of the good—but his notion of evil is mollified by believing that what appears evil today may very well be for good, or in the least, neutralized by the passage of time and the widening of our view. In the 12th Canto of this poem he will assert: "And I will show that there is no imperfection in the present, and can be none in the future, And I will show that whatever happens to anybody it may be turn'd to beautiful results." Emerson would concur:

> A man must thank his defects and stand in some terror to his talents. A transcendent talent draws so largely on his forces as to lame him; a defect pays him revenues on the other side…
>
> If fate is ore and quarry, if evil is good in the making, if limitation is power that shall be, if calamities, oppositions, and weights are wings and means—we are all reconciled.[175]

Each is not for its own sake because each is part of a larger whole (Omnes!). In the end each is discerned to be the other — whole and part — equally Divine.

7.

> I am the credulous man of qualities, ages, races, 95
> I advance from the people in their own spirit,
> Here is what sings unrestricted faith.
>
> Omnes! omnes! let others ignore what they may,
> I make the poem of evil also, I commemorate that part also, 99
> I am myself just as much evil as good, and my nation is — and I say there is in fact no evil,
> (Or if there is I say it is just as important to you, to the land or to me, as any thing else.)
>
> I too, following many and follow'd by many, inaugurate a religion, I descend into the arena, 102
> (It may be I am destin'd to utter the loudest cries there, the winner's pealing shouts,
> Who knows? they may rise from me yet, and soar above every thing.)
>
> Each is not for its own sake,
> I say the whole earth and all the stars in the sky are for religion's sake.

I say no man has ever yet been half
   devout enough, 107
None has ever yet adored or worship'd
   half enough
None has begun to think how divine he
   himself is, and how certain the
   future is. 109

I say that the real and permanent
   grandeur of these States must be
   their religion, 110
Otherwise there is just no real and
   permanent grandeur;
(Nor character nor life worthy the name
   without religion,
Nor land nor man or woman without
   religion.) 113

8.

What are you doing young man? 114
Are you so earnest, so given up to
   literature, science, art, amours?
These ostensible realities, politics,
   points?
Your ambition or business whatever it
   may be?

It is well—against such I say not a word,
   I am their poet also,
But behold! such swiftly subside, burnt
   up for religion's sake,
For not all matter is fuel to heat,
   impalpable flame, the essential life
   of the earth,
Any more than such are to religion. 121

9.

> What do you seek so pensive and silent? 122
> What do you need camerado?
> Dear son do you think it is love?
>
> Listen dear son—listen America, daughter or son,
> It is a painful thing to love a man or woman to excess, and yet it satisfies, it is great, 126
> But there is something else very great, it makes the whole coincide, 127
> It, magnificent, beyond materials, with continuous hands sweeps and provides for all. 128

In Tibetan Buddhism we have the familiar mantra: "Om Mani Padme Hum" It bespeaks the jewel of nirvana in the lotus of samsara—Whitman's spiritual component in the ostensibly material. The mantra also has a sexual link—it refers, as ably, to the link of the "lingam" entering the flowered petals of the "yoni." Whitman's celebration of sexuality is one of the hallmarks of his verse. In Canto 9 he moderates his focus on love: "It is a painful thing to love a man or woman to excess... there is something else very great it makes the whole coincide." The sexual interpretation of the mantra is directed to the same end—two lovers become one—making the whole, coincide.

The 10th Canto is an effort to make an American Trinity: Love, Democracy and Religion. (Line 133 below) Note that the Trinity is also the cartography of his soul. Love is the public persona (Walt Whitman, one of the roughs) created and celebrated in *Song of Myself;* the emergent love of the Me/Myself also embraces the multitudinous

Whitman whereby he absorbs the Democratic multitudes of these United States; and finally Religion is the *Soul*, the transcendental identity that lies behind and within all things in the wide sweeping universe — "Mélange mine own, the unseen and the seen, Mysterious ocean where the streams empty." There is also a correspondence between the Whitman Triad and the Triads of Meister Eckhart and Sigmund Freud. The Dominican priest believed[176] that *Doing, Knowing* and *Being* were the necessary links to bridge human consciousness with the Godhead: "Doing" correlates with *Walt Whitman*, his creation and persona; *Knowing*, with the *Me/Myself*, the interior Whitman; and the "Being "of Eckhart is equivalent to the *Soul* that the poet seeks and so often celebrates. Freud's familiar triad: *Ego, Super-ego & Id* is the basis of his psychoanalytic theory.

10.
>Know you, solely to drop in the earth
>>the germs of a greater religion,   129
>The following chants each for its kind I
>>sing.
>
>My comrade!
>For you to share with me two
>>greatnesses, and a third one rising
>>inclusive and more resplendent,
>The greatness of Love and Democracy,
>>and the greatness of Religion.   133
>
>Mélange mine own, the unseen and the
>>seen,   134
>Mysterious ocean where the streams
>>empty,

> Prophetic spirit of materials shifting and flickering around me,
> Living beings, identities now doubtless near us in the air that we know not of, 137
> Contact daily and hourly that will not release me,
> These selecting, these in hints demanded of me. 139
>
> Not he with a daily kiss onward from childhood kissing me, 140
> Has winded and twisted around me that which holds me to him,
> Any more than I am held to the heavens and all the spiritual world,
> After what they have done to me, suggesting themes.
>
> O such themes—equalities! O divine average! 144
> Warblings under the sun, usher'd as now, or at noon, or setting,
> Strains musical flowing through ages, now reaching hither,
> I take to your reckless and composite chords, add to them, and cheerfully pass them forward. `147

The *seen* of his personal experience and the *Mélange* of the *unseen* universe which is its supporting context are the two components necessary for the revelation of any singularity or isolated entity. Any part is buoyed and inseparable from the whole—each is inconceivable without the other.

The necessity of their congruence renders each as equal. The mysterious ocean where the streams empty is the Godhead of Whitman's Trinity—the ocean of Eckhart's *being*, where we swim in God as fish swim in the sea. The poet is consumed by mystic enchantment. William Blake, as a child, reported seeing God peering through his bedroom window; God was no less present in this report from Whitman:

> ... he with a daily kiss onward from childhood kissing me, / Has winded and twisted around me that which holds me to him... (Lines 140-141 above)

The poet is enfolded in his God as intimately as a newborn is to its mother. No less lovely is "Prophetic spirit of materials shifting and flickering around me," which is followed by the even more tantalizing speculation: *Living beings, identities now doubtless near us in the air that we know not of...* (Lines 133-139 above) Whitman struck a similar note in a poem he later excluded:

> I swear to you that the body of yours give proportions to your Soul somehow to live in other spheres: / I do not know how, but I know it is so. [177]

The democratic ideal is once again demonstrated to be pure ontology: *O such themes—equalities! O divine average!* (Line 144 above) Each individual and action is a manifest or mode in the mind of God.

In the 11th Canto he visits the "he and she-birds" that figure prominently in *Out of the Cradle Endlessly Rocking*. In both instances the tally of the birds is translated by our American Siegfried.

11.

> As I have walk'd in Alabama my morning walk, 148
> I have seen where the she-bird the mocking-bird sat on her nest in the briers hatching her brood.
>
> I have seen the he-bird also,
> I have paus'd to hear him near at hand inflating his throat and joyfully singing. 151
>
> And while I paus'd it came to me that what he really sang for was not there only,
> Nor for his mate nor himself only, nor, all sent back by the echoes,
> But subtle, clandestine, away beyond,
> A charge transmitted and gift occult for those being born. 155

The "away beyond" is, of course, Whitman's projection of thought upon the warble of the bird. Note, as well, that the song of the bird is a "gift occult for those being born," whereas in *Out of the Cradle* and *Lilacs* the song of the bird will be for *death*. The 12th Canto is a statement of another trinity—as sure and strong as any in the canon—sex, death and the soul. Lines 162 through 176 are as concise a statement of the gospel according to Whitman as any you will find in all of his poetry.

He promises to make the true poem of riches and then in the next two stanzas does exactly that. It is a tremendous poetic and philosophic feat. Note, as well, his emphasis on *ensemble*—suffering in Buddhism (dukkha) is the hallmark of the individual—when you enter the emptiness (sunyata) of the Buddha you become the *ensemble* and there is nothing by which suffering can take its measure—*time and events are compact... I find there is not one nor any particle of one but has reference to the soul.*

12.

> Democracy! near at hand to you a throat is now inflating itself and joyfully singing. 156
>
> Ma femme! for the brood beyond us and of us,
> For those who belong here and those to come,
> I exultant to be ready for them will now shake out carols stronger and haughtier than have ever yet been heard upon earth.
>
> I will make the songs of passion to give them their way,
> And your songs outlaw'd offenders, for I scan you with kindred eyes, and carry you with me the same as any.
>
> I will make the true poem of riches, 162
> To earn for the body and the mind whatever adheres and goes forward and is not dropt by death;

I will effuse egotism and show it
underlying all, and I will be the
bard of personality,
And I will show of male and female that
either is but the equal of the other, 165
And sexual organs and acts! do you
concentrate in me, for I am
determin'd to tell you with
courageous clear voice to prove you
illustrious,
And I will show that there is no
imperfection in the present, and can
be none in the future, 167
And I will show that whatever happens
to anybody it may be turn'd to
beautiful results, 168
And I will show that nothing can
happen more beautiful than death, 169
And I will thread a thread through my
poems that time and events are
compact, 170
And that all the things of the universe
are perfect miracles, each as
profound as any. 171

I will not make poems with reference to
parts, 172
But I will make poems, songs, thoughts,
with reference to ensemble, 173
And I will not sing with reference to a
day, but with reference to all days, 174
And I will not make a poem nor the
least part of a poem but has
reference to the soul, 175

> Because having look'd at the objects of
> the universe, I find there is no one
> nor any particle of one but has
> reference to the soul.

In earlier day, Meister Eckhart's sermon was the same:

> God does what he wants for the soul's sake...the soul is what is truly made in God's image, in the image of all that he is according to his nature, according to his Being and according to his outflowing...it is according to this outflowing yet remaining works, that God has made the soul. God is always flowing into the soul and can never escape the soul...There is something in the soul which is only God...for herein the soul takes its whole life and being, for this is totally in God...thus the human nature became God...for your human nature and that of the eternal Word are no different — it's one and the same. The soul, as it were, was created at the point which divides time from eternity; it touches both these points. With its highest faculties the soul touches eternity, with its lowest, however, it is in touch with time — but in accordance with eternity. [178]

Whitman will thread a thread through his poems that things are "compact." Line 171 above) Parmenides' indivisible *One* and the Buddhist's *suchness* approach his meaning here. Compact (as in *compacted)* is the obverse of what the Buddhists' call *discrimination* – the belief of separate items comprising the universe.

His emphasis is on *ensemble:* "I will make poems, songs, thoughts, with reference to ensemble." (Line 173 above) Things and parts have reference to the soul — the soul is everywhere compact and working together in ensemble.

In Eckhart's 23rd Sermon we find:

> I say that in the kingdom of heaven everything is in everything else, and that everything is one and that everything is ours...And so I say that whatever one person has there, another person has too. [179]

I and my brother are one — Death the essential partner in the ensemble of life: "...nothing can happen more beautiful than death." His elegy to Lincoln will affirm that aesthetic claim. The first two lines (177, 178) of the 13th Canto are the most forthright statement of Whitman's equation of the material with the spiritual:

13.

Was somebody asking to see the soul?	177
See, your own shape and countenance, persons, substances, beasts, the trees, the running rivers, the rocks and sands.	178
All hold spiritual joys and afterwards loosen them;	
How can the real body ever die and be buried?	180
Of your real body and any man's or woman's real body,	

> Item for item it will elude the hands of the corpse-cleaners and pass to fitting spheres, 182
> Carrying what has accrued to it from the moment of birth to the moment of death.
>
> Not the types set up by the printer return their impression, the meaning, the main concern,
> Any more than a man's substance and life or a woman's substance and life return in the body and the soul,
> Indifferently before death and after death.
>
> Behold, the body includes and is the meaning, the main concern and includes and is the soul; 187
> Whoever you are, how superb and how divine is your body, or any part of it! 188

Again, the opening of the thirteenth Canto is among the most important in this poem. It can and will bear repetition:

> Was somebody asking to see the soul?
>
> See, your own shape and countenance, persons, substances, beasts, the trees, the running rivers, the rocks and sands.

If an adept dives deeply into his consciousness, the soul will be revealed in "persons, substances, beasts, the trees, the running rivers, the rocks and sands." This is Whitman's *proof* of immortality—if the natural world is the source and substance of the soul—if it is time and space itself—then, wherein will mortality find a footing? Our Dominican friend would agree:

> It is in this life that a person is born as a child of God and to eternal life. And this knowledge is without time and space and without here and now. In this life all things are one, all things are united with one another, all in all and all in all.[180]

In Canto 14 Whitman reverts to a tabulation of his countrymen and the states in which they reside. The canto is in three parts. The first is an introductory single line. The second is four lines announcing a theme and the third is 28 lines presenting it. Generally in Whitman a comma is a bridge between the lines of a stanza—you (almost) never see a line standing alone without punctuation. Below are examples of lines that end with exclamation marks and question marks. They are more the exception—most of his lines are linked by commas and stanzas and are primarily concluded with a period—you *never* see a period in mid-stanza.

14.
> Whoever you are, to you endless announcements! 189
>
> Daughter of the lands did you wait for your poet?

Did you wait for one with a flowing mouth and indicative hand?
Toward the male of the States, and toward the female of the States,
Exulting words, words to Democracy's lands.

Interlink'd, food-yielding lands! 194
Land of coal and iron! land of gold! land of cotton, sugar, rice!
Land of wheat, beef, pork! land of wool and hemp! land of the apple and the grape!
Land of the pastoral plains, the grass-fields of the world! land of those sweet-air'd interminable plateaus!
Land of the herd, the garden, the healthy house of adobie!
Lands where the north-west Columbia winds, and where the south-west Colorado winds!
Land of the eastern Chesapeake! land of the Delaware!
Land of Ontario, Erie, Huron, Michigan!
Land of the Old Thirteen! Massachusetts land! land of Vermont and Connecticut!
Land of the ocean shores! land of sierras and peaks! 103
Land of boatmen and sailors! fishermen's land!
Inextricable lands! the clutch'd together! the passionate ones!
The side by side! the elder and younger brothers! the bony-limb'd!

The great women's land! the feminine!
the experienced sisters and the
inexperienced sisters!
Far breath'd land! Arctic braced!
Mexican breez'd! the diverse! The
compact!
The Pennsylvanian! the Virginian! the
double Carolinian!
O all and each well-loved by me! my
intrepid nations! O I at any rate
include you all with perfect love!
I cannot be discharged from you! not
from one any sooner than another!
O death! O for all that, I am yet of you
unseen this hour with irrepressible
love, 212
Walking New England, a friend, a
traveler,
Splashing my bare feet in the edge of the
summer ripples on Paumanok's
sands, 214
Crossing the prairies, dwelling again in
Chicago, dwelling in every town,
Observing shows, births, improvements,
structures, arts,
Listening to orators and oratresses in
public halls,
Of and through the States as during life,
each man and woman my neighbor,
The Louisianian, the Georgian, as near
to me, and I as near to him and her,
The Mississippian and Arkansian yet
with me, and I yet with any of them,
Yet upon the plains west of the spinal
river, yet in my house of adobie,

> Yet returning eastward, yet in the Seaside State or in Maryland,
> Yet Kanadian cheerily braving the winter, the snow and ice welcome to me,
> Yet a true son either of Maine or of the Granite State, or the Narragansett Bay State, or the Empire State,,
> Yet sailing to other shores to annex the same, yet welcoming every new brother,
> Hereby applying these leaves to the new ones from the hour they unite with the old ones,
> Coming among the new ones myself to be their companion and equal, coming personally to you now,
> Enjoining you to acts, characters, spectacles, with me. 228

Within the above inventory is, once again, his acknowledgement of death: "O death! O for all that, I am yet of you unseen this hour with irrepressible love," (Line 212 above) and my favorite line for the naturalness of its beauty: "Splashing my bare feet in the edge of the summer ripples on Paumanok's sands." (Line 214 above)

15.
> With me with firm holding, yet haste, haste on. 229
> For your life adhere to me,
> (I may have to be persuaded many times before I consent to give myself really to you, but what of that?

> Must not Nature be persuaded many times?)
>
> No dainty dolce affettuoso I,
> Bearded, sun-burnt, gray-neck'd, forbidding, I have arrived,
> To be wrestled with as I pass for the solid prizes of the universe,
> For such I afford whoever can persevere to win them.

In the 16th Canto, the poet pauses to acknowledge Native Americans and their contribution to the naming of the land. In *November Boughs* he reflected:

> There is something about these aboriginal Americans,... something very remote, very lofty, arousing comparisons with our own civilized ideals — something that our literature, (and) portrait painting have never caught, and that almost certainly will never be transmitted to the future, even as a reminiscence.

Their culture has been lamely presented from Buffalo Bill's Wild West carnivals to the *horse operas* of Hollywood. The surviving aboriginals live their lives between the stark contrast of the poverty of the reservation and the luxury of American gaming. The poet's report rings poignantly true: "Leaving such to the states they melt, they depart..." (Line 245 below)

16.

> On my way a moment I pause, 237
> Here for you! and here for America!
> Still the present I raise aloft, still the future of the States I harbinge glad and sublime,
> And for the past I pronounce what the air holds of the red aborigines.
>
> The red aborigines, 241
> Leaving natural breaths, sounds of rain and winds, calls as of birds and animals in the woods, syllabled to us for names,
> Okonee, Koosa, Ottawa, Monongahela, Sauk, Natchez, Chattahoochee, Kaqueta, Oronoco,
> Wabash, Miami, Saginaw, Chippewa, Oshkosh, Walla-Walla,
> Leaving such to the States they melt, they depart, charging the water and the land with names. 245

In the 17th Canto the poet feels *the oceans within stirring, preparing for unprecedented waves and storms.*(Line 252 below) This poem premiered in 1860. The storms are undoubtedly the emotional turbulence of the Calamus section which companioned it. That cluster will be presented and discussed in volume two of *Whitman's Code: A New Bible.* A taste of what is to come is presented in the omitted line of the 19th Canto. Thereafter, as we saw in *Song of Myself*, Whitman saves an intimacy for his close.

17.

Expanding and swift, henceforth, 246
Elements, breeds, adjustments, turbulent, quick and audacious,
A world primal again, vistas of glory incessant and branching,
A new race dominating previous ones and grander far, with new contests,
New politics, new literatures and religions, new inventions and arts. 250

These, my voice announcing—I will sleep no more but arise,
You oceans that have been calm within me! how I feel you, fathomless, stirring, preparing unprecedented waves and storms. 252

18.

See, steamers steaming through my poems, 253
See, in my poems immigrants continually coming and landing,
See, in arriere, the wigwam, the trail, the hunter's hut, the flat-boat, the maize-leaf, the claim, the rude fence, and the backwoods village,
See, on the one side the Western Sea and on the other the Eastern Sea, how they advance and retreat upon my poems as upon their own shores,
See, pastures and forests in my poems— see, animals wild and tame—
See, beyond the Kaw, countless herds of buffalo feeding on short curly grass,

> See, in my poems, cities, solid, vast, inland, with paved streets, with iron and stone edifices, ceaseless vehicles, and commerce,
> See, the many-cylinder'd steam printing-press—see, the electric telegraph stretching across the continent,
> See, through Atlantica's depths pulses American Europe reaching, pulses of Europe duly return'd,
> See, the strong and quick locomotive as it departs, panting, blowing the steam-whistle,
> See, ploughmen ploughing farms—see, miners digging mines—see, the numberless factories,
> See, mechanics busy at their benches with tools—see from among them superior judges, philosophs, Presidents, emerge, drest in working dresses,
> See, lounging through the shops and fields of the States, me well-belov'd, close-held by day and night,
> Hear the loud echoes of my songs there—read the hints come at last. 265

In the concluding Canto, Whitman and an imagined lover almost burst into song celebrating "something ecstatic and undemonstrable. "O camerado close!" suggests his intimacy is shared with a man. This was even more explicit at the poem's premiere in 1860. The five lines between 266 and 267 though passionate and in italics, were excluded from all subsequent editions.

19.

> O camerado close! O you and me at last, and us two only. 266
> *O power, liberty, eternity at last!*
> *O to be relieved of distinctions! to make as much of vices as virtues!*
> *O to level occupations and the sexes! O to bring all to common ground! O adhesiveness!*
> *O the pensive aching to be together — you know not why and I know not why.*
> O a word to clear one's path ahead endlessly! 267
> O something ecstatic and undemonstrable! O music wild!
> O now I triumph — and you shall also;
> O hand in hand — O wholesome pleasure — O one more desirer and lover!
> O to haste firm holding — to haste, haste on with me. 271

2. A Broadway Pageant (1860)

A Broadway Pageant has the distinction of being the only *stand alone* or solo canticle of the twenty-five in *Leaves of Grass* that truly stands alone. It resides uncompanioned between the "Birds of Passage" and "Sea Drift" clusters. In it Whitman celebrates a parade and visit by an embassy from *Niphon* (June 16, 1860) which had come to sign treaty and trade agreements with America. Whitman takes the occasion to celebrate his own world's fair.

The visiting Japanese become symbolic of the whole of the Orient, and then the world:

> For not the envoys nor the tann'd Japanee from his island only,
> Lithe and silent the Hindoo appears, the Asiatic continent itself appears, the past, the dead ...
> The north, the sweltering south, eastern Assyria, the Hebrews, the ancient of ancients...
> Geography, the world, is in it,
> The Great Sea, the brood of islands, Polynesia, the coast beyond...
> The countries there with their populations, the millions en-masse are curiously here...

The poet greets his great visitors with a dutiful respect and then respectfully announces a new *Libertad*. These United States will now answer a summons thousands of years in the making. The New World will return the favor to the Old by reaching out to the great mother from which it has descended.

This is one of Whitman's underappreciated longer poems. Its appearance in the celebrated 1860 edition and its anticipation of *A Passage to India* makes it worthy of the reader's attention and study. The "Pageant" is, rather, a mystic vision in three movements. The first movement places the poet in his place, Broadway; and a particular time, the 16th of June, 1860:

A Broadway Pageant

1.

Over the Western sea hither from
    Niphon come,   1
Courteous, the swart-cheek'd two-
    sworded envoys,
Leaning back in their open barouches,
    bare-headed, impassive,
Ride to-day through Manhattan.   4

Libertad! I do not know whether others
    behold what I behold,
In the procession along with the nobles
    of Niphon, the errand-bearers,
Bringing up the rear, hovering above,
    around, or in the ranks marching,
But I will sing you a song of what I
    behold Libertad.

When million-footed Manhattan unpent
    descends to her pavements,   9
When the thunder-cracking guns arouse
    me with the proud roar love,
When the round-mouth'd guns out of
    the smoke and smell I love spit their
    salutes,
When the fire-flashing guns have fully
    alerted me, and heaven-clouds
    canopy my city with a delicate thin
    haze,
When gorgeous the countless straight
    stems, the forests at the wharves,
    thicken with colors,
When every ship richly drest carries her
    flag at the peak,

> When pennants trail and street-festoons
>   hang from the windows,
> When Broadway is entirely given up to
>   foot-passengers and foot-standers,
>   when the mass is densest,
> When the facades of the houses are alive
>   with people, when eyes gaze riveted
>   tens of thousands at a time,   17
> When the guests from the islands
>   advance, when the pageant moves
>   forward visible,
> When the summons is made, when the
>   answer that waited thousands of
>   years answers,
> I too arising, answering, descend to the
>   pavements, merge with the crowd,
>   and gaze with them.   20

The Second Canto becomes a magic lantern illuminating time and eternity: *As it moves changing, a kaleidoscope divine it moves changing before us. The murky night-morning of wonder and fable inscrutable, the envelop'd mysteries...* (Lines 33, 36, 37)

2.

> Superb-faced Manhattan!   21
> Comrade Americanos! to us, then at last
>   the Orient comes.
>
> To us, my city,
> Where our tall-topt marble and iron
>   beauties range on opposite sides, to
>   walk in the space between,
> To-day our Antipodes comes.   25

The Originatress comes,
The nest of languages, the bequeather of poems, the race of eld,
Florid with blood, pensive, rapt with musings, hot with passion,
Sultry with perfume, with ample and flowing garments,
With sunburnt visage, with intense soul and glittering eyes,
The race of Brahma comes. 31

See my cantabile! these and more are flashing to us from the procession,
As it moves changing, a kaleidoscope divine it moves changing before us. 33

For not the envoys nor the tann'd Japanee from his island only,
Lithe and silent the Hindoo appears, the Asiatic continent itself appears, the past, the dead,
The murky night-morning of wonder and fable inscrutable, 36
The envelop'd mysteries, the old and unknown hive-bees, 37
The north, the sweltering south, eastern Assyria, the Hebrews, the ancient of ancients,
Vast desolated cities, the gliding present, all of these and more are in the pageant-procession.

Geography, the world, is in it, 40
The Great Sea, the brood of islands, Polynesia, the coast beyond,

The coast you henceforth are facing —
you Libertad! from your Western
golden shores,
The countries there with their
populations, the millions en-masse
are curiously here,
The swarming market-places, the
temples with idols ranged along the
sides or at the end, bonze, brahmin,
and llama,
Mandarin, farmer, merchant, mechanic,
and fisherman,
The singing-girl and the dancing-girl,
the ecstatic persons, the secluded
emperors, 46
Confucius himself, the great poets and
heroes, the warriors, the castes, all, 47
Trooping up, crowding from all
directions, from the Altay
mountains,
From Thibet, from the four winding and
far-flowing rivers of China,
From the southern peninsulas and the
demi-continental islands, from
Malaysia,
These and whatever belongs to them
palpable show forth to me, and are
seiz'd by me,
And I am seiz'd by them, and friendlily
held by them,
Till as here them all I chant, Libertad!
for themselves and for you. 53

For I too raising my voice join the ranks
of this pageant,

I am the chanter, I chant aloud over the
  pageant,
I chant the world on my Western sea,
I chant copious the islands beyond,
  thick as stars in the sky,
I chant the new empire grander than
  any before, as in a vision it comes to
  me,
I chant America the mistress, I chant a
  greater supremacy,
I chant projected a thousand blooming
  cities yet in time on those groups of
  sea-islands,
My sail-ships and steam-ships threading
  the archipelagoes,
My stars and stripes fluttering in the
  wind,
Commerce opening, the sleep of ages
  having done its work, races reborn,
  refresh'd,
Lives, works resumed — the object I
  know not — but the old, the Asiatic
  new'd as it must be,
Commencing from this day surrounded
  by the world. 65

The 3rd Canto is a return to that June day in 1860: "The sign is reversing, the orb is enclosed, the ring is circled, the journey is done, the box-lid is but perceptibly open'd, nevertheless the perfume pours copiously out of the whole box."

3.
    And you Libertad of the world! 66

You shall sit in the middle well-pois'd
    thousands and thousands of years,
As to-day from one side the nobles of
    Asia come to you,
As to-morrow from the other side the
    queen of England sends her eldest
    son to you.
The sign is reversing, the orb is
    enclosed,
The ring is circled, the journey is done,
The box-lid is but perceptibly open'd,
    nevertheless the perfume pours
    copiously out of the whole box.   72

Young Libertad! with the venerable
    Asia, the all-mother,
Be considerate with her now and ever
    hot Libertad, for you are all,
Bend your proud neck to the long-off
    mother now sending messages over
    the archipelagoes to you,
Bend your proud neck low for once,
    young Libertad.

Where the children straying westward
    so long? so wide the tramping?
Were the precedent dim ages
    debouching westward from
    Paradise so long?
Were the centuries steadily footing it
    that way, all the while unknown, for
    you, for reasons?
They are justified, they are
    accomplish'd, they shall now be

> turn'd the other way also, to travel
> toward you thence,
> They shall now also march obediently
> eastward for your sake Libertad. 81

The box-lid was but perceptibly open'd, but the perfume remains with us as the poem concludes. (Line 72 above) The pageant that marched to greet the poet on Broadway will turn and circle the world in its "march obediently eastward for your sake Libertad."

3. By Blue Ontario's Shore

(1856)

"By Blue Ontario's Shore" was one of the twenty new poems of the 2nd edition. It is both a hodge-podge of disparate elements and also powerful work that balances the intentions of the poet with the aspirations of his imagined brothers. He suggests that his beloved States will only be compromised from within: "If we are lost, no victor else has destroyed us, it is by ourselves we go down to eternal night."

The theme of the one's availability to all is again taken up: "All is eligible to all. All is for the individual, all is for you, no condition is prohibited, not God's or any... if you would be freer than all that has been before, come listen to me."The sixty-six lines taken from the '55 Preface (Appendix 8) are mainly from Cantos 5 and 6. The '55 Preface was, of course, part of the inspiration that produced that edition's poems. Whitman will return to the preface to glean lines for numerous poems.

Aside from the lines utilized in *By Blue Ontario's Shore*; he would also augment *Song of Prudence*; *Song of the Answerer*; *To You*; *Texts*; *A Child's Amaze*; *Says*; and *Perfections*. A careful study of the Preface will reveal ideas, lines, and poetic sentiments that occur in almost every paragraph and appear in some form in *Leaves of Grass*. It worthwhile to note the salute to Language in Canto 10. It appeared only in 1856 but it shows the poet thinking linguistically about its use in his poems. The deleted lines are reproduced below. In the seventh Canto he has a jingoistic lapse. He returns, however, to more familiar and surer footing in Canto 15: "I swear I begin to see the meaning of these things... the whole theory of the universe is directed unerringly to one single individual—namely to you." There is an acknowledgement that America is far from perfect: "O I see flashing that this America is only you and me... its crimes, lies, thefts, defections are you and me... the war was you and me... I dare not shirk any part of myself, not any part of America good or bad..." Then, by blue Ontario's shore he sees the free souls of poets and the loftiest bards who by his charm are invoked. This is Whitman's poetic manifesto. In the penultimate Canto he conjures the great poets and bards of the past "who had long been unawake but were awaked by me." One recalls the conjuring of the dead prophet Samuel by King Saul and the Witch of Endor. Samuel was as peeved at being awakened from death's repose as Hamlet's father will be down long centuries, thereafter. But here, it is the poet who is aggravated. "O my rapt verse, my call, mock me not! / Not for the bards of the past, not to invoke them have I launch'd you forth, / Not to call even those lofty bards here by Ontario's shores, / Have I sung so capricious and loud my savage song."

By Blue Ontario's Shores received more revisions than any other single poem. This is Whitman's advocacy of himself as a poet, prophet, seer and deliverer of these United States. He had begun the poem shortly after the inaugural publication. The last two cantos were added in 1867. In this pose he, as Emerson had done before him, banishes the earlier poets. In the 20th Canto he awaits the newly arriving voices of the future: *Bards for my own land, only I invoke... Bards of the great Idea! Bards of the peaceful inventions... You by my charm I invoke.* There is greatness in this poem for those who will patiently seek it out. Rather than Athena or Apollo, the Phantom is what it purports to be—a projection from his interior— Ontario's shoreline is the poet's *Me Myself* on the edge of the infinite.

By Blue Ontario's Shore

1.

>By blue Ontario's shore,   1
>As I mused of these warlike days and of peace return'd, and the dead that return no more,
>A Phantom gigantic superb, with stern visage accosted me,   3
>Chant me the poem, it said, that comes from the soul of America, chant me the carol of victory,
>And strike up the marches of Libertad, marches more powerful yet,
>And sing me before you go the song of the throes of Democracy.
>
>(Democracy, the destin'd conqueror, yet treacherous lip-smiles everywhere,
>And death and infidelity at every step.)   8

The poet tempers his patriotism with caution. His beloved union is a destined conqueror, "…yet treacherous lip-smiles everywhere and death and infidelity at every step." (Lines 7-8 above)

2.

> A Nation announcing itself, 9
> I myself make the only growth by which
>   I can be appreciated,
> I reject none, accept all, then reproduce
>   all in my own forms. 10
>
> A breed whose proof is in time and
>   deeds,
> What we are we are, nativity is answer
>   enough to objections,
> We wield ourselves as a weapon is
>   wielded,
> We are powerful and tremendous in
>   ourselves,
> We are executive in ourselves, we are
>   sufficient in the variety of ourselves,
> We are the most beautiful to ourselves
>   and in ourselves,
> We stand self-pois'd in the middle,
>   branching thence over the world,
> From Missouri, Nebraska, or Kansas,
>   laughing attacks to scorn. 19
>
> Nothing is sinful to us outside of
>   ourselves,
> Whatever appears, whatever does not
>   appear, we are beautiful or sinful in
>   ourselves only.

> (O Mother—O Sisters dear!
> If we are lost, no victor else has destroy'd us,   23
> It is by ourselves we go down to eternal night.   24

In the final stanza of the 2nd Canto the poet invokes the feminine to save us: "O Mother—O Sisters dear." The final two lines are cautionary and as true today as when they were written: "If we are lost, no victor else has destroyed us, it is by ourselves we go down to eternal night." (Lines 23-24 above) Part of Whitman's sublime confidence is the assurance of equality: "All is eligible to all… no condition is prohibited…one does not countervail another any more than one eyesight countervails another, or one life countervails another." Democracy for the poet is, once again and always, ontology. Each is not only a citizen of a state but a manifest of *being*, however it's configured. We may find Whitman more artful but rarely as distinctly direct: "The whole theory of the Universe is directed unerringly to one single individual—namely to you."[181]

In Canto 17 we find: "Past, Present and Future, are you and me… I am for those who walk abreast with the whole earth, Who inaugurate one to inaugurate all." Immediately below (Lines 27-28) we find: *All is eligible to all…all is for you.* Again, Joyce will later muse: "As I am. As I am. All or not at all."[182] And, a little later on, during *Bloomsday*: "… dio boia, hangman god, is doubtless all in all in all of us." This poem first appeared in the Second edition of 1856 as *The Poem of the Many and the One*. The poet will tautologically suggest a paradigm—there is no distinction between the many and the one—the *Tautological Paradigm*.

3.
>Have you thought there could be but a single supreme? 25
>There can be any number of supremes — one does not countervail another any more than one eyesight countervails another, or one life countervails another.

>All is eligible to all, 27
>All is for individuals, all is for you,
>No condition is prohibited, not God's or any.
>All comes by the body, only health puts you rapport with the universe. 30

>Produce great Persons, the rest follows. 31

In the 4th Canto he rails as if addressing our own *tweet* and tabloid culture: "Who are you that wanted only to be told what you knew before? Who are you that wanted only a book to join you in your nonsense?" (Line 38 below)

4.
>Piety and conformity to them that like, 32
>Peace, obesity, allegiance, to them that like,
>I am he who tauntingly compels men, women, nations,
>Crying, Leap from your seats and contend for your lives!

> I am he who walks the States with a barb'd tongue, questioning every one I meet,
> Who are you that wanted only to be told what you knew before?
> Who are you that wanted only a book to join you in your nonsense? 38
>
> With pangs and cries as thine own O bearer of many children,
> These clamors wild to a race of pride I give.)
>
> O lands, would you be freer than all that has ever been before?
> If you would be freer than all that has been before, come listen to me.
>
> Fear grace, elegance, civilization, delicatesse,
> Fear the mellow sweet, the sucking of honey—juice,
> Beware the advancing mortal ripening of Nature,
> Beware what precedes the decay of the ruggedness of states and men. 46

Whitman follows Emerson's lead in acknowledging the Old World's precedent but, as well, calling for Americans to make their own mark: "A work remains, the work of surpassing all they have done…America…stands by its own at all hazards… these states are the amplest poem…" (Line 60 below). The poet is at his most outlandish when he suggests that the old is a corpse slowly borne from the house:

> "That its life had descended to the stalwart and well-shaped heir who approaches." (Line 56 below)

The irony of Whitman's arrogance is that it comes so completely near the truth. There have only lived a handful of Americans who could legitimately make the claim to be the old world's heir — and Walter Whitman, Junior is one of that handful.

5.

> Ages, precedents, have long been accumulating undirected materials, 47
> America brings builders, and brings its own styles.
>
> The immortal poets of Asia and Europe have done their work and pass'd to other spheres,
> A work remains, the work of surpassing all they have done.
>
> America, curious toward foreign characters, stands by its own at all hazards, 51
> Stands removed, spacious, composite, sound, initiates the true use of precedents,
> Does not repel them or the past or what they have produced under their forms,
> Takes the lesson with calmness, perceives the corpse slowly borne from the house,

Perceives that it waits a little while in the door, that it was fittest for its days,
That its life has descended to the stalwart and well-shaped heir who approaches, 56
And that he shall be fittest for his days. 57

Any period one nation must lead,
One land must be the promise and reliance of the future.

These States are the amplest poem, 60
Here is not merely a nation but a teeming Nation of nations,
Here the doings of men correspond with the broadcast doings of the day and night,
Here is what moves in magnificent masses careless of particulars,
Here are the roughs, beards, friendliness, combativeness, the soul loves,
Here the flowing trains, here the crowds, equality, diversity, the soul loves. 65

The succeeding 6th Canto of the poem is wildly provocative. The poet imagines himself as the original being that divided itself into the varied components of the world. It is one of the most rarefied and provoking moments of the poem: *Plunging his seminal muscle into its merits and demerits, Making its cities… rivers, lakes bays embouchure in him…* (Lines 73-106 below)

Few things in *Leaves of Grass* are as *seminal* as those lines and those which follow. Yes, the pun is precisely the point. Whitman can as ably strew his seed to the stars as he can proffer it to women, men or simply to himself. The poet sees himself in all things American. He is fecund and a prodigious list of America's waterways, waterfowl, savannahs and prairies, and his fellow Americans round out the inclusiveness of the canto.

6.

> Land of lands and bards to corroborate! 66
> Of them standing among them, one lifts to the light a west-bred face,
> To him the hereditary countenance bequeath'd both mother's and father's,
> His first parts substances, earth, water, animals, trees,
> Built of the common stock, having room for far and near,
> Used to dispense with other lands, incarnating this land,
> Attracting it body and soul to himself, hanging on its neck with incomparable love,
> Plunging his seminal muscle into its merits and demerits, 73
> Making its cities, beginnings, events, diversities, wars, vocal in him,
> Making its rivers, lakes, bays, embouchure in him, 75
> Mississippi with yearly freshets and changing chutes, Columbia, Niagara, Hudson, spending themselves lovingly in him,

If the Atlantic coast stretch or the Pacific coast stretch, he stretching with them North or South,
Spanning between them East and West, and touching whatever is between them,
Growths growing from him to offset the growths of pine, cedar, hemlock, live-oak, locust, chestnut, hickory, cottonwood, orange, magnolia,   79
Tangles as tangled in him as any canebrake or swamp,
He likening sides and peaks of mountains, forests coated with northern transparent ice,
Off him pasturage sweet and natural as savanna, upland, prairie,
Through him flights, whirls, screams, answering those of the fish-hawk, mocking-bird, night-heron, and eagle,
His spirit surrounding his country's spirit, unclosed to good and evil,   84
Surrounding the essences of real things, old times and present times,
Surrounding just found shores, islands, tribes of red aborigines,
Weather-beaten vessels, landings, settlements, embryo stature and muscle,
The haughty defiance of the Year One, war, peace, the formation of the Constitution,   88
The separate States, the simple elastic scheme, the immigrants,

The Union always swarming with blatherers and always sure and impregnable,
The unsurvey'd interior, log-houses, clearings, wild animals, hunters, trappers,
Surrounding the multiform agriculture, mines, temperature, the gestation of new States,
Congress convening every Twelfth-month, the members duly coming up from the uttermost parts,
Surrounding the noble character of mechanics and farmers, especially the young men,
Responding their manners, speech, dress, friendships, the gait they have of persons who never knew how it felt to stand in the presence of superiors,
The freshness and candor of their physiognomy, the copiousness and decision of their phrenology,
The picturesque looseness of their carriage, their fierceness when wrong'd,
The fluency of their speech, their delight in music, their curiosity, good temper and open-handedness, the whole composite make,
The prevailing ardor and enterprise, the large amativeness,
The perfect equality of the female with the male, the fluid movement of the population,

The superior marine, free commerce,
    fisheries, whaling, gold-digging,
Wharf-hemm'd cities, railroad and
    steamboat lines intersecting all
    points,
Factories, mercantile life, labor-saving
    machinery, the Northeast,
    Northwest, Southwest,
Manhattan firemen, the Yankee swap,
    southern plantation life,
Slavery—the murderous, treacherous
    conspiracy to raise it upon the ruins
    of all the rest,   105
On and on to the grapple with it—
    Assassin! then your life or ours be
    the stake, and respite no more.   106

The 7th Canto strikes a rare note of jingoism for the poet. It was added in 1867 so its difficult to know to which enemy his animus was directed: I *mark the new aureola around your head... dazzling and fierce, with war's flames... and your foot on the neck of the menacing one...* (Lines 108 & 113 below) His image is only slightly more appealing if the imagined foe is evil—*the menacing one*. Patriots always imagine themselves haloed and their enemies, serpentine. Johnson famously said that "Patriotism is the last refuge of a scoundrel." The country was feeling its oats. It defeated Mexico in 1848, freeing Texas and securing the southwest and California for its continued manifest destiny. But Whitman goes further than we like when he says of the enemy: *The wide-swelling one, the braggart that would yesterday do so much, To-day a carrion dead and damn'd, the despised of all the earth, An offal rank, to the dunghill maggots spurn'd.* (Lines 117-118 below)

7.

>(Lo, high toward heaven, this day, 107
>Libertad, from the conqueress' field return'd, mark the new aureola around your head, 108
>No more of soft astral, but dazzling and fierce,
>With war's flames and the lambent lightnings playing,
>And your port immovable where you stand,
>With still the inextinguishable glance and the clinch'd and lifted fist,
>And your foot on the neck of the menacing one, the scorner utterly crush'd beneath you, 113
>The menacing arrogant one that strode and advanced with his senseless scorn, bearing the murderous knife,
>The wide-swelling one, the braggart that would yesterday do so much,
>To-day a carrion dead and damn'd, the despised of all the earth,
>An offal rank, to the dunghill maggots spurn'd.) 118

In the 8th Canto he sends *Bravas* to those sending sane children into the next age but damns them who take the responsibility lightly, with no thought of the strain and pain that they are passing on to the next generation.

8.

>Others take finish, but the Republic is ever constructive and ever keeps vista, 119

> Others adorn the past, but you O days
> of the present, I adorn you,
> O days of the future I believe in you — I
> isolate myself for your sake,
> O America because you build for
> mankind I build for you,
> O well-beloved stone-cutters, I lead
> them who plan with decision and
> science,
> Lead the present with friendly hand
> toward the future.
>
> (Bravas to all impulses sending sane
> children to the next age!
> But damn that which spends itself with
> no thought of the stain, pains,
> dismay, feebleness, it is
> bequeathing.) 126

The Phantom returns demanding bards. Here the poet reveals his belief in the power of art (poetry) to bind a nation together: *By them alone can these States be fused into the compact organism of a nation.* (Line 129 below) It should be remembered that in antebellum America, the states were as sacrosanct as their union. Whitman is hoping that his poetry will be the welding force. Even in the volatile late fifties the alternative was increasingly thought to be war. Solutions to the rift presented by the Northern states' industrial concerns and the Southern states' agrarian and slave interests would finally fail as the South began its siege of the Federal ramparts of Fort Sumter. Whitman asserts that treaties are of no use. Rather men are held together by living principles, as are the limbs secured to a body and fibers to a plant. He sees that the Mother of poets has long been barren:

Soul of love and tongue of fire!

9.

> I listened to the Phantom by Ontario's shore, 127
> I heard the voice arising demanding bards,
> By them all native and grand, by them alone can these States be fused into the compact organism of a Nation. 129

> To hold men together by paper and seal or by compulsion is no account,
> That only holds men together which aggregates all in a living principle, as the hold of the limbs of the body or the fibres of plants.

> Of all races and eras these States with veins full of poetical stuff most need poets, and are to have the greatest, and use them the greatest, 132
> Their Presidents shall not be their common referee so much as their poets shall.

> (Soul of love and tongue of fire! 134
> Eye to pierce the deepest deeps and sweep the world!
> Ah Mother, prolific and full in all besides, yet how long barren, barren?) 136

The 10th Canto is a great dilation on the role of the poet. He had outlined the poet's role in the 1855 Preface—that passage follows below. Read it slowly—it is dense but you will hear the echo of lines recently traversed and anticipate lines that shortly will follow.

The 1855 Preface: On Poets

The American poets are to enclose old and new for America is the race of races. Of them a bard is to be commensurate with a people. to him the other continents arrive as contributions ... He gives them reception for their sake and his own sake. His spirit responds to his country's spirit ... He incarnates its geography and natural life and rivers and lakes. Mississippi with annual freshets and changing chutes, Missouri and Columbia and Ohio and St. Lawrence with the Falls and beautiful masculine Hudson, do not embouchure where they spend themselves more than they embouchure into him.

The blue breadth over the inland sea of Virginia and Maryland and the sea off Massachusetts and Maine and over Manhattan Bay and over Champlain and Erie and over Ontario and Huron and Michigan and Superior, and over the Texan and Mexican and Floridian and Cuban seas, and over the seas off California and Oregon, is not tallied by the blue breadth of the waters below more than the breadth of above and below is tallied by him. When the long Atlantic coast stretches longer and the Pacific coast stretches longer he easily stretches with them north or south. He spans between them also from east to west and reflects what is between them. On him rise solid growths that offset the growths of pine and cedar and hemlock and live oak and locust and chestnut and cypress and hickory and limetree and cottonwood and tuliptree and caotus and wildvine and tamarind and persimmon ... and tangles as tangled as any canebrake or swamp ... and forests coated with transparent ice, and icicles hanging from boughs and crackling in the wind ... and sides and peaks of mountains ... and pasturage sweet and free as savannah or upland or prairie ... with flights and songs and screams that answer those of the wild pigeon and high-hold and orchard-oriole and coot and surf-duck and red-shouldered-hawk and fish-hawk and white ibis and Indian-hen and cat-owl and water-pheasant and qua-bird and pied-sheldrake and blackbird and mockingbird and buzzard and condor and night heron and eagle. to him the hereditary countenance descends both mother's and father's. to him enter the essences of the real things and past and present events —

Of the enormous diversity of temperature and agriculture and mines—the tribes of red aborigines—the weather-beaten vessels entering new ports or making landings on rocky coasts—the first settlements north or south—the rapid stature and muscle—the haughty defiance of '76, and the war and peace and formation of the constitution ... the Union always surrounded by blatherers and always calm and impregnable—the perpetual coming of immigrants—the wharf-hem'd cities and superior marine—the unsurveyed interior—the loghouses and clearings and wild animals and hunters and trappers ... the free commerce—the fisheries and whaling and gold-digging—the endless gestation of new states—the convening of Congress every December...The members duly coming up from all climates and the uttermost parts ... the noble character of the young mechanics and of all free American workmen and workwomen ... the general ardor and friendliness and enterprise—the perfect equality of the female with the male ... the large amativeness—the fluid movement of the population—the factories and mercantile life and laborsaving machinery—The Yankee swap—the New York firemen and the target excursion—the Southern plantation life—

> The character of the northeast and of the northwest and southwest—slavery and the tremulous spreading of hands to protect it, and the stern opposition to it which shall never cease till it ceases or the speaking of tongues and the moving of lips cease. For such the expression of the American poet is to be transcendent and new. It is to be indirect and not direct or descriptive or epic. Its quality goes through these to much more. Let the age and wars of other nations be chanted and their eras and characters be illustrated and that finish the verse. Not so the great psalm of the republic. Here the theme is creative and has vista. Here comes one among the well beloved stonecutters and plans with decision and science and sees the solid and beautiful forms of the future where there are now no solid forms.

Whitman latter condensed the 10th Canto in one of his many revisions of the poem. The deleted portions (between lines 153 & 154 & the eight lines succeeding line 159) remain very powerful and are presented in italics below.

10.

> Of these States the poet is the equable man,   137
> Not in him but off from him things are grotesque, eccentric, fail of their full returns,

Nothing out of its place is good, nothing
   in its place is bad,
He bestows on every object or quality its
   fit proportion, neither more nor less,
He is the arbiter of the diverse, he is the
   key, 141
He is the equalizer of his age and land,
He supplies what wants supplying, he
   checks what wants checking,
In peace out of him speaks the spirit of
   peace, large, rich, thrifty, building
   populous towns, encouraging
   agriculture, arts, commerce, lighting
   the study of man, the soul, health,
   immortality, government,
In war he is the best backer of the war,
   he fetches artillery as good as the
   engineer's, he can make every word
   he speaks draw blood,
The years straying toward infidelity he
   withholds by his steady faith,
He is no arguer, he is judgment, (Nature
   accepts him absolutely,) 147
He judges not as the judge judges but as
   the sun failing round a helpless
   thing,
As he sees the farthest he has the most
   faith,
His thoughts are the hymns of the praise
   of things,
In the dispute on God and eternity he is
   silent,
He sees eternity less like a play with a
   prologue and denouement,

He sees eternity in men and women, he does not see men and women as dreams or dots. 153

An American literati fills his own place,

He justifies science – did you think the demonstrable less divine than the mythical?

He stands by liberty according the compact of the first day of the first year of These States,

He concentrates in the real body and soul, and in the pleasure of things,

He possesses the superiority of genuineness over fiction and romance,

As he emits himself, facts are showered over with light,

The day-light is lit with more volatile light – the deep between the setting and rising sun goes deeper many fold,

Each precise object, condition, combination, process, exhibits a beauty – the multiplication-table its, old age its, the carpenter's trade its, the grand opera its, the huge-hulled clean-shaped Manhattan clipper at sea, under steam or full sail, gleams with unmatched beauty,

The national circles and large harmonies of government gleams with theirs,

The commonest definite intentions and actions with theirs.

For the great Idea, the idea of perfect and free individuals, 154

For that, the bard walks in advance, leader of leaders,
The attitude of him cheers up slaves and horrifies foreign despots. 156
Without extinction is Liberty, without retrograde is Equality,
They live in the feelings of young men and the best women,
(Not for nothing have the indomitable heads of the earth been always ready to fall for Liberty.) 159

Language-using controls the rest:
Wonderful is language!
Wonderous the English Language, language of live men,
Language of ensemble, powerful language of resistance,
Language of a proud and melancholy stock, and of all who aspire,
Language of growth, faith, self-estemm, rudeness, justice, friendliness, Amplitude, prudence, decision, exactitude, courage,
Language to well-nigh express the inexpressible,
Language for the modern, language for America.

The 11th Canto was added in 1867. Here flag and war are metaphors for the persuasive power of a poem. *Warlike flag of the great idea – angry cloth I saw there leaping.* (Lines 165-166)

Note that he concludes the canto by repeating line 166, first line of the third stanza.

11.
>   For the great Idea,   160
>   That, O my brethren, that is the mission of poets.
>   Songs of stern defiance ever ready,
>   Songs of the rapid arming and the march,
>   The flag of peace quick-folded, and instead the flag we know,
>   Warlike flag of the great Idea.   165
>
>   (Angry cloth I saw there leaping!   166
>   I stand again in leaden rain your flapping folds saluting,
>   I sing you over all, flying beckoning through the fight—O the hard-contested fight!
>   The cannons ope their rosy-flashing muzzles—the hurtled balls scream,
>   The battle-front forms amid the smoke—the volleys pour incessant from the line,
>   Hark, the ringing word Charge!—now the tussle and the furious maddening yells,
>   Now the corpses tumble curl'd upon the ground,
>   Cold, cold in death, for precious life of you,
>   Angry cloth I saw there leaping.)   174

Whitman provides a qualification form for the would-be poet of these United States. We won't be surprised to find him imminently qualified for the position. The basis for employment continues in the 13th Canto.

12.

> Are you he who would assume a place to teach or be a poet here in the States? 175
> The place is august, the terms obdurate.
>
> Who would assume to teach here may well prepare himself body and mind,
> He may well survey, ponder, arm, fortify, harden, make lithe himself,
> He shall surely be question'd beforehand by me with many and stern questions.
>
> Who are you indeed who would talk or sing to America? 180
> Have you studied out the land, its idioms and men?
> Have you learn'd the physiology, phrenology, politics, geography, pride, freedom, friendship of the land? its substratums and objects?
> Have you consider'd the organic compact of the first day of the first year of Independence, sign'd by the Commissioners, ratified by the States, and read by Washington at the head of the army?
> Have you possess'd yourself of the Federal Constitution?
> Do you see who have left all feudal processes and poems behind them, and assumed the poems and processes of Democracy?

Are you faithful to things? do you teach what the land and sea, the bodies of men, womanhood, amativeness, heroic angers, teach? 187
Have you sped through fleeting customs, popularities?
Can you hold your hand against all seductions, follies, whirls, fierce contentions? are you very strong? are you really of the whole people?
Are you not of some coterie? some school or mere religion?
Are you done with reviews and criticisms of life? animating now to life itself? 191
Have you vivified yourself from the maternity of these States?
Have you too the old ever-fresh forbearance and impartiality? 193
Do you hold the like love for those hardening to maturity? for the last-born? little and big? and for the errant?

What is this you bring my America?
Is it uniform with my country?
Is it not something that has been better told or done before?
Have you not imported this or the spirit of it in some ship?
Is it not a mere tale? a rhyme? a prettiness? — Is the good old cause in it?

Has it not dangled long at the heels of the poets, politicians, literats, of enemies' lands?
Does it not assume that what is notoriously gone is still here? 200
Does it answer universal needs? will it improve manners?
Does it sound with trumpet-voice the proud victory of the Union in that secession war?
Can your performance face the open fields and the seaside? 203
Will it absorb into me as I absorb food, air, to appear again in my strength, gait, face?
Have real employments contributed to it? original makers, not mere amanuenses
Does it meet modern discoveries, calibres, facts, face to face?
What does it mean to American persons, progresses, cities? Chicago, Kanada, Arkansas?

Does it see behind the apparent custodians the real custodians standing, menacing, silent, the mechanics, Manhattanese, Western men, Southerners, significant alike in their apathy, and in the promptness of their love?
Does it see what finally befalls, and has always finally befallen, each temporizer, patcher, outsider,

> partialist, alarmist, infidel, who has
> ever ask'd any thing of America?
> What mocking and scornful negligence?
> The track strew'd with the dust of
> skeletons,
> By the roadside others disdainfully
> toss'd. 212

Line 220 below is a hopeful prognostication that will eventually be proven true. The poet's country will, in time, recognize and absorb the poet. But for his early reviewers his sexual pronouncements were as outrageous as his claim that there shortly would be no more priests, their work is done. (Line 226 below)

13.
> Rhymes and rhymers pass away, poems
> distill'd from poems pass away, 213
> The swarms of reflectors and the polite
> pass, and leave ashes,
> Admirers, importers, obedient persons,
> make but the soil of literature,
> America justifies itself, give it time, no
> disguise can deceive it or conceal
> from it, it is impassive enough,
> Only toward the likes of itself will it
> advance to meet them,
> If its poets appear it will in due time
> advance to meet them, there is no
> fear of mistake,
> (The proof of a poet shall be sternly
> deferr'd till his country absorbs him
> as affectionately as he has absorb'd
> it.) 220

He masters whose spirit masters, he
>   tastes sweetest who results sweetest
>   in the long run,
> The blood of the brawn beloved of time
>   is unconstraint;
> In the need of songs, philosophy, an
>   appropriate native grand-opera,
>   shipcraft, any craft,
> He or she is greatest who contributes
>   the greatest original political
>   example.

> Already a nonchalant breed, silently
>   emerging, appears on the streets,
> People's lips salute only doers, lovers,
>   satisfiers, positive knowers,
> There will shortly be no more priests, I
>   say their work is done,
> Death is without emergencies here, but
>   life is perpetual emergencies here,
> Are your body, days, manners, superb?
>   after death you shall be superb,
> Justice, health, self-esteem, clear the way
>   with irresistible power;
> How dare you place any thing before a
>   man?

Whitman then *tips his hand*. He is, indeed, the man qualified for the job: *Fall behind me States!...Give me the pay I have served for, Give me to sing the songs of the great Idea, take all the rest. I have loved the earth, sun, animals, I have despised riches...I have given alms to every one that ask'd, stood up for the stupid and crazy, devoted my income and labor to others...claimed nothing to myself which I have not carefully claimed for others on the same terms.* (Lines

231-241 below). All of which are true. The years he struggled with this poem is evidence of his own doubts. Here he is pleading with himself to be found worthy. With the grand exception of Emerson, his public in 1856 was minuscule—in the next couple of years Whitman wouldn't necessarily include himself among his admirers. When he asks of the Great Mother: *Say O Mother, have I not to your thought been faithful? Have I not through life kept you and yours before me?* (Lines 248-249 below). We earnestly hope that he hears the answer for which he so longs.

For it is *our* hope—the balm of a Buddha or a Christ to soothe the sundered heart of the spinning world.

14.

> Fall behind me States! 231
> A man before all—myself, typical, before all.
>
> Give me the pay I have served for, 233
> Give me to sing the songs of the great Idea, take all the rest,
> I have loved the earth, sun, animals, I have despised riches,
> I have given alms to every one that ask'd, stood up for the stupid and crazy, devoted my income and labor to others,
> Hated tyrants, argued not concerning God, had patience and indulgence toward the people, taken off my hat to nothing known or unknown,

> Gone freely with powerful uneducated
>   persons and with the young, and
>   with the mothers of families,
> Read these leaves to myself in the open
>   air, tried them by trees, stars, rivers,   239
> Dismiss'd whatever insulted my own
>   soul or defiled my body,
> Claim'd nothing to myself which I have
>   not carefully claim'd for others on
>   the same terms,   241
> Sped to the camps, and comrades found
>   and accepted from every State,
> (Upon this breast has many a dying
>   soldier lean'd to breathe his last,
> This arm, this hand, this voice, have
>   nourish'd, rais'd, restored,
> To life recalling many a prostrate form;)
> I am willing to wait to be understood by
>   the growth of the taste of myself,
> Rejecting none, permitting all.   247
>
> (Say O Mother, have I not to your
>   thought been faithful?
> Have I not through life kept you and
>   yours before me?)   249

In the next five Cantos he hears the answer he sought. He finds his strength in the individual — *Underneath all, individuals*. And if there is any question that any of the *Many* is anything other than the *One*, the poet magnificently avers: *The whole theory of the universe is directed unerringly to one single individual — namely to You.* (Line 259 below)

And then the poet concludes with the dramatic image of *Justice*:

> Mother! with subtle sense severe, with
> naked sword in your hand,

He sees that true Justice *at last refuse(s) to treat but directly with individuals.*

15.

> I swear I begin to see the meaning of
>   these things, 250
> It is not the earth, it is not America who
>   is so great,
> It is I who am great or to be great, it is
>   You up there, or any one,
> It is to walk rapidly through
>   civilizations, governments, theories,
> Through poems, pageants, shows, to
>   form individuals.
>
> Underneath all, individuals, 255
> I swear nothing is good to me now that
>   ignores individuals,
> The American compact is altogether
>   with individuals,
> The only government is that which
>   makes minute of individuals,
> The whole theory of the universe is
>   directed unerringly to one
> single individual—namely to You. 259
>
> (Mother! with subtle sense severe, with
>   the naked sword in your hand, 260

> I saw you at last refuse to treat but
> directly with individuals.)   261

Individuals are produced by sex. *Underneath all is the Expression of love for men and women.* (Line 264 below) In this the poet finds his key: "After this day I take my own modes of expressing love for men and women in myself." He has shown us the key but we must unlock our own secret chambers of the soul.

16.
> Underneath all, Nativity,   262
> I swear I will stand by my own nativity,
>   pious or impious so be it;
> I swear I am charm'd with nothing
>   except nativity,
> Men, women, cities, nations, are only
>   beautiful from nativity.
>
> Underneath all is the Expression of love
>   for men and women,
> (I swear I have seen enough of mean
>   and impotent modes of expressing
>   love for men and women,
> After this day I take my own modes of
>   expressing love for men and
> women.)
>
> I swear I will have each quality of my
>   race in myself,
> (Talk as you like, he only suits these
>   States whose manners favor
> the audacity and sublime turbulence of
>   the States.)

> Underneath the lessons of things,
> spirits, Nature, governments,
> ownerships, I swear I perceive other
> lessons,
> Underneath all to me is myself, to you
> yourself, (the same monotonous old
> song.) 272

He sees that America is only you and me. Its crimes, lies, thefts, defections are you and me. The war was you and me. And perhaps in the next line we see the point of inserting the jingoism of Canto 7. For here he asserts: "...that war so bloody and grim, the war I will henceforth forget." For each of us is: *Past, present, future* (Line 281 below). Henceforth he will be "for those who walk abreast with the whole earth, who inaugurate one to inaugurate all." (Lines 291-292 below)

17.

> O I see flashing that this America is only
> you and me, 273
> Its power, weapons, testimony, are you
> and me,
> Its crimes, lies, thefts, defections, are
> you and me, 275
> Its Congress is you and me, the officers,
> capitols, armies, ships, are you and
> me,
> Its endless gestations of new States are
> you and me,
> The war, (that war so bloody and grim,
> the war I will henceforth forget),
> was you and me, 278
> Natural and artificial are you and me,

Freedom, language, poems, employments, are you and me,
Past, present, future, are you and me. 281

I dare not shirk any part of myself,
Not any part of America good or bad,
Not to build for that which builds for mankind,
Not to balance ranks, complexions, creeds, and the sexes,
Not to justify science nor the march of equality,
Nor to feed the arrogant blood of the brawn belov'd of time.

I am for those that have never been master'd, 288
For men and women whose tempers have never been master'd,
For those whom laws, theories, conventions, can never master.

I am for those who walk abreast with the whole earth, 291
Who inaugurate one to inaugurate all.

I will not be outfaced by irrational things,
I will penetrate what it is in them that is sarcastic upon me,
I will make cities and civilizations defer to me,
This is what I have learnt from America—it is the amount, and it I teach again.

> (Democracy, while weapons were everywhere aim'd at your breast,
> I saw you serenely give birth to immortal children, saw in dreams your dilating form,
> Saw you with spreading mantle covering the world.)   299

He will confront the show of day and night. He now is certain that the gross, tantalizing, and wicked earth is for his sake. He will match his *spirit against yours you orbs, growths, mountains, brutes...*(Line 307 below) What is America isolated but finally himself? (Line 309 below) He tenderly asks the Great Mother to "bend down, bend close to me your face." He confesses that he knows not to what end that wars, plots, deferments, and crime are directed: *But I know... your work goes on, and must yet go on.* The goal of the *Bodhisattva* is to *walk abreast with the whole earth,* inaugurating *one to inaugurate all.* (Lines 291-292 above)

18.

> I will confront these shows of the day and night,   300
> I will know if I am to be less than they,
> I will see if I am not as majestic as they,
> I will see if I am not as subtle and real as they,
> I will see if I am to be less generous than they,
> I will see if I have no meaning, while the houses and ships have meaning,
> I will see if the fishes and birds are to be enough for themselves, and I am not to be enough for myself.

> I match my spirit against yours you orbs, growths, mountains, brutes, 307
> Copious as you are I absorb you all in myself, and become the master myself,
> America isolated yet embodying all, what is it finally except myself? 309
> These States, what are they except myself?
>
> I know now why the earth is gross, tantalizing, wicked, it is for my sake,
> I take you specially to be mine, you terrible, rude forms.
>
> (Mother, bend down, bend close to me your face,
> I know not what these plots and wars and deferments are for,
> I know not fruition's success, but I know that through war and crime your work goes on, and must yet go on.) 315

The poet concludes a tortured but great effort in the final two Cantos of *By Blue Ontario's Shore*. I've noted a few of the poem's more salient lines in our brief traversal. The great *War of Succession* had begun and ended during the lengthy long years the poet labored on this poem — many a solider has died upon his breast (Line 243 above) -- brother need no longer fight brother — the only battle worth fighting is the immortal war for meaning. Emerson had earlier averred that each us has a shorefront to an infinite sea.

Each of us is the *many* who is also the *one*. It is clear, as we earlier noted, that the blue Ontario shore is the edge of the waiting Universe. I will leave the penultimate and concluding Canto to the reader's thoughts of their own.

19.

> Thus by blue Ontario's shore, 316
> While the winds fann'd me and the waves came trooping toward me,
> I thrill'd with the power's pulsations, and the charm of my theme was upon me,
> Till the tissues that held me parted their ties upon me.
>
> And I saw the free souls of poets,
> The loftiest bards of past ages strode before me,
> Strange large men, long unwaked, undisclosed, were disclosed to me. 322

20.

> O my rapt verse, my call, mock me not! 323
> Not for the bards of the past, not to invoke them have I launch'd you forth,
> Not to call even those lofty bards here by Ontario's shores,
> Have I sung so capricious and loud my savage song. 326
>
> Bards for my own land only I invoke,
> (For the war the war is over, the field is clear'd,) 328

Till they strike up marches henceforth
    triumphant and onward,
To cheer O Mother your boundless
    expectant soul.

Bards of the great Idea! bards of the
    peaceful inventions! (for the war,
    the war is over!)
Yet bards of latent armies, a million
    soldiers waiting ever-ready,
Bards with songs as from burning coals
    or the lightning's fork'd stripes!
Ample Ohio's, Kanada's bards—bards
    of California! inland bards— bards
    of the war!
You by my charm I invoke.   335

4. Reversals

(1856)

Reversals is the shortest of Whitman's solo canticles. It originally appeared the 1856 edition as the *Poem of the Propositions of Nakedness*. Three of its lines also find themselves in the solo poem, *Transpositions*. It was enlarged in several subsequent editions as *Respondez*, until it was cut from the *Leaves* in 1881. *Respondez* is one of the most remarkable exclusions from the Canon. Neither *Reversals* nor *Transpositions* can do little more than hint at the power of the original—Whitman's Jeremiads go beyond those of Jeremiah. In the more conservative mood of his final decade the poet decided that the poem was a diatribe too much in contrast to the myth of the *good, gray poet*.

The poem is a raucously violent assault on the mores of the masses he had, heretofore, taken such care to cultivate. It is a fascinating example of bi-polar rage—nineteenth century style. *Repondez* takes its place among the uncounted in *Whitman's Code* as an example of a grand symphony that was lost in Whitman's long editorial process and only hinted at in its surviving bagatelles. In the greater freedom of this compendium it has been freed to soar and sing again. Along with Hamlet's: "O what a rogue and peasant slave am I;" [183] Lear's "Let copulation thrive;" [184] and Donne's "Go and catch a falling star;" [185] it is one of the great literary rants in the world's poetry. *Respondez* is, however, the exact opposite of his own moral stance. It was written in the bitter irony that he had been accused of the very things that his derision scorns in the poem. His salute to sexuality was said to be obscene. Whitman wouldn't countenance any disrespect to women. Any *trash talk* about any woman was anathema to his sensibilities. He had come to the defense of prostitutes as an editor in New York. He will write with overwhelming sympathy of their plight in his prose and poetry. As to charges of inspiring public immorality he proposes in his rant that the laws require monthly, on pain of our lives, that each citizen be stripped naked so as to allow the community free reign to fondle our exposed nakedness. When he suggests that the *earth desert God*, it is an echo of the contumely that claimed him Godless. When he acerbically says "Let there be no God," he knows that the hand of God is the promise of his own and that the spirit of God is the brother of his own; and that he sees God in every hour of the twenty-four. By way of introduction, I've selected nine of my favorite lines below. The reader is free to select favorites of his own from the complete *Respondez*, also following, below.

Respondez Mine! [186]

Let the eminence of meanness, treachery, sarcasm, hate, greed, indecency, impotence, lust, be taken for granted above all!,"

Let the crust of hell be neared and trod on! Let the days be darker than the nights!

Let slumber bring less slumber than waking time brings!

Let slumber bring less slumber than waking time brings!

Let the worst men beget children out of the worst women!

Let churches accommodate serpents, vermin, and the corpses of those who have died of the most filthy of diseases!

Let the earth desert God, nor let there ever henceforth be mentioned the name of God!

Let there be no God!

Let men among themselves talk and think forever obscenely of women! And let women talk and think forever obscenely of men!

Let us all, without missing one, be exposed in public naked, monthly, at the peril of our lives! Let our bodies be freely handled and examined by whoever chooses!

Read the poem aloud. It is a single stanza of 68 lines.

Respondez! Enjoy and be damned!

(1856) RESPONDEZ

RESPONDEZ! Respondez! 1
The war is completed—the price is paid—the title is settled beyond recall;)
Let every one answer! Let those who sleep be waked! Let none evade!
Must we go on with our affections and sneaking?
Let me bring this to a close—I pronounce openly for a new distribution of roles;
Let that which stood in front go behind! And let that which was behind go to the front and speak;
Let murders, bigots, fools, unclean persons, offer new propositions! 6
Let the old propositions be postponed!
Let faces and theories be tuned inside out! Let meanings be freely criminal as well as results!
Let their be no suggestion above the suggestion of drudgery!
Let none be pointed toward his destination! (Say! Do you know your destination?.

Let men and women be mock'd with bodies and mock'd with Souls!

Let the love that waits in them, wait! Let it die, or pass still-born to other spheres!

Let the sympathy that waits in every man, wait! Or let it also pass, a dwarf to other spheres!

Let contradictions prevail! Let one thing contradict another! And let one line of my poems contradict another!

Let the people sprawl with yearning, aimless hands! Let their tongues be broken! Let their eyes be discouraged! Let none descend into their hearts with the fresh lusciousness of love!

(Stifled, O days! O lands! In every private and public corruption!

Smothered in thievery, impotence, shamelessness, mountain-high;

Brazen effrontery, scheming, rolling like the ocean waves around and upon you, O my days! My lands!

For not even those thunderstorms of the war, have purified the atmosphere;)

—Let the theory of America still be management, caste, comparison! (Say or what other theory would you?)

Let them that distrust birth and death still lead the rest! (Say! why shall they not lead you?)

Let the crust of hell be neared and trod on! Let the days be darker than the nights! Let slumber bring less slumber than waking time brings!

Let the world never appear to him or her for whom it was all made!

Let the heart of the young man still exile itself from the heart of the old man!

Let the sun and moon go! Let scenery take the applause of the audience! Let there be apathy under the stars!

Let freedom prove no man's inalienable right! Everyone who can tyrannize, let him tyrannize to his satisfaction!

Let none but infidels be countenanced!

Let the eminence of meanness, treachery, sarcasm, hate, greed, indecency, impotence, lust, be taken for granted above all! Let writers, judges, governments, households, religions, philosophies, take such for granted above all!

Let the worst men beget children out of the worst women!

Let the priest still play at immortality!

Let death be inaugurated!

Let nothing remain but the ashes of teachers, artists, moralists, lawyers, and learn'd and polite persons!

Let him who is without my poems be assassinated!

Let the cow, horse, the camel, the garden-bee — let the mud-fish, the lobster, the mussel, eel, the sting-ray, and the grunting pug-fish — let these, and the like of these be put on perfect equality with man and woman!

Let churches accommodate serpents, vermin, and the corpses of those who have died of the most filthy of diseases!

Let marriage slip down among fools, and be for none but fools!

Let men among themselves talk and think forever obscenely of women! And let women talk and think forever obscenely of men!

Let us all, without missing one, be exposed in public naked, monthly, at the peril of our lives! Let our bodies be freely handled and examined by whoever chooses!

Let nothing but copies at second hand be permitted to exist upon the earth!

Let the earth desert God, nor let there ever henceforth be mentioned the name of God!

Let there be no God!

Let there be money, business, imports, exports, custom, authority, precedents, pallor, dyspepsia, smut, ignorance, unbelief!

Let judges and criminals be transposed! let the prison-keepers be put in prison! let those that were prisoners take the keys! Say! why might they not just as well be transposed?)

Let the slaves be masters! let the masters become slaves!

Let the reformers descend from the stands where they are forever bawling! let an idiot or insane person appear on each of the stands!

Let the Asiatic, the African, the European, the American, and the Australian, go armed against the murderous stealthiness of each other! let them sleep armed! let none believe in good will!

Let there be no unfashionable wisdom! let such be scorn'd and derided off from the earth!

Let a floating cloud in the sky—let a wave of the sea—let growing mint, spinach, onions, tomatoes—let these be exhibited as shows, at a great price for admission!

Let all the men of These States stand aside for a few smouchers! let the few seize on what they choose! let the rest gawk, giggle, starve, obey!

Let shadows be furnish'd with genitals! let substances be deprived of their genitals!

Let there be wealthy and immense cities—but still through any of them, not a single poet, savior, knower, lover!

Let the infidels of These States laugh all faith away!

If one man be found who has faith, let the rest set upon him!

Let them affright faith! let them destroy the power of breeding faith!

Let the she-harlots and the he-harlots be
 prudent! let them dance on, while
 seeming lasts!
(O seeming! seeming! seeming!)
Let the preachers recite creeds! let them
 still teach only what they have been
 taught!
Let insanity still have charge of sanity!
Let books take the place of trees,
 animals, rivers, clouds!
Let the daub'd portraits of heroes
 supersede heroes!
Let the manhood of man never take
 steps after itself!
Let it take steps after eunuchs, and after
 consumptive and genteel persons!
Let the white person again tread the
 black person under his heel!
(Say! which is trodden under heel, after
 all?)
Let the reflections of the things of the
 world be studied in mirrors! let the
 things themselves still continue
 unstudied! 63
Let a man seek pleasure everywhere
 except in himself!
Let a woman seek happiness
 everywhere except in herself!
(What real happiness have you had one
 single hour through your whole
 life?)
Let the limited years of life do nothing for the
 limitless years of death!
(What do you suppose death will do,
 then?) 68

The children of *Respondez* are such shadowed offspring of the parent as to call into question the paternity of the poems derived from it. This is the first of the bastards — that is, bagatelles. The second will appear in the twelve hours between noon and midnight.

Reversals

> Let that which stood in front go behind,   1
> Let that which was behind advance to the front,
> Let bigots, fools, unclean persons, offer new propositions,
> Let the old propositions be postponed,
> Let a man seek pleasure everywhere except in himself,
> Let a woman seek happiness everywhere except in herself.   6

5. Proud Music of the Storm

(1869)

Proud Music of the Storm begins a group of six solo canticles that commence after the *Autumn Rivulets* cluster. Here, more than in any other poem, the poet celebrates his love of opera, in particular, and classical music, in general. For Whitman, music was the incarnation of spirit — the soul's manifest written from the earth to the ear. His greatest spiritual transports, prior to the composition of his *Leaves*, were experienced at the opera.

Rossini's *William Tell,* Meyerbeer's *Huguenots,* Gounod's *Faust,* Mozart's *Don Giovanni*, Haydn's *Creation* and Beethoven's symphonies are all named and celebrated. Aside from these, the poet comments on Verdi's *Il Trovatore* and *Rigoletto,* Meyerbeer's *Le Prophete,* Bellini's *Norma, I Puritani* and *La Somnabula*; Donizetti's *La Favorita, La Felle du Regiments*, and *Lucia di Lammermoor*, Rossini's *Il Barbiere di Siviglia, La Cenerentola* and *Guillaume Tell* and Von Weber's *Der Freischutz.* The list is by no means complete. Whitman returned the musical favor by being the inspiration for hundreds of musical settings in the new century dawning at the end of his life. The British were initially more taken with Whitman than his American compatriots. Delius shared with Whitman the challenges of paralysis. Syphilis also added blindness to the composer's ills. In *Sea Drift,* Delius works with the poet's *Out of the Cradle Endlessly Rocking.* Among his last works is a choral and orchestral rendering of Whitman's *Song of Farewell.* In it, the chorus is blended with the orchestra as if it were another color of the artist's musical palette. Gustav Holst wrote his *Whitman Overture* seven years after the poet's death. Holst then utilized *When Lilacs Last in the Dooryard Bloomed* to eulogize the slain of WWI in his sublime *Ode to Death.* Whitman and music became the basis for a lifelong friendship between Holst and Ralph Vaughan Williams. The latter's *Sea Symphony* incorporated a choral fantasy in its scherzo based on Whitman's *After the Sea Ship*—the concluding poem of the *Sea Drift* cluster. Vaughan Williams also used the lyrics from three Whitman poems in his *Dona Nobis Pacem.* Hitler's Reich was rising in Germany—*Beat! Beat! Drum!*— suggests the martial enthusiasm prevalent prior to the American Civil War; and here, prior to WWII.

Reconciliation is the painful obverse of that excitement for both the poet and the musician:

> For my enemy is dead, a man divine as myself is dead,
> I look where he lies white faced and still in the coffin—
> I draw near, Bend down and touch lightly with my lips the white face in the coffin.

The third song adapted by Vaughan Williams is *Dirge for Two Veterans*. It speaks of a father and son slain the same day in battle: "And the double grave awaits them." As Europe, once again, became a vast bone yard, Paul Hindemith composed his *Lilacs Requiem* – the dead of one war mirroring that of another. *Proud Music of the Storm* is itself a grand piece of music. Five of the six cantos take place in a dream. The poet acknowledges its spiritual import when he suggests that it bridges "the way from Life to Death, vaguely wafted in the night air..." We sense the otherworldly atmosphere in the hum of the forest tree-tops— in the wind of the mountains, in the undertone of rivers, and in the roar of pouring cataracts as the poet queries: *Entering my lonesome slumber-chamber, why have you seize'd me?*

Proud Music of the Storm

1.
> Proud music of the storm,
> Blast that careers so free, whistling across the prairies,
> Strong hum of forest tree-tops—wind of the mountains,

3

> Personified dim shapes—you hidden orchestras,
> You serenades of phantoms with instruments alert,
> Blending with Nature's rhythmus all the tongues of nations;
> You chords left as by vast composers—you choruses,   7
> You formless, free, religious dances—you from the Orient,
> You undertone of rivers, roar of pouring cataracts,
> You sounds from distant guns with galloping cavalry,
> Echoes of camps with all the different bugle-calls,
> Trooping tumultuous, filling the midnight late, bending me powerless,
> Entering my lonesome slumber-chamber, why have you seiz'd me?   13

In the 2nd Canto the music is initially of mankind—a festival song of bridegroom and bride; the drumbeat of war; the songs of the minnesingers and troubadours singing their lays of love. Man is often contrasted with the nature in which he lives. In Canto 2 the dichotomy is fused. The vocalists of the ages are wedded to the sweet trill *of winds and woods and mighty ocean waves...* (Line 46 below). The poet's *blades of grass* appears in line 37. Into nature's chorus he searches for his heart but This *brooding yearning heart...cannot tell itself,* (Line 58 below) until *man and art (are) with Nature fused again.* (Line 51 below)

2.

> Come forward O my soul, and let the rest retire, 14
> Listen, lose not, it is toward thee they tend,
> Parting the midnight, entering my slumber-chamber,
> For thee they sing and dance O soul.
>
> A festival song,
> The duet of the bridegroom and the bride, a marriage-march,
> With lips of love, and hearts of lovers fill'd to the brim with love,
> The red-flush'd cheeks and perfumes, the cortege swarming full of friendly faces young and old,
> To flutes' clear notes and sounding harps' cantabile. 22
>
> Now loud approaching drums,
> Victoria! seest thou in powder-smoke the banners torn but flying? the rout of the baffled?
> Hearest those shouts of a conquering army?
>
> (Ah soul, the sobs of women, the wounded groaning in agony,
> The hiss and crackle of flames, the blacken'd ruins, the embers of cities,
> The dirge and desolation of mankind.)
>
> Now airs antique and mediaeval fill me, 29

I see and hear old harpers with their harps at Welsh festivals,
I hear the minnesingers singing their lays of love,
I hear the minstrels, gleemen, troubadours, of the middle ages.

Now the great organ sounds, 33
Tremulous, while underneath, (as the hid footholds of the earth,
On which arising rest, and leaping forth depend,
All shapes of beauty, grace and strength, all hues we know,
Green blades of grass and warbling birds, children that gambol and play, the clouds of heaven above,) 37
The strong base stands, and its pulsations intermits not,
Bathing, supporting, merging all the rest, maternity of all the rest,
And with it every instrument in multitudes,
The players playing, all the world's musicians,
The solemn hymns and masses rousing adoration,
All passionate heart-chants, sorrowful appeals,
The measureless sweet vocalists of ages,
And for their solvent setting earth's own diapason,
Of winds and woods and mighty ocean waves, 46

> A new composite orchestra, binder of
>   years and climes, ten-fold renewer,
> As of the far-back days the poets tell, the
>   Paradiso,
> The straying thence, the separation long,
>   but now the wandering done,
> The journey done, the journeyman come
>   home,
> And man and art with Nature fused
>   again.   51
> Tutti! for earth and heaven;
> (The Almighty leader now for once has
>   signal'd with his wand.)
>
> The manly strophe of the husbands of
>   the world,
> And all the wives responding.
>
> The tongues of violins,
> (I think O tongues ye tell this heart, that
>   cannot tell itself,
> This brooding yearning heart, that
>   cannot tell itself.)   58

The poet enters the consciousness of a sympathic child attune to all the music in its world. To the child and poet all sounds become music. (Line 60 below) Whitman acknowledges the sweet sound of his mother's voice and also his sisters'. He then acknowledges the natural music of the rain... the measur'd sea-surf... the sounds of birds migrating north and south. He then mentions the songs of various nations: The German airs of friendship; English warbles; Chansons of France; Scotch tunes and Italia's peerless compositions.

We know that mention of Italia will elicit a tally of his favorite operas. He doesn't disappoint as the celebrated Norma, Lucia, Ernani and Fernando of Donizetti's *La Favorita* make their appearance on the poet's stage.

3.

Ah from a little child,   59
Thou knowest soul how to me all sounds became music,   60
My mother's voice in lullaby or hymn,
(The voice, O tender voices, memory's loving voices,
Last miracle of all, O dearest mother's, sister's, voices;)
The rain, the growing corn, the breeze among the long-leav'd corn,
The measur'd sea-surf beating on the sand,
The twittering bird, the hawk's sharp scream,
The wild-fowl's notes at night as flying low migrating north or south,
The psalm in the country church or mid the clustering trees, the open air camp-meeting,
The fiddler in the tavern, the glee, the long-strung sailor-song,
The lowing cattle, bleating sheep, the crowing cock at dawn.

All songs of current lands come sounding round me,
The German airs of friendship, wine and love,

Irish ballads, merry jigs and dances, English warbles,
Chansons of France, Scotch tunes, and o'er the rest,
Italia's peerless compositions. 75

Across the stage with pallor on her face, yet lurid passion,
Stalks Norma brandishing the dagger in her hand. 77

I see poor crazed Lucia's eyes' unnatural gleam, 78
Her hair down her back falls loose and dishevel'd.

I see where Ernani walking the bridal garden, 80
Amid the scent of night-roses, radiant, holding his bride by the hand,
Hears the infernal call, the death-pledge of the horn.

To crossing swords and gray hairs bared to heaven,
The clear electric base and baritone of the world,
The trombone duo, Libertad forever!

From Spanish chestnut trees' dense shade,
By old and heavy convent walls a wailing song,
Song of lost love, the torch of youth and life quench'd in despair,

> Song of the dying swan, Fernando's
>   heart is breaking. 89
>
> Awaking from her woes at last retriev'd
>   Amina sings,
> Copious as stars and glad as morning
>   light the torrents of her joy.
>
> (The teeming lady comes,
> The lustrious orb, Venus contralto, the
>   blooming mother,
> Sister of loftiest gods, Alboni's self I
>   hear.) 94

Canto 4 is a grand list of Grand Opera. Each noted is among his special favorites. He then broadens his reach into the world's repertoire of song: "…religious dances old and new and the sound of the Hebrew lyre; the dervishes spinning ecstatically toward Mecca; the Mussulman's mosque and the muezzin calling the faithful to prayer; Egyptian harps and Hindu flutes round out his orchestra International.

4.

> I hear those odes, symphonies, operas, 95
> I hear in the William Tell the music of
>   an arous'd and angry people,
> I hear Meyerbeer's Huguenots, the
>   Prophet, or Robert, Gounod's Faust,
>   or Mozart's Don Juan. 97
>
> I hear the dance-music of all nations,
> The waltz, some delicious measure,
>   lapsing, bathing me in bliss,
> The bolero to tinkling guitars and
>   clattering castanets.

I see religious dances old and new,
I hear the sound of the Hebrew lyre,
I see the crusaders marching bearing the cross on high, to the martial clang of cymbals,
I hear dervishes monotonously chanting, interspers'd with frantic shouts, as they spin around turning always towards Mecca,
I see the rapt religious dances of the Persians and the Arabs,
Again, at Eleusis, home of Ceres, I see the modern Greeks dancing,
I hear them clapping their hands as they bend their bodies,
I hear the metrical shuffling of their feet.

I see again the wild old Corybantian dance, the performers wounding each other,
I see the Roman youth to the shrill sound of flageolets throwing and catching their weapons,
As they fall on their knees and rise again.

I hear from the Mussulman mosque the muezzin calling,
I see the worshippers within, nor form nor sermon, argument nor word,
But silent, strange, devout, rais'd, glowing heads, ecstatic faces.
I hear the Egyptian harp of many strings,

> The primitive chants of the Nile boatmen,
> The sacred imperial hymns of China,
> To the delicate sounds of the king, (the stricken wood and stone,)
> Or to Hindu flutes and the fretting twang of the vina,
> A band of bayaderes. 120

In the 5th Canto he specifically mentions Rossini, Beethoven, Handel and Haydn. He seems particularly moved by Haydn's *Creation:* "in billows of godhood (it) laves me." We know from the poet's reports that music was one his most intimate and spiritual avocations. The depth of his aesthetic experience was instrumental in opening other windows of contact with the deepest aspects of his being. Music was a template for this exploration—it became his spiritual heart: *Give to hold all sounds… Fill me with all the voices of the universe.* (Lines 138-139 below)

5.
> Now Asia, Africa leave me, Europe seizing inflates me, 121
> To organs huge and bands I hear as from vast concourses of voices,
> Luther's strong hymn Eine feste Burg ist unser Gott,
> Rossini's Stabat Mater dolorosa, 124
> Or floating in some high cathedral dim with gorgeous color'd windows,
> The passionate Agnus Dei or Gloria in Excelsis.
> Composers! mighty maestros!

And you, sweet singers of old lands,
   soprani, tenori, bassi!
To you a new bard caroling in the West,
Obeisant sends his love.

(Such led to thee O soul,
All senses, shows and objects, lead to
   thee,
But now it seems to me sound leads o'er
   all the rest.)

I hear the annual singing of the children
   in St. Paul's cathedral,
Or, under the high roof of some colossal
   hall, the symphonies, oratorios of
   Beethoven, Handel, or Haydn,   136
The Creation in billows of godhood
   laves me.

Give me to hold all sounds, (I madly
   struggling cry,)   138
Fill me with all the voices of the
   universe,   139
Endow me with their throbbings,
   Nature's also,
The tempests, waters, winds, operas and
   chants, marches and dances,
Utter, pour in, for I would take them all!   142

In a piece for *Life Illustrated* he rhapsodized on the art of opera:

> A new world—a liquid world—rushes
> like a torrent through you...this is art!

> You envy Italy, and almost become an enthusiast, you wish an equal art here, and an equal science and style, underlain by a perfect understanding of American realities, and the appropriateness of our national spirit and body also.

The *Life Illustrated* article was published the same year as the first edition of *Leaves of Grass*. He was to write to a friend: "but for the opera, *Leaves of Grass* would not have been written." Whitman was interested in the cultural life of America. He corresponded with other journalists, poets and writers of all types. He was a fine-art enthusiast and wrote several poems inspired by visits to famous shows and galleries. He was also friends with many prominent photographers. Many of his "verse" paintings could be called photo paintings or *snap shots*. Whitman is one the first great artists of whom we have a large photographic history. Niepce developed the first photograph in 1826. Whitman's first known photos are from the early 1840s. In the first two photograph the poet appears dandified and somewhat affected. This is a major contrast to the "rough" of the 1855 frontispiece. Photography also helped focus his philosophic and artistic credo: "In these *Leaves of Grass* everything is literally photographed," and "Time, space, both are annihilated, and we identify the semblances with the reality." [187] These semblances we find throughout his *Leaves*. As a younger man he thrilled to the glory of a tenor's high Cs—the purity of Verdi's legato suggesting the resounding banishment of time. In 1860 he proclaimed opera the origin of his poems.

Poetry aspires to the evocativeness of the musical phrase. The critical point of each is an experience beyond simple meter and akin to a sustained note — a poetic image — caught like a photograph — a defiance of the exigencies of time. Whitman had a keen ear for idioms and a decisive distrust of grammarians: "…to conform to our uses, a far more complete dictionary (needs) to be written — and the grammar boldly compelled to serve the real genius underneath our speech, which is not what the school men would suppose, but wild, intractable, suggestive." He found that suggestiveness in black idioms: "In the South words have sprouted up from the dialect and peculiarities of slaves — the Negroes — the South is full of Negro-words — their idioms and pronunciations are heard everywhere." And then, in prophetic anticipation of *Porgy and Bess,* Jazz, and Rock 'n' Roll, the poet writes:

> The nigger dialect furnishes hundreds of outré words, many of them adapted into common speech of the mass of the people — The nigger dialect has the hints of a future theory of the modification of all words of the English language, for musical purposes, for a native grand opera in America.

Scanning the canon, researcher Robert Faner found over 70 instances of musical terms in the titles of his poems and over one hundred musical terms related to vocal music. "Song" appears over 150 times. In the 1800s the cultured class of NYC were the most likely Americans to be an audience for an opera.

Whitman's experience would not be that different from that of an enthusiast of the twenty first century. His ticket would be cheaper but the operatic thrill would be the same. In the late 1840s Whitman enjoyed most of the European debuts of the great singers appearing in New York. His favorite was Marietta Alboni, one of the great visiting contraltos of the period. He sought her out at every opportunity and reports of her animal intensity suggest a nineteenth century Callas. As with his poetry, Whitman believed that classical music would be embraced by all classes. In both instances he was mistaken. Poetry and opera is the province of a wealthier and more educated class than constitutes his beloved masses. This discrepancy, however, points instead to the overarching greatness of his love. Music and poetry were his guiding lights. It is their spiritual radiance he wished to impart and which would remain his life's work. It was here that he most intimately encountered the *Me myself*—that aspect of himself that allowed him to view the world dispassionately, as if reporting the truth of a simple reflection in a mirror.

Schopenhauer's *The World as Will and Representation* was published during the year of Whitman's birth. The German's fabled pessimism is the obverse of Whitman's all encompassing embrace—yet, in their love of music the two are properly aligned:

> In some men knowledge can break free—and stand free of the will and its aims, sheerly in and for itself—as a clean mirror of the world—which is the order of the consciousness of art. [188]

In the concluding Canto he reviews the insights of his vision. He believes they offer him a clue into the mystery of which every human life is a probe: "I sought so long, let us go forth refresh'd amid the day cheerfully tallying life ... nourish'd henceforth by our celestial dream... to a new rhythmus." It is here that we realize that the poet has not been speaking of orchestra, operas or storms — but rather the aesthetic exploration of the human heart. The new rhythmus of which he speaks is one of the loveliest tropes of his poetic credo: *Poems bridging the way from Life to Death...let us go forth in the bold day and write...* (Lines 163-164 below)

6.

> Then I woke softly, 143
> And pausing, questioning awhile the music of my dream,
> And questioning all those reminiscences, the tempest in its fury,
> And all the songs of sopranos and tenors,
> And those rapt oriental dances of religious fervor,
> And the sweet varied instruments, and the diapason of organs,
> And all the artless plaints of love and grief and death,
> I said to my silent curious soul out of the bed of the slumber-chamber,
> Come, for I have found the clew I sought so long,
> Let us go forth refresh'd amid the day,
> Cheerfully tallying life, walking the world, the real,

> Nourish'd henceforth by our celestial dream. 154
>
> And I said, moreover,
> Haply what thou hast heard O soul was not the sound of winds,
> Nor dream of raging storm, nor sea-hawk's flapping wings nor harsh scream,
> Nor vocalism of sun-bright Italy,
> Nor German organ majestic, nor vast concourse of voices, nor layers of harmonies,
> Nor strophes of husbands and wives, nor sound of marching soldiers,
> Nor flutes, nor harps, nor the bugle-calls of camps,
> But to a new rhythmus fitted for thee,
> Poems bridging the way from Life to Death, vaguely wafted in night air, uncaught, unwritten, 163
> Which let us go forth in the bold day and write. 164

6. Passage to India

(1871)

Whitman is deeply interested in time. This book is predicated on that assertion. His embrace of the past is no less intense than his anticipation of the future. The fear of a time in which he did not exist weighs no more heavily on his consciousness than a future in which he will cease to be.

He sees himself as intimately involved in each as he is firmly enjoined in his present—"the present utterly form'd, impell'd by the past." In this we hear the echo of Eckhart:

> There are two meanings to the 'fullness of time.' For a thing is full when it is at its end, as each day is full in its evening. Therefore the day is full when all time falls from you. The second meaning of fullness of time is when time is at its end—that is, in eternity. For in eternity all time has its end and there is neither before nor after. There everything is present and new... And there you have in present vision everything which ever happened or ever will happen."[189]

For Whitman the past in its entirety is the foundation of all experience—and what we call the present is only a "projectile form'd, impell'd, passing a certain line..." This anticipates Whitehead's conception of time in *Process and Reality*. Therein, the present moment is a subjective moment concluded as it is absorbed into closing encroachment of the past. Whitehead realized that Einstein's paper on the Electrodynamics of Moving bodies (Special Relativity) called into question the constancy of Newtonian Time—the occasion of one person's present moment need not correspond to another's, which existed simultaneously. This intuition is older than Plato and descends down successive centuries through Bergson to Heidegger and beyond. This is Joyce on time—(the past that Faulkner averred was not even *past*):

> These heavy sands are language tide
> and wind have silted here. And there,
> the stone heaps of dead builders, a wren
> of weasel rats. Hide gold there. Try it.
> You have some. Sands and stones.
> Heavy of the past. [190]

And here, Whitman: *The Past—the dark unfathom'd retrospect! The past—the infinite greatness of the past! For what is the present after all but a growth out of the past?* (Lines 10-13 below) *Passage to India* is also his soul's navigation of death's darkling seas—India, indeed, a yonder shore...

Passage to India

1.

> Singing my days,   1
> Singing the great achievements of the present,
> Singing the strong light works of engineers,
> Our modern wonders, (the antique ponderous Seven outvied,)   4
> In the Old World the east the Suez canal,
> The New by its mighty railroad spann'd,
> The seas inlaid with eloquent gentle wires;
> Yet first to sound, and ever sound, the cry with thee O soul,
> The Past! the Past! the Past!
>
> The Past—the dark unfathom'd retrospect!   10

> The teeming gulf—the sleepers and the shadows! 11
> The past—the infinite greatness of the past!
> For what is the present after all but a growth out of the past? 13
> (As a projectile form'd, impell'd, passing a certain line, still keeps on,
> So the present, utterly form'd, impell'd by the past.) 15

The Vedic Hymns and their concluding forest murmurs found in the Upanishads, made their own passage to America's intelligentsia of the nineteenth century. The Emperor Shah Jahan not only left us India's Taj Mahal, but also a son, Prince Darn Shukoh, a Sufi mystic who translated the Upanishads into the Persian of the 17th century. Anquetil Duperron translated this version into the Latin that made its way west at the beginning of the nineteenth century. The great literature of the past and its monumental building projects are also prelude to those of the present as those of the present are prelude to those of the future. None is exclusive to its own time for each is interwoven with all time for the sake of that which is beyond time—the *Soul*. This correspondence of thought from one century to another connects our own in the vast interweaving of the World Wide Web—then as now: *The earth (is) span'd connected by network...* and *All these separations and gaps shall be taken up and hook'd and link'd together"* (Lines 32 and 109 below)

2.

> Passage O soul to India! 16
> Eclaircise the myths Asiatic, the primitive fables.

Not you alone proud truths of the world,
Nor you alone ye facts of modern science,
But myths and fables of held, Asia's, Africa's fables,
The far-darting beams of the spirit, the unloos'd dreams,
The deep diving bibles and legends,
The daring plots of the poets, the elder religions;
O you temples fairer than lilies pour'd over by the rising sun!
O you fables spurning the known, eluding the hold of the known, mounting to heaven!
You lofty and dazzling towers, pinnacled, red as roses, burnish'd with gold!
Towers of fables immortal fashion'd from mortal dreams!
You too I welcome and fully the same as the rest!
You too with joy I sing.

Passage to India!
Lo, soul, seest thou not God's purpose from the first?
The earth to be spann'd, connected by network,
The races, neighbors, to marry and be given in marriage,
The oceans to be cross'd, the distant brought near,
The lands to be welded together.

> A worship new I sing,
> You captains, voyagers, explorers, yours,
> You engineers, you architects, machinists, yours,
> You, not for trade or transportation only,
> But in God's name, and for thy sake O soul. 40

The great engineering feats of his day are celebrated in the third Canto. He salutes his favorite explorer, Columbus, and his dream of circling the globe to encounter India. He then returns to his theme of continents being "welded" together and the great transit of culture from East to West—and in the succeeding sections: "the rondure of the world (is) at last accomplish'd."

3.

> Passage to India! 41
> Lo soul for thee of tableaus twain,
> I see in one the Suez canal initiated, open'd,
> I see the procession of steamships, the Empress Engenie's leading the van,
> I mark from on deck the strange landscape, the pure sky, the level sand in the distance,
> I pass swiftly the picturesque groups, the workmen gather'd,
> The gigantic dredging machines.
>
> In one again, different, (yet thine, all thine, O soul, the same,)

I see over my own continent the Pacific
   railroad surmounting every barrier, 49
I see continual trains of cars winding
   along the Platte carrying freight and
   passengers,
I hear the locomotives rushing and
   roaring, and the shrill steam-
   whistle,
I hear the echoes reverberate through
   the grandest scenery in the world,
I cross the Laramie plains, I note the
   rocks in grotesque shapes, the
   buttes,
I see the plentiful larkspur and wild
   onions, the barren, colorless, sage-
   deserts,
I see in glimpses afar or towering
   immediately above me the great
   mountains, I see the Wind river and
   the Wahsatch mountains,
I see the Monument mountain and the
   Eagle's Nest, I pass the Promontory,
   I ascend the Nevadas,
I scan the noble Elk mountain and wind
   around its base,
I see the Humboldt range, I thread the
   valley and cross the river,
I see the clear waters of lake Tahoe, I see
   forests of majestic pines,
Or crossing the great desert, the alkaline
   plains, I behold enchanting mirages
   of waters and meadows,
Marking through these and after all, in
   duplicate slender lines,

> Bridging the three or four thousand miles of land travel,
> Tying the Eastern to the Western sea,
> The road between Europe and Asia.   64
> (Ah Genoese thy dream! thy dream!   65
> Centuries after thou art laid in thy grave,
> The shore thou foundest verifies thy dream.)   67

The poet's vision of the terrain *tying the Eastern and Western Sea — the road between Europe and Asia* is vivid and a remarkably accurate travelogue from Omaha to San Francisco.[191] Whitman then acknowledges Columbus: *Ah Genoese thy dream! thy dream!* (Line 65 above) and segues to the sea to salute sailors: *along all history down the slopes, as a rivulet running.* (Lines 72-73 below)

4.

> Passage to India!   68
> Struggles of many a captain, tales of many a sailor dead,
> Over my mood stealing and spreading they come,
> Like clouds and cloudlets in the unreach'd sky.
>
> Along all history, down the slopes,   72
> As a rivulet running, sinking now, and now again to the surface rising,   73
> A ceaseless thought, a varied train — lo, soul, to thee, thy sight, they rise,
> The plans, the voyages again, the expeditions;

Again Vasco de Gama sails forth,
Again the knowledge gain'd, the mariner's compass,
Lands found and nations born, thou born America,
For purpose vast, man's long probation fill'd,
Thou rondure of the world at last accomplish'd. 80

Canto 5 was submitted for publication independently of the poem and is one of the most prescient and sublimely spiritual visions of the whole Canon. The poet, as if an Apollo astronaut, sees the: *vast Rondure swimming in space... with inscrutable purpose, some hidden prophetic intention, now first it seems my thought begins to span thee.* (Lines 81-87 below) The messianic Whitman appears here as: *the true son of God...* Line 111 is a second Niacene Creed. The poet declares his own apotheosis: "Trinitas divine shall be gloriously accomplished and compacted by the true son of God, the poet." The fretted children shall be sooth'd, the secret should be told, all these separations and gaps shall be taken up and hook'd and link'd together—this whole earth, this cold impassive, voiceless earth shall be completely justified. (Lines 105-110 below) *The true son of God shall absolutely fuse them.* (Line 115 below) Herein we hear a distant echo of another poet/prophet:

> Comfort ye, comfort ye my people, Saith your God. Speak ye comfortably to Jerusalem, and cry unto her, that her warfare is accomplished, that her iniquity is pardoned; for she hath received the Lord's hand double for her sins...

> All flesh is grass, and all the goodliness thereof is as the flower of the field: the grass witherth, the flower fadeth; Because the spirit of the Lord bloweth upon it. Surely the people is grass...

If Isaiah's metaphor of grass was not specific enough, Whitman's ontology becomes more pointed. Existential man is not distinct from the garden from which he was expelled: *Adam and Eve appear, then their myriad generations after them...Who speaks the secret of impassive earth? Who binds it to us? what is this separate Nature so unnatural? What is this earth to our affections? (unloving earth, without a throb to answer ours, Cold earth, the place of graves.* (Lines 89-98 below)The poet as the *true son of God* shall mend the broken pieces of the world: *He shall indeed pass the straits and conquer the mountains, Nature and Man shall be disjoin'd and diffused no more*, (Lines 112-114 below) is again suggested by Isaiah's:

> Who hath measured the waters in the hollow of his hand, and meted out heaven with the span and comprehended the dust of the earth in a measure, and weighed the mountains in the scales and the hills in a balance.

Earlier in *Song of Myself* the poet had seen that what he had guessed at was true: *My ties and ballasts leave me, my elbows rest in sea gaps, I skirt sierras, my palms cover continents.*[192] In the 13th century as flagellates walked the land in the face of the plague's all devouring maw, Eckhart would conclude a celebrated sermon with a similar beatitude:

> In this ever-present vision, I possess everything. That is, in the fullness of time I am just and so I am truly the proper Son and Christ. God help us that we come to this 'fullness of time.' Amen. [193]

5.

O vast Rondure, swimming in space,   81
Cover'd all over with visible power and beauty,
Alternate light and day and the teeming spiritual darkness,   82
Unspeakable high processions of sun and moon and countless stars above,
Below, the manifold grass and waters, animals, mountains, trees,
With inscrutable purpose, some hidden prophetic intention,
Now first it seems my thought begins to span thee.   87

Down from the gardens of Asia descending radiating,
Adam and Eve appear, then their myriad progeny after them,   89
Wandering, yearning, curious, with restless explorations,
With questionings, baffled, formless, feverish, with never-happy hearts,
With that sad incessant refrain, Wherefore unsatisfied soul? and Whither O mocking life?

Ah who shall soothe these feverish children?
Who Justify these restless explorations?
Who speak the secret of impassive earth?
Who bind it to us? what is this separate Nature so unnatural? 96
What is this earth to our affections? (unloving earth, without a throb to answer ours,
Cold earth, the place of graves.) 98

Yet soul be sure the first intent remains, and shall be carried out,
Perhaps even now the time has arrived.

After the seas are all cross'd, (as they seem already cross'd,)
After the great captains and engineers have accomplish'd their work,
After the noble inventors, after the scientists, the chemist, the geologist, ethnologist,
Finally shall come the poet worthy that name,
The true son of God shall come singing his songs. 105

Then not your deeds only O voyagers, O scientists and inventors, shall be justified,
All these hearts as of fretted children shall be sooth'd, 107
All affection shall be fully responded to, the secret shall be told,

> All these separations and gaps shall be
>   taken up and hook'd and link'd
>   together,   109
> The whole earth, this cold, impassive,
>   voiceless earth, shall be completely
>   Justified,   `110
> Trinitas divine shall be gloriously
>   accomplish'd and compacted by the
>   true son of God, the poet,
> (He shall indeed pass the straits and
>   conquer the mountains,   112
> He shall double the cape of Good Hope
>   to some purpose,)
> Nature and Man shall be disjoin'd and
>   diffused no more,   114
> The true son of God shall absolutely
>   fuse them.   115

Whitman's study of geography is put to excellent use in the 6th Canto. He contemplates the flowing Euphrates, Indus and Ganges. He makes the argument of Volume II by seeing the world in the 365 days of the year: *I see O year in you the vast terraqueous globe given and giving all…* (Line 120 below) From history he takes note of Alexander, Tamerlane, Aurungzebe and Marco Polo. These passages of *Passage* are a balm to the disappointment and loss in the soul's traversal of the sea. Each of us is not only of our own time but of all time. Emerson again is instructive:

> A man ought to compare advantageously with a river, an oak or a mountain…If the Universe has these savage accidents, our atoms are savage in resistance…

> He who sees through the design presides over it, and must will that which must be... the years teach much the days never know. Every calamity is a spur and a valuable hint... until at the last the whole...pleases at a sufficient perspective.[194]

Whitman then sets sail with a famed and consummate hero, his beloved Columbus. (Lines 143-164 below) The Italian navigator of unknown seas mirrors the poet's traversal of mystic oceans. And if the Admiral himself experienced *dejection, poverty and death* (Line 160 below) so also the poet could see his own verse as: ... *a seed unreck'd for centuries... lo, to God's due occasion uprising in the night filling the earth with beauty.* (Lines 162-164) God's due occasion is the hope of any true artist. This poem has the virtues of Whitman's greatest verse and was thought by the poet to launch a new and deeper spiritual odyssey in his career.

6.

> Year at whose wide-flung door I sing!   116
> Year of the purpose accomplish'd!
> Year of the marriage of continents, climates and oceans!
> (No mere doge of Venice now wedding the Adriatic,)
> I see O year in you the vast terraqueous globe given and giving all,   120
> Europe to Asia, Africa join'd, and they to the New World,
> The lands, geographies, dancing before you, holding a festival garland,

As brides and bridegrooms hand in hand.

Passage to India!
Cooling airs from Caucasus far, soothing cradle of man,
The river Euphrates flowing, the past lit up again.

Lo soul, the retrospect brought forward,
The old, most populous, wealthiest of earth's lands,
The streams of the Indus and the Ganges and their many affluents,
(I my shores of America walking to-day behold, resuming all,)
The tale of Alexander on his warlike marches suddenly dying,
On one side China and on the other side Persia and Arabia,
To the south the great seas and the bay of Bengal,
The flowing literatures, tremendous epics, religions, castes,
Old occult Brahma interminably far back, the tender and junior Buddha,
Central and southern empires and all their belongings, possessors,
The wars of Tamerlane, the reign of Aurungzebe,
The traders, rulers, explorers, Moslems, Venetians, Byzantium, the Arabs, Portuguese,
The first travelers famous yet, Marco Polo, Batouta the Moor,

Doubts to be solv'd, the map incognita, blanks to be fill'd,
The foot of man unstay'd, the hands never at rest,
Thyself O soul that will not brook a challenge.

The mediaeval navigators rise before me,
The world of 1492, with its awaken'd enterprise,
Something swelling in humanity now like the sap of the earth in spring,
The sunset splendor of chivalry declining.

And who art thou sad shade?
Gigantic, visionary, thyself a visionary,
With majestic limbs and pious beaming eyes,
Spreading around with every look of thine a golden world,
Enhuing it with gorgeous hues.

As the chief histrion,
Down to the footlights walks in some great scena,
Dominating the rest I see the Admiral himself,
(History's type of courage, action, faith,)
Behold him sail from Palos leading his little fleet,
His voyage behold, his return, his great fame,

> His misfortunes, calumniators, behold him a prisoner, chain'd,
> Behold his dejection, poverty, death.   160
>
> (Curious in time I stand, noting the efforts of heroes,
> Is the deferment long? bitter the slander, poverty, death?
> Lies the seed unreck'd for centuries in the ground? lo, to God's due occasion,   162
> Uprising in the night, it sprouts, blooms,
> And fills the earth with use and beauty.)   164
>
> 7.
>
> Passage indeed O soul to primal thought,   165
> Not lands and seas alone, thy own clear freshness,
> The young maturity of brood and bloom,
> To realms of budding bibles.
>
> O soul, repressless, I with thee and thou with me,
> Thy circumnavigation of the world begin,
> Of man, the voyage of his mind's return,
> To reason's early paradise,
> Back, back to wisdom's birth, to innocent intuitions,   173
> Again with fair creation.   174

In the 7th Canto he speaks of the "innocent intuitions." (Line 173 above) That intuition is the immediate perception of Being, *as it is*. Bodhidharma further dilates:

"...a direct pointing beyond words," and Huang Po is only a single word less succinct: "...that which you see before you." And Joyce is more emphatic still: "What you damn well have to see."[195] Whitman further confirms each of these intuitions: "... the voyage of his mind's return to reason's early paradise." This is also the return of the soul to the original material from which it arose. The Gnostics called this realm the Pleroma. Creation was a fall into separation and inevitable death. Whitman sees the *innocent intuitions* as a twining of life and death—or as Eliot suggests: "the hour of death is in every moment." The poet is addressing the coming fact of his death and, by extension his reader's demise. This is made abundantly clear in the concluding cantos (8&9) of the poem. For each of us is ferried into life and eventually, each is ferried out: "Fearless for unknown shores on waves of ecstasy to sail, / Amid the wafting winds, (thou pressing me to thee, I thee to me, O soul,) / Caroling free, singing our song of God...". (Lines 175-181 below) Albert Einstein's birth (March 14, 1879) is contemporaneous with the decade of this poem. The American and the German shared the world's stage for a dozen years. The poet seems to anticipate the physicist's preoccupation with Space-Time: *Thou matest Time...and fillest the vastness of Space.* (Lines 210-211 below) *Passage to India* is comparatively late among Whitman's masterpieces. He was contemplating a collection of more spiritual poems than those that had preceded it. This was probably a fool's errand because the earlier poems are among the most sublimely spiritual to ever find their way to a printed page. Nonetheless, at this juncture in his journey, *Passage to India* and companion poems warranted a separate volume and were only later incorporated into *Leaves of Grass* proper.

E.M. Forster took the title of his last and greatest novel from Whitman's poem. In *A Passage to India* visitors from England make the passage in question. Forster's inclinations were homosexual. Along with Wilde, Carpenter, Symonds and Stoker, he is another of the distinguished Englishmen who were drawn to Whitman for his other-worldly tendencies in general and perhaps others, less than other-worldly, in the specific. In Forster's imagination the American poet was a blend of the English woman, Mrs. Moore and the Indian Brahmin, Narayad Godbole.

The final two stanzas are among the most remarkable in the poem. Time, space and death are its themes and bear the poet and his readers to regions infinite: "Bathe me O God in thee, mounting to thee, I and my soul to range in range in thee."(Lines 192-193 below) The universe is divided between the singular consciousness of the individual and the infinite consciousness of the divine. Whitman is the first and his *Perfect Comrade* is the other. He finds within his own pulse the motive of this universe and others he would launch himself to pursue:

8.
> O we can wait no longer, 175
> We too take ship O soul,
> Joyous we too launch out on trackless seas,
> Fearless for unknown shores on waves of ecstasy to sail,
> Amid the wafting winds, (thou pressing me to thee, I thee to me, O soul,)
> Caroling free, singing our song of God,
> Chanting our chant of pleasant exploration.

With laugh and many a kiss,
(Let others deprecate, let others weep
    for sin, remorse, humiliation,)
O soul thou pleasest me, I thee.

Ah more than any priest O soul we too
    believe in God,
But with the mystery of God we dare
    not dally.

O soul thou pleasest me, I thee,
Sailing these seas or on the hills, or
    waking in the night,
Thoughts, silent thoughts, of Time and
    Space and Death, like waters
    flowing, 189
Bear me indeed as through the regions
    infinite, 190
Whose air I breathe, whose ripples hear,
    lave me all over,
Bathe me O God in thee, mounting to
    thee, 192
I and my soul to range in range of thee. 193

O Thou transcendent,
Nameless, the fibre and the breath,
Light of the light, shedding forth
    universes, thou centre of them, 196
Thou mightier centre of the true, the
    good, the loving,
Thou moral, spiritual fountain—
    affection's source—thou reservoir,
(O pensive soul of me—O thirst
    unsatisfied—waitest not there?

Waitest not haply for us somewhere there the Comrade perfect?) 200
Thou pulse—thou motive of the stars, suns, systems, 201
That, circling, move in order, safe, harmonious,
Athwart the shapeless vastnesses of space,
How should I think, how breathe a single breath, how speak, if, out of myself,
I could not launch, to those, superior universes? 205

Swiftly I shrivel at the thought of God,
At Nature and its wonders, Time and Space and Death, 207
But that I, turning, call to thee O soul, thou actual Me,
And lo, thou gently masterest the orbs,
Thou matest Time, smilest content at Death, 210
And fillest, swellest full the vastnesses of Space. 211

Greater than stars or suns,
Bounding O soul thou journeyest forth;
What love than thine and ours could wider amplify?
What aspirations, wishes, outvie thine and ours O soul?
What dreams of the ideal? what plans of purity, perfection, strength?
What cheerful willingness for others' sake to give up all?

> For others' sake to suffer all? 218

In Buddhism the opening of the 3rd eye is the occasion of *Prajna*—the interconnection of all things resolved into *the one without second*. As Whitman concludes the 8th Canto he conjures the corollary principle of *Karuna* or compassion. In the West, Karuna is often depicted by the *return of the prodigal son*—also one of Rembrandt's great paintings from his late period. Whitman's image is divided. God the father is also "the Elder Brother found—but the implication is the same whether Father absorbing son or brother embracing brother—the power of the poem approaches the drama and emotion of the painting. For the poet all men are his brothers. What could be more perfect than discovering God to be an elder brother who invites us to an eternal embrace: ...*the elder brother found, the younger brother melts in fondness in his arms.* (Lines 222-223 below)

> Reckoning ahead O soul, when thou, the time achiev'd, 219
> The seas all cross'd, weather'd the capes, the voyage done,
> Surrounded, copest, frontest God, yieldest, the aim attain'd,
> As fill'd with friendship, love complete, the Elder Brother found,
> The Younger melts in fondness in his arms. 223

In the 9th Canto we find a sentiment worthy of the *God-intoxicated* Spinoza: "O daring joy, but safe! Are they not all the seas of God?"; and also the earlier Eckhart:

> This knowledge is without time or space and without here and now. In this life all things are one, and all things are united with one another, all in all and all in all... I say that in the kingdom of heaven everything is in everything else, and that everything is one and that everything is ours.[196]

Passage to India is a watershed poem. It is Whitman at his near greatest but also shows evidence of the beginnings of a poetic decline. It was originally published as a separate book taking the title from the poem itself. There is evidence to suggest that in 1871 he was embarking on a new program. Earlier he had sung the body electric and now he wished to sing the poem of the soul. Note also the reference to Sanskrit and the Vedas. (Line 228 below) The individual Atman merging with the perfection of the Brahmanic whole is also one of the poet's most salient themes. Whitman suggested to his chronicler, Horace Traubel, the importance of the poem: "There is more of me, the essential ultimate me, in that than in any of the poems." The new volume contained seventy-five poems of which about a third were new. He faltered in his resolve to start a new venture—the new book became initially incorporated into *Leaves* as a supplement without altering the pagination. In 1881, *Passage to India* was placed among the resident poems and pages.

9.
>> Passage to more than India! 224
>> Are thy wings plumed indeed for such far flights?

O soul, voyagest thou indeed on voyages like those?
Disportest thou on waters such as those?
Soundest below the Sanscrit and the Vedas? 228
Then have thy bent unleash'd.

Passage to you, your shores, ye aged fierce enigmas! 230
Passage to you, to mastership of you, ye strangling problems!
You, strew'd with the wrecks of skeletons, that, living, never reach'd you.

Passage to more than India! 233
O secret of the earth and sky!
Of you O waters of the sea! O winding creeks and rivers!
Of you O woods and fields! of you strong mountains of my land!
Of you O prairies! of you gray rocks!
O morning red! O clouds! O rain and snows!
O day and night, passage to you! 239

O sun and moon and all you stars! Sirius and Jupiter!
Passage to you!
Passage, immediate passage! the blood burns in my veins!
Away O soul! hoist instantly the anchor! 243
Cut the hawsers—haul out—shake out every sail! 244

> Have we not stood here like trees in the ground long enough?
> Have we not grovel'd here long enough, eating and drinking like mere brutes?
> Have we not darken'd and dazed ourselves with books long enough?
>
> Sail forth — steer for the deep waters only,
> Reckless O soul, exploring, I with thee, and thou with me,
> For we are bound where mariner has not yet dared to go,   250
> And we will risk the ship, ourselves and all.
>
> O my brave soul!
> O farther farther sail!
> O daring joy, but safe! are they not all the seas of God?   254
> O farther, farther, farther sail!   255

7. Prayer of Columbus

(1874)

Prayer of Columbus is one of the poet's most dramatic and personal poems. It was written three years after *Passage to India*. It is a declamation spoken in the first person. As earlier noted, Columbus was one of Whitman's great heroes. By placing the poem immediately after the longer poem he connects the poignant paean to Columbus in *Passage to India*:

> "(Ah Genoese thy dream! Thy dream!
> Centuries after thou art laid in thy
> grave, The shore thou foundest verifies
> thy dream.)"

The pathos of one poem is enlarged and completed in the succeeding poem's central character. The poet saw the navigator's life and work as a metaphor. He confessed to the unrequited Nelly O'Connor: "I shouldn't wonder if I have unconsciously put a sort of autobiographical dash in it." [197] To his friend, another unrequited paramour, Anne Gilchrist, it seemed more than a dash: "You too have sailed over stormy seas to your goal — surrounded with mocking disbelievers — you too have paid the great price of health — our Columbus." — even the uninitiated will find it easy to imagine the prayer as the poet's own. I will highlight a few salient passages. The poem, thereafter, will be presented in its entirety without textural interruption. To begin, the poet describes the Navigator as: *A batter'd wreck'd old man... Sore, stiff with many toils, sicken'd and nigh to death, I am too full of woe! Haply I may not live another day; I cannot rest O God, I cannot eat or drink or sleep, Till I put forth myself, my prayer, once more to Thee, Breathe, bathe myself once more in Thee, commune with Thee, Report myself once more to Thee.* (Lines 1-11)

Columbus cannot rest, eat, drink or sleep. The poem was published in *Harper's* magazine in 1874. The poet was paid sixty dollars. In January of the previous year Whitman had suffered a paralytic stroke. The autobiographical nature of the poem is difficult to doubt. As in the earlier anthem to Deity — *Passage to India*, the poet avers that all seas are *seas of God*.

Like Spinoza and Eckhart, Whitman was accused of Godlessness and heresy. His desire to: *breathe, bathe myself, once more in Thee, commune with Thee...* suggests rather a depth of devotion that rivals the Dutchman in unqualified beneficence, and the German, in the ecstasy of his vision.

Eckhart died shortly before he was condemned in the Papal Bull, *In Argo Dominico* of Pope John XXII. Spinoza was excommunicated from the Jewish community of Amsterdam about the same time that Milton began his blind recitation of *Paradise Lost* during England's Restoration—barely escaping execution for his services to Cromwell.

In Spinoza's synagogue candles were extinguished one by one to symbolize the philosopher's expulsion from the blessedness of light. The German priest, the Dutch philosopher and the English poet might have as duly noted what Whitman suggests of the navigator: "...in disgrace, repining not, accepting all from Thee, as duly come from Thee."

In the guise of Columbus, the poet sails the deep and travels in quest of the *pure land* that is his God: *Thou knowest how before I commenced I devoted all to come to Thee... Thou knowest I have not once lost nor faith nor ecstasy in Thee... In shackles, prison'd, in disgrace, repining not, Accepting all from Thee, as duly come from Thee...* (Lines 12-23 below).

The Jews of Amsterdam denied Spinoza access to the celestial light filtering through their synagogues. Charles II spared Milton his head and exiled his spirit to the Paradise Lost of his London apartments.

Pope John XXII ignored requests to exhume and burn Eckhart's earthly remains—no mischief was allowed to desecrate the body and grave of the deceased Dominican.

Who can doubt that Columbus' prayer was also that of these same three: *That Thou O God, my life has lighted, with ray of light, steady... lighting the very light.* Or that, as well, it was the prayer of the broken poet: *Beyond all signs, descriptions, languages; For that O God, be it my latest word, here on my knees, Old, poor, and paralyzed, I thank Thee. My terminus near... I yield my ships to Thee.* (Lines 40-46 below)

Whitman had no way of knowing that he had eighteen years of life still remaining. After a severe stroke he could indeed believe that his terminus was near. Few lines in American letters are as moving as: "My hands, my limbs grow nerveless, My brain feels rack'd, bewild'd." As Melville invokes the damnable grandeur of Macbeth in the abyss that is Ahab; so Whitman is not far from Lear's "...here I stand, your slave, a poor, infirm, weak, despis'd old man." Indeed, Lear, for Whitman, was the greatness and grandeur of Shakespeare. Albert Johnson related visiting Burroughs' Riverby by the Hudson on the occasion of a Whitman visit:

> I was quite young when I spent a week with 'Uncle Walt' at the home of Burroughs, but two things are imprinted on my memory: the breakfast dips the three of us took on the Hudson, and while drying listening to Walt declaiming from Shakespeare, passage after passage, particularly from 'King Lear...'

He was majestic in the rendering of
whatever character he impersonated.[198]

The poet is also *cut to the brains* and buffeted by storm and wave, in a moment that rivals Lear's recognition of Cordelia: *You are a spirit, I know: When did you die?* Whitman here, as well, conjures the most distinct recognition pathos in all of his poetry: *...Thee, Thee at least I know.* (Line 55 below) Note, as well, that both King and Captain are thought mad: *am I raving?* (Line 56 below)

But as with Shakespeare, the miracles are far from through. For as Lear was *bound upon a wheel of fire so that his own tears did scald like molten lead*, so also here, as Whitman wonders if he is raving. Here Whitman / Columbus doubts all he has proclaimed and come to know: *What do I know of life? what of myself? I know not even my own work past or present, And these things I see suddenly, what mean they?* (Lines 57-62 below). If we felt a partial forcing of his muse in 1871's *Passage to India,* in 1874's *Prayer of Columbus* the poet's confident rapture has returned. Whitman's prayer is one of the finest dramatic monologues in American letters—perhaps, only his contemporary Robert Browning's *My Last Duchess,* of about the same length, can take as respected a pride of place—appearing somewhat earlier (1842) in *Dramatic Lyrics.* At the poem's close we are left with a choice of dismay or triumph. As Lear looks into the dead countenance of Cordelia he imagines that her lips move: "Look on her,...look...look, her lips...look there." And as he dies we wonder if, in fact, her lips did move. And we wonder with Whitman (as new and better worlds mock and perplex him) if a divine hand unseals his eyes.

The poet is one with Shakespeare's monarch—he sees *vast shapes smiling through the air* and we wonder if he might as well conclude:

> ...if it be so, it is a chance that does redeem all sorrows that I have ever felt.

Although, not among his most familiar poems, *Prayer of Columbus* is easily ranked with his greatest. It is a neglected masterpiece that I am pleased to showcase among these rapturous 24. It is presented, as promised, without further interruption:

A Prayer of Columbus:

> A batter'd, wreck'd old man,
> Thrown on this savage shore, far, far from home,   2
> Pent by the sea and dark rebellious brows, twelve dreary months,
> Sore, stiff with many toils, sicken'd and nigh to death,   4
> I take my way along the island's edge,
> Venting a heavy heart.
>
> I am too full of woe!   7
> Haply I may not live another day;
> I cannot rest O God, I cannot eat or drink or sleep,   9
> Till I put forth myself, my prayer, once more to Thee,
> Breathe, bathe myself once more in Thee, commune with Thee,   10
> Report myself once more to Thee.   11

Thou knowest my years entire, my life,   12
My long and crowded life of active work, not adoration merely;
Thou knowest the prayers and vigils of my youth,
Thou knowest my manhood's solemn and visionary meditations,
Thou knowest how before I commenced I devoted all to come to Thee,
Thou knowest I have in age ratified all those vows and strictly kept them,
Thou knowest I have not once lost nor faith nor ecstasy in Thee,   19
In shackles, prison'd, in disgrace, repining not,
Accepting all from Thee, as duly come from Thee.   21

All my emprises have been fill'd with Thee,
My speculations, plans, begun and carried on in thoughts of Thee,
Sailing the deep or journeying the land for Thee;
Intentions, purports, aspirations mine, leaving results to Thee.

O I am sure they really came from Thee,
The urge, the ardor, the unconquerable will,
The potent, felt, interior command, stronger than words,
A message from the Heavens whispering to me even in sleep,
These sped me on.

By me and these the work so far accomplish'd,
By me earth's elder cloy'd and stifled lands uncloy'd, unloos'd,
By me the hemispheres rounded and tied, the unknown to the known.

The end I know not, it is all in Thee, 34
Or small or great I know not—haply what broad fields, what lands,
Haply the brutish measureless human undergrowth I know,
Transplanted there may rise to stature, knowledge worthy Thee,
Haply the swords I know may there indeed be turn'd to reaping-tools,
Haply the lifeless cross I know, Europe's dead cross, may bud and blossom there.

One effort more, my altar this bleak sand; 40
That Thou O God my life hast lighted,
With ray of light, steady, ineffable, vouchsafed of Thee,
Light rare untellable, lighting the very light,
Beyond all signs, descriptions, languages;
For that O God, be it my latest word, here on my knees,
Old, poor, and paralyzed, I thank Thee. 46

My terminus near,
The clouds already closing in upon me, 48

The voyage balk'd, the course disputed,
    lost,
I yield my ships to Thee.
My hands, my limbs grow nerveless,
My brain feels rack'd, bewilder'd,   52
Let the old timbers part, I will not part,
I will cling fast to Thee, O God, though
    the waves buffet me,   54
Thee, Thee at least I know.   55

Is it the prophet's thought I speak, or am
    I raving?   56
What do I know of life? what of myself?   57
I know not even my own work past or
    present,
Dim ever-shifting guesses of it spread
    before me,   59
Of newer better worlds, their mighty
    parturition,
Mocking, perplexing me.

And these things I see suddenly, what
    mean they?   62
As if some miracle, some hand divine
    unseal'd my eyes,
Shadowy vast shapes smile through the
    air and sky,   64
And on the distant waves sail countless
    ships,
And anthems in new tongues I hear
    saluting me.   66

8. The Sleepers

(1855)

The Sleepers is one of twelve inaugural poems of 1855 and aside from *Song of Myself*, the greatest of these — which is to say that along with Wordsworth's *Intimations* and Coleridge's *Ancient Mariner*, one of the great mystic musings of humanity. Freud acknowledged that the great poets had long anticipated his exploration of the unconscious. Poetry is, after all, a waking dream. In this poem, Whitman wanders confused: *lost to myself, ill-assorted, contradictory* — all elements familiar to anyone who remembers wandering all night in a vision — captive of a chimera. The poet's speaks of witnessing life and death — emerging from gates as if waking to a dawn: *the new-born emerging from gates, and the dying emerging from gates...* (Line 9 below) We can forgive the *Good Gray Poet's* "the sick-gray faces of the onanists," because he is the most celebrated onanist (excepting Roth's hapless, lust-ridden hero) of whom we have record. The color-program of his witness succeeds to the white features of corpses, gash'd bodies of soldiers, the livid faces of drunkards, and then onto the insane and the sacred idiots — *the night pervades them and infolds them...* (Lines 8-10 below) as it does us as we descend further and deeper into the dark of:

The Sleepers

1.

> I wander all night in my vision,
> Stepping with light feet, swiftly and noiselessly stepping and stopping,
> Bending with open eyes over the shut eyes of sleepers,

Wandering and confused, lost to myself,
    ill-assorted, contradictory, 4
Pausing, gazing, bending, and stopping. 5

How solemn they look there, stretch'd and still,
How quiet they breathe, the little children in their cradles. 7

The wretched features of ennuyes, the white features of corpses, the livid faces of drunkards, the sick-gray faces of onanists,
The gash'd bodies on battle-fields, the insane in their strong-door'd rooms, the sacred idiots, the new-born emerging from gates, and the dying emerging from gates, 9
The night pervades them and infolds them. 10

The married couple sleep calmly in their bed, he with his palm on the hip of the wife, and she with her palm on the hip of the husband,
The sisters sleep lovingly side by side in their bed,
The men sleep lovingly side by side in theirs,
And the mother sleeps with her little child carefully wrapt.

The blind sleep, and the deaf and dumb sleep,

The prisoner sleeps well in the prison, the
  runaway son sleeps,
The murderer that is to be hung next day, how
  does he sleep?
And the murder'd person, how does he sleep?

The female that loves unrequited sleeps,
And the male that loves unrequited sleeps,
The head of the money-maker that plotted all
  day sleeps,
And the enraged and treacherous dispositions,
  all, all sleep.

199

I stand in the dark with drooping eyes
  by the worst-suffering and the most
  restless,   23

> I pass my hands soothingly to and fro a
> few inches from them, 24
> The restless sink in their beds, they
> fitfully sleep. 25

The preceding stanza presents the poet as *Messiah*. Earlier in the 38th Canto of *Song of Myself* he had written: *That I could look with a separate look on my own crucifixion and bloody crowning.* In a notebook formulation we find: *In vain were nails driven through my hand. I remember my crucifixion and bloody coronation... the sepulcher and the white linen have yielded me up... again I tread the streets after two thousand years.*

The savior stands by the worst-suffering and the most restless: *I pass my hands soothingly to and fro...* (Line 24 above) The rapture continues as he floats beyond the earth and dreams in his dream all *the dreams of the other dreamers.* (Line 30 below) Here the poet goes from Son to *Father* as he becomes omnipresent, Brahman dreaming all the days of all our lives — *I become the other dreamers.* (Line 31 below)

> Now I pierce the darkness, new beings
> appear, 26
> The earth recedes from me into the
> night, 27
> I saw that it was beautiful, and I see that
> what is not the earth is beautiful.
>
> I go from bedside to bedside, I sleep
> close with the other sleepers each in
> turn, 29
> I dream in my dream all the dreams of
> the other dreamers, 30

> And I become the other dreamers. 31
> I am a dance—play up there! the fit is whirling me fast! 32

In *Song of Myself*, we suggested that his "fit" was a trance. As if caught in the rapture of Jalal ad-Din Rumi's dervish whirling, here the poet confirms our suspicion as he becomes a dance: *the fit is whirling me fast!* (Line 32 above)

> I am the ever-laughing—it is new moon and twilight, 33
> I see the hiding of douceurs, I see nimble ghosts whichever way look,
> Cache and cache again deep in the ground and sea, and where it is neither ground nor sea. 35
>
> Well do they do their jobs those journeymen divine,
> Only from me can they hide nothing, and would not if they could,
> I reckon I am their boss and they make me a pet besides,
> And surround me and lead me and run ahead when I walk,
> To lift their cunning covers to signify me with stretch'd arms, and resume the way;
> Onward we move, a gay gang of blackguards! with mirth-shouting music and wild-flapping pennants of joy! 41

Prince Darn Shuoh translated the Upanishads into Persian and authored the celebrated Sufi poem, *The Mystic Path*:

> Nowhere exists anything but God. All that you see or know other than Him, verily is separate in name, but in essence one with God...O you, in quest of God, you seek him everywhere, You verily are the God, not apart from him.

After a war of succession the Prince was declared a heretic and joined Giordano Bruno in martyrdom just six decades after the outspoken Italian's own auto de fe. Whitman would sympathize:

> I am the actor, the actress, the voter, the politician, 42
> The emigrant and the exile, the criminal that stood in the box,
> He who has been famous and he who shall be famous after to-day,
> The stammerer, the well-form'd person, the wasted or feeble person. 45

In a startling reversal the poet becomes a woman (I am she) awaiting a tryst with her love and the darkness: ...*it is dark... receive me darkness... Darkness, you are gentler than my lover... darkness and he are one... I follow, I fade away.* (Lines 47, 48, 53, 58, & 59 below) It is a remarkable conflation of death and sex—anticipating Wagner's apotheosis in the "Liebestod" of *Tristan und Isolde*.

> I am she who adorn'd herself and folded her hair expectantly, 46

My truant lover has come, and it is dark.	47
Double yourself and receive me darkness,	48
Receive me and my lover too, he will not let me go without him.	
I roll myself upon you as upon a bed, I resign myself to the dusk.	50
He whom I call answers me and takes the place of my lover,	
He rises with me silently from the bed.	
Darkness, you are gentler than my lover, his flesh was sweaty and panting,	53
I feel the hot moisture yet that he left me.	54
My hands are spread forth, I pass them in all directions,	
I would sound up the shadowy shore to which you are journeying.	
Be careful darkness! already what was it touch'd me?	57
I thought my lover had gone, else darkness and he are one,	58
I hear the heart-beat, I follow, I fade away.	59

Two of the great expurgations from the original poem are presented as 1A and 6A, respectively. In a typical dream episode the poet imagines that he awakens to find his clothes stolen and himself naked and alone in the night.

Gary Schmidgall's *Walt Whitman, A Gay Life* argues the incident may have had a real life corollary. Be that as it may, the imagery is a nightmare brooking childhood and maturity and anything but typical:

1A

> O hotcheeked and blushing! O foolish hectic!
> O for pity's sake, no one must see me now!... my clothes were stolen while I was abed,
> Now I am thrust forth, where shall I run?
> Pier that I saw dimly last night when I look from the window,
> Pier out form the main, let me catch myself with you and stay... I will not chafe you;
> I feel ashamed to go naked about the world,
> And I am curious to know where my feet stand... and what is this flooding me, childhood or manhood... and the hunger that crosses the bridge between.
> The cloth laps a first sweet eating and drinking,
> Laps life-swelling yolks ... laps ear of rose-corn, milky and just ripened:
> The white teeth stay, and the boss-tooth advances in darkness,
> And liquor is spilled on lips and bosoms by touching glasses, and the best liquor afterward.

It is one of the great ironies of Victorian morality that the poet's obeisance to the gray-faced onanist would pass beyond masturbation into same sex love (the "she" in the poem is, of course, Whitman) with hardly a notice: *...you are gentler than my lover, his flesh was sweaty and panting, I feel the moisture yet that he has left me.* Emerson was more alarmed by the sentiments of "To a Common Prostitute" and the allusions to heterosexual love in *Children of Adam* than he was by the lines from *The Sleepers* and the *Calamus* cluster. Henry Miller's *Tropic of Cancer* was published in 1934 and banned in the United States until the early 1950s. I recently revisited these passages in *Buddha Boogie – The Tautological Paradigm*. I am happy to incorporate them once again. The explicitness of Whitman's eroticism was the progenitor of Miller's equally active literary libido. Miller is one of Whitman's most notorious and celebrated descendants. In Miller's "cunt monologue" his friend Joe Van Norden regards a girl friend's shaved pubis:

> ...shaved it clean...not a speck of hair on it. Did you ever have a women who shaved her twat? It's repulsive, ain't it? And funny too.
>
> Sort of mad like. It doesn't look like a twat anymore: it's like a dead clam or something... I made her hold it open and I trained a flashlight on it. I never in my life looked at a cunt up close.
>
> You'd imagine I'd never seen one before. It's an illusion! Wouldn't it be funny if you found a harmonica inside...or a calendar?

> You get all burned up about nothing...
> about a crack with hair on it; or without
> hair. And the more I looked the less
> interesting it became...all that mystery
> about sex and then you discover that its
> nothing, just a blank...it almost drove
> me mad...[200]

The "cunt monologue" is followed by, well, a *cunt monologue*. This time it is Miller's turn to tour what earlier had been dismissed as a *blank — an illusion*. There is an adage in Mahayana Buddhism: Buddhatvam yosidyoniamsritam, "Buddha resides in the female organ." Miller's companion-in-arms is Whitman's common prostitute — *there* she was *saluted with a significant look* by the poet; here in the heat of the *Tropics*, *the look* drives the author mad in thirteen pages of magnificent prose[201] — Buddhatavam yosidyoniamsritam!

> Suddenly I see a dark, hairy crack in
> front of me set in a bright, polished
> billiard ball; the legs are holding me like
> a pair of scissors. A glance at that dark,
> unstitched wound and a deep fissure in
> my brain opens up...My guts spill out
> in a grand schizophrenic rush, an
> evacuation that leaves me face to face
> with the Absolute...I hear a wild
> hysterical laugh, a room full of lockjaw,
> and the body that was black glows like
> phosphorus... when I look down into
> that crack I see an equation sign, the
> world a balance, a world reduced to
> zero... an Arabian zero... the sign from
> which spring endless mathematical

> worlds, the fulcrum and balance of the stars...if any man dared to translate all that is in his heart, to put down what is really his experience, what is truly his truth, I think then that the world would go smash, that it would be blown to smithereens and no god, no accident, no will could ever assemble the pieces again...Out of nothingness arises the sign of infinity...through endless night the earth whirls toward a creation unknown...today I awoke from a sound sleep with curses of joy on my lips, with gibberish on my tongue, repeating to myself like a litany 'Fay ce que vouldras! Fay ce que vouldras! Do anything but let it produce joy. Do anything but let it yield ecstasy...

What is "I am the dance... the fit is whirling me fast," but *the Arabian zero...the fulcrum that balances the stars*? What is *Fay ce que vouldras*, but Whitman's "Onward we move, a gay gang of blackguards! with mirth-shouting music and wild-flapping pennants of joy!"? The 2nd Canto continues the exotic reverie. The poet becomes an old woman darning her grandson's stockings; then he becomes a sleepless widow looking out on the winter midnight, who sees *sparkles of starshine on the icy and pallid earth*. (Line 65 below) Then, in a Poe-like gesture that only Whitman would attempt: She/He becomes the shroud wrapping the body lying in the coffin: *I wrap a body and lie in the dark coffin*. (Line 66 below) Rather than inspire the terror of being buried alive, Whitman's attempt is rather the opposite:

It is dark here under ground, it is not
evil or pain here, it is blank for reasons.
(Line 67 below)

This is followed by one of the great mahakaptus of the
oeuvre: *Whoever is not in his coffin and the dark grave let
him know he has enough.* (Line 69 below)

2.

I descend my western course, my sinews are flaccid,	60
Perfume and youth course through me and I am their wake.	
It is my face yellow and wrinkled instead of the old woman's,	62
I sit low in a straw-bottom chair and carefully darn my grandson's stockings.	63
It is I too, the sleepless widow looking out on the winter midnight,	64
I see the sparkles of starshine on the icy and pallid earth.	65
A shroud I see and I am the shroud, I wrap a body and lie in the coffin,	66
It is dark here under ground, it is not evil or pain here, it is blank here, for reasons.	67
(It seems to me that every thing in the light and air ought to be happy,	68
Whoever is not in his coffin and the dark grave let him know he has enough.)	69

Cantos 3 through 6 are verse pictures (motion pictures or dreamscapes) and among his finest. It is a maxim of Freud that the variegated cast of a dream is only and always the dreamer. In the first, the poet is a drowning swimmer; in the second, the passengers and crew of a sinking steamship; in the third, Washington bidding his troops farewell; and in the forth, an Indian Squaw who once visited his mother and was never seen again. Each is an archetype with which many a reader will be familiar from behind his own rapid eye movements. Fathers, mothers, siblings, water deaths or what you will, it is an extraordinary collection. Few things are as lovely and forlorn as the beautiful gigantic swimmer with the undaunted eyes who is dashed upon the rocks of the poet's dream. The scene anticipates the celebrated Calamus line: ...*what indeed is finally beautiful except death and love.*[202]

3.

> I see a beautiful gigantic swimmer swimming naked through the eddies of the sea, 70
> His brown hair lies close and even to his head, he strikes out with courageous arms, he urges himself with his legs,
> I see his white body, I see his undaunted eyes, 72
> I hate the swift-running eddies that would dash him head-foremost on the rocks. 73

What are you doing you ruffianly red-trickled waves?

> Will you kill the courageous giant? will
> you kill him in the prime of his
> middle age? 75
>
> Steady and long he struggles,
> He is baffled, bang'd, bruis'd, he holds
> out while his strength holds out,
> The slapping eddies are spotted with his
> blood, they bear him away, they roll
> him, swing him, turn him,
> His beautiful body is borne in the
> circling eddies, it is continually
> bruis'd on rocks, 79
> Swiftly and ought of sight is borne the
> brave corpse. 80

The second dreamscape is even briefer, but is presented to the mind with the deftness of a *Sumi-e* brushstroke. Few lines in American letters equal the pathos of the howls of the dying as: ... *they grow fainter, fainter... I help pick up the dead and lay them in rows in the barn.* (Lines 85-89 below)

4.

> I turn but do not extricate myself, 81
> Confused, a past-reading, another, but
> with darkness yet.
>
> The beach is cut by the razory ice-wind,
> the wreck-guns sound,
> The tempest lulls, the moon comes
> floundering through the drifts. 84
>
> I look where the ship helplessly heads
> end on, I hear the burst as she

>   strikes, I hear the howls of dismay,
>   they grow fainter and fainter. 85
>
> I cannot aid with my wringing fingers,
> I can but rush to the surf and let it
>   drench me and freeze upon me. 87
>
> I search with the crowd, not one of the
>   company is wash'd to us alive, 88
> In the morning I help pick up the dead
>   and lay them in rows in a barn. 89

Whitman was born only a generation from the American Revolution. Some of the soldiers described in the 5th Canto could have been friends of his father.

5.

>   Now of the older war-days, the defeat at
>   Brooklyn, 90
>   Washington stands inside the lines, he
>   stands on the intrench'd hills amid a
>   crowd of officers.
>
>   His face is cold and damp, he cannot
>   repress the weeping drops,
>   He lifts the glass perpetually to his eyes,
>   the color is blanch'd from his
>   cheeks,
>   He sees the slaughter of the southern
>   braves confided to him by their
>   parents. 94
>
>   The same at last and at last when peace
>   is declared,

> He stands in the room of the old tavern, the well-belov'd soldiers all pass through, 96
> The officers speechless and slow draw near in their turns,
> The chief encircles their necks with his arm and kisses them on the cheek,
> He kisses lightly the wet cheeks one after another, he shakes hands and bids good-by to the army. 99

The dream in Canto 6 concerns his mother's affection for an Indian squaw. The visitor arrives in the morning and leaves in the middle of the same afternoon. It is a verse poem of passionate subtlety. It, perhaps, masks the poet's own longings and disappointments. The canto is a masterful minature standing in its own right as a poignant shared memory — and mayhaps, a metaphor for what America has lost in the displacement of its own native population:

6.
> Now what my mother told me one day as we sat at dinner together, 100
> Of when she was a nearly grown girl living home with her parents on the old homestead.
>
> A red squaw came one breakfast-time to the old homestead, 102
> On her back she carried a bundle of rushes for rush-bottoming chairs,
> Her hair, straight, shiny, coarse, black, profuse, half-envelop'd her face,

> Her step was free and elastic, and her
> voice sounded exquisitely as she
> spoke.   105
>
> My mother look'd in delight and
> amazement at the stranger,   106
> She look'd at the freshness of her tall-
> borne face and full and pliant limbs,
> The more she look'd upon her she loved
> her,   108
> Never before had she seen such
> wonderful beauty and purity,   109
> She made her sit on a bench by the jamb
> of the fireplace, she cook'd food for
> her,
> She had no work to give her, but she
> gave her remembrance and
> fondness.
>
> The red squaw staid all the forenoon,
> and toward the middle of the
> afternoon she went away,
> O my mother was loth to have her go
> away,
> All the week she thought of her, she
> watch'd for her many a month,   114
> She remember'd her many a winter and
> many a summer,
> But the red squaw never came nor was
> heard of there again.   116

What I call 6A was in the original 1855 formulation of the poem. This section is discussed in relationship to fifth stanza of *Song of Myself's* 10th Canto.

There, I opined that the next three stanzas are the most powerful of the poet's *deletions*. They are wonderfully dramatic in and of themselves. In the context of Melville's masterpiece of the sea and Whitman's masterpiece of the dream, their force is exponentially enlarged:

6A
> Now Lucifer was not dead ... or if he was I am his sorrowful terrible heir;
> I have been wronged ... I am oppressed ... I hate him that oppresses me.
> I will either destroy him, or he shall release me.
> Damn him! How he does defile me,
> How he informs against my brother and sister and takes pay for their blood,
> How he laughs when I look down the bend after the steamboat that carries away my woman.
> Now the vast bulk that is the whale's bulk ... it seems mine,
> Warily, sportsman! Though I lie so sleepy and sluggish, my tap is death.

An alternative version of the last line is rendered more explicitly as "the tap of my fluke is death." Whitman had also written: "I know the sea of torment, doubt, despair and unbelief. How the flukes splash! How they contort rapid as lightning, with spasms and spouts of blood!" (Lines 1115-1116 , Canto 43, *Song of Myself*) Here the poet is a beleaguered slave, identified as Lucifer, the shining son of morning and the sleepy inverse of Ahab's waking nightmare—a black leviathan whose touch is death—one of the most extraordinary reversals in American Literature.

It is entirely possible that Whitman had, in the least, a cursory awareness of *Moby Dick*. He had read and enjoyed Melville's earlier *Omoo* — the sequel to his popular *Typee*. During the years prior to the publication Melville's classic (1851), Whitman was trying to hawk a twenty-two part serial adaptation of Ingemann's *Erik Menveds Bamdom* (Erik Menved's Childhood) — if Shakespeare enjoyed success with medieval regicides, why not an American journalist and would-be poet? In the late 1840s Whitman visited local libraries on a daily basis. He had a plan (on the Emerson model) of becoming an itinerant teacher and wrote essays and lectures on a remarkable diversity of subjects. With the embarkation of *Leaves* the middle-schooled poet had become the supreme autodidact of his generation.

This is R.M. Bucke on Whitman's acumen:

> These facts and considerations (when we join to them others equally well known and obvious, as that he knew the Bible, Shakespeare and Homer almost by heart) bring out pretty clearly the extraordinary industry of this man, who has generally been considered as easy-going, careless, idle, even "a loafer," but who must have been, in fact, though almost in secret, one of the most indefatigable workers who ever lived in America.[203]

And if more proof were needed I've borrowed a few (admittedly) dense of prose from one of the poet's essays on the remarkable Elias Hicks:

TO BEGIN with, my theme is comparatively featureless. The great historian has pass'd by the life of Elias Hicks quite without glance or touch. Yet a man might commence and overhaul it as furnishing one of the amplest historic and biography's back-grounds... While the foremost actors and events from 1750 to 1830 both in Europe and America were crowding each other on the world's stage—While so many kings, queens, soldiers, philosophs, musicians, voyagers, littérateurs, enter one side, cross the boards, and disappear—amid loudest reverberating names— Frederick the Great, Swedenborg, Junius, Voltaire, Rousseau, Linneus, Herschel—curiously contemporary with the long life of Goethe—through the occupancy of the British throne by George the Third— amid stupendous visible political and social revolutions, and far more stupendous invisible moral ones—while the many quarto volumes of the Encyclopædia Française are being published at fits and intervals, by Diderot, in Paris—While Haydn and Beethoven and Mozart and Weber are working out their harmonic compositions—while Mrs. Siddons and Talma and Kean are acting—while Mungo Park explores Africa, and Capt. Cook circumnavigates the globe— through all the fortunes of the American

Revolution, the beginning, continuation and end, the battle of Brooklyn, the surrender at Saratoga, the final peace of '83—through the lurid tempest of the French Revolution, the execution of the king and queen, and the Reign of Terror—through the whole of the meteor-career of Napoleon—Through all Washington's, Adams's, Jefferson's, Madison's, and Monroe's Presidentiads—amid so many flashing lists of names, (indeed there seems hardly, in any department, any end to them, Old World or New,) Franklin, Sir Joshua Reynolds, Mirabeau, Fox, Nelson, Paul Jones, Kant, Fichte, and Hegel, Fulton, Walter Scott, Byron, Mesmer, Champollion—Amid pictures that dart upon me even as I speak, and glow and mix and coruscate and fade like aurora boreales—Louis the 16th threaten'd by the mob, the trial of Warren Hastings, the deathbed of Robert Burns, Wellington at Waterloo, Decatur capturing the Macedonian, or the sea-fight between the Chesapeake and the Shannon—During all these whiles, I say, and though on a far different grade, running parallel and contemporary with all—a curious quite yet busy life centered in a little country village on Long Island, and within sound on still nights of the mystic surf-beat of the sea. About this life, this Personality—neither soldier, nor scientist, nor littérateur—I propose to occupy a few minutes in fragmentary talk, to give some few melanges, disconnected impressions, statistics, resultant groups, pictures, thoughts of him, or radiating from him.

The preceding paragraph is an interesting catalogue of Hicks' contemporaries. It gives us, as well, an insight into the garrulous depth of Whitman's library studies after his departure from middle school and beyond. Cantos 7 and 8 of *The Sleepers* are summations of the opening sections of the poem. The inventories are brief and the short ruminations will reward the patient reader. The opening of the seventh Canto, the close of the eighth, and Whitman's musings on the deformed, those of twisted skull and the children of the *venerealee* are among the finest lines in the poem. They partake of the same time frame and genius in affirmations from the 43rd Canto of *Leaves of Grass*. Therein we found the same metaphor of a whale that was later deleted (6A) from this poem and then the litany of the *lost* whom the universe could not fail: *Each who passes is consider'd, each who stops is consider'd, no a single one can it fail.* (Lines 1123-1133 *Song of Myself*) Here the poet is even more emphatic: *I swear they are all beautiful. Everyone that sleeps is beautiful, everything in the dim light is beautiful.* (Lines 143-160 below)In Whitman's universe each of us "awaits" our anointed hour. In *Song of Myself* he reported that "Long was I hugg'd close—long and long, immense have been the preparations for me...cycles ferried my cradle, rowing and rowing like cheerful boatmen...all forces have been steadily employ'd to complete and delight me, now on this spot I stand with my robust soul."

This *waiting* is the poet's answer to the problem of evil — evil awaits its resolution into the order and temperament of the universe. Day's soothing night and life's soothing death are restorative agents of time, health, wholeness, and beauty — *a contact of something unseen — an amour of light and air*. His lines: "previously jetting genitals" and "perfect and clean the womb cohering," only escaped the censor because of their wholesome perfection.

7.

> A show of the summer softness — a contact of something unseen — an amour of the light and air, 117
> I am jealous and overwhelm'd with friendliness,
> And will go gallivant with the light and air myself.
>
> O love and summer, you are in the dreams and in me,
> Autumn and winter are in the dreams, the farmer goes with his thrift,
> The droves and crops increase, the barns are well-fill'd.
>
> Elements merge in the night, ships make tacks in the dreams, 123
> The sailor sails, the exile returns home,
> The fugitive returns unharm'd, the immigrant is back beyond months and years,
> The poor Irishman lives in the simple house of his childhood with the well known neighbors and faces,

They warmly welcome him, he is
  barefoot again, he forgets he is well
  off,   127
The Dutchman voyages home, and the
  Scotchman and Welshman voyage
  home, and the native of the
  Mediterranean voyages home,
To every port of England, France, Spain,
  enter well-fill'd ships,
The Swiss foots it toward his hills, the
  Prussian goes his way, the
  Hungarian his way, and the Pole his
  way,
The Swede returns, and the Dane and
  Norwegian return.   131

The homeward bound and the outward
  bound,   132
The beautiful lost swimmer, the ennuye,
  the onanist, the female that loves
  unrequited, the money-maker,
The actor and actress, those through
  with their parts and those waiting to
  commence,
The affectionate boy, the husband and
  wife, the voter, the nominee that is
  chosen and the nominee that has
  fail'd,
The great already known and the great
  any time after to-day,
The stammerer, the sick, the perfect-
  form'd, the homely,   137
The criminal that stood in the box, the
  judge that sat and sentenced him,

the fluent lawyers, the jury, the audience,
The laugher and weeper, the dancer, the midnight widow, the red squaw,
The consumptive, the erysipalite, the idiot, he that is wrong'd, 140
The antipodes, and every one between this and them in the dark,
I swear they are averaged now—one is no better than the other, 142
The night and sleep have liken'd them and restored them. 143

I swear they are all beautiful,
Every one that sleeps is beautiful, every thing in the dim light is beautiful, 145
The wildest and bloodiest is over, and all is peace.
Peace is always beautiful,
The myth of heaven indicates peace and night. 148

The myth of heaven indicates the soul,
The soul is always beautiful, it appears more or it appears less, it comes or it lags behind, 150
It comes from its embower'd garden and looks pleasantly on itself and encloses the world,
Perfect and clean the genitals previously jetting, and perfect and clean the womb cohering,
The head well-grown proportion'd and plumb, and the bowels and joints proportion'd and plumb.

The soul is always beautiful, 154
The universe is duly in order, every thing is in its place, 155
What has arrived is in its place and what waits shall be in its place,
The twisted skull waits, the watery or rotten blood waits,
The child of the glutton or venerealee waits long, and the child of the drunkard waits long, and the drunkard himself waits long,
The sleepers that lived and died wait, the far advanced are to go on in their turns, and the far behind are to come on in their turns, 159
The diverse shall be no less diverse, but they shall flow and unite— they unite now. 160

The 8th and last Canto of the poem is a magnificent paean to the restorative powers of sleep, night and death: *The sleepers are very beautiful as they lie unclothed. The sleepers flow hand and hand over the whole earth from east to west as they lie unclothed.* They flow with the turning of the earth—of night to day. They might be souls awaiting birth. In Whitman night and death is always a prelude to morning and life. The concluding Canto is also an exquisite catalogue of the poet's faith in love and the *restorative chemistry of the night* (Line 176 below). The first half of the first stanza details the love of boy and girl, man and woman, father and son, mother and daughter, scholar and teacher. The second half details the broken becoming whole as they awake to the spreading dawn.

In Whitman's dream the sick, the feverish, the rheumatic and the paralyzed have been healed by the night and awake to the glory that is day. *The Sleepers* might have only been a dream (among the most beautiful of which we have record) but it was also a conviction that the poet aspired to all his waking life.

8.

> The sleepers are very beautiful as they lie unclothed, 161
> They flow hand in hand over the whole earth from east to west as they lie unclothed,
> The Asiatic and African are hand in hand, the European and American are hand in hand,
> Learn'd and unlearn'd are hand in hand, and male and female are hand in hand, 164
> The bare arm of the girl crosses the bare breast of her lover, they press close without lust, his lips press her neck, 165
> The father holds his grown or ungrown son in his arms with measureless love, and the son holds the father in his arms with measureless love,
> The white hair of the mother shines on the white wrist of the daughter,
> The breath of the boy goes with the breath of the man, friend is inarm'd by friend,
> The scholar kisses the teacher and the teacher kisses the scholar, the wrong 'd made right, 169

> The call of the slave is one with the master's call, and the master salutes the slave,
> The felon steps forth from the prison, the insane becomes sane, the suffering of sick persons is reliev'd,   171
> The sweatings and fevers stop, the throat that was unsound is sound, the lungs of the consumptive are resumed, the poor distress'd head is free,
> The joints of the rheumatic move as smoothly as ever, and smoother than ever,
> Stiflings and passages open, the paralyzed become supple,   174
> The swell'd and convuls'd and congested awake to themselves in condition,
> They pass the invigoration of the night and the chemistry of the night, and awake.   176
> I too pass from the night,
> I stay a while away O night, but I return to you again and love you.   178

The mystic rapture of night passes to the serenity of morning. The poem is properly regarded as one of the poet's masterworks. The images are surreal, poignant, profound and beautiful throughout each of its lines — deleted or no. To Whitman movement and flux is the reflective obverse of serenity and oneness. Like a canny Zen master he attempts by indirections to point directions out -- to make us experience the ecstasy of the present moment.

At the end of the 7th Canto the poet had assured us that *the universe is duly in order, every thing is in its place. What has arrived is in its place and what waits shall be in its place... The sleepers that lived and died wait... The diverse shall be no less diverse, but they shall flow and unite – they unite now.*

Whitman concludes the 8th Canto and *The Sleepers* with a final salute to *mother night* to whom, as a loving son, he promises to duly return:

> Why should I be afraid to trust myself to you? 179
> I am not afraid, I have been well brought forward by you,
> I love the rich running day, but I do not desert her in whom I lay so long, 181
> I know not how I came of you and I know not where I go with you, but I know I came well and shall go well. 182
>
> I will stop only a time with the night, and rise betimes,
> I will duly pass the day O my mother, and duly return to you. 184

9. Transpositions

(1856)

In the ninth hour of the Code, Whitman records a rare moment of doubt as if a bitter flotsam arising from the maelstrom of his rejected *Respondez*.

And like *Reversals,* the length of his cavil is inversely proportionate to the depth of his feeling. Both *Reversals* and *Transpositions* are, not surprisingly, lines from the same poem. *Respondez!* is recorded with Reversals, earlier in this volume. What is surprising is that the original poem dates from 1856 and betrays a want of confidence—probably owing to the paucity of sales that the inaugural edition of *Leaves* had experienced.

Transpositions

Let the reformers descend from the stands where they are forever bawling—let an idiot or insane person appear on each of the stands;
Let judges and criminals be transposed—let the prison-keepers be put in prison—let those that were prisoners take the keys;
Let them that distrust birth and death lead the rest.

10. To Think of Time

(1855)

To Think of Time is another masterpiece from the inaugural edition of the masterwork we are considering. It predates the announcement of his plan to write a new Bible—*The Three Hundred and Sixty-Five,* but along with the inaugural edition's preoccupation with time and eternity it was undoubtedly an influence on his grand design. It was initially untitled and was first known as *Burial Poem* in the 1856 edition.

Its present title was acquired for the 1871 edition. Its didactic title belies nine stanzas that were composed during a blaze of brilliance that remains one of the high-water marks of American literature—and that of the world. Time is one of the most elusive of metaphysical constructs. Our clocks seduce us into complacency. Take away a timepiece and then ponder the pieces of time. Augustine felt confident in his understanding of the concept until he subjected it to the scrutiny of thought. Whitman exposes the dreaded hug of mortality:

> Have you guess'd you yourself would not continue?
> Have you dreaded these earth-beetles?
> Have you fear'd the future would be nothing to you?

To Think of Time

1.

> To think of time—of all that retrospection,
> To think of to-day, and the ages continued henceforward.
>
> Have you guess'd you yourself would not continue?
> Have you dreaded these earth-beetles?
> Have you fear'd the future would be nothing to you? 5
>
> Is to-day nothing? is the beginningless past nothing? 6
> If the future is nothing they are just as surely nothing.

> To think that the sun rose in the east—
> that men and women were flexible,
> real, alive—that every thing was
> alive,
> To think that you and I did not see, feel,
> think, nor bear our part,   9
> To think that we are now here and bear
> our part.   10

One of the crucial time-related thoughts is *where were we before our "time" began* and *where will we be after is has ceased to continue?* The first half of that thought is less distressing than the contemplation of the second. Whitman suggests they are the same. In Canto 2 he composes a verse-portrait of a death scene. It is poignant and true. Perhaps only the stark expressionism of Edvard Munch has as faithfully recorded the grief and tenderness associated with dissolution. Note also the curious, though extraordinary, lines that conclude the 2nd Canto: *The living look upon the corpse with their eyesight, But without eyesight lingers a different living and looks curiously on the corpse...* (Lines 23-24 below). Mayhaps, Emerson can suggest a meaning:

> Nothing is dead: men feign themselves dead, and endure mock funerals and mournful obituaries, and there they stand looking out of the window, sound and well, in some new a strange disguise. Jesus is not dead; he is very well alive: nor John, nor Paul, nor Mahomet, nor Aristotle; at times we believe we have seen them all, and could easily tell the names under which they go.[204]

And Borges had a similar epiphany:

> The profile of a Jewish man in the subway may well be the same as Christ's; the hands that make change for us at the ticket window could be identical to the hands that soldiers one day nailed to a cross. Some features of the crucified face may lurk in every mirror. Maybe the face died and faded away so that God could be everyman. Who knows? We might see it tonight in the labyrinths of sleep and remember nothing in the morning.[205]

2.

> Not a day passes, not a minute or second without an accouchement,   11
> Not a day passes, not a minute or second without a corpse.   12
>
> The dull nights go over and the dull days also,
> The soreness of lying so much in bed goes over,
> The physician after long putting off gives the silent and terrible look for an answer,   15
> The children come hurried and weeping, and the brothers and sisters are sent for,
> Medicines stand unused on the shelf, (the camphor-smell has long pervaded the rooms,)
> The faithful hand of the living does not desert the hand of the dying,

> The twitching lips press lightly on the forehead of the dying,
> The breath ceases and the pulse of the heart ceases,
> The corpse stretches on the bed and the living look upon it,
> It is palpable as the living are palpable.   22
>
> The living look upon the corpse with their eyesight,   23
> But without eyesight lingers a different living and looks curiously on the corpse.   24

The most vivid image is reserved for Canto 3: *Slow-moving and black lines creep over the whole earth...* (Lines 31-32 below) Whitman would see more death during the Civil War than any other civilian. The poet even seems to identify with the dead more than their living counterparts: "*we* taking no interest... *we* quite indifferent." [206] Burroughs reports a visit with the poet after one his nightly ministrations to the wounded in Washington: "Death, he says, is a great mystery and fills him with awe. In its presence he is dumb; he walks up and down the room and sees the flame of life hover and flicker, and words are a profanity..." [207]

3.
> To think the thought of death merged in the thought of materials,   25
> To think of all these wonders of city and country, and others taking great interest in them, and we taking no interest in them.   26

> To think how eager we are in building
> our houses,
> To think others shall be just as eager,
> and we quite indifferent. 28
>
> (I see one building the house that serves
> him a few years, or seventy or
> eighty years at most,
> I see one building the house that serves
> him longer than that.)
> Slow-moving and black lines creep over
> the whole earth — they never cease —
> they are the burial lines, 31
> He that was President was buried, and
> he that is now President shall surely
> be buried. 32

There is an uncanny prescience to the final line of Canto 3. Lincoln's death is more closely aligned with Whitman than to any other man of letters. Those *slow moving and black lines* will return a decade hence when *the great star early droops in the western sky,* at the war's conclusion. The black lines are not only the myriad mourners, but also the railroad tracks that will take the President from Washington, D.C. to Springfield, Illinois.

In the 4th Canto, Whitman takes up a reminiscence of a less powerful figure — the funeral of an old Broadway stage driver. In like manner, Leopold Bloom contemplates the death of Paddy Dingham. Joyce had prepared us for his view of death early in *Ulysses*:

> — You were making tea, Stephen said,
> and I went across the landing to get
> more hot water...

> Your mother and some visitor came out of the drawing room. She asked you who was in your room.
> —Yes? Buck Mulligan said. What did I say? I forget.
> —You said, Stephen answered, *O, it's only Dedalus whose mother is beastly dead.*[208]

The two funerals are interspersed, below. Whitman's poem continues unimpeded simply by ignoring the Irishman's delightfully impudent interjections.

Joyce:

> He had a sudden death, poor fellow, he said. —
> The best death, Mr. Bloom said. Their wide open eyes looked at him. [209]

Whitman:

4.

> A reminiscence of the vulgar fate,   33
> A frequent sample of the life and death of workmen,
> Each after his kind.
>
> Cold dash of waves at the ferry-wharf, posh and ice in the river, half-frozen mud in the streets,
> A gray discouraged sky overhead, the short last daylight of December,
> A hearse and stages, the funeral of an old Broadway stage-driver, the cortege mostly drivers.

> Steady the trot to the cemetery, duly rattles the death-bell, 39

Joyce:

> Boom! Upset. A coffin bumped out on to the road. Burst open. Paddy Dingham shot out rolling over stiff in the dust in a brown habit too large for him Red face: grey now. Mouth fallen open. Asking what's up now. Quite right to close it. Looks horrid open. The insides decome quickly. Much better to close up all the orifices. Yes, also. Wax. The sphincter loose. Seal up all... would it bleed if a nail say cut him the knocking about? He would and he wouldn't, I suppose. Depends on where. The circulation stops. Still some might ooze out of an artery. It would be better to bury them in red: a dark red. [210]

Whitman:

> The gate is pass'd, the new-dug grave is halted at, the living alight, the hearse uncloses, 40

Joyce:

> Coffin now. Got here before us, dead as he is. Horse looking round... collar tight on his neck, pressing on a blood vessel or something. Do they know what they cart out here every day? Must be twenty

or thirty funerals every day... Then Mount Jerome for the protestants. Funerals over the world every minute. Shoveling them under by the cartload doublequick. Thousands every hour. Too many in the world...[211]

Whitman:

> The coffin is pass'd out, lower'd and settled, the whip is laid on the coffin, the earth is swiftly shovel'd in,   41
> The mound above is flatted with the spades—silence,
> A minute—no one moves or speaks—it is done,
> He is decently put away—is there any thing more?   44

Joyce:

> Mr. Kernan said with Solemnity: '*I am the resurrection and the life*. That touches a man's inmost heart.'—It does, Mr. Bloom said. Your heart perhaps but what price the fellow in the six feet by two with his toes to the daisies? No touching that. Seat of the affections. Broken heart. A pump after all, pumping thousands of gallons of blood every day. One fine day it gets bunged up and there you are. Lots of them lying around here: lungs, hearts, livers. Old rusty pumps: damn the thing else.[212]

Whitman:

> He was a good fellow, free-mouth'd, quick-temper'd, not bad-looking,   45
> Ready with life or death for a friend, fond of women, gambled, ate hearty, drank hearty…   46

Joyce:

> Blazing face: redhot. Too much John Barleycorn. Cure for a red nose. Drink like the devil till it turns adelite. A lot of money he spent colouring it.Mr. Power gazed at the passing horses with rueful apprehension.[213]

Whitman:

> Had known what it was to be flush, grew low-spirited toward the last, sicken'd, was help'd by a contribution,   47
> Died, aged forty-one years—and that was his funeral.   48

Joyce:

> The resurrection and the life. Once you are dead you are dead. The last day idea. Knocking them all up out of their graves. Come forth, Lazarus! And he came fifth and lost his job.[214]

Whitman:

> Thumb extended, finger uplifted, apron, cape, gloves, strap, wet-weather clothes, whip carefully chosen, 49
> Boss, spotter, starter, hostler, somebody loafing on you, you loafing on somebody, headway, man before and man behind… 50

Joyce:

> Get up! Last day! Then every fellow mousing around for his liver and his lights and the rest of his traps.
> Find damn all of himself that morning. Pennyweight of powder in the skull. Twelve grams one pennyweight. Troy measure.[215]

Whitman:

> Good day's work, bad day's work, pet stock, mean stock, first out, last out, turning-in at night, 51
> To think that these are so much and so nigh to other drivers, and he there takes no interest in them. 52

Whitman finds it odd that the living should take such interest that the dead no longer possess. In that oddity he will begin the formulation of an answer that he will grapple with over the next three and a half decades.

5.

> The markets, the government, the working-man's wages, to think what account they are through our nights and days, 53
> To think that other working-men will make just as great account of them, yet we make little or no account.
>
> The vulgar and the refined, what you call sin and what you call goodness, to think how wide a difference, 55
> To think the difference will still continue to others, yet we lie beyond the difference. 56
>
> To think how much pleasure there is,
> Do you enjoy yourself in the city? or engaged in business? or planning a nomination and election? or with your wife and family?
> Or with your mother and sisters? or in womanly housework? or the beautiful maternal cares?
> These also flow onward to others, you and I flow onward,
> But in due time you and I shall take less interest in them. 61
>
> Your farm, profits, crops — to think how engross'd you are,
> To think there will still be farms, profits, crops, yet for you of what avail? 63

Emerson's *Hamatreya* lurks between the last two lines:

> Where are these men? Asleep beneath
> their grounds;
> And strangers, fond as they, their
> furrows plough;

Whitman's *what will be will be well, for what is, is well* (Line 64 below) harkens back to the fourteenth century's Julian of Norwich [216] whose *All shall be well, and all manner of thing shall be well* was also incorporated into T.S. Eliot's "Little Gidding", the fourth of his *Four Quartets*.

Compare also Section 1 of Eliot's *East Coker:*

> As in their living in the living seasons
> The time of the seas and the
> constellations
> The time of coupling of man and
> women
> And that of beasts, Feet rising and
> falling,
> Eating and drinking. Dung and Death.

Norwich is venerated by both Anglicans and Lutherans although (and perhaps because) she was never canonized as a Saint by the Catholic Church. She is among the most important of English mystics. Her work, however, was not widely known until early in the 20th century.

Her *Revelation of Love* is an early forerunner of Whitman's own attitude. She along with Whitman believed that everything was directed toward good ends and averred: *all will be saved by a merciful God.*

6.
> What will be will be well, for what is is well, 64
> To take interest is well, and not take interest shall be well.
>
> The domestic joys, the daily housework or business, the building of houses, are not phantasms, they have weight, form, location,
> Farms, profits, crops, markets, wages, government, are none of them phantasms,
> The difference between sin and goodness is no delusion,
> The earth is not an echo, man and his life and all the things of his life are well-consider'd. 69

In Emerson's *Worship* we find:

> The solar system has no anxiety about its reputation, and the credit of truth and honesty is as safe... every man takes care that his neighbor shall not cheat him. But a day comes when he begins to care that he does not cheat his neighbor. Then all goes well, he has changed his market cart into a chariot of the sun.

Whitman reiterates that same celebration of the individual spirit here at the conclusion of the 6th Canto:

> You are not thrown to the winds, you
> gather certainly and safely around
> yourself, 70
> Yourself! yourself! yourself, for ever and
> ever! 71

In Canto 7 we also hear the echo of Emerson's essay *Fate:*

> Let us build to Beautiful Necessity, which makes man brave in believing that he cannot shun a danger that is appointed, not incur one that is not.

In one of Emerson's soundest journal entries, some months after the death of Ellen (his first wife), we find: "When I talk with the sick they sometimes think I treat death with unbecoming indifference and do not make the case my own, or, if I do, err in my judgment. I do not fear death...I should lie down in the lap of the earth as trustingly as ever on my own bed." [217]

7.

> It is not to diffuse you that you were
> born of your mother and father, it is
> to identify you, 72
> It is not that you should be undecided,
> but that you should be decided,
> Something long preparing and formless
> is arrived and form'd in you, 74
> You are henceforth secure, whatever
> comes or goes.
>
> The threads that were spun are gather'd,
> the weft crosses the warp, the
> pattern is systematic. 76

> The preparations have every one been justified, 77
> The orchestra have sufficiently tuned their instruments, the baton has given the signal.
>
> The guest that was coming, he waited long, he is now housed,
> He is one of those who are beautiful and happy, he is one of those that to look upon and be with is enough.
>
> The law of the past cannot be eluded, 81
> The law of the present and future cannot be eluded,
> The law of the living cannot be eluded, it is eternal,
> The law of promotion and transformation cannot be eluded,
> The law of heroes and good-doers cannot be eluded,
> The law of drunkards, informers, mean persons, not one iota thereof can be eluded. 86

Joyce feels the same silent necessity of all things:

> Famine, plague and slaughter. Their blood is in me, their lusts my waves. I moved among them on the frozen Liffey, that I a changeling, among the spluttering resin fires. I spoke to no-one: none to me. [218]

The Buddhist notion of impermanence (anicca) comes into play later in the Canto. Here the poet reconciles transient loss with the permanence of eternity. It is a magnificent intuition: *And I have dream'd that the purpose and essence of the known life, the transient, Is to form and decide identity for the unknown life, the permanent.* (Lines 101-102 below) Whitman continues his trope of the funeral lines (Cf. line 31 above) at the beginning of the 8th Canto.

8.

> Slow moving and black lines go ceaselessly over the earth, 87
> Northerner goes carried and Southerner goes carried, and they on the Atlantic side and they on the Pacific,
> And they between, and all through the Mississippi country, and all over the earth.
>
> The great masters and kosmos are well as they go, the heroes and good-doers are well,
> The known leaders and inventors and the rich owners and pious and distinguish'd may be well,
> But there is more account than that, there is strict account of all.
>
> The interminable hordes of the ignorant and wicked are not nothing, 93
> The barbarians of Africa and Asia are not nothing,
> The perpetual successions of shallow people are not nothing as they go.

Of and in all these things,
I have dream'd that we are not to be changed so much, nor the law of us changed,
I have dream'd that heroes and good-doers shall be under the present and past law,
And that murderers, drunkards, liars, shall be under the present and past law,
For I have dream'd that the law they are under now is enough. 100

And I have dream'd that the purpose and essence of the known life, the transient, 101
Is to form and decide identity for the unknown life, the permanent. 102

If all came but to ashes of dung, 103
If maggots and rats ended us, then Alarum! for we are betray'd, 104
Then indeed suspicion of death. 105
Do you suspect death? if I were to suspect death I should die now, 107
Do you think I could walk pleasantly and well-suited toward annihilation?

Pleasantly and well-suited I walk,
Whither I walk I cannot define, but I know it is good, 109
The whole universe indicates that it is good, 110

> The past and the present indicate that it is good.
>
> How beautiful and perfect are the animals!
> How perfect the earth, and the minutest thing upon it!
> What is called good is perfect, and what is called bad is just as perfect, 114
> The vegetables and minerals are all perfect, and the imponderable fluids perfect;
> Slowly and surely they have pass'd on to this, and slowly and surely they yet pass on. 116

Eckhart's 9th Sermon quotes Luke 21:31, "Know that the kingdom of God is near." In his dilation on this theme he continues:

> My being depends on the fact that God is "near" to me and present for me. He is also near and present for a stone or a piece of wood...God is equally near in all creatures. God has his net, his hunter's ploy, spread out over all creatures. Thus all people can find him in everything so long as they can penetrate this net...and recognize God in everything...The one who knows God best is the one who recognizes him equally everywhere...God is near to us but we are very far from him. God is within but we are without. God is at home but we are abroad.

Whitman couples his own notion of the soul with Eckhart's all inclusive 'net' in a final anthem to universal immortality: "I swear I think there is nothing but immortality!" It is one of his most sublime iterations — the hope of the world in which the curious universe finds itself behind the eye of each illumiation.

9.
> I swear I think now that every thing without exception has an eternal soul! 117
> The trees have, rooted in the ground! the weeds of the sea have! the animals!
>
> I swear I think there is nothing but immortality! 119
> That the exquisite scheme is for it, and the nebulous float is for it, and the cohering is for it!
> And all preparation is for it — and identity is for it — and life and materials are altogether for it! 121

11. Thou Mother ...

In 1872 Whitman received an invitation by a group of Dartmouth students to present a poem at that year's commencement. For that occasion he composed *Thou Mother of Thy Equal Brood*. The first line of Canto 2 was originally its opening line and title: "As a Strong Bird With Pinions Free." The first Canto was added nearly a decade later, in the 1881 edition of *Leaves*. The rhetoric is for the poet's beloved democracy:

I sow a seed for thee of endless Nationality.

His concern enlarges to the metaphysical in the 2nd Canto. Note that Plato's "immortal idea!" and Aristotle's "immortal reality!" are blended with God." Only those students worthy the *Paedia* would have caught his inflection: "Thought of man justified, blended with God, through thy idea, lo, the immortal reality; through thy reality, lo, the immortal idea!"

Thou Mother With Thy Equal Brood

1.
>Thou Mother with thy equal brood,
>Thou varied chain of different States, yet
>>one identity only, 2
>A special song before I go I'd sing o'er
>>all the rest,
>For thee, the future.
>I'd sow a seed for thee of endless
>>Nationality,
>I'd fashion thy ensemble including body
>>and soul,
>I'd show away ahead thy real Union,
>>and how it may be accomplish'd. 6
>
>The paths to the house I seek to make,
>But leave to those to come the house
>>itself.
>
>Belief I sing, and preparation;
>As Life and Nature are not great with
>>reference to the present only,
>But greater still from what is yet to
>>come,

Out of that formula for thee I sing. 13

Whitman's democracy is also his notion of "being." As *endless Nationality* blends into the world, so also the democratic man is "justified" by *being blended* into *God*. Whitman reiterates Emerson's call of a national character not indebted to the conceits of other lands. Canto 2 was originally the opening focus of the poem and its initial title: *As a Strong Bird on Pinions Free*. Whitman added the first canto as he later enlarged the poem and its great theme of *the ensemble of body and soul*. In the 2nd Canto he poetically suggests areas of the nation by their fragrance: the odors of pine in the forests of Maine; the smell of the open prairie in Illinois; the fragrance of the glades in Florida; and the glory of Yosemite in California. (Lines 20-22 below) Whitman is one of the world's most beloved and universal of poets because his unifying images embrace all of mankind: *And murmuring under, pervading all, I'd bring the rustling sea-sound, that endlessly sounds from the two Great Seas of the world.* (Lines 25-26 below) At the conclusion of the Canto is, once again, the unmistakable conflation of Plato and Aristotle: *Through thy idea, lo the immortal reality! Through thy reality, lo the immortal idea!* (Lines 32-33 below).

2.
>As a strong bird on pinions free, 14
>Joyous, the amplest spaces heavenward cleaving,
>Such be the thought I'd think of thee America,
>Such be the recitative I'd bring for thee.

The conceits of the poets of other lands
    I'd bring thee not,
Nor the compliments that have served
    their turn so long,
Nor rhyme, nor the classics, nor
    perfume of foreign court or indoor
    library;   20
But an odor I'd bring as from forests of
    pine in Maine, or breath of an
    Illinois prairie,
With open airs of Virginia or Georgia or
    Tennessee, or from Texas uplands,
    or Florida's glades,   22
Or the Saguenay's black stream, or the
    wide blue spread of Huron,
With presentment of Yellowstone's
    scenes, or Yosemite,
And murmuring under, pervading all,
    I'd bring the rustling sea-sound,   25
That endlessly sounds from the two
    Great Seas of the world.   26

And for thy subtler sense subtler
    refrains dread Mother,
Preludes of intellect tallying these and
    thee, mind-formulas fitted
for thee, real and sane and large as these
    and thee,
Thou! mounting higher, diving deeper
    than we knew, thou transcendental
    Union!
By thee fact to be justified, blended with
    thought,
Thought of man justified, blended with
    God,   31

> Through thy idea, lo, the immortal
> reality!
> Through thy reality, lo, the immortal
> idea! 33

Joyce plays with the same dichotomy between Plato and the *Peripatetic* Aristotle:

> Unsheathe your definitions. Horseness
> is the whatness of all horse. Streams of
> tendency and eons they worship. God: a
> noise in the street: very peripatetic.
>
> Space what you damn well have to
> see...Hold to the now, the here, through
> which all future plunges to the past. [219] 33

Whitman then salutes the old world in his praise of the new — the modern and the mighty living present which he sees infolded in the old and ripening as if apples falling into reality: *Thou but the apples, long, long, long a-growing, The fruit of all the Old ripening to-day in thee.* (Lines 45-46 below)

3.
> Brain of the New World, what a task is
> thine, 34
> To formulate the Modern — out of the
> peerless grandeur of the modern,
> Out of thyself, comprising science, to
> recast poems, churches, art,
> (Recast, may-be discard them, end
> them — maybe their work is done,
> who knows?)

> By vision, hand, conception, on the background of the mighty past, the dead,
> To limn with absolute faith the mighty living present. 39
>
> And yet thou living present brain, heir of the dead, the Old World brain,
> Thou that lay folded like an unborn babe within its folds so long, 41
> Thou carefully prepared by it so long—haply thou but unfoldest it, only matures it,
> It to eventuate in thee—the essence of the by-gone time contain'd in thee,
> Its poems, churches, arts, unwitting to themselves, destined with reference to thee;
> Thou but the apples, long, long, long a-growing, 45
> The fruit of all the Old ripening to-day in thee. 46

The theme of time continues in the 4th Canto. He employs the tired image of a *ship* for democracy but imbues it with the gravitas of the *earth's resume—the antecedent nations sink or swim with thee...Venerable priestly Asia sails with thee, and royal feudal Europe sails with thee*. (Lines 51-51 & 56-57 below)

4.
> Sail, sail thy best, ship of Democracy, 47
> Of value is thy freight, 'tis not the Present only,
> The Past is also stored in thee,

> Thou holdest not the venture of thyself
> alone, not of the Western continent
> alone,
> Earth's resume entire floats on thy keel
> O ship, is steadied by thy spars,
> With thee Time voyages in trust, the
> antecedent nations sink or swim
> with thee,
> With all their ancient struggles, martyrs,
> heroes, epics, wars, thou bear'st the
> other continents,
> Theirs, theirs as much as thine, the
> destination-port triumphant;
> Steer then with good strong hand and
> wary eye O helmsman, thou carriest
> great companions,
> Venerable priestly Asia sails this day
> with thee,
> And royal feudal Europe sails with thee. 57

Canto 5 takes up the tautological theme of Shankara's Vedanta as the poet asserts: *World of the real — world of the twain in one, World of the soul, born by world of the real alone, led to identity, body, by it alone...* (Lines 64-65 below) Whitman's Idealism is filtered through Plato, Plotinus. and Emerson:

> The over powering reality is that unity,
> that oversoul within which every man's
> particular being is contained and made
> one with all other... Within man is the
> soul of the whole; the wise silence; the
> universal beauty, to which every part
> and particle is related; the Eternal One.

> And this deep power in which we exist, and whose beatitude is all accessible to us, is not only self-sufficing and perfect in every hour, but the act of seeing and things seen, the seer and the spectacle, the subject and the object are one.

In 1845 Emerson was reading the Bhagavad Gita and Henry Thomas Colebrook's essays on the Upanishads. He was to ingest these ideas and make them his own. There is no more cogent or good humored exegesis of Vedanta in American letters than that of Emerson's.

> The end and the means, the gamester and the game—life is made up of the intermixture and reaction of these two amicable powers, whose marriage appears beforehand monstrous, as each denies and tends to abolish the other. We must reconcile the contradictions as we can, but their discord and their concord introduce wild absurdities into our thinking and speech. No sentence will hold the whole truth, and the only way in which we can be just, is by giving ourselves the lie; speech is better than silence; silence is better than speech: All things are in contact; every atom has a sphere of repulsion; things are, and are not, at the same time; and the like. All the universe over, there is but one thing, this old Two-Face, creator-creature, mind-matter, right-wrong, of which any proposition may be affirmed or denied…

> So the least of its rational children, the most dedicated to his private affair, works out, though as it were under a disguise, the universal problem. We fancy men are individuals; so are pumpkins…We hide this universality if we can but it appears at all points. [220]

In line 71 of the poem, Whitman asks: *How can I pierce the impenetrable blank of the future?* Whitman's new Bible is all-inclusive. If Whitman is a savior then Jesus wasn't uniquely so—*Thy saviors countless, latent within thyself, thy bibles incessant within thyself, equal to any divine as any.* (Line 89 below) When the poet speaks of two great wars and the century's visible growth we could almost believe that he is prophetically anticipating WW1 and WW2 rather than the Revolutionary and the Civil of which he makes reference.

The Norton Critical Edition reports that the poet was invited by the students for his notoriety. Whitman was delighted to be commissioned for his art. He sent press releases to local papers announcing his recitation. He enlarged the poem in later editions. Canto 5 is a beautiful evocation of the poet's optimism—but, as noted above, the commingling of Plato and Aristotle: *World of the real—world of the twain in one,* is the poem's strongest suit.

5.
>> Beautiful world of new superber birth that rises to my eyes, 58
>> Like a limitless golden cloud filling the western sky,

Emblem of general maternity lifted above all,
Sacred shape of the bearer of daughters and sons,
Out of thy teeming womb thy giant babes in ceaseless procession issuing,
Acceding from such gestation, taking and giving continual strength and life,
World of the real—world of the twain in one, 64
World of the soul, born by the world of the real alone, led to identity, body, by it alone,
Yet in beginning only, incalculable masses of composite precious materials, 66
By history's cycles forwarded, by every nation, language, hither sent,
Ready, collected here, a freer, vast, electric world, to be constructed here,
(The true New World, the world of orbic science, morals, literatures to come,)
Thou wonder world yet undefined, unform'd, neither do I define thee,
How can I pierce the impenetrable blank of the future?
I feel thy ominous greatness evil as well as good, 72
I watch thee advancing, absorbing the present, transcending the past,
I see thy light lighting, and thy shadow shadowing, as if the entire globe,

But I do not undertake to define thee,
    hardly to comprehend thee,
I but thee name, thee prophesy, as now,
I merely thee ejaculate!

Thee in thy future, 78
Thee in thy only permanent life, career,
    thy own unloosen'd mind, the
    soaring spirit,
Thee as another equally needed sun,
    radiant, ablaze, swift-moving,
    fructifying all,
Thee risen in potent cheerfulness and
    joy, in endless great hilarity,
Scattering for good the cloud that hung
    so long, that weigh'd so long upon
    the mind of man,
The doubt, suspicion, dread, of gradual,
    certain decadence of man; 83
Thee in thy larger, saner brood of
    female, male — thee in thy athletes,
    moral, spiritual, South, North, West,
    East,
(To thy immortal breasts, Mother of All,
    thy every daughter, son, endear'd
    alike, forever equal,) 85
Thee in thy own musicians, singers,
    artists, unborn yet, but certain,
Thee in thy moral wealth and
    civilization, (until which thy
    proudest material civilization must
    remain in vain,)
Thee in thy all-supplying, all-enclosing
    worship — thee in no single bible,
    saviour, merely, 88

Thy saviours countless, latent within
 thyself, thy bibles incessant within
 thyself, equal to any, divine as any, 89
(Thy soaring course thee formulating,
 not in thy two great wars, nor in thy
 century's visible growth, 90
But far more in these leaves and chants,
 thy chants, great Mother!)
Thee in an education grown of thee, in
 teachers, studies, students, born of
 thee,
Thee in thy democratic fetes en-masse,
 thy high original festivals, operas,
 lecturers, preachers,
Thee in thy ultimate, (the preparations
 only now completed, the edifice on
 sure foundations tied,)
Thee in thy pinnacles, intellect, thought,
 thy topmost rational joys, thy love
 and godlike aspiration, 95
In thy resplendent coming literati, thy
 full-lung'd orators, thy sacerdotal
 bards, kosmic savans,
These! these in thee, (certain to come,)
 to-day I prophesy. 97

6.

Land tolerating all, accepting all, not for
 the good alone, all good for thee, 98
Land in the realms of God to be a realm
 unto thyself,
Under the rule of God to be a rule unto
 thyself.

(Lo, where arise three peerless stars,

> To be thy natal stars my country,
> Ensemble, Evolution, Freedom,
> Set in the sky of Law.)
>
> Land of unprecedented faith, God's faith,
> Thy soil, thy very subsoil, all upheav'd,
> The general inner earth so long so sedulously draped over, now hence, for what it is boldly laid bare,
> Open'd by thee to heaven's light for benefit or bale. 107

The fourth stanza of Canto 6 to the god within is tempered by a litany of a near apocalypse that gives *the devil his due:*

> Not for success alone, 108
> Not to fair-sail unintermitted always,
> The storm shall dash thy face, the murk of war and worse than war shall cover thee all over,
> (Wert capable of war, its tug and trials? be capable of peace, its rtrials,
> For the tug and mortal strain of nations come at last in prosperous peace, not war;)
> In many a smiling mask death shall approach beguiling thee, thou in disease shalt swelter,
> The livid cancer spread its hideous claws, clinging upon thy breasts, seeking to strike thee deep within,

> Consumption of the worst, moral consumption, shall rouge thy face with hectic,   115

The poet cannot long linger on the negative—he continues the 2nd half of the fourth stanza with a fanfare that makes explicit the metaphysical trappings that accompany his notion of Nation and Democracy. Union is not just the coming together of these United States but rather a *mystical Union*—Pantanjali's yoking or *yoga* of the transient with the eternal—the individual with the infinite.

> But thou shalt face thy fortunes, thy diseases, and surmount them all,   116
> Whatever they are to-day and whatever through time they may be,
> They each and all shall lift and pass away and cease from thee,
> While thou, Time's spirals rounding, out of thyself, thyself still extricating, fusing,
> Equable, natural, mystical Union thou, (the mortal with immortal blent,)
> Shalt soar toward the fulfilment of the future, the spirit of the boy and the mind,
> The soul, its destinies.   122

The 5th and concluding stanza of Canto 6 and the poem is a paean to Platonic idealism:

> The soul, its destinies, the real real,   123
> (Purport of all these apparitions of the real;)   123

> In thee America, the soul, its destinies,
> Thou globe of globes! thou wonder nebulous!
> By many a throe of heat and cold convuls'd, (by these thyself solidifying,)
> Thou mental, moral orb—thou New, indeed new, Spiritual World!
> The Present holds thee not—for such vast growth as thine,
> For such unparallel'd flight as thine, such brood as thine,
> The FUTURE only holds thee and can hold thee.   131

The 12th hour or noon of the Whitman *Ante Meridiem* balances the start of the day's *Starting From Paumanok* by ending with the complexity of life and death[221] in a simple verse painting or picture, *A Paumanok Picture*:

12. A Paumanok Picture

(1881)

A Paumanok Picture

> Two boats with nets lying off the sea-beach, quite still,   1
> Ten fishermen waiting—they discover a thick school of mossbonkers—they drop the join'd seine-ends in the water,
> The boats separate and row off, each on its rounding course to the beach, enclosing the mossbonkers,

The net is drawn in by a windlass by
those who stop ashore,
Some of the fishermen lounge in their
boats, others stand ankle-deep in
the water, pois'd on strong legs,
The boats partly drawn up, the water
slapping against them,
Strew'd on the sand in heaps and
windrows, well out from the water,
the green-back'd spotted
mossbonkers. 7

POST   **MERIDIEM**

FROM NOON TO STARRY NIGHT
13. Salut Au Monde!
14. Song of the Open Road
15. Crossing Brooklyn Ferry
16. Song of the Answerer
17. Our Old Fueillage
18. A Song of Joys
19. Song of the Broad-Axe
20. Song of the Exposition
21. Song of the Redwood Tree
22. Song for Occupations
23. A Song of the Rolling Earth
24. Young, Day, Old Age and Night

13. Salut au Monde!

"Salut au Monde!" (1856) is an answer to questions put in the *Book of Job*. One remembers that the voice from the whirlwind questioned the long suffering Uzzite's right to even venture a question. Early in Job, God queries Satan if he has considered his servant Job: "For there is none like him in the earth, a perfect and upright man who feareth God and eschweth evil." Later, after the loss of his servants; sheep; children; and home; Job wonders why *the tents of the robbers prosper and they that provoke God are secure*. These are among the greatest questions that the Bible ponders, but the most celebrated part of the drama is when God confronts Job with a series of questions that each reader of the revered text must leave forever unanswered:

> Where was thou, when I laid the foundations of the earth? Declare, if thou hast understanding. Who determined the measures thereof, if thou knowest? Or who has stretched a line upon it. Whereupon were the foundations thereof fastened?

Skilled as a carpenter, Whitman found each of those queries provocative. More telling still would have been questions concerning mortality:

> Hast thou entered into the springs of the sea? Or hast thou walked in the recesses of the deep? Have the gates of death been revealed unto thee? Or hast thou seen the gates of the shadow of death?...Declare if thou knowest... .

He would have been moved, as Melville had, earlier in the decade, by the evocation of the might and spectacle of the Bible's report of a breaching whale:

> Canst thou draw Leviathan with a fishhook or press down his tongue with a cord? Canst thou put a rope into his nose? Or pierce his jaw with a hook? ...Canst thou fill his skin with barbed irons, or his head with fish spears?... And his eyes are like the eyelids of the morning. Out of his nostrils a smoke goeth, as of a seething pot and burning rushes. His breath kindleth coals and a flame goeth forth from his mouth...he maketh the deep boil like a pot... one would think the deep to be hoary... he is king over the all the sons of pride.

The "Book of Job" is among the highest standards by which the poet could take his measure. *Salut Au Monde!* possesses little of the drama associated with the Biblical classic. It probably was among the *inventory* poems that tried Emerson's patience. Whitman is exploring new forms and beginning a formulation to write "The New Bible." So we shouldn't be surprised to find Deity personally addressing his prophet/poet. Whitman's god tells him to find the world within himself: *What widens within you Walt Whitman? What waves and soils exuding? What climes? what persons and cities are here?* (Lines 5-7 below). As in Job, the drama is a dialogue — but the Deity here is more a comrade than an all consuming and terrible God: *O take my hand Walt Whitman!*

Salut Au Monde!

1.

O take my hand Walt Whitman!
Such gliding wonders! such sights and sound
Such join'd unended links, each hook'd to the next,
Each answering all, each sharing the earth with all.   4

What widens within you Walt Whitman?   5
What waves and soils exuding?   6
What climes? what persons and cities are here?   7
Who are the infants, some playing, some slumbering?   8
Who are the girls? who are the married women?   9
Who are the groups of old men going slowly with their arms about each other's necks?
What rivers are these? what forests and fruits are these?
What are the mountains call'd that rise so high in the mists?
What myriads of dwellings are they fill'd with dwellers?   13

Whitman is up to the challenge. The savvy *Atman* knows that he and *Brahman,* and yes, the very boundaries of the world, are one: *Within me zones, seas, cataracts, forests, volcanoes, groups, Malaysia, Polynesia, and the great West Indian islands.* (Lines 20-21 below)

2.

> Within me latitude widens, longitude
>   lengthens, 14
> Asia, Africa, Europe, are to the east—
>   America is provided for in the west,
> Banding the bulge of the earth winds
>   the hot equator,
> Curiously north and south turn the axis-
>   ends,
> Within me is the longest day, the sun
>   wheels in slanting rings, it does not
>   set for months,
> Stretch'd in due time within me the
>   midnight sun just rises above the
>   horizon and sinks again,
> Within me zones, seas, cataracts, forests,
>   volcanoes, groups, 20
> Malaysia, Polynesia, and the great West
>   Indian islands. 21

The 3rd Canto isolates the sense of hearing. Whitman hears the breath of history: ...the locusts of Syria; the black venerable mother the Nile; the Hebrews; the Greeks; the Romans; the beautiful crucified God; and the Hindoo reporting the injunctions of Krishna to Arjuna three thousand years before. (Lines 37-40 below)

The six italicized lines between 24 and 25 were later rejected for not keeping with the international flavor he was developing in his *Salut Au Monde*. The plague of locusts was transported from Brigham Young's Utah to the farmlands of Syria—he doesn't report if the Syrians were delivered by sea gulls. Lines 33-40 concern Muslims, Jews, Christian and Hindus.

3.

> What do you hear Walt Whitman? 22
>
> I hear the workman singing and the farmer's wife singing, 23
> I hear in the distance the sounds of children and of animals early in the day, 24
> *I hear the inimitable music of the voices of mothers,*
> *I hear the persuasions of lovers,*
> *I hear the quick rifle-cracks from the riflemen of East Tennessee and Kentucky, hunting on the hills...*
> *I hear the Virginia plantation chorus of negroes, of a harvest night,*
> *in the glare of pineknots,*
> *I hear the strong baritone of the 'lone-shore-men of Manahatta, – I hear the stevedores unlading the cargoes and singing,*
> *I hear the screams of the water-fowl of solitary northwest lakes*
> I hear emulous shouts of Australians pursuing the wild horse, 25
> I hear the Spanish dance with castanets in the chestnut shade, to the rebeck and guitar,
> I hear continual echoes from the Thames,
> I hear fierce French liberty songs,
> I hear of the Italian boat-sculler the musical recitative of old poems,

I hear the locusts in Syria as they strike the grain and grass with the showers of their terrible clouds, 30
I hear the Coptic refrain toward sundown, pensively falling on the breast of the black venerable vast mother the Nile,
I hear the chirp of the Mexican muleteer, and the bells of the mule,
I hear the Arab muezzin calling from the top of the mosque, 33
I hear the Christian priests at the altars of their churches, I hear the responsive base and soprano, 34
I hear the cry of the Cossack, and the sailor's voice putting to sea at Okotsk,
I hear the wheeze of the slave-coffle as the slaves march on, as the husky gangs pass on by twos and threes, fasten'd together with wrist-chains and ankle-chains,
I hear the Hebrew reading his records and psalms, 37
I hear the rhythmic myths of the Greeks, and the strong legends of the Romans,
I hear the tale of the divine life and bloody death of the beautiful God the Christ, 39
I hear the Hindoo teaching his favorite pupil the loves, wars, adages, transmitted safely to this day from poets who wrote three thousand years ago. 40

The 4th Canto isolates the sense of vision. He wonderfully anticipates the view afforded the Apollo astronauts of the 1960s: *I see a great round wonder rolling through space, I see diminute farms, hamlets, ruins, graveyards, jails, factories, palaces, hovels, huts of barbarians, tents of nomads upon the surface, I see the shaded part on one side where the sleepers are sleeping and the sunlit part on the other side.* (Lines 43-44 below) Whitman was a fan of astronomy. It is not a great imaginative feat to realize that when half the earth is asleep the other half is awake. But what is remarkable is his anticipation of the speed of a space capsule orbiting the earth: *I see the rapid change of light and shade...* (Line 45 below).

4.

    What do you see Walt Whitman?   41
    Who are they you salute, and that one after another salute you?

    I see a great round wonder rolling through space,   43
    I see diminute farms, hamlets, ruins, graveyards, jails, factories, palaces, hovels, huts of barbarians, tents of nomads upon the surface,   44
    I see the shaded part on one side where the sleepers are sleeping, and the sunlit part on the other side,
    I see the curious rapid change of the light and shade,   45
    I see distant lands, as real and near to the inhabitants of them as my land is to me.   46

The dialogue is hereafter abandoned. Despite my interjections the poem continues apace. The remaining nine Cantos catalog the world that he salutes and which, in turn, will come to salute the poet. And then, in contradistinction to dumbfounded Job, Whitman seems to be flying above the earth, identifying with each mountain peak and sea over which he passes:

> I see plenteous waters,` 47
> I see mountain peaks, I see the sierras of Andes where they range,
> I see plainly the Himalayas, Chian Shahs, Altays, Ghauts,
> I see the giant pinnacles of Elbruz, Kazbek, Bazardjusi,
> I see the Styrian Alps, and the Karnac Alps,
> I see the Pyrenees, Balks, Carpathians, and to the north the Dofrafields, and off at sea mount Hecla,
> I see Vesuvius and Etna, the mountains of the Moon, and the Red mountains of Madagascar, 53
> I see the Lybian, Arabian, and Asiatic deserts, I see huge dreadful Arctic and Antarctic icebergs,
> I see the superior oceans and the inferior ones, the Atlantic and Pacific, the sea of Mexico, the Brazilian sea, and the sea of Peru,
> The waters of Hindustan, the China sea, and the gulf of Guinea,
> The Japan waters, the beautiful bay of Nagasaki land-lock'd in its mountains, 59

> The spread of the Baltic, Caspian,
> Bothnia, the British shores, and the
> bay of Biscay,
> The clear-sunn'd Mediterranean, and
> from one to another of its islands,
> The White sea, and the sea around
> Greenland. 62

The poet then grounds his geography lesson with the human perspective of sailors more personally engaged:

> I behold the mariners of the world, 63
> Some are in storms, some in the night
> with the watch on the lookout,
> Some drifting helplessly, some with
> contagious diseases.
>
> I behold the sail and steamships of the
> world, some in clusters in port,
> some on their voyages,
> Some double the cape of Storms, some
> cape Verde, others capes Guardafui,
> Bon, or Bajadore,
> Others Dondra head, others pass the
> straits of Sunda, others cape
> Lopatka, others Behring's straits,
> Others cape Horn, others sail the gulf of
> Mexico or along Cuba or Hayti,
> others Hudson's bay or Baffin's bay,
> Others pass the straits of Dover, others
> enter the Wash, others the firth of
> Solway, others round cape Clear,
> others the Land's End, 68
> Others traverse the Zuyder Zee or the
> Scheld,

> Others as comers and goers at Gibraltar or the Dardanelles,
> Others sternly push their way through the northern winter-packs,
> Others descend or ascend the Obi or the Lena,
> Others the Niger or the Congo, others the Indus, the Burampooter and Cambodia,
> Others wait steam'd up ready to start in the ports of Australia,
> Wait at Liverpool, Glasgow, Dublin, Marseilles, Lisbon, Naples,
> Hamburg, Bremen, Bordeaux, the Hague, Copenhagen,
> Wait at Valparaiso, Rio Janeiro, Panama. 78

He returns from violent seas to rivers of steel, rivers of wire, and then to the actual "river-stripes" of the earth: (Lines 84-90 below)

5.

> I see the tracks of the railroads of the earth, 79
> I see them in Great Britain, I see them in Europe,
> I see them in Asia and in Africa.
>
> I see the electric telegraphs of the earth,
> I see the filaments of the news of the wars, deaths, losses, gains, passions, of my race.
>
> I see the long river-stripes of the earth, 84
> I see the Amazon and the Paraguay,

> I see the four great rivers of China, the
> Amour, the Yellow River, the Yiang-
> tse, and the Pearl,
> I see where the Seine flows, and where
> the Danube, the Loire, the Rhone,
> and the Guadalquiver flow,
> I see the windings of the Volga, the
> Dnieper, the Oder,
> I see the Tuscan going down the Arno,
> and the Venetian along the Po,
> I see the Greek seaman sailing out of
> Egina bay. 90

The 6th Canto is one of the most extraordinary in the poem. It anticipates the world shaking declaration of Nietzsche's proclamation of the death of God. Note that it precedes the German's *God is dead* by a generation: *I see the temples of the deaths of the bodies of Gods, I see the old signifiers.* (Line 96 below) In our own era Carl Jung suggested something of that same sobriety of requiem[222]:

> That the gods die from time to time is
> due to man's sudden discovery that
> they do not mean anything, that they
> are made by human hands, useless idols
> of wood and stone.[223]

Whitman gives the gods a human touch by the avatars that represent and precede them:

6.

> I see the site of the old empire of
> Assyria, and that of Persia, and that
> of India, 91

I see the falling of the Ganges over the
   high rim of Saukara.
I see the place of the idea of the Deity
   incarnated by avatars in human
   forms, 93
I see the spots of the successions of
   priests on the earth, oracles,
   sacrificers, brahmins, sabians,
   llamas, monks, muftis, exhorters,
I see where druids walk'd the groves of
   Mona, I see the mistletoe and
   vervain,
I see the temples of the deaths of the
   bodies of Gods, I see the old
   signifiers. 96

I see Christ eating the bread of his last
   supper in the midst of youths and
   old persons, 97
I see where the strong divine young
   man the Hercules toil'd faithfully
   and long and then died,
I see the place of the innocent rich life
   and hapless fate of the beautiful
   nocturnal son, the full-limb'd
   Bacchus,
I see Kneph, blooming, drest in blue,
   with the crown of feathers on his
   head,
I see Hermes, unsuspected, dying, well-
   belov'd, saying to the people,
Do not weep for me, This is not my true
   country, I have lived banish'd from my
   true country, I now go back there, 102

*I return to the celestial sphere where every
one goes in his turn.* 103

In the 7th Canto there is a marvelous vision of a Viking resurrection when "the dead men's spirits wearied of their quiet graves might rise up through the mounds and gaze on tossing billows, and be refresh'd by storms, immensity, liberty, action." (Line 111 below)

7.

> I see the battle-fields of the earth, grass grows upon them and blossoms and corn, 104
> I see the tracks of ancient and modern expeditions.
>
> I see the nameless masonries, venerable messages of the unknown events, heroes, records of the earth.
>
> I see the places of the sagas,
> I see pine-trees and fir-trees torn by northern blasts,
> I see granite bowlders and cliffs, I see green meadows and lakes,
> I see the burial-cairns of Scandinavian warriors,
> I see them raised high with stones by the marge of restless oceans, that the dead men's spirits when they wearied of their quiet graves might rise up through the mounds and gaze on the tossing billows, and be refresh'd by storms, immensity, liberty, action. 111

I see the steppes of Asia, 112
I see the tumuli of Mongolia, I see the tents of Kalmucks and Baskirs,
I see the nomadic tribes with herds of oxen and cows,
I see the table-lands notch'd with ravines, I see the jungles and deserts,

I see the camel, the wild steed, the bustard, the fat-tail'd sheep, the antelope, and the burrowing wolf

I see the highlands of Abyssinia,
I see flocks of goats feeding, and see the fig-tree, tamarind, date,
And see fields of teff-wheat and places of verdure and gold.

I see the Brazilian vaquero,
I see the Bolivian ascending mount Sorata,
I see the Wacho crossing the plains, I see the incomparable rider of horses with his lasso on his arm,
I see over the pampas the pursuit of wild cattle for their hides. 123

Whitman returns to geography for the first stanza of Canto 8—he then modifies the vision as he makes himself a random *habitan* (resident) of the cities in his vision. (Lines 130-137 below)

8.
        I see the regions of snow and ice, 124

> I see the sharp-eyed Samoiede and the Finn,
> I see the seal-seeker in his boat poising his lance,
> I see the Siberian on his slight-built sledge drawn by dogs,
> I see the porpoise-hunters, I see the whale-crews of the south Pacific and the north Atlantic,
> I see the cliffs, glaciers, torrents, valleys, of Switzerland—I mark the long winters and the isolation.
>
> I see the cities of the earth and make myself at random a part of them, I am a real Parisian, 130
> I am a habitan of Vienna, St. Petersburg, Berlin, Constantinople,
> I am of Adelaide, Sidney, Melbourne,
> I am of London, Manchester, Bristol, Edinburgh, Limerick,
> I am of Madrid, Cadiz, Barcelona, Oporto, Lyons, Brussels, Berne, Frankfort, Stuttgart, Turin, Florence,
> I belong in Moscow, Cracow, Warsaw, or northward in Christiania or Stockholm, or in Siberian Irkutsk, or in some street in Iceland,
> I descend upon all those cities, and rise from them again. 137

(9.)

The 9th Canto, eventually. was removed from the poem and later became *A Paumanok Picture*. Whitman never replaced or reordered the sequence in the proper numeration. His vision becomes vaporous as he continues his world tour. He sees the picturesque and the defective of the earth and mixes among them indiscriminately: "I see the menials of the earth laboring, I see the defective human bodies of the earth, the blind, the deaf and dumb, idiots hunchbacks lunatics..."His catalogue continues through Cantos 10 – 13 until he arrives at the purport of his inexhaustible list:

> *Each of us inevitable, each of us is limitless – each of us with his or her right upon the earth, each of us allow'd the eternal purports of the earth, Each of us here as divinely as any is here... you will come forward in due time to my side.*

Whitman interpenetrates with mankind and they with him—each interpenetrating through time and space until they arrive at a waiting synapse in the mind of James Joyce:

> "The moment is now. Where then? If Socrates leave his house today, if Judas goes forth tonight. Why? That lies in space which I in time must come to, ineluctably." [224]

10.
> I see vapors exhaling from unexplored countries,
> I see the savage types, the bow and arrow, the poison'd splint, the fetich, and the obi.
> I see African and Asiatic towns,

138

I see Algiers, Tripoli, Derne, Mogadore, Timbuctoo, Monrovia,
I see the swarms of Pekin, Canton, Benares, Delhi, Calcutta, Tokio,
I see the Kruman in his hut, and the Dahoman and Ashantee-man in their huts,
I see the Turk smoking opium in Aleppo,
I see the picturesque crowds at the fairs of Khiva and those of Herat,
I see Teheran, I see Muscat and Medina and the intervening sands, see the caravans toiling onward, 146
I see Egypt and the Egyptians, I see the pyramids and obelisks.
I look on chisell'd histories, records of conquering kings, dynasties, cut in slabs of sand-stone, or on granite-blocks, 147
I see at Memphis mummy-pits containing mummies embalm'd, swathed in linen cloth, lying there many centuries,
I look on the fall'n Theban, the large-ball'd eyes, the side-drooping neck, the hands folded across the breast.

I see all the menials of the earth, laboring, 151
I see all the prisoners in the prisons,
I see the defective human bodies of the earth, 153
The blind, the deaf and dumb, idiots, hunchbacks, lunatics, 154

542

> The pirates, thieves, betrayers, murderers, slave-makers of the earth,
> The helpless infants, and the helpless old men and women.
>
> I see male and female everywhere,
> I see the serene brotherhood of philosophs,
> I see the constructiveness of my race,
> I see the results of the perseverance and industry of my race,
> I see ranks, colors, barbarisms, civilizations, I go among them, I mix indiscriminately,
> And I salute all the inhabitants of the earth. 162

The 11th Canto closes with the justly celebrated lines about inevitability. (Lines 195-198 below)

11.
> You whoever you are! 163
> You daughter or son of England!
> You of the mighty Slavic tribes and empires! you Russ in Russia!
> You dim-descended, black, divine-soul'd African, large, fine-headed, nobly-form'd, superbly destin'd, on equal terms with me!
> You Norwegian! Swede! Dane! Icelander! you Prussian!
> You Spaniard of Spain! you Portuguese!
> You Frenchwoman and Frenchman of France!

You Belge! you liberty-lover of the Netherlands! (you stock whence I myself have descended;)
You sturdy Austrian! you Lombard! Hun! Bohemian! farmer of Styria!
You neighbor of the Danube!
You working-man of the Rhine, the Elbe, or the Weser! you working-woman too!
You Sardinian! you Bavarian! Swabian! Saxon! Wallachian! Bulgarian!
You Roman! Neapolitan! you Greek!
You lithe matador in the arena at Seville!
You mountaineer living lawlessly on the Taurus or Caucasus!
You Bokh horse-herd watching your mares and stallions feeding!
You beautiful-bodied Persian at full speed in the saddle shooting arrows to the mark!
You Chinaman and Chinawoman of China! you Tartar of Tartary!
You women of the earth subordinated at your tasks!
You Jew journeying in your old age through every risk to stand once on Syrian ground!
You other Jews waiting in all lands for your Messiah!
You thoughtful Armenian pondering by some stream of the Euphrates! you peering amid the ruins of Nineveh! you ascending mount Ararat!

You foot-worn pilgrim welcoming the far-away sparkle of the minarets of Mecca!
You sheiks along the stretch from Suez to Bab-el-mandeb ruling your families and tribes!
You olive-grower tending your fruit on fields of Nazareth, Damascus, or lake Tiberias!
You Thibet trader on the wide inland or bargaining in the shops of Lassa!
You Japanese man or woman! you liver in Madagascar, Ceylon, Sumatra, Borneo!
All you continentals of Asia, Africa, Europe, Australia, indifferent of place!
All you on the numberless islands of the archipelagoes of the sea!
And you of centuries hence when you listen to me!
And you each and everywhere whom I specify not, but include just the same!
Health to you! good will to you all, from me and America sent!

Each of us inevitable,	195
Each of us limitless—each of us with his or her right upon the earth,	196
Each of us allow'd the eternal purports of the earth,	197
Each of us here as divinely as any is here.	198

12.

> You Hottentot with clicking palate! you woolly-hair'd hordes! 199
> You own'd persons dropping sweat-drops or blood-drops!
> You human forms with the fathomless ever-impressive countenances of brutes!
> You poor koboo whom the meanest of the rest look down upon for all your glimmering language and spirituality!
> You dwarf'd Kamtschatkan, Greenlander, Lapp!
> You Austral negro, naked, red, sooty, with protrusive lip,
> groveling, seeking your food!
> You Caffre, Berber, Soudanese!
> You haggard, uncouth, untutor'd Bedowee!
> You plague-swarms in Madras, Nankin, Kaubul, Cairo!
> You benighted roamer of Amazonia! you Patagonian! you Feejeeman!
> I do not prefer others so very much before you either,
> I do not say one word against you, away back there where you stand,
> (You will come forward in due time to my side.) 211

In the final canto of the poem the poet becomes one with the vapors of his vision as he is wafted by the very winds that accompanied the deific voice from the poem's commencement:

> You vapors, I think I have risen with
> you, moved away to distant continents,
> and fallen down there, for reasons, I
> think I have blown with you winds.
> (Lines 214-215 below)

In the ecstasy of his vision he has become the very mysteries of which Job was queried. He makes the magnificent signal to all whom he salutes in the whole of his wide world.

13.
> My spirit has pass'd in compassion and determination around the whole earth,   212
> I have look'd for equals and lovers and found them ready for me in all lands,
> I think some divine rapport has equalized me with them.
>
> You vapors, I think I have risen with you, moved away to distant continents, and fallen down there, for reasons,   215
> I think I have blown with you you winds;   216
> You waters I have finger'd every shore with you,
> I have run through what any river or strait of the globe has run through,
> I have taken my stand on the bases of peninsulas and on the high embedded rocks, to cry thence:

Salute au monde! 220
What cities the light or warmth penetrates I penetrate those cities myself, 221
All islands to which birds wing their way I wing my way myself. 222

Toward you all, in America's name,
I raise high the perpendicular hand,
I make the signal,
To remain after me in sight forever,
For all the haunts and homes of men. 227

14. Song of the Open Road

Song of the Open Road is a celebrated and justly popular piece among his masterworks. It partakes of the inspiration that was flagless in the early editions of his *Leaves*. This is one of the twenty poems that were added to the 2nd edition of 1856 and was there entitled *Poem of the Road*. The first line competes with those of *Lilacs* and *Song of Myself* for the immediate force and identity of its lyric. Emerson's *Self Reliance* is a strong precursor and is noted often below. Its greatest strength is the intimacy in which it speaks—few are the readers who believe that the poet is addressing any one other than themselves.

Isadora Duncan was an avid Whitman fan. She based much of her innovation in dance on the inspiration she drew from him. In her autobiography she suggests that she is the spiritual daughter of the poet. Whitman's exaltation of the body gave her the spiritual permission to express all aspects of it in her movement.

At the end of one performance, more was exposed than was planned or expected. She quickly composed herself and challenged the audience to go home and pull Walt Whitman from their library shelves. *Song of the Open Road* was her favorite from among his poems.

Isadora Duncan:

1877-1927
Bayreuth Festival

Whitman's call to rebellion was of particular note to Duncan and a whole cadre of artists who were coming of age in the early decades of the twentieth century. They who would feel *loos'd of limits and imaginary lines; going where they list, their own master total and absolute.* Among them we find Marcel Duchamp, Robert Henri, John Marin and Joseph Stella in painting; Louis Sullivan and Frank Lloyd Wright in architecture; Ezra Pound Gertrude Stein, T.S. Eliot, William Carlos Williams, Wallace Stevens, Hart Crane, John Dos Passos, Henry Miller and Ernest Hemingway in the poetry and literature of the new century.

In the middle decades of the last century *Song of the Open Road* was a favorite among *Beat* poets. Jack Kerouac and Neal Cassidy took up the poet's challenge, and never looked back at the road receding. In their darker moments they might have suspected that Whitman's *Song* was more a pose than a promise. The Dharma Bums discovered that the *Dharma* of Whitman's Open Road was not always one of unencumbered sunlit freedom. Alan Watts became a friend of Kerouac and was featured in *The Dharma Bums* as the character, Arthur Whane. Watts latter disparaged what he called the self-consciousness of *beat-zen*: "a share too self-conscious, too subjective, and too strident to have the flavor of Zen."[225]

Borges rightly intuited that the "mere happy vagabond proposed in the verses of *Leaves of Grass* would have been incapable of writing them." [226] Whitman traveled to New Orleans with his brother Jeff in 1848.

A month after leaving his editorship at the *Brooklyn Eagle* he ran into a J.E. McClure while attending a theatrical performance in New York City. McClure was starting a newspaper in New Orleans, *The New Orleans Crescent*. After a few drinks McClure offered the editor's job to Whitman before their shared intermission had concluded. Theretofore, Whitman's idea of travel had been Brooklyn ferries and Broadway stage buses. The trip to New Orleans would be one of two major trips he would embark upon during his lifetime. The brothers were given two hundred dollars to cover the expense of their journey. They first went by train from Brooklyn to Baltimore. After a night in Baltimore they took another train to Cumberland. And then took a stage coach over the mountains to Wheeling West Virginia. This was an all night journey which was only interrupted for a couple of meals and exchanges of fresh horses. They then boarded a steamship and traveled various waterways for nearly two weeks before sliding down the Mississippi to the Cajun hothouse of New Orleans. This and the return trip to the northeast were recorded in a diary the poet kept. It would be these impressions that would flood in upon him as he romanticized his travels winging across the nation in *Leaves of Grass*. The poet, of course, is using the road as a metaphor for our respective lives. *Song of the Open Road* and *Crossing Brooklyn Ferry* are his two most celebrated poems on this theme. The road or the flowing river of Heraclitus is a traditional trope for change, movement, thought, creation, love and finally, death. Whitman would be largely incapacitated less than two decades after writing this poem but his mental journeys would continue for nearly two additional decades after that first paralytic stroke. The road is an interior formulation.

In Eliot's *Four Quartets* there is a similar trope concerning a river:

> I do not know much about gods; but I think the river
> Is a strong brown god—sullen, untamed and intractable,
> Useful, untrustworthy, as a conveyor of commerce;
> Then only a problem confronting the builder of bridges.
> The problem once solved, the brown god is almost forgotten
> By the dwellers in the city—ever, however, implacable,
> Keeping his seasons and rages, destroyer, reminder
> Of the machine, but waiting, watching and waiting.
> His rhythm was present in the nursery bedroom,
> In the rank ailanthus of the April dooryard,
> In the smell of grapes on the autumn table.
> And the evening circle in the winter gaslite.
> The river is within us the sea is all around us.

The road is within the Poet—there is nothing so small or soft but it makes a *hub for the universe* spinning about him. The Mundaka Upanishad conveys the same message:

> "The flowing river is lost in the sea; the illuminated sage is lost in the Self.
> The flowing river has become the sea.
> The illuminated sage has become the Self."

Eliot's description of the river is not dissimilar to Whitman's description of himself — sullen, untamed, and intractable — but it is to the "sea, death, night and the stars" to which the poet is inevitably drawn. Here we also dimly anticipate a lilac blooming in an April dooryard. Nonetheless, there is a ringing truth to a poet finding the earth sufficient on which to plant his feet as he gazes outward to the stars. Here we find the profound lesson of Whitman's *reception:* to open our minds and senses to a new and ancient Universe that greets us each dawn. The road awaits us, we best not dally...

Song of the Open Road.

1.

>
> Afoot and light-hearted I take to the open road,
> Healthy, free, the world before me,
> The long brown path before me leading wherever I choose. 3
>
> Henceforth I ask not good-fortune, I myself am good-fortune, 4
> Henceforth I whimper no more, postpone no more, need nothing,
> Done with indoor complaints, libraries, querulous criticisms,

> Strong and content I travel the open road.
>
> The earth, that is sufficient,   8
> I do not want the constellations any nearer,   9
> I know they are very well where they are,   10
> I know they suffice for those who belong to them.
>
> (Still here I carry my old delicious burdens,
> I carry them, men and women, I carry them with me wherever I go,
> I swear it is impossible for me to get rid of them,
> I am fill'd with them, and I will fill them in return.)   15

In the first stanza of the 2nd Canto the poet returns to his theme of the unseen: *You road I enter upon and look around, I believe you are not all that is here, I believe that much unseen is also here.* (Line 16 -- See also line 29 below) The slave, the felon, the diseas'd and the illiterate are not to be denied. It is a theme the poet will return to time and again. The road judges them not. The mountains by the roadside are neither better nor worse for being of lesser or greater stature then those that succeed them in the distance — *none can be interdicted*

2.
> You road I enter upon and look around,
>   I believe you are not all that is here,   16
>   I believe that much unseen is also here.   17

> Here the profound lesson of reception, nor preference nor denial, 18
> The black with his woolly head, the felon, the diseas'd, the illiterate person, are not denied;
> The birth, the hasting after the physician, the beggar's tramp, the drunkard's stagger, the laughing party of mechanics,
> The escaped youth, the rich person's carriage, the fop, the eloping couple,
> The early market-man, the hearse, the moving of furniture into the town, the return back from the town,
> They pass, I also pass, any thing passes, none can be interdicted,
> None but are accepted, none but shall be dear to me. 24

3.

> You air that serves me with breath to speak! 25
> You objects that call from diffusion my meanings and give them shape!
> You light that wraps me and all things in delicate equable showers!
> You paths worn in the irregular hollows by the roadsides!
> I believe you are latent with unseen existences, you are so dear to me. 29

The world calls forth the poet's meanings. In his expansiveness the very stones impart impressions from the living and the dead that have trod upon them:

You flagg'd walks of the cities! you
strong curbs at the edges! 30
You ferries! you planks and posts of
wharves! you timber-lined side! you
distant ships!
You rows of houses! you window-
pierc'd facades! you roofs!
You porches and entrances! you copings
and iron guards!
You windows whose transparent shells
might expose so much!
You doors and ascending steps! you
arches!
You gray stones of interminable
pavements! you trodden crossings!
From all that has touch'd you I believe
you have imparted to yourselves,
and now would impart the same
secretly to me,
From the living and the dead you have
peopled your impassive surfaces,
and the spirits thereof would be
evident and amicable with me. 38

4.

The earth expanding right hand and left
hand, 39
The picture alive, every part in its best
light,
The music falling in where it is wanted,
and stopping where it is not
wanted,
The cheerful voice of the public road,
the gay fresh sentiment of the road.

> O highway I travel, do you say to me *Do not leave me?*
> Do you say Venture not—if you leave me you are lost?
> Do you say I am already prepared, I am well-beaten and undenied, adhere to me?
> O public road, I say back I am not afraid to leave you, yet I love you,
> You express me better than I can express myself,
> You shall be more to me than my poem.
>
> I think heroic deeds were all conceiv'd in the open air, and all free poems also,
> I think I could stop here myself and do miracles,   50
> I think whatever I shall meet on the road I shall like, and whoever beholds me shall like me,
> I think whoever I see must be happy.   52

The forth stanza of Canto 4's *I think I could stop here myself and do miracles* and *whoever beholds me shall like me,* is nicely balanced by the pronouncement of freedom of the first line of Canto 5 and his celebration of the compass in stanzas two and three.

The poet marvels at his expansive nature. He *is* the four points of the compass and all they contain: *I inhale great draughts of space, the east and the west are mine, and the north and the south are mine. I am larger, better than I thought.* (Lines 54-60 below)

5.

> From this hour I ordain myself loos'd of
>   limits and imaginary lines, 53
> Going where I list, my own master total
>   and absolute,
> Listening to others, considering well
>   what they say,
> Pausing, searching, receiving,
>   contemplating,
> Gently, but with undeniable will,
>   divesting myself of the holds that
>   would hold me.
>
> I inhale great draughts of space, 58
> The east and the west are mine, and the
>   north and the south are mine.
>
> I am larger, better than I thought, 60
> I did not know I held so much
>   goodness.
>
> All seems beautiful to me, 62
> I can repeat over to men and women
>   You have done such good to me   I
>   would do the same to you,[227]
> I will recruit for myself and you as I go,
> I will scatter myself among men and
>   women as I go,
> I will toss a new gladness and
>   roughness among them,
> Whoever denies me it shall not trouble
>   me,
> Whoever accepts me he or she shall be
>   blessed and shall bless me. 68

6.

> Now if a thousand perfect men were to
> appear it would not amaze me, 69
> Now if a thousand beautiful forms of
> women appear'd it would not
> astonish me.
>
> Now I see the secret of the making of
> the best persons,
> It is to grow in the open air and to eat
> and sleep with the earth.
> Here a great personal deed has room, 73
> (Such a deed seizes upon the hearts of
> the whole race of men,
> Its effusion of strength and will
> overwhelms law and mocks all
> authority and all argument against
> it.)
>
> Here is the test of wisdom,
> Wisdom is not finally tested in schools,
> Wisdom cannot be pass'd from one
> having it to another not having it, 78

Michael Ventura quoted the 3rd stanza of Canto 6 (Line 73 above) in his essay on *The Death of John Wayne*. It came to his mind when he first saw the startling close up of the Ringo Kid in John Ford's *Stagecoach*: "That shot made Wayne a star. In Monument Valley 'a great personal deed has room.' " Few open roads are as worthy a song. We suspect Emerson is, again, close at hand and can easily accompany the younger poet. The remainder of Canto 6 through 13 proceeds in those lines identified as Whitman's

Each of Whitman's sections will be enclosed by numerical notation and each continuing canto identified by its respective number to assist the reader in navigating the *duet*. Song *of the Open Road* concludes unimpaired in Cantos 14 and 15. This is the first of three *Songs* that the two American masters will share. Emerson, as will be seen, was the younger poet's ultimate guide and Comerado, whether on or off the open road.

Emerson:

> The same reality pervades all teaching. The man may teach by doing and not otherwise. If he can communicate himself he can teach, but not by the words. He teaches who gives, and he learns who receives. There is no teaching until the pupil is brought into the same state or principle in which you are; a transfusion takes place; he is in you and you are in he; then is a teaching." [228]

Whitman:
Canto 6 (cont.)

> Wisdom is of the soul, is not susceptible of proof, is its own proof, 79
> Applies to all stages and objects and qualities and is content,
> Is the certainty of the reality and immortality of things, and the excellence of things;

> Something there is in the float of the sight of things that provokes it out of the soul. 82

Emerson:

> Whoso would be a man, must be nonconformist. He who would gather immortal palms must not be hindered by the name goodness, but must explore if it be goodness. Nothing is at last sacred but the integrity of your own mind. Good and bad are but names very ready transferable to that or this; the only right is what is after my constitution; the only wrong what is against it." [229]

Whitman:

> Now I re-examine philosophies and religions, 83
> They may prove well in lecture-rooms, yet not prove at all under the spacious clouds and along the landscape and flowing currents. 84

Emerson:

> In this pleasing contrite wood-life which God allows me, let me record day by day my honest thought without prospect or retrospect...my book should smell of pines and resound with the hum of insects. [230]

Whitman:

> Here is realization, 85
> Here is a man tallied—he realizes here what he has in him,
> The past, the future, majesty, love—if they are vacant of you, you are vacant of them. 86

Emerson:

> No man can learn what he has not preparation for learning however near to his eyes are the object. A chemist may tell his most precious secret to the carpenter and he shall be never the wiser... our eyes are beholden that we can not see things that stare us in the face until the hour arrives when the mind is ripened; then we behold them and the time we saw them not is like a dream.[231]

Whitman:

> Only the kernel of every object nourishes; 87
> Where is he who tears off the husks for you and me?
> Where is he that undoes stratagems and envelopes for you and me?
>
> Here is adhesiveness, it is not previously fashion'd, it is apropos;
> Do you know what it is as you pass to be loved by strangers?

> Do you know the talk of those turning eye-balls? 92

Emerson:

> A just thinker will allow full swing to his skepticism. I dip my pen in the blackest ink because I am not afraid of falling into my inkpot. I have no sympathy with a poor man, I knew, who, when suicides abounded, told me he dared not look at his razor. [232]

Whitman:

7.

> Here is the efflux of the soul, 93
> The efflux of the soul comes from within through embower'd gates, ever provoking questions,
> These yearnings why are they? these thoughts in the darkness why are they? 95
> Why are there men and women that while they are nigh me the sunlight expands my blood?
> Why when they leave me do my pennants of joy sink flat and lank?
> Why are there trees I never walk under but large and melodious thoughts descend upon me? 97
> (I think they hang there winter and summer on those trees and always drop fruit as I pass:) 98

What is it I interchange so suddenly
    with strangers?
What with some driver as I ride on the
    seat by his side?
What with some fisherman drawing his
    seine by the shore as I walk by and
    pause?
What gives me to be free to a woman's
    and man's good-will? what gives
    them to be free to mine?   104

Emerson:

When good is near you, when you have life in yourself, it is not by any known or accustomed way; you shall not discern the footprints of any other; you shall not see the face of any man; you shall not hear any name; the way, the thought, the good, shall be wholly strange and new. It shall exclude example and experience.

You take the way from man, not to man. All persons who have ever existed are its forgotten ministers… the soul raised over passion beholds identity and eternal causation, perceives the self existence of Truth and Right, and calms itself knowing that all things go well. Vast spaces of nature, the Atlantic Ocean, the South Sea; long intervals of time[233], years, centuries, are of no account. [234]

Whitman:

8.
>   The efflux of the soul is happiness, here is happiness, 105
>   I think it pervades the open air, waiting at all times,
>   Now it flows unto us, we are rightly charged. 107

Emerson:

> I am thankful for small mercies. I compared notes with one of my friends who expects everything from the Universe and is disappointed when anything is less then the best, and I found I begin at the other extreme expecting nothing and am always full of thanks for moderate goods...The results of life are uncalculated and uncalcuable. The years teach much that the days never know.

Whitman:

>   Here rises the fluid and attaching character, 108
>   The fluid and attaching character is the freshness and sweetness of man and woman,
>   (The herbs of the morning sprout no fresher and sweeter every day out of the roots of themselves, than it sprouts fresh and sweet continually out of itself.) 110

Emerson:

> God builds his temple in the heart on the ruins of churches and religions…Heaven always bears some proportion to the earth. The god of the cannibals will be a cannibal; of the crusaders, a crusader; of the merchants, a merchant.[235]

Whitman:

> Toward the fluid and attaching character exudes the sweat of the love of young and old,   111
> From it falls distill'd the charm that mocks beauty and attainments,
> Toward it heaves the shuddering longing ache of contact.   113

9.

> Allons! whoever you are come travel with me!   114
> Traveling with me you find what never tires.
>
> The earth never tires,
> The earth is rude, silent, incomprehensible at first, Nature is rude and incomprehensible at first,
> Be not discouraged, keep on, there are divine things well envelop'd,
> I swear to you there are divine things more beautiful than words can tell.   119

Emerson:

> ...that which is coexistent or ejaculated from a deeper cause as yet far from being conscious knows not its own tendency... bear with these distractions, with this coetaneous growth of the parts; they will one day be members and obey one will...Underneath the inharmonious and trivial particulars is a musical perfection; the Ideal journeying always with us, the heaven without rent or seam." [236]

Whitman:

> Allons! we must not stop here,   120
> However sweet these laid-up stores, however convenient this dwelling we cannot remain here,
> However shelter'd this port and however calm these waters we must not anchor here,
> However welcome the hospitality that surrounds us we are permitted to receive it but a little while.   123

Emerson:

> Suffice it for the joy of the universe that we have not arrived at a wall, but at interminable oceans."[237]

Whitman:

10.
> Allons! the inducements shall be greater, 124
> We will sail pathless and wild seas,
> We will go where winds blow, waves dash, and the Yankee clipper speeds by under full sail.
>
> Allons! with power, liberty, the earth, the elements,
> Health, defiance, gayety, self-esteem, curiosity;
> Allons! from all formules!
> From your formules, O bat-eyed and materialistic priests.
>
> The stale cadaver blocks up the passage — the burial waits no longer.
>
> Allons! yet take warning!
> He traveling with me needs the best blood, thews, endurance, 133

Emerson:

> The civilized man has built a coach but has lost the use of his feet. He is supported by crutches but lacks so much muscle. [238]

Canto 10 (concl.)

Whitman:

None may come to the trial till he or she bring courage and health, 134
Come not here if you have already spent the best of yourself,
Only those may come who come in sweet and determin'd bodies,
No diseas'd person, no rum-drinker or venereal taint is permitted here.

(I and mine do not convince by arguments, similes, rhymes,
We convince by our presence.) 139

11.

Listen! I will be honest with you, 140
I do not offer the old smooth prizes, but offer rough new prizes,
These are the days that must happen to you: 142
You shall not heap up what is call'd riches,
You shall scatter with lavish hand all that you earn or achieve, 144
You but arrive at the city to which you were destin'd, you hardly settle yourself to satisfaction before you are call'd by an irresistible call to depart,
You shall be treated to the ironical smiles and mockings of those who remain behind you,
What beckonings of love you receive you shall only answer with passionate kisses of parting,

> You shall not allow the hold of those who spread their reach'd hands toward you. 148

12.

> Allons! after the great Companions, and to belong to them! 149
> They too are on the road — they are the swift and majestic men — they are the greatest women, 150

Emerson:

> Do that which is assigned to you and you can not hope too much or dare too much. There is at this moment for you an utterance brave and grand as that of the colossal chisel of Phidas, or trowel of the Egyptians or the pen of Moses or Dante…[239]

Canto 12 (cont.)

Whitman:

> Enjoyers of calms of seas and storms of seas, 151
> Sailors of many a ship, walkers of many a mile of land,
> Habitues of many distant countries, habitues of far-distant dwellings,
> Trusters of men and women, observers of cities, solitary toilers,
> Pausers and contemplators of tufts, blossoms, shells of the shore,

Dancers at wedding-dances, kissers of brides, tender helpers of children, bearers of children,
Soldiers of revolts, standers by gaping graves, lowerers-down of coffins,
Journeyers over consecutive seasons, over the years, the curious years each emerging from that which preceded it,
Journeyers as with companions, namely their own diverse phases,
Forth-steppers from the latent unrealized baby-days,
Journeyers gayly with their own youth, journeyers with their bearded and well-grain'd manhood,
Journeyers with their womanhood, ample, unsurpass'd, content,
Journeyers with their own sublime old age of manhood or womanhood,
Old age, calm, expanded, broad with the haughty breadth of the universe,
Old age, flowing free with the delicious near-by freedom of death. 165

13.

Allons! to that which is endless as it was beginningless, 166
To undergo much, tramps of days, rests of nights,
To merge all in the travel they tend to, and the days and nights they tend to,
Again to merge them in the start of superior journeys,

To see nothing anywhere but what you may reach it and pass it,	170
To conceive no time, however distant, but what you may reach it and pass it,	171
To look up or down no road but it stretches and waits for you, however long but it stretches and waits for you,	172
To see no being, not God's or any, but you also go thither,	173
To see no possession but you may possess it, enjoying all without labor or purchase, abstracting the feast yet not abstracting one particle of it,	
To take the best of the farmer's farm and the rich man's elegant villa, and the chaste blessings of the well-married couple, and the fruits of orchards and flowers of gardens,	
To take to your use out of the compact cities as you pass through,	
To carry buildings and streets with you afterward wherever you go,	
To gather the minds of men out of their brains as you encounter them, to gather the love out of their hearts,	178
To take your lovers on the road with you, for all that you leave them behind you,	
To know the universe itself as a road, as many roads, as roads for traveling souls.	180
All parts away for the progress of souls,	181

> All religion, all solid things, arts, governments—all that was or is apparent upon this globe or any globe, falls into niches and corners before the procession of souls along the grand roads of the universe.
>
> Of the progress of the souls of men and women along the grand roads of the universe, all other progress is the needed emblem and sustenance. 182

Emerson:

> The consciousness in each man is a sliding scale which identifies him now with the first cause and now with the flesh of his body; life above life in infinite degrees. [240]

Whitman:

> Forever alive, forever forward, 183
> Stately, solemn, sad, withdrawn, baffled, mad, turbulent, feeble, dissatisfied,
> Desperate, proud, fond, sick, accepted by men, rejected by men,
> They go! they go! I know that they go, but I know not where they go,
> But I know that they go toward the best—toward something great. 187
>
> Whoever you are, come forth! or man or woman come forth!

You must not stay sleeping and dallying there in the house, though you built it, or though it has been built for you.

Out of the dark confinement! out from behind the screen!
It is useless to protest, I know all and expose it.

Behold through you as bad as the rest,
Through the laughter, dancing, dining, supping, of people,
Inside of dresses and ornaments, inside of those wash'd and trimm'd faces,
Behold a secret silent loathing and despair. 196

No husband, no wife, no friend, trusted to hear the confession,
Another self, a duplicate of every one, skulking and hiding it goes, 198
Formless and wordless through the streets of the cities, polite and bland in the parlors,
In the cars of railroads, in steamboats, in the public assembly,
Home to the houses of men and women, at the table, in the bedroom, everywhere,
Smartly attired, countenance smiling, form upright, death under the breast-bones, hell under the skull-bones, 202

> Under the broadcloth and gloves, under the ribbons and artificial flowers,
> Keeping fair with the customs, speaking not a syllable of itself,
> Speaking of any thing else but never of itself. 205

14.

> Allons! through struggles and wars! 206
> The goal that was named cannot be countermanded.
>
> Have the past struggles succeeded?
> What has succeeded? yourself? your nation? Nature?
> Now understand me well—it is provided in the essence of things that from any fruition of success, no matter what, shall come forth something to make a greater struggle necessary.
> My call is the call of battle, I nourish active rebellion, 211
> He going with me must go well arm'd,
> He going with me goes often with spare diet, poverty, angry enemies, desertions. 213

Emerson had once suggested: "I am very much struck in literature by the appearance that one person wrote all the books: as if the editor of a journal planned his body of reporters in different parts of the fields of action and relieved some by others from time to time; there is such an equality and identity both of judgment and point of view in the narrative that its is plainly the work of one all-seeing, all-hearing gentleman."[241]

Certainly, in *Song of the Open Road* the two spirits are in accord. In these final Cantos the younger poet finds very much his own voice. Who but Whitman could proclaim of flesh and thought: "death under the breast bones and hell under the skull bones." (Line 202 above) Yet beneath his call to anarchy is a blessed invitation—no more intimate, generous, or tempting offer has ever been extended from author to reader:

15.
> Allons! the road is before us! 214
> It is safe—I have tried it—my own feet
> have tried it well—be not detain'd!
>
> Let the paper remain on the desk
> unwritten, and the book on the self
> unopen'd!
> Let the tools remain in the workshop! let
> the money remain unearn'd!
> Let the school stand! mind not the cry of
> the teacher!
> Let the preacher preach in his pulpit! let
> the lawyer plead in the court, and
> the judge expound the law.
>
> Camerado, I give you my hand! 220
> I give you my love more precious than
> money,
> I give you myself before preaching or
> law;
> Will you give me yourself? will you
> come travel with me?
> Shall we stick by each other as long as
> we live? 224

15. Crossing Brooklyn Ferry

"Sun-Down Poem" followed the titling conceit of all the 1856 poems by having the word, "Poem," in the title. Whitman had been hurt by the reception of the first edition. The critics had wondered if *Leaves of Grass* was more prose than poetry. Whitman wished to boldly assert that each piece was, in fact, a poem. He needn't have concerned himself with the poem that by 1860 would be known as "Crossing Brooklyn Ferry". It is easily one of the greatest poems in the World's Canon.

The theme of time as suggested by the Ferry occurred to the poet in the 7th of his Sunday Dispatch essays called *Letters from a Traveling Bachelor*:

> You and I, reader, and quite all the people who are now alive, won't be much thought of then; but the world will be just as jolly, and the sun will shine as bright, and the rivers off there — the Hudson on one side and the East on the other — will slap along their green waves, precisely as now; and other eyes will look upon them about the same as we do.[242]

This work is among the loveliest, most meditative, and greatest of his poems. In *Song of the Open Road* the poet transcended time to invite us on his journey. *In Crossing Brooklyn Ferry* he is rather in the midst of time's eternity — seeing it pass in the flowing current and the setting sun and in the faces of his fellow passengers. He anticipates my words and those of other chroniclers who gaze back even as the poet had gazed forward.

As noted before, this poem was one of Thoreau's favorites. Whitman had given the author a copy of the 1856 edition of *Leaves of Grass* shortly after it had been published. Thoreau's earlier reservations about the poet were put to rest within a few days of reading the "Sundown Poem":

> He (Whitman) occasionally suggests something a little more than human. You can't confound him with the other inhabitants of Brooklyn or New York. How they must shudder when they read him!... Since I have seen him I find that I am not disturbed by any brag or egoism in his book. He may turn out to be the least braggart of all, having a better right to be confident. He is a great fellow. [243]

The poem's progeny is a distinguished family of poets whose work pays homage to the poem's mythos of Eros and death. Chief among these is the star-crossed Hart Crane. Crane began *The Bridge* in 1923 and finished two years before his suicide in 1932. When Whitman composed *Sundown Poem* the ferry was the main transit between Manhattan and Brooklyn. Crane's epic surveys much the same seascape of yearning as Whitman's poem. The Brooklyn Bridge took the ferry's place as the main connection between the two shores. It also appears in Ginsberg's similarly linked *Howl*:

> ...in the roaring winter dusks of Brooklyn, ashcan rantings and kind king light of mind, who chained themselves to subways for the endless ride from

> Battery to holy Bronx on benzedrineuntil the noise of wheels and children brought them down shuddering mouth-wracked and battered bleak of brain all drained of brilliance in the drear light of Zoo, who sank all night in submarine light of Bickford's floated out and sat through the stale beer afternoon in desolate Fugazzi's, listening to the crack of doom on the hydrogen jukebox, who talked continuously seventy hours from park to pad to bar to Bellevue to museum to the Brooklyn Bridge...

Whitman was ambiguous about industrial expansion. Industries were growing cities but signaling the decline of his agrarian ideals. In *Song of the Exposition* he applauds the arrival of the machine age and the engineering wonders of the Suez Canal and the laying of the Atlantic Cable—the connection of the Old World to the New. His brothers George Washington and Thomas Jefferson eschewed politics (and poetry—none in the family, besides Walt, had much of an ear for it) and became involved in the water works of Brooklyn and New York. Utility companies were a bridge between science and industry. Surviving the Civil War, George later became a member of the New York Metropolitan Water Board and for a Whitman, would die financially relatively well-off. Jeff was a member of the American Society of Civil Engineers. He was initially involved in the design of the celebrated Brooklyn Water Works and later helped design the waterworks of a half dozen facilities across the Midwest.

The Brooklyn Bridge was another wonder of the age. It was built over a period of thirteen years between 1870 and 1883 from a design by John Augustus Roebling. During an early survey of the East River an arriving ferry crushed Roebling's foot against a pylon at the ferry's terminus. His toes were amputated and he died of tetanus within a month of the accident. His son, Washington Roebling took over the project. Twenty-seven men died during the construction of the bridge. Washington Roebling was stricken with the bends during work beneath the river. His wife, Emily Warren Roebling learned engineering and later communicated his instructions to workers on the site. She was the first person to walk across the expanse of the bridge. If she managed to escape death at the hands of an engineering marvel, her son did not. Washington Roebling Jr. died when the Titanic dropped to the bottom of the Atlantic in April of 1912. The metaphor of water in connection with time is (almost) itself, timeless harkening back most famously to Heraclitus, Egyptian papyri and the stone-cut cuneiform of Gilgamesh. Hart Crane uses the bridge as a link in time between the former poet and himself. The bridge is the bridge between their respective eras and longings. In the Cape Hattera's section of his poem he challenges Whitman's relentless optimism when viewing the disappointments that were the reality of Crane's Manhattan prison crypts lining the labyrinthine stone canyons of New York City:

> Walt, tell me Walt Whitman, if infinity
> Be still the same as when you walked
>   the beach
> Near Paumanok—your lone patrol—
>   and heard the wraith

> Through surf, its bird note there a long time falling...
> For you — the panoramas and this breed of towers,
> Of you — the theme that's saturated in the cliff.
> O Saunterer on the free ways still ahead!
> Not this our empire yet, but labyrinth
> Wherein your eyes, like the Great Navigator's without ship,
> Gleam from the great stones of each prison crypt
> Of canyoned traffic...Confronting the Exchange,
> Surviving in a world of stocks, they also range
> Across the hills where second timber strays
> Back over Connecticut farms, abandoned pastures,-
> Sea eyes and tidal, undenying, bright with myth!

Whitman's homosexuality, latent or no, was also a bridge to the tattered soul of Hart Crane. Cape Hatteras is a cape on the North Carolina coastline. It is the point that protrudes the farthest to the southeast along the northeast-to-southwest line. In Whitman's *Song of Myself* (Canto 28) the protruding Cape is called a *headland* and has phallic significance:

> The sentries desert every other part of me,
> They have left me helpless to a red marauder,
> They all come to the headland to witness and assist against me.

> I am given up by traitors,
> I talk wildly, I have lost my wits, I and nobody
>   else am the greatest traitor,
> I went myself first to the headland, my own
> hands carried me there.
> You villain touch! what are you doing? my
> breath tightens in my throat,   Unclench your
> floodgates, you are too much for me.

Whitman reaches forward to Hart Crane even as Crane reaches back to him. The bridge of Crane's *The Bridge* is also "time." The two poets are bound in Crane's apostrophe:

> thou who on boldest heel
> stood up and flung the span on even
>   wing
> Of that great Bridge, our Myth, whereof
>   I sing.

The elements in Whitman's poem are immediately personified: "Flood-tide below me! I see you face to face!" So also with the clouds of the west and the "sun there half an hour high—I see you also face to face." The ferry is the link between his fellow passengers and those he anticipates:

> Crowds of men and women attired in
> the usual costumes, how curious you
> are to me...and you that shall cross from
> shore to shore years hence are more to
> me, and more in my meditations, than
> you might suppose.

As previously, on the *Open Road*, we are now invited to board a ferry between two very different shores. As another poet will come to note:

> You are not the same people who left
> that station or who will arrive at any
> terminus.

The same is true of the Prajnaparamita texts referenced in this volume's concluding chapter — *Passage to India, Redux*. Prajna is the Holy Grail among adepts of Mahayana Buddhism. Simply put, it is Wisdom. But it is wisdom that ties time to eternity, space to the infinite and the many to the One. Emerson and Whitman are America's preeminent mentors of Prajna. Paramita, put simply — is Yonder Shore. Nowhere in Whitman is the sentiment of the Wisdom of the *Yonder Shore* explored more cogently than in the tropes of *Crossing Brooklyn Ferry*:

> Others will enter the gates of the ferry
> and cross from shore to shore,

The thoughtful reader will be transformed — this is a transcendent poem, ascending from sea to sky — while never distant from eternal dockage.

Hart Crane & Brooklyn Bridge:

WHITMAN'S CODE: A NEW BIBLE, VOLUME I
M.C. GARDNER

1899 – 1932

Crossing Brooklyn Ferry

(1855)

1.

Flood-tide below me! I see you face to face!

Clouds of the west—sun there half an hour high—I see you also face to face. 2

Crowds of men and women attired in the usual costumes, how curious you are to me!

On the ferry-boats the hundreds and hundreds that cross, returning home, are more curious to me than you suppose,

And you that shall cross from shore to shore years hence are more
to me, and more in my meditations, than you might suppose. 5

2.

The impalpable sustenance of me from all things at all hours of the day, 6

The simple, compact, well-join'd scheme, myself disintegrated, every one disintegrated yet part of the scheme, 7

The similitudes of the past and those of the future,

The glories strung like beads on my smallest sights and hearings, on the walk in the street and the passage over the river, 9

> The current rushing so swiftly and swimming with me far away,
> The others that are to follow me, the ties between me and them, 11
> The certainty of others, the life, love, sight, hearing of others. 12
>
> Others will enter the gates of the ferry and cross from shore to shore, 13
> Others will watch the run of the flood-tide,
> Others will see the shipping of Manhattan north and west, and the heights of Brooklyn to the south and east,
> Others will see the islands large and small;
> Fifty years hence, others will see them as they cross, the sun half an hour high,
> A hundred years hence, or ever so many hundred years hence, others will see them,
> Will enjoy the sunset, the pouring-in of the flood-tide, the falling-back to the sea of the ebb-tide. 19

Whitman contrasts his impalpable sustenance with an awareness of his palpable disintegration. Living is also at every moment dying—yet between the twain are the *glories strung like beads on* his *smallest sights and hearing.* This an astonishing line set among the beautiful low key observations of his opening salvos. The poet sees his fellow passengers as agents of time—*fifty, one hundred years hence:*

Less than a hundred years later Hart Crane will write of the bridge and the same expanse it spanned:

> Sheerly the eyes, like seagulls stung with rime—
> Slit and propelled by glistening fins of light—
> Pick biting way up towering looms that press
> Sidelong with flight of blade on tendon blade—Tomorrows
> into yesteryear—and link
> What cipher-script of time no traveler reads
> But who, through smoking pyres of love and death,
> Searches the timeless laugh of mythic spears.

Remembering Whitman and anticipating Tennessee Williams, Crane concludes his poem: "Now pity steeps the grass and rainbow ring / The serpent with the eagle in leaves...? / Whispers antiphonal in azure swing." Williams had often stated a desire to be buried at sea at the point where Crane had leapt into the Caribbean. He was, in fact, interred in Calvary Cemetery, St. Louis, Missouri. He had choked to death on an eye-drop cap that he had placed in his mouth while administering medication. Along with these celebrated artists, each of us, as Whitman foresees: "...will enter the gates of the ferry and cross from shore to shore." The 3rd canto continues the theme of commonality between the poet and all men. It is three lines shy of the thirty-one that concludes the poem in the ninth canto.

Whitman believes that his fellow travelers and those in future generations share the loveliness of his poetic vision. There is a lilting sadness to his address to generations hence. His diction is from the grave. His reader's vision is put in the present tense while that of the poet is relegated to the past. He assures us that he is with us but there is a heartbreaking finality to his placement in an earlier time now extinct. We are left with the distinct feeling that the beauty of an image achieves its own immortality:

> The scallop-edged waves in the twilight,
> the ladled cups, the frolic-some crests
> and glistening,

If we had not, heretofore, taken that backward glance, we can surely do so now. Few moments in World Literature are as contemplative as the remarkable 3rd, 4th, and 5th Cantos of this poem. The reader should note that in the five lines of Canto 4, the poet is looking forward to him or her and imagines, as well, the reader looking back to the poet. Whitman knows that we too will avail ourselves of his imaginative conceit and look forward to a progeny reflecting on our own oblivion. The 3rd Canto concludes with an image of less than complete assurance: (Lines 47-48 below)

3.
> It avails not, time nor place—distance
>   avails not,   30
> I am with you, you men and women of
>   a generation, or ever so many
>   generations hence,
> Just as you feel when you look on the
>   river and sky, so I felt,   32

Just as any of you is one of a living crowd, I was one of a crowd,
Just as you are refresh'd by the gladness of the river and the bright flow, I was fresh'd, you stand and lean on the rail, yet hurry with the swift current,
I stood was hurried,
Just as you look on the numberless masts of ships and the thick-stemm'd pipes of steamboats, I look'd. 26

I too many and many a time cross'd the river of old,
Watched the Twelfth-month sea-gulls, saw them high in the air
   floating with motionless wings, oscillating their bodies, 28
Saw how the glistening yellow lit up parts of their bodies and left the rest in strong shadow,
Saw the slow-wheeling circles and the gradual edging toward the south,
Saw the reflection of the summer sky in the water,
Had my eyes dazzled by the shimmering track of beams,
Look'd at the fine centrifugal spokes of light round the shape of my head in the sunlit water,
Look'd on the haze on the hills southward and south-westward,
Look'd on the vapor as it flew in fleeces tinged with violet, 35

Look'd toward the lower bay to notice the vessels arriving,
Saw their approach, saw aboard those that were near me,
Saw the white sails of schooners and sloops, saw the ships at anchor,
The sailors at work in the rigging or out astride the spars,
The round masts, the swinging motion of the hulls, the slender serpentine pennants, 40
The large and small steamers in motion, the pilots in their pilothouses,
The white wake left by the passage, the quick tremulous whirl of the wheels,
The flags of all nations, the falling of them at sunset,
The scallop-edged waves in the twilight, the ladled cups, the frolic-some crests and glistening, 44
The stretch afar growing dimmer and dimmer, the gray walls of the granite storehouses by the docks,
On the river the shadowy group, the big steam-tug closely flank'd on each side by the barges, the hay-boat, the belated lighter,
On the neighboring shore the fires from the foundry chimneys burning high and glaringly into the night, 47
Casting their flicker of black contrasted with wild red and yellow light over the tops of houses, and down into the clefts of streets. 48

The certainty of his vision is as haunting as it is masterfully sure. The 4th Canto is compellingly brief. The eleven lines that succeed it in the 5th Canto are personalized and universally shared.

4.
> These and all else were to me the same as they are to you, 49
> I loved well those cities, loved well the stately and rapid river,
> The men and women I saw were all near to me,
> Others the same—others who look back on me because
> I look'd forward to them,
> (The time will come, though I stop here to-day and to-night.) 54

5.
> What is it then between us? 55
> What is the count of the scores or hundreds of years between us? 56
>
> Whatever it is, it avails not—distance avails not, and place avails not, 57
> I too lived, Brooklyn of ample hills was mine,
> I too walk'd the streets of Manhattan island, and bathed in the waters around it,
> I too felt the curious abrupt questionings stir within me, 60
> In the day among crowds of people sometimes they came upon me,
> In my walks home late at night or as I lay in my bed they came upon me, 62

> I too had been struck from the float
> forever held in solution,
> I too had receiv'd identity by my body,
> That I was I knew was of my body, and
> what I should be I knew I should be
> of my body. 64

When the poet asks: "What then is between us?" (Line 55 above) he posits the simple profundity of memory and anticipation—which is to say, time. In a remarkable anticipation of this great poem, Whitman laid the groundwork for it in his preface to the first edition of *Leaves of Grass*:

> Without effort and without exposing in the least how it is done the greatest poet brings the spirit of any or all events and passions and scenes and persons some more and some less to bear on your individual character as you hear or read. To do this well is to compete with the laws that pursue and follow time. What is the purpose must surely be there and the clue of it must there…and the faintest indication is the indication of the best and then becomes the clearest indication. Past and present and future are not disjoined but joined. The greatest poems form the consistence of what is to be from what has been and is. He drags the dead out of their coffins and stands them again on their feet…he say to the past, Rise and walk before me that I might realize you. He learns the lesson…he places himself where the future becomes the present.[244]

If some of us can't quite conjure the cosmic vision that attends much of his verse, there can be little doubt of our empathy as he contemplates the dark nights in his own transversal: *My great thoughts as I supposed them, were they not in reality meagre?* (Line 68 below)Whitman was to become venerated by much of the same world that earlier had ignored or reviled him. In Bolton, England there once was a church dedicated to his vision. His verse was read each Sunday. Virginia Woolf was familiar with the group. She reported that there was a shared consciousness of which each partook. She envied Whitman his ideal audience. She believed it was very much to the poet's credit that those who visited their seer in America found him a nice man but as nondescript as any of their own local farmers. Among America's stock of great writers his essential affability and goodness is little doubted; so it comes as a shock to hear the confessional tone of the 6th Canto:

6.

> It is not upon you alone the dark patches fall,   65
> The dark threw its patches down upon me also,
> The best I had done seem'd to me blank and suspicious,
> My great thoughts as I supposed them, were they not in reality meagre?   68
> Nor is it you alone who know what it is to be evil,
> I am he who knew what it was to be evil,   70
> I too knitted the old knot of contrariety,
> Blabb'd, blush'd, resented, lied, stole, grudg'd,

Had guile, anger, lust, hot wishes I dared not speak,
Was wayward, vain, greedy, shallow, sly, cowardly, malignant,
The wolf, the snake, the hog, not wanting in me. 75
The cheating look, the frivolous word, the adulterous wish, not wanting,
Refusals, hates, postponements, meanness, laziness, none of these wanting,
Was one with the rest, the days and haps of the rest,
Was call'd by my nighest name by clear loud voices of young men as they saw me approaching or passing,
Felt their arms on my neck as I stood, or the negligent leaning of their flesh against me as I sat,
Saw many I loved in the street or ferry-boat or public assembly, yet never told them a word,
Lived the same life with the rest, the same old laughing, gnawing, sleeping,
Play'd the part that still looks back on the actor or actress,
The same old role, the role that is what we make it, as great as we like,
Or as small as we like, or both great and small. 85

Shortly before his suicide, Crane left us a poetic fragment, *The Broken Tower:*

> And so it was I entered the broken world
> To trace the visionary company of love, its voice
> An instant in the wind (I know not whither hurled)
> But not for long to hold each desperate choice.
> My word I poured. But it was cognate, scored
> Of that tribunal monarch of the air
> Whose thigh embronzes earth, strikes crystal Word
> In wounds pledged once to hope, — cleft to despair?

Whitman survived his despair — Crane was swallowed by the Caribbean at thirty-two. We are each mariners who briefly walk a deck and are, in the end, lost at sea. Our shared solitude is, in an instant, tossed to the wind. This theme is a favorite among poets and philosophers alike. Indeed, we seem to hear the echo of another bard who in the guise of a Magus found that his *actors were spirits that melted into air, into thin air* — "the same old role that is what we make it, as great as we like, or as small as we like, or both great and small" — *and like the baseless fabric of this vision… the great globe itself, yea all which it inherit, shall dissolve and like this insubstantial pageant faded leave not a rack behind.* Canto 7 anticipates the concluding poem of the "Calamus" cluster, *Full of Life Now,* that was composed the following year, 1857. In each poem Whitman suggests the uncanny disposition of attending us as we consider his thought and the elegance of his lines, rough hewn though they be:

7.

>Closer yet I approach you, 86
>What thought you have of me now, I had as much of you—I laid in my stores in advance, 87
>I consider'd long and seriously of you before you were born. 88

>Who was to know what should come home to me?
>Who knows but I am enjoying this?
>Who knows, for all the distance, but I am as good as looking at you now, for all you cannot see me? 91

The 8th Canto continues the poet's mystical fusion with his readers:

8.

>Ah, what can ever be more stately and admirable to me than mast-hemm'd Manhattan? 92
>River and sunset and scallop-edg'd waves of flood-tide?
>The sea-gulls oscillating their bodies, the hay-boat in the twilight, and the belated lighter?
>What gods can exceed these that clasp me by the hand, and with voices I love call me promptly and loudly by my nighest name as I approach?
>What is more subtle than this which ties me to the woman or man that looks in my face?

> Which fuses me into you now, and
> pours my meaning into you? 97
>
> We understand then do we not?
> What I promis'd without mentioning it,
> have you not accepted?
> What the study could not teach — what
> the preaching could not accomplish
> is accomplish'd, is it not? 100

And if there were room for doubt he reiterates a glory of images that he brought to life throughout his poem. Including, again, the reflection in line 112: *Consider, you who peruse me, whether I may not in unknown ways be looking upon you...* Also note the poet's nod to idealism: (Lines 119-120 & 127-128 below)

9.
> Flow on, river! flow with the flood-tide,
> and ebb with the ebb-tide! 101
> Frolic on, crested and scallop-edg'd
> waves!
> Gorgeous clouds of the sunset! drench
> with your splendor me, or the men
> and women generations after me! 103
> Cross from shore to shore, countless
> crowds of passengers!
> Stand up, tall masts of Mannahatta!
> stand up, beautiful hills of
> Brooklyn!
> Throb, baffled and curious brain! throw
> out questions and answers! 106
> Suspend here and everywhere, eternal
> float of solution!

Gaze, loving and thirsting eyes, in the
    house or street or public assembly!
Sound out, voices of young men! loudly
    and musically call me by my nighest
    name!
Live, old life! play the part that looks
    back on the actor or actress!
Play the old role, the role that is great or
    small according as one makes it! 111
Consider, you who peruse me, whether
    I may not in unknown ways be
    looking upon you; 112
Be firm, rail over the river, to support
    those who lean idly, yet haste with
    the hasting current; 113
Fly on, sea-birds! fly sideways, or wheel
    in large circles high in the air; 114
Receive the summer sky, you water, and
    faithfully hold it till all downcast
    eyes have time to take it from you!
Diverge, fine spokes of light, from the
    shape of my head, or any one's
    head, in the sunlit water!
Come on, ships from the lower bay! pass
    up or down, white-sail'd schooners,
    sloops, lighters!
Flaunt away, flags of all nations! be duly
    lower'd at sunset!
Burn high your fires, foundry chimneys!
    cast black shadows at nightfall! cast
    red and yellow light over the tops of
    the houses!
Appearances, now or henceforth,
    indicate what you are, 119

> You necessary film, continue to envelop the soul,   120
> About my body for me, and your body for you, be hung our divinest aromas,
> Thrive, cities — bring your freight, bring your shows, ample and sufficient rivers,
> Expand, being than which none else is perhaps more spiritual,
> Keep your places, objects than which none else is more lasting.
> You have waited, you always wait, you dumb, beautiful ministers,   127
> We receive you with free sense at last, and are insatiate henceforward,   128
> Not you any more shall be able to foil us, or withhold yourselves from us,
> We use you, and do not cast you aside — we plant you permanently within us,
> We fathom you not — we love you — there is perfection in you also,   130
> You furnish your parts toward eternity,
> Great or small, you furnish your parts toward the soul.   132

There is perfection in this poem. An earlier poet suggested we were such stuff as dreams are made on. Here, a later poet rightly guesses that the phantasmagoria behind his vision, he fathoms not — that phantasmagoria was beautifully expressed in lines that introduced the last canto, but were later deleted after the Centennial edition:

> We descend upon you and all things—
> we arrest you all;
> We realize the soul only by you, you
> faithful solids and fluids;
> Through you color, form, location,
> sublimity, ideality;
> Through you every proof, comparison,
> and all suggestions and
> determinations of ourselves.

All things furnish their parts toward eternity—great or small: "...you furnish your parts toward the soul." Before leaving "Crossing Brooklyn Ferry" it would be well to speak of its influence on another poet. T.S. Eliot has little patience with Whitman's poetic theory: "When Whitman speaks of lilacs or the mocking-bird, his theories and beliefs drop away like a needless pretext." He defended Pound against an undue influence by the earlier bard, although Pound would reluctantly acknowledge his debt:

> Personally I might be very glad to conceal my relationship to my spiritual father and brag about my more congenial ancestry...

Pound knew that his relationship with world literature is specifically and beautifully addressed in this poem. Whitman was Ezra Pound's spiritual father as he was Isadora Duncan's paterfamilias. As much as Pound and Eliot might prefer more congenial ancestry they were envisioned by *their* father and look back in paternal debt in "Crossing Brooklyn Ferry".

Ezra Pound
1885-1972

We find in the unrhymed freedom of Eliot's verse, Whitman's definite Echo. Eliot claimed it was rather the echo of Jules Laforgue, but since Laforgue's admits to being highly influenced by Whitman it amounts to the same thing.

> You cannot face it steadily, but this
>   thing is sure,
> That time is no healer: the patient is no
>   longer here.

When the train starts, and the passengers are settled
To fruit, periodicals and business letters
(And those who saw them off have left the platform)
Their faces relax from grief into relief,
To the sleepy rhythm of a hundred hours.
Fare forward, travelers! not escaping from the past
Into different lives, or into any future;
You are not the same people who left that station
Or who will arrive at any terminus,
While the narrowing rails slide together behind you;
And on the deck of the drumming liner
Watching the furrow that widens behind you,
You shall not think "the past is finished"
Or "the future is before us."
At nightfall, in the rigging and the aerial,
Is a voice descanting (though not to the ear,
The murmuring shell of time, and not in any language)
"Fare forward, you who think that you are voyaging;
You are not those who saw the harbor
Receding, or those who will disembark.
Here between the hither and the farther shore
While time is withdrawn, consider the future

> And the past with an equal mind.
> At the moment which is not of action or inaction
> You can receive this: 'on whatever sphere of being
> The mind of a man may be intent
> At the time of death' — that is the one action
> (And the time of death is every moment)
> Which shall fructify in the lives of others:
> And do not think of the fruit of action.
> Fare Forward.[245]

Eliot reveled in the influence of world literature. That he prefers the pedigree of Dante, Shelly, Baudelaire and Laforgue is not surprising. In the same essay in which he famously defined the "objective correlative," he declared Hamlet an "aesthetic failure." Eliot, like Shaw, could never forgive the fates for not being born in Stratford in April of 1565. That said, I should admit to having read and loved Eliot for decades and shall continue for such a stretch of time as I have remaining to me. I shall return to the man from Missouri when lilacs *next* in a dooryard bloom. Until then, remember that all things furnish their parts toward eternity — all things furnish their parts to the soul. Fare Forward.

16. Song of the Answerer

The *Song of the Answer* (1855) is in two parts. It was at one time two separate poems. The first half of the poem was one of the original twelve of the inaugural edition of

Leaves of Grass. That fact alone suggests cause for careful study. The second part was one of the twenty new poems in the 2nd edition of 1856. It was christened one of the collection's least inspired names. Whitman called it *Poem of the Singers and of the Words of Poems*. It was joined with the first part in 1881 and also took its more succinct title at that time. The poem's construction is among the more tortuous of his efforts. He is a little unclear as to the meaning of the young man or his brother. Having read this far in the canon we are not likely to be surprised by the identity of the mysterious *answerer*. The business of the handshakes and the signs also suggest a Masonic encounter. We perceive a clue to what the poet is up to when he suggests he answers for his brother and for men: "… and I answer for him that answers for all, and send these signs."With greater clarity the poet suggested the same sentiment in Canto 17 of *Song of Myself*:

> These are really the thoughts of all men in all ages and lands, they are not original with me,
> If they are not yours as much as mine they are nothing or next to nothing.
> If they are not the riddle and the untying of the riddle they are nothing,
> If they are not just as close as they are distant they are nothing.
> This is the grass that grows wherever the land is and the water is,
> This is the common air that bathes the globe.

I earlier stated that the greatest creation of the poet was the poet himself, an observation made by Borges and other commentators as Whitman receded in the passing decades subsequent to his demise. In *Song of the Answer* we find the character of Walt Whitman in its inchoate form. Whitman imagines a messianic poet that he was to become. Whether the "Answerer" was an earlier formulation of his design in *Song of Myself* or a relapse that occurred after the more seminal poem is surely not the question—the two share the unity and greatness of the first edition as a whole—and there is, of a surety, greatness in each. What the poet says of the *Answerer*— "One part does not counteract another part, he is the joiner, he sees how they join," could have as easily been said about each of the twelve poems of his inaugural effort. As the poet will later add "and sing myself" to *Song of Myself*—so here, he reports his morning's romanza a *song*: "To the cities and farms I sing...

Song of the Answerer

1.

> Now list to my morning's romanza,
>   I tell the signs of the Answerer,
> To the cities and farms I sing as they
>   spread in the sunshine before me.   2
>
> A young man comes to me bearing a
>   message from his brother,
> How shall the young man know the
>   whether and when of his brother?
> Tell him to send me the signs.   5
>
> And I stand before the young man face
>   to face, and take his right hand in

> my left hand and his left hand in my right hand, 6
> And I answer for his brother and for men, and I answer for him that answers for all, and send these signs. 7

Emerson had earlier anticipated the signs and the poet:

> …the experience of each new age requires a new confession, and the world seems always waiting for its poet…I look in vane for the poet whom I describe.
>
> We do not with sufficient plainness or sufficient profoundness address ourselves to life, nor dare we chant our own times and social circumstance. If we filled the day with bravery we would not shrink from celebrating it. Time and nature yield us many gifts, but not yet the timely man, the new religion, the reconciler whom all things await.[246]

The Answerer justifies the anticipation as the first Canto continues:

> Him all wait for, him all yield up to, his word is decisive and final, 8
> Him they accept, in him lave, in him perceive themselves as amid light,
> Him they immerse and he immerses them.

Beautiful women, the haughtiest nations, laws, the landscape, people, animals,
The profound earth and its attributes and the unquiet ocean, (so tell I my morning's romanza,)
All enjoyments and properties and money, and whatever money will buy,
The best farms, others toiling and planting and he unavoidably reaps,
The noblest and costliest cities, others grading and building and he domiciles there,
Nothing for any one but what is for him, near and far are for him, the ships in the offing,
The perpetual shows and marches on land are for him if they are for anybody. 17

He puts things in their attitudes,
He puts to-day out of himself with plasticity and love,
He places his own times, reminiscences, parents, brothers and sisters, associations, employment, politics, so that the rest never shame them afterward, nor assume to command them. 20

He is the Answerer, 21
What can be answer'd he answers, and what cannot be answer'd he shows how it cannot be answer'd. 22

A man is a summons and challenge, 23
(It is vain to skulk—do you hear that mocking and laughter? do you hear the ironical echoes?)

Books, friendships, philosophers, priests, action, pleasure, pride, beat up and down seeking to give satisfaction,
He indicates the satisfaction, and indicates them that beat up and down also.

Whichever the sex, whatever the season or place, he may go freshly and gently and safely by day or by night,
He has the pass-key of hearts, to him the response of the prying of hands on the knobs.

His welcome is universal, the flow of beauty is not more welcome or universal than he is,
The person he favors by day or sleeps with at night is blessed. 30

Every existence has its idiom, every thing has an idiom and tongue,
He resolves all tongues into his own and bestows it upon men, and any man translates, and any man translates himself also,

> One part does not counteract another
> part, he is the joiner, he sees how
> they join.   33

The characteristics of the Answerer are ones that poet will espouse in his creation as the poet-seer of *Leaves of Grass*. Saint Mark created the literary character of Jesus in the earliest of the four gospels. Jesus was one of the *roughs* found among the commoners of Judea. No doubt, the thieves and the prostitutes who he counseled to *go their way and sin no more* were precursors to the rabble that the Answerer walks amongst and transmutes: *...they are not vile anymore, they hardly know themselves they are so grown.* (Line 52 below)

> He says indifferently and alike How are
> you friend? to the President at his
> levee,   34
> And he says Good-day my brother, to
> Cudge that hoes in the sugar-field,
> And both understand him and know
> that his speech is right.
>
> He walks with perfect ease in the
> capitol,   37
> He walks among the Congress, and one
> Representative says to another, *Here
> is our equal appearing and new.*
> Then the mechanics take him for a
> mechanic,
> And the soldiers suppose him to be a
> soldier, and the sailors that he has
> follow'd the sea,
> And the authors take him for an author,
> and the artists for an artist,   40

And the laborers perceive he could labor with them and love them,
No matter what the work is, that he is the one to follow it or has follow'd it,
No matter what the nation, that he might find his brothers and sisters there. 43
The English believe he comes of their English stock, 45
A Jew to the Jew he seems, a Russ to the Russ, usual and near, removed from none.

Whoever he looks at in the traveler's coffee-house claims him,
The Italian or Frenchman is sure, the German is sure, the Spaniard is sure, and the island Cuban is sure,
The engineer, the deck-hand on the great lakes, or on the Mississippi or St. Lawrence or Sacramento, or Hudson or Paumanok sound, claims him.

The gentleman of perfect blood acknowledges his perfect blood,
The insulter, the prostitute, the angry person, the beggar, see themselves in the ways of him, he strangely transmutes them,
They are not vile any more, they hardly know themselves they are so grown. 52

The gestating Walt Whitman of *Song of the Answerer* is the poet of Eternity—he makes a distinction between singers of the words of *the hours and the minutes*, and the maker of the poems that *are the general light and dark*—the Whitman of *Song of Myself* is the Whitman that accepts *time absolutely*—the poet of time and eternity: "Distant and dead resuscitate, they show as the dial or move as the hands of me, I am the clock myself."

In 1881 Whitman joined 1855's first portion of this poem with 1856's *Poem of the Singers and of The Words of Poems*, the 2nd and concluding Canto.

2.

> The indications and tally of time,   53
> Perfect sanity shows the master among philosophs,
> Time, always without break, indicates itself in parts,
> What always indicates the poet is the crowd of the pleasant company of singers, and their words,
> The words of the singers are the hours or minutes of the light or dark, but the words of the maker of poems are the general light and dark,
> The maker of poems settles justice, reality, immortality,
> His insight and power encircle things and the human race,
> He is the glory and extract thus far of things and of the human race.   60
>
> The singers do not beget, only the Poet begets,

The singers are welcom'd, understood, appear often enough, but rare has the day been, likewise the spot, of the birth of the maker of poems, the Answerer,
(Not every century nor every five centuries has contain'd such a day, for all its names.) 63
The singers of successive hours of centuries may have ostensible names, but the name of each of them is one of the singers,
The name of each is, eye-singer, ear-singer, head-singer, sweet-singer, night-singer, parlor-singer, love-singer, weird-singer, or something else.

All this time and at all times wait the words of true poems, 66
The words of true poems do not merely please,
The true poets are not followers of beauty but the august masters of beauty;
The greatness of sons is the exuding of the greatness of mothers and fathers,
The words of true poems are the tuft and final applause of science. 70

Emerson was *a voice crying in the wilderness*:

> All that we call sacred history attests that the birth of a poet is the principal event in chronology...For it is not metres, but a metremaking argument that makes a poem—a thought so passionate and alive that like the spirit of a plant or an animal it has an architecture of its own...things admit of being used as symbols because nature is a symbol in the whole and in every part...We stand before the secret of the world, there where Being passes into Appearance and Unity into variety. The Universe is the externalization of the soul... Since every thing in nature answers to a moral power, if any phenomenon remains brute and dark it is because the corresponding faculty in the observer is not yet active. [247]

The Answer was, thereafter, anointed as Part 2 continues:

> Divine instinct, breadth of vision, the law of reason, health, rudeness of body, withdrawnness,   71
> Gayety, sun-tan, air-sweetness, such are some of the words of poems.
>
> The sailor and traveler underlie the maker of poems, the Answerer,
> The builder, geometer, chemist, anatomist, phrenologist, artist, all these underlie the maker of poems, the Answerer.

> The words of the true poems give you more than poems, 75
> They give you to form for yourself poems, religions, politics, war, peace, behavior, histories, essays, daily life, and every thing else, 76
> They balance ranks, colors, races, creeds, and the sexes,
> They do not seek beauty, they are sought,
> Forever touching them or close upon them follows beauty, longing, fain, love-sick.
> They prepare for death, yet are they not the finish, but rather the outset, 80
> They bring none to his or her terminus or to be content and full,
> Whom they take they take into space to behold the birth of stars, to learn one of the meanings,
> To launch off with absolute faith, to sweep through the ceaseless rings and never be quiet again. 83

In 1855, *Song of the Answer* concluded with the stanza presented below. It was discarded in the 1867 edition of the poem and did not appear again.

> Do you think it would be good to be the writer of melodious verses?
> Well, it would be good to be the writer of melodious verses;
> But what are the verses beyond the flowing character you could have?

> or beyond beautiful manners and behavior?
>
> Or beyond one manly or affectionate deed of an apprentice-boy? or old woman? Or man that has been in prison, or is likely to be in prison?

17. Our Old Feuillage

(1860)

The first impression of *Our Old Feuillage* is that of inventories. In Whitman there are inventories *good* and inventories *bad*. Emerson had praised the one and scorned *t'other*. A journal entry by his friend John Burroughs records Emerson's reflection and Whitman's response to it:

> Walt said a friend of his Mr. Marvin, met Emerson in Boston the other day. When Walt was mentioned, 'Yes,' said Mr. Emerson, 'Walt sends me all his books. But tell Walt I am not satisfied, not satisfied, I expect—him—to make—the songs of the—nation—but he seems contented to—make the inventories.' Walt laughed and said it tickled him much. It was capital. But it did not disturb him at all. 'I know what I am about better than Emerson does. Yet I love to hear what the gods have to say.' And continuing, he said, 'I see how I might easily have wandered into other and easier paths than I did—paths that

would have paid better, and gained me popularity; and I wonder how my feet were guided as they were. I am more satisfied with myself for having the courage to do what I have.' [248]

Manuscript evidence suggests that *Our Old Feuillage* was written as early as 1856 and suggests "inventory good." The poem was offered to and rejected by Harper's in 1860. It is, Harper's aside, a magnificent collection of the fauna and flora of North America. Although he speaks of the continent of Democracy he is careful to include Kanada and soft-breath'd Cuba. The poet of the all inclusive embraces more than the many states united by *Our Old Feuillage*. The word feuillage is French for foliage and embraces the 'old' world as well as the new one that Whitman discovers in each succeeding line. He hints at his method: "All characters, movements, growths, a few noticed, myriads unnoticed, through Mannahatta's streets I walking, these things gathering..."In the penultimate line of the poem the rewarded reader will find an invitation and a poetic wink underlying the whole of Whitman's offerings: "Whoever you are! how can I but offer you divine leaves, that you also be eligible as I am?"

Our Old Feuillage!

Always our old feuillage!
Always Florida's green peninsula—
    always the priceless delta of
    Louisiana—always the cotton-fields
    of Alabama and Texas,
Always California's golden hills and
    hollows, and the silver mountains of

New Mexico—always soft-breath'd
Cuba,

Always the vast slope drain'd by the
Southern sea, inseparable with the
slopes drain'd by the Eastern and
Western seas,

The area the eighty-third year of these
States, the three and a half millions
of square miles, 5

The eighteen thousand miles of sea-
coast and bay-coast on the main, the
thirty thousand miles of river
navigation, 6

The seven millions of distinct families
and the same number of
dwellings—always these, and more,
branching forth into numberless
branches, 7

Always the free range and diversity—
always the continent of Democracy; 8

Always the prairies, pastures, forests,
vast cities, travelers, Kanada, the
snows;

Always these compact lands tied at the
hips with the belt stringing the huge
oval lakes;

Always the West with strong native
persons, the increasing density
there, the habitans, friendly,
threatening, ironical, scorning
invaders;

All sights, South, North, East—all
deeds, promiscuously done at all
times,

All characters, movements, growths, a
few noticed, myriads unnoticed,
Through Mannahatta's streets I walking,
these things gathering,
On interior rivers by night in the glare
of pine knots, steamboats wooding
up, 15
Sunlight by day on the valley of the
Susquehanna, and on the valleys of
the Potomac and Rappahannock,
and the valleys of the Roanoke and
Delaware,
In their northerly wilds beasts of prey
haunting the Adirondacks the hills,
or lapping the Saginaw waters to
drink,
In a lonesome inlet a sheldrake lost from
the flock, sitting on the water
rocking silently,
In farmers' barns oxen in the stable,
their harvest labor done, they rest
standing, they are too tired,
Afar on arctic ice the she-walrus lying
drowsily while her cubs play
around,
The hawk sailing where men have not
yet sail'd, the farthest polar sea,
ripply, crystalline, open, beyond the
floes, 21
White drift spooning ahead where the
ship in the tempest dashes,
On solid land what is done in cities as
the bells strike midnight together,
In primitive woods the sounds there
also sounding, the howl of the wolf,

the scream of the panther, and the hoarse bellow of the elk,
In winter beneath the hard blue ice of Moosehead lake, in summer visible through the clear waters, the great trout swimming, 25
In lower latitudes in warmer air in the Carolinas the large black buzzard floating slowly high beyond the tree tops,
Below, the red cedar festoon'd with tylandria, the pines and cypresses growing out of the white sand that spreads far and flat,
Rude boats descending the big Pedee, climbing plants, parasites with color'd flowers and berries enveloping huge trees,
The waving drapery on the live-oak trailing long and low, noiselessly waved by the wind,
The camp of Georgia wagoners just after dark, the supper-fires and the cooking and eating by whites and negroes,
Thirty or forty great wagons, the mules, cattle, horses, feeding from troughs,
The shadows, gleams, up under the leaves of the old sycamore-trees, the flames with the black smoke from the pitch-pine curling and rising; 32
Southern fishermen fishing, the sounds and inlets of North Carolina's coast, the shad-fishery and the herring-fishery, the large sweep-seines, the

windlasses on shore work'd by horses, the clearing, curing, and packing-houses;
Deep in the forest in piney woods turpentine dropping from the incisions in the trees, there are the turpentine works,
There are the negroes at work in good health, the ground in all directions is cover'd with pine straw;
In Tennessee and Kentucky slaves busy in the coalings, at the forge, by the furnace-blaze, or at the corn-shucking,
In Virginia, the planter's son returning after a long absence, joyfully welcom'd and kiss'd by the aged mulatto nurse,
On rivers boatmen safely moor'd at nightfall in their boats under shelter of high banks,
Some of the younger men dance to the sound of the banjo or fiddle, others sit on the gunwale smoking and talking;
Late in the afternoon the mocking-bird, the American mimic, singing in the Great Dismal Swamp,   40
There are the greenish waters, the resinous odor, the plenteous moss, the cypress-tree, and the juniper-tree;
Northward, young men of Mannahatta, the target company from an excursion returning home at

evening, the musket-muzzles all bear bunches of flowers presented by women;
Children at play, or on his father's lap a young boy fallen asleep, (how his lips move! how he smiles in his sleep!)
The scout riding on horseback over the plains west of the Mississippi, he ascends a knoll and sweeps his eyes around;
California life, the miner, bearded, dress'd in his rude costume, the stanch California friendship, the sweet air, the graves one in passing meets solitary just aside the horse-path;
Down in Texas the cotton-field, the negro-cabins, drivers driving mules or oxen before rude carts, cotton bales piled on banks and wharves;
Encircling all, vast-darting up and wide, the American Soul, with equal hemispheres, one Love, one Dilation or Pride;
In arriere the peace-talk with the Iroquois the aborigines, the calumet, the pipe of good-will, arbitration, and endorsement,
The sachem blowing the smoke first toward the sun and then toward the earth,
The drama of the scalp-dance enacted with painted faces and guttural exclamations,

The setting out of the war-party, the long and stealthy march,
The single file, the swinging hatchets, the surprise and slaughter of enemies;
All the acts, scenes, ways, persons, attitudes of these States, reminiscences, institutions,
All these States compact, every square mile of these States without excepting a particle;
Me pleas'd, rambling in lanes and country fields, Paumanok's fields,
Observing the spiral flight of two little yellow butterflies shuffling between each other, ascending high in the air,
The darting swallow, the destroyer of insects, the fall traveler southward but returning northward early in the spring,
The country boy at the close of the day driving the herd of cows and shouting to them as they loiter to browse by the roadside,
The city wharf, Boston, Philadelphia, Baltimore, Charleston, New Orleans, San Francisco,
The departing ships when the sailors heave at the capstan;
Evening—me in my room—the setting sun,
The setting summer sun shining in my open window, showing the swarm of flies, suspended, balancing in the

> air in the centre of the room, darting
> athwart, up and down, casting swift
> shadows in specks on the opposite
> wall where the shine is;
> The athletic American matron speaking
> in public to crowds of listeners,
> Males, females, immigrants,
> combinations, the copiousness, the
> individuality of the States, each for
> itself—the moneymakers,
> Factories, machinery, the mechanical
> forces, the windlass, lever, pulley,
> all certainties, 65
> The certainty of space, increase,
> freedom, futurity,
> In space the sporades, the scatter'd
> islands, the stars—on the firm earth,
> the lands, my lands, 67

Of his longer Canticles only this one, "Song of Joys" and "Prayer of Columbus" are not broken into separate Cantos. "Our Old Fuelliage" makes a thematic separation at this juncture and reveals its metaphysical intent. Time is suggested in *the darting swallow* and *spiral flight of butterflies,* but here the poet-shaman crosses into the amalgam of eternity. He *becomes* the living landscape he envisions for the remainder of the poem. The poet's identification with the cornered moose is one of my favorites of the poem—and this only a myriad part of a singular whole—eighty-two lines projecting the conceit of *One Identity.* It is an astonishing performance.

> O lands! all so dear to me—what you
> are, (whatever it is,) I putting it at

random in these songs, become a part of that, whatever it is, 68
Southward there, I screaming, with wings slow flapping, with the myriads of gulls wintering along the coasts of Florida,
Otherways there atwixt the banks of the Arkansaw, the Rio Grande, the Nueces, the Brazos, the Tombigbee, the Red River, the Saskatchawan or the Osage, I with the spring waters laughing and skipping and running,
Northward, on the sands, on some shallow bay of Paumanok, I with parties of snowy herons wading in the wet to seek worms and aquatic plants,
Retreating, triumphantly twittering, the king-bird, from piercing the crow with its bill, for amusement—and I triumphantly twittering,
The migrating flock of wild geese alighting in autumn to refresh themselves, the body of the flock feed, the sentinels outside move around with erect heads watching, and are from time to time reliev'd by other sentinels—and I feeding and taking turns with the rest,
In Kanadian forests the moose, large as an ox, corner'd by hunters, rising desperately on his hind-feet, and plunging with his fore-feet, the hoofs as sharp as knives—and I,

plunging at the hunters, corner'd and desperate,
In the Mannahatta, streets, piers, shipping, store-houses, and the countless workmen working in the shops, 75
And I too of the Mannahatta, singing thereof — and no less in myself than the whole of the Mannahatta in itself,
Singing the song of These, my ever-united lands — my body no more inevitably united, part to part, and made out of a thousand diverse contributions one identity, any more than my lands are inevitably united and made ONE IDENTITY; 77
Nativities, climates, the grass of the great pastoral Plains,
Cities, labors, death, animals, products, war, good and evil — these me,
These affording, in all their particulars, the old feuillage to me and to America, how can I do less than pass the clew of the union of them, 80
to afford the like to you?
Whoever you are! how can I but offer you divine leaves, that you also be eligible as I am? 81
How can I but as here chanting, invite you for yourself to collect bouquets of the incomparable feuillage of these States? 82

18. A Song of Joys

(1860)

"A Song of Joys" first entered the canon as "Poem of Joy" in 1860. The *Norton Critical Edition* notes a pre-1855 manuscript: "Poem incarnating the mind of an old man, whose life has been magnificently developed—the wildest and most exuberant joy—-the utterance of hope and floods of anticipation."[249] The poet is developing the persona that will become *Walt Whitman*. In the preceding note he anticipates an alternate project of writing from the standpoint of an old man—this when he was in his early thirties! *Whitman*, of *Song of Myself*; the Answerer, of *Song of the Answer*; and the "old man" from the earlier manuscript of *A Song of Joys,* show that *Project Whitman* was an on-going metamorphosis. Of the thirty-six stanzas in the poem only 5 have resisted the ecstatic "O" that otherwise begins each line. The *ecstatic "O"* of *Pioneers! O Pioneers!* and *O Captain! My Captain!* does not come trippingly from my tongue. I find its use in *Song of Joys* the least egregious of the three. His friend and author R.M. Bucke noted that Whitman:

> ...did not talk much. Sometimes, while remaining cheery and good-natured, he would speak very little a day... When I first knew Walt Whitman I used to think that he watched himself, and did not allow his tongue to give expression to feelings of fretfulness, antipathy, complaint and remonstrance. It did not occur to me as possible that these mental states could be absent in him...

> After long observation, however, and talking to others who had known him for many years, I satisfied myself that such absence or unconsciousness was entirely real. His deep, clear, and earnest voice made a good part, though not all, of the charm of the simplest things he said—a voice not characteristic of any special nationality or dialect. If he said (as he sometimes would involuntarily on stepping to the door and looking out), 'Oh, the beautiful sky! or, 'Oh, the beautiful grass! The words produced the effect of sweet music.

That would have been much too much *Oh-ing* for me. In fairness to our American bard, even Hamlet uses it twice in his address to the players. And as I noted above, the overuse of the convention is at its least offensive in "A Song of Joys". Excepting lines 86 through 93 (where he also becomes an old woman), the poet has given up the original conceit of the joys belonging exclusively to an old man—it is simply the palpable joy of the poet. In his Camden notebooks he speaks of composing his poems. The note is from May 13 of 1881:

> I do the main part of my work out in the woods—I like to try my pieces by negligent, free, primitive Nature, the sky, the sea-shore, the plentiful grass, or dead leaves (as now) under my feet, and the song of some cat-bird wren or russet thrush within hearing—like (as now) the half-shadowed tall-column'd trees,

> with green leaves and branches in relief against the sky...Such is the library, the study, where (seated on a big log) I have sifted out and given some finishing touches to this edition.[250]

The poet, so ensconced, inhabits the souls of all he surveys. A single earth in a single time is not enough—he will have: "...a thousand globes and all time." It is a remarkable ambition. In Borges' Introduction to his own Spanish translation of *Leaves of Grass*, he suggests he succeeded: "Whitman, I insist,, is the modest man he was from 1819 to 1892 and is the man he wanted to be but never fully was, and is each one of us and all those who will populate the earth." The Farmland and the woodland are suggested by his joy "full of grain and trees." Also suggested is the loveliness of nostalgia: "O to go back to the place where I was born, to hear the birds sing once more, to ramble about the house and barn and over the fields once more, and through the orchard and along the old lanes once more." The reader is effectively challenged to catalogue his own list of "joys." How many have you shared with the poet—how many of your own could you share?

A Song of Joys

> O to make the most jubilant song!
> Full of music—full of manhood, womanhood, infancy!
> Full of common employments—full of grain and trees.   3
>
> O for the voices of animals—O for the swiftness and balance of fishes!

O for the dropping of raindrops in a song!
O for the sunshine and motion of waves in a song!

O the joy of my spirit—it is uncaged—it darts like lightning!
It is not enough to have this globe or a certain time,
I will have thousands of globes and all time.

O the engineer's joys! to go with a locomotive!
To hear the hiss of steam, the merry shriek, the steam-whistle, the laughing locomotive!
To push with resistless way and speed off in the distance.

O the gleesome saunter over fields and hillsides!
The leaves and flowers of the commonest weeds, the moist fresh stillness of the woods,
The exquisite smell of the earth at daybreak, and all through the forenoon.
O the horseman's and horsewoman's joys!
The saddle, the gallop, the pressure upon the seat, the cool gurgling by the ears and hair.

O the fireman's joys!
I hear the alarm at dead of night,
I hear bells, shouts! I pass the crowd, I run!
The sight of the flames maddens me with pleasure.

O the joy of the strong-brawn'd fighter, towering in the arena in perfect condition, conscious of power, thirsting to meet his opponent.

O the joy of that vast elemental sympathy which only the human soul is capable of generating and emitting in steady and limitless floods.

O the mother's joys!
The watching, the endurance, the precious love, the anguish, the patiently yielded life.
O the of increase, growth, recuperation,
The joy of soothing and pacifying, the joy of concord and harmony.

O to go back to the place where I was born,
To hear the birds sing once more,
To ramble about the house and barn and over the fields once more,
And through the orchard and along the old lanes once more.

In the next several stanzas the poet imagines the life of a fisherman in its various forms and vicissitudes. Clearly the sea is one of his dearest themes, as are those who spend their days and nights upon it. He also salutes miners and soldiers — the fruit of the one perhaps more benign than the harvest of the other.

> O to have been brought up on bays, lagoons, creeks, or along the coast, 32
> To continue and be employ'd there all my life,
> The briny and damp smell, the shore, the salt weeds exposed at low water,
> The work of fishermen, the work of the eel-fisher and clam-fisher;
> I come with my clam-rake and spade, I come with my eel-spear,
> Is the tide out? I join the group of clam-diggers on the flats,
> I laugh and work with them, I joke at my work like a mettlesome young man; 37
> In winter I take my eel-basket and eel-spear and travel out on foot on the ice — I have a small axe to cut holes in the ice,
> Behold me well-clothed going gayly or returning in the afternoon, my brood of tough boys accompanying me,
> My brood of grown and part-grown boys, who love to be with no one else so well as they love to be with me,

By day to work with me, and by night to sleep with me.

Another time in warm weather out in a boat, to lift the lobster-pots where they are sunk with heavy stones, (I know the buoys,)
O the sweetness of the Fifth-month morning upon the water as I row just before sunrise toward the buoys,
I pull the wicker pots up slantingly, the dark green lobsters are desperate with their claws as I take them out, I insert wooden pegs in the joints of their pincers,
I go to all the places one after another, and then row back to the shore,
There in a huge kettle of boiling water the lobsters shall be boil'd till their color becomes scarlet. 47

Another time mackerel-taking, 48
Voracious, mad for the hook, near the surface, they seem to fill the water for miles;
Another time fishing for rock-fish in Chesapeake bay, I one of the brown-faced crew;
Another time trailing for blue-fish off Paumanok, I stand with braced body,
My left foot is on the gunwale, my right arm throws far out the coils of slender rope,

In sight around me the quick veering
and darting of fifty skiffs, my
companions.

O boating on the rivers, 54
The voyage down the St. Lawrence, the
superb scenery, the steamers,
The ships sailing, the Thousand Islands,
the occasional timber-raft and the
raftsmen with long-reaching sweep-
oars,
The little huts on the rafts, and the
stream of smoke when they cook
supper at evening.

(O something pernicious and dread!
Something far away from a puny and
pious life!
Something unproved! something in a
trance!
Something escaped from the anchorage
and driving free.)

O to work in mines, or forging iron, 62
Foundry casting, the foundry itself, the
rude high roof, the ample and
shadow'd space,
The furnace, the hot liquid pour'd out
and running.

O to resume the joys of the soldier! 65
To feel the presence of a brave
commanding officer — to feel his
sympathy!

> To behold his calmness—to be warm'd
>   in the rays of his smile!
> To go to battle—to hear the bugles play
>   and the drums beat!
> To hear the crash of artillery—to see the
>   glittering of the bayonets and
>   musket-barrels in the sun!
> To see men fall and die and not
>   complain!
> To taste the savage taste of blood—to be
>   so devilish!   71
> To gloat so over the wounds and deaths
>   of the enemy.   72

Undoubtedly, many a solider has tasted the savage taste of blood. I cannot help but feel the wound-dresser of the 1863 would have been appalled at any thought of "gloating so" over the wounds and deaths of the enemy. If we are all Walt Whitman, then, also here—nonetheless, we are *less*, rather than more for it. We can more ably isolate the joy of killing whales to the nineteenth century and hope that *there* it will primarily remain. The killing of hundred of thousands of dolphins remains a regrettable fact of the twenty-first century. If the world's fishing industry continues its unchecked harvest of the sea, large portions of the world's fisheries will be completely depleted before the light falls on the barren oceans of the twenty-second. The morality of one era is not necessarily congruent with that of another.

If Melville can have his Moby Dick, I'll not deny Whitman the whaleman's joys:

> O the whaleman's joys! O I cruise my
>   old cruise again!   73

I feel the ship's motion under me, I feel
the Atlantic breezes fanning me,
I hear the cry again sent down from the
mast-head, There—she blows!
Again I spring up the rigging to look
with the rest—we descend, wild
with excitement,
I leap in the lower'd boat, we row
toward our prey where he lies,
We approach stealthy and silent, I see
the mountainous mass, lethargic,
basking,
I see the harpooneer standing up, I see
the weapon dart from his vigorous
arm;
O swift again far out in the ocean the
wounded whale, settling, running to
windward, tows me,
Again I see him rise to breathe, we row
close again,
I see a lance driven through his side,
press'd deep, turn'd in the wound,
Again we back off, I see him settle
again, the life is leaving him fast,
As he rises he spouts blood, I see him
swim in circles narrower and
narrower, swiftly cutting the
water—I see him die,
He gives one convulsive leap in the
centre of the circle, and then falls
flat and still in the bloody foam.   85
O the old manhood of me, my noblest
joy of all!   86
My children and grand-children, my
white hair and beard,

My largeness, calmness, majesty, out of
   the long stretch of my life.   88

O ripen'd joy of womanhood! O
   happiness at last!
I am more than eighty years of age, I am
   the most venerable mother,   90
How clear is my mind — how all people
   draw nigh to me!
What attractions are these beyond any
   before? what bloom more than the
   bloom of youth?
What beauty is this that descends upon
   me and rises out of me?   93

O the orator's joys!
To inflate the chest, to roll the thunder
   of the voice out from the rib and
   throat,
To make the people rage, weep, hate,
   desire, with yourself,
To lead America — to quell America with
   a great tongue.

O the joy of my soul leaning pois'd on
   itself, receiving identity through
   materials and loving them,
   observing characters and absorbing
   them,   98
My soul vibrated back to me from them,
   from sight, hearing, touch, reason,
   articulation, comparison, memory,
   and the like,
The real life of my senses and flesh
   transcending my senses and flesh,   100

My body done with materials, my sight
    done with my material eyes,   101
Proved to me this day beyond cavil that
    it is not my material eyes which
    finally see,   102
Nor my material body which finally
    loves, walks, laughs, shouts,
    embraces, procreates.

O the farmer's joys!
Ohioan's, Illinoisian's, Wisconsinese',
    Kanadian's, Iowan's, Kansian's,
    Missourian's, Oregonese' joys!
To rise at peep of day and pass forth
    nimbly to work,
To plough land in the fall for winter-
    sown crops,
To plough land in the spring for maize,
To train orchards, to graft the trees, to
    gather apples in the fall.

O to bathe in the swimming-bath, or in a
    good place along shore,
To splash the water! to walk ankle-deep,
    or race naked along the shore.   111

O to realize space!   112
The plenteousness of all, that there are
    no bounds,
To emerge and be of the sky, of the sun
    and moon and flying clouds, as one
    with them.   114

The expansive Whitman emerges to be of the sky, *the sun and moon and flying clouds.* Returning to the earth he contemplates the joy of manhood, youth, pensive thought and the beautiful touch of death..

> O the joy a manly self-hood! 115
> To be servile to none, to defer to none, not to any tyrant known or unknown,
> To walk with erect carriage, a step springy and elastic,
> To look with calm gaze or with a flashing eye,
> To speak with a full and sonorous voice out of a broad chest,
> To confront with your personality all the other personalities of the earth. 120
>
> Knowist thou the excellent joys of youth?
> Joys of the dear companions and of the merry word and laughing face?
> Joy of the glad light-beaming day, joy of the wide-breath'd games?
> Joy of sweet music, joy of the lighted ball-room and the dancers?
> Joy of the plenteous dinner, strong carouse and drinking?
>
> Yet O my soul supreme!
> Knowist thou the joys of pensive thought?
> Joys of the free and lonesome heart, the tender, gloomy heart?

Joys of the solitary walk, the spirit
  bow'd yet proud, the suffering and
  the struggle?
The agonistic throes, the ecstasies, joys
  of the solemn musings day or night?   130
Joys of the thought of Death, the great
  spheres Time and Space?   131
Prophetic joys of better, loftier love's
  ideals, the divine wife, the sweet,
  eternal, perfect comrade?
Joys all thine own undying one, joys
  worthy thee O soul.

O while I live to be the ruler of life, not a
  slave,
To meet life as a powerful conqueror,
No fumes, no ennui, no more
  complaints or scornful criticisms,
To these proud laws of the air, the water
  and the ground, proving my interior
  soul impregnable,
And nothing exterior shall ever take
  command of me.

For not life's joys alone I sing,
  repeating—the joy of death!   139
The beautiful touch of Death, soothing
  and benumbing a few moments, for
  reasons,   140
Myself discharging my excrementitious
  body to be burn'd, or render'd to
  powder, or buried,   141
My real body doubtless left to me for
  other spheres,

> My voided body nothing more to me,
> returning to the purifications,
> further offices, eternal uses of the
> earth.
>
> O to attract by more than attraction!
> How it is I know not—yet behold! the
> something which obeys none of the
> rest,
> It is offensive, never defensive—yet how
> magnetic it draws.
>
> O to struggle against great odds, to meet
> enemies undaunted!
> To be entirely alone with them, to find
> how much one can stand!
> To look strife, torture, prison, popular
> odium, face to face!
> To mount the scaffold, to advance to the
> muzzles of guns with perfect
> nonchalance!
> To be indeed a God!   151

Briefly the poet is intoxicated by strife, torture, and execution. The mayhem is accepted with such perfect nonchalance that it is prelude to a remarkable transformation: "To be indeed a God!" (Line 151 above) Less ambitious is his desire to take to ship and become the ship itself: "see indeed these sails I spread to the sun and air." Note that he uses "indeed" for both God and ship.

> O to sail to sea in a ship!   152
> To leave this steady unendurable land,

To leave the tiresome sameness of the streets, the sidewalks and the houses,
To leave you O you solid motionless land, and entering a ship,
To sail and sail and sail! 156

O to have life henceforth a poem of new joys!
To dance, clap hands, exult, shout, skip, leap, roll on, float on!
To be a sailor of the world bound for all ports,
A ship itself, (see indeed these sails I spread to the sun and air,)
A swift and swelling ship full of rich words, full of joys. 161

19. Song of the Broad-Axe

(1856)

Song of the Broad-Axe is an early "Song," initially known as *Broad-Axe Poem* in the '56 or the 2nd edition of *Leaves*. It is comprised of twelve cantos. It was edited over the poet's expanding editions from its largest rendition of 390 lines to its final formulation of 254 lines. The poet's evocation of the axe is one of his most tortured metaphors: "Head from the mother's bowels drawn." He is trying to suggest the axe's formation from the earth—and mother's bowels is certainly an earthy image, if less than felicitous. We forgive him the prologue of the first stanza for the grand adventure of the verse that succeeds it.

WHITMAN'S CODE: A NEW BIBLE, VOLUME I
M.C. GARDNER

The poet in his "Songs" aims for epic gestures on the model of his beloved grand opera or as he suggests in the 2nd stanza: "skipping staccato over the keys of the great organ." The trochaic meter of the first lines give it a chopping rhythm appropriate for its subject. The axe is the poem's protagonist and it is from the axe that Whitman's catalogues will ensue and from which the energetic *shapes* will arise later in the poem.

Song of the Broad-Axe

1.

> Weapon shapely, naked, wan,
> Head from the mother's bowels drawn, 2
> Wooded flesh and metal bone, limb only one and lip only one,
> Gray-blue leaf by red-heat grown, helve produced from a little seed sown,
> Resting the grass amid and upon,
> To be lean'd and to lean on.
>
> Strong shapes and attributes of strong shapes, masculine trades, sights and sounds.
> Long varied train of an emblem, dabs of music, 8
> Fingers of the organist skipping staccato over the keys of the great organ. 9

The 2nd Canto bids America welcome…

2.

> Welcome are all earth's lands, each for its kind, 10
> Welcome are lands of pine and oak,
> Welcome are lands of the lemon and fig,

> Welcome are lands of gold,
> Welcome are lands of wheat and maize, welcome those of the grape,
> Welcome are lands of sugar and rice,
> Welcome the cotton-lands, welcome those of the white potato and sweet potato,
> Welcome are mountains, flats, sands, forests, prairies,
> Welcome the rich borders of rivers, table-lands, openings,
> Welcome the measureless grazing-lands, welcome the teeming soil of orchards, flax, honey, hemp;
> Welcome just as much the other more hard-faced lands,
> Lands rich as lands of gold or wheat and fruit lands,
> Lands of mines, lands of the manly and rugged ores,
> Lands of coal, copper, lead, tin, zinc,
> Lands of iron—lands of the make of the axe. 24

At sixty-eight lines, Canto 3 is the longest of the twelve which make up the poem. From the simple image of the axe resting on a log, the poet catalogues a vast array of workers across the land and down through time. Most of the images are in some sense related to the axe: "the space clear'd for garden... cutting away of masts... lumbermen in day camps... woodmen with their untrimmed faces." Other images are perhaps a tad beyond the original metaphor: "The American contempt for statutes and ceremonies, the boundless impatience of restraint, the loose drift of character, the inkling through random types, the solidification."

Yet even in the remembered quiet of a campsite one can imagine the axe nearby: "The blazing fire at night, the sweet taste of supper, the talk, the bed of hemlock-boughs and the bear-skin."

3.
>
> The log at the wood-pile, the axe supported by it, 25
> The sylvan hut, the vine over the doorway, the space clear'd for garden,
> The irregular tapping of rain down on the leaves after the storm is lull'd, 27
> The walling and moaning at intervals, the thought of the sea,
> The thought of ships struck in the storm and put on their beam ends, and the cutting away of masts,
> The sentiment of the huge timbers of old-fashion'd houses and barns,
> The remember'd print or narrative, the voyage at a venture of men, families, goods,
> The disembarkation, the founding of a new city,
> The voyage of those who sought a New England and found it, the outset anywhere,
> The settlements of the Arkansas, Colorado, Ottawa, Willamette,
> The slow progress, the scant fare, the axe, rifle, saddle-bags; 35
> The beauty of all adventurous and daring persons,

> The beauty of wood-boys and wood-men with their clear untrimm'd faces,
> The beauty of independence, departure, actions that rely on themselves,
> The American contempt for statutes and ceremonies, the boundless impatience of restraint,
> The loose drift of character, the inkling through random types, the solidification;
> The butcher in the slaughter-house, the hands aboard schooners and sloops, the raftsman, the pioneer,
> Lumbermen in their winter camp, daybreak in the woods, stripes of snow on the limbs of trees, the occasional snapping,
> The glad clear sound of one's own voice, the merry song, the natural life of the woods, the strong day's work,
> The blazing fire at night, the sweet taste of supper, the talk, the bed of hemlock-boughs and the bear-skin; 44

The next twenty-one lines (Lines 45-66 below) might be called the *Song of the Carpenter*. Whitman affectionately recalls some apprentice years with his father, Walter Whitman Sr., who was a house builder. "Spar-makers in the spar-yard, the swarming row of well-grown apprentices, The swing of their axes on the square-hew'd log shaping it toward the shape of a mast, The brisk short crackle of the steel driven slantingly into the pine, the butter-color'd chips flying off in great flakes and slivers." The poet also betrays his eye for masculine beauty:

"The limber motion of brawny young
arms and hips in easy costumes."

But, for the most part, he sticks to the business at hand:

> The house-builder at work in cities or anywhere, 45
> The preparatory jointing, squaring, sawing, mortising,
> The hoist-up of beams, the push of them in their places, laying them regular,
> Setting the studs by their tenons in the mortises according as they were prepared,
> The blows of mallets and hammers, the attitudes of the men, their curv'd limbs,
> Bending, standing, astride the beams, driving in pins, holding on by posts and braces,
> The hook'd arm over the plate, the other arm wielding the axe,
> The floor-men forcing the planks close to be nail'd,
> Their postures bringing their weapons downward on the bearers,
> The echoes resounding through the vacant building:
> The huge storehouse carried up in the city well under way,
> The six framing-men, two in the middle and two at each end, carefully bearing on their shoulders a heavy stick for a cross-beam,

The crowded line of masons with trowels in their right hands rapidly laying the long side-wall, two hundred feet from front to rear,
The flexible rise and fall of backs, the continual click of the trowels striking the bricks,
The bricks one after another each laid so workmanlike in its place, and set with a knock of the trowel-handle,
The piles of materials, the mortar on the mortar-boards, and the steady replenishing by the hod-men;
Spar-makers in the spar-yard, the swarming row of well-grown apprentices,
The swing of their axes on the square-hew'd log shaping it toward the shape of a mast,
The brisk short crackle of the steel driven slantingly into the pine,
The butter-color'd chips flying off in great flakes and slivers,
The limber motion of brawny young arms and hips in easy costumes,
The constructor of wharves, bridges, piers, bulk-heads, floats, stays against the sea;
The city fireman, the fire that suddenly bursts forth in the
close-pack'd square,
The arriving engines, the hoarse shouts, the nimble stepping and daring,
The strong command through the fire-trumpets, the falling in line, the rise

> and fall of the arms forcing the water,
> The slender, spasmic, blue-white jets, the bringing to bear of the hooks and ladders and their execution,
> The crash and cut away of connecting wood-work, or through floors if the fire smoulders under them,
> The crowd with their lit faces watching, the glare and dense shadows;   72

Whitman celebrates firemen here as he had in *Song of Myself*—he seems as excited by the spectacle of a fire as "the crowd with their lit faces watching..." From that reverie he contemplates the making of the axe in ages past and the uses just and unjust as he imagines the siege of a city: *Roar, flames, blood, drunkenness, madness...* (Line 88 below) With *the hell of war and cruelties of creeds* we can't help but think of the religious wars of the sixteenth century or the Albegensian campaign of the thirteenth: "Kill them all, for God knows his own." [251]

> The forger at his forge-furnace and the user of iron after him,   73
> The maker of the axe large and small, and the welder and temperer,
> The chooser breathing his breath on the cold steel and trying the edge with his thumb,
> The one who clean-shapes the handle and sets it firmly in the socket;
> The shadowy processions of the portraits of the past users also,
> The primal patient mechanics, the architects and engineers,

> The far-off Assyrian edifice and Mizra edifice,
> The Roman lictors preceding the consuls,
> The antique European warrior with his axe in combat,
> The uplifted arm, the clatter of blows on the helmeted head,
> The death-howl, the limpsy tumbling body, the rush of friend and foe thither, 83
> The siege of revolted lieges determin'd for liberty,
> The summons to surrender, the battering at castle gates, the truce and parley,
> The sack of an old city in its time,
> The bursting in of mercenaries and bigots tumultuously and disorderly,
> Roar, flames, blood, drunkenness, madness, 88
> Goods freely rifled from houses and temples, screams of women in the gripe of brigands,
> Craft and thievery of camp-followers, men running, old persons despairing,
> The hell of war, the cruelties of creeds, 91
> The list of all executive deeds and words just or unjust,
> The power of personality just or unjust. 93

The poet takes up the theme of life and death in the 4th Canto. The dead are not so much vanquished as they are invigorated by the life they left behind. The curious line:

"And the dead advance as much as the living advance," (Line 96 below) is explained essentially in a question:

> "What do you think endures?" (Line 100 below)

Once, at a writer's seminar, author A.J. Langguth addressed the same issue. "As a writer you do your work—and then you die." Few writers are as concise or as truthful.

4.
>> Muscle and pluck forever!   94
>> What invigorates life invigorates death,
>> And the dead advance as much as the living advance,   96
>> And the future is no more uncertain than the present,
>> For the roughness of the earth and of man encloses as much as the delicatesse of the earth and of man,
>> And nothing endures but personal qualities.
>>
>> What do you think endures?   100
>> Do you think a great city endures?
>> Or a teeming manufacturing state? or a prepared constitution? or the best built steamships?
>> Or hotels of granite and iron? or any chef-d'oeuvres of engineering, forts, armaments?   103

The end of Canto 4 and the succeeding Cantos 5 & 6 anticipate Nietzsche's *Ubermensch* by three decades:

"All does very well till one flash of defiance." is the poet's opening salvo of the theme and the determination of what constitutes a great city — and Whitman's utopian dream of a readership that embraces it.

> Away! these are not to be cherish'd for themselves, 104
> They fill their hour, the dancers dance, the musicians play for them,
> The show passes, all does well enough of course,
> All does very well till one flash of defiance.
>
> A great city is that which has the greatest men and women,
> If it be a few ragged huts it is still the greatest city in the whole world. 109

5.

> The place where a great city stands is not the place of stretch'd wharves, docks, manufactures, deposits of produce merely, 110
> Nor the place of ceaseless salutes of new-comers or the anchor-lifters of the departing,
> Nor the place of the tallest and costliest buildings or shops selling goods from the rest of the earth,
> Nor the place of the best libraries and schools, nor the place where money is plentiest,
> Nor the place of the most numerous population.

Where the city stands with the brawniest breed of orators and bards,

Where the city stands that is belov'd by these, and loves them in return and understands them,

Where no monuments exist to heroes but in the common words and deeds,

Where thrift is in its place, and prudence is in its place,

Where the men and women think lightly of the laws,

Where the slave ceases, and the master of slaves ceases,

Where the populace rise at once against the never-ending audacity of elected persons,

Where fierce men and women pour forth as the sea to the whistle of death pours its sweeping and unript waves,

Where outside authority enters always after the precedence of inside authority,

Where the citizen is always the head and ideal, and President, Mayor, Governor and what not, are agents for pay,

Where children are taught to be laws to themselves, and to depend on themselves,

Where equanimity is illustrated in affairs,

> Where speculations on the soul are encouraged, 127
> Where women walk in public processions in the streets the same as the men,
> Where they enter the public assembly and take places the same as the men;
> Where the city of the faithfulest friends stands,
> Where the city of the cleanliness of the sexes stands,
> Where the city of the healthiest fathers stands,
> Where the city of the best-bodied mothers stands,
> There the great city stands. 134

Whitman anticipates the great German. So also were they both students of Emerson. Nietzsche not only called Emerson the "American Socrates" but was to write: "To no other book have I felt as close as to the books of Emerson; I do not have the right to praise them." [252] And Whitman, in a notebook entry, *At Emerson's grave*: "A just man, poised on himself, all-loving, all-inclusive, and sane and clear as the sun." We are doubly moved by the lines from Emerson's essay, *Experience*, when we recall that one of Whitman's sobriquets is the vagabond poet :

Emerson:

> I carry the keys to my castle in my hand ready to throw them at the feet of my lord, whenever and in what disguise wheresoever he shall appear...

I know he is in the neighborhood,
hidden among vagabonds.[253]

Emerson and Nietzsche will briefly reverberate in the 6th Canto of Whitman's *Song of the Broad-Axe*. As is the practice, Whitman's *Song* can be studied as a solo canticle by simply following the linear numeration.

6.
>How beggarly appear arguments before a defiant deed! 135
>How the floridness of the materials of cities shrivels before a man's or woman's look! 136

Whitman:

>All waits, or goes by default, till a strong being appears; 137
>A strong being is the proof of the race, and of the ability of the universe;
>When he or she appears, materials are overaw'd, 139
>The dispute on the Soul stops,
>The old customs and phrases are confronted, turn'd back, or laid away. 141

Nietzsche:

>Man is a rope stretched between the animal and the Superman—a rope over an abyss...What is great in man is that he is a bridge and not a goal: what is lovable in man is that he is an over-going and a down-going...

> I love the great despisers, because they are the great adorers, and arrows longing for the other shore.[254]

Whitman:

> What is your money-making now? what
>   can it do now? 142
> What is your respectability now?
> What are your theology, tuition, society,
>   traditions, statute-books, now?
> Where are your jibes of being now?
> Where are your cavils about the Soul
>   now? 146

In Canto 7 the axe has been displaced by a pick as the poet travels through time to the *time out of mind* when artists applied pigment to the granite walls of the ancient necropoli of Lascaux and Altamira.

7.
> A sterile landscape covers the ore, there
>   is as good as the best for all the
>   forbidding appearance. 147
>
> There is the mine, there are the miners,
> The forge-furnace is there, the melt is
>   accomplish'd, the hammersmen are
>   at hand with their tongs and
>   hammers,
> What always served and always serves
>   is at hand.
>
> Than this nothing has better served, it
>   has served all,

Served the fluent-tongued and subtle-sensed Greek, and long ere the Greek,
Served in building the buildings that last longer than any,
Served the Hebrew, the Persian, the most ancient Hindustanee,
Served the mound-raiser on the Mississippi, served those whose relics remain in Central America,
Served Albic temples in woods or on plains, with unhewn pillars and the druids,
Served the artificial clefts, vast, high, silent, on the snow-cover'd hills of Scandinavia,
Served those who time out of mind made on the granite walls rough sketches of the sun, moon, stars, ships, ocean waves,
Served the paths of the irruptions of the Goths, served the pastoral tribes and nomads,
Served the long distant Kelt, served the hardy pirates of the Baltic,
Served before any of those the venerable and harmless men of Ethiopia,
Served the making of helms for the galleys of pleasure and the making of those for war,
Served all great works on land and all great works on the sea,
For the mediaeval ages and before the mediaeval ages,

> Served not the living only then as now,
> but served the dead. 165

The less savory aspect of the heroic axe is addressed in Canto 8. The poet reviews the martyrs who met their end on the headsmen's scaffold and telegraphs his defiance: *Mind you O foreign kings. O priests, the crop shall never run out.* (Line 177 below)

8.
> I see the European headsman, 166
> He stands mask'd, clothed in red, with
> huge legs and strong naked arms,
> And leans on a ponderous axe.
>
> (Whom have you slaughter'd lately
> European headsman?
> Whose is that blood upon you so wet
> and sticky?) 170
>
> I see the clear sunsets of the martyrs,
> I see from the scaffolds the descending
> ghosts,
> Ghosts of dead lords, uncrown'd ladies,
> impeach'd ministers, rejected kings,
> Rivals, traitors, poisoners, disgraced
> chieftains and the rest.
>
> I see those who in any land have died
> for the good cause, 175
> The seed is spare, nevertheless the crop
> shall never run out, (Mind you O
> foreign kings, O priests, the crop
> shall never run out.) 176

> I see the blood wash'd entirely away from the axe,
> Both blade and helve are clean,
> They spirt no more the blood of European nobles, they clasp no more the necks of queens. 179
>
> I see the headsman withdraw and become useless,
> I see the scaffold untrodden and mouldy, I see no longer any axe upon it,
> I see the mighty and friendly emblem of the power of my own race, the newest, largest race. 183

The concluding four Cantos celebrate the fruit of the axe which follows: "The axe leaps," with the equally demonstrative: "The Shapes arise," which is a repeated refrain throughout the remaining sixty-nine lines of the poem. It is instructive to read some of it aloud — it is a solid and stirring performance and easily approaches the poet's ideal of music and the grandness of Grand Opera. Listen to the cadence of words "tumbling forth": hut, tent, pick, spade, rail, prop, lamb, lath, tub, hoop, vane, sash, hoe, rake saw, mallet, wedge and rounce.

9.

> (America! I do not vaunt my love for you, 184
> I have what I have.)
>
> The axe leaps! 186
> The solid forest gives fluid utterances,
> They tumble forth, they rise and form,

Hut, tent, landing, survey,
Flail, plough, pick, crowbar, spade,
Shingle, rail, prop, wainscot, lamb, lath, panel, gable,
Citadel, ceiling, saloon, academy, organ, exhibition-house, library,
Cornice, trellis, pilaster, balcony, window, turret, porch,
Hoe, rake, pitchfork, pencil, wagon, staff, saw, jack-plane, mallet, wedge, rounce,
Chair, tub, hoop, table, wicket, vane, sash, floor,
Work-box, chest, string'd instrument, boat, frame, and what not,
Capitols of States, and capitol of the nation of States,
Long stately rows in avenues, hospitals for orphans or for the poor or sick,
Manhattan steamboats and clippers taking the measure of all seas.

The shapes arise!
Shapes of the using of axes anyhow, and the users and all that neighbors them,
Cutters down of wood and haulers of it to the Penobscot or Kenebec,
Dwellers in cabins among the Californian mountains or by the little lakes, or on the Columbia,
Dwellers south on the banks of the Gila or Rio Grande, friendly gatherings, the characters and fun,

Dwellers along the St. Lawrence, or north in Kanada, or down by the Yellowstone, dwellers on coasts and off coasts,
Seal-fishers, whalers, arctic seamen breaking passages through the ice.

The shapes arise! 207
Shapes of factories, arsenals, foundries, markets,
Shapes of the two-threaded tracks of railroads,
Shapes of the sleepers of bridges, vast frameworks, girders, arches,
Shapes of the fleets of barges, tows, lake and canal craft, river craft,
Ship-yards and dry-docks along the Eastern and Western seas, and in many a bay and by-place,
The live-oak kelsons, the pine planks, the spars, the hackmatack-roots for knees,
The ships themselves on their ways, the tiers of scaffolds, the workmen busy outside and inside,
The tools lying around, the great auger and little auger, the adze, bolt, line, square, gouge, and bead-plane. 215

Note how the 2nd half of the 10th Canto is contrasted with the first. In the first *the shapes that arise* are decidedly PG in presentation. This is not to disparage the virtues praised. He specifically references their wholesomeness:

> "friendly parents…happy young man and woman, well-married, supper joyously cooked, joyously eaten, chaste young wife and chaste husband."

Then follows the R rated list: "prisoners placed in the court room; the liquor bar leaned against by the rum drinkers, young and old; shamed and angry stairs; the unwholesome adulterous couple; the gambling board and the devilish winnings and losings; the step ladder to the scaffold, the dangling rope; the convicted murdered with haggard face and pinion'd arms."

And then, finally, the return of the prodigal son:

> The door whence the son left home confident and puff'd up,
> The door he enter'd again from a long and scandalous absence, diseas'd, broken down, without innocence, without means;

I've contrasted these stanzas to give the obvious lie to the charges of immorality inherent in his poetry. *Song of the Broad-Axe* first appeared in the 2nd edition (1856) of *Leaves*. His morality is, by contemporary standards, of an elevated order. The poet, perhaps loads the deck in his plea for the conventional—but if his intention was to deny the blue noses their righteous thunder he largely succeeds, although remaining largely unheralded and unread.

10.
> The shapes arise!   216

The shape measur'd, saw'd, jack'd, join'd, stain'd,
The coffin-shape for the dead to lie within in his shroud, 218
The shape got out in posts, in the bedstead posts, in the posts of the bride's bed,
The shape of the little trough, the shape of the rockers beneath, the shape of the babe's cradle,
The shape of the floor-planks, the floor-planks for dancers' feet,
The shape of the planks of the family home, the home of the friendly parents and children,
The shape of the roof of the home of the happy young man and woman, the roof over the well-married young man and woman,
The roof over the supper joyously cook'd by the chaste wife, and joyously eaten by the chaste husband, content after his day's work.
The shapes arise! 225
The shape of the prisoner's place in the court-room, and of him or her seated in the place, 226
The shape of the liquor-bar lean'd against by the young rum-drinker and the old rum-drinker, 227
The shape of the shamed and angry stairs trod by sneaking foot- steps, 228
The shape of the sly settee, and the adulterous unwholesome couple, 229

> The shape of the gambling-board with its devilish winnings and losings, 230
> The shape of the step-ladder for the convicted and sentenced murderer, the murderer with haggard face and pinion'd arms, 231
> The sheriff at hand with his deputies, the silent and white-lipp'd crowd, the dangling of the rope. 232
>
> The shapes arise! 233
> Shapes of doors giving many exits and entrances,
> The door passing the dissever'd friend flush'd and in haste,
> The door that admits good news and bad news,
> The door whence the son left home confident and puff'd up,
> The door he enter'd again from a long and scandalous absence, diseas'd, broken down, without innocence, without means. 238

The next lines originally appeared in the 1856 edition of *Leaves of Grass* but were excluded in the 1867 edition, and thereafter. Aside from the sexual innuendo of his poems, the most stridently offended critics decried the poet's egoism. It took the better part of a century for them to recognize that his ego was attached to the character he created and not the poet himself. Egoism belies its name when it is equally projected to the readers of his poems: "For every atom belonging to me as well belongs to you."

Self-aggrandizement was presumed by virtue of self-reviews that he submitted to the press. Traubel recorded a conversation he had with the poet on this very point:

> Walt, some people think you blew your own horn a lot — wrote puffs on yourself — sort of attitudinized and called attention to yourself quite a bit...
>
> 'Do they say so? Do they? Who are "some people"? what are "puffs"? I have often talked of myself as I would of you — blamed and praised just the same; looked at myself as I would if I was somebody else. I am not ashamed of it. I have never praised myself where I would not if it had been somebody else; I have merely look myself over, and repeated candidly what I saw — the mean things and the good things. I did so in the "Leaves"; I have done so in other places — candidly faced the life in myself — my own possibilities, probabilities; reckoned up my account, so to speak. I know this is unusual, but is it wrong? Why should not everybody do it? You, anybody? If you did it for the sake of aggrandizing yourself, that would be another thing, but doing it simply for the purpose of getting your own weight and measure, is as right done for you, by yourself, as done for another.'[255]

WHITMAN'S CODE: A NEW BIBLE, VOLUME I

M.C. GARDNER

The following lines are less a biography of the poet than of his poetic creation—the rowdy boisterous *Walt Whitman* swaggering through his poems. He decided to delete them as a provocation that would add to that perception—the lines are so much a part of the accepted Whitman mythos, that the risk is minimal:

> His shape arises,
>
> > Arrogant, masculine, naïve, rowdish,
> > Laughter, weeper, worker, idler, citizen, countrymen,
> > Saunterer of woods, stander upon hills, summer swimmer in rivers or by the sea,
> > Of pure American breed, of reckless health, his body perfect, free from taint from top to toe, free forever from headache and dyspepsia, clean-breathed,
> > Attitudes lithe and erect, costume free, neck gray and open, of slow movement on foot,
> > Passer of his right arm round the shoulders of his friends, companion of the street,
> > Persuader always of people to give him their sweetest touches, and never their meanest,
> > A Manhattanese bred, fond of Brooklyn, fond of Broadway, fond of life of the wharves and the great ferries,
> > Enterer everywhere, welcomed everywhere, easily understood after all.

> Never offering others, always offering himself, corroborating in his phrenology,
> Voluptuous, inhibitive, combative, conscientious, ailmentive, esteem, comparison, individuality, form, locality, eventuality,
> Arrowing by life, manners, works, to contribute illustrations of results of the States.
> Teacher of the unquenchable creed, namely egoism,
> Inviter of others continually henceforth to try their strength against his.

Note that the poet as man is followed by the shape of woman. Perhaps he was correct in thinking that others would assume that he assumed too much.

11.

> Her shape arises, 239
> She less guarded than ever, yet more guarded than ever,
> The gross and soil'd she moves among do not make her gross and soil'd,
> She knows the thoughts as she passes, nothing is conceal'd from her,
> She is none the less considerate or friendly therefore,
> She is the best belov'd, it is without exception, she has no reason to fear and she does not fear,
> Oaths, quarrels, hiccupp'd songs, smutty expressions, are idle to her as she passes,

> She is silent, she is possess'd of herself,
> they do not offend her,
> She receives them as the laws of Nature
> receive them, she is strong,
> She too is a law of Nature—there is no
> law stronger than she is. 248

The concluding canto embodies the shapes to which the previous eleven were directed:

12.
> The main shapes arise! 249
> Shapes of Democracy total, result of
> centuries,
> Shapes ever projecting other shapes,
> Shapes of turbulent manly cities,
> Shapes of the friends and home-givers
> of the whole earth,
> Shapes bracing the earth and braced
> with the whole earth. 254

20. Song of the Exposition

(1871)

Song of the Exposition was written for a reading by the poet at the Fortieth Annual Exhibition of the American Institute in 1871. It is a poem of great erudition and demonstrates a remarkable depth to poet's extensive studies. He almost *out-Milton's* Milton in classical allusions. The poem was published in a number of newspapers, many which had critical reviews of the poet and his poem.

Sixteen years after the inaugural edition of *Leaves*, Whitman was still a controversial poet seeking a sympathetic audience. The poem's original first line and title were demoted to the fourth line by 1881: *After All Not to Create Only*. The poet evokes the muse of the old world to visit these *united states* as he articulates a song of industry on behalf of the American worker: "To exalt the present and the real, to teach the average man the glory of his daily walk and trade." The first Canto is remarkably terse given the grandeur of its subject: "Ah little recks the laborer how near his work is holding him to God." We are not only the fruit of our own effort but, as well, the leavings of "the loving Laborer through space and time." Our results are the trust of times we know not of and as little acknowledge: "While how little the New after all, how much the Old, Old World... long and long has the grass been growing, long and long has the rain been falling, long has the globe been rolling round."

Song of the Exposition

1.

(Ah little recks the laborer,
How near his work is holding him to God, 2
The loving Laborer through space and time.)

After all not to create only, or found only,
But to bring perhaps from afar what is already founded, 5
To give it our own identity, average, limitless, free, 6

> To fill the gross the torpid bulk with vital religious fire,
> Not to repel or destroy so much as accept, fuse, rehabilitate, 8
> To obey as well as command, to follow more than to lead,
> These also are the lessons of our New World; 10
> While how little the New after all, how much the Old, Old World!
>
> Long and long has the grass been growing, 12
> Long and long has the rain been falling,
> Long has the globe been rolling round. 14

In the Second Canto, the poet has fun with Emerson's pronouncements in *The American Scholar*: First, he invites the old-world Muse to America. "Cross out the immensely overpaid accounts...Placard 'Removed' and 'To Let' on the rocks of snowy Parnassus...repeat at Jerusalem, place the notice high on Jaffa Gate and on Mount Moriah."

2.

> Come Muse migrate from Greece and Ionia, 15
> Cross out please those immensely overpaid accounts,
> That matter of Troy and Achilles' wrath, and Aeneas', Odysseus' wanderings,
> Placard "Removed" and "To Let" on the rocks of your snowy Parnassus,

> Repeat at Jerusalem, place the notice high on Jaffa's gate and on Mount Moriah,
> The same on the walls of your German, French and Spanish castles, and Italian collections,
> For know a better, fresher, busier sphere, a wide, untried domain awaits, demands you.   21

In the Third Canto the invited muse arrives and the poet *amuses* himself imagining the rustle of her dress and projects his own smile on her face as she's "installed amid the kitchen ware!" Before her "installation" the poet evokes the inspiration of Virgil, Dante and Tennyson. His love of Shakespeare was without bounds. One suspects that " Shakespeare's purple page" (Line 52 below) is as likely the "royal robe" of the *Prince of Poets*, than the *purple prose* of an old world rival.

3.
> Responsive to our summons,   22
> Or rather to her long-nurs'd inclination,
> Join'd with an irresistible, natural gravitation,
> She comes! I hear the rustling of her gown,   25
> I scent the odor of her breath's delicious fragrance,
> I mark her step divine, her curious eyes a-turning, rolling,
> Upon this very scene.
>
> The dame of dames! can I believe then,

Those ancient temples, sculptures classic, could none of them retain her?
Nor shades of Virgil and Dante, nor myriad memories, poems, old associations, magnetize and hold on to her?
But that she's left them all — and here?

Yes, if you will allow me to say so,
I, my friends, if you do not, can plainly see her,
The same undying soul of earth's, activity's, beauty's, heroism's expression,
Out from her evolutions hither come, ended the strata of her former themes,
Hidden and cover'd by to-day's, foundation of to-day's,
Ended, deceas'd through time, her voice by Castaly's fountain,
Silent the broken-lipp'd Sphynx in Egypt, silent all those century-baffling tombs,
Ended for aye the epics of Asia's, Europe's helmeted warriors, ended the primitive call of the muses,   40
Calliope's call forever closed, Clio, Melpomene, Thalia dead,
Ended the stately rhythmus of Una and Oriana, ended the quest of the holy Graal,
Jerusalem a handful of ashes blown by the wind, extinct,

The Crusaders' streams of shadowy midnight troops sped with the sunrise,
Amadis, Tancred, utterly gone, Charlemagne, Roland, Oliver gone,
Palmerin, ogre, departed, vanish'd the turrets that Usk from its waters reflected,
Arthur vanish'd with all his knights, Merlin and Lancelot and Galahad, all gone, dissolv'd utterly like an exhalation;
Pass'd! pass'd! for us, forever pass'd, that once so mighty world, now void, inanimate, phantom world,
Embroider'd, dazzling, foreign world, with all its gorgeous legends, myths, 49
Its kings and castles proud, its priests and warlike lords and courtly dames,
Pass'd to its charnel vault, coffin'd with crown and armor on,
Blazon'd with Shakspere's purple page, 52
And dirged by Tennyson's sweet sad rhyme. 53

I say I see, my friends, if you do not, the illustrious emigre, (having it is true in her day, although the same, changed, journey'd considerable,)
Making directly for this rendezvous, vigorously clearing a path for herself, striding through the confusion,

> By thud of machinery and shrill steam-whistle undismay'd,
> Bluff'd not a bit by drain-pipe, gasometers, artificial fertilizers,
> Smiling and pleas'd with palpable intent to stay,
> She's here, install'd amid the kitchen ware! 59

The poet forgets his manners (not among his chief concerns) and then introduces the Muse to Dame Columbia — ever henceforth sisters dear be both. He then assures the muse as to America's worthiness:

4.

> But hold — don't I forget my manners? 60
> To introduce the stranger, (what else indeed do I live to chant for?) to thee Columbia;
> In liberty's name welcome immortal! clasp hands,
> And ever henceforth sisters dear be both.
>
> Fear not O Muse! truly new ways and days receive, surround you,
> I candidly confess a queer, queer race, of novel fashion,
> And yet the same old human race, the same within, without,
> Faces and hearts the same, feelings the same, yearnings the same,
> The same old love, beauty and use the same. 68

WHITMAN'S CODE: A NEW BIBLE, VOLUME I
M.C. GARDNER

Whitman is careful not to completely dispel Europe and Asia. In the first stanza of the 5th Canto, he presents a magic show to further acquaint the muse with the occupations and products of America:

5.

    We do not blame thee elder World, nor really separate ourselves from thee,   69
    (Would the son separate himself from the father?)
    Looking back on thee, seeing thee to thy duties, grandeurs, through past ages bending, building,
    We build to ours to-day.

    Mightier than Egypt's tombs,
    Fairer than Grecia's, Roma's temples,
    Prouder than Milan's statued, spired cathedral,   75
    More picturesque than Rhenish castle-keeps,
    We plan even now to raise, beyond them all,
    Thy great cathedral sacred industry, no tomb,
    A keep for life for practical invention.
    As in a waking vision,
    E'en while I chant I see it rise, I scan and prophesy outside and in,
    Its manifold ensemble.   82

    Around a palace, loftier, fairer, ampler than any yet,
    Earth's modern wonder, history's seven outstripping,

High rising tier on tier with glass and
    iron facades,
Gladdening the sun and sky, enhued in
    cheerfulest hues,
Bronze, lilac, robin's-egg, marine and
    crimson,
Over whose golden roof shall flaunt,
    beneath thy banner Freedom,
The banners of the States and flags of
    every land,
A brood of lofty, fair, but lesser palaces
    shall cluster.   90

Somewhere within their walls shall all
    that forwards perfect human life be
    started,
Tried, taught, advanced, visibly
    exhibited.

Not only all the world of works, trade,
    products,
But all the workmen of the world here
    to be represented.
Here shall you trace in flowing
    operation,
In every state of practical, busy
    movement, the rills of civilization,
Materials here under your eye shall
    change their shape as if by magic,
The cotton shall be pick'd almost in the
    very field,
Shall be dried, clean'd, ginn'd, baled,
    spun into thread and cloth before
    you,

You shall see hands at work at all the
    old processes and all the new ones,   100
You shall see the various grains and
    how flour is made and then bread
    baked by the bakers,
You shall see the crude ores of
    California and Nevada passing on
    and on till they become bullion,
You shall watch how the printer sets
    type, and learn what a composing-
    stick is,   103
You shall mark in amazement the Hoe
    press whirling its cylinders,
    shedding the printed leaves steady
    and fast,
The photograph, model, watch, pin,
    nail, shall be created before you.

In large calm halls, a stately museum
    shall teach you the infinite lessons
    of minerals,
In another, woods, plants, vegetation
    shall be illustrated—in another
    animals, animal life and
    development.

One stately house shall be the music
    house,
Others for other arts—learning, the
    sciences, shall all be here,
None shall be slighted, none but shall
    here be honor'd, help'd, exampled.   110

6.

(This, this and these, America, shall be
    your pyramids and obelisks,   111

> Your Alexandrian Pharos, gardens of
>   Babylon,
> Your temple at Olympia.)
> The male and female many laboring not,
> Shall ever here confront the laboring
>   many,
> With precious benefits to both, glory to
>   all,
> To thee America, and thee eternal Muse.
>
> And here shall ye inhabit powerful
>   Matrons!
> In your vast state vaster than all the old,
> Echoed through long, long centuries to
>   come,
> To sound of different, prouder songs,
>   with stronger themes,
> Practical, peaceful life, the people's life,
>   the People themselves,
> Lifted, illumin'd, bathed in peace — elate,
>   secure in peace.   123

The wound dresser of the 1860s imagines a utopia that does away with war and remembers it with as startling an image as Shakespeare's *Universal wolf*: "...never more return that show of blacken'd, mutilated corpses! That hell unpent and raid of blood, fit for tigers or for lop-tongued wolves, not reasoning men." (Lines 125-126 below)

7.

> Away with themes of war! away with
>   war itself!   124

> Hence from my shuddering sight to never more return that show of blacken'd, mutilated corpses! 125
> That hell unpent and raid of blood, fit for wild tigers or for lop-tongued wolves, not reasoning men, 126
> And in its stead speed industry's campaigns,
> With thy undaunted armies, engineering,
> Thy pennants labor, loosen'd to the breeze,
> Thy bugles sounding loud and clear. 130

Whitman, among the most romantic of poets, has little patience for romance—the poet's creation was believed by the poet to be a realistic vision—something seen, not only just believed.

> Away with old romance, 131
> Away with novels, plots and plays of foreign courts,
> Away with love-verses sugar'd in rhyme, the intrigues, amours of idlers,
> Fitted for only banquets of the night where dancers to late music slide,
> The unhealthy pleasures, extravagant dissipations of the few,
> With perfumes, heat and wine, beneath the dazzling chandeliers.
>
> To you ye reverent sane sisters, 137
> I raise a voice for far superber themes for poets and for art,

To exalt the present and the real,
To teach the average man the glory of his daily walk and trade, 140
To sing in songs how exercise and chemical life are never to be baffled,
To manual work for each and all, to plough, hoe, dig,
To plant and tend the tree, the berry, vegetables, flowers,
For every man to see to it that he really do something, for every woman too;
To use the hammer and the saw, (rip, or cross-cut,) 145
To cultivate a turn for carpentering, plastering, painting,
To work as tailor, tailoress, nurse, hostler, porter,
To invent a little, something ingenious, to aid the washing, cooking, cleaning,
And hold it no disgrace to take a hand at them themselves.

I say I bring thee Muse to-day and here, 150
All occupations, duties broad and close,
Toil, healthy toil and sweat, endless, without cessation,
The old, old practical burdens, interests, joys,
The family, parentage, childhood, husband and wife,
The house-comforts, the house itself and all its belongings,
Food and its preservation, chemistry applied to it,

> Whatever forms the average, strong, complete, sweet-blooded man or woman, the perfect longeve personality,
> And helps its present life to health and happiness, and shapes its soul,
> For the eternal real life to come.   159
>
> With latest connections, works, the inter-transportation of the world,
> Steam-power, the great express lines, gas, petroleum,
> These triumphs of our time, the Atlantic's delicate cable,
> The Pacific railroad, the Suez canal, the Mont Cenis and Gothard and Hoosac tunnels, the Brooklyn bridge,
> This earth all spann'd with iron rails, with lines of steamships threading in every sea,
> Our own rondure, the current globe I bring.   165

When the poet speaks of *the eternal real life to come* he is also speaking of the eternal life that we each experience under the notion of time. Plato rightly saw that time was the moving image of eternity. Wittgenstein further noted that timelessness was not the same as perpetual endurance. Whitman's soul, as is each our own, is eternal—Whitman and Tom, Dick, and Harry are, however, mortal and subject to dissolution. In the logic of Vedanta these two statements are not contradictory—each, in fact, confirms the other.

The same can be said of Buddhists and Hindus who are popularly believed to countenance an eternity of transmigration. Alan Watts was curiously skeptical:

> I wish, therefore, to commend what to many students of these doctrines may seem a startling thesis: that Buddhists and Vedantists who understand their own doctrines profoundly, who are in fact liberated, do not believe in reincarnation in any literal sense."[256]

Whitman makes as much a distinction between himself and his creation as he does between his *Me myself* and the Soul. Clearly the one is subject to illness, infirmary, old age and death—while the other attended the first great nothing and will attend Universal dissolution in the confidence that all will surely commence again.

The first half of that equation is, however, subject to the same fears and hopes of any mortal. He could, at times, harbor the ambition of traveling between the stars without personal forfeiture, upon shuffling off his mortal coil. Coomaraswamy reiterates Watts' pronouncement. If we substitute eternal life with reincarnation we can see that the two are essentially the same:

> The notion of a "reincarnation" in the popular sense of the return of deceased individuals to rebirth on this earth represents only a misunderstanding of the doctrines of heredity, transmigration and regeneration.[257]

The key, perhaps, is in the Mahayana Buddhist notion of sunyata—or what we translate as void or emptiness. It had been suggested by earlier Buddhist schools that particulars were an illusion and only the *One* was real. Emerson (who had no knowledge of the yet to be translated *Prajnaparamita Sutras*) was forceful and quick in his critique:

> Though the uninspired man certainly finds persons a convenience in household matters, the divine man does not respect them; he sees them as a rack of clouds, or a fleet of ripple which the wind drives over the surface of the water. But this is flat rebellion. Nature will not be Buddhist, she resents generalizing; and insults the philosopher in every moment with a million fresh particulars. It is all idle talking, as much as a man is a whole so is he also a part: and it were partial not to see it. What you say in your pompous distribution only distrusts you into your class and section. You have not got rid of parts by denying them, but are the more partial. [258]

The first Buddhist scriptures were assembled by the 2nd council in 383 B.C. This was concurrent with the assemblage of the Hebrew scripture into the *Tanakh*—what the Christians call the Old Testament when they wish to distinguish *wisdom past its sell date* from the *fresh* or New Testament notions newly available for your philosophical predilection. The Buddhists were not exempt from this same type of name game.

The earliest Buddhists were known as Theravadins. These were the devoted monks who kept an oral tradition of the Buddha subsequent to his Parinirvana. During a early council of his followers a schism developed between two major factions, the Theravadins and the Mahasanghikas. For the first group the revelation was complete with the advent and conclusion of the Buddha's teachings. The second group believed that the Buddha's revelation was on-going to those who were open to receiving it. By 80 B.C. the Tipitaka had been recorded on scrolls and placed in baskets. These included the Buddha's celebrated points of doctrine or Dhammapada. This was among the first scriptures translated for the west and would have been Emerson's point of contact. The Mahasanghikas during these centuries were also collecting a body of scripture that had been transmitted since the Buddha's death. The authors of these collections suggested they were further teachings of the Buddha — but teaching disseminated by the Buddha in his spiritual body — the Sambhogakaya. The first translators thought these claims fantastical and were initially reluctant to give them relevance. These were the Sutras of the Mahayana — the Greater ship or vehicle as opposed to the Hinayana (the Theravadins) who were designated the Lesser or smaller vehicle. The Mahayanas saw the Buddha in all things whereas the "Hinayanas," preferred that their master remain restricted his historical incarnation. The Mahayana had beaten Emerson to the punch by two thousand years. They well knew that in designating the *particular* as illusionary and the *One* as sacrosanct, they were simply creating another duality. The Mahayana took an additional step by asserting *Particulars* and the *One* to be completely empty concepts. The individual was designated "anatman" or without self.

The rest of existence was declared sunyata, void—completely empty. Whitman knew little of the Hinayana and nothing of the Mahayana but throughout *Leaves of Grass* was to suggest a conflation of them both. He is at his most *Mahayana* during his "witness" poems. Here he gazes at the world without judgment in what he calls "the divine average." That average is 0 or the sunyata of which we have been speaking. This vision is moderated by the opening of the 3rd *eye*, or Prajna. And although that might seem cold and unfeeling it is always companioned by compassion (Karuna) for the suffering it beholds. Prajna is the philosophic pole of the Mahayana and Karuna is the religious. Whitman might *see and watch and be silent* but he also nursed tens of thousand of soldiers during the Civil War. But since I have taken this digression to critique Emerson's critique, I will give him the last word, where, as one might suspect, he is bemused and serenely beyond refutation:

> How sincere and confidential we can be, saying all that lies in the mind, and yet go away feeling that all is yet unsaid, from the incapacity of the parties to know each other, although they use the same words! My companion assumes to know my mood and habit of thought, and we go on from explanation to explanation until all is said which words can, and we leave matters just as they were at first, because of that vicious assumption. Is it that every man believes every other to be an incurable partialist, and himself a universalist? I talked yesterday with a pair of philosophers:

> I endeavored to show my good men that I like everything by turns and nothing long; that I loved the centre, but doated on the superficies; that I love *man*, if men seemed to me mice and rats; that I revered saints, but woke up glad that the old pagan world stood its ground and died hard; that I was glad of men of every gift and nobility, but would not live in their arms. Could they but once understand that I loved to know they existed and heartily wished them God-speed, yet, out of my poverty of life and thought, had no word or welcome for them when they came to see me, and could well consent to their living in Oregon for any claim I felt on them—it would be a great satisfaction. [259]

8.

> And thou America,   166
> Thy offspring towering e'er so high, yet higher Thee above all towering,
> With Victory on thy left, and at thy right hand Law;
> Thou Union holding all, fusing, absorbing, tolerating all,
> Thee, ever thee, I sing.
>
> Thou, also thou, a World,
> With all thy wide geographies, manifold, different, distant,
> Rounded by thee in one—one common orbic language,
> One common indivisible destiny for All.   174
>
> And by the spells which ye vouchsafe to those your ministers in earnest,

> I here personify and call my themes, to make them pass before ye. 176

In a magnificent pastoral the poet bids the muse to witness America:

> Behold, America! (and thou, ineffable guest and sister!) 177
> For thee come trooping up thy waters and thy lands;
> Behold! thy fields and farms, thy far-off woods and mountains,
> As in procession coming. 180
>
> Behold, the sea itself,
> And on its limitless, heaving breast, the ships;
> See, where their white sails, bellying in the wind, speckle the green and blue, 183
> See, the steamers coming and going, steaming in or out of port,
> See, dusky and undulating, the long pennants of smoke.
>
> Behold, in Oregon, far in the north and west,
> Or in Maine, far in the north and east, thy cheerful axemen,
> Wielding all day their axes.
>
> Behold, on the lakes, thy pilots at their wheels, thy oarsmen,
> How the ash writhes under those muscular arms!

There by the furnace, and there by the anvil,
Behold thy sturdy blacksmiths swinging their sledges,
Overhand so steady, overhand they turn and fall with joyous clank,
Like a tumult of laughter.

Mark the spirit of invention everywhere, thy rapid patents,
Thy continual workshops, foundries, risen or rising,
See, from their chimneys how the tall flame-fires stream.

Mark, thy interminable farms, North, South,
Thy wealthy daughter-states, Eastern and Western,
The varied products of Ohio, Pennsylvania, Missouri, Georgia, Texas, and the rest,
Thy limitless crops, grass, wheat, sugar, oil, corn, rice, hemp, hops,
Thy barns all fill'd, the endless freight-train and the bulging store-house,
The grapes that ripen on thy vines, the apples in thy orchards,
Thy incalculable lumber, beef, pork, potatoes, thy coal, thy gold and silver,
The inexhaustible iron in thy mines.

All thine O sacred Union!

> Ships, farms, shops, barns, factories, mines,
> City and State, North, South, item and aggregate,
> We dedicate, dread Mother, all to thee!
>
> Protectress absolute, thou! bulwark of all!
> For well we know that while thou givest each and all, (generous as God,)
> Without thee neither all nor each, nor land, home,
> Nor ship, nor mine, nor any here this day secure,
> Nor aught, nor any day secure. 214

Whitman closes with a moving evocation to the nation's flag filtered through the memory of war: "For the blood of children, what is it, only the blood maternal? For the sake that, my beauty, that thou might's dally, as now, secure up there, many a good man I have seen go under." Also of note, is a stab at the capitalist grab for wealth to the detriment of the *electric* spirit: "While we rehearse our measureless wealth, it is for thee, dear Mother, we own it all and several to-day indissoluble in thee; think not our chant, our show, merely for products gross or lucre— it is for thee, the soul in thee, electric, spiritual!"

9.

> And thou, the Emblem waving over all! 215
> Delicate beauty, a word to thee, (it may be salutary,)

Remember thou hast not always been as here to-day so comfortably ensovereign'd,
In other scenes than these have I observ'd thee flag,
Not quite so trim and whole and freshly blooming in folds of stainless silk,
But I have seen thee bunting, to tatters torn upon thy splinter'd staff,
Or clutch'd to some young color-bearer's breast with desperate hands,
Savagely struggled for, for life or death, fought over long,
'Mid cannons' thunder-crash and many a curse and groan and yell, and rifle-volleys cracking sharp,
And moving masses as wild demons surging, and lives as nothing risk'd,
For thy mere remnant grimed with dirt and smoke and sopp'd in blood,
For sake of that, my beauty, and that thou might'st dally as now secure up there,
Many a good man have I seen go under. 227

Now here and these and hence in peace, all thine O Flag!
And here and hence for thee, O universal Muse! and thou for them!
And here and hence O Union, all the work and workmen thine!
None separate from thee — henceforth One only, we and thou,
(For the blood of the children, what is it, only the blood maternal?

And lives and works, what are they all at last, except the roads to faith and death?)

While we rehearse our measureless wealth, it is for thee, dear Mother,
We own it all and several to-day indissoluble in thee;
Think not our chant, our show, merely for products gross or lucre — it is for thee, the soul in thee, electric, spiritual!
Our farms, inventions, crops, we own in thee! cities and States in thee!
Our freedom all in thee! our very lives in thee! 239

21. Song of the Redwood-Tree

(1874)

Song of the Redwood-Tree is a strangely moving elegy to and about a dying redwood giant. Whitman becomes the otherwise stoic and silent tree. In the manner of Out of the Cradle Endlessly Rocking he uses italics to distinguish his own voice from that of the coastal colossus. The "Song" is relatively brief with 105 lines dispersed in three cantos — eighty-two in the first canto alone. Nearly half of the lines (46 of 105) are a monologue from the dying old tree. In *Cradle* the ratio is 71 to 183. Twenty-five years separate the two poems. The dying redwood will never compete with the popularity of the earlier poem. The bird's loss of its mate is more tender material. But it is interesting to align the two.

Cradle is a childhood memory. *Redwood* is rather the song of an old man. Whitman might well have assumed its voice. He had suffered a stroke earlier in the year (1873) and his mother had died in May. He had accepted his father's death with equanimity but was devastated by the loss of his mother, Louisa Van Velsor Whitman: "...the only staggering, blow & trouble I have had — but unspeakable — my physical sickness, bad as it is, is nothing to it." [260] He stayed up all night next to her coffin, refusing to leave her until the burial. Burroughs wondered if the poet might soon follow his mother, so weak was his constitution and so deep was his grief.[261] The poem was, however, restorative. Whitman, the shape-shifter and Shaman, returns from the private pain of the poet. In a lovely nod to the age of the great tree the poet imagines ancient wood spirits arriving to hear the tree's final chants. The poet makes us believe that there are more things between heaven and earth than we might have otherwise *dreamt of in (our) philosophy*.

> As the wood-spirits came from their haunts of a thousand years to join the refrain, but in my soul I plainly heard. Murmuring out of its myriad leaves, down from its lofty top rising two hundred feet high, out of its stalwart trunk and limbs, out of its foot-thick bark, that chant of the seasons and time, chant not of the past only but the future.

I find that I have interrupted the poem more than is my usual wont. Those wishing to follow the poem exclusive of the commentary should note that line numbers both begin and conclude each portion of the poem's three cantos.

Song of the Redwood Tree is among his most magnificent late raptures. It was published in *Harper's* in February of 1874.

Song of the Redwood Tree

1.

    A California song,
    A prophecy and indirection, a thought impalpable to breathe as air,
    A chorus of dryads, fading, departing, or hamadryads departing,
    A murmuring, fateful, giant voice, out of the earth and sky,   4
    Voice of a mighty dying tree in the redwood forest dense.   5

    Farewell my brethren,   6
    Farewell O earth and sky, farewell ye neighboring waters,
    My time has ended, my term has come.   8
    Along the northern coast,
    Just back from the rock-bound shore and the caves,
    In the saline air from the sea in the Mendocino country,
    With the surge for base and accompaniment low and hoarse,
    With crackling blows of axes sounding musically driven by strong arms,
    Riven deep by the sharp tongues of the axes, there in the redwood forest dense,
    I heard the mighty tree its death-chant chanting.   15

The mystical hearing employed in *Cradle* and *Lilacs* returns to the soul of the poet:

> The choppers heard not, the camp shanties echoed not,   16
> The quick-ear'd teamsters and chain and jack-screw men heard not,
> As the wood-spirits came from their haunts of a thousand years to join the refrain,
> But in my soul I plainly heard.   19
> Murmuring out of its myriad leaves,   20
> Down from its lofty top rising two hundred feet high,   21
> Out of its stalwart trunk and limbs, out of its foot-thick bark,   22
> That chant of the seasons and time, chant not of the past only but the future.   23

The succeeding stanzas (Lines 25-72) are Whitman's pronouncement of Swedenborg's *correspondences*. Emerson and Henry James Sr. were avid Swedenborgians. Emerson had written an Essay on Swedenborg in *Representative Men:*

> For by being assimilated to the original soul, by whom and after whom all things subsist, the soul of man does easily flow into all things, and all things flow into it, they mix; and he is present and sympathetic with their structure and law.

And again, in *Experience:*

Spirit is matter reduced to an extreme thinness.

Swedenborg was born in 1688 and died late in the eighteenth century at the age of 85. He was a scientist of some note and at the age of 54 began having a series of *Illuminations*. Basically, he testified of seeing into the spiritual realm—a realm that was side by side with the natural one. Everything in nature had it spiritual correspondence. In 1850 the American Swedenborg Printing and Publishing Society was formed.

In 1852 Whitman wrote an article on Swedenborg for the *Daily Times* in which declared that Swedenborg would one day have: "The deepest and broadest influence upon the religions of the future ages here, of any man that ever walked the earth."[262] Emerson, in 1854, declared: "This is the age of Swedenborg."

Also of the times was the former Swedenborgian minister Thomas Lake Harris. In 1854 Harris, while in a trance, was dictated a 4,000 line poem by a spirit claiming to be Dante Alighieri. It was later published as *An Epic of the Starry Heavens*. Harris would speed through space to distant Heavens beyond the stars where he would witness immortal men and women in ecstatic sexual embrace. By the late 1850s Harris became even more elitist and reported having regular conversations with God.

The poem begins in the minor key before quickly ascending to the major. Here is the beginning of the Harris vision into the Star bejeweled heavens:

Cries from its hollow depths, " No more, no more."
Death sits, calm browed, upon the snow-white shore
In love with Immortality, whose breast
Pillows its form to its eternal rest.
Now Death is pillowed on the lap of Life,
And dies in happy dreams. There is no Deep,
Hungry and dark, with agonizing strife,
To swallow up Love's argosy, and sweep
All the great Past into its sunless caves.
God smites the tomb, and saith, " Ye hollow graves
So still and secret, ope your lips and tell
The Nations that My children do not dwell,
Nor fade, nor crumble in your drear abyss,
But share the vast dominions of My bliss."
God's heavens to earth have spoken. In the glow
Of the New Era's dawning it is sweet
To wake and see dull Night from Nature go.
The cycle of the ages shines complete.
Man came from God; he goes to Him again.
From Him came down to Him aspires the flame
The friendly Angels ope Love's Eden door ;

Man enters in departs not ever more.
The seers and saints of all the centuries past
Have set their seal unto the sacred page
Earth disappeared, and I arose and stood
On the bright summit of Earth's Seventh Sphere.
I saw the spirit-sky I felt the flood
Of music lift me to that region clear
Of endless morning, where the Man of Sorrows
Shines from the Infinite, and every knee
Is bent in living adoration there,
And every face immortal glory borrows
From His own countenance. The very air
Thrilled me with ecstasy,

Ffor Love Divine
Flowed in it. Through the vastness of that shrine
The constellated spirits burned and shone.
I bowed in worship at the Spirit-Throne ;
And, as I prayed, me thought an answer came.
My heart impulsed the warm blood through my frame,
Till the shrunk channels overflowed, and then
Celestial voices breathed a low " Amen."

Whitman reported to Horace Traubel: "I think Swedenborg was right when he said there was a close connection—a very close connection—between the state we call religious ecstasy and the desire to copulate. I find it confirmed in all my experience." Whitman's Redwood Tree continues its plaint:

> *You untold life of me,* 25
> *And all you venerable and innocent joys,*
> *Perennial hardy life of me with joys 'mid rain and many a summer sun,*
> *And the white snows and night and the wild winds;*
> *O the great patient rugged joys, my soul's strong joys unreck'd by man,*
> *(For know I bear the soul befitting me, I too have consciousness, identity,*
> *And all the rocks and mountains have, and all the earth,)* 30
> *Joys of the life befitting me and brothers mine,*
> *Our time, our term has come.* 32

Whitman had earlier written:

> Because having look'd at the objects of the universe, I find that there is not one nor any particle of one but has reference to the soul. Was anyone asking to the soul? See, your own shape and countenance, persons, substances, beasts, the trees, the running rivers, the rocks and sands.[263]

And, as if to prove a somewhat abstruse metaphysical speculation, the redwood continues its plaintive reverie:

> *Nor yield we mournfully majestic brothers,*   33
> *We who have grandly fill'd our time,*
> *With Nature's calm content, with tacit huge delight,*   35
> *We welcome what we wrought for through the past,*
> *And leave the field for them.*
>
> *For them predicted long,*
> *For a superber race, they too to grandly fill their time,*
> *For them we abdicate, in them ourselves ye forest kings.'*
> *In them these skies and airs, these mountain peaks, Shasta, Nevadas,*
> *These huge precipitous cliffs, this amplitude, these valleys, far Yosemite,*
> *To be in them absorb'd, assimilated.*   43

Then to a loftier strain,
Still prouder, more ecstatic rose the chant,
As if the heirs, the deities of the West,
Joining with master-tongue bore part.   47

> *Not wan from Asia's fetiches,*   48
> *Nor red from Europe's old dynastic slaughter-house,*   48
> *(Area of murder-plots of thrones, with scent left yet of wars and scaffolds everywhere,*

*But come from Nature's long and harmless
    throes, peacefully builded thence,*
*These virgin lands, lands of the Western
    shore,*
*To the new culminating man, to you, the
    empire new,*
You promis'd long, we pledge, we dedicate.

You occult deep volitions, 55
*You average spiritual manhood, purpose of
    all, pois'd on yourself, giving not taking
    law,*
*You womanhood divine, mistress and source
    of all, whence life and love and aught
    that comes from life and love,*
*You unseen moral essence of all the vast
    materials of America, age upon age
    working in death the same as life,)*
*You that, sometimes known, oftener
    unknown, really shape and mould the
    New World, adjusting it to Time and
    Space,*
*You hidden national will lying in your
    abysms, conceal'd but ever alert,*
*You past and present purposes tenaciously
    pursued, may-be unconscious of
    yourselves,*
*Unswerv'd by all the passing errors,
    perturbations of the surface;*
*You vital, universal, deathless germs,
    beneath all creeds, arts, statutes,
    literatures,* 63
*Here build your homes for good, establish
    here, these areas entire, lands of the
    Western shore,*
We pledge, we dedicate to you.

For man of you, your characteristic race,
Here may he hardy, sweet, gigantic grow,
here tower proportionate to Nature,
Here climb the vast pure spaces unconfined,
uncheck'd by wall or roof,
Here laugh with storm or sun, here joy, here
patiently inure,
Here heed himself, unfold himself, (not
others' formulas heed,)
here fill his time,
To duly fall, to aid, unreck'd at last,
To disappear, to serve. 72

The ending stanza of the first Canto is a magnificent effort, ten lines in length where the poet makes us catch our breath as he concludes with the subject of his thought—the parentheticals, each preceding:

> Thus on the northern coast, 73
> In the echo of teamsters' calls and the clinking chains, and the music of choppers' axes,
> The falling trunk and limbs, the crash, the muffled shriek, the groan,
> Such words combined from the redwood-tree, as of voices ecstatic, ancient and rustling,
> The century-lasting, unseen dryads, singing, withdrawing,
> All their recesses of forests and mountains leaving,
> From the Cascade range to the Wahsatch, or Idaho far, or Utah,
> To the deities of the modern henceforth yielding,

> The chorus and indications, the vistas of
>   coming humanity, the settlements,
>   features all,
> In the Mendocino woods I caught.[264]   82

Cantos 2 & 3 anticipate the role of California in the future of the states. He speaks with great familiarity of a state he never visited. The second Canto is dedicated to the rich valleys and mountains of the state, the third to the future citizens who will populate it.

2.
> The flashing and golden pageant of
>   California,   83
> The sudden and gorgeous drama, the
>   sunny and ample lands,
> The long and varied stretch from Puget
>   sound to Colorado south,
> Lands bathed in sweeter, rarer, healthier
>   air, valleys and mountain cliffs,
> The fields of Nature long prepared and
>   fallow, the silent, cyclic chemistry,
> The slow and steady ages plodding, the
>   unoccupied surface ripening, the
>   rich ores forming beneath;
> At last the New arriving, assuming,
>   taking possession,
> A swarming and busy race settling and
>   organizing everywhere,
> Ships coming in from the whole round
>   world, and going out to the whole
>   world,
> To India and China and Australia and
>   the thousand island paradises of the
>   Pacific,

Populous cities, the latest inventions, the steamers on the rivers, the railroads, with many a thrifty farm, with machinery,
And wool and wheat and the grape, and diggings of yellow gold.   94

3.

But more in you than these, lands of the Western shore,   95
(These but the means, the implements, the standing-ground,)
I see in you, certain to come, the promise of thousands of years, till now deferr'd,
Promis'd to be fulfill'd, our common kind, the race.

The new society at last, proportionate to Nature,
In man of you, more than your mountain peaks or stalwart trees imperial,
In woman more, far more, than all your gold or vines, or even vital air.

Fresh come, to a new world indeed, yet long prepared,
I see the genius of the modern, child of the real and ideal,
Clearing the ground for broad humanity, the true America, heir of the part so grand,
To build a grander future.   105

22. A Song of Occupations

Song for Occupations was the 2nd poem of the '55 edition's untitled twelve—that alone would suggest close scrutiny. It underwent extensive revision in each subsequent *Leaves* up until 1881. In the 1856 edition it was titled the ungainly, *Poem of the Daily Work of the Workmen and Workwomen of These States*. The poem takes an ironic stance toward the occupations that it celebrates—it suggests that these are grand in and of themselves, but in the context of the soul they take on a greater grandeur. In these final "hours" we will call upon Emerson to buttress the very grandeur of which the younger poet speaks. Emerson asks:

> Why should we not also enjoy an original relation to the universe? Why should we not have a poetry and philosophy of insight and not of tradition, and a religion by revelation to us, and not the history of theirs?...Why should we grope among the dry bones of the past, or put the living generation into masquerade out of its faded wardrobe? The sun shines today also...Let us demand our own works and laws and worship...Everyman's condition is a solution in hieroglyphic to those inquiries he would put. He acts it as life before he apprehends it as truth. In like manner, nature is already, in its forms and tendencies, describing it from design. Let us interrogate the great apparition that shines so peacefully

around us. Let us inquire, to what end
nature? [265]

As if in a whisper the poet answers. In the inaugural edition there was a more intimate opening which seems more sympathetically in line with Emerson's queries. It is sorely missed in the poem's final presentation and is offered as a prelude immediately below:

> Come closer to me,
> Push close my lovers and take the best I possess,
> Yield closer and closer and give the best you possess,
> This is unfinished business with me…how is it with you?
> I was chilled with the cold types and cylinder and wet paper between us.
> I pass so poorly with paper and types…
> I must pass with the contact of bodies and souls.
> I do not thank you for liking me as I am, and liking the touch of me…
> I know it is good for you to do so.

A Song of Occupations!

(1855)

1.

A song for occupations!
In the labor of engines and trades and the labor of fields I find the developments,
And find the eternal meanings. 3

Workmen and Workwomen!

Were all educations practical and ornamental well display'd out of me, what would it amount to? 5
Were I as the head teacher, charitable proprietor, wise statesman, what would it amount to?
Were I to you as the boss employing and paying you, would that satisfy you?

The learn'd, virtuous, benevolent, and the usual terms,
A man like me and never the usual terms.

Neither a servant nor a master I,
I take no sooner a large price than a small price, I will have my own whoever enjoys me,
I will be even with you and you shall be even with me.

If you stand at work in a shop I stand as nigh as the nighest in the same shop,
If you bestow gifts on your brother or dearest friend I demand as good as your brother or dearest friend,
If your lover, husband, wife, is welcome by day or night, I must be personally as welcome,
If you become degraded, criminal, ill, then I become so for your sake,
If you remember your foolish and outlaw'd deeds, do you think I

> cannot remember my own foolish
> and outlaw'd deeds?
> If you carouse at the table I carouse at
> the opposite side of the table,
> If you meet some stranger in the streets
> and love him or her, why
> I often meet strangers in the street and
> love them. 19

The greasy, pimpled drunks, thieves and prostitutes are assured of their immortality. Whitman is, once again, a *Christ* among the publicans and sinners:

> Why what have you thought of
> yourself? 20
> Is it you then that thought yourself less?
> Is it you that thought the President
> greater than you? 22
> Or the rich better off than you? or the
> educated wiser than you?
>
> (Because you are greasy or pimpled, or
> were once drunk, or a thief,
> Or that you are diseas'd, or rheumatic,
> or a prostitute,
> Or from frivolity or impotence, or that
> you are no scholar and never saw
> your name in print,
> Do you give in that you are any less
> immortal?) 27

The final eight lines of Canto 2 suggest the illumination that the poet experienced sometime after 1850: "I bring you what you much need yet always have" begins the declension. Advocates of Zen Buddhism often quote

Huang Po's assertion of enlightenment: "That which you see before you." Whitman is only a little less succinct: "…it is no farther from you than your hearing and sight are from you."

2.

> Souls of men and women! it is not you I call unseen, unheard, untouchable and untouching, 28
> It is not you I go argue pro and con about, and to settle whether you are alive or no,
> I own publicly who you are, if nobody else owns.
>
> Grown, half-grown and babe, of this country and every country, in-doors and out-doors, one just as much as the other, I see,
> And all else behind or through them.
>
> The wife, and she is not one jot less than the husband, 33
> The daughter, and she is just as good as the son,
> The mother, and she is every bit as much as the father. 34
> Offspring of ignorant and poor, boys apprenticed to trades, 35
> Young fellows working on farms and old fellows working on farms,
> Sailor-men, merchant-men, coasters, immigrants,
> All these I see, but nigher and farther the same I see,

> None shall escape me and none shall wish to escape me.
>
> I bring what you much need yet always have, 40
> Not money, amours, dress, eating, eruditon, but as good,
> I send no agent or medium, offer no representative of value, but offer the value itself.
>
> There is something that comes to one now and perpetually, 43
> It is not what is printed, preach'd, discussed, it eludes discussion and print, 44
> It is not to be put in a book, it is not in this book, 45
> It is for you whoever you are, it is no farther from you than your hearing and sight are from you, 46
> It is hinted by nearest, commonest, readiest, it is ever provoked by them. 48

Emerson, as well, is ever provoked by it:

> In good health, the air is cordial of incredible virtue. Crossing a bare common, in snow puddles, at twilight under a clouded sky, without having in my thoughts any occurrence of special good fortune, I have enjoyed perfect exhilaration. I am glad to the point of fear...

> In the woods, too, a man casts off his years, as the snake his slough, and at whatsoever period of life is always a child. In the woods is perpetual youth. Within these plantations of God, a decorum and sanctity reign, a perennial festival is dressed, and the guest sees not how he should tire of them in a thousand years. In the woods, we return to reason and faith. There I feel that nothing can befall me in life—no disgrace, no calamity…which nature can not repair. Standing on the bare ground—my head bathed by the blithe air and uplifted into infinite space—all mean egoism vanishes. I become a transparent eyeball; I am nothing, I see all; the currents of the Universal Being circulate through me; I am part and parcel of God.[266]

Whitman continues the thought in his song:

> You may read in many languages, yet read nothing about it,   49
> You may read the President's message and read nothing about it there,
> Nothing in the reports from the State department or Treasury department, or in the daily papers or weekly papers,
> Or in the census or revenue returns, prices current, or any accounts of stock.   52

The poet's vision does not flag in Canto 3. The mystery of being is palpable: "I do not know what it is except that it is grand, and that it is happiness." The whole of Canto 3 is an invitation to enlightenment. Vincent Van Gogh wrote to his sister about his affection for the author:

> He sees in the future, even in the present, a world of health, carnal love, strong and frank—of friendship—of work—under the great starlit vault of heaven a something which after all one can only call God—an eternity in its place above the world. [267]

The letter was dated 1888. In May of 1889 Van Gogh committed himself to the hospital Saint-Paul-de-Mausole, near Arles. In June of 1889 he painted *The Starry Night*. The artist had seen *the sun and the stars that float in the open air...surely the drift of them is something grand*. Whitman's assertions and counter assertions are as canning as any Zen master's paradoxical koans. The English poet, Edward Carpenter, testified to their use and effectiveness—a list of the international readership over the last century and a half would make a long list of illuminati, indeed.

3.
> The sun and stars that float in the open air, 53
> The apple-shaped earth and we upon it, surely the drift of them is something grand,
> I do not know what it is except that it is grand, and that it is happiness, 55

> And that the enclosing purport of us here is not a speculation or bon-mot or reconnoissance,
> And that it is not something which by luck may turn out well for us, and without luck must be a failure for us,
> And not something which may yet be retracted in a certain contingency.
>
> The light and shade, the curious sense of body and identity, the greed that with perfect complaisance devours all things,
> The endless pride and outstretching of man, unspeakable joys and sorrows,
> The wonder every one sees in every one else he sees, and the wonders that fill each minute of time forever, 61
> What have you reckon'd them for, camerado? 62

It is a question Emerson poses as often as he proposes an answer:

> We are taught by great actions that the universe is the property of every individual in it. Every rational creature has all nature for his dowry and estate. It is his, if he will. He may divest himself of it, he may creep into a corner and abdicate his kingdom as most men do, but he is entitled to the world by his constitution. In proportion to his energy and thought he takes the world into himself.[268]

Whitman readily concurs as he continues the same sentiment in the third canto and concludes it in the fourth with a series of observations and ironies (Lines 63-97) designed to tempt us into the seamless light of *Satori*.

> Have you reckon'd them for your trade or farm-work? or for the profits of your store? 63
> Or to achieve yourself a position? or to fill a gentleman's leisure, or a lady's leisure?
>
> Have you reckon'd that the landscape took substance and form that it might be painted in a picture? 65
> Or men and women that they might be written of, and songs sung?
> Or the attraction of gravity, and the great laws and harmonious combinations and the fluids of the air, as subjects for the savans?
> Or the brown land and the blue sea for maps and charts?
> Or the stars to be put in constellations and named fancy names?
> Or that the growth of seeds is for agricultural tables, or agriculture itself?
>
> Old institutions, these arts, libraries, legends, collections, and the practice handed along in manufactures, will we rate them so high?
> Will we rate our cash and business high? I have no objection,

> I rate them as high as the highest—then
> a child born of a woman and man I
> rate beyond all rate.
>
> We thought our Union grand, and our
> Constitution grand,
> I do not say they are not grand and
> good, for they are,
> I am this day just as much in love with
> them as you,
> Then I am in love with You, and with all
> my fellows upon the earth.
>
> We consider bibles and religions
> divine—I do not say they are not
> divine, 78
> I say they have all grown out of you,
> and may grow out of you still,
> It is not they who give the life, it is you
> who give the life, 80
> Leaves are not more shed from the trees,
> or trees from the earth,
> than they are shed out of you. 81

The fourth Canto continues the Idealism that is one pole of his ardent dialectic. Whitman understands that the purport of the universe is in the present moment of sentient experience. It is as fine a demonstration of the notion as you will find in Plotinus or the Bhagavad Gita.

4.
> The sum of all known reverence I add
> up in you whoever you are, 82

The President is there in the White
  House for you, it is not you who are
  here for him,
The Secretaries act in their bureaus for
  you, not you here for them,
The Congress convenes every Twelfth-
  month for you,
Laws, courts, the forming of States, the
  charters of cities, the going and
  coming of commerce and malls, are
  all for you.
List close my scholars dear,
Doctrines, politics and civilization
  exurge from you,
Sculpture and monuments and any
  thing inscribed anywhere are tallied
  in you,
The gist of histories and statistics as far
  back as the records
  reach is in you this hour, and myths
  and tales the same, 90
If you were not breathing and walking
  here, where would they all be? 91
The most renown'd poems would be
  ashes, orations and plays would be
  vacuums.

All architecture is what you do to it
  when you look upon it, 93
(Did you think it was in the white or
  gray stone? or the lines of the arches
  and cornices?) 94

> All music is what awakes from you
>   when you are reminded by the
>   instruments,
> It is not the violins and the cornets, it is
>   not the oboe nor the beating drums,
>   nor the score of the baritone singer
>   singing his sweet romanza, nor that
>   of the men's chorus, nor that of the
>   women's chorus,
> It is nearer and farther than they.   97

Is there nothing greater or more than your present experience? Is your vocation sung between Lines 103-135.? When you look in the mirror do you believe there is nothing greater or more? Does all sit there with you, with the mystic unseen soul? These are essential questions. Here the two sides of a dialectic begun in an Academy in Athens are given a single voice in the fifth canto. They are two of the most important lines in the Canon: *Strange and hard that paradox true I give. Objects gross and the unseen soul are one.* (Lines 101-102 below).

And if we have trouble imagining that these *cloud-capp'd towers, the gorgeous palaces, the solemn temples, the great globe itself... shall dissolve and, like this insubstantial pageant faded, Leave not a rack behind* — let us give Lord Bertrand Arthur William Russell, 3rd Earl Russell of Kingston Russell, Viscount Amberley of Amberley and of Ardsalla — aka Bertie, a piece of the speculative floor. Russell's lifetime spanned the Presidential administrations from U. S. Grant to R. M. Nixon. He was a consummate analyst, critic, philosopher, logician, mathematician, social pioneer and provocateur. He was a student at Cambridge at the time of the poet's death:

Matter, for common sense, is something which persists in time and moves in space. But for modern relativity-physics this view is no longer tenable. A piece of matter has become, not a persistent thing with varying states, but a system of inter-related events. The solidity is gone, and with it the characteristics that, to the materialist, made matter seem more real than fleeting thoughts. Nothing is permanent, nothing endures; the prejudice that the real is persistent must be abandoned.[269]

5.

Will the whole come back then?	98
Can each see signs of the best by a look in the looking-glass? is there nothing greater or more?	
Does all sit there with you, with the mystic unseen soul?	99
Strange and hard that paradox true I give,	101
Objects gross and the unseen soul are one.	102

House-building, measuring, sawing the boards,
Blacksmithing, glass-blowing, nail-making, coopering, tin-roofing, shingle-dressing,
Ship-joining, dock-building, fish-curing, flagging of sidewalks by flaggers,

The pump, the pile-driver, the great derrick, the coal-kiln and brick-kiln,
Coal-mines and all that is down there, the lamps in the darkness, echoes, songs, what meditations, what vast native thoughts looking through smutch'd faces, 107
Iron-works, forge-fires in the mountains or by river-banks, men around feeling the melt with huge crowbars, lumps of ore, the due combining of ore, limestone, coal,
The blast-furnace and the puddling-furnace, the loup-lump at the bottom of the melt at last, the rolling-mill, the stumpy bars of pig-iron, the strong clean-shaped Trail for railroads,
Oil-works, silk-works, white-lead-works, the sugar-house, steam-saws, the great mills and factories,
Stone-cutting, shapely trimmings for facades or window or door-lintels, the mallet, the tooth-chisel, the jib to protect the thumb,
The calking-iron, the kettle of boiling vault-cement, and the fire under the kettle,
The cotton-bale, the stevedore's hook, the saw and buck of the sawyer, the mould of the moulder, the working-knife of the butcher, the ice-saw, and all the work with ice,
The work and tools of the rigger, grappler, sail-maker, block-maker, 114

Goods of gutta-percha, papier-mache, colors, brushes, brush-making, glazier's implements,
The veneer and glue-pot, the confectioner's ornaments, the decanter and glasses, the shears and flat-iron,
The awl and knee-strap, the pint measure and quart measure, the counter and stool, the writing-pen of quill or metal, the making of all sorts of edged tools,
The brewery, brewing, the malt, the vats, every thing that is done by brewers, wine-makers, vinegar-makers,
Leather-dressing, coach-making, boiler-making, rope-twisting, distilling, sign-painting, lime-burning, cotton-picking, electroplating, electrotyping, stereotyping,
Stave-machines, planning-machines, reaping-machines, ploughing-machines, thrashing-machines, steam wagons,
The cart of the carman, the omnibus, the ponderous dray,
Pyrotechny, letting off color'd fireworks at night, fancy figures and jets;
Beef on the butcher's stall, the slaughter-house of the butcher, the butcher in his killing-clothes,
The pens of live pork, the killing-hammer, the hog-hook, the scalder's tub, gutting, the cutter's cleaver, the

packer's maul, and the plenteous winter work of pork-packing, 124
Flour-works, grinding of wheat, rye, maize, rice, the barrels and the half and quarter barrels, the loaded barges, the high piles on wharves and levees, 125
The men and the work of the men on ferries, railroads, coasters, fish-boats, canals;
The hourly routine of your own or any man's life, the shop, yard, store, or factory,
These shows all near you by day and night—workman! whoever you are, your daily life!
In that and them the heft of the heaviest—in that and them far more than you estimated, (and far less also,)
In them realities for you and me, in them poems for you and me, 130
In them, not yourself-you and your soul enclose all things, regardless of estimation,
In them the development good—in them all themes, hints, possibilities.
I do not affirm that what you see beyond is futile, I do not advise you to stop,
I do not say leadings you thought great are not great,
But I say that none lead to greater than these lead to. 135

Some of the lines of the sixth canto compare nicely with the affirmations of *Song of Myself*. They are from the same inspiration. For the poet there is no greener grass than that which grows presently under his own feet: *Will you seek afar off? You will sure come back at last…Happiness, knowledge, not in another place but this place, not for another hour but this hour.* (Lines 136-139) The concluding Canto of the 10th hour, smiles like the night-watchman's daughter of line 149 below:

6.

> Will you seek afar off? you surely come back at last,   136
> In things best known to you finding the best, or as good as the best,
> In folks nearest to you finding the sweetest, strongest, lovingest,
> Happiness, knowledge, not in another place but this place, not for another hour but this hour,   139
> Man in the first you see or touch, always in friend, brother, nighest neighbor — woman in mother, sister, wife,
> The popular tastes and employments taking precedence in poems or anywhere,
> You workwomen and workmen of these States having your own divine and strong life,
> And all else giving place to men and women like you.
>
> When the psalm sings instead of the singer,

> When the script preaches instead of the preacher,
> When the pulpit descends and goes instead of the carver that carved the supporting desk,
> When I can touch the body of books by night or by day, and when they touch my body back again,
> When a university course convinces like a slumbering woman and child convince, 148
> When the minted gold in the vault smiles like the night-watchman's daughter, 149
> When warrantee deeds loafe in chairs opposite and are my friendly companions,
> I intend to reach them my hand, and make as much of them as I do of men and women like you. 151

23. A Song of the Rolling Earth

(1856)

In the 23rd hour of the poet's night he continues his Idealism. *Song of the Rolling Earth* was one of the twenty he added to *Leaves* in 1856. As a prelude to yet another of his greatest *Songs*, let us hold two counsels. The first, with the most certain of his mentors, R.W. Emerson:

> The materialist, secure in the certainty of sensation, mocks at fine-spun theories, at star-gazers and dreamers, and

believes that his life is solid, that at least takes nothing for granted, but knows where he stands, and what he does. Yet how easy it is to show him that he also is a phantom walking and working amid phantoms and that he only need ask a question or two beyond his daily questions to find his solid universe growing dim and impalpable before his sense. The sturdy capitalist, no matter how deep and square on blocks of Quincy granite he lays the foundation of his banking-house or Exchange, must set it, at last, not on a cube corresponding to the angles of his structure, but on a mass of unknown materials and solidity, red-hot or white-hot perhaps at the core, which rounds off to an almost perfect sphericity, and lies floating in soft air, and goes spinning away, dragging bank and banker with it a rate of thousands of miles the hour, he knows not whither — a bit of a bullet, now glimmering, now darkling through a small cubic space on the edge an unimaginable pit of emptiness.

And this wild balloon, in which his whole venture is embarked is just a symbol of his whole state and faculty...ask him why he believes that an uniform experience will continue uniform, or on what grounds he founds his faith in figures and he will perceive

> that his mental fabric is built up on just as strange and quaking foundation as his proud edifice of stone.[270]

And for the second, Lord Russell:

> Both mind and matter seem to be composite, and the stuff of which they are compounded lies in a sense between the two, in a sense above them both, like a common ancestor.[271]

> I conclude that while mental events and their qualities can be known without inference, physical events are known only as regards their space-time structure.

> The qualities that compose such events are unknown—so completely unknown that we cannot say either that they are or that they are not different from the qualities that we know as belonging to mental events.[272]

Russell's composite of mind and matter is very similar to Emerson's notion of mind being very thin material. In other words the distinction between the two is called into question. Russell's brilliant student, Wittgenstein, questioned it further: "At the basis of the whole modern view of the world lies the illusion that the so-called laws of nature are the explanations of natural phenomenon."
I have argued that Emerson's influence on the poet was of the first importance.

WHITMAN'S CODE: A NEW BIBLE, VOLUME I
M.C. GARDNER

As late as 1876, the editor of *Scribner's Monthly*, J.G. Holland, decried Whitman's poems as a "mixture of rhapsodical passages of...Emerson's prose...we believe in his theories and performances he is radically wrong — that he is doing nothing but advertize himself as a literary eccentric, and that he ought to have and will have no following." [273]

Whitman was sensitive to the charge and at varying times in his career ambivalent about the depth of his debt to the Concord lion. To his great credit, Emerson had hailed *Leaves of Grass* as "...the most extraordinary gift of wit and wisdom that America has yet produced." To Whitman's credit, despite his sensitivity, he regarded "Emerson as one of the great, eternal men, there is not another living, nor has there lived (another as great) for two or three centuries." [274]

I will suggest that as aesthetically challenged as Mr. Holland now presents himself, he was in fairness, partially correct. He perceived Whitman's debt to Emerson but missed the more definite conflation of Plato and Aristotle that his works reveal. To the first half of that conflation, Emerson will comment, now and again, as before. Whitman, the great lover of grand opera, would perhaps smile as we formulate *A Song of the Rolling Earth*, as another duet harmoniously blended by their respective voices.

Note also that principal numbers connected with the argument of this book (twenty-four & three hundred sixty-five) appear in lines 55 and 63 of the first canto and another Zen exposition in lines 108-109.

Song of the Rolling Earth

Whitman:

1.

> A song of the rolling earth, and of words according,
> Were you thinking that those were the words, those upright lines?
> those curves, angles, dots?
> No, those are not the words, the substantial words are in the ground and sea,
> They are in the air, they are in you. 4

Emerson:

> In my utter impotence to test the authenticity of the report of my senses, to know whether the impressions they make on me correspond with the outlying objects, what difference does it make, whether Orion is up there in the heaven or some god paints the image in the firmament of the soul…
>
> Whether nature enjoys a substantial existence without, or is only an apocalypse of the mind, it is alike useful and alike venerable to me.[275]

Whitman:

> Were you thinking that those were the words, those delicious sounds out of your friends' mouths? 5
> No, the real words are more delicious than they. 6

Emerson:

> A man conversing in earnest, if he watch his intellectual processes, will find that a material image more or less luminous arises in his mind, contemporaneous with every thought, which furnishes the vestment of that thought.

Whitman:

> Human bodies are words, myriads of words, 7
> (In the best poems re-appears the body, man's or woman's, well-shaped, natural, gay,
> Every part able, active, receptive, without shame or the need of shame.)
>
> Air, soil, water, fire—those are words,
> I myself am a word with them—my qualities interpenetrate with theirs—my name is nothing to them,

> Though it were told in the three thousand languages, what would air, soil, water, fire, know of my name?
>
> A healthy presence, a friendly or commanding gesture, are words, sayings, meanings,
> The charms that go with the mere looks of some men and women, are sayings and meanings also.
>
> The workmanship of souls is by those inaudible words of the earth,
> The masters know the earth's words and use them more than audible words.
> Amelioration is one of the earth's words,
> The earth neither lags nor hastens,
> It has all attributes, growths, effects, latent in itself from the jump,
> It is not half beautiful only, defects and excrescences show just as much as perfections show. 20

Emerson:

> The world thus exists to the soul to satisfy the desire of beauty. This element I call an ultimate end. No reason can be asked or given why the soul seeks beauty. Beauty in its largest sense, is one expression for the universe. God is the all-fair. Truth, and goodness and beauty are different faces of the same all.[276]

Whitman:

> The earth does not withhold, it is generous enough,   21
> The truths of the earth continually wait, they are not so conceal'd either,
> They are calm, subtle, untransmissible by print,
> They are imbued through all things conveying themselves willingly,
> Conveying a sentiment and invitation, I utter and utter,
> I speak not, yet if you hear me not of what avail am I to you?
> To bear, to better, lacking these of what avail am I?
>
> (Accouche! accouchez!
> Will you rot your own fruit in yourself there?
> Will you squat and stifle there?)   30

Emerson:

> Know then that the world exists for you. For you is the phenomenon perfect. What we are only that can we see. All that Adam had and Caesar could, you have and can do. Adam called his house heaven and earth; Caesar called his house, Rome; you perhaps call yours a cobbler's trade; a hundred acres of ploughed land; or a scholar's garret. Yet line for line and point for point your dominion is as great as theirs, though

without fame or names. Build therefore your own world.²⁷⁷

Whitman:

> The earth does not argue, 31
> Is not pathetic, has no arrangements,
> Does not scream, haste, persuade, threaten, promise,
> Makes no discriminations, has no conceivable failures,
> Closes nothing, refuses nothing, shuts none out,
> Of all the powers, objects, states, it notifies, shuts none out. 36

Emerson:

> All loss, all pain, is particular; the universe remains to the heart unhurt... For it is only the finite that has wrought and suffered, the infinite lies stretched in smiling repose.²⁷⁸

Whitman:

> The earth does not exhibit itself nor refuse to exhibit itself, possesses still underneath, 37
> Underneath the ostensible sounds, the august chorus of heroes, the wail of slaves,
> Persuasions of lovers, curses, gasps of the dying, laughter of young people, accents of bargainers,

> Underneath these possessing words that never fall.
>
> To her children the words of the eloquent dumb great mother never fail,
> The true words do not fail, for motion does not fail and reflection does not fail,
> Also the day and night do not fall, and the voyage we pursue does not fail. 43

Emerson:

> For seen in the light of thought, the world always is phenomenal: and virtue subordinates it to the mind. Idealism sees the world in God. It beholds the whole circle of persons and things, of actions and events, of country and religion, not as painfully accumulated, atom after atom, act after act, in an aged and creeping past, but as one vast picture which God paints on the instant eternity for the contemplation of the soul.[279]

Whitman:

> Of the interminable sisters, 44
> Of the ceaseless cotillons of sisters,
> Of the centripetal and centrifugal sisters, the elder and younger sisters,
> The beautiful sister we know dances on with the rest.

> With her ample back towards every beholder,
> With the fascinations of youth and the equal fascinations of age,
> Sits she whom I too love like the rest, sits undisturb'd,
> Holding up in her hand what has the character of a mirror, while her eyes glance back from it,
> Glance as she sits, inviting none, denying none,
> Holding a mirror day and night tirelessly before her own face. 53

Emerson:

> The supreme being does not build up nature around us, but puts it forth through us, as the life of a tree puts forth new branches and leaves through the pores of the old. As a plant upon the earth, so a man rests upon the bosom of God; he is nourished by unfailing fountains and draws at his need inexhaustible power.
>
> Who can set the bounds to the possibilities of man. Once inhale the upper air... and we learn that man has access to the entire mind of the Creator...[280]

Whitman:

> Seen at hand or seen at a distance, 54

Duly the twenty-four appear in public every day, 55
Duly approach and pass with their companions or a companion,
Looking from no countenances of their own, but from the countenances of those who are with them,
From the countenances of children or women or the manly countenance,
From the open countenances of animals or from inanimate things,
From the landscape or waters or from the exquisite apparition of the sky,
From our countenances, mine and yours, faithfully returning them,
Every day in public appearing without fall, but never twice with the same companions.

Embracing man, embracing all, proceed the three hundred and
 sixty-five resistlessly round the sun; 63
Embracing all, soothing, supporting, follow close three hundred and sixty-five offsets of the first, sure and necessary as they.

Tumbling on steadily, nothing dreading,
Sunshine, storm, cold, heat, forever withstanding, passing, carrying,
The soul's realization and determination still inheriting,

The fluid vacuum around and ahead still entering and dividing,

> No balk retarding, no anchor anchoring,
>   on no rock striking,
> Swift, glad, content, unbereav'd, nothing
>   losing,
> Of all able and ready at any time to give
>   strict account,
> The divine ship sails the divine sea.   72

2.

> Whoever you are! motion and reflection
>   are especially for you,   73
> The divine ship sails the divine sea for
>   you.

Emerson:

> What are we? And whither we tend? Here we drift, kite the white sail across the wild ocean—but from what port did we sail? Or to what port are we bound? Who knows! There is no one to tell us but such poor weather-tossed mariners as our selves, whom we speak as we pass, or who have hoisted some signal, or floated to us some letter in a bottle from far.[281]

Whitman:

> Whoever you are! you are he or she for
>   whom the earth is solid and liquid,   75
> You are he or she for whom the sun and
>   moon hang in the sky,
> For none more than you are the present
>   and the past,
> For none more than you is immortality.

> Each man to himself and each woman to herself, is the word of the past and present, and the true word of immortality;
> No one can acquire for another — not one,
> Not one can grow for another — not one. 81

Emerson:

> Today is a king in disguise. Today always looks mean to the thoughtless, in the face of a uniform experience that all good and great and happy actions are made up precisely of these blank to-days. Let us not be so deceived. Let us unmask the king as he passes. Let us not see the foundations of a new and better order of things laid, with roving eyes and an attention preoccupied with trifles.[282]

Whitman:

> The song is to the singer, and comes back most to him, 82
> The teaching is to the teacher, and comes back most to him,
> The murder is to the murderer, and comes back most to him,
> The theft is to the thief, and comes back most to him,
> The love is to the lover, and comes back most to him,

> The gift is to the giver, and comes back most to him—it cannot fail,
> The oration is to the orator, the acting is to the actor and actress not to the audience,
> And no man understands any greatness or goodness but his own, or the indication of his own. 89

3.

> I swear the earth shall surely be complete to him or her who shall be complete, 90
> The earth remains jagged and broken only to him or her who remains jagged and broken. 91

Emerson:

> Each man has his own vocation. The talent is the call. There is one direction in which all space is open to him. He has faculties silently inviting him thither to endless exertion. He is like a ship in a river; he runs against obstructions on every side but one; on that side all obstruction is take away and he sweeps serenely over a deeping channel into an infinite sea.[283]

Whitman:

> I swear there is no greatness or power that does not emulate those of the earth, 92

> There can be no theory of any account
> unless it corroborate the theory of
> the earth,
> No politics, song, religion, behavior, or
> what not, is of account, unless it
> compare with the amplitude of the
> earth,
> Unless it face the exactness, vitality,
> impartiality, rectitude of the earth. 95

Emerson:

> What a man does that he has. What has
> he to do with hope or fear? In himself is
> his might. Let him regard no good as
> solid but that which is in his nature and
> which must grow out of him as long as
> he exists; The goods of fortune may
> come and go like summer leaves; let
> him scatter them on every wind as the
> momentary signs of his infinite
> productiveness.[284]

Whitman:

> I swear I begin to see love with sweeter
> spasms than that which
> responds love, 96
> It is that which contains itself, which
> never invites and never refuses.
>
> I swear I begin to see little or nothing in
> audible words,
> All merges toward the presentation of
> the unspoken meanings of the earth,

> Toward him who sings the songs of the
> body and of the truths of the earth,
> Toward him who makes the dictionaries
> of words that print cannot touch.
>
> I swear I see what is better than to tell
> the best,
> It is always to leave the best untold.
>
> When I undertake to tell the best I find I
> cannot,
> My tongue is ineffectual on its pivots,
> My breath will not be obedient to its
> organs,
> I become a dumb man. 107

Emerson:

> When the eye of Reason opens to the outline and surface are at once added grace and expression. These proceed from imagination and affection and abate somewhat of the angular distinctness of objects. If Reason be stimulated to more earnest vision, outline and surfaces become transparent and are no longer seen, causes and spirits are seen through them. The best moments of life are these delicious awakenings of the higher powers.[285]

Whitman:

> The best of the earth cannot be told
> anyhow, all or any is best, 108

It is not what you anticipated; it is cheaper, easier, nearer,   109
Things are not dismiss'd from the places they held before,

The earth is just as positive and direct as it was before,
Facts, religions, improvements, politics, trades, are as real as before,
But the soul is also real, it too is positive and direct,
No reasoning, no proof has establish'd it,
Undeniable growth has establish'd it.   115

4.

These to echo the tones of souls and the phrases of souls,   116
(If they did not echo the phrases of souls what were they then?
If they had not reference to you in especial what were they then?)
I swear I will never henceforth have to do with the faith that tells the best,
I will have to do only with that faith that leaves the best untold.   120

Emerson:

> Words are finite organs of the infinite mind. They can not cover the dimensions of what is in truth. They break, chop, and impoverish it…

> Every universal truth which we express in words implies or supposes every other truth…It is like a great circle on a sphere, comprising all other circles: which, however, may be drawn and comprise it in like manner. Every such truth is the absolute *Ens* seen from one side. But it has innumerable sides.

Whitman:

> Say on, sayers! sing on, singers! 121
> Delve! mould! pile the words of the earth!
> Work on, age after age, nothing is to be lost,
> It may have to wait long, but it will certainly come in use,
> When the materials are all prepared and ready, the architects shall appear. 125
>
> I swear to you the architects shall appear without fall,
> I swear to you they will understand you and justify you,
> The greatest among them shall be he who best knows you, and encloses all and is faithful to all,
> He and the rest shall not forget you, they shall perceive that you are not an iota less than they,
> You shall be fully glorified in them. 130

24. Youth, Day, Old Age ...

The poet accommodates our argument of time in the 24th of the Solo Canticles. This short poem is of interest because it is all that remains of the only poem of the 1855 edition that was eliminated in the 1881 and Deathbed formulations.

That poem ended the 1855 *twelve* and was in later editions known as *Great Are the Myths*. For now it is appropriate that the poem that concluded the 1855 edition here concludes the 24 Canticles assembled in this volume. In the previous duet we gave Plato and Emerson their eternal due. The clock now concludes the final hour of Whitman's day with an appropriate summation:

Youth, Day, Old Age and Night

Youth, large, lusty, loving—youth full of grace, force, fascination,
Do you know that Old Age may come after you with equal grace, force, fascination? 2

Day full-blown and splendid-day of the immense sun, action, ambition, laughter,
The Night follows close with millions of suns, and sleep and restoring darkness. 4

Each Hour

of
the Twenty-Four

Since our poet/prophet professed to see *something of God each hour of the twenty-four*, it is perhaps appropriate to review some of highlights of the same. Like the fragment just visited from "Great Are the Myths" – "Reversals" and "Transpositions" are fragments from a deleted poem. That poem is *Respondez* (reproduced earlier in this volume). "Reversals" is six lines and appears with "By Blue Ontario's Shore" after the *Drum-Taps* cluster. "Transpositions" is four lines long and appears with the six solo canticles after the Autumn Rivulets cluster. "Youth, Day, Old Age and Night" is the concluding poem of the twelve solo poems appearing after the *Calamus* cluster. Each of these fragments only hint at the power of the larger poems that the poet later deleted. The only fragment of these four that stands substantially on its own is "A Paumanok Picture". It is the deleted original eighth canto of *Salut au Monde*. Whitman then moved the ninth canto into the eighth position and never replaced the then missing 9th. It is curious that Whitman never recalculated the canto count after the deletion and movement. Perhaps it says something of his affection for this short poem that "Salut au Monde" was permanently left with no canto between Canto VIII and X. The poet begins his day with the more epic of his two *Paumnaok* portraits. He awakens with "Starting From Paumanok" – 19 cantos of biography and Idealism. Whitman will make the poems for the living materials of his body and their dispersal in a serenely anticipated death: *For I think I shall then supply myself with the poems of my soul and immortality…*

Then, in his most striking conflation of Plato and Aristotle—Idealism and Materialism, he writes: *Was someone asking to see the soul? See, your own shape and countenance, persons, substances, beasts, the trees, the running rivers, the rocks and sands... I find there is not one nor any particle of one but has reference to the soul.* This statement (among many others) makes *Starting From Paumanok* one of the signature poems of the canon.

"By Blue Ontario Shores" is Whitman's poetic manifesto. It is a grand experiment in form and language. It first appeared in 1856 but many of it lines were present in the preface to the 1855 edition. He continued to work on the poem until 1881. It is most memorable for the *Phantom gigantic superb,* that charges the poet to *chant me the poem.* The Phantom has many precedents in literature but here it is Whitman's soul calling him to chant the carol of victory for Democracy. Democracy here is less a political pose than an ontological assertion: *Have you thought there could be but a single supreme? There can be any number of supremes... All is eligible to all.* The poetic manifesto begins in the tenth canto: *Of these states the poet is the equable man* and continues through the poem's conclusion in the twentieth. When we read: *For the war is over, the field is clear'd*, we realize he has carried this effort through the Civil War. He will continue to revise it for an additional sixteen years. The triumph of the poem comes in fifteenth canto: *The whole theory of the Universe is directed unerringly to one single individual — namely to you.*

A Broadway Pageant celebrates a visit by emissaries from Japan. It is a mystic vision presented in three movements. The 1st establishes the poet at the parade in June of 1860.

By what will become a literary coincidence it happened to be the 16th of June, known to lovers of Joyce as *Bloomsday* — the remarkable 24 hours recorded in *Ulysses*. The second movement and canto is a phantasmagoria where the history of the East floods the mind of the poet — a mini *Finnegans Wake* for the nineteenth century: *See my cantabile! These and more are flashing to us from the procession as it moves changing, a kaleidoscope divine it moves changing before us... vast desolated cities, the gliding present, all of these and more are in the pageant procession... geography, the world is in it... the countries there with their populations, the millions enmasse* [sic] *are curiously here...* The final movement returns the poet to the crush of humanity and Manhattan's Broadway where his pageant and reverie began. *Proud Music of the Storm* is a paean to his love of music. In the first canto he hears the music of nature — that of a storm whistling across the prairies, tree tops and mountains. He reveals the music as a dream in the final line of the first canto: *Entering my lonesome slumber-chamber, why have you seiz'd me?* The answer to that question is this poem in particular and all the poems that follow, in general. Music was Whitman's key to the sublime and spiritual in his life. He was able to take the rapture that music inspired and see it in the world of his experience. The world became his opera and his poetry its libretto. In the end, the music of his life bridges *the way from Life to Death, vaguely wafted in the night air, uncaught, unwritten, which lets us go forth in the bold day and write.* Handel, Haydn, Mozart, Beethoven and Verdi are just a few of the luminaries featured in the poem. *Passage to India* is a spiritual manifesto voyaging beyond the poet's mortality. It also celebrates the grand accomplishments of mankind's mortal achievements. Whitman's prophetical performance is fully in evidence:

O vast Rondure, swimming in space, Covered all over with visible power and beauty... Unspeakable high processions of sun and moon and countless stars ... suggests the American Apollo program of the 60s & 70s. Even more impressive is his understanding that any road, rail or arcing span connects one point of the earth with every other. Today we see that the point of a single PC is fantastically woven into a world wide web—*the earth... spanned by network.*

Yet even beyond these techno wonders is his shared ascension to the trinity: *Trinitas divine shall be gloriously accomplished... the voyage of ... mind's return, To reason's early paradise, Back, back to wisdom's birth, to innocent intuitions... For we are bound where mariner has not yet dared to go... O daring joy, but safe! Are they not all the seas of God?*

The mystical announcement of *Passage to India* is followed by one of his most neglected masterpieces. *Prayer of Columbus* is among the most personal pronouncements of the poet. It is also one of the most moving dramatic monologues in American Letters.

In January of 1873 the poet suffered a paralytic stroke. In speaking as Columbus it is clear that with: *My hands, my limbs grow nerveless, My brain feels rack'd and bewild'd,* he is speaking for himself. There are few lines as exquisitely pathetic in all the world's poetry. We hear, as well, the echo of his favorite Shakespearean character: "... here I stand, your slave, a poor, infirm, weak, despis'd old man."[286] The same heart severing doubt that attends the *Calamus* and *Sea Drift* clusters is masterfully in evidence throughout this little read masterwork.

"The Sleepers" has had a more celebrated exposure. It partakes of the poet's inaugural inspiration and is one of the most surreal of his *Leaves*. In Whitman's dream he imagines himself a Christ-figure bending over and healing the tortured and restless of the earth. He also sees himself dreaming the dream of Vishnu — the Hindu God who dreams the universe: *I dream in my dream all the dreams of the other dreamers, And I become the other dreamers.* In one of his most magnificent reversals he imagines himself as a woman awaiting her lover.

> I am she who adorn'd herself and folded her hair expectantly, My truant lover has come, and it is dark.
> Double yourself and receive me darkness, Receive me and my lover too, he will not let me go without him.
> I roll myself upon you as upon a bed, I resign myself to the dusk.
> He whom I call answers me and takes the place of my lover, He rises with me silently from the bed.
> Darkness, you are gentler than my lover, his flesh was sweaty and panting, I feel the hot moisture yet that he left me.
> My hands are spread forth, I pass them in all directions, I would sound up the shadowy shore to which you are journeying.
> Be careful darkness! already what was it touch'd me?
> I thought my lover had gone, else darkness and he are one,

I hear the heart beat, I follow, I fade
away.[287]

There are few moments in Whitman as vividly imagined—few moments as ineffably beautiful as: *I hear the heart beat, I follow, I fade away*. Add to this the *beautiful gigantic swimmer swimming naked through the eddies of the sea* of Canto III and the shipwreck of Canto IV and I can do little more than send the reader back to experience the poem anew—for thus it will long remain for you.

"To Think of Time" precedes "The Sleepers" in the remarkable '55 edition. It is the third of the inaugural twelve. It shares with "The Sleepers" the poet's prophetic anticipation of the Civil War. In the previous poem he was a healer. In this poem he imagines a President's death and *the Slow moving and black lines (that) creep over the whole earth*.

In the eighth canto we find: *How perfect the earth and, the minutest thing upon it*. In the ninth—the incomparable: *I swear I think that everything without exception has an immortal soul!... I swear I think there is nothing but immortality*. The poet leaves us little room for doubt.

"Thou Mother With Thy Equal Brood" shares with Shakespeare's *Troilus and Cressida* a performance written for a more specifically educated audience. Shakespeare gives Homer's Iliad a run for its money. Anticipating Joyce by a half-century, Whitman specifically plays with the ultimate archetypes—the Platonic Ideas:

> Preludes of intellect tally these and thee,
> mind-formulas fitted for thee, real

> and sane and large as these and thee,
> Thou! Mounting higher, diving deeper than we knew, thou transcendental Union! By thee fact to be justified, blended with thought, Thought of man justified, blended with God, Through the idea, lo, the immortal reality!
> Through thy reality, lo, the immortal idea! [288]
> World of the real—world of the twain in one, World of the soul, born by the world of the real alone, led to identity, body, by it alone. [289]

"Song of the Answerer" is two separate poems joined together in 1881. The first poem is part of the 1855 edition—reason alone to spend time with either of its pieces. *The Answerer* is he who will provide the solution to mankind's ceaseless queries. He is, of course, the poet—he will relinquish this pose to the more personal creation of *Walt Whitman*—his most compelling literary creation. Here he toys with an inchoate or variation of that character: *He is the Answerer, What can be answer'd he answers, and what cannot be answered he shows how it cannot be answered... Every existence has its idiom, everything has an idiom and tongue, He resolves all tongues, into his own and bestows it upon men... One part does not counteract another part, he is the joiner, he sees how they join.*

The Sixty-eight lines "Our Old Feuillage" is an inventory of the flora and fauna of these United States. As inventories go, it is one of his best. It takes on a *shape-shifting* mode in its sixty-ninth line:

> O lands! All so dear to me—what you
> are, (whatever it is,) I putting it at
> random in these song, become a
> part of that, whatever it is.
> Southward there, I screaming, with
> wings slow flapping, with the
> myriad gulls, wintering along the
> coasts of Florida...
> Northward, on the sands, on some
> shallow bay by Paumanok, I with
> parties of snowy herons wading in
> the wet to seek worms and aquatic
> plants.

Note the poet's theme of divine ignorance: *what you are, (whatever it is,)* — is an echo of *How could I answer the child? I do not know what it is any more than he.*[290] Note that its conclusion is also an invitation to his readers:

> Whoever you are! How can I but offer you divine
> leaves, that you also be as eligible as I am.
>
> How can I but as here chanting, invite you
> for yourself to collect bouquets of the in
> comparable feuillage of these states?

"A Song of Joys" is another inventory. It is less successful than "Our Old Feuillage" primarily because he uses the creaky exclamation of "O" to launch into each of the respective stanzas.[291] It is a long poem of joyous life relieved, ironically, in its praise of death: *For not life's joys alone I sing, repeating — the joy of death! The beautiful touch of Death, soothing and benumbing a few moments for reasons.*

"Song of the Broad-Axe" is 12 cantos of 254 lines. The poem is an historical account of mankind's use of the axe. In the third canto Whitman pays homage to his early work as a carpenter. He assisted his father in building homes on speculation. That enterprise failed for the father but helped launch Whitman into journalism and poetry. Whitman's carpenter mythos is reminiscent of an earlier sage. Here we will find hammers, beams and studs aplenty as he raises structures of words in the spiritual dynamism of his verse. The last three cantos are punctuated with the line: "The shapes arise!" These have a musical cadence that harkens back to the poet's devotion to Grand Opera.

Song of the Exposition was another poem written for a specific audience. This was the audience attending the American Institute's 40th Exhibition in New York City. Here the poet invokes Homer and Virgil in much the same way Shakespeare played with the Trojan War in his *Troilus and Cressida*. Whitman even has a *go* at Ulysses' "Degree" speech[292] that concludes with humanity becoming a universal wolf that last eats up itself. Here is Whitman's take:

> Away with themes of war! away with war itself! Hence from my shuddering sight to never more return that show of blacken'd, mutilated corpses!
>
> That hell unpent and raid of blood, fit for wild tigers or for lop-tongued wolves, not reasoning men…[293]

"Song of the Redwood Tree" was written after his stroke of January '73 and his mother's death in May of the same year. Whitman came close to death at both of these perilous milestones. In this poem he *shape-shifts* into a dying redwood giant of the Northern California coast. It is a strangely moving lyric. The redwood's voice is identified by italics:

> *Farewell my brethren,*
> *Farewell O earth and sky, farewell ye neighboring waters,*
> *My time has ended my term has come.*

Whitman started the poem as nearly immobile as the old tree. But his effort was restorative. The last lines of the first canto are reminiscent of and as masterful as the *Coffin Canto* (Canto V) of "When Lilacs Last in the Dooryard Bloomed." I can think of little by way of higher praise:

> Thus on the northern coast,
> In the echo of teamsters' calls and the clinking chains, and the music of choppers' axes,
> The falling trunk and limbs, the crash, the muffled shriek, the groan,
> Such words combined from the redwood-tree, as of voices ecstatic, ancient and rustling,
> The century-lasting, unseen dryads, singing, withdrawing,
> All their recesses of forests and mountains leaving,
> From the Cascade range to the Wasatch, or Idaho far, or Utah,

> To the deities of the modern henceforth yielding,
> The chorus and indications, the vistas of coming humanity, the settlements, features all,
> In the Mendocino woods I caught.

"A Song for Occupations" follows *Song of Myself* in the 1855 edition. It was extensively revised throughout the poet's lifetime. These lines remained from the original:

> Why what have you thought of yourself?
> Is it you then that thought yourself less?
> Is it you that thought the President greater than you?
> Or the rich better off than you? or the educated wiser than you?
>
> (Because you are greasy or pimpled, or were once drunk, or a thief,
> Or that you are diseas'd, or rheumatic, or a prostitute,
> Or from frivolity or impotence, or that you are no scholar and never saw your name in print,
> Do you give in that you are any less immortal?)

Also in the original is one of Whitman's efforts to use language to move beyond language. It is, therefore, one of his finest *Zen* moments:

> I bring what you much need yet always have,
> Not money, amours, dress, eating, erudition, but as good,
> I send no agent or medium, offer no representative of value, but offer the value itself.
> There is something that comes to one now and perpetually,
> It is not what is printed, preach'd, discussed, it eludes discussion and print,
> It is not to be put in a book, it is not in this book,
> It is for you whoever you are, it is no farther from you than your hearing and sight are from you,
> It is hinted by nearest, commonest, readiest, it is ever provoked by them.
>
> What is there ready and near you now?

The last line was later removed from the poem. It is, however, one of the most profound of his *invitations*. He invites the reader into enlightenment: "What is there ready and near you now?" Later in Canto 5 he will ask another of his most profound questions:

> Does all sit there with you, with the mystic unseen soul?

Yes, answers the sage:

> All the laws of nature may be read in the smallest fact.[294]

And Whitman at his most profound:

> Strange and hard that paradox true I give,
> Objects gross and the unseen soul are one.

These lines alone place *Song of Occupations* in the upper echelon of Whitman's thought. *Song of the Rolling Earth* is another of his greatest solo efforts. Here in this 1856 poem he expands on the paradoxes suggested above:

> A song of the rolling earth, and of words according,
> Were you thinking that those were the words, those upright lines? those curves, angles, dots?
>
> No, those are not the words, the substantial words are in the ground and sea,
> They are in the air, they are in you.

Whitman the wordsmith asks us to move away from words and to embrace life and living each of which is greater than any words a poet might conjure:

> The earth does not withhold, it is generous enough,
> The truths of the earth continually wait, they are not so concealed either, They

> are calm, subtle, untransmissible by print...
> The best of the earth cannot be told anyhow, all or any is best, It is not what you anticipated; it is cheaper, easier, nearer...

"Salut au Monde" opens the grand 12 Canticles that commence after *Calamus*. It is an answer to questions posed by the *Book of Job*. The poet picked a Biblical masterpiece to measure himself against. We can forgive an occasional reach that exceeds his grasp. But yet, is it not wonderful to imagine a Deity that invites him to this remarkable vision: *What widens within you Walt Whitman?* What widens within him is the world of *Salut au Monde*: *Within me latitude widens, longitude lengthens...* What widens within him is the interpenetrating grasp of his soul through time and space. He recognizes that he interpenetrates the world as it, as well, interpenetrates him — this two are one. *As I am. I am. All or not at all.*[295] By the poem's end: *My spirit has pass'd in compassion and determination around the whole earth... You vapors, I think I have risen with you, moved away to distant continents, and fallen down there for reasons...*

Of greater inspiration is "Song of the Open Road". The road of which he speaks is mapped in the interior of his soul: *Here the profound lesson of reception, nor preference nor denial... None but are accepted, none but shall dear to me.* The opening of Canto V was to become the aesthetic manifesto of the succeeding century: *From this hour I ordain myself loos'd of limits and imaginary lines, Going where I list my own master total and absolute.* The concluding stanza of the 15th canto is one of the greatest invitations his readers will ever receive:

> Comerado, I give you my hand! I give
> you my love more precious than money,
> I give you myself before preaching and
> law, Will you give me yourself? Will
> you come travel with me? Shall we stick
> by each other as long as we live?

"Crossing Brooklyn Ferry" is perhaps of a higher order still, which is to say it is one of the greatest of his poems. It belongs to a select group that includes: *Song of Myself, The Sleepers, Song of the Open Road, Song of Occupations, Song of the Rolling Earth, I Sing the Body Electric, Prayer of Columbus, Out of the Cradle Endlessly Rocking, As I Ebbed With the Ocean of Life, Come Up From the Fields Father, The Wound Dresser* and *When Lilacs Last in the Dooryard Bloom'd*. This is a short list that could perhaps, be extended to a dozen others. *Crossing Brooklyn Ferry* is surely on any list extending beyond *Song of Myself* and *Lilacs*. Not bad company, they.

Flood-tide below me begins the Crossing. He sees the tide below and the clouds of the west—face to face. These are reflections of his own face. As all things are Buddha-things for the Buddhist—all things are Whitman-things to the poet. Whereas he extended his love to travelers of the open road in his time—here, he extends it to our time: *And you that shall cross from shore to shore years hence are more to me, and more in my meditations, than you might suppose.* The similitude of the past and future are *The glories strung out like beads on the smallest sights and hearings… Others that are to follow me, the ties between me and them… A hundred years hence… Just as you feel when you look on the river, I felt…* The poet bridges time and invites us to share his rapture of eternity:

We use you, and do not cast you aside — we plant you permanently within us, We fathom you not — we love you — there is perfection in you also, You furnish the parts toward eternity, Great or small, you furnish your parts to the soul. In an earlier book[296] I averred that the poem was one of the great thought experiments of the 19th Century. This is a highly condensed paraphrase of the nine cantos and 132 lines of the poem. I've purposely jumbled the order of the 24 *hours* in this *day* so I could conclude this summation with its greatest poems. The poet's output took place over a lifetime. The proper study of his *poem* takes place over the lifetime of his readers. *Great or small they furnish the parts to the soul.*

PASSAGE TO INDIA REDUX

The Past — the dark unfathom'd retrospect!
The teeming gulf — the sleepers and the shadows!
The past — the infinite greatness of the past!
For what is the present after all but a growth out of the past?

Whitman was fascinated by history and spent long hours at the Egyptian Museum on New York's upper Broadway. One of the earliest documents concerning the relativity of the gods is Egyptian in origin. [297] At the inception of the Old Kingdom is found a religious ceremony known as the *Sod Festival*. The Pharaoh wears a crown which symbolizes the Upper and Lower Kingdoms over which he presides. But beneath the duality of the two kingdoms is a scroll which symbolizes their unity in the *Will of Maat* — the unifying principle of the Universe. Whitman, who loved visiting Egyptian artifacts in a N.Y. museum, is only a laterly exponent of the equation in question.

The *Will of Maat* is also known as the *Secret of the Two Partners*. The Pharaoh is a God-King believed to be an incarnation of Horus. Horus enters the mouth of the Cow Goddess, Hathor at dusk to bring down the curtain of the day. The Pharaoh is born each morning to herald the dawn. Like a good Christian he is both God the Father and God the Son — in this case the Son is also the *Sun*. Rather than paraphrase myself and the late Joseph Campbell I'll simply quote from *Buddha Boogie: The Tautological Paradigm:*

> On engravings and paintings that survive this time beyond time the Pharaoh is shown on equal footing with his dreaded nemesis, Seth, the slayer of the god Osiris, father of the Pharaoh. Four thousand years before Hamlet we find another son decrying a father slain by a plotting uncle. In the earlier of the two dramas the father and the uncle have a clearer understanding of their respective roles. Horus needs no 'mousetrap' to determine the guilt of his Claudius. That guilt, the necessity of night to follow day and death to follow life, is understood to underlie the Will of Maat in this cosmology. It also underlines *Me* in the Sumerian Sphere, *Rita* in the Vedic, *Dharma* among the Buddhists and the familiar *Tao* in the far Eastern enactment. The animal connected with each is the sacred cow. With each there is a tacit understanding of the necessity of opposites to fire the eternal engines of the cosmos. The intuition of the infinite occurs in the nexus of any pair of opposites that the mind can conceive. Its apprehension is at hand at any moment where the finite has lost its limitations. [298]

WHITMAN'S CODE: A NEW BIBLE, VOLUME I
M.C. GARDNER

Hinduism (Sanatana Dharma) is an amalgam of the ancient Dravidian cosmologies and that of migrating Aryans who conquered them sometime after 1500 BCE. The word Veda is related to the word *Vid* — to know. The earliest writings collected by the Aryans were songs to the various deities of their Pantheon. These were called Samhitas and were collected in groups of Ten 'Mandalas' associated with Indra, Agni, Soma, Varuna and variety of lesser deities. Annexed to the Vedas are the preeminent scriptures of Hinduism, the Upanishads. The Upanishads are translated into Persian in the 17th Century. This is then translated into Latin at the beginning of the nineteenth century. It is this translation that soothed the pessimistic scowl of Schopenhauer, who avers it to be the solace of his life and would, as well, be the solace of his death. Schopenhauer's masterwork, *The World as Will and Idea,* is published in Germany the year of Whitman's birth, 1819. Emerson is studying Henry Thomas Colebrook's essays on the Upanishads in 1845 and has, a decade earlier, written his essay *The Oversoul*, from promptings urged from the *Bhagavad Gita*.

The *Upanishads* are part of a much larger group of musings than the few pages assembled here to complement Walt Whitman. There are also extended interpretations of the Brahmans and rhapsodic evocations of the Samhitas that would please any group in need of personal gods or God. Mankind feels more deeply about its symbols than any abstraction lying behind them. One can as ably cull passages from the *Upanishads* that are the inspiration for the worship of many of India's more popular deities. The end of life to a devotional Hindu is *Bhatia* or the adoring meditation of a chosen *diva*.

What is known as the *Uttar Mimamsa* or Vedanta is more precisely rendered by the *Upanishads*, the *Bhagavad Gita* and *Badarayana's Sutras on the Upanishads*. Attached to the epical *Mahabharata* and preserved for the centuries (somewhat as the *Upanishads* have been attached to the Vedas) is the 'Song of God' or *Bhagavad Gita*. Along with the Vedas it is the most highly revered among the copious record of the Indian Spirit. Sir Charles Wilkins' 1785 English translation of the *Bhagavad Gita* predates Duperron's Latin translation of the *Upanishads* in the early nineteenth century. Later, this translation makes contact with Emerson and Thoreau.

From *A Week on the Concord and Merrimac River* we find:

> I would say to the readers of Scripture, if they wish for a good book read the Bhagavat-Geeta—it deserves to be read with reverence even by Yankees.

Mahatma Gandhi's first encounter with the Scripture is in an English translation which he reads while he studying law in Great Britain. Some years after his return to India he reflects:

> My life has been full of external tragedies and if they have not left any visible and indelible effect on me, I owe it to the teaching of the Bhagavad Gita.

The *Bhagavad Gita* profoundly influences Thoreau. He in turn is a major influence for Gandhi's stand of non-violent civil disobedience. The *Gita* concerns an interview with Arjuna (one of the five pale faced Pandavas) and Lord Krishna—an incarnation of the god Vishnu.

The scene is on a field before the battle of Kurukshetra. In the distance is the enemy, his cousins the Karuavas and their armies. Arjuna doubts the value of the coming conflict knowing that so many must die. He wonders if it might be better to lose the battle if the suffering could be mitigated. Krishna, who is sometimes referred to as the *Christ of India*, councils his young charge in an allegorical wisdom that is definitely from the *yonder shore*. Emerson, Thoreau, and Whitman make an American literary Trinity. Each was deeply affected by the council of Krishna. Their writings are, in turn, embraced by the *yonder shores* of the Asias.

> Sri Krishna:
>
> Your words are wise, Arjuna, but your sorrow is for nothing: The truly wise mourn neither for the living nor the dead. There was never a time when I did not exist, nor you, nor any of these kings. Nor is there any future in which you will cease to be.
>
> That which is non-existent can never come into being, and that which *is* can never cease to be.
>
> Knowing it is birthless, knowing it is deathless, knowing it endless, forever unchanging, dream not you do the deed of a killer, dream not it is yours to command it.
>
> He who dwells within all living bodies remains forever indestructible.

Therefore you should never mourn for anyone.

Realize that pleasure and pain, gain and loss, victory and defeat, are the one and the same: then go into battle. Do this and you cannot commit any sin.

When the whole country is flooded, the reservoir becomes superfluous. So, to the illuminated seer, the Vedas are all superfluous.

When your intellect has cleared itself of its delusion, you will become indifferent to the results of all actions, present or future.

A man has found delight and satisfaction and peace in Atman, then he is no longer obliged to perform any kind of action. He has nothing to gain in this world by action and nothing to lose by refraining from action.

Consider me: I am not bound by any sort of duty. There is nothing in all the three worlds, which I do not already possess; nothing I have yet to acquire.

Whatever path men travel is my path; No matter where they walk it leads to me.

> When you have reached enlightenment, ignorance will delude you no longer. In the light of that knowledge you will see the entire creation within your own Atman and in me.
>
> The blazing fire turns wood to ashes: The fire of knowledge turns all karmas to ashes.
> The Lord is everywhere and always perfect: What does he care for man's sin or the righteousness of man?
>
> Now I shall tell you that innermost secret: Knowledge of God which is nearer than knowing, open vision direct and instant. Understand this and be free forever from birth and dying with all their evil.
>
> Some see me one with themselves, or separate: Some bow to the countless gods that are my million faces.[299]

Whitman was a voracious reader and famously autodidactic. If he was unfamiliar with Colebrook's work such could not be said of his familiarity with the *Sage of Concord*, R.W. Emerson. Sri Ramakrishna was thought by many to be an avatar of Krishna — if one were to make the same claim for either Emerson or Whitman, those that know their work would not be surprised. There are no Americans who have as assiduously reported the countless gods that are *their* million faces. The Trinity is a theological construct not exclusive to Christianity.

Whitman's own cartography includes *Walt Whitman*, the *Me / Myself*, and the *Soul*. The Hindus revere Brahma, the Creator, Vishnu, the Preserver and Shiva, the Destroyer — a triad subsumed in Brahman, the underlying reality of the three. In Buddhism, the Buddha is said to be comprised of three lotus bodies: Nirmanakaya, his earthly body; Sambhogakaya, his celestial teaching body; and the Dharmakaya — the body he shares with all living creatures — including he or she whose eyes move from word to word upon this page. Underlying each of these *Trinities* is a tautology — the Tautological Paradigm. Each separate entity is a *Godhead* — the whole masquerading as a part in search of Union with itself. The Nirmanakaya body is of primary interest to the Theravadin monks. Their theology is based on the rich collection of teachings that were collected during the Buddha's lifetime. These were written on palm leaves. They were compiled in *Pitakas* or baskets. The Pali Canon was assembled eighty years before the birth of Christ. This collection is known as the *Tripitaka*. The *Viayapitaka* recorded the rules for the monastic order. The *Suttapitaka* is comprised of five collections or nikayas of the Buddha's sermons. Chief among these is the celebrated points of doctrine, *Dhammapada*. The third Pitaka is the *Abhidhamma* — an abstruse collection of seven volumes detailing the illusory dharmas or elements comprising the Maya of the physical world. Yoga is an ancient Indian attempt at linkage between the *Many* and the *One*. Whitman's *I Sing the Body Electric* is one of his most compelling statements of this theme. Here the chains on the beings in question are not metaphorical — they press indelibly against the anguished flesh of slaves: *O I say now these are the soul!* is one of the greatest indictments of slavery that the poet will ever deliver — it is also a tautological directive to liberation.

The Mahayana school of Buddhist thought is primarily focused on the *Sambhogakaya* of the Buddha. It is in this body Buddha's inspiration continues in the long centuries succeeding the Buddha's earthly sojourn. The oldest of the Mahayana Sutras are the Prajnaparamita texts. Many of the original Sanskrit texts have been lost to the millennia. However, translations of these scriptures proceeded apace in China, Tibet and Japan. Their influence corresponds to a remarkable flowering of genius in these respective cultures: The Theravadins had originally asserted that objects were real and subjects illusory. The Mahayana school then asserted the emptiness of anything, whatsoever. The subject was *Anatman* (without self) and the objective world was *sunyata* or void. This double void was to be the impetus of an incredible *much ado about nothing*. Its out-flowing of literary, philosophic and artistic creation has had few rivals in the creative history of the race. It is only in recent decades that the major Mahayana Sutras have found themselves the subject of Western translation and study. The earlier efforts of the nineteenth century were drawn to the more orderly presentation of the Pali texts of Southern Buddhism. The Theravadins, in something of a huff about being declared the "lesser" vehicle, went on offence and declared the Mahayana texts *heretical*. Their admittedly late date of composition put them beyond the oral memory of the Buddha's original teaching. The historical advocates like to suggest that the Mahayana texts were secret teachings by the Buddha and only accessible to a select group of his followers. This is a pretty myth but these late additions to the Buddha's teaching are of such surpassing beauty and profundity that the argument of their veracity has become a moot historical point.

Suzuki has rightly argued that texts that have enriched the lives of millions down the millennia have already established a veracity of their own. When scholars freed themselves from the prejudice of reporting the historical teachings of a 6th century Hindu saint they were open to a vision beyond that of any country or time. Their findings for Occidental thought of the twenty-first century are as profound as the Arabic transfusion of Athens had been on the medieval mind.[300] There is no complete consensus among Buddhists of a Mahayana canon.

Among the most revered are the *Ananta-nirdesa Sutra*, the *Lalitavistara Sutra*, the *Lankavatara Sutra*, the *Lotus Sutra*, the *Vimalakirti-nirdesa Sutra*, the *Platform Sutra*, the *Amitabha Sutra*, the *Avatamsaka Sutra* and the *Prajnaparamita Sutras*. This last is a group of sutras of devoted to the development of *Prajna* or wisdom—the opening of a vision to the true nature of reality—the opening of the third eye. Among the most celebrated of these is the *Prajnaparamitahridaya*, the *Heart Sutra*; and the *Vajracchedika*, the *Diamond Sutra*.

The import of all these works is to see beyond the moral and physical distinctions with which we have divided the world and our lives. The chief principles guiding this pursuit are *anicca* (impermanence) and *anatta* (absence of substance). The vision appropriated by the successful adept is that of *sunyata*. This is simply seeing the world as a witness. It is a stance we find throughout *Leaves of Grass*: *The suicide sprawls on the bloody floor of the bedroom, I witness the corpse with its dabbled hair, I note where the pistol has fallen*. When you see the world in this fashion you see it as it *is* in the moment that it *is*.

There is no moral prerogative of right or wrong. There is no casual link explaining the present moment, for the present moment is believed to be without precondition—as non-originating as the universe, itself. There is not even a *self* attending the witness at hand—there is no definitional distance between the witness and the observed—the witness is the observation. This is very much the argument of the great Scottish skeptic, David Hume. Hume did not believe in cause and effect because he could not discern any necessary connection between the two. He argued that an iron ball placed within a fire would at one moment be golden and at another be red. He believed these were simply two different states and bridging the twain with a cause called heat or fire could never be empirically demonstrated. He also believed there was nothing that could be shown to be identity. What you believed to be yourself was simply the memory of a kaleidoscopic series bundled together by force of habit. This argument awakened Immanuel Kant from his *dogmatic slumbers*. It was also the foundational argument devised by a thinker that preceded the Scotsman by a millennium and a half: In the manner of a grand Mahayana myth, Nagarjuna is invited by the Nagas, (serpents who ruled under the seas) to open vast storehouses of secret knowledge that had been lost to the world since the death of the Buddha—six hundred years before. The Sutras he retrieves are the Prajnaparamita texts. It is unclear whether Nagarjuna was the author of these texts or their greatest interpreter. His understanding of *Madhyamika*, the Buddha's famed *Middle Way* is subsumed in *Sunyavada*, the doctrine of the void—the absurdity of any proposition, whatsoever. He is remembered for a famed logical construction called the *Eight-fold Negation*:

1. Nothing comes into being.
2. Nor does anything disappear.
3. Nothing is eternal.
4. Nor does anything have an end.
5. Nothing is identical.
6. Nor is anything capable of differentiation.
7. Nothing moves hither.
8. Nor anything thither.

The first two are connected to creation: A. Creation did not occur. B. Dissolution is a myth: (Nothing that *is* can become an *isn't*). The 2nd pair concerns A. Eternity and B. Time: (The proposition of eternity is as absurd as that of time—one can argue for the one as ably as the other, therefore each is sunyata). The 3rd opposition concerns the A. One: (Nothing is capable of differentiation, therefore there is only one entity that exists). B. Many: (No two things can said to be identical, therefore the world is a multiple construct.). The fourth duo is an argument for A. Movement: (Nothing *comes* hither). B. Repose: (nor *moves* thither). And in the manner of David Hume (fifteen centuries to the future)—the canny Indian asserted that consciousness is *nihsvabhavata*, which is to say, *without self-existence*. In Zen, you meditate to discover the face you possessed before you were born. That is, to see reality without the glaze of the ego—to see it as it is without the discriminations that have, heretofore, defined its parameters. Whitman suggests it is as simple as looking in a mirror:

> Can each see signs of the best by a look
>   in the looking glass?
> Is their nothing greater or more?

> Does all sit there with you, with the
>   mystic unseen soul?
> Strange and hard that paradox true I
>   give,
> Objects gross and the unseen soul are one.

If *objects gross and the unseen soul are one,* then there is no distance between yourself and anything in your experience. At that juncture we discover language is powerless to truthfully convey any position we might otherwise choose to assert—for the contrary position is just as logically tenable. We are left perhaps with the smile of the Buddha or Wittgenstein's proposition 6.521 of The Tractatus:

> The solution of the problem of life is seen in the vanishing of the problem. Is not this the reason why those who have found, after a long period of doubt, that the sense of life became clear to them — have been unable to say what constituted that clarity?

Wherein, we might hear the echo of Whitman: *Do I contradict myself? Very well then I contradict myself, (I am large, I contain multitudes).* Hui Neng would also tautologically opine that there is no difference between an enlightened man and an ignorant one. Joseph Campbell was fascinated by these profoundly enigmatic texts:

> In these we are told that just as there never has been any world, so, also, there never was a historical Buddha to redeem it. The Buddha and the world are equally void; sunyam: empty, without being.

> From the transcendental standpoint of the released consciousness they are on one and the same plane of illusoriness...The illusory historical Buddha, who through bodhi entered into nirvana yet until his parinirvana continued to live for the eyes of the world, may consequently be represented as though alive in the illusory world. Thus the Mahayana, "The Great Ferry," is a vessel on which all may ride — in fact are riding — going absolutely nowhere.

The prospect of going absolutely nowhere may seem a dubious enterprise until we reflect that the other shore is one to which we need never depart for we have already arrived. And as to the meaning of it all? We might safely assert with Joyce:

> ...everything in fine, in nature's workshop from the extinction of some remote sun to the blossoming of one of the countless flowers which beautify our public parks is subject to a law of numeration as yet unascertained.[301]

And conclude with Whitman

> A child said *What is the grass?* Fetching it to me with full hands.
> How could I answer the child? I do not know any more than he. [302]

Perhaps the only answer (as in the sound of one hand clapping) is in the handful itself.

ANATOMY OF A CODE

The terrain on which I plant my flag is new,[303] although it has had a long foreground (nearing four decades) and I have been rubbing my eyes a little now to see if the sunbeams of which I write are not illusions.[304] Whitman published his inaugural volume in July, 1855. He continued to work on *Leaves of Grass* and its enigmatic structure for the remaining thirty seven years of his life—completing its design in the final 1891-92 collection. On the 8th of June, 2008 I unraveled a code in that *Deathbed* edition. *Whitman's Code: A New Bible* is based on deciphering a simple numerical scheme that the poet devised and implemented into his masterpiece over a century ago.

The time frame of my thought is similar to that which the poet took to write the poems of the first through the last edition.[305] The poet was brought to a boil by a careful reading of Emerson in the early 1850s ("I had Emerson on the brain."[306]) and his percolation continued with in-depth readings and memorizations of the Bible, the Greeks and Shakespeare until his demise in 1892.

In preparation for this exegesis I consulted the *Textual Variorum of the Printed Poems,* [307] his notebooks, prose and various editions and supplements of *Leaves of Grass*. The literati among my readers will recall that 1855's first edition consisted of a preface and twelve unnamed poems—over half the poetry consisting of what would later be called *Song of Myself*. Emerson rightly declared the volume to be "the most extraordinary piece of wit and wisdom that America has yet contributed."[308] This, given the literature of the period, was a remarkable assertion. Emerson's inaugural works: *Nature, The American Scholar* and *The Harvard Divinity School Address* were, respectively, from 1836, 1837 and 1838.

His Essay Series (I & II) followed in 1841 and '44. Hawthorne's *Scarlet Letter* was published in 1850, Melville's *Moby Dick* in 1851 and Thoreau's *Walden* in 1854. Emerson was reported to be somewhat taken aback when Whitman published his praise without permission, but it was an assertion he maintained. [309]

The author of the '55 edition neither named himself as poet[310], nor titled his poems. Walter Whitman was listed as the owner of the copyright on the obverse of the slender volume's title page:

> Entered according to Act of Congress, in the year 1855, by WALTER WHITMAN, in the Clerk's office of the District Court of the United States for the Southern District of New York.

The seemingly anonymous author presented himself only as a photographic image in the most famous frontispiece ever to companion an American publication. The Samuel Hollyer or John C. McRae engraving (from a lost daguerreotype taken by Gabriel Harrison in 1854) presents the poet truncated at the knees yet arising as if from an aperture in the earth. He has one hand in his left pocket and the right hand on his hip. He stares unapologetically at his readers.[311] He sports a wide brimmed hat and his head is cocked in an insouciance of shadow. Aside from the benevolent and discerning praise of *America's Socrates*[312] Whitman himself submitted fulsome reviews that might have best been left to more disinterested parties. The acclaim is so obviously by the poet himself that the editors of the *Brooklyn Daily Times*, September 29, 1855, must have scratched their heads in wonderment surveying the meter and meat of this single sentence:

> No dilettante democrat—a man who is art-and-part with the commonalty, and with immediate life—loves the street—loves the docks—loves the free rasping talk of men—likes to be called by his given name, and nobody at all needs Mr. him—can laugh with laughers—likes the ungenteel ways of laborers—is not prejudiced one mite against the Irish talks readily with them—talks readily with niggers—does not make a stand on being a gentleman, nor on learning or manners—eats cheap fare—likes the strong flavored coffee of the coffee-stands in the market, at sunrise—likes supper of oysters fresh from the oyster-smack—likes to make one at he crowed table among sailors and work-people—would leave a select soiree of elegant people any time to go with tumultuous men, roughs receive their caresses and welcome, listen to their noise, oaths, smut, fluency, laughter, repartee—and can preserve his presence perfectly among these, and the like of these.[313]

William Swinton of the New York Times had written favorably of Whitman. He was amused to realize that Whitman was his own best critic:

> On subsequently comparing the critiques from the *United States Review* and the *Phrenological Journal* with the preface of *Leaves of Grass* we discovered unmistakable evidence that Mr. Walt Whitman, true to the character of a

> Kosmoswas not content with writing a book, but was also determined to review it, so Mr. Walt Whitman has concocted both those criticisms of his own work, treating it we need not say how favorably.[314]

Charles Eliot Norton was less certain than Swinton on Whitman's claim of Kosmos:

> We learn on page 29, that our poet is "Walt Whitman, an American, one of the roughs, a Kosmos." That he was an American, we knew before, for, aside from America there is no quarter of the universe where such a production could have had a genesis. That he was one of the roughs is tolerably plain; but that he was a Kosmos, is a piece of news we were hardly prepared for. Precisely what a Kosmos is, we trust Mr. Whitman will take an early occasion to inform the impatient public.

The poem, however, was *of* a piece—the dozen poems presented as a single poem. In the 2nd edition of 1856 Whitman added an additional twenty poems and gave up the lofty (though cumbersome) conceit of a single poem. Whitman became sensitive to the charge of formlessness. No one had seen a book quite like the first edition. Critics weren't even sure it should be considered poetry. Whitman's response to the charge was to include the word "Poem" in each of the titles of the respective poems in the new volume. This was not a satisfactory solution for nomenclature or structure.

WHITMAN'S CODE: A NEW BIBLE, VOLUME I
M.C. GARDNER

The poem we know as *Song of Myself* was then called, "Poem of Walt Whitman". That was fine as far as it went but it also led to such unsatisfactory results as *Poem of The Daily Work of The Workmen and Workingwomen of These States;* and *Liberty Poem for Asia, Africa, Europe, America, Australia, Cuba and the Archipelagoes of the Sea*. Say what you might, it doesn't fall trippingly from the tongue.

Whitman was in great haste to publish a second edition of his poems. Emerson's praise was a marketing tool that he felt must be used immediately. The dew on that remarkable lily might not linger. I will treat the controversy concerning the use of Emerson's name later in these volumes. Suffice it to say, that Whitman saw fit not only to advertise the encomium but, as well, to have a line from it stamped on the spine of the 2nd Edition. (Emerson's initial letter and a photo of the offending "spine," can be apprehended in Appendices 9 & 11).

Whitman approached the 3rd Edition with a cooler head. One of the most tantalizing notes we have from the period appears in R.M. Bucke's *Notes and Fragments*. In the 14th fragment of chapter 2 we find:

> The Great Construction of the New Bible. Not to be diverted from the principal object—the main life work—the three hundred and sixty-five—It ought to be ready in 1859 (June '57).

The date in parentheses is Bucke's conjecture of the note's origin. The "It ought to be ready in 1859," is Whitman's anticipated date of completion. It is from this arcane suggestion that *Whitman's Code: A New Bible* has been constructed.

1860's edition of one-hundred thirty-six [315] poems fell well short of his planned three-hundred sixty-five.[316] As we shall see, the remainder of that total was to be the work of a lifetime. It is in the 3rd edition that Whitman begins the imaginative groupings of his "clusters," *Calamus* and *Enfans d'Adam*, among them. One of his most celebrated poems, "Out of the Cradle Endlessly Rocking", is also premiered, although with its more abbreviated, though lovely, title: *A Word Out of the Sea*.

The 1860 edition is a poetic masterpiece; however, any careful reading of his work reveals that Walt Whitman was the poet's most imaginative creation:

> Whitman extracted from his noble experiment the vivid and personal figure who is one of the few great things in modern literature: the figure of himself.[317]

The poem and its poet are as tightly entwined as any of the lassies (or lads) frolicking in its ardent reveries. Whitman lost a government job when Interior Secretary James Harlan chanced upon the poet's erotic compendium originally known as *Enfans d'Adam* while rifling through Whitman's desk early in his employment.

Separating Whitman from his public and private personas has been the subject of learned speculation since the poet and poem appeared in 1855. Harlan, of course, separated the poet from his job in Indian Affairs. J. Hubley Ashton and William Douglas O'Connor placed the poet in another clerkship in the Attorney General's office on the day following his dismissal.

WHITMAN'S CODE: A NEW BIBLE, VOLUME I
M.C. GARDNER

Whitman was more bemused by his employer than seriously rebuffed: "He was only a fool, there was only a dim light in his noodle, he had to steer by that light, what else could he do? Yet, he had the courage of his convictions; he didn't allow Ashton's eloquence to shake him; he threw me out; his heart said 'Throw Whitman out,' so out I went. I have always had a latent sneaking admiration for his cowardly despicable act."[318]

O'Connor, however, was so incensed at Harlan that he wrote an extended biographical essay defending "the good gray poet." The sobriquet struck a note with the public and despite the excesses of his forty-six page essay the poet has been known, as such, ever there after. Throughout *Leaves of Grass* Whitman identifies himself with the total expanse of time and space. His friend, author Dr. R.M. Bucke[319], believed this identification to be a result of what he termed *Cosmic Consciousness*[320]. Whitman became the preeminent subject of a book by Bucke of the same name. In the 33rd section of *Song of Myself*. Whitman imagines that the:

> Distant and dead resuscitate,
> They show as the dial or move as the
>   hands of me, I am the clock myself.

The suggestiveness of this *messianic time piece* is wherein I first chanced upon the *code* found hidden within *Leaves of Grass* — the basis for *Whitman's Code: A New Bible*. I had begun work on a book concerning the *Unseen* Walt Whitman—*Whitman between the lines* and it was there that I discovered a numeric code far different than the one used to disguise his notebook entries[321] concerning his passion and anguish over his relationship with the street car conductor Peter Doyle.

Rather, this was a lovely metaphor underpinning the whole of his *poem* and the basis for this essay. If Spinoza was considered a "God-intoxicated man" we may as faithfully assert that Whitman was a "Time-intoxicated-poet." For to fully immerse oneself in the time of one's becoming is to, as well, be baptized into the eternity of one's being — time's primordial companion.

Depending on the count criteria, *Leaves of Grass* was published in six or nine[322] editions in Whitman's lifetime. Aside from his newspaper reportage and editing, the prose of the *Prefaces*, *Specimen Days* and *Democratic Vistas*, *Leaves of Grass* was his life and his life's work.

This is from a fragment dated June 21, 1856:

> It seems to me quite clear and determined that I should concentrate my powers {on} "*Leaves of Grass*" — not diverting my means, strength, interest to the construction of anything else — of any other book.[323]

He was to refine, retool and rework the poems, ultimately collected in the canonical *Deathbed* edition of 1891-92 until his actual demise in March of '92.[324] His shuffling of supplements, and work from one cluster to another and his minute attention to single lines and individual words show a devotion that might only be rivaled by his continental contemporary, Flaubert. Much of this constituted the overall structure of what he originally desired to be a single poetic utterance.

The question remained how to transform an ungainly colossus into a unified work of art. In order to envision *Leaves* as a whole I set about tabulating the so called "clusters" of poems and those poems not thematically so collected yet segregated as "stand-alone" poems for the canon. I ask the reader's indulgence as I try to unravel a complicated matter as simply as the matter permits.

What constitutes the Whitman Canon depends, of course, on which poems are thought to be canonical. I fear a tautology in that construction, but I will let it stand. The Variorum suggests (page XX, Vol. I) that *Leaves of Grass* first assumed its permanent form in the 1881-82 edition: *This represented the final selection and grouping by cluster of what we call the 'canon.'* The Variorum goes on to say (page XXIV, Vol. I): *The copy-text for Leaves of Grass, then, is not 1881 as is generally assumed, but with the addition of the prefatory poem missing from 1889, which otherwise would have had the designation, the 1891-2 Leaves, the so-called 'Deathbed edition.'* Those convolutions are the Variorum's — mine are of an altogether different order. The Variorum acknowledges the two *Deathbed* annexes (*Sands at Seventy* and *Good-Bye My Fancy*) but shows less affection for *Old Age Echoes* (13 poems collected by Horace Traubel after the poet's death) which is relegated to Appendix A of the Variorum. The prefatory poem, referenced above, is called *Come Said My Soul*. It had appeared as early as 1871 and subsequently disappeared in later editions and then reappeared as a signed epigraph on the title page of the *Deathbed* collection. "Inscriptions" as a cluster first appeared as 9 poems in the 1871 edition. In the 1881 and the *Deathbed* edition, it begins the volume and the number of *Inscriptions* was finalized at 24.

Twenty-five poems were listed outside of the *clusters*. These I call *stand alone or solo poems* as a consequence of their exclusivity and "canticles" to designate their sonorous, spiritual nature.[325] These include the major "Song" poems, the most celebrated being *Song of Myself, Song of the Open Road*, the evocative *Night Poem*, later *The Sleepers*; and also the lovely *Sundown Poem* of the '56 edition, which we now know as *Crossing Brooklyn Ferry*. The poems accorded this singular *stand-alone* treatment are among his greatest but not exclusively so. The poem that Swinburne proclaimed: "the most sweet and sonorous nocturne ever chanted in the church of the world, "When Lilacs Last in the Dooryard Bloomed" is included in the four poem cluster, *Memories of President Lincoln*. "Out of the Cradle Endlessly Rocking" appears in the cluster, *Sea Drift*; "I Sing the Body Electric" appears in the *Children of Adam* grouping; and the *Drum-Taps* cluster is of such surpassing beauty that one could easily cull a half dozen of his most haunting poems from that collection alone. Whitman moved the poems of the clusters throughout the various editions of his work. Sometimes given clusters were published initially as separate books. These supplementary volumes, *Drum-Taps* and *Passage to India* among them, were later stitched into new editions of the parent epic with separate pagination. Other supplements were *Songs Before Parting, As a Strong Bird on Pinions Free, Two Rivulets, November Boughs* and *Good-Bye My Fancy*. Some appear more congruent then others but it is clear, as he reintroduced them into *Leaves of Grass*, that they became a major attempt at unifying the whole of his rambling opus. Two *Canticles* follow the opening Inscriptions. The first is *Starting from Paumanok*. The 2nd is the aforementioned *Song of Myself*. *Paumanok* contains nineteen cantos and balances the last *stand alone* poem in the volume—the seven lines limning *A Paumanok Picture*.

When we come to the former first poem of the 1855 edition we somewhat lament its secondary placement in the final edition. *Song of Myself* is arguably the greatest poem the poet ever penned—perhaps one or two others might justifiably compete for its celebrated preeminence. For many it will always, at least figuratively, stand at the beginning of the volume as it did in the inaugural '55 edition. Mark Van Doren was not alone in asserting:

> It was and is one of Whitman's masterpieces, if not the chief one it had the right position for the book... [326]

Whitman divided *Song of Myself* into 52 sections or cantos in 1867. Now were I to have the audacity to remove and segregate *Song of Myself* from the twenty-five *Canticles*, we might imaginatively discern that there were now twenty-four stand-alone poems beneath it. That is, I've simply swapped the first poem, *Starting from Paumanok* with the 2nd poem, *Song of Myself*. *Starting from Paumanok* still suggests the incipient stirrings of the poet's Long Island prelude, (undoubtedly the reason for its placement by the poet) and stands as the first of the 24 *Canticles* while still balancing *A Paumanok Picture*, the concluding poem found outside a cluster. I've only given *Song of Myself* something of the status of the '55 edition by making it a separate entity fronting the body of the other canticles—first among equals. The clusters of *Leaves of Grass* proper number twelve—the same number as the original group of untitled poems in the inaugural 1855 edition, and the same number of uncollected poems known as "Live Oak with Moss"—the precursor to the *Calamus* cluster. Whitman also collected two further annexes: *Sands at Seventy* and

Farewell My Fancy for the concluding *Deathbed* edition of his *Leaves*. Either subconsciously or by deliberation, the poet is working with the numbers 12, 24 and 52 in several of the major groupings in his chief d'oeuvre. The uncertainty of the final poems is owing to the fact that the poet was still composing within weeks of his demise.

It was determined that whatever these leavings, they would be designated as *Old Age Echoes*. This group was the least certain of any of his collections. He had no way of knowing how many poems remained to him. Given this uncertainty, *Old Age Echoes* was the least likely group to make its way cogently into the poet's conception (unconscious or otherwise). As earlier noted, in the *Variorum of the Printed Poems* it is relegated to an appendix—so also here. Indeed, it can be reasonably asserted that in the weeks preceding his death he might have had little interest in keeping with any early or late design, whatsoever. The poet was, in fact, seized by the notion of calling a truncated anthology of his work, *Leaves of Grass, Junior*: "I want the Junior spelled out, made unmistakable."

This obstinacy suggests a mental deterioration that was, in fact, prelude to a complete physical collapse: *His body shrank and caved in. His legs turned strange colors and became scaly. He coughed continually and he was so weak he couldn't even lift a knife or fork.*[327] Preceding that collapse, Whitman authored his final prose address to his readers in the *Preface Note to 2nd Annex* of the *Deathbed* 91/92 edition. In that note Whitman suggests that *Goodbye My Fancy* is the conclusion of his clusters:

In answer, or rather defiance, to that kind of well-put interrogation, here comes this little cluster, and conclusion of my preceding clusters.

The leavings beyond *Goodbye My Fancy* were tabulated by friend and chronicler, Horace Traubel to be thirteen at the death of the poet. They appeared as *Old Age Echoes* in the 10th edition of 1897 which together with the solo canticles and the clusters and annexes of the *Deathbed* edition totaled a count of 402 poems.

The twenty-five *Canticles* (*solo* poems) were purposely segregated from the clusters by the poet. So we begin with the 52 cantos of *Song of Myself*—metaphorically reflecting the fifty two weeks of the year. The twelve poems beginning with *Starting from Paumanok* and the eleven others dispersed adjacent to diverse clusters suggest the 12 hours from midnight till noon of the Ante Meridiem. The twelve *stand-alone* poems following the "Calamus" cluster conjure the subsequent 12 hours of one of his own titles, *From Noon to Starry Night*. The 12 clusters also mirror the 12 Houses of the Zodiac and the 12 months of the calendar year. Allusion to other time frames is also suggested: the four seasons or weeks of the month by the 4 poems in *Memories of President Lincoln*, the week's "seven days" in the 7 poems of the *Birds of Passage* cluster; the thirty-one day month in the concluding 31 poems of the 2nd annex cluster, *Goodbye My Fancy*; and even a "leap-year month" if the 29 poems of *By the Roadside* are so designated. All this was well enough, but other arrangements might suggest different values—as constellations will appear as different figures by incorporating additional stars or deleting others.

The 402 count (of the poems collected in and out of cluster, exclusive of the Epigraph) didn't seem to represent anything except a tabulation of the greatest body of American poetry in the nineteenth century. That aside, I again looked at the numbers. If I subtracted the segregated *stand-alone* poems (solo canticles) and the malleable 13 poems of *Old Age Echoes*, what might we find? The math is simple (402-38). Once preformed the number 364 stood certain and sure. 7 days X 52 weeks = 364 or, by including the opening Epigraph, *Come Said My Soul* — 365 days of that early notebook's lifetime projection. With the addition of his grand *solo* poems *Whitman's Code: A New Bible* had come into view — time and space revealing the simple grandeur of the poet's poem and the staggering constellation of the poet himself.

Critics of the *Code* will claim that there is a certain caprice that selects certain numbers to the exclusion of others. I would argue *that a man's reach should exceed his grasp...* and that my grasp corresponds to the numbers in the *Deathbed* assemblage. Over 93% of Whitman's poems are confined by cluster. The order of the clusters and the order of the poems within the clusters are exactly as the poet decreed. He labored over thirty- five years on his *Leaves*. Anyone suggesting alterations in his book must contend with two late exhortations as to its disposition. The first was made to his young chronicler Horace Traubel:

> So far as you may have anything to do with it I place upon you the injunction that whatever may be added to the *Leaves* shall be supplementary, avowed

> as such, leaving the book complete as I left it, consecutive to the point I left off, marking always an unmistakable, deep down, unobliteratable division line. In the long run the world will do as it pleases with the book. I am determined to have the world know what I was pleased to do. [328]

Except for acknowledging that "the world will do as it pleases with the book," it is a strong statement of his satisfaction in its completeness—which is to say he would hope that his poems be left intact and their order preserved. The 2nd statement concerning his poems is less adamantine and would appear to grant greater latitude in how we might approach his life's *leavings*, as it were. It is a statement appearing in 1888's *A Backward Glance O'er Traveled Roads* (Appendix 15, page 886) :

> The word I myself put primarily for them (the poems) as they stand at the last, is the word suggestiveness. I round and finish little, if anything; and could not consistently with my scheme. The reader will always have his or her part to do, just as much as I have had mine. I seek less to state or display any theme or thought and more to bring you the reader into the atmosphere of the theme or thought—there to pursue your own thought. [329]

R.W.French speaks to that very suggestiveness:

> "... many placements of poems may seem arbitrary rather than purposeful, as appropriate to one place as to another—indeed, a significant number of poems had already *been* in other places, since the arrangements of poems within and without the clusters had been so frequently revised over the course of more than twenty years. Thus the structure of *Leaves of Grass* will always be open to differing perceptions." [330]

Pursuing my own thought and arguably, a new perception, I am presenting the argument to readers of my own. James E. Miller's *A Critical Guide to Leaves of Grass* put the problem this way:

> Perhaps the solution to the dilemma is to find a metaphorical structure—a structure resembling some object other than a book of poems. Almost every critic who has ever talked about Whitman has at some point or other lapsed into metaphor to convey his meaning. And although an analogy does not prove the presence of an element, such a comparison aids in understanding the thing if it really exists.[331]

Ed Folsom of The Walt Whitman Archive took an even more expansive view of consolidating the whole of the Whitman opus in his essay, *Projecting Whitman*.[332] By essay's end Folsom suggests a "hypotext" archive that grows with each new reader. Amusingly enough, the figure *twelve*, once again, manages to find itself evoked in relation to Whitman:

So in the mid-1950s a relatively young group of **twelve** scholars joined together to devote a major part of their professional lives to a multi-volume, multi-year project named the *Collected Writings of Walt Whitman*... Today, nearly a half-century after those announcements, the *Whitman Collected Writings*... remains incomplete, and even the finished individual volumes have turned out not to be nearly as finished as everyone back then assumed they would be... But the key for a hyper text archive... is that finally it makes available a true facsimile of each edition of the poem... so that the user becomes a co-creator, a co-editor, everytime he or she comes to the archive...[333]

Ultimately, the légerdemain of my central thesis (even at two thousand pages) will remain incomplete and can only be predicated on a foundational statement, already noted, by the poet himself:

> The Great Construction of the New Bible. Not to be diverted from the principal object—the main life work—the three hundred and sixty-five—it ought to be ready in 1859." (June '57).

Whitman's Code: A New Bible is a loving assessment of *Leaves of Grass*, set slightly askew. I've divided the new Bible, fittingly into 2 volumes. The 25 Solo Canticles of Vol. I and Vol. II—the *Three Hundred Sixty-Five* poems collected in the clusters, annexes and opening epigraph of the *Deathbed* edition *of 91/92*.

I have interspersed his poetry with photographs, biography, literary materials influenced by his works and brought to bear a large body critical acumen intended to illuminate the legacy of a nineteenth century colossus.

Whitman's work is a great literate joy (despite its faults) for any who judiciously take the time to apprehend it. Care has been taken keep the poet's stanzas intact. Generally when a stanza is interrupted by a page break the poetic line will conclude with a comma — if the poetic line ends with a period it almost always ends the stanza, as well. I have taken the liberty to add occasional lines that once graced earlier editions but which were ultimately excluded by the poet. These are noted in the text and referenced by line number. It remains my fervent wish to acquaint the reader with the whole of Whitman's poetic output — not just the more celebrated pieces that may have chanced his or her way. The two volumes of poetry and commentary allow for an intimate visit with his work. Whitman is one of the world's more subtle poets despite his oft reported desire to be the bard of the common man.

These poems will reward many readings through the course of a lifetime.[334] If his meaning seems obscure at one juncture, the light of another day may yet prove illuminating. It is only as I neared completion of the second book that I discovered an even more essential and numinous numbering scheme that had also managed to elude the scholarly investigations that have steadfastly attended his lifetime's offering. The entrancing and evocative details of that discovery I have left to the *Forward* and *Addendum* of the succeeding and concluding volume of *Whitman's Code*.

WHITMAN'S CODE: A NEW BIBLE, VOLUME I

M.C. GARDNER

Whether by unconscious design or early literary conceit, we find hidden in the tabulations of the poet's beloved *Leaves,* evidence of a recondite schemata—a key or code to the construction of a *New Bible... dropt as if a handkerchief bearing the owner's name someway in the corners, that we may see and remark, and say whose?*

APPENDIX

1. Birthplace
West Hills, Long Island, New York
Library of Congress

2. Parents

Walter Whitman Sr.
d. 1855
Library of Congress

Louisa von Velsor
Whitman
d. 1873
Library of Congress

3. 328 Mickle Street
Residence: 1884 -1892
Library of Congress

4. Circle

John Burroughs
1837 -1921

. Richard Maurice Bucke
1837 -1902

. William O' Connor
d. 1889

Horace Traubel
1859 -1919

Photographs: Library of Congress

5. Anne Gilchrist
d. 1885
Gutenberg.org

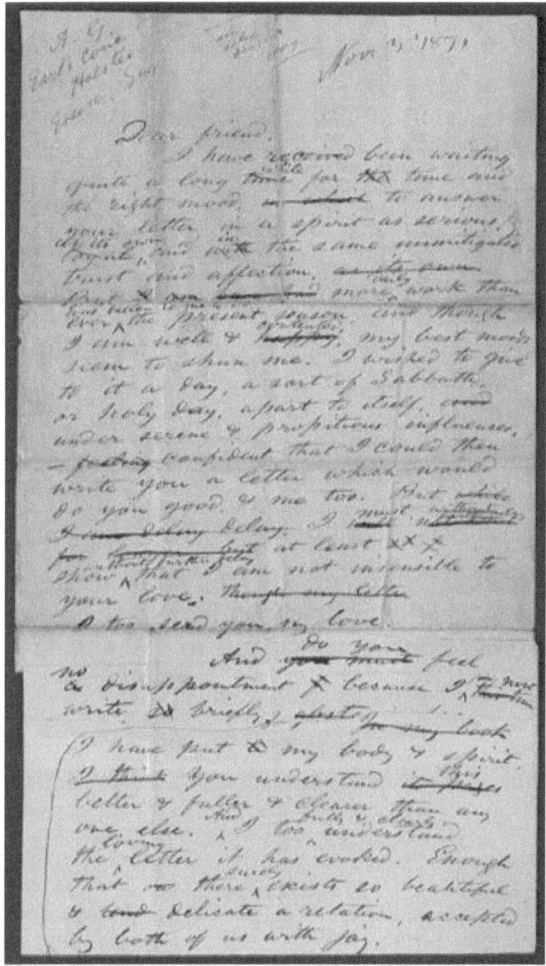

6. Whitman letter to Anne Gilchrist

7. Preface to Preface

Whitman's Prefaces bear an inverse relationship to the acceptance of his poetry. The poems rankled many a self-styled aesthetician. The rambling nature of his prose was not subjected to the same criticism that befell the verse.

Certainly, after a century that gave us Joyce, Eliot and Woolf, the beleaguered poems of Whitman have lost something of their scandal. Readers of Whitman in the Twenty-first century are more likely to have difficulty with his prose stylings.[335] Facsimilies of each of the prefaces can easily be scanned at The Walt Whitman Achive. Here, some of the longer paragraphs have been divided to assist their placement and meaning on any given page.

The Whitman Prefaces remain worthy and are duly celebrated in their own right—but they will never win the affectionate legions that the poems command. The prose is solidly grounded whereas the poetry soars.

The best that can be said of the 1855 Preface is that the lion's share of it will find its way into the *Leaves of Grass* editions that will grace the remaining decades of the poet's life.

The primary beneficiary of the preface is 1856's *Poem of Many in One*, of which 25% was drawn from the preface. Whitman will edit and revise this poem more than any other in the canon. It, like the preface on which it is based, is his aesthetic credo. It will eventually (1881) be known as *By Blue Ontario's Shore*.

Some lines from below will demonstrate the poet's method:

> America, curious toward foreign characters, stands by it own at all hazards,
> Stands removed, spacious, composite, sound, initiates the true use of precedents,
> Does not repel them or the past or what they have produced under their forms.
> Takes the lesson with calmness, perceives the corpse slowly borne from the house,
> Perceives that it waits a little while in the door, that it was fittest for its days,
> That its life has descended to the stalwart and well-shaped hier, who approaches,
> And that he shall be fittest for his days.
> Any period one nation must lead,
> One land must be the promise and reliance of the future,
> These States are the amplest poem,
> Here is not merely a nation but a teeming Nation of nations,
> Here the doings of men correspond with the broadcast doings of day and night,
> Here is what moves in magnificent masses careless of particulars...

Here are the roughs, beards, friendliness, combativeness, the soul loves,
Here the flowing trains, here the crowds, equality, diversity the soul loves.

8. Preface to 1855's *Leaves of Grass*

America does not repel the past or what it has produced under its forms or amid other politics or the idea of castes or the old religions ... accepts the lesson with calmness ... is not so impatient as has been supposed that the slough still sticks to opinions and manners and literature while the life which served its requirements has passed into the new life of the new forms ... perceives that the corpse is slowly borne from the eating and sleeping rooms of the house ... perceives that it waits a little while in the door ... that it was fittest for its days ... that its action has descended to the stalwart and well shaped heir who approaches ... and that he shall be fittest for his days.

The Americans of all nations at any time upon the earth have probably the fullest poetical nature. The United States themselves are essentially the greatest poem. In the history of the earth hitherto the largest and most stirring appear tame and orderly to their ampler largeness and stir. Here at last is something in the doings of man that corresponds with the broadcast doings of the day and night. Here is not merely a nation but a teeming nation of nations. Here is action untied from strings necessarily blind to particulars and details magnificently moving in vast masses. Here is the hospitality which forever indicates heroes.... Here are the roughs and beards and space and ruggedness and nonchalance that the soul loves. Here the performance disdaining the trivial unapproached in the tremendous audacity of its crowds and groupings and the push of its perspective spreads with crampless and flowing breadth and showers its prolific and splendid extravagance.

One sees it must indeed own the riches of the summer and winter, and need never be bankrupt while corn grows from the ground or the orchards drop apples or the bays contain fish or men beget children upon women. Other states indicate themselves in their deputies ... but the genius of the United States is not best or most in its executives or legislatures, nor in its ambassadors or authors or colleges or churches or parlors, nor even in its newspapers or inventors ... but always most in the common people. Their manners, speech, dress, friendship — the freshness and candor of their physiognomy — the picturesque looseness of their carriage ... their deathless attachment to freedom — their aversion to anything indecorous or soft or mean — the practical acknowledgment of the citizens of one state by the citizens of all other states — the fierceness of their roused resentment — their curiosity and welcome of novelty — their self-esteem and wonderful sympathy — their susceptibility to a slight — the air they have of persons who never knew how it felt to stand in the presence of superiors — the fluency of their speech — their delight in music, the sure symptom of manly tenderness and native elegance of soul ... their good temper and open handedness — the terrible significance of their elections — the President's taking off his hat to them, not they to him — these too are unrhymed poetry. It awaits the gigantic and generous treatment worthy of it.

The largeness of nature or the nation were monstrous without a corresponding largeness and generosity of the spirit of the citizen. Not nature nor swarming states nor streets and steamships nor prosperous business nor farms nor capital nor learning may suffice for the ideal of man ... nor suffice the poet.

No reminiscences may suffice either. A live nation can always cut a deep mark and can have the best authority the cheapest ... namely from its own soul. This is the sum of the profitable uses of individuals or states and of present action and grandeur and of the subjects of poets. — As if it were necessary to trot back generation after generation to the eastern records! As if the beauty and sacredness of the demonstrable must fall behind that of the mythical! As if men do not make their mark out of any times! As if the opening of the western continent by discovery and what has transpired since in North and South America were less than the small theatre of the antique or the aimless sleep-walking of the middle ages! The pride of the United States leaves the wealth and finesse of the cities and all returns of commerce and agriculture and all the magnitude of geography or shows of exterior victory to enjoy the breed of full sized men or one full sized man unconquerable and simple. The American poets are to enclose old and new for America is the race of races. of them a bard is to be commensurate with a people. to him the other continents arrive as contributions ... he gives them reception for their sake and his own sake. His spirit responds to his country's spirit ... he incarnates its geography and natural life and rivers and lakes. Mississippi with annual freshets and changing chutes, Missouri and Columbia and Ohio and St. Lawrence with the Falls and beautiful masculine Hudson, do not embouchure where they spend themselves more than they embouchure into him. The blue breadth over the inland sea of Virginia and Maryland and the sea off Massachusetts and Maine and over Manhattan Bay and over Champlain and Erie and over Ontario and Huron and Michigan and Superior, and over the Texan and Mexican and Floridian and Cuban seas, and over the seas off California and Oregon, is not tallied by the blue breadth of the waters below more than the breadth of above and below is tallied by him. When the long Atlantic coast stretches longer and the Pacific coast stretches longer he easily stretches with them north or south. He spans between them also from east to west and reflects what is between them. On him rise solid growths that offset the growths of pine and cedar and hemlock and live oak and locust and chestnut and cypress and hickory and limetree and cottonwood and tuliptree and caotus and wildvine and tamarind and persimmon ... and tangles as tangled as any canebrake or swamp ... and forests coated with transparent ice, and icicles hanging from boughs and crackling in the wind ... and sides and peaks of mountains ... and pasturage sweet and free as savannah or upland or prairie ... with flights and songs and screams that answer those of the wild pigeon and high-hold and orchard-oriole and coot and surf-duck and red-shouldered-hawk and fish-hawk and white ibis and Indian-hen and cat-owl and water-pheasant and qua-bird and pied-sheldrake and blackbird and mockingbird and buzzard and condor and nightheron and eagle. to him the hereditary countenance descends both mother's and father's. to him enter the essences of the real things and past and present events — of the enormous diversity of temperature and agriculture and mines — the tribes of red aborigines — the weather-beaten vessels entering new ports or making landings on rocky coasts — the first settlements north or south — The rapid stature and muscle — the haughty defiance of '76, and the war and peace and formation of the constitution ... the Union always surrounded by blatherers and always calm and impregnable — the perpetual coming of immigrants — the wharf-hem'd cities and superior marine —

the unsurveyed interior—the loghouses and clearings and wild animals and hunters and trappers ... the free commerce—the fisheries and whaling and gold-digging—the endless gestation of new states—the convening of Congress every December, the members duly coming up from all climates and the uttermost parts ... the noble character of the young mechanics and of all free American workmen and workwomen ... the general ardor and friendliness and enterprise—the perfect equality of the female with the male ... the large amativeness—the fluid movement of the population—the factories and mercantile life and laborsaving machinery—the Yankee swap—the New York firemen and the target excursion—the Southern plantation life—the character of the northeast and of the northwest and southwest—slavery and the tremulous spreading of hands to protect it, and the stern opposition to it which shall never cease till it ceases or the speaking of tongues and the moving of lips cease. For such the expression of the American poet is to be transcendent and new. It is to be indirect and not direct or descriptive or epic. Its quality goes through these to much more. Let the age and wars of other nations be chanted and their eras and characters be illustrated and that finish the verse. Not so the great psalm of the republic. Here the theme is creative and has vista. Here comes one among the well beloved stonecutters and plans with decision and science and sees the solid and beautiful forms of the future where there are now no solid forms.

Of all nations the United States with veins full of poetical stuff most need poets and will doubtless have the greatest and use them the greatest. Their Presidents shall not be their common referee so much as their poets shall. of all mankind the great poet is the equable man.

Not in him but off from him things are grotesque or eccentric or fail of their sanity. Nothing out of its place is good and nothing in its place is bad. He bestows on every object or quality its fit proportions neither more nor less. He is the arbiter of the diverse and he is the key. He is the equalizer of his age and land ... he supplies what wants supplying and checks what wants checking. If peace is the routine out of him speaks the spirit of peace, large, rich, thrifty, building vast and populous cities, encouraging agriculture and the arts and commerce—lighting the study of man, the soul, immortality—federal, state or municipal government, marriage, health, freetrade, intertravel by land and sea ... nothing too close, nothing too far off ... the stars not too far off. In war he is the most deadly force of the war. Who recruits him recruits horse and foot ... he fetches parks of artillery the best that engineer ever knew. If the time becomes slothful and heavy he knows how to arouse it ... he can make every word he speaks draw blood. Whatever stagnates in the flat of custom or obedience or legislation he never stagnates. Obedience does not master him, he masters it. High up out of reach he stands turning a concentrated light ... he turns the pivot with his finger ... he baffles the swiftest runners as he stands and easily overtakes and envelopes them. The time straying towards infidelity and confections and persiflage he withholds by his steady faith ... he spreads out his dishes ... he offers the sweet firmfibred meat that grows men and women. His brain is the ultimate brain. He is no arguer ... he is judgment. He judges not as the judge judges but as the sun falling around a helpless thing. As he sees the farthest he has the most faith. His thoughts are the hymns of the praise of things. In the talk on the soul and eternity and God off of his equal plane he is silent.

He sees eternity less like a play with a prologue and denouement ... he sees eternity in men and women ... he does not see men or women as dreams or dots. Faith is the antiseptic of the soul ... it pervades the common people and preserves them ... they never give up believing and expecting and trusting. There is that indescribable freshness and unconsciousness about an illiterate person that humbles and mocks the power of the noblest expressive genius. The poet sees for a certainty how one not a great artist may be just as sacred and perfect as the greatest artist... . The power to destroy or remould is freely used by him, but never the power of attack. What is past is past. If he does not expose superior models and prove himself by every step he takes he is not what is wanted. The presence of the greatest poet conquers ... not parleying or struggling or any prepared attempts. Now he has passed that way see after him! There is not left any vestige of despair or misanthropy or cunning or exclusiveness or the ignominy of a nativity or color or delusion of hell or the necessity of hell ... and no man thenceforward shall be degraded for ignorance or weakness or sin.

The greatest poet hardly knows pettiness or triviality. If he breathes into anything that was before thought small it dilates with the grandeur and life of the universe. He is a seer ... he is individual ... he is complete in himself ... the others are as good as he, only he sees it and they do not.

He is not one of the chorus ... he does not stop for any regulation ... he is the president of regulation. What the eyesight does to the rest he does to the rest. Who knows the curious mystery of the eyesight?

The other senses corroborate themselves, but this is removed from any proof but its own and foreruns the identities of the spiritual world. A single glance of it mocks all the investigations of man and all the instruments and books of the earth and all reasoning. What is marvellous? what is unlikely? what is impossible or baseless or vague? after you have once just opened the space of a peachpit and given audience to far and near and to the sunset and had all things enter with electric swiftness softly and duly without confusion or jostling or jam.

The land and sea, the animals, fishes, and birds, the sky of heaven and the orbs, the forests, mountains, and rivers, are not small themes ... but folks expect of the poet to indicate more than the beauty and dignity which always attach to dumb real objects ... they expect him to indicate the path between reality and their souls. Men and women perceive the beauty well enough ... probably as well as he. The passionate tenacity of hunters, woodmen, early risers, cultivators of gardens and orchards and fields, the love of healthy women for the manly form, seafaring persons, drivers of horses, the passion for light and the open air, all is an old varied sign of the unfailing perception of beauty and of a residence of the poetic in outdoor people. They can never be assisted by poets to perceive ... some may but they never can. The poetic quality is not marshalled in rhyme or uniformity or abstract addresses to things nor in melancholy complaints or good precepts, but is the life of these and much else and is in the soul. The profit of rhyme is that it drops seeds of a sweeter and more luxuriant rhyme, and of uniformity that it conveys itself into its own roots in the ground out of sight.

WHITMAN'S CODE: A NEW BIBLE, VOLUME I

M.C. GARDNER

The rhyme and uniformity of perfect poems show the free growth of metrical laws and bud from them as unerringly and loosely as lilacs and roses on a bush, and take shapes as compact as the shapes of chestnuts and oranges and melons and pears, and shed the perfume impalpable to form. The fluency and ornaments of the finest poems or music or orations or recitations are not independent but dependent. All beauty comes from beautiful blood and a beautiful brain. If the greatnesses are in conjunction in a man or woman it is enough ... the fact will prevail through the universe ... but the gaggery and gilt of a million years will not prevail. Who troubles himself about his ornaments or fluency is lost. This is what you shall do: Love the earth and sun and the animals, despise riches, give alms to every one that asks, stand up for the stupid and crazy, devote your income and labor to others, hate tyrants, argue not concerning God, have patience and indulgence toward the people, take off your hat to nothing known or unknown or to any man or number of men, go freely with powerful uneducated persons and with the young and with the mothers of families, read these leaves in the open air every season of every year of your life, re-examine all you have been told at school or church or in any book, dismiss whatever insults your own soul; and your very flesh shall be a great poem and have the richest fluency not only in its words but in the silent lines of its lips and face and between the lashes of your eyes and in every motion and joint of your body... . The poet shall not spend his time in unneeded work. He shall know that the ground is always ready ploughed and manured ... others may not know it but he shall. He shall go directly to the creation. His trust shall master the trust of everything he touches ... and shall master all attachment.

The known universe has one complete lover and that is the greatest poet. He consumes an eternal passion and is indifferent which chance happens and which possible contingency of fortune or misfortune and persuades daily and hourly his delicious pay. What baulks or breaks others is fuel for his burning progress to contact and amorous joy. Other proportions of the reception of pleasure dwindle to nothing to his proportions. All expected from heaven or from the highest he is rapport with in the sight of the daybreak or a scene of the winter woods or the presence of children playing or with his arm round the neck of a man or woman. His love above all love has leisure and expanse ... he leaves room ahead of himself. He is no irresolute or suspicious lover ... he is sure ... he scorns intervals. His experience and the showers and thrills are not for nothing. Nothing can jar him ... suffering and darkness cannot — death and fear cannot. to him complaint and jealousy and envy are corpses buried and rotten in the earth ... he saw them buried. The sea is not surer of the shore or the shore of the sea than he is of the fruition of his love and of all perfection and beauty.

The fruition of beauty is no chance of hit or miss ... it is inevitable as life ... it is as exact and plumb as gravitation. From the eyesight proceeds another eyesight and from the hearing proceeds another hearing and from the voice proceeds another voice eternally curious of the harmony of things with man. to these respond perfections not only in the committees that were supposed to stand for the rest but in the rest themselves just the same.

These understand the law of perfection in masses and floods ... that its finish is to each for itself and onward from itself ... that it is profuse and impartial ... that there is not a minute of the light or dark nor an acre of the earth and sea without it—nor any direction of the sky nor any trade or employment nor any turn of events. This is the reason that about the proper expression of beauty there is precision and balance ... one part does not need to be thrust above another. The best singer is not the one who has the most lithe and powerful organ ... the pleasure of poems is not in them that take the hand-somest measure and similes and sound.Without effort and without exposing in the least how it is done the greatest poet brings the spirit of any or all events and passions and scenes and persons some more and some less to bear on your individual character as you hear or read. to do this well is to compete with the laws that pursue and follow time. What is the purpose must surely be there and the clue of it must be there ... and the faintest indication is the indication of the best and then becomes the clearest indication. Past and present and future are not disjoined but joined. The greatest poet forms the consistence of what is to be from what has been and is. He drags the dead out of their coffins and stands them again on their feet ... he says to the past, Rise and walk before me that I may realize you. He learns the lesson ... he places himself where the future becomes present. The greatest poet does not only dazzle his rays over character and scenes and passions ... he finally ascends and finishes all ... he exhibits the pinnacles that no man can tell what they are for or what is beyond ... he glows a moment on the extremest verge.

He is most wonderful in his last half-hidden smile or frown ... by that flash of the moment of parting the one that sees it shall be encouraged or terrified afterward for many years.

The greatest poet does not moralize or make applications of morals ... he knows the soul. The soul has that measureless pride which consists in never acknowledging any lessons but its own. But it has sympathy as measureless as its pride and the one balances the other and neither can stretch too far while it stretches in company with the other. The inmost secrets of art sleep with the twain. The greatest poet has lain close betwixt both and they are vital in his style and thoughts.

The art of art, the glory of expression and the sunshine of the light of letters is simplicity. Nothing is better than simplicity ... nothing can make up for excess or for the lack of definiteness. to carry on the heave of impulse and pierce intellectual depths and give all subjects their articulations are powers neither common nor very uncommon. But to speak in literature with the perfect rectitude and insouciance of the movements of animals and the unimpeachableness of the sentiment of trees in the woods and grass by the roadside is the flawless triumph of art. If you have looked on him who has achieved it you have looked on one of the masters of the artists of all nations and times. You shall not contemplate the flight of the gray gull over the bay or the mettlesome action of the blood horse or the tall leaning of sunflowers on their stalk or the appearance of the sun journeying through heaven or the appearance of the moon afterward with any more satisfaction than you shall contemplate him.

WHITMAN'S CODE: A NEW BIBLE, VOLUME I
M.C. GARDNER

The greatest poet has less a marked style and is more the channel of thoughts and things without increase or diminution and is the free channel of himself. He swears to his art, I will not be meddlesome, I will not have in my writing any elegance or effect or originality to hang in the way between me and the rest like curtain s. I will have nothing hang in the way not the richest curtains. What I tell I tell for precisely what it is. Let who may exalt or startle or fascinate or soothe I will have purposes as health or heat or snow has and be as regardless of observation. What I experience or portray shall go from my composition without a shred of my composition. You shall stand by my side and look in the mirror with me.

The old red blood and stainless gentility of great poets will be proved by their unconstraint. A heroic person walks at his ease through and out of that custom or precedent or authority that suits him not. of the traits of the brotherhood of writers savans musicians inventors and artists, nothing is finer than silent defiance advancing from new free forms. In the need of poems, philosophy, politics, mechanism, science, behavior, the craft of art, an appropriate native grand-opera, shipcraft, or any craft, he is greatest for ever and for ever who contributes the greatest original practical example. The cleanest expression is that which finds no sphere worthy of itself and makes one. The messages of great poets to each man and woman are, Come to us on equal terms, Only then can you understand us, We are no better than you, What we enclose you enclose, What we enjoy you may enjoy. Did you suppose there could be only one Supreme?

We affirm there can be unnumbered Supremes, and that one does not countervail another any more than one eyesight countervails another ... and that men can be good or grand only of the consciousness of their supremacy within them. What do you think is the grandeur of storms and dismemberments and the deadliest battles and wrecks and the wildest fury of the elements and the power of the sea and the motion of nature and the throes of human desires and dignity and hate and love? It is that something in the soul which says, Rage on, Whirl on, I tread master here and everywhere, Master of the spasms of the sky and of the shatter of the sea, Master of nature and passion and death, and of all terror and all pain.

The American bards shall be marked for generosity and affection and for encouraging competitors... . They shall be kosmos ... without monopoly or secrecy ... glad to pass anything to any one ... hungry for equals night and day. They shall not be careful of riches and privilege ... they shall be riches and privilege ... they shall perceive who the most affluent man is. The most affluent man is he that confronts all the shows he sees by equivalents out of the stronger wealth of himself. The American bard shall delineate no class of persons nor one or two out of the strata of interests nor love most nor truth most nor the soul most nor the body most ... and not be for the eastern states more than the western or the northern states more than the southern. Exact science and its practical movements are no checks on the greatest poet but always his encouragement and support. The outset and remembrance are there ... there the arms that lifted him first and brace him best ... there he returns after all his goings and comings.

The sailor and traveller ... the anatomist, chemist, astronomer, geologist, phrenologist, spiritualist, mathematician, historian, and lexicographer, are not poets, but they are the lawgivers of poets and their construction underlies the structure of every perfect poem. No matter what rises or is uttered they sent the seed of the conception of it ... of them and by them stand the visible proofs of souls ... always of their fatherstuff must be begotten the sinewy races of bards.

If there shall be love and content between the father and the son and if the greatness of the son is the exuding of the greatness of the father there shall be love between the poet and the man of demonstrable science. In the beauty of poems are the tuft and final applause of science.

Great is the faith of the flush of knowledge and of the investigation of the depths of qualities and things. Cleaving and circling here swells the soul of the poet yet is president of itself always. The depths are fathomless and therefore calm. The innocence and nakedness are resumed ... they are neither modest nor immodest.

The whole theory of the special and supernatural and all that was twined with it or educed out of it departs as a dream. What has ever happened ... what happens and whatever may or shall happen, the vital laws enclose all ... they are sufficient for any case and for all cases ... none to be hurried or retarded ... any miracle of affairs or persons inadmissible in the vast clear scheme where every motion and every spear of grass and the frames and spirits of men and women and all that concerns them are unspeakably perfect miracles all referring to all and each distinct and in its place.

It is also not consistent with the reality of the soul to admit that there is anything in the known universe more divine than men and women.Men and women and the earth and all upon it are simply to be taken as they are, and the investigation of their past and present and future shall be unintermitted and shall be done with perfect candor. Upon this basis philosophy speculates ever looking towards the poet, ever regarding the eternal tendencies of all toward happiness never inconsistent with what is clear to the senses and to the soul.

For the eternal tendencies of all toward happiness make the only point of sane philosophy. Whatever comprehends less than that ... whatever is less than the laws of light and of astronomical motion ... or less than the laws that follow the thief the liar the glutton and the drunkard through this life and doubtless afterward ... or less than vast stretches of time or the slow formation of density or the patient upheaving of strata—is of no account. Whatever would put God in a poem or system of philosophy as contending against some being or influence is also of no account. Sanity and ensemble characterize the great master ... spoilt in one principle all is spoilt. The great master has nothing to do with miracles. He sees health for himself in being one of the mass ... he sees the hiatus in singular eminence. to the perfect shape comes common ground. to be under the general law is great, for that is to correspond with it. The master knows that he is unspeakably great and that all are unspeakably great ... that nothing for instance is greater than to conceive children and bring them up well ... that to be is just as great as to perceive or tell.

In the make of the great masters the idea of political liberty is indispensable. Liberty takes the adherence of heroes wherever men and women exist ... but never takes any adherence or welcome from the rest more than from poets. They are the voice and exposition of liberty. They out of ages are worthy the grand idea ... to them it is confided and they must sustain it. Nothing has precedence of it and nothing can warp or degrade it. The attitude of great poets is to cheer up slaves and horrify despots. The turn of their necks, the sound of their feet, the motions of their wrists, are full of hazard to the one and hope to the other.

Come nigh them awhile and though they neither speak nor advise you shall learn the faithful American lesson. Liberty is poorly served by men whose good intent is quelled from one failure or two failures or any number of failures, or from the casual indifference or ingratitude of the people, or from the sharp show of the tushes of power, or the bringing to bear soldiers and cannon or any penal statutes.

Liberty relies upon itself, invites no one, promises nothing, sits in calmness and light, is positive and composed, and knows no discouragement. The battle rages with many a loud alarm and frequent advance and retreat ... the enemy triumphs ... the prison, the handcuffs, the iron necklace and anklet, the scaffold, garrote and leadballs do their work ... the cause is asleep ... the strong throats are choked with their own blood ... the young men drop their eyelashes toward the ground when they pass each other ... and is liberty gone out of that place? No never. When liberty goes it is not the first to go nor the second or third to go ... it awaits for all the rest to go ... it is the last... .

WHITMAN'S CODE: A NEW BIBLE, VOLUME I
M.C. GARDNER

When the memories of the old martyrs are faded utterly away ... when the large names of patriots are laughed at in the public halls from the lips of the orators ... when the boys are no more christened after the same but christened after tyrants and traitors instead ... when the laws of the free are grudgingly permitted and the laws for informers and bloodmoney are sweet to the taste of the people ... when I and you walk abroad upon the earth stung with compassion at the sight of numberless brothers answering our equal friendship and calling no man master—and when we are elated with noble joy at the sight of slaves ... when the soul retires in the cool communion of the night and surveys its experience and has much extasy over the word and deed that put back a helpless innocent person into the gripe of the gripers or into any cruel inferiority ... when those in all parts of these states who could easier realize the true American character but do not yet—when the swarms of cringers, suckers, doughfaces, lice of politics, planners of sly involutions for their own preferment to city offices or state legislatures or the judiciary or congress or the presidency, obtain a response of love and natural deference from the people whether they get the offices or no ... when it is better to be a bound booby and rogue in office at a high salary than the poorest free mechanic or farmer with his hat unmoved from his head and firm eyes and a candid and generous heart ... and when servility by town or state or the federal government or any oppression on a large scale or small scale can be tried on without its own punishment following duly after in exact proportion against the smallest chance of escape ... or rather when all life and all the souls of men and women are discharged from any part of the earth—then only shall the instinct of liberty be discharged from that part of the earth.

As the attributes of the poets of the kosmos concentre in the real body and soul and in the pleasure of things they possess the superiority of genuineness over all fiction and romance. As they emit themselves facts are showered over with light ... the daylight is lit with more volatile light ... also the deep between the setting and rising sun goes deeper many fold. Each precise object or condition or combination or process exhibits a beauty ... the multiplication table its—old age its—the carpenter's trade its—the grand opera its—the hugehulled cleanshaped New-York clipper at sea under steam or full sail gleams with unmatched beauty ... the American circles and large harmonies of government gleam with theirs ... and the commonest definite intentions and actions with theirs. The poets of the kosmos advance through all interpositions and coverings and turmoils and stratagems to first principles. They are of use ... they dissolve poverty from its need and riches from its conceit. You large proprietor, they say, shall not realize or perceive more than any one else. The owner of the library is not he who holds a legal title to it having bought and paid for it. Any one and every one is owner of the library who can read the same through all the varieties of tongues and subjects and styles, and in whom they enter with ease and take residence and force toward paternity and maternity, and make supple and powerful and rich and large. These American states strong and healthy and accomplished shall receive no pleasure from violations of natural models and must not permit them. In paintings or mouldings or carvings in mineral or wood, or in the illustrations of books and newspapers, or in any comic or tragic prints, or in the patterns of woven stuffs or anything to beautify rooms or furniture or costumes, or to put upon cornices or monuments or on the prows or sterns of ships, or to put anywhere before the human eye indoors or out, that which distorts honest shapes or which creates unearthly beings or places or contingencies, is a nuisance and revolt. of the human form especially, it is so great it must never be made ridiculous. of ornaments to a work nothing outré can be allowed ... but those ornaments can be allowed that conform to the perfect facts of the open air, and that flow out of the nature of the work and come irrepressibly from it and are necessary to the completion of the work. Most works are most beautiful without ornament ... Exaggerations will be revenged in human physiology. Clean and vigorous children are jetted and conceived only in those communities where the models of natural forms are public every day ... Great genius and the people of these states must never be demeaned to romances. As soon as histories are properly told there is no more need of romances.

The great poets are also to be known by the absence in them of tricks and by the justification of perfect personal candor. Then folks echo a new cheap joy and a divine voice leaping from their brains: How beautiful is candor! All faults may be forgiven of him who has perfect candor. Henceforth let no man of us lie, for we have seen that openness wins the inner and outer world and that there is no single exception, and that never since our earth gathered itself in a mass have deceit or subterfuge or prevarication attracted its smallest particle or the faintest tinge of a shade—and that through the enveloping wealth and rank of a state or the whole republic of states a sneak or sly person shall be discovered and despised ... and that the soul has never once been fooled and never can be fooled ... and thrift without the loving nod of the soul is only a fœtid puff ...

and there never grew up in any of the continents of the globe nor upon any planet or satellite or star, nor upon the asteroids, nor in any part of ethereal space, nor in the midst of density, nor under the fluid wet of the sea, nor in that condition which precedes the birth of babes, nor at any time during the changes of life, nor in that condition that follows what we term death, nor in any stretch of abeyance or action afterward of vitality, nor in any process of formation or reformation anywhere, a being whose instinct hated the truth.

Extreme caution or prudence, the soundest organic health, large hope and comparison and fondness for women and children, large alimentiveness and destructiveness and causality, with a perfect sense of the oneness of nature and the propriety of the same spirit applied to human affairs ... these are called up of the float of the brain of the world to be parts of the greatest poet from his birth out of his mother's womb and from her birth out of her mother's. Caution seldom goes far enough. It has been thought that the prudent citizen was the citizen who applied himself to solid gains and did well for himself and for his family and completed a lawful life without debt or crime. The greatest poet sees and admits these economies as he sees the economies of food and sleep, but has higher notions of prudence than to think he gives much when he gives a few slight attentions at the latch of the gate.

The premises of the prudence of life are not the hospitality of it or the ripeness and harvest of it. Beyond the independence of a little sum laid aside for burial-money, and of a few clapboards around and shingles overhead on a lot of American soil owned, and the easy dollars that supply the year's plain clothing and meals,

the melancholy prudence of the abandonment of such a great being as a man is to the toss and pallor of years of money-making with all their scorching days and icy nights and all their stifling deceits and underhanded dodgings, or infinitesimals of parlors, or shameless stuffing while others starve ... and all the loss of the bloom and odor of the earth and of the flowers and atmosphere and of the sea, and of the true taste of the women and men you pass or have to do with in youth or middle age, and the issuing sickness and desperate revolt at the close of a life without elevation or naivete,
and the ghastly chatter of a death without serenity or majesty, is the great fraud upon modern civilization and forethought, blotching the surface and system which civilization undeniably drafts, and moistening with tears the immense features it spreads and spreads with such velocity before the reached kisses of the soul.

Still the right explanation remains to be made about prudence. The prudence of the mere wealth and respectability of the most esteemed life appears too faint for the eye to observe at all when little and large alike drop quietly aside at the thought of the prudence suitable for immortality. What is wisdom that fills the thinness of a year or seventy or eighty years to wisdom spaced out by ages and coming back at a certain time with strong reinforcements and rich presents and the clear faces of wedding-guests as far as you can look in every direction, running gaily toward you? Only the soul is of itself ... all else has reference to what ensues. All that a person does or thinks is of consequence. Not a move can a man or woman make that effects him or her in a day or a month or any part of the direct lifetime or the hour of death but the same affects him or her onward afterward through the indirect lifetime.

The indirect is always as great and real as the direct. The spirit receives from the body just as much as it gives to the body. Not one name of word or deed ... not of venereal sores or discolorations ... not the privacy of the onanist ... not of the putrid veins of gluttons or rumdrinkers ... not peculation or cunning or betrayal or murder ... no serpentine poison of those that seduce women ... not the foolish yielding of women ... not prostitution ... not of any depravity of young men ... not of the attainment of gain by discreditable means ... not any nastiness of appetite ... not any harshness of officers to men or judges to prisoners or fathers to sons or sons to fathers or of husbands to wives or bosses to their boys ... not of greedy looks or malignant wishes ... nor any of the wiles practised by people upon themselves ... ever is or ever can be stamped on the programme but it is duly realized and returned, and that returned in further performances ... and they returned again. Nor can the push of charity or personal force ever be anything else than the profoundest reason, whether it bring argument to hand or no. No specification is necessary ... to add or subtract or divide is in vain. Little or big, learned or unlearned, white or black, legal or illegal, sick or well, from the first inspiration down the windpipe to the last expiration out of it, all that a male or female does that is vigorous and benevolent and clean is so much sure profit to him or her in the unshakable order of the universe and through the whole scope of it for ever. If the savage or felon is wise it is well ... if the greatest poet or savan is wise it is simply the same ... if the President or chief justice is wise it is the same ... if the young mechanic or farmer is wise it is no more or less ... if the prostitute is wise it is no more nor less. The interest will come round ... all will come round.

All the best actions of war and peace ... all help given to relatives and strangers and the poor and old and sorrowful and young children and widows and the sick, and to all shunned persons ... all furtherance of fugitives and of the escape of slaves ... all the self-denial that stood steady and aloof on wrecks and saw others take the seats of the boats ... all offering of substance or life for the good old cause, or for a friend's sake or opinion's sake ... all pains of enthusiasts scoffed at by their neighbors ... all the vast sweet love and precious sufferings of mothers ... all honest men baffled in strifes recorded or unrecorded ... all the grandeur and good of the few ancient nations whose fragments of annals we inherit ... and all the good of the hundreds of far mightier and more ancient nations unknown to us by name or date or location ... all that was ever manfully begun, whether it succeeded or no ... all that has at any time been well suggested out of the divine heart of man or by the divinity of his mouth or by the shaping of his great hands ... and all that is well thought or done this day on any part of the surface of the globe ... or on any of the wandering stars or fixed stars by those there as we are here ... or that is henceforth to be well thought or done by you whoever you are, or by any one—these singly and wholly inured at their time and inure now and will inure always to the identities from which they sprung or shall spring... . Did you guess any of them lived only its moment? The world does not so exist ... no parts palpable or impalpable so exist ... no result exists now without being from its long antecedent result, and that from its antecedent, and so backward without the farthest mentionable spot coming a bit nearer the beginning than any other spot...

Whatever satisfies the soul is truth. The prudence of the greatest poet answers at last the craving and glut of the soul, is not contemptuous of less ways of prudence if they conform to its ways, puts off nothing, permits no let-up for its own case or any case, has no particular sabbath or judgment-day, divides not the living from the dead or the righteous from the unrighteous, is satisfied with the present, matches every thought or act by its correlative, knows no possible forgiveness or deputed atonement … knows that the young man who composedly perilled his life and lost it has done exceeding well for himself, while the man who has not perilled his life and retains to old age in riches and ease has perhaps achieved nothing for himself worth mentioning … and that only that person has no great prudence to learn who has learnt to prefer real longlived things, and favors body and soul the same, and perceives the indirect assuredly following the direct, and what evil or good he does leaping onward and waiting to meet him again—and who in his spirit in any emergency whatever neither hurries or avoids death.

The direct trial of him who would be the greatest poet is to-day. If he does not flood himself with the immediate age as with vast oceanic tides … and if he does not attract his own land body and soul to himself, and hang on its neck with incomparable love and plunge his semitic muscle into its merits and demerits … and if he be not himself the age transfigured … and if to him is not opened the eternity which gives similitude to all periods and locations and processes and animate and inanimate forms, and which is the bond of time, and rises up from its inconceivable vagueness and infiniteness in the swimming shape of to-day, and is held by the ductile anchors of life, and makes the present spot the passage from what was to what shall be, and commits itself to the representation of this wave of an hour and this one of the sixty beautiful children of the wave—let him merge in the general run and wait his development.

Still the final test of poems or any character or work remains. The prescient poet projects himself centuries ahead and judges performer or performance after the changes of time. Does it live through them? Does it still hold on untired? Will the same style and the direction of genius to similar points be satisfactory now? Has no new discovery in science or arrival at superior planes of thought and judgment and behavior fixed him or his so that either can be looked down upon? Have the marches of tens and hundreds and thousands of years made willing detours to the right hand and the left hand for his sake? Is he beloved long and long after he is buried? Does the young man think often of him? and the young woman think often of him? and do the middle aged and the old think of him?A great poem is for ages and ages in common, and for all degrees and complexions, and all departments and sects, and for a woman as much as a man and a man as much as a woman. A great poem is no finish to a man or woman but rather a beginning. Has any one fancied he could sit at last under some due authority and rest satisfied with explanations and realize and be content and full? to no such terminus does the greatest poet bring ... he brings neither cessation or sheltered fatness and ease. The touch of him tells in action. Whom he takes he takes with firm sure grasp into live regions previously unattained ... thenceforward is no rest ... they see the space and ineffable sheen that turn the old spots and lights into dead vacuums.

The companion of him beholds the birth and progress of stars and learns one of the meanings. Now there shall be a man cohered out of tumult and chaos ... the elder encourages the younger and shows him how ... they too shall launch off fearlessly together till the new world fits an orbit for itself and looks unabashed on the lesser orbits of the stars and sweeps through the ceaseless rings and shall never be quiet again.

There will soon be no more priests. Their work is done. They may wait awhile ... perhaps a generation or two ... dropping off by degrees. A superior breed shall take their place ... the gangs of kosmos and prophets *en masse* shall take their place. A new order shall arise and they shall be the priests of man, and every man shall be his own priest. The churches built under their umbrage shall be the churches of men and women. Through the divinity of themselves shall the kosmos and the new breed of poets be interpreters of men and women and of all events and things. They shall find their inspiration in real objects to-day, symptoms of the past and future... . They shall not deign to defend immortality or God or the perfection of things or liberty or the exquisite beauty and reality of the soul. They shall arise in America and be responded to from the remainder of the earth.

The English language befriends the grand American expression ... it is brawny enough and limber and full enough ... on the tough stock of a race who through all change of circumstance was never without the idea of political liberty, which is the animus of all liberty, it has attracted the terms of daintier and gayer and subtler and more elegant tongues. It is the powerful language of resistance ... it is the dialect of common sense.

It is the speech of the proud and melancholy races and of all who aspire. It is the chosen tongue to express growth faith self-esteem freedom justice equality friendliness amplitude prudence decision and courage. It is the medium that shall well nigh express the inexpressible.

No great literature nor any like style of behavior or oratory or social intercourse or household arrangements or public institutions or the treatment of bosses of employed people, nor executive detail or detail of the army and navy, nor spirit of legislation or courts or police or tuition or architecture or songs or amusements or the costumes of young men, can long elude the jealous and passionate instinct of American standards.
Whether or no the sign appears from the mouths of the people, it throbs a live interrogation in every freeman's and freewoman's heart after that which passes by or this built to remain. Is it uniform with my country? Are its disposals without ignominious distinctions? Is it for the ever growing communes of brothers and lovers, large, well-united, proud beyond the old models, generous beyond all models? Is it something grown fresh out of the fields or drawn from the sea for use to me today here? I know that what answers for me an American must answer for any individual or nation that serves for a part of my materials. Does this answer? or is it without reference to universal needs? or sprung of the needs of the less developed society of special ranks? or old needs of pleasure overlaid by modern science or forms? Does this acknowledge liberty with audible and absolute acknowledgment, and set slavery at nought for life and death? Will it help breed one goodshaped and wellhung man, and a woman to be his perfect and independent mate? Does it improve manners?

Is it for the nursing of the young of the republic? Does it solve readily with the sweet milk of the nipples of the breasts of the mother of many children? Has it too the old ever-fresh forbearance and impartiality? Does it look for the same love on the last born and on those hardening toward stature, and on the errant, and on those who disdain all strength of assault outside their own?

The poems distilled from other poems will probably pass away. The coward will surely pass away. The expectation of the vital and great can only be satisfied by the demeanor of the vital and great. The swarms of the polished deprecating and reflectors and the polite float off and leave no remembrance. America prepares with composure and goodwill for the visitors that have sent word.

It is not intellect that is to be their warrant and welcome. The talented, the artist, the ingenious, the editor, the statesman, the erudite ... they are not unappreciated ... they fall in their place and do their work. The soul of the nation also does its work. No disguise can pass on it ... no disguise can conceal from it. It rejects none, it permits all. Only towards as good as itself and toward the like of itself will it advance half-way. An individual is as superb as a nation when he has the qualities which make a superb nation. The soul of the largest and wealthiest and proudest nation may well go half-way to meet that of its poets. The signs are effectual. There is no fear of mistake. If the one is true the other is true. The proof of a poet is that his country absorbs him as affectionately as he has absorbed it.

9. Emerson's Inaugural Letter

Emerson's profoundly simple critique of *Leaves of Grass* is the most important critical document of the nineteenth century. The career and poetical output Walt Whitman balances on its singular pivot. Emerson became immersed in the book's controversies for the praise he pronounced. If you pronounced Whitman a devil you had to address Emerson's praise (see Rufus W. Griswold's Criterion review).

Emerson and Whitman would have their differences over the course of the 2nd half of the nineteenth century. Emerson claimed he might have written a more qualified review had he known that his letter would be published — which is to say he would have preferred not to have been embroiled in controversies that were to plague the younger poet. Despite such speculative qualifications, Emerson remained steadfast in his defense of Whitman's "brave thought."

I was pleased to discover that the Library of Congress had possession of the original letter — the Magna Carta of American Literature. It is presented below with a readable text, following.

Concord, 21 July
Mass[tts] } 1855

Dear Sir,

I am not blind to the worth of the wonderful gift of "Leaves of Grass." I find it the most extraordinary piece of wit & wisdom that America has yet contributed. I am very

must have had a long foreground somewhere, for such a start. I rubbed my eyes a little to see if this sunbeam were no illusion; but the solid sense of the book is a sober certainty. It has the best merits, namely, of fortifying & encouraging.

I did not know until I, last night, saw

DEAR SIR—

I am not blind to the worth of the wonderful gift of "LEAVES OF GRASS." I find it the most extraordinary piece of wit and wisdom that America has yet contributed. I am very happy in reading it, as great power makes us happy. It meets the demand I am always making of what seemed the sterile and stingy nature, as if too much handiwork, or too much lymph in the temperament, were making our western wits fat and mean

I give you joy of your free and brave thought. I have great joy in it. I find incomparable things said incomparably well, as they must be. I find the courage of treatment which so delights us, and which large perception only can inspire.

I greet you at the beginning of a great career, which yet must have had a long foreground somewhere, for such a start. I rubbed my eyes a little, to see if this sunbeam were no illusion; but the solid sense of the book is a sober certainty. It has the best merits, namely, of fortifying and encouraging.

I did not know until I last night saw the book advertised in newspaper that I could trust the name as real and available for a post-office. I wish to see my benefactor, and have felt much like striking my tasks, and visiting New York to pay you my respects.

        R.W. EMERSON
        Concord, Massachusetts, 21 July, 1855

The Emerson Preface :
1856 Edition of Leaves of Grass

The '56 Preface is often called the 'Emerson Preface'. Whitman, at last, acknowledges Emerson's letter from the preceding year. Whitman had made a private letter a public one. He returns the dubious favor by making his reply a public one, as well. We wince a bit at the first paragraph's appellation of *Master*—although, surely the more celebrated of the two is clearly that. We doubly wince when the poet uses it twice again in the second paragraph. Emerson's "masterhood" would acquire more bite when it was passed to Whitman with the arrival of Bram Stoker. The creator of Dracula would abjectly acknowledge Whitman as his "master." Where the hell is Van Helsing when you need him?

The younger poet stretches the truth when he speaks of the first edition readily selling. Readily *gifted* is closer to the truth. But beyond these quibblings the preface is well worth a read. "Master," only returns again at the close. At that juncture it happily feels more heartfelt and genuinely appropriate.

10. Preface, 1856 Edition

BROOKLYN, August, 1856.

HERE are thirty-two Poems, which I send you, dear Friend and Master, not having found how I could satisfy myself with sending any usual acknowledgment of your letter. The first edition, on which you mailed me that till now unanswered letter, was twelve poems—

I printed a thousand copies, and they readily sold; these thirty-two Poems I stereotype, to print several thousand copies of. I much enjoy making poems. Other work I have set for myself to do, to meet people and The States face to face, to confront them with an American rude tongue; but the work of my life is making poems. I keep on till I make a hundred, and then several hundred — perhaps a thousand. The way is clear to me. A few years, and the average annual call for my Poems is ten or twenty thousand copies — more, quite likely. Why should I hurry or compromise? In poems or in speeches I say the word or two that has got to be said, adhere to the body, step with the countless common footsteps, and remind every man and woman of something.

Master, I am a man who has perfect faith. Master, we have not come through centuries, caste, heroisms, fables, to halt in this land today. Or I think it is to collect a tenfold impetus that any halt is made. As nature, inexorable, onward, resistless, impassive amid the threats and sereams of disputants, so America. Let all defer. Let all attend respectfully the leisure of These States, their politics, poems, literature, manners, and their free-handed modes of training their own offspring. Their own comes, just matured, certain, numerous and capable enough, with egotistical tongues, with sinewed wrists, seizing openly what belongs to them. They resume Personality, too long left out of mind. Their shadows are projected in employments, in books, in the cities, in trade; their feet are on the flights of the steps of the Capitol; they dilate, a larger, brawnier, more candid, more democratic, lawless, positive native to The States, sweet-bodied, completer, dauntless, flowing, masterful, beard-faced, new race of men.

Swiftly, on limitless foundations, the United States too are founding a literature. It is all as well done, in my opinion, as could be practicable. Each element here is in condition. Every day I go among the people of Manhattan Island, Brooklyn, and other cities, and among the young men, to discover the spirit of them, and to refresh myself. These are to be attended to; I am myself more drawn here than to those authors, publishers, importations, reprints, and so forth. I pass coolly through those, understanding them perfectly well. and that they do the indispensable service, outside of men like me, which nothing else could do. In poems, the young men of The States shall be represented, for they out-rival the best of the rest of the earth.

The lists of ready-made literature which America inherits by the mighty inheritance of the English language—all the rich repertoire of traditions, poems, historics, metaphysics, plays, classics, translations, have made, and still continue, magnificent preparations for that other plainly signified literature, to be our own, to be electric, fresh, lusty, to express the full-sized body, male and female—to give the modern meanings of things, to grow up beautiful, lasting, commensurate with America, with all the passions of home, with the inimitable sympathies of having been boys and girls together, and of parents who were with our parents.

What else can happen The States, even in their own despite? That huge English flow, so sweet, so undeniable, has done incalculable good here, and is to be spoken of for its own sake with generous praise and with gratitude. Yet the price The States have had to lie under for the same has not been a small price.

Payment prevails; a nation can never take the issues of the needs of other nations for nothing. America, grandest of lands in the theory of its politics, in popular reading, in hospitality, breadth, animal beauty, cities, ships, machines, money, credit, collapses quick as lightning at the repeated, admonishing, stern words, Where are any mental expressions from you, beyond what you have copied or stolen? Where the born throngs of poets, literats, orators, you promised? Will you but tag after other nations? They struggled long for their literature, painfully working their way, some with deficient languages, some with priest-craft, some in the endeavor just to live—yet achieved for their times, works, poems, perhaps the only solid consolation left to them through ages afterward of shame and decay. You are young, have the perfectest of dialects, a free press, a free government, the world forwarding its best to be with you.

As justice has been strictly done to you, from this hour do strict justice to yourself. Strangle the singers who will not sing you loud and strong. Open the doors of The West. Call for new great masters to comprehend new arts, new perfections, new wants. Submit to the most robust bard till he remedy your barrenness. Then you will not need to adopt the heirs of others; you will have true heirs, begotten of yourself, blooded with your own blood.

With composure I see such propositions, seeing more and more every day of the answers that serve. Expressions do not yet serve, for sufficient reasons; but that is getting ready, beyond what the earth has hitherto known, to take home the expressions when they come, and to identify them with the populace of The States, which is the schooling cheaply procured by any outlay any number of years. Such schooling The States extract from the swarms of reprints, and from the current authors and editors. Such service and extract are done after enormous, reckless, free modes, characteristic of The States. Here are to be attained results never elsewhere thought possible; the modes are very grand too. The instincts of the American people are all perfect, and tend to make heroes. It is a rare thing in a man here to understand The States. All current nourishments to literature serve. Of authors and editors I do not know how many there are in The States, but there are thousands, each one building his or her step to the stairs by which giants shall mount. Of the twenty-four modern mammoth two-double, three-double, and four-double cylinder presses now in the world, printing by steam, twenty-one of them are in These States. The twelve thousand large and small shops for dispensing books and newspapers—the same number of public libraries, any one of which has all the reading wanted to equip a man or woman for American reading—the three thousand different newspapers, the nutriment of the imperfect ones coming in just as usefully as any—the story papers, various, full of strong-flavored romances, widely circulated—the onecent and two-cent journals—the political ones, no matter what side—the weeklies in the country—the sporting and pictorial papers—the monthly magazines, with plentiful imported feed—the sentimental novels, numberless copies of them—the low-priced flaring tales, adventures, biographies—all are prophetic; all waft rapidly on. I see that they swell wide, for reasons. I am not troubled at the movement of them, but greatly pleased.

I see plying shuttles, the active ephemeral myriads of books also, faithfully weaving the garments of a generation of men, and a generation of women, they do not perceive or know. What a progress popular reading and writing has made in fifty years! What a progress fifty years hence! The time is at hand when inherent literature will be a main part of These States, as general and real as steam-power, iron, corn, beef, fish. First-rate American persons are to be supplied. Our perennial materials for fresh thoughts, histories, poems, music, orations, religions, recitations, amusements, will then not be disregarded, any more than our perennial fields, mines, rivers, seas. Certain things are established, and are immovable; in those things millions of years stand justified.

The mothers and fathers of whom modern centuries have come, have not existed for nothing; they too had brains and hearts. Of course all literature, in all nations and years, will share marked attributes in common, as we all, of all ages, share the common human attributes. America is to be kept coarse and broad. What is to be done is to withdraw from precedents, and be directed to men and women — also to The States in their federalness; for the union of the parts of the body is not more necessary to their life than the union of These States is to their life.

A profound person can easily know more of the people than they know of themselves. Always waiting untold in the souls of the armies of common people, is stuff better than anything that can possibly appear in the leadership of the same.

That gives final verdicts. In every department of These States, he who travels with a coterie, or with selected persons, or with imitators, or with infidels, or with the owners of slaves, or with that which is ashamed of the body of a man, or with that which is ashamed of the body of a woman, or with any thing less than the bravest and the openest, travels straight for the slopes of dissolution. The genius of all foreign literature is clipped and cut small, compared to our genius, and is essentially insulting to our usages, and to the organic compacts of These States.

Old forms, old poems, majestic and proper in their own lands here in this land are exiles; the air here is very strong. Much that stands well and has a little enough place provided for it in the small scales of European kingdoms, empires, and the like, here stands haggard, dwarfed, ludicrous, or has no place little enough provided for it. Authorities, poems, models, laws, names, imported into America, are useful to America today to destroy them, and so move disencumbered to great works, great days.

Just so long, in our country or any country, as no revolutionists advance, and are backed by the people, sweeping off the swarms of routine representatives, officers in power, book-makers, teachers, ecclesiastics, politicians, just so long, I perceive, do they who are in power fairly represent that country, and remain of use, probably of very great use. To supersede them, when it is the pleasure of These States, full provision is made; and I say the time has arrived to use it with a strong hand.

Here also the souls of the armies have not only overtaken the souls of the officer, but passed on, and left the souls of the officers behind out of sight many weeks' journey; and the souls of the armies now go en-masse without officers. Here also formulas, glosses, blanks, minutiæ, are choking the throats of the spokesmen to death. Those things most listened for, certainly those are the things least said. There is not a single History of the World. There is not one of America, or of the organic compacts of These States, or of Washington, or of Jefferson, nor of Language, nor any Dictionary of the English Language. There is no great author; every one has demeaned himself to some etiquette or some impotence. There is no manhood or life-power in poems; there are shoats and geldings more like. Or literature will be dressed up, a fine gentleman, distasteful to our instincts, foreign to our soil. Its neck bends right and left wherever it goes. Its costumes and jewelry prove how little it knows Nature.

Its flesh is soft; it shows less and less of the indefinable hard something that is Nature. Where is any thing but the shaved Nature of synods and schools? Where is a savage and luxuriant man? Where is an overseer? In lives, in poems, in codes of law, in Congress, in tuitions, theatres, conversations, argumentations, not a single head lifts itself clean out, with proof that it is their master, and has subordinated them to itself, and is ready to try their superiors. None believes in These States, boldly illustrating them in himself. Not a man faces round at the rest with terrible negative voice, refusing all terms to be bought off from his own eye-sight, or from the soul that he is, or from friendship, or from the body that he is, or from the soil and sea.

To creeds, literature, art, the army, the navy, the executive, life is hardly proposed, but the sick and dying are proposed to cure the sick and dying. The churches are one vast lie; the people do not believe them, and they do not believe themselves; the priests are continually telling what they know well enough is not so, and keeping back what they know is so. The spectacle is a pitiful one. I think there can never be again upon the festive earth more bad-disordered persons deliberately taking seats, as of late in These States, at the heads of the public tables—such corpses' eyes for judges—such a rascal and thief in the Presidency.

Up to the present, as helps best, the people, like a lot of large boys, have no determined tastes, are quite unaware of the grandeur of themselves, and of their destiny, and of their immense strides—accept with voracity whatever is presented them in novels, histories, newspapers, poems, schools, lectures, every thing. Pretty soon, through these and other means, their development makes the fibre that is capable of itself, and will assume determined tastes. The young men will be clear what they want, and will have it. They will follow none except him whose spirit leads them in the like spirit with themselves. Any such man will be welcome as the flowers of May. Others will be put out without ceremony. How much is there anyhow, to the young men of These States, in a parcel of helpless dandies, who can neither fight, work, shoot, ride, run, command—some of them devout, some quite insane, some castrated—all second-hand, or third, fourth, or fifth hand—waited upon by waiters, putting not this land first, but always other lands first, talking of art, doing the most ridiculous things for fear of being called ridiculous, smirking and skipping along, continually taking off their hats—no one behaving, dressing, writing, talking, loving, out of any natural and manly tastes of his own, but each one looking cautiously to see how the rest behave, dress, write, talk, love—pressing the noses of dead books upon themselves and upon their country—favoring no poets, philosophs, literats here, but dog-like danglers at the heels of the poets, philosophs, literats, of enemies'lands—favoring mental expressions, models of gentlemen and ladies, social habitudes in These States, to grow up in sneaking defiance of the popular substratums of The States? Of course they and the likes of them can never justify the strong poems of America. Of course no feed of theirs is to stop and be made welcome to muscle the bodies, male and female, for Manhattan Island, Brooklyn, Boston, Worcester, Hartford, Portland, Montreal, Detroit, Buffalo, Cleaveland, Milwaukee, St. Louis, Indianapolis, Chicago, Cincinnati, Iowa City, Philadelphia, Baltimore, Releigh, Savannah, Charleston, Mobile, New Orleans, Galveston, Brownsville, San Francisco, Havana, and a thousand equal cities, present and to come. Of course what they and the likes of them have been used for, draws toward its close, after which they will all be discharged, and not one of them will ever be heard of any more. America, having duly conceived, bears out of herself offspring of her own to do the workmanship wanted. To freedom, to strength, to poems, to personal greatness, it is never permitted to rest, not a generation or part of a generation. To be ripe beyond further increase is to prepare to die. The architects of These States laid their foundations, and passed to further, spheres.

What they laid is a work done; as much more remains. Now are needed other architects, whose duty is not less difficult, but perhaps more difficult. Each age forever needs architects. America is not finished, perhaps never will be; now America is a divine true sketch. There are Thirty-Two States sketched — the population thirty millions. In a few years there will be Fifty States.

Again in a few years there will be A Hundred States, the population hundreds of millions, the freshest and freest of men. Of course such men stand to nothing less than the freshest and freest expression. Poets here, literats here, are to rest on organic different bases from other countries; not a class set apart, circling only in the circle of themselves, modest and pretty, desperately scratching for rhymes, pallid with white paper, shut off, aware of the old pictures and traditions of the race, but unaware of the actual race around them — not breeding in and in among each other till they all have the scrofula. Lands of ensemble, bards of ensemble! Walking freely out from the old traditions, as our politics has walked out, American poets and literats recognize nothing behind them superior to what is present with them — recognize with joy the sturdy living forms of the men and women of These States, the divinity of sex, the perfect eligibility of the female with the male, all The States, liberty and equality, real articles, the different trades, mechanics, the young fellows of Manhattan Island, customs, instincts, slang, Wisconsin, Georgia, the noble Southern heart, the hot blood, the spirit that will be nothing less than master, the filibuster spirit, the Western man, native-born perceptions, the eye for forms, the perfect models of made things, the wild smack of freedom, California, money, electrictelegraphs, free-trade, iron and the iron mines — recognize without demur those splendid resistless black poems, the steam-ships of the sea-board states, and those other resistless splendid poems, the locomotives, followed through the interior states by trains of rail-road cars.

A word remains to be said, as of one ever present, not yet permitted to be acknowledged, discarded or made dumb by literature, and the results apparent. To the lack of an avowed, empowered, unabashed development of sex, (the only salvation for the same,) and to the fact of speakers and writers fraudulently assuming as always dead what every one knows to be always alive, is attributable the remarkable non-personality and indistinctness of modern productions in books, art, talk; also that in the scanned lives of men and women most of them appear to have béen for some time past of the neuter gender; and also the stinging fact that in orthodox society today. if the dresses were changed, the men might easily pass for women and the women for men.

Infidelism usurps most with foetid polite face; among the rest infidelism about sex. By silence or obedience the pens of savans, poets, historians, biographers, and the rest, have long connived at the filthy law, and books enslaved to it, that what makes the manhood of a man, that sex, womanhood, maternity, desires, lusty animations, organs, acts, are unmentionable and to be ashamed of, to be driven to skulk out of literature with whatever belongs to them. This filthy law has to be repealed — it stands in the way of great reforms. Of women just as much as men, it is the interest that there should not be infidelism about sex, but perfect faith.

Women in These States approach the day of that organic equality with men, without which, I see, men cannot have organic equality among themselves. This empty dish, gallantry, will then be filled with something. This tepid wash, this diluted deferential love, as in songs, fictions, and so forth, is enough to make a man vomit; as to manly friendship, everywhere observed in The States, there is not the first breath of it to be observed in print. I say that the body of a man or woman, the main matter, is so far quite unexpressed in poems; but that the body is to be expressed, and sex is. Of bards for These States, if it come to a question, it is whether they shall celebrate in poems the eternal decency of the amativeness of Nature, the motherhood of all, or whether they shall be the bards of the fashionable delusion of the inherent nastiness of sex, and of the feeble and querulous modesty of deprivation. This is important in poems, because the whole of the other expressions of a nation are but flanges out of its great poems. To me, henceforth, that theory of any thing, no matter what, stagnates in its vitals, cowardly and rotten, while it cannot publicly accept, and publicly name, with specific words, the things on which all existence, all souls, all realization, all decency, all health, all that is worth being here for, all of woman and of man, all beauty, all purity, all sweetness, all friendship, all strength, all life, all immortality depend. The courageous soul, for a year or two to come, may be proved by faith in sex, and by disdaining concessions. To poets and literats — to every woman and man, today or any day, the conditions of the present, needs, dangers, prejudices, and the like, are the perfect conditions on which we are here, and the conditions for wording the future with undissuadable words. These States, receivers of the stamina of past ages and lands, initiate the outlines of repayment a thousand fold.

They fetch the American great masters, waited for by old worlds and new, who accept evil as well as good, ignorance as well as erudition, black as soon as white, foreign-born materials as well as home-born, reject none, force discrepancies into range, surround the whole, concentrate them on present periods and places, show the application to each and any one's body and soul, and show the true use of precedents.

Always America will be agitated and turbulent. This day it is taking shape, not to be less so, but to be more so, stormily, capriciously, on native principles, with such vast proportions of parts! As for me, I love screaming, wrestling, boiling-hot days.

Of course, we shall have a national character, an identity. As it ought to be, and as soon as it ought to be, it will be. That, with much else, takes care of itself, is a result, and the cause of greater results. With Ohio, Illinois, Missouri, Oregon—with the states around the Mexican sea—with cheerfully welcomed immigrants from Europe, Asia, Africa—with Connecticut, Vermont, New Hampshire, Rhode Island—with all varied interests, facts, beliefs, parties, genesis—there is being fused a determined character, fit for the broadest use for the freewomen and freemen of Tho States, accomplished and to be accomplished, without any exception whatever—each indeed free, each idiomatic, as becomes live states and men, but each adhering to one enclosing general form of politics, manners, talk, personal style, as the plenteous varieties of the race adhere to one physical form. Such character is the brain and spine to all, including literature, including poems.

Such character, strong, limber, just, open-mouthed, American-blooded, full of pride, full of ease, of passionate friendliness, is to stand compact upon that vast basis of the supremacy of Individuality—that new moral American continent without which, I see, the physical continent remained incomplete,

may-be a carcass, a bloat—that newer America, answering face to face with The States, with ever-satisfying and ever-unsurveyable seas and shores.

Those shores you found. I say you have led The States there—have led Me there. I say that none has ever done, or ever can do, a greater deed for The States, than your deed. Others may line out the lines, build cities, work mines, break up farms; it is yours to have been the original true Captain who put to sea, intuitive, positive, rendering the first report, to be told less by any report, and more by the mariners of a thousand bays, in each tack of their arriving and departing, many years after you.

Receive, dear Master, these statements and assurances through me, for all the young men, and for an earnest that we know none before you, but the best following you; and that we demand to take your name into our keeping, and that we understand what you have indicated, and find the same indicated in ourselves, and that we will stick to it and enlarge upon it through These States.

WALT WHITMAN.

11. 1856 Cover Art & Spine

of
Leaves of Grass

12. 1856 Edition of *Leaves of Grass*, TOC

1 — Poem Of Walt Whitman, An American
2 — Poem Of Women
3 — Poem Of Salutation
4 — Poem Of The Daily Work Of The Workmen And Workwomen Of These States
5 — Broad-Axe Poem
6 — Poem Of A Few Greatnesses
7 — Poem Of The Body
8 — Poem Of Many In One.
9 — Poem Of Wonder At The Resurrection Of The Wheat
10 — Poem Of You, Whoever You Are
11 — Sun-Down Poem
12 — Poem Of The Road
13 — Poem Of Procreation
14 — Poem Of The Poet
15 — Clef Poem
16 — Poem Of The Dead Young Men Of Europe, The 72d And 73d Years Of These States
17 — Poem Of The Heart Of The Son Of Manhattan Island
18 — Poem Of The Last Explanation Of Prudence
19 — Poem Of The Singers, And Of The Words Of Poems
20 — Faith Poem

21 – Liberty Poem For Asia, Africa, Europe, America, Australia, Cuba, And The Archipelogoes Of The Sea
22 – Poem Of Apparitions In Boston, The 78th Year Of These States
23 – Poem Of Remembrances For A Girl Or A Boy Of These States
24 – Poem Of Perfect Miracles.
25 – Poem Of The Child That Went Forth, And Always Goes Forever And Forever
26 – Night Poem
27 – Poem Of Faces
28 – Bunch Poem
29 – Lesson Poem
30 – Poem Of The Propositions Of Nakedness
31 – Poem Of The Sayers Of The Words Of The Earth
32 – Burial Poem

13. "The Swimmers"

Thomas Eakins
1885

Also known as "The Swimming Hole." Eakins' 1885 painting is reminiscent of the 11th canto of *Song of Myself.* Eakins will later be among the last to photograph the poet before his death and mould his final image in the portrait of his *death mask.*

A series of nude shots (see conclusion of Volume II) of an old man (surmised by some to be the poet) was taken by the artist during this same time frame.

14. Deathbed Edition, TOC
of
Leaves of Grass

KEY: Clusters In Bold
Poems of the Clusters Indented
Solo Canticles Numbered

INSCRIPTIONS:
    One's-Self I Sing
    As I Ponder'd In Silence
    In Cabin'd Ships At Sea
    To Foreign Lands
    To A Historian
    To Thee Old Cause
    Eidólons
    For Him I Sing
    When I Read The Book
    Beginning My Studies
    Beginners
    To The States
    On Journeys Through The States
    To A Certain Cantatrice
    Me Imperturbe
    Savantism
    The Ship Starting
    I Hear America Singing
    What Place Is Besieged?
    Still Though The One I Sing
    Shut Not Your Doors
    Poets To Come
    To You
    Thou Reader

Starting From Paumanok (1)
Song Of Myself (2)

CHILDREN OF ADAM
    To The Garden The World
    From Pent-Up Aching Rivers
    I Sing The Body Electric
    A Woman Waits For Me
    Spontaneous Me
    One Hour To Madness And Joy
    Out Of The Rolling Ocean The Crowd
    Ages And Ages Returning At Intervals
    We Two, How Long We Were Fool'd
    O Hymen! O Hymenee!
    I Am He That Aches With Love
    Native Moments
    Once I Pass'd Through A Populous City
    I Heard You Solemn-Sweet Pipes Of The Organ
    Facing West From California's Shores
    As Adam Early In The Morning

CALAMUS
    In Paths Untrodden
    Scented Herbage Of My Breast

WHITMAN'S CODE: A NEW BIBLE, VOLUME I
M.C. GARDNER

Whoever You Are Holding Me Now In Hand

For You O Democracy

These I Singing In Spring

Not Heaving From My Ribb'd Breast Only

Of The Terrible Doubt Of Appearances

The Base Of All Metaphysics

Recorders Ages Hence

When I Heard At The Close Of The Day

Are You The New Person Drawn Toward Me?

Roots And Leaves Themselves Alone

Not Heat Flames Up And Consumes

Trickle Drops

City Of Orgies

Behold This Swarthy Face

I Saw In Louisiana A Live-Oak Growing

To A Stranger

This Moment Yearning And Thoughtful

I Hear It Was Charged Against Me

The Prairie-Grass Dividing

When I Peruse The Conquer'd Fame

We Two Boys Together Clinging

A Promise To California

Here The Frailest Leaves Of Me

No Labor-Saving Machine

A Glimpse

WHITMAN'S CODE: A NEW BIBLE, VOLUME I
M.C. GARDNER

A Leaf For Hand In Hand
Earth, My Likeness
I Dream'd In A Dream
What Think You I Take My Pen In Hand?
To The East And To The West
Sometimes With One I Love
To A Western Boy
Fast Anchor'd Eternal O Love!
Among The Multitude
O You Whom I Often And Silently Come
That Shadow My Likeness
Full Of Life Now

Salut Au Monde! (3)
Song Of The Open Road (4)
Crossing Brooklyn Ferry (5)
Song Of The Answerer (6)
Our Old Feuillage (7)
A Song Of Joys (8)
Song Of The Broad-Axe (9)
Song Of The Exposition (10)
Song Of The Redwood-Tree (11)
A Song For Occupations (12)
A Song Of The Rolling Earth (13)
Youth, Day, Old Age And Night (14)

BIRDS OF PASSAGE
>	Song Of The Universal
>	Pioneers! O Pioneers!
>	To You
>	France
>	Myself And Mine
>	Year Of Meteors
>	With Antecedents

A Broadway Pageant. (15)
SEA-DRIFT
>	Out Of The Cradle Endlessly Rocking
>	As I Ebb'd With The Ocean Of Life
>	Tears
>	To The Man-Of-War-Bird
>	Aboard At A Ship's Helm
>	On The Beach At Night
>	The World Below The Brine
>	On The Beach At Night Alone
>	Song For All Seas, All Ships
>	Patroling Barnegat
>	After The Sea-Ship

BY THE ROADSIDE
>	A Boston Ballad
>	Europe

WHITMAN'S CODE: A NEW BIBLE, VOLUME I
M.C. GARDNER

A Hand-Mirror

Gods

Germs

Thoughts

When I Heard The Learn'd Astronomer

Perfections

O Me! O Life!

To A President

I Sit And Look Out

To Rich Givers

The Dalliance Of The Eagles

Roaming In Thought

A Farm Picture

A Child's Amaze

The Runner

Beautiful Women

Mother And Babe

Thought

Visor'd

Thought

Gliding O'er All

Hast Never Come To Thee An Hour

Thought

To Old Age

Locations And Times

Offerings

To The States

DRUM-TAPS

First O Songs For A Prelude

Eighteen Sixty-One

Beat! Beat! Drums!

From Paumanok Starting I Fly Like A Bird

Song Of The Banner At Daybreak

Rise O Days From Your Fathomless Deeps

Virginia—The West

City Of Ships

The Centenarian's Story

Cavalry Crossing A Ford

Bivouac On A Mountain Side

An Army Corps On The March

By The Bivouac's Fitful Flame

Come Up From The Fields Father

Vigil Strange I Kept On The Field One Night

A March In The Ranks Hard-Prest, And The Road Unknown

A Sight In Camp In The Daybreak Gray And Dim

As Toilsome I Wander'd Virginia's Woods

Not The Pilot

Year That Trembled And Reel'd Beneath Me

The Wound-Dresser

Long, Too Long America

Give Me The Splendid Silent Sun

Dirge For Two Veterans

Over The Carnage Rose Prophetic A Voice

I Saw Old General At Bay

The Artilleryman's Vision

Ethiopia Saluting The Colors

Not Youth Pertains To Me

Race Of Veterans

World Take Good Notice

O Tan-Faced Prairie-Boy

Look Down Fair Moon

Reconciliation

How Solemn As One By One

As I Lay With My Head In Your Lap Camerado

Delicate Cluster

To A Certain Civilian

Lo, Victress On The Peak

Spirit Whose Work Is Done

Adieu To A Soldier

Turn O Libertad

To The Leaven'd Soil They Trod

MEMORIES OF PRESIDENT LINCOLN

    When Lilacs Last In The Dooryard Bloom'd
    O Captain! My Captain!
    Hush'd Be The Camps To-Day
    This Dust Was Once The Man

By Blue Ontario's Shore (16)
Reversals (17)

AUTUMN RIVULETS

    As Consequent, Etc.
    The Return Of The Heroes
    There Was A Child Went Forth
    Old Ireland
    The City Dead-House
    This Compost
    To A Foil'd European Revolutionaire
    Unnamed Lands
    Song Of Prudence
    The Singer In The Prison
    Warble For Lilac-Time
    Outlines For A Tomb
    Out From Behind This Mask
    Vocalism
    To Him That Was Crucified
    You Felons On Trial In Courts

Laws For Creations

To A Common Prostitute

I Was Looking A Long While

Thought

Miracles

Sparkles From The Wheel

To A Pupil

Unfolded Out Of The Folds

What Am I After All

Kosmos

Others May Praise What They Like

Who Learns My Lesson Complete?

Tests

The Torch

O Star Of France

The Ox-Tamer

An Old Man's Thought Of School

Wandering At Morn

Italian Music In Dakota

With All Thy Gifts

My Picture-Gallery

The Prairie States

Proud Music Of The Storm (18)
Passage To India (19)

Prayer Of Columbus (20)
The Sleepers (21)
Transpositions (22)
To Think Of Time (23)

WHISPERS OF HEAVENLY DEATH
        Darest Thou Now O Soul
        Whispers Of Heavenly Death
        Chanting The Square Deific
        Of Him I Love Day And Night
        Yet, Yet, Ye Downcast Hours
        As If A Phantom Caress'd Me
        Assurances
        Quicksand Years
        That Music Always Round Me
        What Ship Puzzled At Sea
        A Noiseless Patient Spider
        O Living Always, Always Dying
        To One Shortly To Die
        Night On The Prairies
        Thought
        The Last Invocation
        As I Watch'd The Ploughman Ploughing
        Pensive And Faltering

Thou Mother With Thy Equal Brood (24)

A Paumanok Picture (25)

FROM NOON TO STARRY NIGHT

    Thou Orb Aloft Full-Dazzling

    Faces

    The Mystic Trumpeter

    To A Locomotive In Winter

    O Magnet-South

    Mannahatta

    All Is Truth

    A Riddle Song

    Excelsior

    Ah Poverties, Wincings, And Sulky Retreats

    Thoughts

    Mediums

    Weave In, My Hardy Life

    Spain, 1873-74

    By Broad Potomac's Shore

    From Far Dakota's Cañons

    Old War-Dreams

    Thick-Sprinkled Bunting

    What Best I See In Thee

    Spirit That Form'd This Scene

    As I Walk These Broad Majestic Days

A Clear Midnight

SONGS OF PARTING

As The Time Draws Nigh
Years Of The Modern
Ashes Of Soldiers
Thoughts
Song At Sunset
As At Thy Portals Also Death
My Legacy
Pensive On Her Dead Gazing
Camps Of Green
The Sobbing Of The Bells
As They Draw To A Close
Joy, Shipmate, Joy!
The Untold Want
Portals
These Carols
Now Finalè To The Shore
So Long!

FIRST ANNEX: SANDS AT SEVENTY

Mannahatta
Paumanok
From Montauk Point

To Those Who've Fail'd

A Carol Closing Sixty-Nine

The Bravest Soldiers

A Font Of Type

As I Sit Writing Here

My Canary Bird

Queries To My Seventieth Year

The Wallabout Martyrs

The First Dandelion

America

Memories

To-Day And Thee

After The Dazzle Of Day

Abraham Lincoln, Born Feb. 12, 1809

Out Of May's Shows Selected

Halcyon Days

Fancies At Navesink

The Pilot In The Mist

Had I The Choice

You Tides With Ceaseless Swell

Election Day, November, 1884

With Husky-Haughty Lips, O Sea!

Death Of General Grant

Red Jacket (From Aloft.)

Washington's Monument, February, 1885

Of That Blithe Throat Of Thine

Broadway

To Get The Final Lilt Of Songs

Old Salt Kossabone

The Dead Tenor

Continuities

Yonnondio

Life

"Going Somewhere"

Small The Theme Of My Chant

True Conquerors

The United States To Old World Critics

The Calming Thought Of All.

Thanks In Old Age

Life And Death

The Voice Of The Rain

Soon Shall The Winter's Foil Be Here

While Not The Past Forgetting

The Dying Veteran

Stronger Lessons

A Prairie Sunset

Twenty Years

Orange Buds By Mail From Florida

Twilight

You Lingering Sparse Leaves Of Me

WHITMAN'S CODE: A NEW BIBLE, VOLUME I
M.C. GARDNER

Not Meagre, Latent Boughs Alone

The Dead Emperor

As The Greek's Signal Flame

The Dismantled Ship

Now Precedent Songs, Farewell

An Evening Lull

Old Age's Lambent Peaks

After The Supper And Talk

SECOND ANNEX: GOOD BYE MY FANCY

Preface Note To 2d Annex

Sail Out For Good, Eidólon Yacht!

Lingering Last Drops

Good-Bye My Fancy

On, On The Same, Ye Jocund Twain!

My 71st Year

Apparitions

The Pallid Wreath

An Ended Day

Old Age's Ship & Crafty Death's

To The Pending Year

Shakspere-Bacon's Cipher

Long, Long Hence

Bravo, Paris Exposition!

Interpolation Sounds

To The Sun-Set Breeze

Old Chants

A Christmas Greeting

Sounds Of The Winter

A Twilight Song

When The Full-Grown Poet Came

Osceola

A Voice From Death

A Persian Lesson

The Commonplace

"The Rounded Catalogue Divine Complete"

Mirages

L. Of G.'S Purport

The Unexpress'd

Grand Is The Seen

Unseen Buds

Good-Bye My Fancy!

Essay: A Backward Glance O'er Travel'd Roads.

So Long...

What was to become Whitman's first annex to *Leaves of Grass* was published as sixty-four poems in an 1888 prose and poetry volume called *November Boughs*. That collection was also included in a 1888 compendium called *Complete Poems & Prose* and The 1889 70th birthday edition of *Leaves of Grass*. *November Boughs'* preface (below) was both a beginning and an end. It introduced the 1888 volume and the poet selected it, as well, as a farewell pronouncement and afterword to the *Deathbed* edition of '91 & '92.

15. A Backward Glance
O'er Travel'd Roads

PERHAPS the best of songs heard, or of any and all true love, or life's fairest episodes, or sailors', soldiers' trying scenes on land or sea, is the *résumé* of them, or any of them, long afterwards, looking at the actualities away back past, with all their practical excitations gone. How the soul loves to float amid such reminiscences!

So here I sit gossiping in the early candle-light of old age—I and my book—casting backward glances over our travel'd road. After completing, as it were, the journey—(a varied jaunt of years, with many halts and gaps of intervals—

or some lengthen'd ship-voyage, wherein more than once the last hour had apparently arrived, and we seem'd certainly going down—yet reaching port in a sufficient way through all discomfitures at last)—After completing my poems, I am curious to review them in the light of their own (at the time unconscious, or mostly unconscious) intentions, with certain unfoldings of the thirty years they seek to embody. These lines, therefore, will probably blend the weft of first purposes and speculations, with the warp of that experience afterwards,always bringing strange developments.

Result of seven or eight stages and struggles extending through nearly thirty years, (as I nigh my three-score-and-ten I live largely on memory,) I look upon "Leaves of Grass," now finish'd to the end of its opportunities and powers, as my definitive *carte visite* to the coming generations of the New World,* if I may assume to say so.

> *When Champollion, on his deathbed, handed to the printer the revised proof of his "Egyptian Grammar," he said gayly, "Be careful of this—it is my *carte de visite* to posterity."

That I have not gain'd the acceptance of my own time, but have fallen back on fond dreams of the future — anticipations — ("still lives the song, though Regnar dies") — That from a worldly and business point of view "Leaves of Grass" has been worse than a failure — that public criticism on the book and myself as author of it yet shows mark'd anger and contempt more than anything else — ("I find a solid line of enemies to you everywhere," — letter from W. S. K., Boston, May 28, 1884) — And that solely for publishing it I have been the object of two or three pretty serious special official buffetings — is all probably no more than I ought to have expected. I had my choice when I commenc'd. I bid neither for soft eulogies, big money returns, nor the approbation of existing schools and conventions. As fulfill'd, or partially fulfill'd, the best comfort of the whole business (after a small band of the dearest friends and upholders ever vouchsafed to man or cause — doubtless all the more faithful and uncompromising — this little phalanx! — for being so few) is that, unstopp'd and unwarp'd by any influence outside the soul within me, I have had my say entirely my own way, and put it unerringly on record — the value thereof to be decided by time.

In calculating that decision, William O'Connor and Dr. Bucke are far more peremptory than I am. Behind all else that can be said, I consider "Leaves of Grass" and its theory experimental — as, in the deepest sense, I consider our American republic itself to be, with its theory. (I think I have at least enough philosophy not to be too absolutely certain of any thing, or any results.) In the second place, the volume is a *sortie* — whether to prove triumphant, and conquer its field of aim and escape and construction, nothing less than a hundred years from now can fully answer. I consider the point that I have positively gain'd a hearing, to far more than make up for any and all other lacks and withholdings. Essentially, *that* was from the first, and has remain'd throughout, the main object. Now it seems to be achiev'd, I am certainly contented to waive any otherwise momentous drawbacks, as of little account. Candidly and dispassionately reviewing all my intentions, I feel that they were creditable — and I accept the result, whatever it may be. After continued personal ambition and effort, as a young fellow, to enter with the rest into competition for the usual rewards, business, political, literary, &c. — to take part in the great *mèlée* , both for victory's prize itself and to do some good.

WHITMAN'S CODE: A NEW BIBLE, VOLUME I
M.C. GARDNER

After years of those aims and pursuits, I found myself remaining possess'd, at the age of thirty-one to thirty-three, with a special desire and conviction. Or rather, to be quite exact, a desire that had been flitting through my previous life, or hovering on the flanks, mostly indefinite hitherto, had steadily advanced to the front, defined itself, and finally dominated everything else. This was a feeling or ambition to articulate and faithfully express in literary or poetic form, and uncompromisingly, my own physical, emotional, moral, intellectual, and æsthetic Personality, in the midst of, and tallying, the momentous spirit and facts of its immediate days, and of current America—and to exploit that Personality, identified with place and date, in a far more candid and comprehensive sense than any hitherto poem or book.Perhaps this is in brief, or suggests, all I have sought to do. Given the Nineteenth Century, with the United States, and what they furnish as area and points of view, "Leaves of Grass" is, or seeks to be, simply a faithful and doubtless self-will'd record. In the midst of all, it gives one man's—the author's—identity, ardors, observations, faiths, and thoughts, color'd hardly at all with any decided coloring from other faiths or other identities.

Plenty of songs had been sung—beautiful, matchless songs—adjusted to other lands than these—another spirit and stage of evolution; but I would sing, and leave out or put in, quite solely with reference to America and to-day. Modern science and democracy seem'd to be throwing out their challenge to poetry to put them in its statements in contradistinction to the songs and myths of the past. As I see it now (perhaps too late,) I have unwittingly taken up that challenge and made an attempt at such statements—which I certainly would not assume to do now, knowing more clearly what it means.

For grounds for "Leaves of Grass," as a poem, I abandon'd the conventional themes, which do not appear in it: none of the stock ornamentation, or choice plots of love or war, or high, exceptional personages of Old-World song; nothing, as I may say, for beauty's sake—no legend, or myth, or romance, nor euphemism, nor rhyme. But the broadest average of humanity and its identities in the now ripening Nineteenth Century, and especially in each of their countless examples and practical occupations in the United States to-day.

One main contrast of the ideas behind every page of my verses, compared with establish'd poems, is their different relative attitude towards God, towards the objective universe, and still more (by reflection, confession, assumption, &c.) the quite changed attitude of the ego, the one chanting or talking, towards himself and towards his fellow-humanity. It is certainly time for America, above all, to begin this readjustment in the scope and basic point of view of verse; for everything else has changed. As I write, I see in an article on Wordsworth, in one of the current English magazines, the lines. "A few weeks ago an eminent French critic said that, owing to the special tendency to science and to its all-devouring force, poetry would cease to be read in fifty years." But I anticipate the very contrary. Only a firmer, vastly broader, new area begins to exist—nay, is already form'd—to which the poetic genius must emigrate. Whatever may have been the case in years gone by, the true use for the imaginative faculty of modern times is to give ultimate vivification to facts, to science, and to common lives, endowing them with the glows and glories and final illustriousness which belong to every real thing, and to real things only.

Without that ultimate vivification—which the poet or other artist alone can give—reality would seem incomplete, and science, democracy, and life itself, finally in vain.

Few appreciate the moral revolutions, our age, which have been profounder far than the material or inventive or war-produced ones. The Nineteenth Century, now well towards its close (and ripening into fruit the seeds of the two preceding centuries*)—the uprisings of national masses and shiftings of boundary-lines—the historical and other prominent facts of the United States—the war of attempted Secession—the stormy rush and haste of nebulous forces—never can future years witness more excitement and din of action—never completer change of army front along the whole line, the whole civilized world. For all these new and evolutionary facts, meanings, purposes, new poetic messages, new forms and expressions, are inevitable. My Book and I—what a period we have presumed to span! those thirty years from 1850 to '80—and America in them! Proud, proud indeed may we be, if we have cull'd enough of that period in its own spirit to worthily waft a few live breaths of it to the future!

Let me not dare, here or anywhere, for my own purposes, or any purposes, to attempt the definition of Poetry, nor answer the question what it is. Like Religion, Love, Nature, while those terms are indispensable, and we all give a sufficiently accurate meaning to them, in my opinion no definition that has ever been made sufficiently encloses the name Poetry; nor can any rule or convention ever so absolutely obtain but some great exception may arise and disregard and overturn it.

Also it must be carefully remember'd that first-class literature does not shine by any luminosity of its own; nor do its poems. They grow of circumstances, and arc evolutionary.

The actual living light is always curiously from elsewhere—follows unaccountable sources, and is lunar and relative at the best. There are, I know, certain controling themes that seem endlessly appropriated to the poets—as war, in the past—in the Bible, religious rapture and adoration—always love, beauty, some fine plot,

*The ferment and germination even of the United States to-day, dating back to, and in my opinion mainly founded on, the Elizabethan age in English history, the age of Francis Bacon and Shakspere. Indeed, when we pursue it, what growth or advent is there that does not date back, back, until lost — perhaps its most tantalizing clues lost — in the receded horizons of the past? or pensive or other emotion. But, strange as it may sound at first, I will say there is something striking far deeper and towering far higher than those themes for the best elements of modern song. Just as all the old imaginative works rest, after their kind, on long trains of presuppositions, often entirely unmention'd by themselves, yet supplying the most important bases of them, and without which they could have had no reason for being, so "Leaves of Grass," before a line was written, presupposed something different from any other, and, as it stands, is the result of such presupposition. I should say, indeed, it were useless to attempt reading the book without first carefully tallying that preparatory background and quality in the mind. Think of the United States to-day — the facts of these thirty-eight or forty empires solder'd in one — sixty or seventy millions of equals, with their lives, their passions, their future — these incalculable, modern, American, seething multitudes around us, of which we are inseparable parts! Think, in comparison, of the petty environage and limited area of the poets of past or present Europe, no matter how great their genius. Think of the absence and ignorance, in all cases hitherto, of the multitudinousness, vitality, and the unprecedented stimulants of to-day and here. It almost seems as if a poetry with cosmic and dynamic features of magnitude and limitlessness suitable to the human soul, were never possible before. It is certain that a poetry of absolute faith and equality for the use of the democratic masses never was.In estimating first-class song, a sufficient Nationality, or, on the other hand, what may be call'd the negative and lack of it, (as in Goethe's case, it sometimes seems to me,) is often, it not always, the first element. One needs only a little penetration to see, at more or less removes, the material facts of their country and radius, with the coloring of the moods of humanity at the time, and its gloomy or hopeful prospects, behind all poets and each poet, and forming their birth-marks. I know very well that my "Leaves" could not possibly have emerged or been fashion'd or completed, from any other era than the latter half of the Nineteenth Century, nor any other land than democratic America, and from the absolute triumph of the National Union arms.And whether my friends claim it for me or not, I know well enough, too, that in respect to pictorial talent, dramatic situations, and especially in verbal melody and all the conventional technique of poetry, not only the divine works that to-day stand ahead in the world's reading, but dozens more transcend (some of them immeasurably transcend) all I have done, or could do. But it seem'd to me, as the objects in Nature, the themes of æstheticism, and all special exploitations of the mind and soul, involve not only their own inherent quality, but the quality, just as inherent and important, of *their point of view,* * the time had come to reflect all themes and things, old and new, in the lights thrown on them by the advent of America and democracy—to chant those themes through the utterance of one, not only the grateful and reverent legatee of the past, but the born child of the New World—to illustrate all through the genesis and ensemble of to-day; and that such illustration and ensemble are the chief demands of America's prospective imaginative literature.

*(According to Immanuel Kant, the last essential reality, giving shape and significance to all the rest.)

Not to carry out, in the approved style, some choice plot of fortune or misfortune, or fancy, or fine thoughts, or incidents, or courtesies — all of which has been done overwhelmingly and well, probably never to be excell'd — but that while in such æsthetic presentation of objects, passions, plots, thoughts, &c., our lands and days do not want, and probably will never have, anything better than they already possess from the bequests of the past, it still remains to be said that there is even towards all those a subjective and contemporary point of view appropriate to ourselves alone, and to our new genius and environments, different from anything hitherto; and that such conception of current or gone-by life and art is for us the only means of their assimilation consistent with the Western world. Indeed, and anyhow, to put it specifically, has not the time arrived when, (if it must be plainly said, for democratic America's sake, if for no other) there must imperatively come a readjustment of the whole theory and nature of Poetry? The question is important, and I may turn the argument over and repeat it: Does not the best thought of our day and Republic conceive of a birth and spirit of song superior to anything past or present?

WHITMAN'S CODE: A NEW BIBLE, VOLUME I
M.C. GARDNER

To the effectual and moral consolidation of our lands (already, as materially establish'd, the greatest factors in known history, and far, far greater through what they prelude and necessitate, and are to be in future) — to conform with and build on the concrete realities and theories of the universe furnish'd by science, and henceforth the only irrefragable basis for anything, verse included — to root both influences in the emotional and imaginative action of the modern time, and dominate all that precedes or opposes them is not either a radical advance and step forward, or a new verteber of the best song indispensable? The New World receives with joy the poems of the antique, with European feudalism's rich fund of epics, plays, ballads — seeks not in the least to deaden or displace those voices from our ear and area — holds them indeed as indispensable studies, influences, records, comparisons. But though the dawn-dazzle of the sun of literature is in those poems for us of to-day — though perhaps the best parts of current character in nations, social groups, or any man's or woman's individuality, Old World or New, are from them — and though if I were ask'd to name the most precious bequest to current American civilization from all the hitherto ages,

I am not sure but I would name those old and less old songs ferried hither from east and west—some serious words and debits remain; some acrid considerations demand a hearing. Of the great poems receiv'd from abroad and from the ages, and to-day enveloping and penetrating America, is there one that is consistent with these United States, or essentially applicable to them as they are and are to be? Is there one whose underlying basis is not a denial and insult to democracy? What a comment it forms, anyhow, on this era of literary fulfilment, with the splendid day-rise of science and resuscitation of history, that our chief religious and poetical works are not our own nor adapted to our light, but have been furnish'd by far-back ages out of their arriere and darkness, or, at most, twilight dimness! What is there in those works that so imperiously and scornfully dominates all our advanced civilization, and culture? Even Shakspere, who so suffuses current letters and art (which indeed have in most degrees grown out of him,) belongs essentially to the buried past. Only he holds the proud distinction for certain important phases of that past, of being the loftiest of the singers life has yet given voice to.

All, however, relate to and rest upon conditions, standards, politics, sociologies, ranges of belief, that have been quite eliminated from the Eastern hemisphere, and never existed at all in the Western. As authoritative types of song they belong in America just about as much as the persons and institutes they depict True, it may be said, the emotional, moral, and æsthetic natures of humanity have not radically changed — that in these the old poems apply to our times and all times, irrespective of date; and that they are of incalculable value as pictures of the past. I willingly make those admissions, and to their fullest extent; then advance the points herewith as of serious, even paramount importance.

I have indeed put on record elsewhere my reverence and eulogy for those never-to-be-excell'd poetic bequests, and their indescribable preciousness as heirlooms for America. Another and separate point must now be candidly stated. If I had not stood before those poems with uncover'd head, fully aware of their colossal grandeur and beauty of form and spirit, I could not have written "Leaves of Grass."

My verdict and conclusions as illustrated in its pages are arrived at through the temper and inculcation of the old works as much as through anything else—perhaps more than through anything else. As America fully and fairly construed is the legitimate result and evolutionary outcome of the past, so I would dare to claim for my verse. Without stopping to qualify the averment, the Old World has had the poems of myths, fictions, feudalism, conquest, caste, dynastic wars, and splendid exceptional characters and affairs, which have been great; but the New World needs the poems of realities and science and of the democratic average and basic equality, which shall be greater. In the centre of all, and object of all, stands the Human Being, towards whose heroic and spiritual evolution poems and everything directly or indirectly tend, Old World or New. Continuing the subject, my friends have more than once suggested—or may be the garrulity of advancing age is possessing me—some further embryonic facts of "Leaves of Grass," and especially how I enter'd upon them. Dr. Bucke has, in his volume, already fully and fairly described the preparation of my poetic field, with the particular and general plowing, planting, seeding, and occupation of the ground, till everything was fertilized, rooted, and ready to start its own way for good or bad. Not till after all this, did I attempt any serious acquaintance with poetic literature. Along in my sixteenth year I had become possessor of a stout, well-cramm'd one thousand page octavo volume (I have it yet,) containing Walter Scott's poetry entire — an inexhaustible mine and treasury of poetic forage (especially the endless forests and jungles of notes) — has been so to me for fifty years, and remains so to this day.*

Later, at intervals, summers and falls, I used to go off, sometimes for a week at a stretch, down in the country, or to Long Island's seashores — there, in the presence of outdoor influences, Lockhart's 1833 (or '34) edition with Scott's latest and copious revisions and annotations. (All the poems were thoroughly read by me, but the ballads of the Border Minstrelsy over and over again.)

> *Sir Walter Scott's COMPLETE POEMS; especially including BORDER MINSTRELSY; then Sir Tristrem; Lay of the Last Minstrel; Ballads from the German; Marmion; Lady of the Lake; Vision of Don Roderick; Lord of the Isles; Rokeby; Bridal of Triermain; Field of Waterloo; Harold the Dauntless; all the Dramas; various Introductions, endless interesting Notes, and Essays on Poetry, Romance, &c.

WHITMAN'S CODE: A NEW BIBLE, VOLUME I
M.C. GARDNER

I went over thoroughly the Old and New Testaments, and absorb'd (probably to better advantage for me than in any library or indoor room — it makes such difference *where* you read,) Shakspere, Ossian, the best translated versions I could get of Homer, Eschylus, Sophocles, the old German Nibelungen, the ancient Hindoo poems, and one or two other masterpieces, Dante's among them. As it happen'd, I read the latter mostly in an old wood. The Iliad (Buckley's prose version,) I read first thoroughly on the peninsula of Orient, northeast end of Long Island, in a shelter'd hollow of rocks and sand, with the sea on each side. (I have wonder'd since why I was not overwhelm'd by those mighty masters. Likely because I read them, as described, in the full presence of Nature,

under the sun, with the far-spreading landscape and

vistas, or the sea rolling in.)

Toward the last I had among much else look'd over Edgar Poe's poems — of which I was not an admirer, tho' I always saw that beyond their limited range of melody (like perpetual chimes of music bells, ringing from lower b flat up to g) they were melodious expressions, and perhaps never excell'd ones, of certain pronounc'd phases of human morbidity. (The Poetic area is very spacious — has room for all — has so many mansions!)

But I was repaid in Poe's prose by the idea that (at any rate for our occasions, our day) there can be no such thing as a long poem. The same thought had been haunting my mind before, but Poe's argument, though short, work'd the sum out and proved it to me.

Another point had an early settlement, clearing the ground greatly. I saw, from the time my enterprise and questionings positively shaped themselves (how best can I express my own distinctive era and surroundings, America, Democracy?) that the trunk and centre whence the answer was to radiate, and to which all should return from straying however far a distance, must be an identical body and soul, a personality — which personality, after many considerations and ponderings I deliberately settled should be myself — indeed could not be any other. I also felt strongly (whether I have shown it or not) that to the true and full estimate of the Present both the Past and the Future are main considerations.

These, however, and much more might have gone on and come to naught (almost positively would have come to naught,) if a sudden, vast, terrible, direct and indirect stimulus for new and national declamatory expression had not been given to me.

It is certain, I say, that, although I had made a start before, only from the occurrence of the Secession War, and what it show'd me as by flashes of lightning, with the emotional depths it sounded and arous'd (of course, I don't mean in my own heart only, I saw it just as plainly in others, in millions) — that only from the strong flare and provocation of that war's sights and scenes the final reasons-for-being of an autochthonic and passionate song definitely came forth.

I went down to the war fields in Virginia (end of 1862), lived thenceforward in camp — saw great battles and the days and nights afterward — partook of all the fluctuations, gloom, despair, hopes again arous'd, courage evoked — death readily risk'd — *the cause* , too — along and filling those agonistic and lurid following years, 1863-'64-'65 — the real parturition years (more than 1776-'83) of this henceforth homogeneous Union. Without those three or four years and the experiences they gave, "Leaves of Grass" would not now be existing. But I set out with the intention also of indicating or hinting some point-characteristics which I since see (though I did not then, at least not definitely) were bases and object-urgings toward those "Leaves" from the first.

The word I myself put primarily for the description of them as they stand at last, is the word Suggestiveness. I round and finish little, if anything; and could not, consistently with my scheme. The reader will always have his or her part to do, just as much as I have had mine. I seek less to state or display any theme or thought, and more to bring you, reader, into the atmosphere of the theme or thought—there to pursue your own flight.

Another impetus-word is Comradeship as for all lands, and in a more commanding and acknowledg'd sense than hitherto. Other word-signs would be Good Cheer, Content, and Hope. The chief trait of any given poet is always the spirit he brings to the observation of Humanity and Nature—the mood out of which he contemplates his subjects. What kind of temper and what amount of faith report these things? Up to how recent a date is the song carried? What the equipment, and special raciness of the singer—what his tinge of coloring? The last value of artistic expressers, past and present—Greek æsthetes, Shakspere—or in our own day Tennyson, Victor Hugo, Carlyle, Emerson—is certainly involv'd in such questions.

WHITMAN'S CODE: A NEW BIBLE, VOLUME I
M.C. GARDNER

I say the profoundest service that poems or any other writings can do for their reader is not merely to satisfy the intellect, or supply something polish'd and interesting, nor even to depict great passions, or persons or events, but to fill him with vigorous and clean manliness, religiousness, and give him *good heart* as a radical possession and habit. The educated world seems to have been growing more and more ennuyed for ages, leaving to our time the inheritance of it all. Fortunately there is the original inexhaustible fund of buoyancy, normally resident in the race, forever eligible to be appeal'd to and relied on. As for native American individuality, though certain to come, and on a large scale, the distinctive and ideal type of Western character (as consistent with the operative political and even money-making features of United States' humanity in the Nineteenth Century as chosen knights, gentlemen and warriors were the ideals of the centuries of European feudalism) it has not yet appear'd. I have allow'd the stress of my poems from beginning to end to bear upon American individuality and assist it—not only because that is a great lesson in Nature, amid all her generalizing laws, but as counterpoise to the leveling tendencies of Democracy—

and for other reasons. Defiant of ostensible literary and other conventions, I avowedly chant "the great pride of man in himself," and permit it to be more or less a *motif* of nearly all my verse. I think this pride indispensable to an American. I think it not inconsistent with obedience, humility, deference, and self-questioning.

Democracy has been so retarded and jeopardized by powerful personalities, that its first instincts are fain to clip, conform, bring in stragglers, and reduce everything to a dead level. While the ambitious thought of my song is to help the forming of a great aggregate Nation, it is, perhaps, altogether through the forming of myriads of fully develop'd and enclosing individuals. Welcome as are equality's and fraternity's doctrines and popular education, a certain liability accompanies them all, as we see. That primal and interior something in man, in his soul's abysms, coloring all, and, by exceptional fruitions, giving the last majesty to him—something continually touch'd upon and attain'd by the old poems and ballads of feudalism, and often the principal foundation of them—modern science and democracy appear to be endangering, perhaps eliminating. But that forms an appearance only; the reality is quite different.

The new influences, upon the whole, are surely preparing the way for grander individualities than ever. To-day and here personal force is behind everything just the same. The times and depictions from the Iliad to Shakspere inclusive can happily never again be realized—but the elements of courageous and lofty manhood are unchanged. Without yielding an inch the working-man and working-woman were to be in my pages from first to last. The ranges of heroism and loftiness with which Greek and feudal poets endow'd their god-like or lordly born characters—indeed prouder and better based and with fuller ranges than those—I was to endow the democratic averages of America. I was to show that we, here and to-day, are eligible to the grandest and the best—more eligible now than any times of old were. I will also want my utterances (I said to myself before beginning) to be in spirit the poems of the morning. (They have been founded and mainly written in the sunny forenoon and early midday of my life.) I will want them to be the poems of women entirely as much as men. I have wish'd to put the complete Union of the States in my songs without any preference or partiality whatever.

Henceforth, if they live and are read, it must be just as much South as North—just as much along the Pacific as Atlantic—in the valley of the Mississippi, in Canada, up in Maine, down in Texas, and on the shores of Puget Sound.

From another point of view "Leaves of Grass" is avowedly the song of Sex and Amativeness, and even Animality—though meanings that do not usually go along with those words are behind all, and will duly emerge; and all are sought to be lifted into a different light and atmosphere. Of this feature, intentionally palpable in a few lines, I shall only say the espousing principle of those lines so gives breath of life to my whole scheme that the bulk of the pieces might as well have been left unwritten were those lines omitted. Difficult as it will be, it has become, in my opinion, imperative to achieve a shifted attitude from superior men and women towards the thought and fact of sexuality, as an element in character, personality, the emotions, and a theme in literature. I am not going to argue the question by itself; it does not stand by itself. The vitality of it is altogether in its relations, bearings, significance—like the clef of a symphony.

At last analogy the lines I allude to, and the spirit in which they are spoken, permeate all "Leaves of Grass," and the work must stand or fall with them, as the human body and soul must remain as an entirety.

Universal as are certain facts and symptoms of communities or individuals all times, there is nothing so rare in modern conventions and poetry as their normal recognizance. Literature is always calling in the doctor for consultation and confession, and always giving evasions and swathing suppressions in place of that "heroic nudity"* on which only a genuine diagnosis of serious cases can be built. And in respect to editions of "Leaves of Grass" in time to come (if there should be such) I take occasion now to confirm those lines with the settled convictions and deliberate renewals of thirty years, and to hereby prohibit, as far as word of mine can do so, any elision of them.

*"Nineteenth Century," July, 1883.

Then still a purpose enclosing all, and over and beneath all. Ever since what might be call'd thought, or the budding of thought, fairly began in my youthful mind, I had had a desire to attempt some worthy record of that entire faith and acceptance ("to justify the ways of God to man" is Milton's well-known and ambitious phrase) which is the foundation of moral America. I felt it all as positively then in my young days as I do now in my old ones; to formulate a poem whose every thought or fact should directly or indirectly be or connive at an implicit belief in the wisdom, health, mystery, beauty of every process, every concrete object, every human or other existence, not only consider d from the point of view of all, but of each.

While I can not understand it or argue it out, I fully believe in a clue and purpose in Nature, entire and several; and that invisible spiritual results, just as real and definite as the visible, eventuate all concrete life and all materialism, through Time. My book ought to emanate buoyancy and gladness legitimately enough, for it was grown out of those elements, and has been the comfort of my life since it was originally commenced.

WHITMAN'S CODE: A NEW BIBLE, VOLUME I
M.C. GARDNER

One main genesis-motive of the "Leaves" was my conviction (just as strong to-day as ever) that the crowning growth of the United States is to be spiritual and heroic. To help start and favor that growth—or even to call attention to it, or the need of it—is the beginning, middle and final purpose of the poems. (In fact, when really cipher'd out and summ'd to the last, plowing up in earnest the interminable average fallows of humanity—not "good government" merely, in the common sense—is the justification and main purpose of these United States.)Isolated advantages in any rank or grace or fortune—the direct or indirect threads of all the poetry of the past—are in my opinion distasteful to the republican genius, and offer no foundation for its fitting verse. Establish'd poems, I know, have the very great advantage of chanting the already perform'd, so full of glories, reminiscences dear to the minds of men. But my volume is a candidate for the future. "All original art," says Taine, anyhow, "is self-regulated, and no original art can be regulated from without; it carries its own counterpoise, and does not receive it from elsewhere—lives on its own blood"—a solace to my frequent bruises and sulky vanity.

As the present is perhaps mainly an attempt at personal statement or illustration, I will allow myself as further help to extract the following anecdote from a book, "Annals of Old Painters," conn'd by me in youth. Rubens, the Flemish painter, in one of his wanderings through the galleries of old convents, came across a singular work. After looking at it thoughtfully for a good while, and listening to the criticisms of his suite of students, he said to the latter, in answer to their questions (as to what school the work implied or belong'd,) "I do not believe the artist, unknown and perhaps no longer living, who has given the world this legacy, ever belong'd to any school, or ever painted anything but this one picture, which is a personal affair—a piece out of a man's life."

"Leaves of Grass" indeed (I cannot too often reiterate) has mainly been the outcropping of my own emotional and other personal nature—an attempt, from first to last, to put *a Person* , a human being (myself, in the latter half of the Nineteenth Century, in America,) freely, fully and truly on record. I could not find any similar personal record in current literature that satisfied me.

But it is not on "Leaves of Grass" distinctively as *literature* , or a specimen thereof, that I feel to dwell, or advance claims. No one will get at my verses who insists upon viewing them as a literary performance, or attempt at such performance, or as aiming mainly toward art or æstheticism.

I say no land or people or circumstances ever existed so needing a race of singers and poems differing from all others, and rigidly their own, as the land and people and circumstances of our United States need such singers and poems to-day, and for the future. Still further, as long as the States continue to absorb and be dominated by the poetry of the Old World, and remain unsupplied with autochthonous song, to express, vitalize and give color to and define their material and political success, and minister to them distinctively, so long will they stop short of first-class Nationality and remain defective.

In the free evening of my day I give to you, reader, the foregoing garrulous talk, thoughts, reminiscences,

As idly drifting down the ebb,
Such ripples, half-caught voices, echo from the shore.

Concluding with two items for the imaginative genius of the West, when it worthily rises —

First, what Herder taught to the young Goethe, that really great poetry is always (like the Homeric or Biblical canticles) the result of a national spirit, and not the privilege of a polish'd and select few; Second, that the strongest and sweetest songs yet remain to be sung.

DUSK

To the vapor and the dusk…

BIBLIOGRAPHY

Allen, B. (1980). *Leaves of Grass A Textural Variorum of the Printed Poems V 1,2,3*. New York, NYU Press.

Allen, G. W. (1972). *The Merrill Studies in Leaves of Grass* Columbus: Charles E. Merrill Publishing Company.

Allen, G. W. (1955). *The Solitary Singer*. New York: The MacMillian Company.

Allen, G. (1981). *Waldo Emerson*. New York: Penguin.

Augustine, *City of God*

Aurelius, M. *The Meditations of Marcus Aurelius*.

Belasco, S; Folsom, E.; Price, K.M.; Leaves of Grass the Sesqucentennial Essays, University of Nebraska, 2007.

Barrus, C. (1931). *Whitman and Burroughs Comrades*. New York: Houghton Mifflin Company.

Blake, W. (1946). *The Portable Blake*. N.Y. Viking Press.

Blofield, J. *The Teachings of Huang Po*.

Bloom, H. (2003). *Bloom's Modern Critical Interpretations, Whitman's Song of Myself*.

Bloom, H. *Genius*. (2002). Warner Books, N.Y.

Bloom, H. (1994). *The Western Canon*. New York: Riverhead Books.

Boheme, J. *The Way to Christ*.

Borges, J. L. *In Praise of Darkness*.

Borges, J. L. *Other Inquisitions*.

Brodie, F. *No Man Knows My History*.

Bucke, R. *Cosmic Consciousness*.

Bucke, R. (1899). *Notes and Fragments*.

Cambell, J. *The Masks of God*.

Camus, A. *The Rebel*.

Carpenter, E. (1906). *Days with Walt Whitman*. London.

Carpenter, E. *Towards Democracy*

Chan, G. *The Buddhist Teaching of Totality*.

Cleary, T. *The Avatamsaka Sutra*.

Deussen, P. *The System of Vedanta*.

Eckhart, Meister. *Sermons*

Easwaran, E. *The Bhagavad Gita*.

Easwaran, E. *The Upanishads.*

Eliade, M. *The History of Religious Ideas.*

Eliot, T. S. (1958). *The Complete Poems and Plays.* New York: Harcourt Brace and Company.

Emerson, R. W. (1929). *Complete Writings.* New York: Wm. H. Wise and Co.

Emerson, R.W. *Heart of Emerson's Journals*, ed., Bliss Perry

Epictetus. *The Discourses of Epictetus.*

Faner, R. D. (1951). *Walt Whitman and Opera.* London: Feffer and Simons, Inc.

Friedrich, C. J. (1953). *The Philosophy of Hegel.* New York: Random House / The Modern Library.

Gardner, M. (2000). *Buddha Boogie, The Tautological Paradigm.* Los Angeles: Another America.

Genoways, T. *"One goodshaped and wellhung man": Accentuated Sexuality and the Uncertain Authorship to the 1855 Edition of Leaves of Grass; Leaves of Grass, The Sesquicentennial Essays*, University of Nebraska, 2007

Goddard, Harold 1950 The Meaning of Shakespeare

Greenspan, E. (1995). *The Cambridge Companion to Walt Whitman.* Cambridge: Cambridge Univ. Press.

Gregory, P. *Studies in Ch'an and Hua-Yen.*

Grier, E. (1984). *Notebooks and Unpublished Prose Manuscripts Vol. II Washington.* New York: NYU Press.

Grier, E. (1984). *Notebooks and Unpublished Prose Manuscripts Vol. III Camden.* New York: NYU Press.

Grossman, J. *"Profession of the Calamus": Whitman, Eliot, Matthiessen. Leaves of Grass, The Sesquicentennial Essays*, University of Nebraska, 2007

Heidegger, M. *Being and Time.*

Heidegger, M. *Poetry, Language, Thought.*

Hume, D. *An Enquiry Concerning Human Understanding.*

Hurley, A. (1998). *Jorge Luis Borges Collected Fictions.* New York: Penguin.

Isherwood, C. *Vedanta For the Western World.*

Jowett, B. *Works of Plato.*

Kant, I. *Critique of Pure Reason.*

Kaplan, J. (1980). *Walt Whitman: A Life.* New York: Simon and Schuster.

Katz, D. Mark. 1991. *Witness to an Era. The Life and Photography of Alexander Gardner.*

Katz, J. N. *Love Stories: Sex Between Men Before Homosexuality*. The University of Chicago Press, 2001.

Loving, J. (1999) *Walt Whitman, The Song of Himself*

Lowenfels, W. (1960). *Walt Whtiman's Civil War*. New York: A Da Capo Paperback.

McPherson, J. *Battle Cry of Freedom, The Civil War Era*.

Melville, H. *Billy Budd*.

Melville, H. *Moby Dick*.

Miller, E. H. (1969). *A Century of Whitman Criticism*. Indiana: Indiana University Press.

Miller, H. *Stand Still Like the Hummingbird*.

Miller, H. *The Books In My Life*.

Miller, H. *The Tropic of Cancer*.

Miller, J. E. (1957). *A Critical Guide to Leaves of Grass*. Chicago: The University of Chicago Press.

Miller, J. E. (1962). *Walt Whitman*. New York: Twayne Publishers, Inc.

Milton, J. (1949). *The Protable Milton*. Clinton: Penguin Books.

Monegal, E. R. (1981). *Borges A Reader*. E.P. Dutton.

Moon, M. (1973). *Leaves of Grass and Other Writings, Walt Whitman*. New York: W.W. Norton and Company, Ltd.

Morris, R. J. (2000). *The Better Angel*. Oxford: Oxford University Press.

Nietzsche, F. (1928). *Thus Spake Zarathustra*. New York: Tudor Publishing.

Odin, S. *Process Metaphysics and Hua-Yen Buddhism*.

Pine, R. *Zen Teachings of Bodhidharma*.

Reynolds, D. S. (1995). *Walt Whtiman's America, A Cultural Biography*. New York: Alfred A. Knoph.

Rilke, R. M. (1939). *Duino Elegies*. New York: W.W. Norton Company.

Roper, R. (2008). *Now the Drum of War*. New York: Waller and Company.

Russell, B. *Human Knowledge*.

Schmidgall, G. (1997). *Walt Whitman, A Gay Life*. New York: Dutton.

Schopenhauer, A. *The World As Will and Representation*.

Schyberg, F. (1951). *Walt Whitman*. New York: Columbia University Press.

Shakespeare, W. *Henry IV Parts 1 & II, Henry V, Hamlet, King Lear, Macbeth, Othello, Coriolanus, Measure For Measure, Trolis and Cresida, Julius Caesar.*

Sharpe, E. *The Universal Gita.*

Spinoza, B. *Ethics.*

Stacy, Jason Editor, Leaves of Grass 1860, 150th Anniversary Facimile Edition.

Stoker, B (1897/ 2003). *Dracula.* London / New York: Barnes and Noble Classics.& Norton Critical Edition, Editors Auerbach and Seal.

Suzuki, D. *Essays in Zen Buddhism 1st Series, 3rd Series.*

Symonds, J. A. (1893). *Walt Whitman, A Study.* London: John C. Nimmo.

Tarnas, R. (1991)*The Passion of the Western Mind*

Thoreau, H. D. *Walden, or Life in the Woods*

Thoreau, H.D. *Civil Disobedience*

Thoreau, H.D. *A Week on the Concord and Merrimac Rivers.*

Traubel, H. *With Walt Whitman in Camden*

Weinberger, E. (1999). *Jorge Luis Borges Selected Non-Fictions.* New York: Penguin.

Whitehead, A. *Process and Reality.*

Whitman, W. (1912). *Democratic Vistas*. Letchworth: Temple Press.

Whitman, W. (1855). *Leaves of Grass*. Brooklyn.

Whitman, W. (1856). *Leaves of Grass*. Brooklyn.

Whitman, W. (1860). *Leaves of Grass*. Brooklyn.

Whitman, W. (1867). *Leaves of Grass*. New York.

Whitman, W. (1881). *Leaves of Grass*. Boston.

Whitman, W. (1882). *Speciman Days*. Philadelphia.

Williams, T. *The Night of the Iguana*.

Young, Elizabeth & Anthony Lee *On Alexander Gardner's Photographic Sketch Book of the Civil War*

INDEX

'55 edition, 781
'55 edition of *Leaves*, 110
'55 edition of the poem, 66
10th edition of 1897, 783
12 months of the calendar year, 783
1855 edition, 36, 771
1855 frontispiece, 425
1856 Edition
   2nd part of Song of the Answerer, 605
1856's Sundown Poem, 320
2nd longest section in the poem, 87
4,000 line poem by the Poet Dante., 695
a bright, polished billiard ball
   Miller's vision, 471
A Broadway Pageant, 357
A Call, 220
A Child Said to Me, What is the Grass?, 49
A great city is...
   Song of the Broad Axe, 652
a hub for the wheel'd, 245
a liquid world—rushes like a torrent through you...this is art!
   Life Illustrated article on opera, 424
A morning-glory at my window, 152

A Paumanok Picture, 524, **780**
A Song of Joys, 627
A Song of the Rolling Earth, 722
A Week on the Concord and Merrimac Rivers, 277
Abhidhamma
   Illusionary elements of the world, 764
ability to time travel, 215
accepting him that was crucified,, 226
Acropolis, 260, 261
Advaita Vedanta, 44
Aeneas, 670
Afar down I see the huge first Nothing, 229, 231
Afoot and light-hearted I take to the open road
   Song of the Open Road, 554
After All Not to Create Only
   Original title of Song of Exposition, 669
Agonies are one of my changes of garments,, 193
Agonies are one of my garments, 198
Ahab's waking nightmare, 479
Alan Watts
   On time and reincarnation, 682

Alboni, Marietta, 427
   Great Diva, 156
Alcott, Amos Bronson, 278
Alcott, Louisa May, 278
Alexander, 441
Alexandrian Pharos, 678
All is eligible to all, 365
All these I feel or am., 193
All Truths, 165
All truths wait in all things, 180
Alone Far in the Wilds, 63
America is only you and me, 398
America's Socrates, 772
American Civil War, 71
American Institute in 1871, 668
American Revolution, 476
American Siegfried, 343
American Socrates, 654
American Swedenborg Printing and Publishing Society
   Formed in 1850, 695
American Trinity, 339
Amida, 335
Amitabha, 335
Amitabha Sutra, 766
Amitayus, 335
amusing *mahatakyus*, 58
An Address Delivered to Divinity College, 175
An Epic of the Starry Heavens, 695
An inevitable dualism bisects nature, 35
anamnesis
   Platonic memory of archetypes, 257
Ananta-nirdesa Sutra, 766
And am stucco'd with quadrupeds and birds all over, 174
And any thing I have I bestow, 214
And As To You Death, 247
And I become the other dreamers.
   The Sleepers, 466
And nothing, not God, is greater to one than one's self is,, 244
And such as it is to be of these more or less I am, 101
And what is reason? and what is love? and what is life?, 223
Answerer
   An early formulation of the Whitman Character, 606
Apollo astronaut, 437
Are they my poor, 105
Aristotle, 99
   Substance, 257
arriving ferry crushed his foot
   John Augustus Roebling, 581
art of opera, 424
As a Strong Bird With Pinions Free
   Thou Mother of Thy Equal Brood, 510
As God comes a loving bedfellow, 36, 39, 41
Ashton, J Hubley
   Harlan Affair, 776
assimilated to the original soul

Emerson's essay on Swedenborg, 694
At the Mountains of Madness, 197
Atman, 44, 528
Augustine
   City of God, 260
   On "time", 492
Aurelius, Marcus, 28
   To see all things, 170
Aurungzebe, 441
autograph
   Never sent the two dollars, 111
autograph fellows
   Used their requests for the stove, 111
Avatamsaka Sutra, 250
   Tower of Maitreya, 167
Averroes, 260
Avicenna, 260
Away with old romance
   Song of Exposition, 679
Baader, Franz von, 263
baboons, 68
Be at peace bloody flukes of doubters, 227
Beautiful Necessity, 510
beautiful uncut hair of graves, 50
Beecher, Henry Ward, 181
Beethoven, 413
Beghards, 264
Beguines, 264
being, 512
Being, 43
Being passes into Appearance, 614
Belonging to the winders of the circuit of circuits, 226
Bergson, 430
Bhagavad Gita, 29, 108, 254, 760
Binns, H. B., 38
Bipolarism, 404
Birthplace, Whitman
   Photo, 790
black idioms
   Whitman's ear for, 426
black leviathan, 479
Blackwoodtown Insane Asylum, 107
Blake, 133
Blake, William
   Design of Whitman's Tomb, 110
Blind Loving Wrestling Touch, 165
blood of Christ
   Elias Hick Sermon, 269
Bloom, Leopold
   Joyce lost in the stars..., 239
Bodhidharma, 445
Bolton, England, 594
Book of Job, 526
Borges, 72
Borges, Jorge Luis
   Faces, 293
Borges' Introduction, 629
Botticelli, 264
bound upon a wheel of fire, 457
Brahman, 44, 528
Bramante, 264
Bridge, The
   Hart Crane's poem, 583
Broken Tower, The
   Hart Crane's last poem, 595
Brook Farm, 273

Social experiment, 129
Brooklyn Daily Times, 772
Brooklyn's Plymouth, 181
Brown, John
　Harper's Ferry, 67
Brown's execution, 325
Browning, 457
Browning, Robert, 457
Bruno, Giordano, 467
Bryan, William Jennings
　Scopes Trial, 135
Bryon, Lord, 281
Bucke, 104
Bucke, Dr. R.M., 777
Bucke, R.M.
　On Whitman's observation and speech, 627
Bucke, Richard Maurice
　Photo, 793
Buddha, 218
Buddhatvam
　yosidyoniamsritam,, 471
Buddhism, 450
Buddhist's *suchness*, 346
Buddhists, 682
Buddhists and Vedantists, 682
Buddhists' call *discrimination*, 346
Buffalo Bill's Wild West carnivals, 353
Burroughs, 104
Burroughs, John
　Photo, 793
By Blue Ontario's Shore, 365
By God, you shall not go down!, 215
Caesarea Borgia, 265
Call me, Ishmael, 23
Callas, 427
Camden notebooks
　Observation of nature, 628
camel and the eye of the needle:, 110
Canst thou draw Leviathan with a fishhook
　Job, 527
Canto 3 of the '55 edition, 47
Cape Hatteras
　Hart Crane, 582
Carlyle on Christianity, 94
Carlyle's "It availeth a man little, 85
Carlyle's books, 94
Carlyle's Herr Teufelsdrockh, 95
Carpenter, 104
Carpenter, Edward, 37, 711
cartography, Whitman's
　Me Mysef / Soul, 131
Cassidy, Neal
　Friend of Jack Kerouac, 551
Chandogya Upanishad, 52
Channing, Ellery
　Poet, 271
Channing, William Ellery
　Remarks on American Literature, 270
charity
　Worst of Charity, 106
Chartres, 261
Chateaubriand, Francois-Rene de
　The Genius of Christianity, 136

Chemistry in Its Application to Physiology and Agriculture, 175
Childhood, 480
Cho-Butsu-Ossono-Dan, 243
Chuang Tzu, 100
Colebrook, Henry Thomas
    Gita Essays, Emerson studied, 517
Columbus, 265, 434
Columbus., 442
Come closer to me
    Original opening line in A Song of Occupations, 705
Come Said My Soul, **779**
Comfort ye, comfort ye my people, 437
complexity of life and death
    A Paumanok Picture, 524
conclusion of my preceding clusters.", 783
consciousness of each man is a sliding scale, 44
Constable's *The Hay Wain*, 62
convergence of Milton and Shakespeare, 67
Coomaraswamy
    On reincarnation, 682
Copernicus, 265
Copulation is no more rank to me than death is., 150
Cordelia, 457
Corpse I think you are good manure, 247
Cosmic Consciousness, 777
Cosmos: A sketch of a Physical Description of the Universe, 134
Cowley, Malcom
    55 Edition is superior, 156
crack in everything God hath made
    Emerson on Dualism, 35
Crane, Hart, 551
    Eros and death, 579
Crossing Brooklyn Ferry, 578
cunt monologue, 470
d tire of them in a thousand years.
    Emerson's Nature Essay, 710
Daguerre, 425
Daguerre, Louis-Jacque-Mande
    Dagurreotype, 291
Daily times
    Whitman article on Swedenborg, 695
Daily Times, September 29, 1855, 772
dark matter, 101
dark patches fall, 594
Darkness, you are gentler than my lover
    The Sleepers, 468
Darrow, Clarence
    Scopes Trial, 135
Dartmouth, 510
Darwin, 137
Dazzling and Tremendous, 153
Death Bed" edition of 1891-92, **778**
Death's Valley, 65
Deism
    Founding Fathers, 182
Deity, Joyce's

no nickel and dime bum show, 244
Delius, 413
Democratic Vistas, 778
developmental biography, 43
Dhammapada
    Early teachings of Buddha, 684
Dhammapada.
    Points of doctrine, 764
Dharmakaya
    All living creatures, 764
Diorama
    Dagurrerre show, 291
directed unerringly to one single individual—namely to you, 396
distrust of grammarians, 426
Do you give in that you are any less immortal?)
    A Song of Occupations, 707, 752
Do you take it I would astonish?, 116
Don Giovanni, 413
Dona Nobis Pacem, 413
Donne, John, 404
Dos Passos, John, 551
Doyle, Peter, 37, 104, 777
Dravidian
    Pre-aryan Indians, 759
Drums Taps, 780
DuBois, Blanche, 81
Duncan, Isadora
    Inspired by, 548
Duperron, Anquetil, 432
Durer,, 264

Each moment and whatever happens thrills me with joy,, 152
Earth of the slumbering liquid trees...rich apple-blossomed earth.", 118
Ecclesiastes, 117
Ecclesiastes on death, 117
Eckhart
    Condemnation, 262
Eckhart, Meister, 260
    All in all and all in all, 170
    Any flea as it is in God..., 48
    Death & Condemnation, 455
    Dying in God, 56
    Emptiness, Unity, God's Wealth, 27
    Empty yourself, 114
    God as bride, 58
Eckhart's 9th Sermon
    God is equally near in all creatures, 509
Écrasez l'Infâme, 265
Edition of 1856, 774
Edward's seizures, 107
Einstein, 430
elder, mullein and poke weed., 48
Eliot, T.S.
    On Whitman, 601
    River is a strong brown god, 553
Eliot's *Four Quartets*, 503
Emerson, 104, **771**
    Death of, 34
    Ellen's death, 34
    Resigns as minister, 273
    Signs of the Poet, 607

Emerson of *The American Scholar*, 330
Emerson was *a voice crying in the wilderness:*, 613
Emerson, Bulkely
    Emerson's retarded brother, 108
Emerson, R.W.
    Nature Essay & Transcendentalism, 129
Emerson's Cause and effect, 101
Emerson's essay *Fate:*, 505
Emerson's Hamatreya, 502
Emerson's *Self-Reliance*, 33
Emerson's *Worship*, 504
Emperor Shah Jahan, 432
empiricism, 58
Encompass worlds, but never try to encompass me,
    Song of Myself, 154
Endless Unfolding, 147
Enfans d'Adam, 776
engineering feats, 434
Englishman's war with Newton, 133
Enough!, 209
Epictetus, 28
epistemology, 48
erotic encounter with Whitman, 37
Essay on Swedenborg, 694
Eternal One, 516
Every one that sleeps is beautiful
    The Sleepers, 486
fakes of death
    Operatic image, 156
Faner, Robert
    musical terms in Whiman, 426
Farewell My Fancy, 782
father
    Whitman Sr.'s death, 110
Faulkner, William
    On Time, 430
Faust, Goethe's
    Linger a while, thou art so fair..., 160
Fay ce que vouldras
    Whitman and Henry Miller, 472
fireman scene
    Suggestive of Passion, 198
Flaunt of Sunshine, 212
Flaunt of the Sunshine, 213
Flood-tide below me! I see you face to face!
    Crossing Brooklyn Ferry, 586
Folsom, Dr. Ed
    Editor, Whitman Quaterly, 293
for tigers or for lop-tongued wolves
    War, 678
Ford, John
    Stagecoach, 560
four hundred and twelve, 200
Fox, George, 264
    Divine Light, 123
Frankenstein's monster incarnate, 38
Franklin, Benjamin
    Deist, 182
Freud, Sigmuend
    dreaming, 474

Frolic on, crested and scallop-edg'd waves
  Crossing Brooklyn Ferry, 598
Fruitlands, 273
Full of Life
  Anticipation of, 596
Fuller, Margaret
  Photo, 283
  Woman in the 19th Century, 281
Gandavyhua Sutra
  39th Chapter of Avatamsaka, 166
Gandi, Mahatma, 277
gardens of Babylon,, 678
Gardner, Alexander, 293
  Photo, 300
Gardner's Studio, 307
Gardner's Washington D.C. Studio
  Photo, 306
ghost written letter, 212
Gilchrist, Anne
  Photo, 794
  Unrequited paramour, 454
Ginsberg, Allen
  Howl, 579
Giorgione,, 264
Glasgow Sentinel, 301
glories strung like beads, 587
God had slipped stealthily from his bed, 47
God intoxicated Spinoza
  all the seas of God..., 450
God is the all-fair, 728
God queries Satan
  In Job, 526
God: noise in the street:
  Joyce, 514
God-intoxicated, 137
Godlessness and blasphemy.
  Whitman and Spinoza, 455
Goethe, Johan Wolfgang
  Sorrows of Young Werther, 53
Good and bad are but names very ready transferable, 562
good, evil and religion, 336
Gottlieb, Rabbi David
  Age of the earth, 136
Gounod, 413
grand opera, 643
Great Awakening, 265
  2nd, 265
Great or small, you furnish your parts toward the soul.
  Crossing Brooklyn Ferry, 600
Grosse, Phillip Henry
  British Zoologist, 135
guise of a Magus, 596
Hamlet, 628
hangman god
  dio boia
    all in all in all of us., 247
  J. Joyce, 247
Harlan James, 776
Harned, Thomas
  Paid balance on Whitman's tomb, 112
Harper's Magazine, 454, 693
Harris, Thomas Lake., 695
Harrison Gabriel, 772

Harrison, Gabriel
    Photographer, 297
Has Anyone supposed?, 56
Hawthorne, **772**
Hawthorne, Nathaiel
    Brook Farm, 273
Haydn, 413
headland
    Whitman's phallic symbol, 582
headland, the
    28th Canto, 161
heaven without rent or seam.
    Emerson's Experience, 568
Hegel, 119
    & Eckhart, 263
Hegelian dialectic, 35
Heidegger, 430
Hemingway, Ernest, 551
Henry James Jr.emulate the wound dresser, 104
Henry Jr., 104
Heraclitus.
    Metaphor of the river, 584
Hicks, Elias, 268
    Radical Quakerism, 123
Hinayana Buddhism
    Lesser Vehicle, 684
Hindemith, Paul, 414
Hindus, 682
His sister Mary, 39
Holbrook, Josiah
    American Lyceum, 134
Hollyer S, 772
Hollyer, Samuel
    Frontispiece engraving, 297
Holst, Gustave, 413
homosexual inferences, 38
horribly in a pail
    Anticipation of Civil War, 87
horse operas, 353
Houses and Rooms, 30
how quick the sun-rise would kill me,, 153
How the flukes splash!, 227
how there can be a mean man or an, 147
Hua Yen
    Buddhism, 166
Hua Yen Buddhism, 246
Huang Po, 446
    Non attachment, 171
    On Enlightenment, 708
Hugh, of Saint Victor
    First Summae, 261
Humboldt, Alexander von, 134
Hume, David
    Lame performance of an infant deity, 243
    radical skepticism, 271
    Scottish skeptic, 767
Huxley, Aldous
    Perennial Philosophy, 254
I am, 44
I am an acme of things accomplish'd,, 230
I Am He Bringing Help, 217
I am large, I contain multitudes, 251
I Am of the Old and Young, 98
I am part and parcel of God
    Emerson's Nature Essay, 710

WHITMAN'S CODE: A NEW BIBLE, VOLUME I
M.C. GARDNER

I am thankful for small mercies, 566
I am the clock myself., 199
I am the man, I suffer'd, I was there, 192
I Am the Poet, 144
I am the poet of the woman the same as the man,, 144
I Am the Teacher, 240
I an encloser of things to be, 230
I Believe, 173
I Believe In You My Soul, 45
I carry the plenum of proof and every thing else in my face, 154
I Celebrate Myself, 23
I chant the chant of dilation or pride, 144
I dilate you with tremendous breath, 215
I do not call one greater and one smaller,, 230
I Do Not Despise, 225
I exist as I am, that is enough, 143
I fly those flights of a fluid and swallowing soul, 190
I had Emerson on the brain., 771
I Have Heard, 39
I have no chair, no church, no philosophy, 237
I Have Said, 244
I hear and behold God in every object, 245
I hear from the Mussulman mosque the muezzin calling, 422
I heard the mighty tree its death-chant chanting.
Song of the Redwood-tree, 693
I help pick up the dead and lay them in rows in a barn.
The Sleepers, 476
I help pick up the dead and lay them in rows in the barn.", 475
I Know, 237
I know I am deathless, 142
I know I have the best of time and space, 237
I know perfectly well my own egotism,, 220
I know the amplitude of time, 143
I know the sea of torment, doubt, despair, 227
I laid in my
Crossing Brooklyn Ferry, 597
I laugh at what you call dissolution, 143
I make holy whatever I touch, 151
I myself become the wounded person.
Song of Myself, 198
I never in my life looked a cunt up close
Cunt monologue, Henry Miller, 470
I nourish active rebellion
Song of Open Road, 576
I refuse putting from me what I really
Song of Myself, 154

I say no man has ever yet been half devout enough,, 338
I see a great round wonder rolling through space
Salut au Monde, 532
I see Christ eating the bread of his last supper
Salut au Monde, 537
I sound my barbaric yawps, 252
I swear I begin to see the meaning of these things,, 396
I Think, 176
I think I could stop here myself, 558
I think I could turn and live with animals,, 176
I too am of one phase and of all phases, 146
I too knitted the old knot of contrariety
Crossing Brooklyn Ferry, 594
I wear my hat as I please indoors or out, 118
I wholly confound the skeptic
Song of Myself, 154
I will show that there is no imperfection in the present, 336, 345
Idealism, 714
Immense have been the preparations for me, 229, 231, 232
In the Mendocino woods I caught.
Song of Redwood-tree,, 702

Inness, George, 65
Inscriptions, 783
interminable oceans, 568
Is he waiting for civilization, or past it and mastering it?, 211
Is This Then a Touch?, 163
Isaiah, 438
it is a word unsaid, 249
It is by ourselves we go down to eternal night, 369
It is for the wicked just same as the righteous, 115
It Is Time, 229
It is time to explain myself—let us stand up, 228
it keeping tally with the meaning of all
Song of Myself, 154
its turn prove sufficient, and cannot fail., 227
Jackson, Lydia
Emerson's 2nd wife, 34
James, Henry Sr., 104
Jefferson, Thomas
Deist, 182
Jefferson, Wayland, 38
Jehovah, 216
Jelkes, Hannah, 75
Jesus
also one of the "roughs, 610
Jesus Christ, 68
Johnson, President Andrew, 67
Jones, John Paul, 203
Joyce on time
Ulysses, 430

Jung, Carl, 536
Just as you feel when you look on the river and sky, so I felt
    Crossing Brooklyn Ferry, 589
Kafka, 72
Kant, Immanuel, 129
    structures of mind, 133
Kant's *thing in itself*, 30
Karuna, 450
    Religious Aspect of Buddhism, 685
Keats, John, 462
Kennedy, William Sloane
    loaferish portrait, 298
Kerouac, Jack
    On the Road, 551
King James, 55
King, Martin Luther, 277
Know then that the world exists for you
    Emerson, 729
Koran,, 226
Korzybski, Alfred, 100
Kronos and Zeus, 216
Laforgue, Jules
    Whitman's influence, 602
Lalitavistara Sutra, 766
Langguth, A. J.
    Author, 651
Langguth, A.J.
    Writer's work, 651
Lankavatara Sutra, 766
Lascaux and Altimira, 656
Lawerence, D. H.
    lower and higher selves, 162
le Bègue, Lambert, 264
Lear, King, 404, 457

    Whitman recitinng, 456
Leaves of Grass, Junior:, 782
Leonardo, 264
Let the physician and the priest go home, 216
Liebig, Justus, 175
Life Illustrated, 424
Lincoln's assassination, 68
lingam, 339
Live Oak with Moss
    12 poems, 781
living in Orgeon
    Emerson's sarcasm, 686
Locke, John
    tabula rasa, 271
look of the bay mare shames silliness out of me., 85
Lord Krishna
    Incarnation of Vishnu, 760
Lotus Sutra, 766
Lovecraft, H. P., 197
Lucifer Was Not Dead, 66
Lucifer's portrait
    A Black Man from "Pictures", 67
Luther, Martin, 265
Maat
    Will of, 757
Macbeth, 456
Machiavelli, 265
Magellan, 265
Magnus, Albert, 260
mahatakyu, 53
Mahayana Buddhism, 246, 335, 471
    Greater Vehicle, 684
Mahsandhikas
    Early Mahayana Buddhism, 684

Making its cities, 374
Making its rivers, lakes, bays, 374
Man is a rope stretched between the animal and the Superman
   Nietzsche's Zarathustra, 655
Margaret and Katherine Fox, 215
Marin, John, 551
materialism
   Emerson on,, 722
Me
   Sumerian, 758
Me myself, 43
Melville, 67
   Ahab, 67
Melville and Whitman announce, 23
Melville, Herman, 456, 527, 772
Me-myself, plunges its tongue to Whitman's bare-stript heart, 47
Menved, Erik, 480
messianic time piece, 777
Meyerbeer, 413
Meyerbeer's Huguenots, 421
Michelangelo, 264
Miller, Henry, 470, 551
   Indictment of Western Civilization, 124
Miller, Jacob Miller, 65
Millerites, 266
Millet, Jean Francois
   Whitman's gallery visit, 63
Milton, John, 67
   Invocation of Muse, 24

Milton,, John, 455
Mind you O foreign kings. O priests, the crop shall never run out Defiance, 658
miracle of *being*, 30
Mirandolla, Pico della
   Oration on the Dignity of Man, 264
Moby Dick, 480, 772
Mormon
   Book of, 266
Mormon tenet, 220
Moses, 44
most famous frontispiece, 772
Mount's *Farmer's Nooning*, 62
Mozart, 413
Mundaka, Upanishad
   Indian Scripture, 553
My course runs below the soundings of plummets, 190
My faith is the greatest of faiths and the least of faiths, 225
my fire-locked lean'd in the corner., 65
My messengers continually cruise away or bring their returns to me, 190
my own crucifixion and bloody crowning., 209
My real body doubtless left to me for other spheres, Song of Joys, 640
My voice is the wife's voice, 197
My voided body nothing more to me,

Song of Joys, 641
Myerson, Joel
   Transcendentalism, A Reader, 271
mystical hearing, 694
Nagarjuna
   Indian Logician, 767
namu Amida butsu, 335
Natural Theology, 135
Nature, Emerson's, 29
New Bible, 787, 789
New York Times, 773
Newtonian Time, 430
Niepce, Joseph Nicephore
   1st Photo, 290
Nietzche, Friedrich
   On Emerson, 654
Nietzsche, 536
Nietzsche's *Ubermensch*, 651
Nietzsche's will to power, 30
nigger dialect, 426
Night follows close with millions of suns
   Song of the Rolling Earth, 741
Night of south winds—night of the large few stars!, 145
Night of the Iguana, 75
nine editions in Whitman's lifetime, 778
Nirmanakaya
   Earthly body of the Buddha, 764
no prouder than the level I plant my house by, 143
None has ever yet adored or worship'd half enough, 338
nonsense
   Join you in your nonsense, 371
not worth preserving
   Emerson, 106
November Boughs, 353
Now I Will Do Nothing, 157
Now on this spot I stand with my robust soul, 232
Nowhere exists anything but God
   Shuoh, Prince Darn, 467
O' Connor, Nelly
   falls in love with Whitman, 213
O divine average!
   Starting from Paumanok, 341
O foreign kings, O priests, the crop shall never run out.)
   Song of the Broad Axe, 658
O hotcheeked and blushing!, 469
O Span of Youth, 233
O take my hand Walt Whitman
   Salut au Monde!, 528
O' Connor, William
   10 year breach with Whitman, 68
   Photo, 793
O'Connor, 104
O'Connor, W. D., 776
O'Connor, William, 212
objects of the universe perpetually flow, 142
Odysseus, 670

Of every hue and caste am I, of every rank and religion, 99
Old Age Echoes, 782
Old age superbly rising!, 233
Om Mani Padme Hum, 339
Omoo
    Melville's sequel to Typee, 480
Omphalos Argument
    P. H. Grosse, 135
Omphalos, An Attempt to Untie the Geological Knot
    P.H. Grosse, 135
On Heroes, Hero-worship and Heroic in History, 94
On the Same Picture, 65
onanist, 470
onanists, 462
one holocaust anticipates another, 202
one of the most indefatigable workers
    Bucke on Whitman, 480
ontology, 48
opera, 426
    Enraptured and prelude, 155
oppositions in Emerson, 96
Others will enter the gates of the ferry and cross from shore to shore,
    Crossing Brooklyn Ferry, 587
Our Old Feuillage, 616
out of that lesson until it becomes omnific, 166
Out of the Cradle Endlessly Rocking, 83

Oversoul, 130
paean to Idealism, 722
Paine, Thomas
    Deist, 182
Paine, Thomas Paine
    Friend of Whitman Sr., 265
Paine, Tom
    The Age of Reason, 123
Paley, William, 135
Pantanjali, 523
    Mystical union, yoga, 523
Pantheism, 137
Paradise Lost, 455
Parmenides, 346
Parthenon, 260
Passage to India, 429
    late among masterpieces, 446
Penn
    William, 124
Phantom by Ontario's shore, 380
photographic history, 425
Photographic Sketchbook of the Civil War, 304
Phrenological Journal, 773
Pinter's silence meets Ginsberg's *Howl*., 60
Pizarro,, 265
Platform Sutra, 766
Plato, 260, 430
    Archetypes, 257
    Emerson's Essay on, 129
    On time, 681
Play the old role, the role that is great or small
    Crossing Brooklyn Ferry, 599

Play'd the part that still looks back on the actor or actress,
    Crossing Brooklyn Ferry, 595
Plotinus, 260
Plunging his seminal muscle into its merits and demerits, 374
pocketless of a dime may purchase the pick of the earth, 245
Poem of Joy, 627
Poem of the Daily Work of the Workmen and Workwoman of These States, 704
Poem of the Propositions of Nakedness, 403
Poem of the Road, 548
Poem of Walt Whitman, 320
poet as *Messiah*, 465
Poetry and opera
    masses, 427
poet-shaman *becomes* the living landscape he envisions
    2nd Half of Our Old Feuillage, 624
Polo, Marco, 441
Porgy and Bess, 426
Portnoy, 462
Poughkeepsie Seer, 215
Pound, Ezra
    Debt to Whitman, 601
Prajna, 450
    Opening of 3rd eye, 685
Prajnaparamita, 254
    Oldest Mahayana Texts, 765
Prajnaparamitahridaya
    Heart Sutra, 766
Prayer of Columbus, 453
premier signature line in all of Whitman, 48
Premonitions, 325
President is a trifle, 118
problem of evil, 484
Process and Reality, 430
prodigal son, 450
Proto-Leaf., 325
Proud Music of the Storm, 412
Pure Land, 335
purport of the universe
    A Song of Occupations Canto 4, 714
Put God in your debt, 102
pyramids, 677
Queequeg, 37
quotidian and the tragic, 202
Raphael
    School of Athens, 258
red marauder
    Whitman phallic symbol, 582
regicides set in Denmark, 480
reincarnation, 682
Rembrandt, 290, 450
Respondez!, 406
Reversals, 403
Rhineland Mysticism, 263
Ripley, George
    Transcendentalism, 129
Rita
    Vedic, 758
Riverby by the Hudson
    Burrough's farm, 456

Roar, flames, blood, drunkenness, madness, 649
Roebling Jr., Washington
  Death on Titanic, 581
Roebling, Emily Warren
  Wife of Washington Sr. First woman to walk across Brooklyn Bridge., 581
Roebling, John Augustus
  death by tetanus, 581
  Designer, Brooklyn Bridge, 581
Roebling, Washington
  Son of John Augustus Roebling, 581
  Stricken with the Bends, 581
roses under my window, Emerson's, 59
Rossini', 413
Rossini's Stabat Mater, 423
Rumi, Jalal ad-Din
  Persian mystic, 466
Russell, Bertrand
  the five minute universe, 136
Russell, Russell
  Cyclical History, 160
Russell's composite of mind and matter, 724
Salut au Monde!, 526
Sambhogakaya
  Celestial Teaching Body, 764
samsara, 339
Sanatana Dharma
  Hinduism, 759
Sands at Seventy, 781
sane and clear as the sun.

Whitman at Emerson's grave, 654
Sartor Resartus, 95
Saunders, Henry Scholey, 292
School of Athens
  Painting, 259
Schopenhauer was *the will*, 30
Schopenhauer, Arthur, 427
Schulze, Johan Heinrich
  Photography beginnings, 290
Scopes Trial
  1925, 135
Seas of bright juice suffuse heaven
  Song of Myself, 153
seduced by the poetry, 83
Sen T'sen
  Oneness, 60
Seuse Heinrich, 263
Shakespeare, 457
Shakespeare's *Universal wolf*, 678
Shakspere's purple page, 673
Shankara,, 44
Shankara's Vedanta, 516
Shannon, Reverend T., 75
Shastas, 226
sheath'd hooded sharp-tooth'd touch, 162, 165
Shelley
  death at sea, 281
Shukoh, Prince Darn, 432
Shuoh, Prince Darn, 467
Sinai, 44
Slifkin, Rabbi Nathan
  on Scientific vs. Revealed history, 137

Slow-moving and black lines creep over the whole earth
  To Think of Time, 495
Smith, Joseph, 215, 266
Socrates
  dialectic, 271
Sod Festival, 757
Soft doctrine as steady help as stable doctrine, 147
Song of the Answerer, 604
Song of the Broad-Axe, 642
Song of the Carpenter, 646
Song of the Exposition, 668
Song of the Open Road, 554
Song of the Redwood-Tree, 691
Space and Time, 183
sparkles of starshine on the icy and pallid earth, 472
Special Relativity, 430
Specimen Days, **778**
Spinoza, 137
Spinoza, Baruch, 455
  Pantheism, 54
Spinoza, Benedict, 778
Splashing my bare feet in the edge of the summer ripples on
  14th Canto Starting from Paumanok, 351
St. Denis Basilica, 260
St. Denis, Abbey of, 260
St. Peters, 264
Stafford, Harry, 104
star-child reverie, 196
Starting from Paumanok, **780**
Starting From Paumanok, 325

States are the amplest poem
  By Blue Ontario's Shore, 373
Steep'd amid honey'd morphine, my windpipe throttled in fakes of
  Song of Myself, 159
Stella, Joseph, 551
Stevens, Wallace, 551
  The Blue Guitar, 133
stop with fugitives and them that, 149
Strectch'd and Still, 205
students of Whitman in 1840, 38
Such is the library, the study, where (seated on a big log) I have sifted out
  Camden notebook entry, 629
Sudhana visits 52, 250
Suhhavati, 335
Sullivan, Louis
  architect, 551
Sun-Down Poem
  Crossing Brooklyn Ferry, 578
supplementary volumes, 780
Suttapitaka
  5 Collections of sermons, 764
Suzuki, D.T.
  Ceases to be a mystery, 171
Swedenborg, 695
swimmer swimming naked through the eddies
  The Sleepers, 474

Swinburne, Algernon, 780
Swinton William,, **773**
Symonds, John Addington, 332
Taj Mahal, 432
Tamerlane, 441
Tantric, 35
Tao., 254
Taoist, 35
Tat Tvam asi, 53
Tell Walt I am not satisfied, not satisfied
   Emerson on Inventories, 616
Tennyson's sweet sad rhyme, 673
the agents that emptied and broke my brother, 107
the beautiful gentle God by my side, 189
The Big Doors, 62
The Bridge
   Hart Crane, 579
The Butcher Boy, 82
The Creation in billows of godhood laves me., 424
The earth does not argue
   Song of the Rolling Earth, 730
The earth does not withhold, it is generous enough
   Song of the Rolling Earth, 729
The earth, that is sufficient
   Song of the Open Road, 555
the elementary laws never apologize, 143
The Friendly and Flowing Savage, 211
the gnawing teeth of his saw, 207
the gods die from time to time
   Carl Jung, 536
The goods of fortune may come and go like summer leaves, 737
The hiss of the surgeon's knife, 207
The insignificant is as big to me as any,, 166
the journey work of the stars, 173
The Little One Sleeps, 60
the long swim to China, 75
The most delicate and even conventional lady only need to know him to love him., 213
The mysterious ocean, 342
The Mystic Path, 467
The nearest gnat is an explanation, 240, 241
the nothing of life to the nothing of death., 106
the order of the consciousness of art
   Schopenhauer, 427
The others that are to follow me,
   Crossing Brooklyn Ferry, 587
The Past and Present, 251
the poet is the equable man, 384
The Pure Contralto, 87
the riddle and the untying of the riddle, 103
the sacs merely floating with open mouths, 228

The saints and sages in history—but you yourself?, 223
The same reality pervades all teaching
    Emerson, 561
The scallop-edged waves in the twilight,
    Crossing Brooklyn Ferry, 589, 591
The Shapes arise, 659
The Sleepers, 462
The smallest sprout, 51
the solid prizes of the universe
    Canto 15 Starting from Paumanok, 353
The Spotted Hawk, 252
The Starry Night, 711
the threads that connect the stars, 150
the trees, the running rivers, the rocks and sands, 347
The true son of God, 437, 441
The true son of God shall come singing his songs, 440
The Valley of the Shadow of Death, 65
the Whitman clock, 93
the whole theory of the universe, 366
The Wild Gander, 85
The World as Will and Representation, 427
The years teach much that the days never know.
    Emerson's Self Reliance, 566

Theologia Germanica
    Goodness and the soul, 59
There Is That In Me, 249
These Are Really the Thoughts, 102
These States are the amplest poem, 373
They are not vile any more, they hardly know themselves
    Song of the Answer, 611
They do not lie awake in the dark and weep for their sins,, 177
They do not make me sick discussing their duty to God,, 177
thirty-one day month, 783
This hour I will tell you things in confidence, 115
This Is the Meal, 115
This is the meal equally set, 115
Thoreau, 104
Thoreau, Henry David, 320
    Walden, 772
Thoreau's favorite, 579
Tibetan Buddhism, 339
time and extension (space) were structures of the mind., 133
time is the moving image of eternity, 133
Time, space and death, 447
Time, space, both are annihilated
    Photography, 425
To Be, 163
To be indeed a God!, 641

to feel the puzzle of puzzles,, 159
To gloat so over the wounds and deaths of the enemy
    Antipathetical Joy in Song of Joys, 635
To limn with absolute faith the mighty living present.
    Thou Mother of thy Equal Brood, 515
To see no possession but you may possess
    Song of Open Road, 573
To Think of Time, 491
Today is a king in disguise, 735
tomb, Whitman, 110
tomb, Whitman's
    Size of tomb, 112
Transpositions, 490
Trapper's Bride, 65
Traubel, Horace, 698
    Photo, 793
trinity of victims, 71
Trippers and Askers, 41
Tristan und Isolde
    Liebestod, 467
Tropic of Cancer, 470
    I love everything that flows, 157
true doctrine of omnipresence, 180
Turner
    My tap is death, 67
twenty five *stand alone* poems, 783
two funerals
    Joyce and Whitman, 497
Two Partners
    Secret of, 758
Unitarianism
    Emerson & Ripley ministers of, 129
universe is the property of every individual in it.
    Emerson's Nature Essay, 712
Upanishads, 432
Vajracchedika, the Diamond Sutra, 766
Van Gogh, Vincent
    Affection for Whitman, 711
Vasco de Gama, 437
Vaughan, Fred, 37
Vedas, 53, 226
Vedic Hymns, 432
Viayapitaka
    Monastic rules, 764
Viking resurrection, 538
Vimalakirti –nirdesa Sutra, 766
Virgina Woolf
    On Bolton Groop, 594
Volney, Count
    Ruins or Mediation on Revolutions, 123
Voltaire, 265
Wagner, Richard
    Sensuality, 162
    Tristan und Isolde, 467
Walden, 274
Walden: or Life in the Woods, 277
Waldo Emerson
    Death of, 34
walks to his own grave dressed in a shroud, 244
Wall Street, 109

Walt Whitman at Southold, 38
Walter Whitman Jr.'s most imaginative creation:, 776
Was somebody asking to see the soul?, 347
Washington bidding his troops farewell, 474
Washington, George
   Deist, 182
Watts, Alan
   Beat-Zen, 551
week's "seven days", 783
What gods can exceed these that clasp me by the hand
   Crossing Brooklyn Ferry, 597
What is a man anyhow?, 141
What is less or more than a touch?, 166
wheeze, cluck, swash of falling blood, 207
When the full-grown poet came, 269
Whitman
   Comments on Swedenborg, 698
Whitman as supreme poet of autoerotic, 81
Whitman as watcher, 44
Whitman authored his final prose, 782
Whitman Codex, 784
Whitman equates the material with the spiritual, 334
Whitman his own best critic, **773**

Whitman identifies himself, 777
Whitman is patient, 195
Whitman on aboriginal Americans, 353
Whitman the carpenter, 526
Whitman the grand egalitarian became a reactionary, 68
Whitman, Andrew Jackson, 93
Whitman, at Emerson's grave, 654
Whitman, Hanna, 93
Whitman, Jesse, 93
Whitman, Louisa Van Velsor
   Death of Whitman's mother, 692
Whitman, Walt
   Indictment of United States, 127
Whitman, Walter Sr.
   Carpenter father, 646
Whitman's democracy, 512
Whitman's expressed permission, 785
Whitman's new Bible, 518
Whitman's Vedanta was filtered through Emerson:, 516
Whitman's opposition of life and death, 54
Whitman's physical collapse, 782
Who Goes There?, 141
Who were "the saints and sages in history but you yourself.", 223

Whoever degrades another degrades me,, 149
Whoever is not in his coffin The Sleepers, 473
Wilde, 104
Wilde, Oscar, 37
Williams, Ralph Vaughan, 413
Williams, Tennesse
    Hart Crane anticipating Williams, 588
Williams, Tennessee, 75
    Photo, 73
Williams, William Carlos, 551
with a New Orleans woman, 38
With Music Strong, 108
Within me latitude widens, longitude lengthens
    Salut au Monde, 529
Witness scenes, 59
Wittgenstein, 681, 724
    6.521, 769
wolf, the snake, the hog, 595
word sketches, 63
words are in the ground
    Song of the Rolling Earth, 726, 754
Wordsworth, William, 462
World Wide Web, 432
worst chief executive., 67
Would You Hear, 203
wound dresser in the civil war, 65
Wright, Fanny
    A Few Days in Athens, 124
Wright, Frank Lloyd, 551
yoga, 523
yoni., 339
You must travel it for yourself, 238
You Sea!, 145
You shall not heap up what is call'd riches
    Song of Open Road, 570
You take the way from man, not to man
    Emerson's Experience, 565
Zen Buddhism, 243, 249, 707
Zen master's paradoxical koans, 711

WHITMAN'S CODE: A NEW BIBLE, VOLUME I
M.C. GARDNER

NOTES

[1] *Walt Whitman's America*, page 588. David S. Reynolds' notes that the poet was pronounced dead by Dr. Alex MacAllister at 6:43 p.m.and that "an early spring rain was falling as the dusk settled."

[2] Canticle, after the Latin canticum for "Song." Over 1/3 of Whitman's poetry lies outside his formal clusters and are identified as a "Song" in their titles. It is telling to note that in his final address to his readers – a reprint for his 91-92 edition of *A Backward Glance O'er Travel'd Roads* (in the concluding sentence and paragraph of that address) he references "Biblical canticles" in a parenthetical.

[3] R.M. Bucke; *Notes and Fragments*; 1899; Chapter 2, Fragment 14.

[4] Horace L. Traubel and Thomas B. Harned were the other two.

[5] Ibid.

[6] From *Forword, Volume II*: "Initially I began this compendium, as Whitman had in the *Deathbed* edition, with the *Inscriptions* cluster. The 24 Inscriptions made a good argument for the twenty-four hours of the *Code*. You can equally arrive at 365 by assuming the Inscriptions to be a twenty-four piece introduction (not included in the count) which concludes with the invitation: 'Therefore for thee the following Chants.' The 365 count then begins with *Starting From Paumanok*. This has the advantage of keeping the poet's placement of his poems in precisely the arrangement of the *Deathbed* edition. The poems starting with *Starting From Paumanok* through the final poem, *Goodbye My Fancy* become the 365 to which he alluded in an early notebook fragment. But as I progressed in the effort I came to believe that *Song of Myself* should inaugurate Book I. Aside from the greatness of his inaugural '55 poem is the fact that he later divided it into 52 cantos--the weeks of the year. I also believe that the remaining 24 solo canticles are given a fresh perspective when grouped as a cluster. It was with some reluctance that I took this course because, for the most part, I believe deference should be given an author's final design and desire. But as earlier stated in *Anatomy of*

a Code the poet also desired, near the end of his life 'to bring you the reader into the atmosphere of the theme or thought—there to pursue your own thought.'"

[7] Whitman often refers to his opus as his "poem": *To formulate a poem whose every thought or fact should directly or indirectly be or connive to at an implicit belief in the wisdom, health, mystery, beauty of every process, every concrete object, every human or other existence, not only consider'd from the point of view of all, but of each.* "A Backward Glance"

[8] Whitman's poems are not numbered. I discovered the count of 365 simply by assembling the numbers of each cluster as a mnemonic device to better my comprehension of the whole of his opus. The Bradley and Blodgett's *Textural Variorum Edition of the Printed Poems*, lists 437 poems in the order of their composition. The *Deathbed* edition lists a total of 390 poems including the opening Epigraph. Subsequent editions often include 13 Poems collected posthumously as "Old Age Echoes"—a total of 403 poems. The Norton Critical Edition of *Leaves of Grass* lists the canonical 390 of the *Deathbed* edition and 45 *Excluded* Poems, poems that once appeared in *Leaves of Grass* or its supplements but were not included in the *Deathbed* edition. It further lists a total of 44 published but uncollected poems; 28 Passages excluded from *Leaves of Grass* Poems; 22 Unpublished Poems; and 60 Uncollected Manuscript Fragments. This Compendium assembles the 25 Solo Poems not collected in Cluster for Book I; and the Epigraph and 364 Poems collected in thematic cluster for Book II. These numbers together constitute the 390 of the *Deathbed* edition.

[9] Whitman's poetic line will often resemble that of an Old Testament prophet—the division of Old and New Testament is, however, only figurative.

[10] "The book he knew best was the Bible, the prophetical parts of which stirred in him a vague desire to be the bard or prophet of his own time and country." John Townsend

Trowbridge's account in an *Atlantic Monthly* article, *Reminiscences of Walt Whitman*, 1902

[11] W. Whitman; "The Sleepers", Section 1

[12] W. Whitman; *Leaves of Grass*, "Song of Myself", 15th Canto (Line 271, 1855 edition)

[13]. Ibid., *Drum-Taps*; "The Wound Dresser"; Conclusion of 2nd Canto.

[14] Ibid.; Opening lines, "Song of Myself".

[15] With the exception of the Universe, Whitman was a man of few possessions — compare with Emerson's: "I am my brother and my brother is me" from *Compensation*.

[16] Cf., W. Whitman; *Leaves of Grass*, "Song at Sunse"t: To be the incredible God I am. / To go forth among other Gods, these men and women I love.

[17] R.W. Emerson; a paraphrase

[18] R.W. Emerson; *Nature*, Section 1

[19] June 16, Bloomsday — the day he met his future wife, Nora.

[20] James Joyce, *Ulysses,* page 25, Random House, 1934

[21] Ibid., page 409

[22] R.W. Emerson; *Conduct of Life*, "Illusions"

[23] Ibid., *Essays, First Series*; "Intellect"

[24] Sartor Resartus Book 1 Chapter XI

[25] W. Whitman; "Song of Myself", Conclusion of 5th Canto

[26] T.S. Eliot; *Four Quartets*; "Burnt Norton", Section II

[27] Emerson; "The Natural History of the Intellect": *I owe to genius always the same debt, of lifting the curtain from the common and showing me that gods are sitting disguised in every company.*

[28] Reference is made to the *poems* of 91/92 *Deathbed* edition — 364 vs. 25 (93.14%).

[29] A titled grouping of poems, primarily, by theme.

[30] Most of the Solo poems are of extensive length. The 364 vs. 25 refers only to individual poems and not the mass and matter of the poetry.

[31] The major exceptions are during "conversations" between Whitman & a variety of invited *guests*.

[32] Ed Folsom of The Walt Whitman Archive has pointed out that the conciseness of saying the poems of the '55 edition are untitled should be qualified. The first six poems are preceded by the title: "Leaves of Grass". The six poems after the last of these (later "Faces") are delineated by a simply centered line dividing the remaining poems: _____

[33] The author is pictured in a famed frontispiece engraving by Samuel Hollyer from a picture by Gabriel Harrison.

[34] W. Whitman; *Leaves of Grass*; 1855 edition; line 499

[35] Ibid.; line 709

[36] Ibid., line 852

[37] Initially untitled; 1856, *Poem of Walt Whitman, an American*; 1860 and later, *Walt Whitman*; 1881, *Song of Myself*. Word's grammar application lists this last as a misuse of reflexive pronouns. It recommends in its stead: *Song of Me* — we can be grateful the Whitman's construction predated Microsoft.

[38] W. Whitman; Leaves of Grass, 1867 edition

[39] Cf., James Joyce's *Finnegans Wake*: Joyce uses the Italian philosopher's ricorso schemata from *La Scienza Nuova* to undergird the crazed and magnificent pageantry of his text. The number 4 is the four sections of the Joyce's book; the four weeks of the month; the four gospelers, Matthew, Mark, Luke and John; and the four bedposts of the innkeeper's bed where the book is dreamed. The number 12 is the twelve patrons of the inn; the twelve apostles; the twelve members of the jury; the twelve signs of the zodiac; and the twelve months of the year.

[40] The clusters and annexes contain 364 poems (7 days X 52 weeks) — the poet added a poetic Epigraph to the *Deathbed* edition

culminating the count at 365. a good argument for the twenty-four hours of the Code.

[41] Obscuring the count for most investigators are the poems inserted in editions after the poet's death. Originally I followed the *Variorum's* lead by placing these 13 *Old Age Echoes* in the Appendix of Vol. II but space considerations only allowed the inclusion of the last of those thirteen.

[42] "Old Age Echoes" first made its first appearance in the 1897 edition of *Leaves of Grass*.

[43] Care has been taken to preserve the stanzas of 91/92 edition. When a stanza is interrupted by a page's end it continues as a stanza if the concluding line ends in a comma.

[44] "Full of Life Now"; Originally, 1860's Calamus 45

[45] Twain: *Persons attempting to find a motive in this narrative will be prosecuted; persons attempting to find a moral in it will be banished; persons attempting to find a plot will be shot.*

[46] Other line numbers reference salient points of text.

[47] The inaugural 1336 lines of *Leaves of Grass* would later be christened "Song of Myself" in the 1881 edition of *Leaves of Grass*. The 1855 edition of *Leaves of Grass* contained a prose preface of 827 lines and an untitled collection of verse of 2315 lines. Of the poetry represented by those twenty-three hundred over 1900 of the inaugural lines ended up *outside* the poems collected in the 1881 clusters. 5 of the 25 solo poems in his final collection were from the original untitled 12 (12 again!) of the first edition.

[48] James E. Miller Jr. sees the poem as a dramatic presentation of the mystical experience. He doesn't fault the poet for what he sees as a feint or pose because all artists are congenitally so presupposed—"*which is to say that all artists are liars.*" He sees the first five cantos as preparation to entry into the mystical state, followed by cantos six through forty-nine as manifests of the mystical state and the final two Cantos as the return from it. He further relates this scheme to the Evelyn Underhill's 1926 *Mystic Way* in which seven different stages are delineated. In

this expanded schemata Cantos 1-5, Entry into the mystical state; Cantos 6-16, Awakening of the self; Cantos 17-32, Purification of the self; Cantos 33-37, Illumination and the dark night of the soul; Cantos 38-43, Union (faith and love); Cantos 44-49, Union (perception); and Cantos 50-52, Emergence from the mystical state. Harold Bloom takes a more abstract literary approach by relating the poem to "...the model of the British Romantic crisis-poem." In this schemata Cantos 1-6 are designated *Clinamen*, Irony of presence and absence; Cantos 7-27, *Tessera*, senecdoche of part for whole; Cantos 28-30, *Kenosis*, metonymy of empting out; Cantos 31-38, *Daemonization*, hyperbole of high and low; Cantos 39-49, *Askesis*, metaphor of inside and outside; and concluding with *Apopbrades*, metalepsis reversing early and late. Malcolm Cowley, also no slouch at this sort of game, suggests: Cantos 1-4, *Introduction of Poet*; Canto 5, *The Ecstasy*; Cantos 6-19 *The Grass*; Cantos 20-25, *The Poet in Person*; Cantos 26-29 *The Ecstasy Through Senses*; Cantos 30-38, *The Power of Identification*; Cantos 39-41, *The Superman*; Cantos 42-50, *The Sermon*; Cantos 51-52, *The Poet's Farewell*.

[49] Had I not resisted complicating my own schemata the two volumes would have also suggested the cartography of Whitman's sonorous consciousness: Vol. 1 Prologue: 52 Cantos of *Walt Whitman*; Vol. I: 24 Canticles of the *Me Myself*; and Vol. II: 365 Lyrics of *The Soul*. These designations are discussed throughout these volumes but they seemed rather, a more difficult approach to the poet.

[50] Meister Eckhart, Sermon Eleven.

[51] "Backward Glance O'er Travel'd Road"

[52] *Walt Whitman in Camden* Vol. II, Horace Traubel.

[53] R.W. Emerson; *Essays, First Series*; "Self-Reliance".

[54] As the foundational and ultimate Deity—*God* would be just as appropriate.

[55] Frank Sanborn to Horace Traubel. Sanborn also has the dubious distinction of losing the copy of *Leaves of Grass* that was originally sent to Emerson by Whitman.

[56] My insertion.

[57] "A Backward Glance Over Well-Traveled Roads", from Whitman's *November Boughs*.

[58] Threnody, lines 11-14 Emerson's Collected Poem

[59] Both amative and adhesive are phrenological terms.

[60] Cf. Leonard Cohen's "Anthem": *Forget your perfect offering. There is a crack in everything. That's how the light gets in.*

[61] Emerson' essay, "Compensation".

[62] God, of course, could be an expansive metaphor for the lover, himself.

[63] Wilde's "discovery" was shared by hundreds of wounded soldier who wouldn't have given it a second thought.

[64] *Walt Whitman, A Study*; Chapter 5 page 67; John Addington Symonds

[65] Ibid; page 197

[67] Emerson, essay: "The Method of Nature".

[68] R.W. Emerson, *Essays Second Series*, "Experience".

[69] Ibid., *Nature*, Section VI

[70] Cf., J. Boehme: *While in this state, as I was walking through a field of flowers, in fifteen minutes, I saw through the mystery of creation, the original of this world and of all creatures. . . . Then for seven days I was in a continual state of ecstasy, surrounded by the light of the Spirit, which immersed me in contemplation and happiness. I learned what God is, and what is his will. . . . I knew not how this happened to me, but my heart admired and praised the Lord for it!*

[71] Ibid., *Essays, First Series*, "Compensation".

[72] M. Fox; *Breakthrough, Meister Eckhart's Creation Spirituality*.

[73] Ecclesiastes

[74] Meister Eckhart; primarily Sermon 23.

[75] J. Joyce; *Ulysses,* page 50; Random House.

[76] R.W. Emerson; *Conduct of Life*; Worship

[77] Meister Eckhart, Sermon Four

[78] Isaiah, Chapter 40

[79] Meister Eckhart, Sermon Four

[80] Meister Eckhart

[81] William Law, Cited by Huxley, *The Perennial Philosophy,* page 2.

[82] Meister Eckhart, Sermon 5.

[83] *Emerson Essays*

[84] Cited by Aldous Huxley, page 14, *The Perennial Philosophy.*

[85] *Specimen Days*

[86] Lines 127-133, the forth unnamed poem of the '55 edition, *Leaves of Grass*

[87] Lines 66, 67 Pictures; Uncollected Poems, Norton Critical Edition, *Leaves of Grass and Other Writings*; editor, Michael Moon

[88] *Walt Whitman's America,* Cited by David S. Reynolds page 470.

[89] *Whitman and Burroughs, Comrades* by Clara Barrus from a conversation with John Burroughs.

[90] Ibid., page 97

[91] *The Perennial Philosophy* by Aldous Huxley, Time and Eternity.

[92] J. Joyce; *Ulysses*, page 370; Random House

[93] *Sartor Resartus*, Book 1 Chapter XI

[94] R.W. Emerson's "Compensation"

[95] Emerson, "Self Reliance"

[96] Emerson, "Considerations by the Way" from *Conduct of Life*

[97] "Faces", lines 26-29, *Leaves of Grass*; Walt Whitman
[98] Ibid; line 43
[99] Ibid; line 41
[100] *Leaves of Grass, Autumn Rivulets*, "Thought"
[101] "Hast Never Come to Thee an Hour", *By the Roadside*, *Leaves of Grass*; Walt Whitman
[102] *Whitman and Burroughs, Comrades* by Clara Barrus page 189
[103] Ibid., page 248
[104] *Walt Whitman's America* by David S. Reynolds page 570
[105] *Whitman and Burroughs, Comrades* by Clara Barrus page 341
[106] Meister Eckhart Sermons 2 and 11
[107] "Starting From Paumanok", Canto 12, lines 167-168
[108] Emory Holloway, *The Uncollected Poetry and Prose of Walt Whitman*
[109] Cited by G.A. Wilson in *The Solitary Singer* pages 48-49
[110] Ibid. page 53
[111] Cited by Jerome Loving: *Walt Whitman, The Song of Himself* page 146
[112] Henry Miller, *Tropic of Cancer*
[113] *Democratic Vistas*, lines 48-60
[114] *The Passion of the Western Mind* by Richard Tarnas page 417
[115] Emerson, "Natural History of the Intellect".
[116] Stevens, *Collected Poetry and Prose*, "The Man with the Blue Guitar".
[117] Cited by David S. Reynolds's *Walt Whitman's America*, page 242
[118] *The Analysis of Mind*, 9th Chapter, Bertrand Russell
[119] *Génie du christianisme* (Part I Book IV Chapter V), Chateaubriand, 1802
[120] J. Joyce; *Ulysses;* page 39, Random House
[121] Rabbi David Gottlieb

[122] G. Safran, "Gedolei Yisroel Condemns Rabbi Nosson Slifkin's Books". Dei'ah veDibur, January 12, 2005..

[123] W. Whitman; 1855 edition, line 499: *Walt Whitman, an American, one of the roughs, a kosmos...*

[124] B. Russell; "An Inquiry into Meaning and Truth" The Contemporaneous whole of a given quality is every other quality — If that whole is preceded by the same, the eternal return is set in eternal tautological motion.

[125] R.W. Emerson; *Essays, First Series*; "Intellect"

[126] *The Avatamsaka Sutra*, Thomas Cleary translation, cited in *Buddha Boogie, The Tautological Paradigm*, M. C. Gardner

[127] *The Reflections of Marcus Aurielus* Volume VI

[128] Meister Eckhart primarily from Sermon 23

[129] D.T. Suzuki, *Essays in Zen Buddhism, 3rd Series*

[130] J. Joyce; *Ulysses*, page 407; Random House

[131] *An Address*, The conclusion of the Divinity College Address at Cambridge by R.W. Emerson

[132] Job 39: 19-25

[133] Emerson Essay, "Compensation"

[134] Emerson Essay, "The Over-soul"

[135] Emerson Essay, "Experience"

[136] Eckhart 2nd Sermon

[137] David S. Reynolds' *Walt Whitman's America* page 237

[138] W. Whitman; *Leaves of Grass*; Line 702 of '55 edition: *Swift wind! Space! My Soul! Now I know it is true what I guessed at...*

[139] J. Joyce; *Ulysses*, page 210

[140] B. Russell; "What I Believe"

[141] I added (who) for clarity.

[142] J. Joyce; *Ulysses*, page 231; Random House

[143] "Dialogues Concerning Natural Religions" V; David Hume.

[144] Meister Eckhart's Sermon 9

[145] J. Joyce, *Ulysses,* page 421; Random House

[146] Ibid., page 210; Random House

[147] Greg Stanford reminds me that Bach's "Goldberg Variations" repeats its opening Aria da capo at the conclusion of its thirty variationsEarlier this same afternoon I had been enjoying Gould's luminous performance of the same. What the pianist said of Bach's variations could also be said of Whitman's fifty two cantos: *It is, in short, music which observes neither end nor beginning ... it has, then, unity through intuitive perception... revealed to us here ... in the vision of subconscious design exulting upon a pinnacle of potency."*

[148] *Four Quartets,* "Little Gidding", Section V, T.S. Eliot

[149] B. Spinoza; 8th Definition in his foundational chapter of *The Ethics.*

[150] C. Hitchens; "God Is Not Great: The Case Against Religion."

[151] Raphael moves back and forth in time. Nothing would restrict him from giving the famous Florentine two roles in his remarkable composition. The title was not Raphael's, indeed, most of those pictured were not Athenians. Leonardo and Michelangelo often competed for the commissions that would become the hallmarks of the Renaissance—Raphael would have been well aware of a competition in which he, as well, was intimately involved.

[152] The followers of Harold Camping of the *Family Radio Network* suffered a similar disappointment shortly after 6:00 pm, May 21, 2011—Jesus was, once again, a no-show. Camping's unique calculation is worth noting: Jesus was crucified on Friday, April 1, 33 A.D. It takes exactly 365.2422 days for the earth to complete one orbit of the sun. On April 1, 2011, Jesus was crucified exactly 722,449.07 days ago. Add 51 days to this to get to May 1, and you get a figure of 722,500.07. Round that down to the nearest integer, and you get 722,500, which is an important number because it is the square of 5 x 17 x 10. To a Christian numerologist the number 5 represents

atonement; 10 represents completeness; and 17 represents heaven. Multiply all these together – twice – and you get 722,500. Ergo, the apocalypse kicks off on Saturday, May 21. I'm indebted to Eoin O'Carroll of the Christian Science Monitor for reportage on the mathematics and metaphors in question. Camping's followers found themselves less than enraptured without their Rapture—however, the following day a volcano erupted in Iceland and category 5 Tornado hit Joplin, Missouri on the 22nd—close, but no loaded cigar for Camping. The Reverend released a revised computation the following Tuesday— the Apocalypse had been rescheduled for October 21, 2011! Take note. Take cover. The Mayan's "long calendar," ending date of the December 21, 2012 missed by a few weeks the 17,200 mile fly-by of asteroid 2012 DA 14. At the size of a 10 story building (50 meters) it is larger than the asteroid that struck Tungustan Russia on June 30, 1908. That event leveled 800 square miles of forest--DA 14 was also close, but, once again, no cigar.

[153] *November Boughs* by Walt Whitman, 2nd note on Elias Hicks

[154] Ibid.

[155] Quoted by Whitman in *November Boughs*, Hick's Notes #2

[156] The Soul invites each to expand to the full measure of the Universe. R.W.E.

[157] Joel Myerson; *Transcendentalism, A Reader*; Introduction, page xxvi

[158] A short compendium from R.W.E.

[159] His plainclothesman, William Henry Crook reported that Lincoln spoke of this as a multiple dream of that same week, the latest on the eve of the Assassination. Elsewhere the same story was reported as a pale image in a mirror.

[160] W. Whitman; "When the Full Born Poet Came"; 1876

[161] E. Schrödinger; "My View of the World"

[162] Among Mormons there is certain pride of place among Smiths who imagine a genealogy in common with the founding prophet of their faith—if so there, so also here. I

have, however, traced the shared genealogy to Robert Gardner of the late 1600s.

[163] K. Burn's; *The Civil War*: "Secretly almost blind, he took few photographs himself. The highly regarded 'Photographs by Brady' were mainly the work of his assistants, including Alexander Gardner and Timothy O'Sullivan."

[164] Dr. Ed Folsom and Dr. Kenneth Price are co-directors of The Walt Whitman Archive. Dr. Folsom is also the editor of The Whitman Quarterly.

[165] Ted Genoways makes an excellent case for the engraving being produced by the artist John C. McRae. Whitman identified McRae as the engraver in 1876. Hollyer's first claimed credit five years after Whitman was pushing leaves of grass out of his Harleigh mausoleum:, *"One goodshaped and wellhung man": Accentuated Sexuality and the Uncertain Authorship of the Frontpiece of the 1855* edition *of Leaves of Grass*. See *Leaves of Grass The Sesquicentennial Essays;* Belasco, Folsom, and Price, editors. 1997 University of Nebraska Press.

[166] Alexander and Margret Gardner's children did not have natural children of their own. Daughter Eliza never married. His son Laurence and wife Elizabeth adopted two children but had none of their own. Going the other way his parents were James and Jean Glenn Gardner. Three generations earlier we find that Robert Gardner and Janet Blair's eldest son is named Alexander. This Alexander was born in 1718 and is the older brother to William Gardner—my family's branch of the pedigree. If there is a direct link (beyond the fact they all hail from the Renfreshire area of the Scottish lowlands) it is likely with the aforementioned Alexander or one of his other brothers: Robert (1722); James (1727) or John (1730). Robert and Janet are the earliest progenitors I can trace—all the Gardners and Gardiners (of which there are many) undoubtedly share a common ancestor of an earlier era.

[167] Third Volume of Horace Traubel's *Walt Whitman in Camden* pgs. 234, 236; cited by D. Mark Katz in *Witness To An Era: The Life and Photographs of Alexander Gardner*; Rutledge Hill Press, Nashville, Tenn.

[168] W. Whitman, *Leaves of Grass*, "Song of the Rolling Earth", Line 56

[169] J.E. Miller; *A Critical Guide to Walt Whitman*; University of Chicago; 1957 — A worthy try but I believe no brass ring or what you will.

[170] The first 1336 lines of the 1855 edition would be called "Song of Myself" by the 1881 edition

[171] H. D. Thoreau; Letter to Harrison Blake; 1856

[172] "Year of Meteors", lines 4-6; Walt Whitman, *Leaves of Grass*

[173] From a self-promotional letter by Whitman to the New York Times

[174] Lines 78-89 of 1855 edition; later to become 2nd Stanza of Canto 5, "Song of Myself", *Deathbed* text.

[175] R.W. Emerson; *Conduct of Life*; "Fate".

[176] *Breakthrough: Meister Eckhart's Creation Spirituality* by Matthew Fox

[177] The concluding lines of *Poem of Remembrances for a Girl or Boy of These States*, later excluded.

[178] Eckhart's 7th and 6th Sermons

[179] Ibid., Sermons

[181] W. Whitman; *Leaves of Grass*; "By Blue Ontario's Shore"; Canto 15

[182] J. Joyce, *Ulysses*, page 50; Random House

[183] Act II Scene II *Hamlet, Prince of Denmark*; William Shakespeare

[184] Act IV Scene VI *King Lear*, William Shakespeare

[185] Song: *Go and Catch a Falling Star*; John Donne

[186] My title

[187] Cited by David S. Reynolds's; *Walt Whitman's America* page 282

[188] Schopenhauer, *The World as Will and Idea*

[189] Meister Eckhart, Sermon 6

[190] J. Joyce; *Ulysses*, page 45

[191] Norton Critical Edition, Note 9 for "Passage to India".

[192] "Song of Myself", 33rd Canto, lines 714-715

[193] Meister Eckhart; Sermon 6

[194] R.W. Emerson; *Conduct of Life*; "Fate"

[195] Words page 11, My own *Buddha Boogie: The Tautological Paradigm*

[196] Meister Eckhart; Sermon 23

[197] *Walt Whitman, A Life; Justin* Kaplan, Passages Chapter page 348.

[198] *Whitman and Burroughs, Comrades* by Clara Barrus page 176-177

[199] This is my favorite Whitman portrait. Scholars who attribute it to William Kurtz date it after 1866-68. R. M. Bucke dates the photo to the beginning of the war which would suggest Gardner. (See Gardner's Whitman portraits from 1862, where the attire is similar.) Most of Brady's portraits of the poet were postbellum. Bucke writes that Whitman's *attitude and aspect betokened the shadow of the national catastrophe, which was to crush him as well as so many thousand others . . . already falling upon him and darkening his life.*

[200] Henry Miller, *Tropic of Cancer*, cited in author's own *Buddha Boogie: The Tautological Paradigm*

[201] The passage quoted is, of course, a brief collection of assorted fragments.

[202] "Scented Herbage From My Breast"

[203] R.M. Bucke's Notes and Fragments

[204] *Essays 2nd Series*, "Nominalist and Realist", by R.W. Emerson

[205] J.L. Borges; "Paradiso XXXL"

[206] Italics mine.

[207] *Whitman and Burroughs, Comrades* by Clara Barrus page 16.

[208] J. Joyce; *Ulysses,* page 10; Random House. For an earlier satire see Charles Dicken's 1844 *Martin Chuzzlet*—the death and burial of the elder Chuzzlewit's brother.

[209] Ibid., page 94

[210] Ibid., page 97

[211] Ibid., page 99-100

[212] Ibid., page 104

[213] Ibid., page 94

[214] Ibid., page 104

[215] Ibid., page 104

[216] Julian of Norwich, 1342-1416

[217] *Emerson's Journals*, Boston, December 19

[218] J. Joyce; *Ulysses*, page 46, Random House

[219] Ibid., page 184

[220] R.W. Emerson; *Essays 2nd Series*, "Nominalist and Realist".

[221] One can easily imagine a Winslow Homer presentation. When we contemplate the *green* of the poet's celebrated grass, *as* the uncut hair of graves we see that "The green-back'd spotted mossbonkers" is one of the poet's most succinct and subtle handlings of his theme.

[222] *Buddha Boogie, The Tautological Paradigm,* "Coda"; M.C. Gardner

[223] C. Jung; *The Archetypes of the Collective Unconscious*

[224] J. Joyce; *Ulysses,* page 214; Random House

[225] A. Watts; *Beat Zen, Square Zen and Zen*

[226] *Borges, A Reader*; Monegal and Reid ed., Note on Walt Whitman page 192

[227] Italics mine.

[228] "Spiritual Laws", R.W. Emerson

[229] "Self Reliance", R.W. Emerson

[230] "Self Reliance", R.W. Emerson

[231] "Spiritual Laws", R.W. Emerson

[232] *Conduct of Life*, "Worship", by R. W. Emerson

[233] "Experience", R.W. Emerson

[234] "Self Reliance", R.W. Emerson

[235] *Conduct of Life*, "Worship", R.W. Emerson

[236] "Experience"; R.W. Emerson

[237] Ibid.

[238] "Self Reliance"; R.W. Emerson

[239] "Self Reliance", R.W. Emerson

[240] "Experience", R.W. Emerson

[241] "Nominalist and Realist", R.W. Emerson

[242] Cited: Jerome Loving's *Walt Whitman, A Song of Himself*

[243] Cited in *Walt Whitman A Life*, pg 222; Justin Kaplan

[244] 1855 Preface to *Leaves of Grass* (Paragraph 10)

[245] T.S. Eliot, *Four Quartets*, "Dry Salvages", Section III

[246] "The Poet", R.W. Emerson

[247] "The Poet", R.W. Emerson

[248] *Whitman and Burroughs* by Clara Barrus, page 64

[249] Norton Critical Edition; Michael Moon, ed., Note #1 "A Song of Joys", page 149

[250] *Notebooks and Unpublished Prose Manuscripts Volume III, Camden*, page 1102, ed., Edward F. Grier,

[251] **Early 13th Century:** It was attributed by Caesar of Heisterbach, a papal representative, to Arnaud-Amaury, Abbot of Citeaux and military leader of the Cathar Crusade, during the abbot's sack of Beziers in southern France. Around 10,000 residents were massacred because the city had been officially allied with the **Cathars or Cathari.**

[252] Cited by Borges in *Selected Non-fictions*; Prologues, page 417

[253] "Experience", *Essays 2nd Series*, R.W. Emerson.

[254] *Also Sprach Zarathustra*; Freidrich Nietzsche Zarathustra's Prologue part IV

[255] Cited by Clara Barrus, *Whitman and Burroughs*, page 112

[256] *Psychotherapy East and West*; Alan Watts

[257] *Hinduism and Buddhism*; Anada Coomarswamy

[258] *Essays, 2nd Series*, "Nominalist and Realist", R.W. Emerson

[259] Ibid.

[260] Spoken to Abbey Price at the time of his mother's death.

[261] *Walt Whitman, A Life*; Justin Kaplan page 347

[262] Cited by Justin Kaplan; *Walt Whitman, A Life* page 265

[263] "Starting From Paumonok", end of 14th Canto and beginning of the 15th.

[264] Compare with the extended six lines of Canto 5 in "When Lilacs Last in the Dooryard Bloomed".

[265] *Nature*, Part 1; R.W. Emerson

[266] *Nature*, Part 1; R.W. Emerson

[267] *Complete letters of Vincent Van Gogh*, Vol. III page 445

[268] *Nature*, Part III; R.W. Emerson

[269269] Materialism, Past and Present by Bertrand Russell

[270] *The Transcendentalist, Nature Addresses and Lectures*; R.W. Emerson

[271] *The Analysis of Mind*; Bertrand Russell, 1921

[272] *Human Knowledge, Its Scope and Limits*; Bertrand Russell, 1948 "Mind and Matter" page 231

[273] *Is It Poetry?*, J.G. Holland, Scribner's Monthly, May 1876, Vol. 12 pages 123-25

[274] Letter to Benton by John Burroughs

[275] *Nature*, Part IV, "Idealism", R.W. Emerson,

[276] *Nature*, Part III, "Beauty", R.W. Emerson

[277] *Nature*, Part VIII, "Prospects", R.W. Emerson

[278] "Spiritual Laws"; R.W. Emerson

[279] *Nature*, Part VI, "Idealism"; R.W. Emerson.

[280] R.W. Emerson's *Nature*, Section VII

[281] "The Times", *Nature Addresses and Lectures*, R.W. Emerson

[282] Ibid

[283] "Spiritual Laws", R.W. Emerson

[284] Ibid.

[285] *Nature*, Part IV, "Idealism"

[286] W. Shakespeare; *King Lear*

[287] W. Whitman; *Leaves of Grass*; "The Sleepers", Conclusion of Canto I

[288] Ibid., "Thou Mother of thy Equal Brood", Conclusion of Canto II

[289] Ibid., lines 7 & 8 of Canto V

[290] Ibid., "Song of Myself," 1st Stanza of Canto VI

[291] Ibid., In truth, 5 of the Stanzas resist the *joyous* O

[292] W. Shakespeare; *Troilus and Cressida*:

> Then every thing includes itself in power,
> Power into will, will into appetite;
> And appetite, a universal wolf,
> So doubly seconded with will and power,
> Must make perforce a universal prey,
> And last eat up himself.

[293] Ibid., "Song of the Exposition", 1st stanza of Canto VII

[294] R.W. Emerson; *Essays, First Series*, "Intellect"

[295] J. Joyce; *Ulysses*, page 50; Random House.

[296] *Buddha Boogie: The Tautological Paradigm*

[297] Following the bliss of Joseph Campbell's *Masks of God*, "Oriental Mythology"

[298] *Buddha Boogie: The Tautological Paradigm*, Part III Chapter 2, "Forest of the Mind", M.C. Gardner

[299] C. Isherwood & Prabhavananda; *Bhagavad Gita*; Trans. 1944

WHITMAN'S CODE: A NEW BIBLE, VOLUME I

M.C. GARDNER

300 *Buddha Boogie, The Tautological Paradigm*, Part III, Entr'acte, M.C. Gardner

301 J. Joyce, *Ulysses*, page 412; Random House

302 W.Whitman; *Leaves of Grass*, "Song of Myself", Canto 6

303 Alas, several scholars have walked up to the address of the code but not gone through the door. W.C. Harris essay: *Whitman's Leaves of Grass and the Writing of a New American Bible* is the most worthy of those that my research has come to survey.

304 Emerson's note to Whitman after the publication of the inaugural *Leaves*.

305 Whitman lived with his *Leaves* from 1855 'til his passing in 1892--at this juncture in my life I also approach four decades of its companionship.

306 J.Townsend Trowbridge's report of an 1860 conversation with Whitman, Atlantic Monthly 1902: Whitman talked frankly on the subject, that day on Prospect Hill, and told how he became acquainted with Emerson's writings. He was at work as a carpenter (his father's trade before him) in Brooklyn, building with his own hands and on his own account small and very plain houses for laboring men; as soon as one was finished and sold, beginning another, — houses of two or three rooms. This was in 1854; he was then thirty-five years old. He lived at home with his mother; going off to his work in the morning and returning at night, carrying his dinner pail like any common laborer. Along with his pail he usually carried a book, between which and his solitary meal he would divide his nooning. Once the book chanced to be a volume of Emerson; and from that time he took with him no other writer. His half-formed purpose, his vague aspirations, all that had lain smoldering so long within him, waiting to be fired, rushed into flame at the touch of those electric words, — the words that burn in the prose-poem *Nature*, and in the essays on *Spiritual Laws, The Over-Soul, Self-Reliance*. The sturdy carpenter in his working-day garb, seated on his pile of boards; a poet in that rude disguise, as yet but dimly conscious of his powers; in one

hand the sandwich put up for him by his good mother, his other hand holding open the volume that revealed to him his greatness and his destiny,—this is the picture which his simple narrative called up, that Sunday so long ago, and which has never faded from my memory. He freely admitted that he could never have written his poems if he had not first "come to himself," and that Emerson helped him to "find himself." I asked if he thought he would have come to himself without that help. He said, "Yes, but it would have taken longer." And he used this characteristic expression: "I was simmering, simmering, simmering; Emerson brought me to a boil."

[307] Bradley, Blodgett, Golden, & White Editors; 3 Volumes, University Press 1965

[308] Emerson's celebrated letter to the, as of yet unknown, poet (1855).

[309] Whitman used Emerson's letter to promote his book in The *New York Herald Tribune* and published it himself in the appendix of the 2nd edition (1856) of Leaves of Grass and printed a laudatory line from the letter on the spine of the 1856 edition—in all instances without Emerson's permission. Whitman had been the editor of the *Brooklyn Eagle* (1846-48) and was likely aware of the improprieties in question.

[310] Near the 500th line the poet identifies himself as *Walt Whitman, an American...*

[311] I am reminded of a bit of dialogue from Marlon Brando's *The Wild One*: Mildred: Hey Johnny, are you rebelling against something? Johnny: Whadda ya got?

[312] Nietzsche's sobriquet of R.W.E.

[313] A portion of an unsigned review from Whitman to Brooklyn *Daily Times*.

[314] *Walt Whitman, A Life*, Justin Kaplan pg 209

[315] Whitman details the number of poems (individually and in groups) in the 1860 Table of Contents. I count 136 poems. However, the single listed poem *Says* has eight numbered entities and the single listed poem *Debris* is divided into 14

sections. This (158) brings the total close to the Norton Critical Edition's count of 156. The numbers are further complicated and enlarged by Whitman's conceit of numbering each of the stanzas of each of the poems, as if they were chapters and verses of the Bible. The poem *Walt Whitman* (Later, *Song of Myself*) ends of with a count of 372 sections.

[316] The Clusters were like Biblical books with individual poems posing as Chapters and Stanzas invidually numbered as if Biblical verses , the succeeding lines of each stanza were left for the readers to ignore or number themselves.

[317] Lascelles Abercrombie, Note on Walt Whitman. *Borges, A Reader*, ed. Monegal and Reid, pg 191

[318] *Whitman and Burroughs, Comrades* by Clara Barrus, pages 34-35

[319] Head of London, Ontario Asylum for the Insane. Read Whitman in 1868 and became his friend in 1877. Hegel's "Absolute Idea" and Emerson's "Oversoul" were influences and precursors to the thought of the poet.

[320] Published in 1901

[321] The number 164 was used instead of Peter Doyle. P=16th letter of the alphabet, D=4th letter of the alphabet.

[322] The nine count was from Whitman's own reckoning. The *Textual Variorum of the Printed Poems* argues for six. It excludes editions (impressions) that were printed from earlier plates. R.W. French suggests that the major changes that required new plate settings are found in the editions of 1855, 1856, 1860, 1867, 1871, and 1881. The *Deathbed* edition of 1891-92 primarily used the Osgood plates of the 1881 Edition. That being said the *Deathbed* edition included numerous corrections of spelling and two "annexes" which he also called "clusters." To further convolute the evolution of Whitman's *Leaves* I'll give Mr. French a further dilation: "The first annex was printed initially in the varied collection entitled *November Boughs*, published in 1888 by David McKay in Philadelphia. In its 140 pages the volume included a long prefatory essay entitled "A Backward

Glance O'er Travel'd Roads" and sixty-four new poems, all short, as well as a collection of prose works. *November Boughs* appeared in its entirety as part of the *Complete Poems & Prose* of 1888; and then, under the title "Sands at Seventy," the poems of *November Boughs* were annexed first to the 1888 and 1889 impressions of *Leaves of Grass*, and finally to the 1891-1892 impression as pages [383]-404. "A Backward Glance O'er Travel'd Roads" was published in the 1889 *Leaves of Grass* and then was made the concluding text of the 1891-1892 volume as pages [423]-438. Between the poems and the essay, filling pages 405-422, appeared the second annex, "Good-Bye my Fancy," a collection of thirty-one short poems taken from the gathering of prose and poetry published under that title by McKay in 1891." As might be expected from an underappreciated poet whose early training was as a printer-- Whitman was himself his primary publisher. In an early version of *Print by Demand* -- the poet-publisher could put together editions of his "poem" from Leaves and cluster that were left over from earlier printings. This accounts for various incarnations where poems were stitched into a volume with no regard to the volume's pagination. Gay Allen has suggested that no one knows how many "editions" of this sort might have been struck by the poet simply for the eyes of a friend or admirer whom he thought might enjoy a presentation of the "current" evolution of his *Leaves*.

[323] *Notes and Fragments*, R.M. Bucke pg 84, Part 3 Fragment 22

[324] Horace Traubel suggests his "last deliberate composition" to have been "*A Thought of Columbus*", dated December of '91.

[325] In the last sentence he wished his readers to read in the *Deathbed* edition of 1891-92: we find "...that really great poetry is always (like the Homeric or Biblical canticles) ... the strongest and sweetest songs yet remain to be sung."

[326] Mark Van Doren, *The Happy Critic and Other Essays*.

[327] *Walt Whitman's America*, David S. Reynolds page 587

[328] Horace Traubel: An Executor's Diary Note, 1891. Preface to the 1897 edition of *Leaves of Grass*.

[329] 1888's essay, "A Backward Glance O'er Traveled Roads" (Lines 389-396.) Traubel's report of an 1891 conversation with the poet would seem to be the last word on the subject excepting that the poet selected the earlier essay to conclude the 1891-92 *Deathbed* edition: pages 423-438. You can construct an argument with either pronouncement and neither would be definitive.

[330] (Whitman Archive, Selected Criticism: R.W. French, *Leaves of Grass* 1891-92 edition).

[331] *A Critical Guide to Walt Whitman*, James E.

Miller Jr. Exploration of a Structure page 168

[332] Ed Folsom; *Projecting Whitman: The Eolution and Remediation of the Collected Writings of Walt Whitman*

[333] Taken from the second and last paragraph of Folsom's essay.

[334] As a last note to these many notes, I am amused to acknowledge a thanks that should have come at its inception. In my youth I was given the gift of Walt Whitman by Nancy Sinclair as *I arose in rainy autumn and walked abroad in a shower of all my days...*

M.C. Gardner has produced plays on both T.S. Eliot *(The Man From Lloyd's)* and Elvis Presley *(A Presley Passion).* His two-volume Walt Whitman study, *Whitman's Code: A New Bible,* was elicited by unraveling a numeric puzzle within the poetic clusters of *Leaves of Grass. Whitman's Code* is available in a variety of formats through major booksellers. Gardner resides in Los Angeles with his wife Barbara and their cat Sky. He is the principal editor of the literary website Another America (www.anotheramerica.org).

A grateful acknowledgment is owed to Greg Stanford for proofing the Whitman series of which this volume is a part. Greg is the author of Another America's "Operatic Ear," and his word-by-word survey of these pages has spared its readers errata of epic proportions.

www.ingramcontent.com/pod-product-compliance
Lightning Source LLC
Chambersburg PA
CBHW031406230426
43668CB00007B/227